PEARSON   ALWAYS LEARNING

Charles L. Ballard
Michigan State University

Real Economics
for Real People

Sixth Edition

Pearson Education, Inc., 330 Hudson Street, New York, New York 10013
A Pearson Education Company
www.pearsoned.com

Printed in the United States of America

1 16

000200010272044188

EEB

ISBN 10: 1-323-42317-6
ISBN 13: 978-1-323-42317-2

Contents

Chapter 1

What Is Economics, Anyway?

ECONOMICS AND YOU:
DECISIONS, DECISIONS, DECISIONS

The alarm clock just went off. Amy Neyland is lying in bed, struggling to decide whether to get up. She can stay in bed, or she can get up and get ready for work. If she stays in bed, she'll get a little more rest, but she won't have time for a shower and a cup of coffee. On the other hand, if she gets up, she'll be able to take the shower, drink the coffee, have some toast, and maybe even read the paper. But she will be a little more tired than she would have been, if she had stayed in bed.

Amy has only a limited amount of time. If she decides to spend the time in bed, she won't be able to have breakfast. If she decides to have breakfast, she won't be able to spend the time in bed. So, she will have to make a decision. She doesn't know it, but Amy is about to make an *economic* decision. Economics is fundamentally concerned with how people make decisions. We only have a limited amount of resources, and we have to make choices about how to use those resources, in an attempt to do our best in life. That is what economics is all about.

In fact, Amy will be making economic decisions all day long. At work, she'll have to decide whether to get a task done "in house",

or to contract with another company. On her lunch hour, she will have to decide whether to have a burger and fries, or a salad, or a burrito. After work, she'll go to the grocery store, and she will have to decide whether to buy more, or less, of each of thousands of items.

And so it goes all through the day. We all make decisions. Those decisions are central to the discipline called economics. In this book, you will have the opportunity to learn a lot about one important branch of economics, which is called microeconomics. Of course, whether you learn will depend on the decisions you make. No one is holding a gun to your head, forcing you to learn economics. You can choose to do nothing but eat, sleep, and watch TV. If so, you won't learn much economics. On the other hand, you can choose to read the book, and work the questions and problems. If so, you might not get to watch as much TV. It's your choice. And choice is one of the most important topics of economics.

Before this book is over, we will study the ways in which people make all sorts of choices. These include choices about what to buy, how much to save, how much to work, and how much education to get, as well as many other choices. We'll also study the ways in which business firms make choices about what to produce, how much to produce, how many workers to hire, how many machines to use, and what prices to charge.

The decisions made by consumers, workers, and business owners are not made in a vacuum. If Amy wants to buy a slice of pepperoni pizza for lunch, she will be able to find one. (Like most Americans, Amy lives in a town with restaurants that sell pizza, and just about every pizza place sells pepperoni.) However, if Amy wants a pizza that is made with organic goat cheese and morel mushrooms, it may be hard to find.

Thus the choices made by some people (such as what kind of pizza to buy) are interwoven with the choices made by other people (such as what kind of pizza to sell). In this book, we will emphasize the ways in which people *interact* with each other. The economic world that we observe is the result of the *interactions* among the decisions of different people.

The decisions made by consumers, workers, and business owners are also affected by laws and regulations. Every well-functioning society has some form of government. It is unfortunate, but true, that people sometimes cheat, steal, and kill. At a minimum, governments can play an important role in establishing and enforcing laws, with an eye toward reducing these bad behaviors. Moreover, even perfectly honest people can have disagreements. Thus every well-functioning society has some sort of legal system, to resolve contract disputes and other disagreements peacefully.

In many countries, including the United States, governments engage in many other activities that go beyond the basics of maintaining order. In this book, we will discuss government policies regarding education, poverty, air pollution, and many other issues. We will also look at some of the ways in which government policies affect the decisions made by consumers, workers, and business owners.

Important Issues Covered by This Book

Our study of decision making will prepare us to confront many of the most important policy issues of our time. For example, in Chapters 2 and 5, we will study international economics. *International economics* deals with why we import some goods from other countries, and export different goods to other countries. What will happen if the government imposes a tariff, which is a tax on imports? What will happen if the government imposes an import quota, which is a strict limit on the amount of imports?

In Chapters 9–12, we will study the economics of industrial organization. For example, the *economics of industrial organization* deals with how the behavior of the firms in an industry would change, if they were to merge into one giant firm. What happens when the government regulates the firms in an industry? What types of industry are best for consumers?

Another important field of study is labor economics, which we will consider in Chapter 13. *Labor economics* is concerned with the interactions between workers and their employers. Why do some people earn high wages, while the wages of others are much lower? What are the effects of labor unions? What happens as a result of a minimum-wage law?

Toward the end of this book, in Chapter 16, we will take a look at public economics. *Public economics* deals with the causes and effects of government spending, and the taxes that are used to pay for government operations. Which goods and services should be provided by government, and which should be provided by private markets? Would it be better to tax the wages of workers, or to tax corporate profits, or to raise tax revenues from other sources?

The final chapter of the book, Chapter 17, deals with environmental economics. Using the tools of *environmental economics*, we will discuss how economic principles can be used to find effective ways to clean up pollution.

How to Read This Book

Many of the people who read this book will be reading about economics for the first time. When you're exploring a new subject, it's important to have some idea of what approach to take. It is important for you to know that *it won't make sense to read this book like a novel*. Usually, when you read a novel, you can go fast. However, if you try to go too fast in this book, everything will be a blur, and your understanding will be mushy, at best.

Some people think it's OK to settle for a superficial understanding. However, understanding economics at a superficial level is often the same as not understanding it at all. You may have to stop from time to time, to make sure that you *really* understand what you have read. For this reason, each chapter has "Interim Review Questions". It may be tempting to skip over these questions, but you'll be better off if you tackle them. The only way to be sure that you understand is to see whether you can answer the questions. At the end of each chapter, you will find more Questions and Problems. You are urged to do these, too. As in most activities, the more you practice, the better you will be. The answers to the Interim Review Questions are at the end of the book, as are the answers to the end-of-chapter Questions and Problems.

Often, the concepts introduced in one chapter will build on the concepts that were developed in earlier chapters. Thus, it is really important to have a solid understanding of each chapter, before moving on to the next chapter. Going forward in a steady, methodical way is the best way to master the material.

Different people have different backgrounds and learning styles. Thus some readers may find the material in this book to be very intuitive and easy to follow, while others

may not. If you don't get it the first time, don't be afraid to go over the material again. There is nothing wrong with repetition. It is universally accepted that football coaches and basketball coaches will run the same play again and again in practice. The reason for this is that practice helps to improve performance. Just as a basketball team will get better by practicing and repeating, an economics student will also get better by practicing and repeating.

The last few paragraphs have stressed the importance of being steady and careful. However, we hope that it has been possible to stress these things without making it seem that economics is extremely difficult. In fact, most students will find that this material is not terribly hard. It just takes work. Almost everyone who is serious about studying this material will be able to learn it. Introductory microeconomics is not rocket science.

Quantitative Skills

Since introductory microeconomics is not rocket science, it does not require sophisticated mathematics. This book does not have any calculus, or matrix algebra, or differential equations. However, we will use some basic algebra. We will also use *lots* of graphs.

Most people who read a book like this are college students. Almost all of these students have had a few years of algebra and geometry in middle school and high school. In most cases, students find that their mathematical background is more than enough to do well in an introductory microeconomics course.

However, a few of you may have been the kind of person who limped through high-school algebra. Then, at the end of your sophomore or junior year of high school, you closed the algebra book and said "Hallelujah! I'll never have to do that again!". Now, it's three or four or five years later, and your quantitative skills are very rusty. If that's you, then it will be really important for you to brush up on your quantitative skills. The appendix to this chapter is designed to help you to accomplish that. Even if you are pretty strong with algebra and graphs, it might be a good idea to look at the appendix. If you are weak with algebra and graphs, it is *essential* that you study the appendix.

WHAT IS *ECONOMICS*?

Economics can be defined in several different ways. Here's one: *Economics* is the study of how people use their limited resources to satisfy unlimited wants. Here's another definition: Economics is the study of how a society chooses to use its scarce resources to produce, exchange, and consume goods and services.

The two definitions are not identical, but they have a lot in common. At the center of each definition is the idea that our resources are *scarce,* or *limited.* However, our desires are unlimited. The human imagination has an infinite capacity to dream. Wouldn't it be great to be sunning yourself on the beach in Hawaii, and eating a gourmet meal at a restaurant in Paris, and watching a Broadway play, all at the same time? Yes, it would be great. However, for better or worse, it can't be done. Each of us only has 24 hours in a day, and we can only be in one place at one time. Moreover, some of us would have trouble getting to Broadway, or Hawaii, or Paris because we may not be able to get enough time off from work, and because airfare and hotels cost a lot of money. We are *constrained* by the limits on our resources. Therefore, we have to *choose.*

Three Fundamental Choices

In the chapters to come, we will discuss all sorts of choices. However, every society must make three *fundamental* choices. The three fundamental choices are (1) what to produce, (2) how to produce, and (3) for whom to produce.

What to Produce. Every society has to make choices about what to produce. Since our resources are scarce, we can't have everything that we would like. We can build more passenger aircraft, but devoting more resources to airliners may mean that we won't be able to build as many automobiles. So, one question is whether we shall build more airliners or more automobiles. Similarly, we can raise more chickens, but devoting more resources to raising chickens may mean that we won't be able to produce as much asparagus. Do we produce more chickens or more asparagus? How many leather handbags should we produce? How many smart phones? How much electricity? How much bacon? Different societies make these choices in different ways. In simple tribal societies, many economic decisions are made by a chief, or by a council of tribal elders. In some countries, such as North Korea, most economic decisions are made by government officials. However, in the United States and most other countries, most decisions are made by individual households and/or businesses. Much of this book will be devoted to describing the process by which a modern industrial nation, such as the United States, makes its decisions about what to produce.

The issue of what to produce will come up in every chapter of this book.

How to Produce. If a new highway were to be built in the United States, it would be built by a relatively small number of workers. Each worker would have a tremendous amount of equipment to work with, including graders, bulldozers, and trucks. On the other hand, if a new highway were to be built in a country like India, which has less heavy equipment but a very large population, it would probably be built with a relatively large number of workers. The workers would be more likely to use shovels and wheelbarrows, instead of gigantic earthmoving machines. This example illustrates the fact that it's possible to produce the same good or service in many different ways. Therefore, it is necessary to make choices about how to produce.

Once again, different societies may make these choices in different ways. In this book, we will focus primarily on the way in which choices about how to produce are made in a modern industrial economy. Usually, these choices are made by business firms, in a process that involves interactions with workers, and with the owners of machinery, equipment, buildings, energy, materials, and land.

The question of how to produce will be addressed throughout this book, but especially in Chapter 8.

For Whom to Produce.   In parts of medieval Europe, the local lord was very wealthy, and the serfs had very little. In most countries today, the gap between rich and poor is not as great as it was then, but there are still huge differences between those at the top and those at the bottom. The distribution of income is largely determined by the interaction between employers and workers. Highly skilled workers can earn a lot of money, while less-skilled workers earn less. The distribution of income is also determined by other interactions in the private economy, and by governments. When a government raises taxes from some people, and makes payments of Social Security, Medicare, Medicaid, and food stamps to other people, the government has an effect on the distribution of income. The distribution of income will be at center stage in Chapters 13–16.

One of the biggest trends in the U.S. economy in the last 40 years or so has been a large increase in income inequality. College-educated workers have always earned more than those with only a high-school education, but the gap between the two groups has increased a great deal since the 1970s. At the very top of the income distribution, corporate executives, Wall Street bankers, and top athletes and entertainers have done extraordinarily well. But the average family has not done nearly as well. We will discuss these trends on several occasions, especially in Chapters 13 and 15.

There is no way to escape these three fundamental choices. *Every* society must decide what to produce, how to produce, and for whom to produce.

Microeconomics

Economics is divided into two broad branches—*micro*economics and *macro*economics. This book focuses on microeconomics. **Microeconomics** is concerned with the behavior of households and business firms, and the way in which they interact with each other in markets. The phrase "micro" means "very small". Microeconomics is concerned with households and business firms, because these are usually the smallest units that make decisions in the economy.

Just because microeconomics is concerned with the smallest decision-making units in the economy, it does *not* follow that microeconomics is somehow trivial or unimportant. In this chapter, we have already mentioned some of the topics that can be studied using the tools of microeconomic analysis. These issues include taxes, imports and exports, government spending, regulation of businesses, environmental pollution, and the wage differences among workers. These are *not* small issues. These issues are often covered on the front page of the newspaper, or the lead story in a television news program.

In addition, even though microeconomics deals with the smallest decision-making units in the economy, some of the units are very large indeed. Companies like Walmart, Microsoft, Exxon Mobil, General Electric, and AT&T have hundreds of thousands of employees, and they generate hundreds of *billions* of dollars of sales every year.

Macroeconomics

The other big branch of economics is macroeconomics. **Macroeconomics** is concerned with the aggregates for the economy as a whole, such as the overall rate of economic growth, the overall rate of unemployment, and the overall rate of inflation. "Macro" means very large, and so it makes sense that macroeconomics would deal with the totals for the economy.

However, even when we study macroeconomics, microeconomics is never far away. After all, what are the totals? They are the sum of all of the little pieces. We get the overall unemployment rate by counting the individual people who are unemployed, and dividing that number by the total number of people who are in the labor force. We get the overall inflation rate by finding the change in price for each of thousands of individual goods and services, and then averaging all of those individual inflation rates.

It would be wrong to think that microeconomics is completely different from macroeconomics. In many cases, microeconomics and macroeconomics use very similar tools. Since the macroeconomic totals come from the microeconomic pieces, we can say that macroeconomics rests on a microeconomic foundation. Often, we can use the tools of microeconomic analysis to understand macroeconomic events. For example, the deep recession of 2007–09, which featured the worst financial crisis since the 1930s, is definitely a macroeconomic phenomenon. However, as we will see in Chapter 4, we can use the tools of microeconomics to get a better understanding of the sequence of events that led to the recession and financial crisis.

Reality Check:
Interim Review Questions

IR1-1. What is economics?

IR1-2. Describe the difference between microeconomics and macroeconomics.

IR1-3. What are the three fundamental choices that every society must make?

THE ANALYTICAL PERSPECTIVE OF ECONOMICS

Before we go any further, it will be useful to give you a few ideas about how economists approach the world.

Positive Economics and Normative Economics

In most of this book, we are concerned with understanding how the economy works. When we think about the *actual workings* of the economy, we are concerned with *positive economics*. Here is an example of a prediction that could come from positive economics: "If the minimum wage is raised, there will be an increase in unemployment among teenagers." This is a *statement of fact*. If we can gather enough data, and analyze the data properly, we can show the statement to be correct or incorrect.

Positive economics deals with what *is*. In other words, positive economics deals with the *actual* workings of the economy. On the other hand, **normative economics** deals with what ought to be. Here is a statement that could come from normative economics: "It would be immoral for the minimum wage to be anything less than $15 per hour. Therefore, we should raise the minimum wage now." Clearly, this normative statement involves a value judgment. As such, this statement cannot be shown to be correct or incorrect. Some people may agree with it, and some may disagree. However, if one person insists that the minimum wage should be raised from its current level ($7.25 throughout the United States in 2016, but higher in some states) to $15 per hour, and another person disagrees, there is no way for one of them to prove that the other is wrong. For a person with one set of values, an increase in the minimum wage may well be the right thing to do. But for another person, with a different set of values, it may be best to keep the minimum wage where it is. Different values are consistent with different policy preferences. However, it is very hard to "prove" that one set of values is correct. Thus if two people have different values, they can reach different normative conclusions, even if they have the same understanding of the positive facts.

To summarize, positive economics is concerned with what is, while normative economics is concerned with what ought to be. Normative statements often include words like "should" or "ought to", whereas positive statements do not.

Economists have value judgments, like everyone else. Thus, economists can reach normative conclusions, just like everyone else. However, normative statements are not the economist's strong suit: Our normative opinions aren't necessarily any better than anyone else's normative opinions. Instead, our strength is in the area of positive economics. There are good reasons to give special weight to economists' views about *positive* economics. Over the years, economists have developed a very useful framework for thinking about the actual, positive workings of the economy.

Since economists are on stronger ground when they talk about positive economics than when they offer normative opinions, and since this book is written by an economist, it is not surprising that this book will concentrate mostly on positive economics. Of course, value judgments will inevitably creep into the book. However, we will spend most of this book thinking about why prices are what they are. We won't spend as much time thinking about whether a price is "just" or "unjust", or "fair" or "unfair".

Even though this book is mainly concerned with positive economics, it would be silly to pretend that value judgments are unimportant. Every person makes value judgments, and many people believe in their values with great passion and fervor. Thus it is appropriate to say a little more about values.

It turns out that normative values often tend to show certain patterns. Among other things, "conservatives" tend to prefer lower taxes on high-income people, less public support for health insurance, and weaker labor unions. "Liberals" tend to prefer higher taxes on high-income people, more public support for health insurance, and stronger labor unions.

The Role of Government

It is often said that the main difference between "conservatives" and "liberals" has to do with their attitudes toward government, with conservatives favoring smaller government, and liberals favoring bigger government. But this distinction between "big-government liberals" and "small-government conservatives" is very simplistic, and thus it can be misleading. For example, many conservatives are in favor of *increased* government spending on the military. Moreover, the stark differences between conservatives and liberals regarding taxes on high-income people don't have anything to do with the size of government: We can finance the same size of government with a tax system that takes relatively more from those with high incomes, as with a tax system that takes relatively less from them.

Despite the fact that the division between "small-government conservatives" and "big-government liberals" can be misleading, it is probably still true that conservatives in 21st-century America are more likely than liberals to prefer a relatively small degree of government regulation of the private economy. If that is the case, then you will find that this book has some messages that give comfort to conservatives, and some messages that give comfort to liberals.

Early in the book, we emphasize the amazing ability of private markets to deliver goods and services, with relatively little direction from government officials. Thus the early chapters of the book may appeal to readers who consider themselves to be conservative.

As the book progresses, however, we find that there are many situations in which private markets may lead to outcomes that aren't very good for society. For example, a monopoly is a situation in which there is only one seller of a good or service. Monopolies often charge higher prices than those that would be charged if there were many sellers. These higher prices can be good for the monopoly but bad for consumers, and bad for the society as a whole. In Chapter 12, we consider government policies to restrain monopolies. This part of the book may appeal to readers who consider themselves to be liberal or progressive.

Also, if private companies are left to their own devices, with no government regulations, they may produce a lot of air pollution and water pollution. In Chapter 17, we consider government policies to reduce pollution.

Private markets often do a great job, with minimal government regulation. But private markets can sometimes create problems that governments may be able to fix. Thus it's not all one thing, or all the other. By the time you have finished reading this book, it is hoped that you will have a nuanced understanding of both the strengths and weaknesses of government intervention in the private economy.

The Role of Models and Assumptions

The economy of the United States has more than 320 million people, divided into more than 121 million households. Each of these households makes dozens of economic decisions every day: Do we pay cash or use a credit card? Do we buy hamburger or steak? Do we fill the tank with regular gasoline, or with premium? Do we buy another pair of jeans, or save the money for the future? Do we make a sandwich and take it to work, or buy lunch at a restaurant?

The economy that we observe is the result of *billions* of decisions that are made every day. There is no way to describe every one of these decisions in complete detail, or with complete accuracy. Because the economy is so large and so complex, we will have to rely on *models* of the economy.

Before we describe *economic* models, let's think about other kinds of models. If you go to a hobby store, you can buy a kit for a model automobile, such as a model version of a Porsche Carrera GT sports car. If you follow the instructions, and glue the pieces of the model together carefully, you will end up with a stylized representation of a Porsche Carrera GT. It won't be a *real* Porsche. (For example, it won't be able to drive 140 miles per hour.) However, it will look a lot like a real Porsche. It will have two wheels on the front axle, and two wheels on the rear axle. The model will have the sleek styling that Porsche is famous for. Some models will be designed in such a way that you can get the model's wheels to turn by turning the steering wheel. So, even though the model Porsche is not a real Porsche, it can still give a fairly decent idea of what a real Porsche is like.

Just as a model sports car is not a real sports car, an economic model is not a real economy. And yet, just as a model sports car can provide us with some idea of what a real sports car is like, an economic model can give some idea of what a real economy is like. An *economic model* is a stylized representation of some aspect of the real economy.

When we construct an economic model, we know that we cannot hope to predict every single detail of what happens in the real economy. Thus an economic model can be a good economic model, even if it doesn't get every single detail correct. Instead, we say that an economic model does a good job if it gives us a useful guide to thinking about an economic issue. If the model makes predictions that are pretty close to the mark, much of the time, it is a good model.

To decide whether a model is doing a good job, we have to see whether it is consistent with the facts. If we were physicists or chemists, we would test our theoretical models in the laboratory. In a laboratory setting, it is possible to hold everything else constant, so that we can focus on one relationship. Physicists can perform laboratory experiments, because they are dealing with photons, or neutrons, or other particles and forces from the natural world. Chemists are able to perform laboratory experiments because they are dealing with chemical compounds. However, for better or worse, economists are trying to understand the behavior of *people*. Therefore, economists are usually unable to perform laboratory experiments. Instead, we have to rely on statistical techniques to test our models. Economists gather data from a wide variety of sources, and analyze the data. Often, the data reveal facts that aren't consistent with the models. In that case, it is necessary to refine our models, and test the new models against the data.

Thus, as economic science develops, there is a constant interplay between economic models and economic data. We develop models, and test them against data. Then we develop new models based on insights gained from the data. Then we test the new models against data. And so the process continues.

An Example of the Relationship Between Model and Data. Here is a story that illustrates the interplay between a model and the data that can be used to test the model. An economist tells the story of his younger daughter, Meredith, from the time when she was three years old. Meredith learned that she would soon be going to see her grandmother. She didn't remember ever having seen Grandma before. Meredith began to ask questions of her father, in an attempt to get a better understanding of what Grandma might be like.

First, Meredith verifies her own age: Meredith is three years old. Then she asks about her older sister, Stephanie, and learns that Stephanie is 10 years old. Then she asks "How old is Mommy?", and learns that her mother is 35. Then she asks "How old are you, Daddy?", and learns that her father is 38. Finally, she asks "How old is Grandma?", and learns that her grandmother is 63.

Meredith thinks about all of this information, and says "Wow. Grandma must be VERY tall."

Let's think about Meredith's thought process. (1) She had probably developed her theory before she started to ask questions. Roughly speaking, her theory was that people continue to grow taller throughout their lives, so that older people are always taller than younger people. (2) With a theory in mind, Meredith collected data. She already knew that her father was the tallest member of her immediate family, followed by her mother, followed by her older sister, and she knew that she was the shortest member of the family. Then she got the data on the ages of the individuals. (3) Next, Meredith tested her model against the data. In fact, the data provided support for her model: Among these four people, a larger age was always accompanied by a larger height. (4) On the basis of her model, Meredith formed a prediction about her grandmother's height. Since her model predicts that older people are taller, and since her grandmother is older, the model predicts that Grandma must be very tall.

Now, it turns out that Meredith's model was incomplete. But that doesn't mean it was a bad model. In fact, it was a very good starting point. For one thing, Meredith's theoretical model has implications that are easy to test against data. For another thing, her model *is* consistent with much of the data on the heights and ages of people. Sooner or later, however, Meredith would observe data that do not fit well with her simple model. For one thing, she would find that her Grandma was *not* as tall as her father, even though her model would predict that Grandma would be much taller than Daddy. To explain these data, it would be necessary to develop a more refined model. A more complete model would need to account for a variety of facts, such as (1) most people stop growing taller in their late teens or early 20s, (2) on average, men reach an adult height that is taller than the adult height of women, and (3) at any age, and for either gender, there is considerable variation in heights.

We have just described a process of scientific thought. The scientist begins by observing some facts, and develops a model to explain those facts. Then the scientist tests the model against data. The scientist will often find that the model is consistent with some aspects of the data, but that some aspects of the data don't correspond very well to the model. Then the scientist must go back and refine the model, and the process repeats itself.

Another Example. A similar process is followed in the economic literature. For example, since 1938, the United States has had minimum-wage laws, and economists have long been interested in the effects of these laws. The most popular theory (which will be developed in Chapter 4 of this book) goes like this: Lots of people won't be affected by the minimum wage at all. If the minimum wage is $7.25 per hour, and if your employer is already paying you $10 per hour, then the law won't have any effect on you. However, if the wage that you would be paid (in the absence of the minimum-wage law) is $4 per hour, then the minimum-wage law might cause your employer to decide to let you go (or not hire you in the first place). In other words, the minimum-wage law might lead to unemployment.

Over the years, dozens of research studies have attempted to get an idea of the size of the employment losses. These research studies have used all sorts of data. A few studies have even reached the odd conclusion that the minimum wage *increases* employment. However, most studies have found that the minimum wage does reduce employment. When the minimum wage is increased, some workers do keep their jobs, and their wages go up. However, some workers lose their jobs, or can't find a job in the first place.

Each time a new study comes out, it gives us new evidence, and it forces economists to refine their models. The economic models of the minimum wage have been refined over the years, to consider (1) the fact that the law is sometimes ignored, (2) the fact that not all workers are covered by the minimum-wage law, (3) the fact that some States have higher minimum-wage laws than other States. The economy is very complex, and we can never hope to have a model that will explain every effect of the minimum-wage laws. However, as we continue to gather more information, we can continue to gain a stronger understanding of the effects.

The Assumption of "All Else Equal"

When a natural scientist performs a laboratory experiment, the goal is to look at one relationship in isolation, while holding everything else constant. However, as we said earlier, it is often impossible for economists to perform controlled laboratory experiments. But we still want to concentrate on one influence at a time. Instead of holding everything else constant in a laboratory setting, we have to hold everything else constant in other ways.

In this book, we will develop a number of economic models. In virtually every case, we will employ the *assumption* that all other things are equal. This is called the *ceteris-paribus* assumption. **Ceteris paribus** is the Latin phrase that means "all other things equal".

In fact, all sorts of things are changing every day. If we did not employ the assumption of *ceteris paribus*, the world would be a jumble, and it would be extremely difficult to make sense of things. Here is an example. In Chapter 13, we will see that people who work at dirty, dangerous jobs tend to earn higher wages, *all else equal*. However, this does *not* mean that people who work at dirty, dangerous jobs always earn more than people who work in clean, safe jobs. The reason is that wages are determined by *many* influences, including the skill level that is required on the job. Many of the most unpleasant jobs are also jobs that don't require a lot of skill. So, if we compare a worker in a poultry-processing plant (whose work is very unpleasant) with an accountant (whose work is clean and safe), we find that the accountant earns a higher wage. This is because it takes a lot more education, training, and skill to be an accountant than to be a poultry-plant worker.

Therefore, if we want to test the idea that people who work at dirty, dangerous jobs tend to earn higher wages, *all else equal*, we need to hold constant the skill level of the job. In statistical studies, this is done by including data on a whole host of variables, so we can assess the influence of each variable, while holding constant all of the other influences.

Reality Check:
Interim Review Questions

IR1-4. Which of the following is a normative statement, and which is a positive statement? (a) If it gets too hot in the chicken-growing regions of Arkansas this summer, some chickens will die from the heat, and the price of chicken will increase. (b) Everyone should eat two pounds of chicken per week.

IR1-5. What does *ceteris paribus* mean?

IR1-6. Why is the *ceteris-paribus* assumption important?

WHAT THIS BOOK DOESN'T COVER

This is an introductory textbook. Most of the people who read it are enrolled in a first college course in microeconomics. The book provides an introduction to a very wide range of topics. However, it's impossible to cover every topic in a great deal of depth.

For example, many of the chapters deal with the decisions of business firms. We will discuss how firms set prices (if they are able to set prices), how they decide how many workers to hire, and how they decide how much to produce and sell. But all of this discussion will be at a very basic level. The book will not describe the details of how to develop a business plan, or how to get financing for your new business.

If you want a really complete understanding of how businesses operate, this book is only a start; you will probably also want to take courses in accounting, finance, marketing, management, and business law.

But even though this book doesn't cover *everything*, it still covers a lot of very interesting and important things.

ECONOMICS AND YOU: DECISIONS, DECISIONS, DECISIONS

This chapter began by emphasizing that economics is concerned with how people make decisions, and with how those decisions interact with one another. Then we surveyed some of the questions that can be addressed, using the tools of microeconomics. These include the behavior of large and small businesses, the buying behavior of consumers, the determination of wages and prices, the effects of taxes, tariffs, minimum-wage laws, and much, much more.

The next decision is up to you, the reader. You have to decide whether to read the rest of this book, or whether to devote your time to other activities. It is hoped that this chapter has stimulated your interest. Reading this book is like taking a journey. You'll find lots of interesting things along the way. Here's an invitation: Let's take this journey together.

Chapter Summary

1. Economics is the study of how people use their limited resources to satisfy unlimited wants. Similarly, economics can be defined as the study of how a society chooses to use its scarce resources to produce, exchange, and consume goods and services.

2. Microeconomics is the study of the decisions of households and business firms, and the interactions of those decisions. The actions of households and business firms take place within the context of a system of laws, which are established and enforced by governments. Thus microeconomic decisions are affected by government policies.

3. The tools of microeconomic analysis can be used to study international economics (which deals with international trade, and the effects of policies that interfere with international trade), the economics of industrial organization (which deals with the way in which business firms interact with one another and with their customers, and with government policies to control businesses), and labor economics (which deals with wage rates, participation in the labor force, labor unions, and policies such as minimum-wage laws). The tools of microeconomic analysis can also be used to study public economics (which deals with taxes and government spending) and environmental economics.

4. Macroeconomics is the study of the economy-wide aggregates, such as the overall rate of economic growth, or the overall rate of unemployment, or the overall rate of inflation. Since the macroeconomic aggregates are made from microeconomic pieces, we say that macroeconomics rests on a microeconomic foundation.

5. Every society must make three fundamental choices: (a) What to produce, (b) How to produce, and (c) For whom to produce.

6. Positive economics is concerned with understanding the actual workings of the economy. In principle, positive statements can be proven to be true or false.

7. Normative economics is concerned with what ought to be. Therefore, normative statements involve value judgments. People can disagree about normative judgments, but it is not possible to prove normative statements to be correct or incorrect.

8. Because the economy is very complex, economists use models to represent some of the workings of the economy. These models are tested against data, using statistical techniques. Then the models are refined, and tested again.

9. In economics, it is often impossible to perform controlled laboratory experiments. Therefore, it is especially important to perform thought experiments in which one variable is changed, while holding everything else constant. The assumption that all other things are the same is called the *ceteris-paribus* assumption.

Key Terms

International Economics

Economics of Industrial Organization

Labor Economics

Public Economics

Economics

Microeconomics

Macroeconomics

Environmental Economics

Positive Economics

Normative Economics

Economic Model

The Ceteris-Paribus Assumption

Questions and Problems

QP1-1. Which of these is a subject of microeconomics? Which is a subject of macroeconomics?

a. The overall rate of inflation.
b. The choice made by an individual household, regarding how many tacos to buy.
c. The overall rate of economic growth.
d. The wages paid by high-tech firms.

QP1-2. What is the difference between positive analysis and normative analysis?

QP1-3. What kinds of question are addressed by international economics? What about labor economics? How about the economics of industrial organization?

Appendix to Chapter 1:
A Brief Review of Graphs and Algebra

A few pages ago, we discussed the quantitative skills that are important for success in understanding introductory microeconomics. Here is part of what was said: "Since introductory microeconomics is not rocket science, it does not require sophisticated mathematics. This book does not have any calculus, or matrix algebra, or differential equations. However, we will use some basic algebra. We will also use *lots* of graphs."

Many readers of this book are very well-prepared in basic algebra, and are able to understand graphs. However, some readers may be rusty with algebra, and others may have trouble digesting information that is presented in the form of a graph. This appendix is designed to help anyone who wants to use this book, but it is especially aimed at those who may need to brush up on their quantitative skills. We begin with fractions, proportions, and percentages, and we review how to multiply and divide fractions. Then we discuss the techniques for solving equations. Finally, we consider graphs. If you are strong in these areas, you may want to go through this appendix fairly quickly. However, if your skills are out of shape, it will definitely be worthwhile to go through this appendix in detail.

FRACTIONS, PROPORTIONS, AND PERCENTAGES

In economics, we often relate the size of one quantity to the size of some other quantity. This can be done in different ways. In this book, we will use fractions, proportions, and percentages.

A *fraction* is one number divided by another number. For example, 1/2 and 3/4 are fractions. The number on top of a fraction is called the *numerator*. The number on the bottom is called the *denominator*. For example, in the fraction 1/2, the 1 is the numerator, and the 2 is the denominator.

A *proportion* expresses a fraction in decimal terms. For example, if we were to express 1/2 as a proportion, it would be 0.5. This is because 1/2 is equal to 1 divided by 2. When we divide 1 by 2, we get 0.5. If we were to express 3/4 as a proportion, it would be 0.75.

A *percentage* is a proportion multiplied by 100. For example, if we were to express 0.5 as a percentage, we would multiply 0.5 by 100, which gives us (0.5)x(100) = 50 percent, or 50%. If we were to express 0.75 as a percentage, it would be (0.75)x(100), which is 75 percent, or 75%.

In the preceding paragraphs, we have seen that 1/2 = 0.5 = 50%, and that 3/4 = 0.75 = 75%. Here are some other relationships:

$1/20 = 0.05 = 5\%$
$1/10 = 0.1 = 10\%$
$1/5 = 0.2 = 20\%$
$1/4 = 0.25 = 25\%$
$1/3 = 0.3333 = 33.33\%$ (approximately)
$2/5 = 0.4 = 40\%$
$3/5 = 0.6 = 60\%$
$2/3 = 0.6666 = 66.66\%$ (approximately)
$4/5 = 0.8 = 80\%$

Reality Check:
Interim Review Questions

IR1A-1. Express 0.37 as a percentage.

IR1A-2. Express 9/10 as a proportion, and as a percentage.

MULTIPLICATION AND DIVISION OF FRACTIONS

To multiply one fraction by another, we multiply the two numerators by each other, and multiply the two denominators by each other, and then divide the product of the numerators by the product of the denominators. For example, $(1/3)x(1/2) = (1x1)/(3x2) = 1/6$. Also, $(2/5)x(3/4) = (2x3)/(5x4) = 6/20$. If we divide both the numerator and the denominator of 6/20 by 2, we have $6/20 = (6/2)/(20/2) = 3/10$.

To divide one fraction by another, it is useful to understand the concept of the reciprocal. The *reciprocal* of a fraction is the number which, when multiplied by the fraction, gives one. Thus, since $(1/2)x2 = 1$, we say that two is the reciprocal of one-half. Since $(2/3)x(3/2) = 1$, we say that 3/2 is the reciprocal of 2/3.

Now, let's divide by a fraction. Let's say that we want to divide one by one-half: $1 \div (1/2)$. In this case, the numerator is 1, and the denominator is 1/2. We have seen that 2 is the reciprocal of 1/2. What would happen if we were to multiply both the numerator and the denominator of our expression by 2? This would preserve the value of the expression, because multiplying both the numerator and the denominator by 2 is the same as multiplying the entire expression by $(2/2) = 1$, and multiplying an expression by 1 will preserve its value.

So, our goal is to take $[1 \div 1/2]$, and multiply both the numerator and the denominator by 2. After multiplying by 2, the numerator would be $(1)x(2) = 2$. The denominator would be $(1/2)x(2) = 1$. This simplifies things greatly! When we multiply the denominator by its reciprocal, we get 1.

Since we now have a numerator of 2, and a denominator of 1, we can now divide the numerator by the denominator, which gives us $2 \div 1 = 2$. Therefore, the value of the entire expression is equal to the numerator multiplied by the reciprocal of the denominator: $[1 \div 1/2] = 2$.

Sometimes, this procedure is called "invert and multiply". The more correct way to say it is "multiply by the reciprocal of the fraction in the denominator". Regardless of what we call it, the easiest way to divide by a fraction is to multiply both the numerator and the denominator by the reciprocal of the fraction. For example, $(1/2) \div (3/4) = (1/2)x(4/3)$, because $(4/3)$ is the reciprocal of $(3/4)$. If we carry through with the multiplication, we have $(1/2)x(4/3) = 4/6$. If we then divide both the numerator and denominator by 2, we see that $4/6 = 2/3$.

Reality Check:
Interim Review Questions

IR1A-3. What is the reciprocal of 3/7? What is the reciprocal of 9/4?

IR1A-4. What is $(2/3) \div (3/4)$?

SOLVING EQUATIONS

An Example

In this book, we will sometimes need to solve equations. For example, let's say that we want to solve the following equation for x:

$$z = x/2.$$

To solve for x, we need to get the x all by itself, so that it is no longer divided by 2. Note that another way to write this equation is as follows: $z = (1/2)x$. In the original version, we had $z = x/2$; that is, z is equal to x divided by 2. In the new version, we have $z = (1/2)x$; that is, z is equal to one-half multiplied by x. Dividing by 2 is exactly the same as multiplying by $(1/2)$. Therefore, the way to get x all by itself is to multiply by the reciprocal of $(1/2)$. Since 2 is the reciprocal of $(1/2)$, we multiply both sides of the equation by 2. In that way, x will be multiplied by $(2/2)$. Since $2/2=1$, we will just have x:

$$2z = x(2/2) = x. \text{ Therefore, } x = 2z.$$

We can check our work by using an actual number for z. Let's say that $z = 4$. In that case, we can insert $z = 4$ into the original equation. This gives us $z = x/2$, which becomes $4 = x/2$. We have just found that, if we solve that original equation for x, we get $x = 2z$. If $z = 4$, then $x = 2z = (2)(4) = 8$. Therefore, the original equation ($z = x/2$) becomes $4 = 8/2$, which is indeed correct. This verifies that we have solved the equation correctly.

Example No. 2

Here is another type of equation that we will want to solve on occasion. Let's solve the following for y:

$$z = 3/y.$$

In this case, it will take two steps to solve for y. First, we need to get y out of the denominator of the right-hand side of the equation. Note that another way to write this equation is as follows: $z = (1/y)3$. In the original version, we had $z = 3/y$; that is, z is equal to 3 divided by y. In the new version, we have $z = (1/y)3$; that is, z is equal to 3 multiplied by $(1/y)$. Dividing by y is exactly the same as multiplying by $(1/y)$. Therefore, the way to get y out of the denominator of the right-hand side of the equation is to multiply by the reciprocal of $(1/y)$. Since y is the reciprocal of $(1/y)$, we multiply both sides of the equation by y:

$$zy = 3y/y = 3.$$

Now, we have $zy = 3$. To finish the job of solving for y, we divide both sides of the equation by z:

$$zy/z=3/z,$$

therefore, $y=3/z$.

Example No. 3

Finally, it will sometimes be useful to solve more than one equation at the same time. For example, let's say that we have the following two equations:

(1) $y = 100 – x$

and

(2) $y = 3x.$

In order to solve this system of two equations, we need to recognize that $(100–x)$ and $3x$ are both equal to y. Therefore, we can form a new equation by substituting equation (2) into equation (1):

$$3x = 100 – x.$$

To solve this equation, the first step is to get all of the "x" terms on the same side of the equation. Notice that the right-hand side of the equation contains $(–x)$. If we add x to this, we get $(–x + x) = 0$. Thus one way to get all of the "x" terms on the same side of the equation is to add x to both sides of the equation:

3x + x = 100 − x + x.

This can be simplified to say that 4x = 100. Now, to solve for x, we divide both sides of the equation by 4:

4x/4 = x = 100/4 = 25.

So, x = 25 is the value of x that satisfies both equation (1) and equation (2). To check our work, we can substitute x = 25 into equation (1) and equation (2). In equation (1), we have:

y = 100 − x = 100 − 25 = 75.

In equation (2), we have

y = 3x = (3)(25) = 75.

This verifies that we have done the arithmetic properly. There is only one combination of values of x and y that satisfy both equation (1) and equation (2) at the same time. These values are x = 25 and y = 75.

Reality Check:
Interim Review Questions

IR1A-5. $y = (x/2) + 3$. Solve for x.

IR1A-6. $y = 10/x$. Solve for x.

IR1A-7. (a) $y = 10 − x$

(b) $y = x$

Solve for the values of x and y that satisfy the equations (a) and (b).

GRAPHS

Often, a picture is worth a thousand words. Economists find it useful to represent the relationships between variables in graphs, and we will use a large number of graphs in this book. For example, we will draw graphs of the relationship between the price of a good and the quantity of that good that buyers are willing and able to buy. We will also draw graphs of the relationship between the quantity of a good and the total cost of production. These are just two of the many relationships that we will draw.

This book is printed on pieces of paper that are flat, which means that they are two-dimensional. Therefore, all of the graphs in this book will be in two dimensions. In a two-dimensional graph, we represent the value of one variable on the *horizontal axis*, or *x-axis*, and we represent the value of another variable on the *vertical axis*, or *y-axis*. (Some people have trouble remembering the difference between horizontal and vertical. A good mem-

ory aid involves seeing that "horizontal" has the same root as "horizon". The horizon is flat, and the horizontal axis is flat, whereas the vertical axis goes straight up.)

Let's begin by writing down the values of two variables in a table, and then representing those values with a graph. To keep our focus on graphing techniques, we will use a (very) simple example. Table 1.1 shows the relationship between the number of motorcycles in a parking lot and the number of motorcycle wheels in the parking lot. If zero motorcycles are in the parking lot, then zero motorcycle wheels are in the parking lot. If one motorcycle is in the parking lot, then two motorcycle wheels are in the parking lot. If two motorcycles are in the parking lot, then four motorcycle wheels are in the parking lot. And so on.

Now, let's graph the information from Table 1.1. We put the number of motorcycles on the horizontal axis, or x-axis. We put the number of wheels on the vertical axis, or

Table 1.1 The Relationship Between the Number of Motorcycles and the Number of Motorcycle Wheels

Number of Motorcycles	Number of Motorcycle Wheels
0	0
1	2
2	4
3	6
4	8
5	10
6	12
7	14
8	16

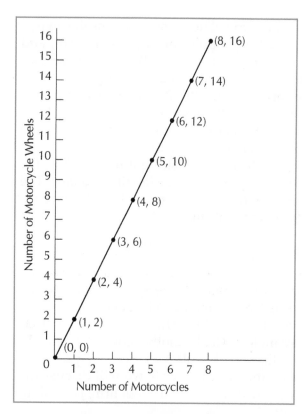

Figure 1.1 A Straight-Line Graph with Positive Slope

The number of motorcycles in a parking lot is on the horizontal axis, and the number of motorcycle wheels is on the vertical axis. Because each motorcycle has two wheels, the value on the vertical axis always increases by two, whenever the value on the horizontal axis increases by one. Therefore, the slope of the line is $(2 \div 1) = 2$.

y-axis. The first point that we graph is the point that corresponds to zero motorcycles and zero wheels. This point is labeled as (0,0) in Figure 1.1. The first number in parentheses stands for the value of the variable on the x-axis, and the second number in parentheses stands for the value of the variable on the y-axis. The point (0,0) is called the *origin*.

Next, we graph the point that corresponds to one motorcycle and two wheels. This point is labeled as (1,2) in Figure 1.1. The rest of the points in Figure 1.1 are graphed in a similar manner.

The Slope of a Line

Every time the number of motorcycles in the parking lot increases by one, the number of motorcycle wheels in the parking lot increases by two. In other words, the ratio of the change in the number of wheels to the change in the number of motorcycles is always two. This is an example of an important concept in graphing. When we interpret graphs, we are often interested in comparing the rate of change of one variable with the rate of change in another variable.

The *slope of a line* is equal to the change in the value of the variable on the y axis, divided by the change in the value of the variable on the x axis. In other words,

$$\text{slope} = \Delta y / \Delta x,$$

where Δ (the Greek letter delta) stands for the change in the value of a variable. Another popular way to define the slope is to say that

$$\text{slope} = \text{rise/run},$$

where the "rise" is the change in the value of the y variable, and the "run" is the change in the value of the x variable.

Let's calculate the slope for the line in Figure 1.1. One point on the line is (0,0), and another point is (1,2). Between these two points, the rise (the change in the value of the y variable) is (2 – 0) = 2. The run (the change in the value of the x variable) is (1 – 0) = 1. If we divide the rise by the run, we see that the slope of the line in Figure 1.1 is 2 ÷ 1 = 2.

In the case of a straight line, such as the one in Figure 1.1, the slope is constant. The slope of this line is 2, regardless of where we look along the line.

The Meaning of "Per"

On many occasions in this book, we will use the word "per". If we were to refer to the example of motorcycles and motorcycle wheels, we could say that there are two wheels *per* motorcycle. In another context, we might say that a basketball star is averaging 22 points *per* game. In Chapter 8, we will discuss the costs incurred by a business firm, *per* unit of output.

In every case, "per" means "divided by". If we have five motorcycles and ten motorcycle wheels, we would divide the number of wheels by the number of motorcycles, and this would show us that there are 10/5 = two wheels per motorcycle. To calculate the number of points per game for the basketball star, we divide the total number of points by the number of games played. Thus if a player has played in 16 games, and has scored a total of 352 points, he or she is scoring 352/16 = 22 points per game. Similarly, to find the firm's costs per unit of output, we divide the total costs by the number of units produced.

The Equation for a Line

We have used a graph to represent the relationship between the number of motorcycles and the number of motorcycle wheels. We can also represent the same information with an equation. In this case, the equation is

$$y = 2x,$$

where y is the y variable (the number of wheels), and x is the x variable (the number of motorcycles).

Table 1.2 has a set of numbers that are similar to those in Table 1.1. The only difference is that, if we use the same x value that was used in Table 1.1, the value of the y variable is always greater in Table 1.2. The difference is always three.

Figure 1.2 is a graph of the numbers in Table 1.2. Once again, we have a straight line, with a slope of 2. However, the y values in Figure 1.2 are always three greater than the corresponding values in Figure 1.1.

It's especially important to focus on the value of y that occurs when the value of x is zero. In Figure 1.2, when x = 0, y = 3. When x = 0, the value of the y variable is called the *y intercept*, or *vertical intercept*.

We can express the line in Figure 1.2 using an equation. In this case, the equation is

$$y = 2x + 3.$$

In fact, any straight line can be expressed by an equation of this form. The general form for the equation for a straight line is

$$y = mx + b,$$

where y is the value of the variable on the vertical axis, m is the slope of the line, x is the value of the variable on the horizontal axis, and b is the vertical intercept. This equation can be used to describe *any* straight line.

Table 1.2	
x value	y value
0	3
1	5
2	7
3	9
4	11
5	13
6	15
7	17
8	19

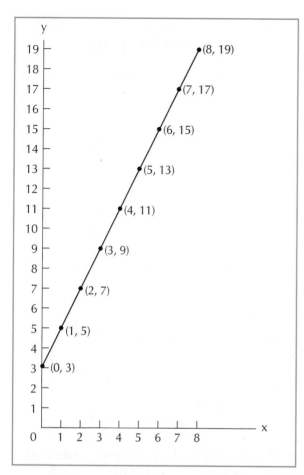

Figure 1.2 Another Straight-Line Graph with Positive Slope

This graph is similar to the graph in Figure 1.1. In each of these graphs, the slope of the line is 2. The difference is that the vertical intercept is zero in Figure 1.1, while the vertical intercept is three in Figure 1.2.

A Straight Line with Negative Slope

In Tables 1.1 and 1.2, when the x value increases, the y value also increases. As a result, the graphs in Figures 1.1 and 1.2 slope upward as we move from left to right across the diagram. However, Table 1.3 shows the relationship between two variables, in which an increase in the x variable is accompanied by a *decrease* in the y variable.

The numbers in Table 1.3 are graphed in Figure 1.3. Since there is an inverse rela-

Table 1.3

x value	y value
0	40
1	36
2	32
3	28
4	24
5	20
6	16
7	12
8	8

tionship between the x variable and the y variable in Table 1.3, the graph in Figure 1.3 slopes downward as we move from left to right across the diagram. In Table 1.3, whenever the x variable increases by one, the y variable decreases by 4. Therefore, the slope of the line is $\Delta y / \Delta x = -4/1 = -4$. When x = 0 in Table 1.3 and Figure 1.3, y = 40. Therefore, the vertical intercept of this line is 40. If we take the slope of –4 and the vertical intercept of 40, and put them into the equation for a straight line, the equation for this line is

$$y = -4x + 40.$$

Curved Lines

So far, all of our graphs have been straight lines, in which the slope does not change. However, many relationships cannot be graphed as straight lines. An example can be found in Table 1.4 and Figure 1.4. Earlier in this chapter, we discussed the relationship between age and height. Table 1.4 shows this relationship for Kelly Morrison, and Figure 4 is a graph of the information in Table 1.4. At birth, Kelly's height is 21 inches. She grows rapidly during childhood. However, the number of inches by which she grows is not constant. In the first year (between birth and age 1), she grows from 21 inches to 27 inches, which is an increase of (27 – 21) = 6 inches. In the second year, she

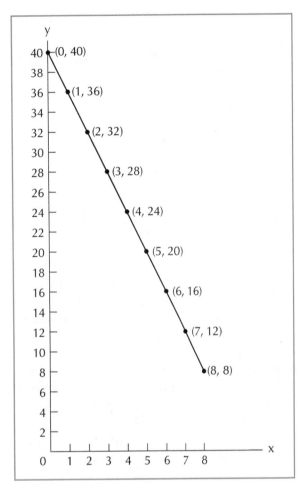

**Figure 1.3 A Straight-Line Graph
with Negative Slope**

In this graph, whenever the value of the variable on the horizontal axis *increases* by one, the value of the variable on the vertical axis *decreases* by four. Therefore, the slope of the line is (–4 ÷ 1) = –4.

**Table 1.4 The Relationship Between Age
and Height for Kelly Morrison**

Age	Height (in inches)
0 (birth)	21
1	27
2	33
3	37
4	40
5	43
6	46
7	48
8	52
9	54
10	56
11	58
12	62
13	66
14	67
15	67
16	67

grows from 27 inches to 33 inches, which is an increase of (33 – 27) = 6 inches for the second year in a row. However, in the third year, she grows from 33 inches to 37 inches, which is an increase of only (37 – 33) = 4 inches. Therefore, the slope of the graph in Figure 1.4 is not constant.

In Figures 1.1, 1.2, and 1.3, we can calculate the slope at any point, and we will get the same number, because the slope is constant. However, in Figure 1.4, the slope changes. This

means that we must be careful to say *where* we are calculating the slope.

We have seen that Kelly grew by six inches in her first year of life. If we calculate the slope of the line in Figure 1.4 that corresponds to that first year of life, we find that the slope is $\Delta y / \Delta x$ = (27 – 21)/(1 – 0) = 6/1 = 6. Thus the slope of the graph in Figure 1.4 reveals exactly the same information that is in Table 1.4: Between birth and the age of 1, Kelly grew at a rate of 6 inches per year. Table 1.4 also indicates that, between age 10 and age 11, Kelly grew from 56 inches to 58 inches. This is a rate of growth of 2 inches per year. If we calculate the slope of the line in Figure 1.4 that corresponds to this part of her life, we have $\Delta y / \Delta x$ = (58 – 56)/(11 – 10) = 2/1 = 2. Since Kelly grew six inches in her first year, but only two inches between age 10 and age 11, it follows that the slope of the graph in Figure 1.4 is not constant. In other words, the graph is not a straight line.

Kelly reaches her adult height at age 14. After that, she doesn't grow any more. This is reflected in Figure 1.4, where the graph becomes horizontal after the age of 14 is reached. If we

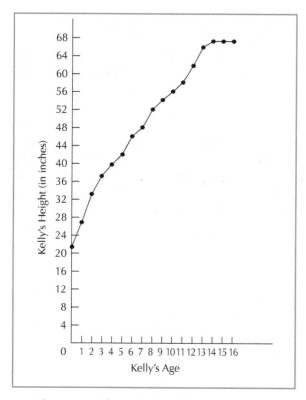

Figure 1.4 The Relationship Between Age and Height for Kelly Morrison

The graphs in Figures 1.1 through 1.3 have all been straight lines. However, this graph of the age-height relationship is not a straight line, since Kelly does not grow by the same number of inches in every year. Kelly eventually stops growing, so that the slope is zero after the age of 14.

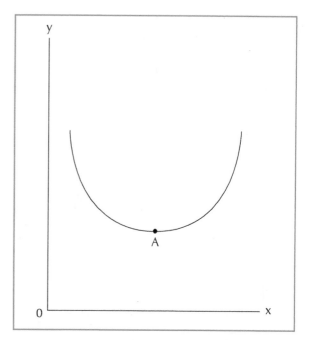

Figure 1.5 A Graph of a "U-Shaped" Curve

At low values of the variable on the horizontal axis, this curve has negative slope. (In other words, the curve slopes downward as we move from left to right.) By point A, however, the curve flattens out, and has a slope of zero. To the right of point A, the curve has positive slope. The value of the y variable is minimized at point A.

were to calculate the slope of the line after Kelly reaches her adult height, we would have $\Delta y / \Delta x = 0 =$ zero. When the variable on the y axis is unchanging, the slope of the line is zero.

Figures 1.5 and 1.6 show two other lines, of kinds that we will often see in this book. Figure 1.5 shows what we might call a "U-shaped" curve. At first, at low values of the x variable, the slope of the line in Figure 1.5 is negative. (In other words, at low values of the x variable in Figure 1.5, an *increase* in the x variable is associated with a *decrease* in the y variable.) But then the curve flattens out. The curve reaches its minimum point at point A.

At that point, the slope of the line is zero. (In other words, at point A, the value of the y variable is not changing.) As we move to the right of point A, the slope of the line is positive. (In other words, at higher values of the x variable in Figure 1.5, an *increase* in the x variable is associated with an *increase* in the y variable.)

Figure 1.6 is what we might call an "inverse-U-shaped" curve. At low values of the x variable, the slope of the line in Figure 1.6 is positive. But then the curve flattens out, and reaches its maximum point at point B. At point B in Figure 1.6, the slope of the line is zero, just as it was zero at point A in Figure 1.5. As we move to the right of point B, the slope of the line is negative.

Note that the y variable reaches its *minimum* at point A in Figure 1.5, and the

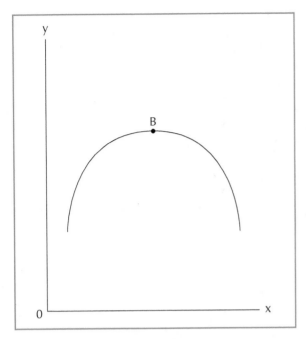

**Figure 1.6 A Graph
of an "Inverse-U-Shaped" Curve**

At low values of the variable on the horizontal axis, this curve has positive slope. (In other words, the curve slopes upward as we move from left to right.) By point B, however, the curve flattens out, and has slope of zero. To the right of point B, the curve has negative slope. The value of the y variable is maximized at point B.

y variable reaches its *maximum* at point B in Figure 1.6. At each of these points, the slope of the curve is zero. Whenever the slope of a curve is equal to zero, the variable on the y axis is either maximized or minimized.

Two Intersecting Lines

Earlier in this appendix, we solved two equations simultaneously. The two equations were

(1) $y = 100 - x$

and

(2) $y = 3x$.

We used algebra to find that $x = 25$ and $y = 75$ are the values that satisfy both equation (1)

and equation (2). We can also use graphs to find these values of x and y.

In Figure 1.7, we draw graphs of equations (1) and (2). The vertical intercept of equation (1) is 100, and its slope is –1. The vertical intercept of equation (2) is zero (which means that the graph of equation (2) goes through the origin), and its slope is 3. Since equation (1) has negative slope and equation (2) has positive slope, it is not surprising that the lines cross. They cross at the point (25,75). Thus, the two lines cross at the unique values of x and y that satisfy both equations at the same time. In other words, we can solve the system of two equations in two ways—we can use algebra, or we can draw graphs and find the point at which the two lines cross.

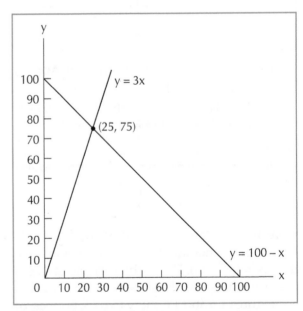

Figure 1.7 Graphs of Two Intersecting Lines

The equation for the upward-sloping line is $y = 3x$. The equation for the downward-sloping line is $y = 100 - x$. We can use algebra to find that $x = 25$ and $y = 75$ are the values of x and y that satisfy both equations at the same time. By drawing the graphs carefully, we can see that the two lines cross where $x = 25$ and $y = 75$. Therefore, the intersection of two lines gives us a graphical representation of the values of x and y that satisfy both equations at the same time.

Finding the Areas
of Rectangles and Triangles

On several occasions in this book, we will represent economic information by the area of a rectangle or the area of a triangle. Figure 1.8 shows a rectangle whose vertices are A, B, C, and D. The coordinates of these vertices are A: (2,2), B: (2,6), C: (7,6), D: (7,2). Figure 1.8 is drawn with a grid of small squares. The area of each small square is one square unit. Since the rectangle ABCD consists of 20 small squares, it must be that the area of ABCD is 20 square units.

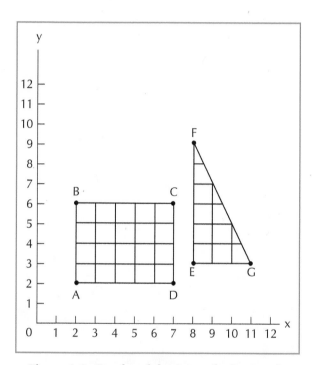

Figure 1.8 Graphs of the Area of a Rectangle and the Area of a Triangle

The height of the rectangle ABCD is 4, and the base of the rectangle is 5. The area of the rectangle is equal to the base multiplied by the height. Therefore, the area of the rectangle is (4)(5) = 20. The height of the triangle EFG is 6, and the base of the triangle is 3. The area of the triangle is one-half times the base times the height. Therefore, the area of the triangle is 0.5(3)(6) = 0.5(18) = 9.

However, we don't have to count squares to calculate the area of a rectangle. *The easier way to calculate the area of the rectangle is to multiply the base of the rectangle by its height:*

Area of Rectangle = bh,

where b = base of the rectangle, and h = height of the rectangle.

The base of the rectangle is (7–2) = 5, and the height is (6–2) = 4. Therefore, the area of the rectangle is (5)x(4) = 20.

Figure 1.8 also includes a triangle, which is defined by the vertices E, F, and G. The coordinates of these vertices are E: (8,3), F: (8,9), G: (11,3). Once again, it's possible to determine the area by counting squares. By counting squares (and parts of squares), we can determine that the area of the triangle is nine square units. However, there is once again an easier way to find the area of the triangle. The easier way to calculate the area of the triangle is to multiply the base by the height, and then divide by two: (or multiply by (1/2), which is exactly the same as dividing by 2):

Area of Triangle = 1/2 bh,

where b = base of the triangle, and h = height of the triangle. The base of the triangle is (11 – 8) = 3, and the height of the triangle is (9 – 3) = 6. Therefore, the area of the triangle is (1/2)bh = (1/2)(3)(6) = 9.

Reality Check:
Interim Review Questions

IR1A-8. Find the slope of the line that is defined by the points (1,3) and (2,7).

IR1A-9. Find the slope of the line that is defined by the points (3,6) and (5,4).

IR1A-10. A rectangle has height of 10 and base of 8. What is the area of the rectangle?

IR1A-11. A triangle has height of 9 and base of 4. What is the area of the triangle?

Chapter 2

Opportunity Cost 机会成本
and Comparative Advantage 比较利益

ECONOMICS AND YOU:
SHOULD YOU BUILD YOUR OWN HOUSE?

About two-thirds of American households own their own homes. You may not own a home now, but there is probably a good chance that you will own one, sooner or later. Most of the time, when a family acquires a home for the first time, they either buy an existing home, or they buy a newly built home from a builder. Some people do build their own homes, but that doesn't happen often.

Why? Why don't most people build their own homes? The reason is that, for most people, it is cheaper to let someone else build the home than to build it yourself. Consider Anthony Varelli, who is a marketing manager for a consumer-products company. Anthony knows just about everything there is to know about toothpaste. He can quote you all of the latest sales figures for his company's five brands of toothpaste, for every region of the country, for the past five years. He knows which brands of toothpaste appeal to women, which to men, and which to teenagers. He makes $90,000 per year.

Now, Anthony is a smart guy, and he probably *could* build his own house. If he were to spend several years at it, he could probably develop his skills in carpentry, and plumbing, and masonry, and electrical wiring, and roofing, to the point where he could build a house. But what would it cost him to do so? To build his own house, Anthony would have to quit his job for several years. Let's say he could build a nice house in three years. If so, then he would have to give up his salary in the amount of ($90,000 per year)x(3 years) = $270,000. And that's before he even buys the land and materials for the house. Let's say the materials cost $30,000, and the land costs $50,000. Then, the total cost of the house would be $30,000 for materials, plus $50,000 for land, plus $270,000 for the cost of Anthony's time. This comes to a total of $350,000.

On the other hand, if Anthony were to buy his home from a builder, he could get it for $200,000, and the workmanship would be better than he could have done by himself. It makes sense for Anthony to buy the house, rather than build it himself, because it's cheaper to do so. It's cheaper for Anthony to specialize in marketing toothpaste, and to let other people specialize in carpentry, plumbing, and roofing.

That's the way it is for most people. Most people specialize in one profession. For example, the author of this book specializes in teaching and research in economics. Relatively speaking, I am much better at economics teaching and research than at growing food, or making clothes, or producing automobiles. Instead of growing my own food, and making my own clothes, and building my own car, I let other people specialize in those activities. The farmers who grow the food that ends up on my table are relatively good at growing food, so they specialize in that activity. The auto workers who built my car are relatively good at making cars, so they specialize in that activity.

All over the world, we see people specializing in the activities at which they are relatively highly skilled. Steph Curry and LeBron James specialize in playing basketball. Tom Hanks and Julia Roberts specialize in acting in motion pictures. Beyoncé specializes in one kind of music, and the New York Philharmonic Orchestra specializes in another kind. If it weren't for this specialization, the world would be a much poorer place, because everyone would have to provide everything for himself or herself.

In fact, it's hard even to imagine a world in which people only consume the goods that they themselves have produced. In such a world, every person would have to grow or gather his or her own food, make his or her own clothes, and provide his or her own shelter. Modern technologies would be out of the question, because modern technologies could never have been invented without the cooperation of large numbers of people. The best way to describe a world in which all people consume only the goods that they have produced is "poor, very, very poor".

Specialization is extremely important to the modern economy. When people specialize a lot, it's necessary for them to exchange goods and services with each other. The exchanges made between people who specialize in different activities are also extremely important. Specialization and exchange are absolutely essential for a rising standard of living. In this chapter, we will begin to develop an understanding of the workings of specialization and exchange. Before this chapter is over, you will have an idea of why specialization and exchange are so beneficial to the economy, and you will have developed a vocabulary for thinking about these concepts.

OPPORTUNITY COST

In the introduction to this chapter, we discussed what it would cost for Anthony Varelli to build his own home. The biggest part of the cost was associated with the fact that, in order to build a house, he would have to quit his job. As a result, if he were to build the house himself, he would have to give up his salary for three years. In order to do one thing, he would have to give up something else.

In order to do one thing, we all have to give up something else. If you spend an hour reading this book, then you won't be able to spend the hour playing football. If you stay up late watching TV, you won't have as much time for sleep. If you spend $5 on a burger, fries, and a drink, you won't have those five dollars to spend on a movie download, or a pair of underwear, or the lunch special at a Chinese restaurant. If you spend $10,000 on college tuition, you won't have those ten thousand dollars to spend on something else.

Again and again, we bump into the same idea. Our resources are scarce. If we devote a portion of our resources to one activity, or one purchase, then those resources will not be available for another activity, or another purchase. The poet Robert Frost had it right: "Two roads diverged in a yellow wood, And sorry I could not travel both . . . ". The narrator of that poem could take one road, or he could take the other, but he could not take both. Consequently, it is necessary to make choices. We must make choices because our resources are scarce. This idea is so fundamental to economics that we put it in our definition of economics, in Chapter 1.

In Frost's poem "The Road Not Taken", the narrator makes a choice. He chooses the road less traveled. As a result, he doesn't get to take the other road. It would have been nice to do both, but it just wasn't possible. And at the end of the poem, it's clear that the narrator believes he has made the right decision. "Two roads diverged in a wood, and I, I took the one less traveled by, and that has made all the difference."

We do have to make choices, but that isn't a reason for sadness. Doing everything is not a reasonable goal. Instead, our goal should be to do the best we can, with the resources that are available to us. To do the best we can, we have to make the correct choices.

Economics is all about finding ways to make the correct choices. How do we do that? How do we make the right choices instead of the wrong ones? The economist's idea is to compare the benefits and costs of the decisions that we might possibly make. If the benefits of one course of action are greater than the costs, then we should take that course of action. However, if the costs are greater than the benefits, we shouldn't do it.

Of course, comparing the benefits and costs is easier said than done. Much of this book is concerned with how to identify and quantify the relevant benefits and costs. The key is to include *all* of the relevant benefits, and *all* of the relevant costs. If we ignore some of the benefits, or if we ignore some of the costs, then we will be more likely to make bad decisions. Similarly, if we include some benefits and costs that should *not* be included, we will be more likely to make wrong decisions.

One of the big goals of this chapter is to begin helping you to understand how to think about including *all* of the relevant costs. We want to define costs in such a way that they provide a good guide for making correct decisions.

Economists have a phrase that captures the idea that, by doing one thing, we must give up another thing. The phrase is "opportunity cost". The *opportunity cost* of one activity is the value of the next-best alternative. If you spend an hour watching TV, the amount of time available for other activities will be reduced by one hour. Thus, the opportunity cost of spending an extra hour watching TV is the value of the next-best activity to which you could have devoted that hour. If the next-best alternative to an hour of TV is an hour of playing volleyball, then the opportunity cost of spending the hour in front of the TV set is that you give up the possibility of spending that hour on the volleyball court.

Often, it is easy to measure opportunity cost in dollars. What is the opportunity cost of spending $40 on a pair of jeans? The opportunity cost is that those $40 will not be available to be spent on something else. Forty dollars can buy five movie tickets, or eight burrito combos, or any number of other things. Therefore, it probably doesn't make sense to try to figure out the next-best way to spend the $40. Instead, we just say that the opportunity cost of spending $40 on a pair of jeans is $40.

However, there are some circumstances under which it is not so easy to measure opportunity cost in dollars. For instance, let's say you decide to go to a Taylor Swift concert. (If you don't like Taylor Swift, substitute Kanye West, or Carrie Underwood, or U-2, or whoever.) Certainly, one big part of the cost will be the price of the ticket. However, tickets for popular musical groups often sell out very quickly. Because of this, the really devoted fans often spend a long time waiting in line for tickets. For example, let's say that you decide to spend the night outside the box office, waiting for the office to open.

This long wait is certainly a part of the opportunity cost of going to the concert. (Presumably, if you did not go to the concert, you would not have spent the night sleeping on the sidewalk next to the box office.) But it may not be easy to put a dollar value on spending the night sleeping on the sidewalk. In fact, the opportunity cost may vary greatly from person to person. If you have to be at work the next morning, then spending the night on the sidewalk might be very costly because it might affect your performance on the job. If you fall asleep at your desk and get fired from your job, then the concert will have been very expensive indeed. In addition, sleeping on the sidewalk isn't the most comfortable thing to do. You will probably be a little bit stiff when you wake up. The older you are, the more likely you are to have sore muscles the next day.

Based on the preceding paragraph, we can develop an understanding of one important fact about the people who spend the night waiting in line for concert tickets: Most of these people are young. Young people are less likely to have a steady job, and they won't be as sore in the morning. Therefore, we can say that the opportunity cost of spending the night in line for tickets is likely to be smaller for a young person than for a middle-aged or elderly person.

We can put opportunity costs into a variety of categories. One good way to deal with opportunity costs is to divide them into the "explicit" costs and the "implicit" costs. An explicit cost involves an actual financial transaction, by cash or check or credit card or debit card. In the case of an explicit cost, it would be possible for one person to issue a receipt to another. In our example of the concert, the money spent to buy the concert ticket is an explicit cost. On the other hand, an implicit cost does not involve an outright financial transaction. In the concert example, the cost of waiting in line is an implicit cost. Even though the time spent waiting in line imposes a very real cost on the individual, no money changes hands, and no one issues a receipt. Explicit costs are easy to measure, because they are already in dollars. Implicit costs can be measured (at least in principle) but it may be difficult to do so.

So far, we have identified two opportunity costs of the concert. You have to spend time waiting in line for tickets, and, when you get to the front of the line, you have to spend money to buy the tickets. There are other opportunity costs, as well. If the concert is a long way from your home, you will have to drive there, or perhaps take a train or bus. Either way, it will take money (for gasoline, or train fare, or bus fare), and it will take time. Once you get to the concert site, you may need to pay for parking. And, of course, when you are actually at the concert, there is an opportunity cost of your time. You could have done something else.

In *Real Economics for Real People 2.1*, we discuss the opportunity cost of going to college.

Reality Check:
Interim Review Questions

IR2-1. What is the opportunity cost of going to a professional baseball game?

IR2-2. What is the opportunity cost of spending $15 on a bouquet of flowers?

Real Economics for Real People 2.1: How Much Does It Cost to Go to College?

Erin Van Nuys is trying to decide whether to go to college. She's been accepted at a publicly supported college that offers her in-state tuition. She gets a letter saying that the estimated cost of tuition, books, room, and food is $25,000 for the year.

But Erin wonders whether these figures really represent the true opportunity cost of spending a year at college. The answer is that some of the "costs" are true opportunity costs of college, and some are not. In addition, there is at least one important opportunity cost that is *not* included in the numbers.

The best way for Erin to think about whether an item is an opportunity cost of college is to compare (a) what she would do if she goes to college, with (b) what she would do if she doesn't go to college. On this basis, it is reasonable to include tuition as a cost of going to college. After all, Erin's family would not choose to write a big check to the college every semester, unless she were registered for classes.

The same is true for most of the books that Erin will have to buy. Of course, she might have bought a few books, even if she weren't attending college. But it's likely that she would not have bought many of the books, except for the fact that they are required for one of her college courses. For example, let's say that Erin would spend $800 per year on books if she were to go to college, but only $100 per year on books if she were not to go to college. In this case, the opportunity cost of going to college would include $(800 − 100) = $700 for books.

The official numbers also include expenses for room and food, but it's highly questionable whether these expenses should be included among the true opportunity costs of college. Let's begin by thinking about the food expenses. Very few people can function effectively for more than a few days without eating some food. Regardless of whether she goes to college, Erin will have to eat. Consequently, for the most part, it is *not* appropriate to think of food expenses as a true opportunity cost of going to college. For one reason or another, it's possible that food expenses could be a little higher at college. In this case, the true opportunity cost of college should include the *difference* between the cost of food at college and the cost of the food that Erin would have eaten if she had not gone to college. For example, let's say that Erin would spend $5000 per year on food if she were to go to college, and $4000 per year on food if she doesn't go to college. In that case, the food portion of the opportunity cost of going to college would be $(5000 − 4000) = $1000.

On the other hand, it's possible that the cost of food at college will be a little *less* than the food costs that Erin would have incurred, if she had not gone to college. This is especially likely to be true if Erin's home is in a high-cost area. In this case, the difference between the two costs would be a *negative* opportunity cost of going to college.

If the cost of food at college is exactly the same as the cost of food away from college, then the food portion of the opportunity cost of college would be zero.

Similar reasoning applies to Erin's room expenses. Regardless of whether she goes to college, she will want to have a roof over her head. If the monthly cost of renting an apartment at college is the same as the cost of renting an apartment in Erin's hometown, then room should not be included as a true opportunity cost of college. If it costs a little more to rent an apartment at college, then the *difference* between the college rental and the hometown rental would be a true opportunity cost. If it costs less to rent an apartment at college than in the hometown, then the room-rent portion of the opportunity cost of college would actually be negative.

Finally, we come to the most important cost of all, even though it is *not* included in the estimate of $25,000. If Erin doesn't go to college, she can get a full-time job for $12 per hour. At 40 hours per week, and 50 weeks per year, this job will pay $24,000 for the year. If Erin goes to college, she will only be able to work part time. Her earnings for the year will be $4000 if she goes to college. Therefore, if Erin goes to college, her *foregone earnings* will be $(24,000 – 4000) = $20,000. **Foregone earnings** are the additional wages and salaries that could be earned if a person were to go to work right after high school, instead of going to college. The foregone earnings are a true opportunity

cost of going to college. If Erin doesn't go to college, she will definitely earn more during the years when she would have been enrolled.

The remarkable thing about foregone earnings is that they are the largest cost of all for some students, in spite of the fact that they aren't included in the official numbers on college costs. The problem is that the official numbers are not based on the idea of opportunity cost. Instead, they are just an accounting of the explicit, out-of-pocket costs of going to college. For students at the more expensive private colleges, the out-of-pocket costs of college can be more than foregone earnings. However, for students at less expensive institutions, foregone earnings may be the biggest cost of all.

THE PRODUCTION-POSSIBILITIES FRONTIER

Economists have a graphical tool for representing scarcity, choice, and opportunity cost. The *production-possibilities frontier* is a graphical representation of the combinations of outputs that can be produced, if all of the available resources are used as well as possible.

A Straight-Line Production-Possibilities Frontier

We will start with a very simple production-possibilities frontier (or p.p.f. for short). Figure 2.1 shows the p.p.f. for red flannel shirts and green flannel shirts, which are produced at a factory owned by the Red Green Company. In this graph, we put red shirts on the horizontal axis and green shirts on the vertical axis. (However, this is not an important choice. We could have put green shirts on the horizontal axis and red shirts on the vertical, and we would still have been able to develop the same ideas.)

This is an especially simple example, because red shirts and green shirts use virtu-

ally identical resources. They both use cotton cloth. They both require that the cloth must be cut and sewn, and buttons added. The only difference is that red shirts use red dye, while green shirts use green dye. If the shirt factory is to change from producing red shirts to producing green shirts, it's only necessary to flip a switch.

If the factory devotes all of its resources to producing red shirts, it can produce 100 red shirts per hour. Of course, if it devotes all of its resources to producing red shirts, it won't be able to produce any green shirts. Thus, one of the points on the production-possibilities frontier is (100,0). At the other extreme, the factory could devote all of its resources to producing green shirts. In this case, it would produce 100 green shirts and no red shirts. Therefore, another point on the p.p.f. is (0,100). Let's say the Red Green Company is currently producing only green shirts, which corresponds to the point (0,100) in Figure 2.1. If it wants to produce one red shirt, it can do so, but it will have to give up production of one green shirt.

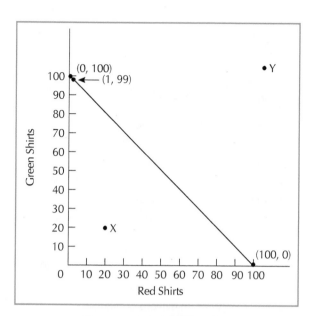

Figure 2.1 A Straight-Line Production-Possibilities Frontier

Green shirts and red shirts use the same resources and technology. As a result, the trade-off between red shirts and green shirts is always at the same rate, and the production-possibilities frontier is a straight line. The slope of the frontier is –1, which means that the opportunity cost of one red shirt is one green shirt. Point X is below the frontier, which means that producing at X involves waste, or inefficiency. Point Y is above the frontier. This means that, given the current resources and technology, point Y is unattainable, or infeasible.

Thus another point on the p.p.f. is the point (1,99), representing one red shirt and 99 green shirts. If the company wants to produce more red shirts, it can do so. But producing more red shirts means that the company must produce fewer green shirts.

In fact, every time the company increases its output of red shirts by one shirt, it must reduce its output of green shirts by one shirt. In other words, the opportunity cost of one additional red shirt is one green shirt. The reverse is also true: The opportunity cost of one additional green shirt is one red shirt.

Opportunity Cost and the Slope of the P.P.F. The p.p.f. for red shirts and green shirts is a downward-sloping line. This illustrates the

concept of scarcity. The available resources are limited. When we are on the p.p.f., the only way to get more of one good is to give up some of another good.

The slope of any line is the change in the quantity on the vertical axis, divided by the change in the quantity on the horizontal axis. In this case, the slope of the p.p.f. is the change in the number of green shirts, divided by the change in the number of red shirts. Let's calculate the slope of the p.p.f. as we go from (0, 100) to (1, 99). The number of green shirts *decreases* from 100 to 99. Therefore, the change in the number of green shirts is $99 - 100 = -1$. The number of red shirts *increases* from 0 to 1, so that the change in the number of red shirts is $1 - 0 = +1$. Thus, the slope of the p.p.f. is $(-1/+1) = -1$. The p.p.f. doesn't just slope downward in Figure 2.1; its slope is exactly –1. This is not a coincidence. Whenever the number of red shirts increases by one, the number of green shirts must decrease by one. Therefore, the slope must be –1.

There is a close connection between the slope of the p.p.f. and the opportunity costs. For any production-possibilities frontier, the slope of the p.p.f. is the negative of the opportunity cost of the good on the horizontal axis. The opportunity cost of the good on the horizontal axis is measured in terms of the number of units of the good on the vertical axis that must be given up, in order to get one more unit of the good on the horizontal axis.

In the case of a straight-line p.p.f., like the one in Figure 2.1, the slope is always the same. No matter where we evaluate the slope in Figure 2.1, we will always find its value to be –1. However, in the next section, we will see that it is common for production-possibilities frontiers to be curved. When the p.p.f. is not a straight line, the slope will change as we move along the frontier.

Waste. By definition, every point on the p.p.f. represents a combination of outputs that can be produced, *if all of the available resources are used as well as possible.* Another way to say this is to say that, if we are on the p.p.f., we are producing "efficiently". Of course, any point *under* the p.p.f. can also be produced, but a point under the p.p.f involves waste, or inefficiency. For example, in Figure 2.1, point X involves only 20 green shirts and 20 red shirts. Thus, at point X, a total of (20 + 20) = 40 shirts are produced, whereas 100 shirts are produced at any of the points on the p.p.f. How could we end up at a point like X? It might happen because the factory manager makes lots of mistakes. Or it might happen because some of the workers don't come to work on time, or because workers are not assigned to the jobs that make the best use of their skills. In any event, a point below the p.p.f. involves incomplete or inefficient use of the available resources.

Figure 2.1 also includes point Y, which is *above* the p.p.f. With today's resources and technology, point Y simply cannot be produced. A point like Y may be available at some time in the future, but for today it is unattainable, or infeasible. 做不到的

不行的.

A Curved Production-Possibilities Frontier

We started with the simple case of a straight-line p.p.f., because it is easy to show some important concepts with a straight p.p.f. But you should understand that the straight-line p.p.f. is a very special case. A straight-line p.p.f occurs when the two goods use the same resources and technology. It is much more common to consider goods that do *not* use the same resources and technology. When the production processes are different, we will get a curved p.p.f.

To illustrate a curved p.p.f., we use an example in which the two goods are wine and wool. These two goods definitely *don't* use the same resources and technology. Some resources are better suited for producing wine, while other resources are better suited for pro-

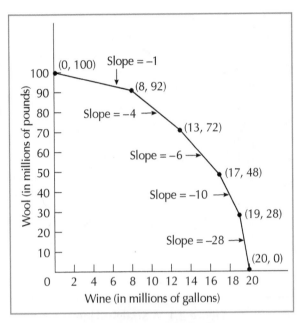

Figure 2.2 A Curved Production-Possibilities Frontier

Since wine and wool use different resources and technologies, the production-possibilities frontier is bowed outward, or concave with respect to the origin. The absolute value of the slope of the frontier increases as we move downward and to the right. This means that the production-possibilities frontier exhibits the Principle of Increasing Opportunity Cost: As we increase the amount of wine, the opportunity cost of further increases in wine production will become greater and greater.

ducing wool. People with nimble fingers are better suited for producing wine because they can pick grapes quickly, without doing a lot of damage to the grapes. On the other hand, big, strong guys are better suited for producing wool, because they can wrestle a sheep to the floor at shearing time. Some soils and climates are better for growing grapes, while other soils and climates are better for raising sheep.

Figure 2.2 is a p.p.f. for wine and wool. We have put wine on the horizontal axis and wool on the vertical axis. Once again, however, these choices don't make any difference. We could show the same information with wool on the horizontal axis and wine on the vertical. If all of the available resources are devoted to producing wool, 100 million pounds per year can be produced. Of course, if all of the available resources are devoted to producing wool, then no wine can be produced. Thus, one of the points on the p.p.f. in Figure 2.2 is (0,100). (We are using one million pounds as our unit of measurement for wool.)

If all of the available resources are devoted to producing wool, it would be necessary to produce wool with many resources that are really much better suited to producing wine. If we produce only wool, that means we would use nimble-fingered grape pickers to wrestle with sheep. We would take hillsides that are well suited for growing grapes, and use them for raising sheep. Consequently, if we decide to produce the first few units of wine, we would use the resources that are relatively best for producing wine. Therefore, in order to produce the first few units of wine, we won't have to give up a relatively large amount of wool. Figure 2.2 shows that if we give up eight million pounds of wool (so that production of wool is now 92 million pounds, instead of 100 million pounds), we get 8 million gallons of wine.

What is the opportunity cost of these first units of wine? To get 8 million gallons of wine, we have to give up 8 million pounds of wool. Therefore, the opportunity cost of an additional 8 million gallons of wine is 8 million pounds of wool. We can express this in the form of an equation:

8 wine = 8 wool

In this equation, wine is measured in millions of gallons, and wool is measured in millions of pounds, so we can say that 8 units of wine are equivalent to 8 units of wool.

The equation shows us the opportunity cost of *eight* units of wine. If we divide both sides of this equation by 8, we can get the opportunity cost of *one* unit of wine:

(8/8)wine = (8/8)wool ⇒ 1 wine = 1 wool

Note that the opportunity cost of one additional unit of wine is one unit of wool, and the opportunity cost of one additional unit of wool is one unit of wine. This isn't an accident. In fact, for any two goods, *the opportunity cost of good A in terms of good B is the reciprocal of the opportunity cost of good B in terms of good A.*

So far, we have seen the movement from the point (0,100) to the point (8,92) in Figure 2.2. Now, what happens if we want to produce *even more* wine? In producing the first 8 million gallons of wine, we have already used the resources that are best suited for wine production. The people with the nimblest fingers, and the land with the best climate and soil for growing grapes, and the best chemists, have all been pulled from wool production into wine production. If we want even more wine, we will have to begin using resources that aren't quite so well suited for wine production. The next point identified in Figure 2.2 is (13,72), which means that it is possible to produce 13 million gallons of wine and 72 million pounds of wool. We get an additional (13 – 8) = 5 units of wine. To get those units of wine, we have to give up an additional (92 – 72) = 20 units of wool. The opportunity cost of an additional five units of wine is 20 units of wool.

Thus in this region of the production-possibilities frontier, the opportunity cost of 5 units of wine is 20 units of wool. As before, we can express this relationship in the form of an equation:

5 wine = 20 wool

If we divide both sides of this equation by 5, we can get the opportunity cost of one unit of wine:

(5/5)wine = (20/5)wool ⇒ 1 wine = 4 wool

Thus, in this portion of the production-possibilities frontier, the opportunity cost of one additional unit of wine is 4 units of wool.

Let's recap what we have seen so far: For the first few units of wine, the opportunity cost was *one* unit of wool per unit of wine. For the next few units of wine, the opportunity cost was *four* units of wool per unit of wine. The opportunity cost of an additional unit of wine increases as we produce more and more wine. As we go to other points on the p.p.f. in Figure 2.2, we see that this trend continues. The opportunity cost of an additional unit of wine increases to six units of wool, and then to 10 units of wool, and finally to 28 units of wool.

The p.p.f. in Figure 2.2 has the usual shape for a production-possibilities frontier. In most cases, p.p.f.'s are bowed outward, or "concave with respect to the origin". This shape is a result of the fact that wine and wool (unlike green shirts and red shirts) use different resources and different technologies. When the p.p.f. has this shape, we say it obeys the *Principle of Increasing Opportunity Cost*. The **Principle of Increasing Opportunity Cost** (also known as the Law of Increasing Opportunity Cost) says that the opportunity cost of producing one additional unit of a good will increase, as we produce more and more of the good.

In other words, the following three statements all mean the same thing: (1) resources and technology are different; (2) the production-possibilities frontier is bowed outward from the origin; (3) the Principle of Increasing Opportunity cost holds.

Reality Check: Interim Review Questions

IR2-3. Why are some production-possibilities frontiers straight, whereas others are bowed outward?

IR2-4. What is the relationship between opportunity cost and the slope of the production-possibilities frontier?

IR2-5. Define the Principle of Increasing Opportunity Cost.

IR2-6. What is happening when a country produces below its p.p.f.?

CHANGES IN THE PRODUCTION-POSSIBILITIES FRONTIER

So far, we have shown two production-possibilities frontiers, in Figures 2.1 and 2.2. These p.p.f.'s, like all p.p.f.'s, are defined at a particular moment in time. They show the maximum amount that can be produced, given the resources that are available at one time. However, p.p.f.'s can shift over time. In fact, the productive capacity of the world's economy has improved tremendously over the last few hundred years.

Figure 2.3 shows an outward shift in the production-possibilities frontier for the United States economy. The p.p.f. is defined over manufactured goods and services, which are two broad categories of production. Over the years, our ability to produce both goods and services has increased dramatically.

The productive capacity of the economy can increase over time, as a result of any of several influences. The first of these is tech-

nological improvements. *Technological improvements* include new inventions, as well as new techniques that allow us to produce more or better goods from a given amount of resources. A century ago, there were no televisions, no radios, no computers, no antibiotics, no microwave ovens, and no Internet browsers. Far more inventions have occurred in the last 100 years than in all the rest of the history of the world. Technological improvements are occurring at an especially rapid rate in digital electronics and computers. As technology improves, the p.p.f. shifts outward.

For most of history, people relied on technologies that are remarkably primitive by today's standards. Our ancestors learned how to control fire at least 100,000 years ago, and possibly much earlier than that. Using technologies such as fire and stone tools, early

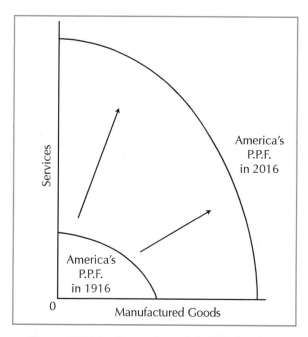

Figure 2.3 The Expansion of the Production-Possibilities Frontier in the United States

Over time, the productive capacity of the United States economy has expanded greatly. This is represented as an outward shift of the production-possibilities frontier. This outward shift has occurred as a result of improved technologies, capital investment, and increases in the size and quality of the labor force.

humans were able to live more safely and comfortably than ever before. But even then they were incredibly poor. However, the pace of technological change began to pick up in the last 10,000 years, and especially in the last 500 years. Technological improvements, more than anything else, have allowed modern people to achieve a standard of living that was once unimaginable. Table 2.1 lists some of the important advances in technology.

The second source of improved production is *capital investment*. When economists use the phrase "capital investment", their meaning is somewhat different from one of the common meanings of the phrase. In ordinary conversation, people often talk about "capital investments" in purely financial terms. They refer to stocks, bonds, checking accounts, savings accounts, cash, and so forth. However, when an economist refers to *capital investment*, he or she refers to the real, long-lasting, man-made inputs into the production process, such as factories, pieces of equipment, computers, and office buildings. In the economist's dictionary, "capital" includes *machinery and equipment*, such as computers, drill presses, drop forges, and circular saws. "Capital" also includes *structures*, such as office buildings, factory buildings, stores, and warehouses. And capital also refers to moving capital, such as delivery vans and railroad cars.

Each year, many people save a part of their income. These savings are put into financial institutions, which then lend the money to businesses. In turn, the businesses acquire new capital and replace old capital. When the amount of capital increases, there is an improvement in the productive capacity of the economy, and the p.p.f. will shift outward.

So far, we have mentioned two sources of improved production—technological improvement and capital investment. Although these two sources of improved production are not the same thing, they are often closely related. This is because many technological improvements are embodied in new capital. Thus when a team of chemists and engineers comes up with a new process for making propylene oxide, they demonstrate the new technology by getting a chemical company to build a new factory, which uses the new process.

The last (but not least) of our three sources of improved productivity is increases in the size and quality of the work force. Very little can be produced in the economy, unless someone does some work. Therefore, if the size of the labor force grows, we can expect that the production-possibilities frontier will shift outward. In fact, in the United States, the labor force has grown enormously over the years. For example, the population has more than doubled since 1940. In addition, the proportion of the population that is working has also

Table 2.1 Some Important Improvements in Technology

c. 6000 B.C.	Potter's wheel (Mesopotamia)
c. 4000 B.C.	Plow (Mesopotamia)
c. 3500 B.C.	Wheel (Mesopotamia)
c. 3200 B.C.	Sail (Egypt)
c. 1100 B.C.	Phoenician alphabet
c. 700 B.C.	Coins (Asia Minor)
c. 200 B.C.	Magnetic compass (China)
c. 200 B.C.	Stirrup (India)
c. 100 B.C.	Paper (China)
1044	Gunpowder (China)
c. 1280	Eyeglasses (Italy)
1455	Printing press (Germany—Johannes Gutenberg)
1590	Microscope (Netherlands)
1608	Telescope (Netherlands—Hans Lippershey)
1643	Barometer (Italy—Evangelista Torricelli)
1656	Pendulum clock (Netherlands—Christiaan Huygens)
1769	Water-powered spinning frame (England—Richard Arkwright)
1781	Steam engine (England—James Watt)
1800	Electric battery (Italy—Alessandro Volta)
1804	Steam locomotive (England—Richard Trevithick)
1807	Steamboat (United States—Robert Fulton)
1827	Photograph (France—Joseph Nicephore Niepce)
1834	Mechanical reaper (United States—Cyrus McCormick)
1837	Electrical telegraph (United States—Samuel Morse)
1876	Telephone (United States—Alexander Graham Bell)
1879	Incandescent light bulb (United States—Thomas Edison)
1886	Gasoline-powered automobile (Germany—Karl Benz)
1885	Radio (Italy—Guglielmo Marconi)
1895	Motion-picture camera and projector (France—Louis Lumière)
1895	X-rays (Germany—Wilhelm Conrad Roentgen)
1902	Air conditioning (United States—Willis Carrier)
1903	Heavier-than-air aircraft (United States—Wright brothers)
1928	Penicillin, the first antibiotic (England—Alexander Fleming)
1935	Nylon (United States—Wallace Carothers)
1946	Microwave oven (United States—Percy Spencer)
1947	Transistor (United States—John Bardeen, Walter Brattain, William Shockley)
1949	Stored-program electronic computer (England—Maurice Wilkes)
1949	Photocopier (United States—Xerox Corporation)
1957	Orbital satellite (Soviet Union)
1958	Integrated circuit (United States—Jack Kilby)
1965	Desktop personal computer (Italy—Pier Giorgio Perotto)
1969	First computer-to-computer message—beginning of Internet (United States)
1973	First cellular telephone call (United States)
1981	Microsoft Corporation introduces its MS-DOS operating system (United States)
1996	Algorithm for much faster Internet searches (United States—Larry Page and Sergey Brin)
2007	iPhone, first mass-production touch-screen smart phone (United States—Apple Computer)

increased, as women have increased their labor-force participation.

In addition to the increases in the *size* of the labor force, the *quality* of the labor force has also increased. As recently as 1910, only a little more than 10 percent of Americans completed high school. The figure reached about 60 percent by 1940, and today more than

80 percent of American adults have a high-school diploma or its equivalent. The proportion of the work force with a college education has also increased dramatically. Nowadays, more than one-fourth of American adults have a college degree. Because of these increases in education, the work force is much more highly skilled than it was before.

We have identified several sources of increased productivity: technological advances, capital investment, increases in the size of the labor force, and increases in the quality of the labor force. The education and skills of the labor force are the most important of these. After all, new technologies are invented by skilled workers, and capital investments are designed and built by skilled workers.

Of course, it is also possible for the productive capacity of an economy to *decrease*. As an example, let's consider the change in the size of the German economy from 1942 to 1945. In 1942, German armies controlled an empire that stretched from Norway to Tunisia to Greece, and on through much of western Russia. The German economy was in high gear, producing huge quantities of war materials, as well as consumer goods. Three years later, at the end of World War II, the German economy lay in ruins. Many of its factories had been bombed to rubble. Five million Germans had been killed, along with millions of farm animals. Millions of others had been injured. These losses can be represented by an inward shift in the production-possibilities frontier, as shown in Figure 2.4.

Earlier in this section, we saw that an economy's p.p.f. can *grow,* as a result of improved technology, capital investment, and growth of the labor force. From 1942 to 1945, the German economy *shrank,* because of the destruction of much of its capital stock and population.

Natural disasters can also reduce the productive capacity of the economy. The earthquake and tsunami that devastated parts of Japan in March 2011 could be represented as pushing the Japanese p.p.f. downward and to the left. In fact, that earthquake also damaged the U.S. economy, because of the many trade

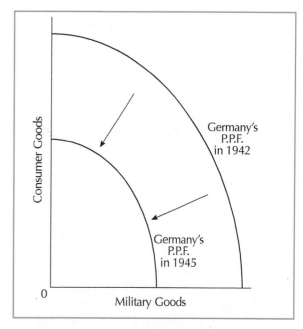

Figure 2.4 The Shrinkage of the German Production-Possibilities Frontier, 1942–1945

Between 1942 and 1945, millions of Germans were killed in the Second World War. Factories, cities, and farms were devastated by the war. As a result, the productive capacity of the German economy decreased. This is represented by an inward shift of the production-possibilities frontier.

relationships between the two countries. In October 2012, Hurricane Sandy caused widespread destruction in New York, New Jersey, and Connecticut. This could be represented as a downward shift in the p.p.f. of that region. We can think of droughts and fires in the same way.

On a happier note, *Real Economics for Real People 2.2* discusses the expansion of the p.p.f. in the United States.

Reality Check: Interim Review Question

IR2-7. What are the main ways in which an economy's production-possibilities frontier can expand outward?

We have identified several ways in which production-possibilities frontiers can expand. The economy can grow as a result of technological improvements, capital investments, and increases in the quantity and quality of the labor force. The United States economy has been fortunate to have an abundance of all of these sources of growth. Let's get an idea of the magnitude of the changes over the last five decades.

First of all, the labor force has expanded greatly. In 1960, the U.S. population was nearly 181 million. By 2016, the population had grown to about 324 million, for an increase of almost 80%. The labor force has grown even more rapidly than the population. In 1960, the civilian labor force was about 70 million. By 2016, the labor force had grown to about 159 million, for an increase of about 125%. The labor force grew faster than the population, because there was an increase in the proportion of the population that is in the labor force. This period saw an exceptional increase in the labor-force participation of women. (Some of the people in the labor force are unemployed. However, out of a labor force of about 159 million, about 151 million were working.)

Not only did the number of workers increase, but their productivity increased, as well. Productivity increased for a variety of reasons. Education levels increased, so workers had better skills. Worker productivity was also enhanced by technological improvements and growth of the capital stock. Output per hour in the business sector is estimated to have increased by more than 200% from 1960 to 2016! (For the entire economy, the rate of growth of output per hour is not quite this fast, because output tends to grow faster in the business sector than in the government sector. Still, the economy has experienced major productivity improvements.)

Since the labor force doubled over this period, and since output per worker also increased substantially, it should not come as a surprise that workers were able to make more money. In 1960, employee compensation was about $302 billion. (Employee compensation includes wages, salaries, and fringe benefits.) By 2016, employee compensation had grown to about $10 *trillion*. This represents an increase by a factor of more than 30! However, much of the increase is more of an illusion than a reality, because of inflation. But even if we adjust for inflation, we still find that real employee compensation increased by a factor of about 5.2.

The overall picture is one of substantial economic growth, driven by a variety of sources. Expansion of production possibilities is the key to prosperity.

COMPARATIVE ADVANTAGE AND TRADE

At the beginning of this chapter, we asked whether a man should build his own house, or get other people to build it for him. More recently, we have introduced the idea of the production-possibilities frontier. Now, it's time to put these two thoughts together. We can do this by asking the following question: What happens if two people, or two nations, have p.p.f.'s that are shaped differently? As it turns out, it will make sense for them to specialize in the activities in which they are relatively more productive, and then trade with each other.

We begin by defining two important terms, "absolute advantage" and "comparative advantage".

Absolute Advantage

Mark and Jason run a 100-yard dash. Mark wins. In other words, Mark can produce an output (traveling 100 yards) using fewer resources (less time) than Jason. We say that Mark has absolute advantage over Jason, in terms of running the 100-yard dash. In general, one person has *absolute advantage* over another person, if he or she can produce a given output using fewer resources than the other person. We can also say that one person has absolute advantage over another if he or she can produce a larger output, or an output of higher quality.

Absolute advantage is defined with reference to only *one* activity. A calculation of absolute advantage only looks at one activity at a time.

Let's consider a further example. Gwen and Cecil are both cooks in a diner. Gwen can make 60 stacks of pancakes per hour, but Cecil can make only 48 stacks of pancakes per hour. Therefore, Gwen has absolute advantage over Cecil in the production of pancakes, because it takes her less time to produce the same number of pancakes.

Gwen can also make 60 hamburgers per hour. Just as Cecil was slower in making pancakes, he is also slower when it comes to making hamburgers. He can make 36 hamburgers in one hour. Gwen has absolute advantage over Cecil in the production of hamburgers, because it takes her less time to produce the same number of hamburgers.

Comparative Advantage

Even though Gwen has absolute advantage over Cecil in both activities, the *proportion* by which she is better is different in the two activities. The next step in our analysis involves determining the activity at which Gwen is *relatively* better, and the activity at which Cecil is *relatively* better. The way to do this is by comparing the opportunity cost of each activity for the two people.

Remember that Gwen can produce 60 hamburgers per hour, or she can produce 60 stacks of pancakes per hour. Therefore, for Gwen, the opportunity cost of 60 hamburgers is 60 stacks of pancakes. If we express this as an equation, we have

$$60H = 60P$$

where H stands for hamburgers and P stands for pancakes. If we divide both sides of this equation by 60, we find that, for Gwen, *the opportunity cost of one hamburger is one stack of pancakes*. Our next step is to calculate the opportunity cost for Cecil. Recall that Cecil can make 36 hamburgers per hour, or he can make 48 stacks of pancakes per hour. We can express this relationship as

$$36H = 48P.$$

Thus for Cecil, the opportunity cost of 36 hamburgers is 48 stacks of pancakes. Now, let's find the opportunity cost of *one* hamburger. To do this, we divide both sides of the equation by 36:

$$(36/36)H = 1H = (48/36)P = 1.3333 \ P.$$

For Cecil, the opportunity cost of one hamburger is one and one-third stacks of pancakes.

We can now determine the activities at which Gwen and Cecil are *relatively* better. For Gwen, the opportunity cost of one hamburger is one stack of pancakes. For Cecil, the opportunity cost of one hamburger is one and one-third stacks of pancakes. The opportunity cost of a hamburger is lower for Gwen. We say that Gwen has "comparative advantage" in the production of hamburgers, because she has lower opportunity cost of producing hamburgers. Following similar reasoning, we find that Cecil has comparative advantage in the production of pancakes. Generally, an individual has *comparative advantage* in an activity if his or her opportunity cost of that activity is lower than the opportunity cost of that activity for anyone else.

Notice that, although Gwen has *absolute* advantage in both activities, she only has *comparative* advantage in hamburger production. It's possible to be absolutely better than another person in every single activity, but it is not possible to be *relatively* better at everything.

Earlier, we said that absolute advantage can be defined with respect to only one activity. On the other hand, we need at least two activities to define comparative advantage.

Comparative Advantage and Opportunities for Beneficial Trade

If you were the owner of the diner where Gwen and Cecil work, you would notice that Gwen is relatively better at hamburger production, and Cecil is relatively better at pancake production. As it turns out, this means that the diner could operate more efficiently by having Gwen specialize (as much as possible) in hamburgers, and by having Cecil specialize (as much as possible) in pancakes.

This is basically the same as the idea that we introduced at the very beginning of this chapter. Anthony Varelli's comparative advantage is as a marketing manager for toothpaste. He does *not* have comparative advantage in building houses. Instead of attempting to build his own house, Anthony should specialize in being a marketing manager, and he should let other people specialize in building houses. If we want to use the available resources to produce as much as we can, the people who should build houses are the ones who have comparative advantage in building houses.

An Example of Comparative Advantage and Trade, with Production-Possibilities Frontiers

Now we are ready to demonstrate the gains that can occur, when people specialize in the activity in which they have comparative advantage, and then trade with each other. To develop this idea, we'll use another numerical example, and we will draw production-possibilities frontiers, based on the numbers.

Kenny lives alone on a desert island. On this island, the only two things to do are to catch fish or gather coconuts. Kenny is great at catching fish. If he devotes all of his energies to fishing, he can catch 60 fish per month. On the other hand, Kenny can only gather 12 coconuts per month. We graph Kenny's production-possibilities frontier in Figure 2.5. (Note that, to keep the analysis simple, we assume that Kenny's p.p.f. is a straight line.)

For Kenny, the opportunity cost of 12 coconuts is 60 fish. Another way to put this is as follows:

$$12\ C = 60\ F,$$

where C stands for coconuts, and F stands for fish.

To calculate the opportunity cost of *one* coconut, divide both sides of the equation by 12. This gives us $(12/12)\ C = 1C = (60/12)\ F = 5F$. For Kenny, the opportunity cost of one coconut is five fish. If we follow the same procedure again, we will find that Kenny's opportunity cost of one fish is 0.2 coconuts. (Note that Kenny's opportunity cost of one coconut is 5 fish, and his opportunity cost of one fish is $1/5 = 0.2$ coconuts. The reciprocal of 5 is $1/5$, or 0.2. The opportunity cost of good A in terms of good B is always the reciprocal of the opportunity cost of good B in terms of good A.)

Let's assume that Kenny always likes to consume fish and coconuts in equal proportions. In other words, every time Kenny eats one fish, he prefers to eat exactly one coconut. There is only one point on his p.p.f. that has equal proportions, and that is the point (10,10). Therefore, Kenny will catch and eat 10 fish, and he will gather and eat 10 coconuts. Since Kenny lives alone, his only choice is to consume a combination of outputs that he can produce himself.

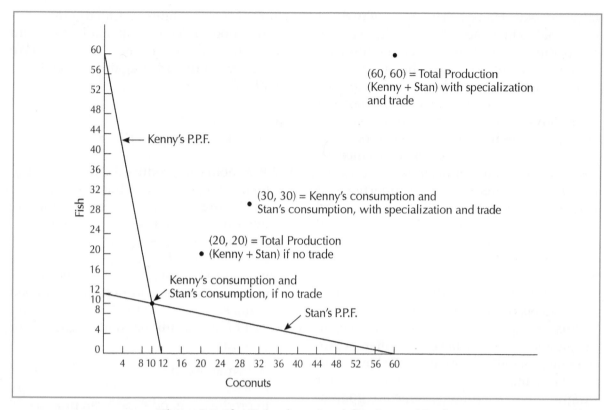

Figure 2.5 The Gains from Specialization and Trade

If Kenny and Stan do not cooperate, each of them will produce 10 coconuts and 10 fish, and each will consume what he produces. Therefore, if they do not cooperate, the total production of the two people is 20 coconuts and 20 fish. However, Kenny has comparative advantage in production of fish, and Stan has comparative advantage in production of coconuts. If they specialize in the activity in which they have comparative advantage, Kenny will produce 60 fish and Stan will produce 60 coconuts. This would allow each of them to consume 30 coconuts and 30 fish. Thus, as a result of specialization and trade, the two people are able to increase production and consumption by a factor of three.

Now, Stan washes up on the same desert island. However, Stan's productive capacities are very different from Kenny's. Kenny could produce either 12 coconuts or 60 fish, but Stan can produce either 60 coconuts or 12 fish. Earlier, we found that Kenny's opportunity cost of one coconut is five fish. By following the same method, we find that Stan's opportunity cost of one coconut is one-fifth of a fish. Stan has lower opportunity cost in coconut production, and Kenny has lower opportunity cost in fish production. Therefore, Kenny has comparative advantage in fish production, and Stan has comparative advantage in

coconut production. Stan's p.p.f. is also graphed in Figure 2.5.

By coincidence, Stan has the same preferences as Kenny. Stan also likes to eat fish and coconuts in equal proportions. This means that, if Stan stays to himself, with no communication with Kenny, he will also choose the point (10,10). If Kenny and Stan don't communicate with each other, then Stan, like Kenny, will catch and eat 10 fish, and he will gather and eat 10 coconuts.

However, if one of these guys is smart, he will notice that their productive capacities are different. Let's say that Kenny is the first to raise the issue. He says "Hey, Stan, why don't we specialize in the activities in which we have comparative advantage, and then trade with each other?" (You see, Kenny has already had an economics course, so he knows the lingo.)

The two shake hands. From that moment on, Kenny specializes in fish production, and Stan specializes in the production of coconuts. Kenny produces 60 fish, and Stan produces 60 coconuts. Since both of them like to consume fish and coconuts in equal proportions, it makes sense that they will divide the food equally. Kenny ends up with 30 fish and 30 coconuts, and so does Stan.

By specializing and trading, each man is able to *triple* his consumption!

If everyone had exactly the same production possibilities, then the kind of gains shown in this example could not occur. However, people and nations do have very different production possibilities. Some people have a talent for fixing cars, some have a talent for programming computers, some are good at delivering packages, and so on. Some nations have a lot of oil, others have a lot of good agricultural land, others have highly educated workers, and so on. The message of this example is that it is possible to improve living standards dramatically, by specializing in the activities in which we have comparative advantage, and then trading. In other words, the people and nations of the world have very diverse talents and resources. We can improve our standard of living by taking advantage of the diversity.

Obviously, this has been a simplified example. Nevertheless, it captures many of the most important ideas in all of economics. First of all, our resources are scarce, which means that we have to make choices. (We

will return to this idea repeatedly throughout this book.) Second, specialization and trade can make everyone better off. (We will return to this idea again, especially in Chapter 5.)

Reality Check: Interim Review Questions

IR2-8. Arnold can produce 5 units of good A, if he devotes all of his time and energy to producing good A. He can produce 10 units of good B, if he devotes all of his time and energy to producing good B. Between these two end-points, Arnold's p.p.f. is a straight line. What is the opportunity cost of one additional unit of good A for Arnold? What is the opportunity cost of one additional unit of good B for Arnold?

IR2-9. Lynnette can produce 15 units of good A, if she devotes all of her time and energy to producing good A. She can produce 20 units of good B, if she devotes all of her time and energy to producing good B. Between these two end-points, Lynnette's p.p.f. is a straight line. What is the opportunity cost of one additional unit of good A for Lynnette? What is the opportunity cost of one additional unit of good B for Lynnette?

IR2-10. If we refer to the preceding two questions, does Arnold or Lynnette have *absolute* advantage in the production of good A? Who has *absolute* advantage in the production of good B? Who has *comparative* advantage in the production of good A? Who has *comparative* advantage in the production of good B?

ECONOMICS AND YOU:
LET SOMEBODY ELSE BUILD THE HOUSE FOR YOU

At the beginning of this chapter, we posed the question of whether Anthony Varelli should build his own home. The answer is that he should not do so, because the opportunity cost of building it himself is bigger than the opportunity cost of letting someone else do it for him.

The same principle pervades every aspect of our lives. If you are a lawyer, you have comparative advantage in the production of legal services. It makes sense to specialize in that activity, and to let others specialize in other activities. The lawyer will make money from providing legal expertise, and he or she will then be able to use that money to buy groceries, gasoline, appliances, video games, and all manner of other things, from people who have comparative advantage in those activities. If you're a loan officer at a bank, it makes sense to specialize in that activity, and to let other people provide the food you eat and the clothes you wear. Of course, the loan officer might keep a small garden because it's nice to have fresh vegetables in the summer. However, when compared with a bank loan officer, a farmer will have comparative advantage in providing most food items.

Here's the bottom line: We can get more out of our resources by taking advantage of specialization. People should specialize in the activities in which they have comparative advantage, and then they should trade with each other. Comparative advantage, specialization, and trade are at the very heart of the success of the modern world economy.

Chapter Summary

1. The opportunity cost of one activity is the value of the next-best alternative. Often, opportunity cost can be measured easily by the dollar price of a good or service. However, it is important to define opportunity cost broadly. For example, the opportunity cost of going to a concert includes the value of time spent waiting in line for tickets. Another example is that the opportunity cost of going to college includes the "foregone earnings", which are the wages and salaries that could have been earned if the person had gone to work right after high school.

2. The production-possibilities frontier (p.p.f.) is a graphical representation of the combinations of outputs that can be produced, if all of the available resources are used as well as possible. The p.p.f. slopes downward as we go from left to right in the graph. This illustrates the concept of scarcity—if we are on the p.p.f, as we increase production of one good, we must decrease production of another good.

3. The slope of the p.p.f. is the negative of the opportunity cost of the good on the horizontal axis. The opportunity cost of good A (in terms of the amount of good B that must be given up) is the reciprocal of the opportunity cost of good B (in terms of the amount of good A that must be given up.)

4. If two goods use the same resources and technology, then the p.p.f. for those two goods will be a straight line. In this special case, each good has constant opportunity cost. In the more common case, in which two goods use different resources and technology, the p.p.f. will be bowed outward. In other words, when two goods use different resources and technology, the p.p.f. will be concave with respect to the origin. When the p.p.f. has this shape, we say that it obeys the "Principle of Increasing Opportunity Cost" or "Law of Increasing Opportunity Cost": As we increase production of one good, the opportunity cost of producing additional amounts of that good will increase.

5. Any combination of outputs that is on the p.p.f. involves "efficient" production. A combination of outputs that is below and to the left of the p.p.f. is associated with wasteful or "inefficient" use of the available resources. A combination of outputs that is above and to the right of the p.p.f. is infeasible, given the current resources and technology.

6. The p.p.f. describes the production possibilities that are available at a particular moment in time. However, over time, the p.p.f. can shift. The production-possibilities frontier can shift outward, due to technological improvements, or capital investments, or increases in the size of the labor force, or improvements in the quality of the labor force. On the other hand, if the productive capacity of the economy is reduced by war, earthquake, fire, flood, or other disaster, the p.p.f. will shift inward.

7. One person has absolute advantage over another person in the production of some output, if he or she can produce a given amount of output using fewer resources than the other person. Absolute advantage is defined with respect to any one good or activity.

8. One person has comparative advantage over another person in the production of some output, if he or she has lower opportunity cost for that output. In order to define comparative advantage, it is necessary to consider at least two goods or activities.

9. If people specialize in the activities in which they have comparative advantage, and then trade with each other, total production can be increased.

Key Terms

Opportunity Cost

Foregone Earnings

Production-Possibilities Frontier

Principle of Increasing Opportunity Cost

Technological Improvements

Capital Investment

Machinery and Equipment

Structures

Absolute Advantage

Comparative Advantage

Questions and Problems

QP2-1. Taco Town and The Taco Joint are next door to each other. You've been to both places before, and you consider the tacos to be equally good at either place. However, you were planning to get your lunch at Taco Town, because their tacos are only 79 cents each, whereas the tacos are 99 cents each at The Taco Joint. When you arrive, you notice that there is a long line at Taco Town, but no line at The Taco Joint. Use the idea of opportunity cost to discuss the circumstances under which it would make sense to change your mind and go to The Taco Joint, as well as the circumstances under which it would make sense to wait in line at Taco Town.

QP2-2. Use the idea of opportunity cost to explain why a highly paid business executive might choose not to mow his own lawn.

QP2-3. Draw a production-possibilities frontier for any two goods of your choosing. Now, put point A above and to the right of the p.p.f. What can be said about the production possibilities depicted at point A?

QP2-4. Once again, use the p.p.f. that you drew for the previous question. This time, put point B below and to the left of the frontier. What can be said about the production possibilities depicted at point B?

QP2-5. Now, put point C on the production-possibilities frontier, so that point C has more of both goods than point B. In moving from point B (below the frontier) to point C (on the frontier), would it be necessary for the total available supply of resources to increase?

QP2-6. If Jane devotes all of her time to making gazpacho, she can produce 8 gallons of gazpacho in a day. If she devotes all of her time to making blintzes, Jane can produce 16 dozen blintzes in a day. Between these endpoints, Jane's production-possibilities frontier is a straight line.

a. Draw a graph of Jane's production-possibilities frontier, with gazpacho on the horizontal axis and blintzes on the vertical axis. (In making the axes, you can assume that a gallon is the unit of measurement for gazpacho, and one dozen is the unit of measurement for blintzes.)

b. What is the slope of Jane's production-possibilities frontier?

c. What is the opportunity cost of one additional gallon of gazpacho for Jane?

d. If Jane were producing six gallons of gazpacho per day, what is the maximum number of dozens of blintzes that she could produce?

e. If Jane were producing 12 dozen blintzes per day, would it be possible for her to produce four gallons of gazpacho per day?

QP2-7. If Samantha devotes all of her time to making gazpacho, she can produce 6 gallons of gazpacho in a day. If she devotes all of her time to making blintzes, Samantha can produce 8 dozen blintzes in a day. Between these endpoints, Samantha's production-possibilities frontier is a straight line.

a. Draw a graph of Samantha's production-possibilities frontier, with gazpacho on the horizontal axis and blintzes on the vertical axis. (You can use the same units of measurement that were used in the previous question.)
b. What is the slope of Samantha's production-possibilities frontier?
c. What is the opportunity cost of one additional gallon of gazpacho for Samantha?
d. If Samantha were producing three gallons of gazpacho per day, what is the maximum number of dozens of blintzes that she could produce?
e. If Samantha were producing six dozen blintzes per day, would it be possible for her to produce four gallons of gazpacho per day?

QP2-8. Based on the information in the previous two questions, who has comparative advantage in gazpacho production? Who has comparative advantage in the production of blintzes?

Chapter 3

Supply and Demand: The Basics

ECONOMICS AND YOU: WHERE DO CAR PRICES COME FROM?

When you shop for a car, you are faced with a tremendous variety of models and prices. In 2016, you could buy a new General Motors Sierra 1500 pickup truck for anywhere from about $27,000 to more than $40,000, depending on which features are included. A Ford Focus would start at about $17,000. A Honda Civic Coupe would begin at about $19,000, with higher prices if more features are included. A Ferrari or a Lamborghini would cost you a whole lot more.

Why do some cars sell for so much more than others? One reason is that some cars are more expensive to build: A high-performance luxury car uses costlier materials, and requires more workmanship. Other things also influence prices. For example, a car may become popular because of an exciting design, or because it gets great reviews in magazines such as *Road and Track* or *Consumer Reports.* When a car is very popular, dealers may be able to charge higher prices. However, if a particular model isn't selling very well, the sellers may have to cut prices to stimulate sales.

The number of sellers can also have an effect: If you live in an area with lots of auto dealerships, the dealers may be willing to cut prices in an attempt to win your business. On the other hand, if there's only one dealership within 100 miles, the dealer may not feel much pressure to keep prices down.

Price determination is one of the most important topics in economics. Whether you're buying a car, a cheeseburger, a T-shirt, or a house, it's important to think clearly about how prices are determined. In this chapter, we will begin to learn how prices are determined by the interaction of buyers and sellers in markets. We will see:

- how the behavior of buyers is affected by prices, incomes, and other factors,

- how the behavior of sellers is affected by prices, technologies, and other factors, and

- how buyers and sellers come together to determine the price of a good, and the quantity that will be bought and sold.

MARKETS

In everyday language, we use the word "market" to refer to a particular place where groceries and other items are bought and sold. But economists define markets in a broader way. A *market* is defined as *any organized system of exchange of a good or service between buyers and sellers*. Another way to say this is that a market is *any institution or mechanism that allows people to interact, for the purpose of buying and selling some good or service*. It was once true that transactions required face-to-face contact, but that is no longer the case. As a result of the growth of online shopping, the buyers and sellers in many transactions don't know each other, and never see each other.

Each good or service has its own market. There is a market for decaffeinated coffee, and a market for AA batteries, and a market for computer spreadsheet programs. There's one market for the services of emergency-room doctors, and another for the services of welders. There is a market for Iowa farmland. The market for hairstyling services in the Cincinnati area is a local market, in the sense that it probably isn't greatly affected by the hairstyling markets in other regions of the country. On the other hand, the market for automobiles is a global market. The sellers come from the United States, Japan, Germany, Korea, and other countries, and they sell their products all around the world.

The details differ from one market to another, but all markets have one thing in common: In every case, there is regular communication between buyers and sellers, for the purpose of buying and selling some good or service.

In order to have an economic transaction in a market, we need both a willing buyer and a willing seller. The word "willing" is very important. Our purpose here is to describe *voluntary* transactions. If there is a willing seller, but no one is willing to buy, then there is no sale. Similarly, if there is a willing buyer, but no one is willing to sell, there is no sale. Every transaction has to have two voluntary participants. We look at the behavior of buyers in the next section. After that, we look at the behavior of sellers. Finally, we put them together, to see how market outcomes are determined by the *interaction* between buyers and sellers.

DEMAND

We use the word *demand* to refer to the behavior of buyers. The identity of the buyer depends on which market we are considering. For example, in the market for running shoes, the buyers are people who want to wear the shoes themselves, or who are buying shoes for family or friends. In the market for the services of computer programmers, the buyers are companies that want to employ the programmers in their businesses. In the market for helicopter gunships, the buyers are the armed forces of various countries around the world. In this chapter, we will focus mostly on markets in which the buyers are consumer households.

There are a great number of influences on the behavior of buyers. For example, in the market for motorcycles, buyers are influenced by incomes, because low-income people may not be able to afford a motorcycle. Buyers are also influenced by "tastes" or "preferences", because some people enjoy riding a motorcycle but others do not. Buyers are also influenced by the prices of other goods. For example, if the prices of passenger cars were to increase, some people might decide to buy a motorcycle instead of a passenger car. Also, buyers are influenced by the current price of motorcycles. In this chapter, we introduce a way of thinking about these various influences.

We separate the influences into two categories: one category is the current price of the good, and the other category includes all other influences. We will analyze the two categories in very distinct ways. This is an absolutely crucial distinction. We will analyze changes in the current price of the good in one way, and we will analyze all other potential influences on buyers in a different way. It is essential to distinguish between changes in the current price of the good, and changes in other influences on buyer behavior.

The *quantity demanded* is the amount of some good or service that buyers are willing and able to buy, at a specific price, in a given period of time. It's important to be specific about the time period we are considering. For example, there is a vast difference between the quantity of gasoline demanded per week and the quantity of gasoline demanded per year.

The Law of Demand

Red-delicious apples often sell for about $1.50 per pound. What would happen if the price were to rise to $2.00 per pound, while everything else stays the same? Most likely, the quantity demanded would decrease. Some people would switch to pears or bananas, and others would just eat less fruit. On the other hand, if the price of apples were to drop to $1.00 per pound, consumers would be willing and able to buy more apples. In other words, when price decreases, quantity demanded will rise.

This type of relationship occurs so frequently that we call it the *Law of Demand.*

The Law of Demand states that:

When the price of a good or service increases, the quantity demanded will decrease, all else equal. In a similar way, when the price decreases, the quantity demanded will increase, all else equal.

In other words, the Law of Demand states that quantity demanded is *inversely related* to the current price, all else equal. The phrase "all else equal" is extremely important. The Law

of Demand describes the relationship between price and quantity demanded, *when all variables other than the price of the good are unchanged*. If the price of apples goes up while all other variables remain the same, the Law of Demand says that the quantity of apples demanded will go down. However, if the price of apples goes up while incomes or tastes or other variables are changing, there's no guarantee that people would want to buy fewer apples.

There may be some price ranges over which the quantity demanded for certain goods is constant. This would appear to be a violation of the Law of Demand. For example, if the price of a hamburger goes up from $4.98 to $4.99, the change in price may be so small that it doesn't have any effect on the quantity demanded. For some goods that people really depend on, even a relatively large increase in the price may have little effect on quantity demanded. But if the price of a good increases far enough, the quantity demanded will have to decrease, because the buyers only have a limited budget. Therefore, in this book we will almost always assume that the Law of Demand is obeyed.

The Demand Schedule and the Demand Curve

There are several ways to represent the relationship between quantity demanded and price. Two of these are the demand schedule and the demand curve. A *demand schedule* is a table showing the quantity of a good or service that would be demanded, at a number of different prices. When constructing a demand schedule, we assume that *all other influences on consumers are held constant*. Thus, when we go from one entry in a demand schedule to the next, we assume that there are no changes in incomes, or in the prices of other products, or in any of the other variables that might have an influence on demand.

Table 3.1 is Rhonda's demand schedule for red-delicious apples. Since it is a demand

Table 3.1 Rhonda's Demand Schedule for Red-Delicious Apples

Price per pound	Quantity Demanded (pounds per year)
$2.00	16
1.75	18
1.50	20
1.25	22
1.00	24

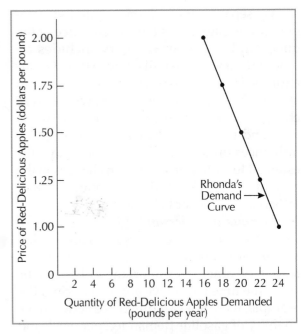

Figure 3.1 Rhonda's Demand Curve for Red-Delicious Apples

This demand curve shows the relationship between the price of red-delicious apples and the quantity of these apples that Rhonda is willing and able to buy, holding constant all other influences on her buying behavior. For example, when the price of apples is $1.50 per pound, Rhonda will buy 20 pounds per year. If the price were to drop to $1.00 per pound, she would be willing to buy 24 pounds per year. The demand curve slopes downward as we move from left to right, which indicates that Rhonda obeys the Law of Demand.

schedule for a single person, it is called an *individual demand schedule*. (Later in this chapter, we will look at a *market demand schedule*, which describes the quantities demanded for all of the buyers in the market.)

At the store where Rhonda shops, red-delicious apples have been selling for $1.50 per pound. Table 3.1 tells us that, if the price were to stay at $1.50 per pound, Rhonda would buy 20 pounds of red-delicious apples per year.

However, if the price were to change, Rhonda would change her quantity demanded. In the top row of Table 3.1, we see that she would buy only 16 pounds per year if the price were to rise to $2.00 per pound. On the other hand, if the price were to fall to $1.00 per pound, she would buy 24 pounds per year. Rhonda obeys the Law of Demand: When there is an increase in the price of red-delicious apples, she demands a smaller quantity.

A *demand curve* is a graph of the information in a demand schedule. In other words, a demand curve is a graph of the relationship between the price of a good and the quantity demanded, holding all else equal. Figure 3.1 shows Rhonda's demand curve for red-delicious apples. Figure 3.1 represents the same information that was shown in Table 3.1. Because Rhonda obeys the Law of Demand, *the demand curve slopes downward as we move from left to right.* In this particular case, the demand curve is a straight line. However, the demand curve doesn't have to be straight to

obey the Law of Demand. It can be curved in almost any way, as long as it slopes downward as we move from left to right across the diagram.

Note that, in Figure 3.1, quantity demanded is on the horizontal axis and price is on the vertical axis. In the natural sciences, it's common to put the independent variable on the horizontal axis. However, for better or worse, economists traditionally put price, which is the independent variable, on the vertical axis. Quantity demanded goes on the horizontal axis.

Individual Demand and Market Demand

Figure 3.1 deals with the demands of a single consumer. However, we are usually more interested in *market* demand. To get market demand, we add up the individual demands for all of the individuals in the market, as shown in Figure 3.2.

In Figure 3.2, we assume that Rhonda and Brian are the only two people in the market. To determine the market demand curve, we add Rhonda's quantity demanded and Brian's quantity demanded. When the price of red-delicious apples is $2.00 per pound, Brian doesn't buy any, so that the entire quantity demanded by the two people is Rhonda's 16 pounds per year. When the price is $1.75, Brian is willing to buy four pounds and Rhonda is willing to buy 18 pounds, so that the total quantity demanded by the two people is (4 + 18) = 22 pounds. We follow this same method in calculating all of the other points shown in Figure 3.2.

Both of the individual demand curves in this example slope downward as we go from left to right across the diagram. In other words, both of the individual demand curves obey the Law of Demand. When we combine two or more downward-sloping individual demand curves, we get a downward-sloping market demand curve. Thus when the individual demand curves obey the Law of Demand, the market demand curve will also obey the Law of Demand.

In order to plot a point on the market demand curve, we first locate the relevant price on the vertical axis. Then we move across the graph horizontally, and add up the quantities demanded by all of the consumers. In other words, we add the individual demand curves *horizontally* to get the market demand curve.

We use the same techniques, regardless of how many consumers are in the market. In Figure 3.2, we add the demands of two people. If there were three people, we would add the demands of all three, and if there were 100 mil-lion people, we would add the demands of them all.

For the rest of this chapter, we will emphasize *market* demand. We show a market demand schedule and a market demand curve for red-delicious apples in Figure 3.3.

Movements Along the Demand Curve vs. Shifts in the Demand Curve

When we construct a demand curve for red-delicious apples, the price of red-delicious apples is the *only* thing that is allowed to change. Everything else is held constant. If there were a change in the price of red-delicious apples, the price change would cause a movement along the existing demand curve for these apples. The same holds true for any demand curve: *If there is a change in the price of a good or service, the change in price will cause a movement along the existing demand curve for that good or service.*

The market demand curve shows the *willingness to pay* of the consumers in the market. At point A in Figure 3.3, if the price is $1.50 per pound, people are willing and able to buy 800 million pounds of red-delicious apples per year. If the price of red-delicious apples were to decrease from $1.50 per pound to $1.25 per pound, some consumers would react by increasing their quantity demanded. Figure 3.3 shows that when the price drops from $1.50 per pound to $1.25 per pound, quantity demanded increases from 800 million pounds per year to 1000 million pounds per year. This is graphed as a movement downward and to the right along the existing demand curve, from point A to point B. The entire demand curve shown in Figure 3.3 slopes downward as we move from left to right. This indicates that the Law of Demand is obeyed by consumers in the market for red-delicious apples.

When we constructed the demand curve in Figure 3.3, we held everything constant,

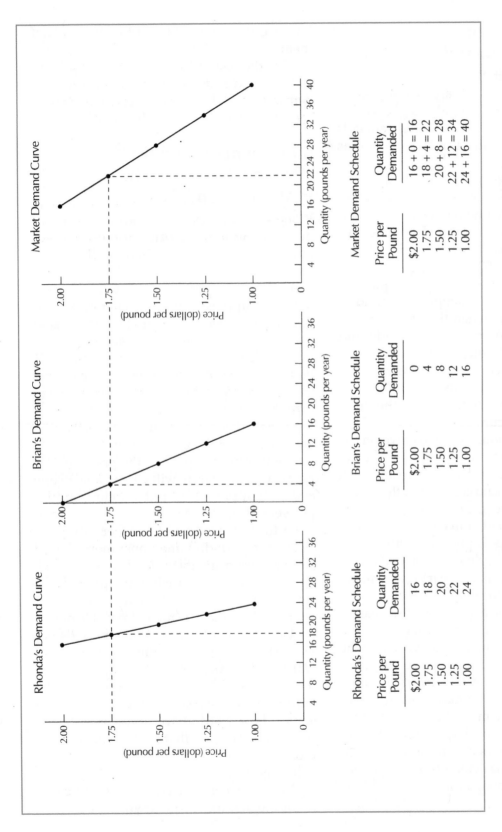

Figure 3.2 Combining Rhonda's Demand and Brian's Demand to Get Market Demand

This figure shows how we combine individual demand curves to get a market demand curve. For example, if the price of red-delicious apples is $1.75 per pound, we add Rhonda's quantity demanded of 18 pounds to Brian's quantity demanded of 4 pounds, and this gives us a total quantity demanded of 22 pounds. In a more realistic setting, with millions of buyers, we would still follow the same basic procedure, except we would add over millions of buyers, instead of only two. Each point on the market demand curve is found by choosing a price, and then moving horizontally across the demand curves for the individuals. Thus, we say that we form market demand curves by adding horizontally. Since Rhonda's demand curve slopes downward as we move from left to right, and Brian's demand curve does the same, the market demand curve will also slope downward as we move from left to right. This indicates that the market demand curve obeys the Law of Demand.

– 54 –

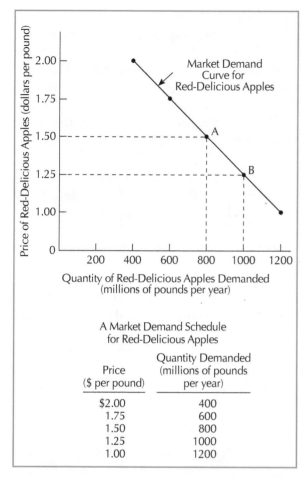

Figure 3.3 A Market Demand Schedule and Demand Curve for Red-Delicious Apples

A Market Demand Schedule
for Red-Delicious Apples

Price ($ per pound)	Quantity Demanded (millions of pounds per year)
$2.00	400
1.75	600
1.50	800
1.25	1000
1.00	1200

If we add together the quantities demanded for everyone in the market, we find a market demand curve. For example, at point A, the price is $1.50 per pound, and consumers are willing and able to buy 800 million pounds per year. If the price were to fall to $1.25 per pound, consumers would increase their quantity demanded from 800 million pounds per year to 1000 million pounds per year. This is shown by the movement from point A to point B. The market demand curve slopes downward as we move from left to right, which indicates that the apple market obeys the Law of Demand.

except for the price of red-delicious apples. What if there is a change in something other than the price of red-delicious apples? If a change occurs in some other influence on buyers of apples, such as consumer incomes, or the prices of bananas and pears, we no longer move along the existing demand curve. Instead, we shift to a different demand curve. *If any influence on buyers other than the current price of the good changes, the change will cause a shift to an entirely new demand curve.*

This is a VERY important distinction. It's crucial to understand the difference between *moving along* an existing demand curve and *shifting* to a new demand curve. Movements along an existing demand curve are caused by changes in the price of the good; shifts to a new demand curve are caused by changes in other influences on buyers.

Changes in Quantity Demanded vs. Changes in Demand

We have distinguished between (1) movements along an existing demand curve, which are caused by changes in price, and (2) shifts to a new demand curve, which are caused by changes in other variables. We can also use a different terminology to describe these two events. A *change in quantity demanded* refers to a movement along an existing demand curve. A *change in demand* refers to a shift to a new demand curve.

Thus, if the price of gasoline goes up, we could refer to a movement along the existing demand curve for gasoline, or we could refer to a change in the quantity of gasoline demanded. Each phrase has the same meaning. On the other hand, if *incomes* go up, we could refer to a shift to a new demand curve for gasoline, or we could refer to a change in demand for gasoline. Once again, each of these phrases has the same meaning.

Some of the forces that can lead to shifts in demand curves are:

- changes in the incomes of consumers,

- changes in the "tastes" or "preferences" of consumers,

- changes in the prices of other goods,

- changes in expectations of future prices,
- changes in expectations of future incomes, and
- changes in the size and composition of the buying population.

We now take a more detailed look at these influences.

The Effect of a Change in Incomes: Normal Goods 正常商品 and Inferior Goods 劣等物品

If you're like most people, you will respond to an increase in your income by spending more on a wide variety of goods. For example, if there is an increase in consumer incomes, many buyers will increase their demand for red-delicious apples. In other words, when consumer incomes go up, the market demand curve for red-delicious apples will shift *to the right*. This is shown in Figure 3.4(a). The original demand curve is D_0. When incomes rise, the result is a new demand curve, D_1. At any given price, the quantity that consumers are willing and able to buy has increased.

Normal Goods. If demand for a good increases when incomes increase, we call the good a *normal good*. Apples are normal goods, as are concert tickets, new cars, and most other goods. For all of these goods, an increase in income leads to an increase in demand. In Figure 3.4(a), when incomes rise, the demand curve shifts *to the right*, because we are dealing with a normal good. It follows

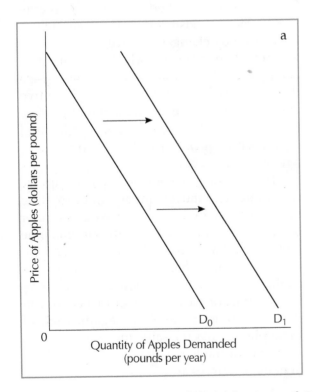 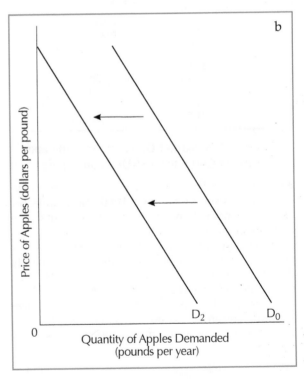

Figure 3.4 Shifts in the Demand Curve, Caused by Changes in Income

Red-delicious apples are normal goods. This means that an increase in incomes will lead to an increase in the demand for such apples. This is shown as a rightward shift in the demand curve for apples, from D_0 to D_1.

For a normal good such as red-delicious apples, a decrease in incomes will lead to a decrease in demand. This is shown as a leftward shift in the demand curve for apples, from D_0 to D_2.

that, if incomes were to fall, the demand curve would shift *to the left* for a normal good. This is shown as a shift from D_0 to D_2 in Figure 3.4(b). At any given price, the quantity that consumers are willing and able to buy has decreased.

Inferior Goods. Most goods are normal goods. However, for some goods, demand responds to a change in income in a different way. If you want to buy a car and your income is very low, you may feel that you can only afford an old used car. If your income increases, you'll probably decide to buy a better car. If there is an increase in incomes, the demand for old used cars will fall; that is, the market demand curve for old used cars will shift *to the left*. Similarly, if there is a *decrease* in incomes, we expect the market demand curve for old used cars to shift *to the right*. In fact, this is exactly what happened during the deep economic recession that began in 2007. Millions of people lost their jobs. As a result, the demand for new cars decreased dramatically, but the demand for used cars was much stronger. If demand for a good decreases when incomes increase, we call the good an ***inferior good***. Some types of used clothes may be inferior goods, while higher-quality new clothes are normal goods. One study indicates that butter is a normal good, but margarine is an inferior good. Can you think of any good that might be an inferior good for you?

The Effect of a Change in Tastes or Preferences

Once again, it's important to remember that a demand curve is constructed by allowing the price to vary, *while everything else remains constant*. If there is a change in another influence, such as consumer tastes or preferences, the demand curve will shift.

In recent years, the American public has become much more aware of the need for a healthy diet. Doctors urge their patients to eat five servings of fruits or vegetables per day, as a way to reduce the risk of cancer. Because of this, consumer preferences have changed, and consumers have increased their demand for many fruits and vegetables, including red-delicious apples. This would be represented by a rightward shift in the demand curve for red-delicious apples, as with the shift from D_0 to D_1 in Figure 3.4(a). Some changes in preferences can lead to increased demand for some goods, but other changes in preferences can lead to *decreased* demand for certain goods. In *Real Economics for Real People 3.1*, we discuss several cases of changes in tastes.

The Effect of a Change in the Price of Another Good: Substitutes and Complements

If there is a change in the price of red-delicious apples, we move along the existing demand curve for these apples. However, if the price of any *other* good changes, the demand curve for red-delicious apples may shift.

Substitutes. If there is an increase in the price of Granny Smith apples, then some people may increase their demand for red-delicious apples. In a case like this, where an increase in the price of one good leads to an increase in the demand for a different good, we say that the two goods are ***substitutes***. In other words, two goods are substitutes if the demand curve for one good shifts to the right when the price of the other good rises. We say that red-delicious apples and Granny Smith apples are substitutes, since an increase in the price of Granny Smith apples will lead to a rightward shift in the demand curve for red-delicious apples. Similarly, we say that two goods are substitutes if the demand curve for one good will shift to the left when the price of the other good falls. The word "substitutes" comes from the fact that consumers will *substitute* away from the good that has become

Jacquelyn Mitchard is the author of a novel called *The Deep End of the Ocean*. Some 100,000 copies of this book were in print by September, 1996. Then, however, the book was recommended on "Oprah's Book Club", a monthly feature of Oprah Winfrey's television talk show. Within a few months, 850,000 copies were in print. Economists would say that the publicity from the Oprah Winfrey Show caused the demand curve for *The Deep End of the Ocean* to shift to the right.

The shift in demand for Jacquelyn Mitchard's book was caused by a change in "preferences" or "tastes". Preferences can change for many reasons. For example, since the 1960s, medical reports have suggested that smoking cigarettes is unhealthy, and this has caused many people to decrease their demand for cigarettes. In other words, the demand curves for many brands of cigarettes have shifted to the left. However, there has been some increase in the demand for cigarettes that are low in "tar", because these are perceived as less unhealthy than other cigarettes. The demand curves for some low-tar brands of cigarette have shifted to the right.

There is nothing new about changes in preferences. In 1934, "It Happened One Night" was a very popular movie. Audiences were amazed by one scene in which the actor Clark Gable took off his shirt. In so doing, he revealed that he wasn't wearing an undershirt. This was considered very unusual and daring because most men wore undershirts at that time. As a result of Gable's dressing habits, undershirts suddenly became much less popular than they had been before. Sales of undershirts decreased dramatically. Economists would say that the demand for undershirts decreased; that is, the demand curve for undershirts shifted to the left.

Toy manufacturers are especially aware of shifts in demand. Every year, some new product will capture the imagination of buyers. Teenage Mutant Ninja Turtles were a hot item for a few years. In one year, the big fad was Beanie Babies. In another year, it was Tickle Me Elmo. In each case, the preferences of consumers changed, leading to large shifts in the demand curves for particular products.

These examples have shown just a few of the ways in which tastes or preferences can change. When an item becomes more popular, its demand curve will shift to the right. When an item becomes less popular, demand will decrease, which means that the demand curve will shift to the left.

relatively more expensive, when there is a change in the price of one of the goods. Consumers will then substitute toward the good that has become relatively cheaper. *When two goods are substitutes, the price of one good and the demand for the other good will move in the* **same** *direction.*

The increase in the demand for red-delicious apples, brought about by the increase in the price of Granny Smith apples, is represented as a rightward shift in the demand curve for red-delicious apples, as in Figure 3.4(a). On the other hand, if the price of Granny Smith apples had *fallen*, the demand curve for red-delicious apples would have shifted to the *left*, as in Figure 3.4(b).

Coffee and tea are substitutes. Vacations at the beach and vacations in the mountains are substitutes. Similarly, vacations in Europe are a substitute for vacations in the United States. Other pairs of substitutes include butter and margarine, and oranges and grapefruit. In every case, consumers are likely to use one or the other, but not both at the same time. Therefore, consumers will tend to substitute from one good to the other when prices change. In *Real Economics for Real People 3.2*, we take a look at another example of substitutes.

Complements. Many people like to consume bread and butter together. If the price of *butter* goes up substantially, these people will probably decide to buy less *bread*. It is as if people don't really desire either bread or butter: Instead, they want to consume the "bread-butter composite." Therefore, if the price of butter goes up, it is as if the entire composite becomes more expensive. We say that bread and butter are *complements*. Two goods are *complements* if an increase in the price of one good leads to a decrease in the demand for the other good. Here's another way to say the same thing: Two goods are complements if the demand curve for one good shifts to the left when the price of the other good increases. We say that bread and butter are complements, since an increase in the price of butter will lead to a leftward shift in the demand curve for bread. Similarly, two goods are complements if the demand curve for one good shifts to the right when the price of the other good decreases. *When two goods are complements, the price of one good and the demand for the other good will move in* **opposite** *directions.*

The decrease in demand for bread that is caused by the increase in the price of butter is represented as a leftward shift in the demand curve for bread. This is similar to the leftward shift shown in Figure 3.4(b). On the other hand, if the price of butter had *fallen*, the demand curve for bread would have shifted to the *right*. This is similar to the rightward shift shown in Figure 3.4(a).

There are many examples of goods that are complements. Coffee beans are complementary with several goods, including donuts, cream, sugar, coffee filters, and coffee makers. Automobiles and gasoline are complements, as are computers and printers.

Of course, many pairs of goods are neither substitutes nor complements. When the price of milk goes up, there is probably no effect on the demand for umbrellas. When the demand for one good is unaffected by the price of another good, we say that the two goods are *independent in demand*.

Other Influences on Demand

So far, we have identified three variables that can lead to shifts in demand curves. These are (1) incomes, (2) tastes or preferences, and (3) the prices of other goods. In this section, we'll look at a few other influences.

Expectations of Future Prices. Suppose you're thinking of buying airline tickets for a vacation. If you believe today's ticket prices will continue for the foreseeable future, you may not have a strong feeling about whether to buy today, or tomorrow, or next week. However, if you come to believe the airlines will begin to offer discounted airfares in a few weeks, it might make sense for you *not* to buy today. Since you have decided that prices will decrease in the future, your demand curve for *today's* purchases will shift to the left.

If you decide prices are about to go *down*, you may delay your purchases, in order to take advantage of the lower prices in the future. On the other hand, if you think prices are about to go *up*, you may hurry to buy now. Another way to think of this is that buying now is usually a fairly close substitute with buying in the near future. *The expected future price of a good and the current demand for that good move in the* **same** *direction, just as we would expect for substitutes.*

Real Economics for Real People 3.2:
Going South of the Border in Search of Cheap Gas

Drivers in the San Diego area usually buy their gasoline in the San Diego area, and pay little attention to the prices in Los Angeles, or across the border in Tijuana, Mexico. However, in 1996, gasoline prices increased substantially in the San Diego area. Eventually, the price of regular gasoline was 22 cents per gallon higher in San Diego than in Tijuana. For diesel fuel, the price difference was 64 cents per gallon! When the price differences got this large, some San Diegans began to drive across the border to buy their gasoline.

We can analyze this example, along with some similar examples, to get a better idea of how consumers make their buying decisions. Let's say that an Exxon station and a Texaco station are right across the street from each other. Furthermore, let's say that each sells regular gasoline for $2.40 per gallon. Some people go to the Texaco station, some go to the Exxon station, and each station sells a large volume of gasoline.

What will happen if the Exxon station keeps its price at $2.40, and the Texaco station lowers its price to $2.30 per gallon? In all likelihood, many more people will buy from the Texaco station because it is now selling gasoline for a lower price. If the two stations are very close to each other, and if they sell gasoline that is of similar quality, why pay more? This example indicates that Texaco gasoline and Exxon gasoline are substitutes: When the price of Texaco gasoline falls, the demand for Exxon gasoline falls. In fact, an economist would say that the Texaco gasoline is a *very close* substitute for the Exxon gasoline because the two stations are so close to each other, and they sell very similar products. When two stations are right

across the street from each other, their prices may not be identical. One station may have friendlier service, or a reputation for gasoline of slightly better quality. However, the prices at two adjacent stations are usually not different by more than a few cents per gallon.

If two goods are close substitutes, it is very easy for buyers to switch from one good to the other. Let's assume that the gasoline at one station is a very close substitute for the gasoline at another nearby station. If the prices diverge from each other, buyers can easily reduce their purchases at the station with the higher price, and increase their purchases at the station with the lower price. But this will put downward pressure on the price at the higher-priced station, and it will put upward pressure on the price at the lower-priced station. Thus, although their prices may not be identical, they will always stay close together.

This is not just true in the case of gasoline stations. Whenever two goods are close substitutes, their prices will stay close to each other.

The situation is a little different if the two stations are farther apart from each other. The true opportunity cost of buying gasoline includes the price charged at the pump, but it also includes the time and trouble that it takes to get there. If the Exxon station is right around the corner, and the Texaco station is miles away, you still might be willing to buy from the Exxon station, even if it sells for a few cents more per gallon. When the two stations are farther apart, economists would say that their products are substitutes, but not necessarily very close substitutes.

If two stations are quite far apart, it will take a large price difference before the prices can have an effect on each other. If Tijuana gasoline is only cheaper than San Diego gasoline by one cent per gallon, no one would take the trouble to cross the border to buy gasoline. However, as we have seen, people may cross the border to buy gasoline if the price difference is large enough. San Diego gasoline and Tijuana gasoline are substitutes, although not very close substitutes. In recent years, the opportunity cost of crossing the border has increased. The terrorist attacks on September 11, 2001, led to heightened concern about border security. In addition, the smuggling of drugs and people from Mexico has led to big increases in security concerns along the U.S. border with Mexico. In many cases, this has led to long lines at border crossings. In this setting, it would take a *very* large price difference to induce people to cross the border in search of cheap gasoline.

These examples remind us that consumers are always on the lookout for a bargain. If they can buy one product for a lower opportunity cost than a substitute product, they will shift their demand from one product to the other, even if it's necessary to cross international borders.

Expectations of Future Incomes. If you believe your income will be higher in the future, you may consume more now. For example, a woman who is just finishing medical school may be poor right now, but she can reasonably expect to have a much higher income in the future. She may be willing to borrow money in order to consume more now.

On the other hand, if you believe that your income will be lower in the future, you may want to consume less now. For instance, as people approach retirement, they know that their incomes are about to decrease. In response, they will typically spend less than their current income. That is, they will save. By saving, people increase the amount they can spend during retirement. *For most goods, current demand will move in the **same** direction as expected future income.*

Size and Composition of the Buying Population. All else equal, market demands are affected by the size of the buying population. When there are more consumers, we would expect more demand. Populations around the world have been rising steadily for centuries, and the demand curves for many goods have shifted to the right over the years.

Market demands are also affected by the *composition* of the population. For example, the elderly population has grown very rapidly in recent years. This has led to increases in the demand for retirement communities, nursing-home care, and so on. As the population continues to get older, these demand shifts are likely to continue.

The various influences on demand are summarized in Figure 3.5, on p. 62.

Reality Check: Interim Review Questions

IR3-1. Let's say that digital cameras are a normal good, and that incomes increase. What will happen to the demand curve for digital cameras?

IR3-2. Assume that there is a decrease in the price of digital cameras, because of a government price control. Would we represent this as a shift in the demand curve for digital cameras, or a movement along the existing demand curve?

IR3-3. Consumers learn that a local furniture store is having a sale next week. That is, next week's prices will be lower than this week's prices. What will happen to *this week's* demand curve for furniture?

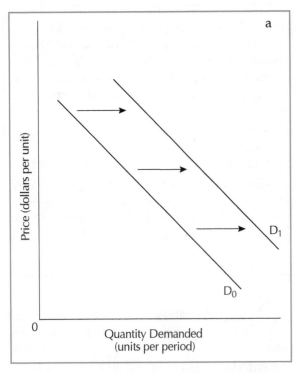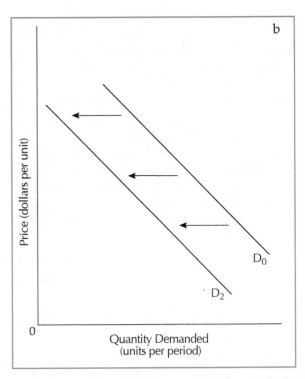

Figure 3.5 Summary of the Influences That Can Shift Demand Curves

An increase in demand (that is, a rightward shift in the demand curve) can be caused by:
- An increase in incomes, if the good is a normal good.
- A decrease in incomes, if the good is an inferior good.
- A change in consumer tastes or preferences, so that the good becomes "more popular".
- An increase in the price of a substitute good.
- A decrease in the price of a complement good.
- Expectations of higher prices in the future.
- Expectations of higher incomes in the future.
- An increase in the size of the buying population.
- A change in the composition of the population.

A decrease in demand (that is, a leftward shift in the demand curve) can be caused by:
- A decrease in incomes, if the good is a normal good.
- An increase in incomes, if the good is an inferior good.
- A change in consumer tastes or preferences, so that the good becomes "less popular".
- A decrease in the price of a substitute good.
- An increase in the price of a complement good.
- Expectations of lower prices in the future.
- Expectations of lower incomes in the future.
- A decrease in the size of the buying population.
- A change in the composition of the population.

SUPPLY 供应品

When we talk about the behavior of sellers, we use the term *supply*. In many markets, the sellers are business firms. For example, Boeing is a supplier of commercial aircraft, Sony is a supplier of consumer electronics, and Volkswagen is a supplier of automobiles. However, in labor markets, the sellers are workers. For example, in the market for the services of accountants, the suppliers are individual people who have

been trained to provide such services. In this chapter, we will concentrate primarily on markets in which the sellers are business firms. Chapter 13 is devoted to labor markets.

In the previous section, we discussed the many influences on the behavior of buyers. We separated these influences into two groups: (1) the price of the good, and (2) anything else, such as incomes, tastes, the prices of other

-62-

goods, expectations of future prices, and so on. In this section, we will follow the same procedure. The behavior of sellers is influenced by all sorts of things. We will separate these influences into two groups: (1) the price of the good, and (2) anything else, such as the technology of production or the prices of inputs.

The *quantity supplied* is the amount of some good or service that sellers are willing and able to sell, at a specific price, in a given period of time.

The Law of Supply

As mentioned before, economists think about supply and demand in similar ways. Many things can affect the quantity supplied, just as many things can affect the quantity demanded. However, economists single out the current price of the good for special attention. We will focus on the current price of the good when we think about supply, just as we focused on price when thinking about demand.

The *Law of Supply* states that:

When the price of a good or service increases, the quantity supplied will increase, all else equal. In a similar way, when the price decreases, the quantity supplied will decrease, all else equal.

In other words, the Law of Supply states that sellers have a *direct, positive relationship* between the current price and quantity supplied, all else equal.

We have two main reasons to expect sellers to obey the Law of Supply. First, *when production of a good increases, the costs of additional production will often increase*. If apple growers try to increase their production, they will have to use more intensive methods of cultivation. For example, they may use more pesticides and fertilizer. These may succeed in increasing the size of the apple crop, but they will also increase costs.

The second reason for suppliers to obey the Law of Supply is that *price is a powerful signal of opportunities for profit*. Consider a business firm

that makes contact lenses and plastic packaging. What happens if there is an increase in the price of contact lenses, while the price of plastic packaging stays the same? The firm will see that it can increase profits by putting more of its production into contact lenses.

Earlier in this chapter, we said that we will almost always assume that the Law of Demand is obeyed. Although we will *usually* assume that the Law of Supply is obeyed, the Law of Supply is not as strong as the Law of Demand. Thus we will encounter several situations in which the Law of Supply is violated.

For example, anything that cannot be reproduced will violate the Law of Supply. In 1601, the Italian painter Caravaggio painted the "Supper at Emmaus", which is now owned by the National Gallery in London. Caravaggio died in 1610, and most experts agree that he is not creating any more paintings (at least not here on earth). If the "Supper at Emmaus" were to be put up for sale, the price could go up and up and up, and the quantity supplied would always be exactly one painting. That doesn't fit with the Law of Supply, which says that an increase in price is associated with an increase in quantity supplied.

Later in this book, we will see some other situations in which the Law of Supply is not obeyed. However, the Law of Supply is strong enough that it is our default option: In most cases, we will assume that the Law of Supply is obeyed.

The Supply Schedule and the Supply Curve

A *supply schedule* is a table that lists different prices for a good or service, and shows the quantity that would be supplied at each price. When we construct a supply schedule, we allow the current price of a good to change, but we assume that *all other influences on suppliers are held constant*. Thus the technology of production is assumed to be unchanged. The prices of the materials used in the production process are also assumed to be unchanged, as are all other influences. In a supply schedule, the *only* thing that we allow to vary is the price of the good.

A *supply curve* is a graph of the information in a supply schedule. In other words, a supply curve is a graph of the relationship between the price of a good and the quantity supplied, all else equal. Figure 3.6 shows a market supply schedule for red-delicious apples, as well as the corresponding market supply curve. *Because of the Law of Supply, the supply curve slopes upward as we move from left to right.*

We construct a market supply curve, such as the one in Figure 3.6, by adding together the supply curves of the individual business firms. We won't actually show any supply curves for individual firms here, although we will study firm supply curves in a later chapter. For the rest of this chapter, we focus on market supply curves.

Movements Along the Supply Curve vs. Shifts in the Supply Curve

When we construct a supply curve, the *only* thing that changes is the price of the good. Everything else is held constant. If there is a change in the price of red-delicious apples, we move along the existing supply curve for red-delicious apples. The same holds true for the supply curve for running shorts, or for floorlamps, or for any other good or service. *A change in the price of a good will cause a movement along the existing supply curve for that good or service.*

This can be seen in Figure 3.6. At point C, the price is $1.25 per pound of apples, and the quantity supplied is 750 million pounds per year. When the price goes up to $1.50 per pound, sellers respond by increasing their quantity supplied. In this example, the sellers of red-delicious apples increase their quantity supplied to 800 million pounds per year, as a result of the increase in price. In Figure 3.6,

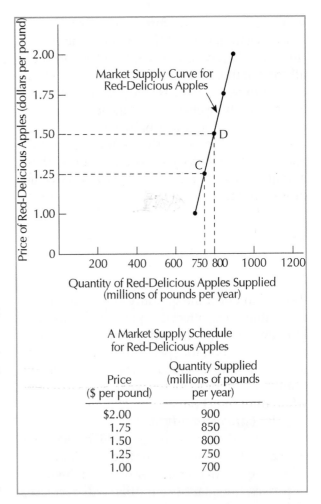

A Market Supply Schedule
for Red-Delicious Apples

Price ($ per pound)	Quantity Supplied (millions of pounds per year)
$2.00	900
1.75	850
1.50	800
1.25	750
1.00	700

Figure 3.6 A Market Supply Schedule and Supply Curve for Red-Delicious Apples

If we add together the quantities supplied by all of the sellers in the market, we find a market supply curve. For example, at point C, the price of red-delicious apples is $1.25 per pound, and sellers are willing to supply 750 million pounds per year. If the price were to increase to $1.50 per pound, sellers would increase their quantity supplied from 750 million pounds per year to 800 million pounds per year. This is shown by the movement from point C to point D. The market supply curve slopes upward as we move from left to right, which indicates that apple sellers obey the Law of Supply.

this is seen as a movement from point C to point D. The entire supply curve shown in Figure 3.6 slopes upward as we move from left to right across the graph. This indicates that the Law of Supply is obeyed by the firms in the market for red-delicious apples.

When we constructed the supply curve in Figure 3.6, we held everything constant, except for the price of red-delicious apples. What if there were a change in something other than the price of red-delicious apples? If there is a change in any other influence on sellers of apples, such as the price of pesticides, we would no longer move along the existing supply curve. Instead, we would shift to a different supply curve. *If there is a change in any influence on sellers other than the current price of the good, the change will cause a shift to an entirely new supply curve.*

This is a crucial distinction. *Movements along* an existing supply curve are caused by changes in the price of the good; *shifts* to a new supply curve are caused by changes in other influences on sellers.

Changes in Quantity Supplied vs. Changes in Supply

In the last few paragraphs, we have distinguished between (1) movements along an existing supply curve, which are caused by changes in price, and (2) shifts to a new supply curve, which are caused by changes in other variables. We can also use a different terminology. A *change in quantity supplied* refers to a movement along an existing supply curve. A *change in supply* refers to a shift to a new supply curve.

Thus, if the price of MP3 players were to go down, we could refer to a movement along the existing supply curve for these devices, or we could refer to a change in the quantity of MP3 players supplied. Each phrase has the same meaning. On the other hand, consider what would happen if there were an increase in the price of the plastics that are necessary

to produce MP3 players. This would make it more costly to produce MP3 players, and it would cause a shift to a *new* supply curve for the devices. Alternatively, instead of referring to a shift to a new supply curve, we could refer to a change in the supply of MP3 players. Once again, each of these phrases has the same meaning.

We can identify some of the forces that can lead to shifts in supply curves, including:

- changes in input prices,
- changes in technology,
- changes in the prices of other goods,
- changes in taxes, subsidies, or regulations, and
- changes in the number of sellers.

We will now take a more detailed look at some of these influences.

The Effect of a Change in Input Prices

Fertilizer is used in the production of apples. In Figure 3.7(a), we show what happens to the supply curve for red-delicious apples, when there is an increase in the price of fertilizer. When the price of fertilizer goes up, it becomes more expensive to produce apples. After an increase in the price of an important input, such as fertilizer, the cost of bringing any given quantity of apples to market will be greater than before. Therefore, the supply curve for red-delicious apples will shift *to the left* when there is an increase in the price of fertilizer. In Figure 3.7(a), this is shown as a shift from the old supply curve, S_0, to the new supply curve, S_1. We can interpret this shift in two ways. First, at any given price, there has been a decrease in the quantity that sellers are willing and able to bring to market. Second, for any given quantity, there has been an increase in the price that firms need to receive, in order to be willing and able to supply that quantity to the market.

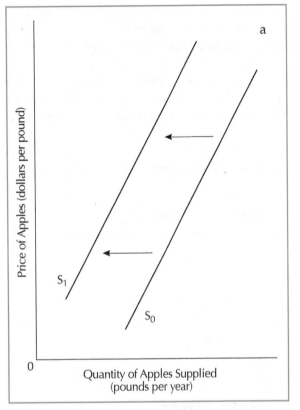

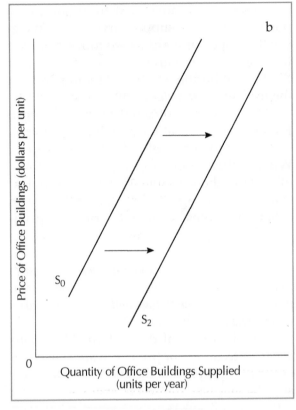

Figure 3.7 Shifts in the Supply Curve, Caused by Changes in the Price of an Input

An increase in the price of any input will cause a decrease in supply. In this case, the price of fertilizer increases, and the supply of red-delicious apples decreases. This is shown as a leftward shift of the supply curve for apples.

A decrease in the price of any input will cause an increase in supply. In this case, the price of steel goes down, and the supply of office buildings increases. This is shown as a rightward shift of the supply curve for office buildings.

When an office building is built, the construction firm uses bulldozers, welding equipment, steel, and lumber, as well as the labor of engineers and construction workers. If any of these inputs were to become cheaper, the supply curve for office buildings would shift to the right. This is shown in Figure 3.7(b). When the price of steel goes down, there is a rightward shift in the supply curve for office buildings, from S_0 to S_2.

The Effect of a Change in Technology

The *technology* of production is society's pool of knowledge about how to produce. In the last hundred years, many industries have experienced rapid improvements in technology. For example, agriculture has gone from using horse-drawn plows to using massive tractors. Another example is that the accounting profession has changed with the introduction of hardware and software for high-speed data processing, such as computer spreadsheet programs.

When there is an improvement in production technology, producers are able to supply products more cheaply, without having to reduce the quality of their products. Thus, technological improvements will shift supply curves *to the right*. Consider a new production process that allows firms to produce more flat-screen TVs, without increasing the amount of inputs that must be used. This would cause a rightward shift in the supply curve, much like the shift from S_0 to S_2 in Figure 3.7(b). At any given price, there has been an increase in the quantity that firms will supply. Alternatively, for any given quantity, there has been a decrease in the price that firms need to receive, in order to be willing and able to supply that quantity to the market.

The last few thousand years, and especially the last few hundred years, have been marked by amazingly rapid technological improvements. These improvements, which we represent as rightward shifts in the supply curve, have been the driving force behind increasing standards of living. However, sometimes technologies can deteriorate as a result of wars, earthquakes, fires, floods, and other such events. We represent a deterioration of technology as a *leftward* shift in the supply curve.

Other Influences on Supply

We've highlighted the effects of input prices and technology on supply. These are certainly among the most important influences on supply. However, there are several other important influences, and we discuss them briefly here.

Prices of Other Goods. Consider a publishing house that produces a variety of books and magazines. If there is an increase in the price of magazines, the publisher may reduce its output of books, in order to devote more resources to the production of magazines. This would be shown as a leftward shift of the supply curve for books. On the other hand, if the price of magazines were to fall, there could be a rightward shift in the supply curve for books.

In some cases, one good is a by-product of the production of another good. For example, the main product of a sawmill is finished lumber. However, sawmills also create by-products such as sawdust and wood chips. These by-products can be used to make packaging, cat litter, and other products. Consequently, when the price of lumber goes up, there is an increase in the quantity of lumber supplied, and the supply curve of wood chips will shift to the right.

Taxes, Subsidies, and Regulations. From the point of view of the business firm, a tax is just like any other cost of doing business. Thus, an increase in a property tax, or a corporation income tax, or a business license fee is much like an increase in the price of an input, which we discussed above. If a tax goes up, the supply curve will shift to the left. If a tax goes down, the supply curve will shift to the right. (In later chapters, we will discuss the effects of taxes in more detail.)

A subsidy is the opposite of a tax. Sometimes, governments provide subsidies to businesses, in an effort to encourage certain kinds of behavior. If a subsidy goes up, the supply curve will shift to the *right*. If a subsidy goes down, the supply curve will shift to the *left*.

Regulations also affect supply. Firms face a number of regulations relating to product

From the late 1930s until the late 1970s, if a company wanted to enter the commercial airlines industry, it had to get approval from a government agency called the Civil Aeronautics Board (CAB). Since the CAB turned down every application, it was effectively impossible for new firms to enter the industry. As a result, the supply of airline flights was restricted. In other words, the supply curve of airline flights was kept farther to the left than it would have been. We would expect that this restriction of supply would keep the quantity of airline trips down, relative to what it might have been.

During the 1970s, there was more and more dissatisfaction with the CAB and its policy of keeping new airlines out of the business. Finally, in 1978, Congress passed a law that allowed new airlines to offer their services. One of the biggest success stories has been that of Southwest Airlines, which has had a dramatic effect on air travel in the United States in recent decades. Southwest tended to concentrate on smaller airports, such as the ones at Burbank and San Jose, California, instead of larger ones, such as those at Los Angeles and San Francisco. By offering more flights, Southwest Airlines pushed the industry supply curve to the right. One study of the West Coast airlines market indicates that the amount of traffic increased by 60 percent, while prices fell by an average of one-third. Southwest may not have been responsible for all of these changes in price and quantity, but it certainly had an important effect.

In the 1990s and 2000s, Southwest Airlines expanded its service throughout the country. By 2016, Southwest provided service in 41 of the 50 states. In many cases, Southwest continued to use smaller airports, such as Chicago's Midway Airport, or Love Field in Dallas, However, Southwest Airlines has also provided competitive service in larger airports.

In almost every market, the entry of new firms can bring benefits. When supply curves are pushed to the right, consumers will be able to enjoy a higher quantity. Thus economists tend to be very skeptical about artificial restrictions on entry into an industry, such as those that were once enforced by the Civil Aeronautics Board.

safety, occupational health and safety, employee benefits, and the environment. For example, firms that process meat or poultry are required to follow a number of government regulations, in an attempt to ensure that the nation's food supply is safe. The federal government requires automobile manufacturers to meet a standard, in terms of the number of miles per gallon that can be achieved by the average car. Dental hygienists, barbers, psychologists, and doctors are all required to obtain government licenses before they can practice their professions. Many of these regulations may produce benefits, but it's also important to realize that they are not free. In many cases, the regulations raise costs, and lead to reductions in supply.

The Number of Sellers. If we hold constant the amount produced by each firm in a market, then the market supply curve will shift to the right when more firms enter the market (all else equal). Similarly, when firms exit from the industry, the market supply curve will shift to the left (all else equal). In *Real Economics for Real People 3.3*, we discuss the increase in the

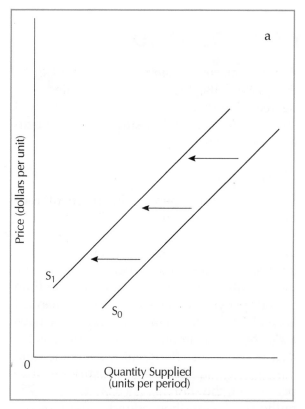
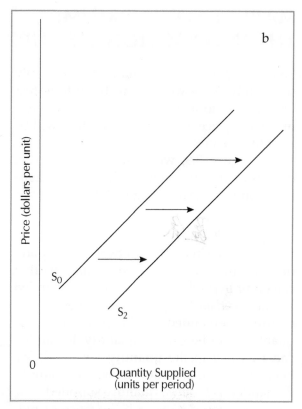

Figure 3.8 Summary of the Influences That Can Shift Supply Curves

A decrease in supply (that is, a leftward shift in the supply curve) can be caused by:
- An increase in the price of an input.
- A deterioration of technology. (Fortunately, this doesn't happen very often.)
- Certain types of change in the price of another good.
- An increase in a tax, or a decrease in a subsidy.
- An increase in a regulation.
- A decrease in the number of sellers.

An increase in supply (that is, a rightward shift in the supply curve) can be caused by:
- A decrease in the price of an input.
- A technological advance.
- Certain other types of change in the price of another good.
- A decrease in a tax, or an increase in a subsidy.
- A decrease in a regulation.
- An increase in the number of sellers.

number of sellers in the commercial airlines industry.

We summarize some of the influences on supply curves in Figure 3.8.

Reality Check:
Interim Review Questions

IR3-4. One type of plastic is an important input in the production of office chairs.

There is an increase in the price of this type of plastic. What effect will this have on the supply curve for office chairs?

IR3-5. Scientists come up with a new invention, which makes it possible to produce steel with fewer inputs than were necessary before. What will happen to the supply curve for steel?

MARKET EQUILIBRIUM:
THE INTERACTION OF SUPPLY AND DEMAND

So far, we've looked at demand and supply separately. Now we can put them together. Our goal is to learn how the market determines the price and the quantity that will be bought and sold.

In Figure 3.9, we combine the market demand curve from Figure 3.3 and the market supply curve from Figure 3.6.

Surpluses 屋条

We can see the interaction between supply and demand by examining three situations that can occur in markets. The quantity demanded can be *less than* the quantity supplied, or the quantity demanded can be *greater than* the quantity supplied, or the quantity demanded can be *equal to* the quantity supplied. We begin with the situation in which quantity demanded is *less than* quantity supplied.

What would happen if the price of red-delicious apples were $2.00 per pound? At this price, Figure 3.9 shows that the quantity supplied is 900 million pounds per year, but the quantity demanded is only 400 million pounds per year. When the quantity demanded is less than the quantity supplied, we have a *surplus*. The amount of the surplus is the difference between the quantity supplied and the quantity demanded. In this case, there is a surplus of (900 million – 400 million) = 500 million pounds of red-delicious apples per year.

The surplus means that crates of unsold apples will accumulate. At a price of $2.00 per pound, the surpluses would pile up, week after week after week. Pretty soon, stores and warehouses would be bursting with surplus apples that can't be sold.

This creates an expensive problem for the sellers, because it costs a lot to carry large inventories. Very quickly, sellers will have a bright idea: "If we charge a lower price, we can sell some of that stuff in the warehouse."

A surplus creates pressure for the price to fall. As the price falls, the quantity supplied will decrease, and the quantity demanded will increase. Because of this, surpluses don't usually last for very long.

Shortages

What would happen if the price of red-delicious apples were only $1.25 per pound? At this price, Figure 3.9 shows that the quantity demanded is 1000 million pounds per year (that is, one billion pounds per year). However, the quantity supplied is only 750 million pounds per year. When the quantity demanded is greater than the quantity supplied, we have a *shortage*. The amount of the shortage is the difference between the quantity demanded and the quantity supplied. When the price is $1.25 per pound, the shortage is (1000 million – 750 million) = 250 million pounds of apples per year. In this situation, some buyers will not find any apples at all, even though they are willing to pay to buy apples at that price.

A shortage is a difficult situation. When a shortage occurs, consumers are willing and able to pay for goods or services, but they are unable to find them. For example, in the 1970s, the United States experienced widespread gasoline shortages. Gasoline stations would put out signs, saying "All out. Please come back next week." This is psychologically difficult for buyers, who are used to being able to buy what they want to buy.

Shortages create uncertainty, as buyers wonder when (if ever) the next shipment will arrive. During the gasoline shortages of the 1970s, people would wait in long lines to get gasoline, even if their tanks were mostly full. This is because they were afraid of running out of gas, and uncertain about whether they could count on being able to buy gasoline a few days later.

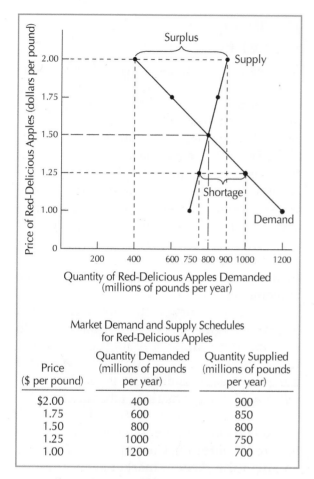

Market Demand and Supply Schedules
for Red-Delicious Apples

Price ($ per pound)	Quantity Demanded (millions of pounds per year)	Quantity Supplied (millions of pounds per year)
$2.00	400	900
1.75	600	850
1.50	800	800
1.25	1000	750
1.00	1200	700

**Figure 3.9 Equilibrium in the Market
for Red-Delicious Apples**

If the price of red-delicious apples is $2.00 per pound, the quantity supplied is 900 million pounds per year, but the quantity demanded is only 400 million pounds per year. This means that we have a surplus of (900 million – 400 million) = 500 million pounds per year. The surplus will create pressure for the price to fall. If the price of apples is $1.25 per pound, the quantity demanded is 1000 million pounds per year, but the quantity supplied is only 750 million pounds per year. This means that we have a shortage of (1000 million – 750 million) = 250 million pounds per year. The shortage will create pressure for the price to rise. If the price of red-delicious apples is $1.50 per pound, the quantity demanded will be 800 million pounds and the quantity supplied will also be 800 million pounds. This is an equilibrium. When the quantity demanded is equal to the quantity supplied, there is no reason for the price to change, because both buyers and sellers are satisfied.

Shortages were an everyday occurrence in the old Soviet Union. There, consumers became accustomed to waiting in long lines, without any assurance that they would be able to find anything when they got to the front of the line. People would often line up, even in the middle of the night, on the basis of mere rumors of the possibility that a new shipment of soap or toilet paper might be coming to town.

Before long, buyers will begin to offer more money for apples. Since many people are willing and able to pay more than $1.25 per pound, sellers will guess that they can increase their profits by raising the selling price. *A shortage creates pressure for the price to rise.* As the price increases, the quantity supplied will increase, and the quantity demanded will fall. Because of this, shortages don't usually last for very long.

Equilibrium 平衡

An interesting thing happens when the price of red-delicious apples is $1.50 per pound. At this price, the quantity demanded is 800 million pounds per year, and the quantity supplied is also 800 million pounds per year! We have neither a surplus nor a shortage. Instead, quantity demanded and quantity supplied are equal. When quantity demanded is equal to quantity supplied, economists say that the market is in *equilibrium.* When the market is in equilibrium, there is no incentive for buyers or sellers to change their behavior. Both buyers and sellers are satisfied.

The equilibrium has two parts—a price and a quantity. The *equilibrium price* is the price at which quantity supplied is equal to quantity demanded. The phrase *equilibrium quantity* can be used to refer to either the quantity supplied or the quantity demanded, since quantity supplied is equal to quantity demanded when the market is in equilibrium.

Equilibrium is a truly astonishing occurrence. At the equilibrium price, the quantity that sellers voluntarily bring to the market is exactly equal to the quantity that buyers voluntarily desire to buy. Neither buyers nor sellers are being coerced. Instead, both sides of the market are the beneficiaries of an exchange that is satisfactory for buyers and for sellers.

Clearly, an equilibrium has some big advantages, but these advantages can only be realized if the market is able to find the equilibrium price. If markets were unable to find the equilibrium price, then the idea of equilibrium would only be a theoretical oddity. Fortunately, *powerful market forces push toward equilibrium*. When the market price is higher than the equilibrium price, there is a surplus, and we have seen that surpluses lead to pressure for price to fall. When the market price is lower than the equilibrium price, there is a shortage, which leads to pressure for price to rise. Thus, the price will tend to fall when it is above equilibrium, and it will tend to rise when it is below equilibrium. Most markets move toward equilibrium very quickly.

Remember that the demand curve shows the relationship between price and quantity demanded, while the supply curve shows the relationship between price and quantity supplied. In Figure 3.9, we have plotted a supply curve and a demand curve on the same graph. The equilibrium price is $1.50 per pound of apples. If you go to the place where the supply curve crosses the demand curve in Figure 3.9, and then follow the dashed line to the left, to the vertical axis, you will find the equilibrium price of $1.50 per pound. *Graphically, the equilibrium can be found at the intersection of the demand curve and the supply curve.*

Whenever you see a supply-demand diagram, such as Figure 3.9, you can easily find the equilibrium price and quantity by locating the place where the supply curve intersects the demand curve. From that point, if you go straight to the left, you will find the equilibrium price. If you go straight down, you'll find the equilibrium quantity.

The Beauty of Market Equilibrium

No one sets out with the goal of achieving market equilibrium. Buyers just want to get the most for their money, and sellers just want to make a profit. And yet, the interaction of buyers and sellers leads the market to equilibrium. This is a remarkable fact, and it is one of the most important concepts in all of economics. In equilibrium, both buyers and sellers are satisfied. This is a very good outcome, and markets achieve it without government intervention. There is no need for a dictator or a bureaucracy to tell people what to do. Instead, the market achieves a desirable outcome on its own.

The 18th-century Scottish economist Adam Smith used the phrase *invisible hand* to describe the beauty of market equilibrium. Even though no one sets out with the goal of achieving market equilibrium, it is as if an invisible hand leads the market in that direction.

The invisible hand is extremely powerful. Markets usually move quickly and strongly toward equilibrium. Consequently, if there is an attempt to keep a market away from its equilibrium price and quantity, lots of problems can occur. In the next chapter, we will learn about some of the problems that happen when governments try to keep prices away from their equilibrium levels.

Reality Check: Interim Review Questions

IR3-6. The equilibrium price of one type of spiral-bound notebook is $2.50. If the price were $1, would there be a shortage or a surplus? What would happen if the price were $4?

IR3-7. In a supply-demand diagram, what is special about the point at which the demand curve crosses the supply curve?

ECONOMICS AND YOU:
SUPPLY, DEMAND, AND AUTOMOBILE PRICES

At the beginning of this chapter, we asked why different automobile models are sold for different prices. The ideas developed in this chapter should help us to answer the question. *Prices are determined by the interaction of supply and demand.*

Supply is clearly important to the determination of prices. One reason that a Ferrari 360 Spider is more expensive than a Ford Taurus is that the Ferrari is costlier to build. The Ferrari uses more expensive materials, and more labor is required.

Taxes also have an effect on supply. Any tax will effectively raise the costs of production. All else equal, a car buyer will have to pay a greater total price if the car is taxed than if it is not taxed. One form of tax is a tariff, which is a tax on items that are imported from one country to another. Since cars are subject to tariffs, the price of an imported car will be higher than the price of a domestically produced car, as long as all other influences on price are the same.

In the determination of prices, demand is just as important as supply. Some Mercedes-Benz models are sold at higher prices in the United States than in Germany. In some cases, the price in the U.S. is more than twice as high! Shipping costs and tariffs aren't large enough to explain such a big difference in prices. The reason for the difference is that some Americans are willing to pay more than some Germans, for the same car.

Supply and demand are both essential for understanding prices and quantities. A British economist, Alfred Marshall, popularized a way of thinking about the interaction of supply and demand. Marshall compared supply and demand to a pair of scissors. For one thing, an intersecting supply curve and demand curve look a little like a pair of scissors. Moreover, you can't cut a piece of paper very easily unless you have *both* blades of the pair of scissors. And you can't explain prices and quantities unless you have *both* supply and demand.

In this chapter, we have set out the basics of supply and demand. In the next chapter, we will apply the supply-demand framework in a variety of ways. We'll look closely at what happens when there are shifts in the supply and demand curves, and we will study the effects of price controls.

Chapter Summary

1. A market is an organized system of exchange of a good or service between buyers and sellers. Markets can be local, national, or international.

2. Demand refers to the behavior of buyers in a market. The Law of Demand states that when there is an increase in the price of a good or service, the quantity demanded will decrease, *all else equal*. Similarly, the Law of Demand states that a decrease in price is associated with an increase in quantity demanded, *all else equal*.

3. A demand schedule is a table that shows the combinations of price and quantity demanded. A demand curve is a graph of the combinations of price and quantity demanded. Thus a demand schedule and a demand curve show the same information; the only difference is that the demand schedule is a table, while the demand curve is a graph. A demand curve is constructed by allowing the price of a good to change, while holding constant all other influences on buyers. The Law of Demand means that the graph of a demand curve will slope downward as we move from left to right.

4. If there is a change in the price of a good, we move along the existing demand curve. If there is a change in any other influence on buyers, we shift to a new demand curve. Many influences can shift demand curves; the most important of these are consumer incomes, the prices of other goods, tastes or preferences, expectations, and the size and composition of the buying population.

5. Supply refers to the behavior of sellers in a market. The Law of Supply states that, *all else equal*, the quantity supplied will increase in response to an increase in the price of a good or service. Similarly, the Law of Supply states that a decrease in price is associated with a decrease in quantity supplied, *all else equal*.

6. A supply schedule is a table that shows the combinations of price and quantity supplied. A supply curve is a graph of the combinations of price and quantity supplied. Thus a supply schedule and a supply curve show the same information; the only difference is that the supply schedule is a table, while the supply curve is a graph. The supply curve is constructed by allowing the price of the good to change, while holding constant all other influences on sellers. The Law of Supply means that the graph of a supply curve will slope upward as we move from left to right.

7. If there is a change in the price of a good, then we move along the existing supply curve. If there is a change in any other influence on sellers, we shift to a new supply curve. The most important influences that shift supply curves are the prices of inputs, the technology of production, the prices of other goods, taxes, subsidies, regulations, and the number of sellers in the market.

8. If the quantity demanded is greater than the quantity supplied, we have a shortage. If the quantity supplied is greater than the quantity demanded, we have a surplus. Equilibrium is achieved when the quantity supplied is equal to the quantity demanded. Graphically, equilibrium is found at the point where the supply curve intersects the demand curve.

9. If the price is below its equilibrium level, the resulting shortages will put upward pressure on price. If the price is above its equilibrium level, the resulting surpluses will create pressure for price to fall. Thus, the market will tend to move toward equilibrium.

10. For a normal good, an increase in income will lead to a rightward shift in the

demand curve, and a decrease in income will cause the demand curve to shift to the left. In other words, for a normal good, an increase in income will lead to an increase in demand, and a decrease in income will cause a decrease in demand.

11. For an inferior good, an increase in income will lead to a leftward shift in the demand curve, and a decrease in income will cause the demand curve to shift to the right. In other words, for an inferior good, an increase in income will lead to a decrease in demand, and a decrease in income will cause an increase in demand.

12. When two goods are substitutes, an increase in the price of one good will lead to a rightward shift in the demand curve for the other good.

13. When two goods are complements, an increase in the price of one good will lead to a decrease in demand for the other good.

14. When the price of an input goes up, the supply curve will shift to the left. When the price of an input falls, the supply curve will shift to the right. In other words, when an input price rises, there is a decrease in supply, and when an input price falls, there is an increase in supply.

15. An improvement in technology will cause the supply curve to shift to the right. A deterioration in technology (perhaps as a result of a war or a hurricane) will cause the supply curve to shift to the left. In other words, an improvement in technology leads to an increase in supply, and a deterioration in technology leads to a decrease in supply.

Key Terms

Market

Demand

Quantity Demanded

Law of Demand

Demand Schedule

Individual Demand Schedule

Market Demand Schedule

Demand Curve

Change in Quantity Demanded

Change in Demand

Normal Good

Inferior Good

Substitutes

Complements

Independent in Demand

Supply

Quantity Supplied

Law of Supply

Supply Schedule

Supply Curve

Change in Quantity Supplied

Change in Supply

Technology

Surplus

Shortage

Market Equilibrium

Equilibrium Price

Equilibrium Quantity

Invisible Hand

Key Figure

The key figure for this chapter is Figure 3.9, showing the equilibrium of supply and demand.

Questions and Problems

QP3-1. Throughout much of the 20th century, practicing Catholics were prohibited from eating meat on Fridays, but they were allowed to eat fish. In the 1960s, this requirement was removed. As a result of this change, what do you expect happened to the demand for codfish?

QP3-2
a. Explain the Law of Demand.
b. Explain the difference between a change in demand (i.e., a shift in the demand curve) and a change in the quantity demanded (i.e., a movement along an existing demand curve).

QP3-3. In 2012, the price of corn increased. Corn is an important input into the production of fatted hogs. As a result of the increase in the price of corn, what do you expect happened to the supply curve of fatted hogs?

QP3-4
a. Explain the Law of Supply.
b. Explain the difference between a change in supply (i.e., a shift in the supply curve) and a change in the quantity supplied (i.e., a movement along an existing supply curve).

QP3-5. Japanese automobile companies raise the prices of the cars that they are selling in North America. What would this do to the demand for American-produced cars? Why?

QP3-6. Analyze the following statement: "The worldwide reserves of oil are fixed, but the size of the economy keeps increasing. Sooner or later, demand will just outrun supply."

QP3-7. Which of the following will shift the *supply curve* for blue jeans? If the supply curve will be shifted, will it shift to the left or to the right?
a. A decrease in the price of cotton, which is an input in the production of blue jeans.
b. A government price control, mandating that the price of blue jeans must be above its equilibrium level.
c. A technological improvement which allows manufacturers to dye blue jeans with less blue dye than before.
d. An increase in the price of blue dye.
e. An increase in the price of cowboy boots, which are a complement of blue jeans.
f. An increase in the number of firms that produce blue jeans. You may assume that the technology of production of blue jeans is unchanged, so each individual firm has the same costs as before.

QP3-8. Which of the following will shift the *demand curve* for raisins? If the demand curve will be shifted, will it shift to the left or to the right?
a. A government price control, mandating that the price of raisins must be below its equilibrium level.
b. An increase in consumer incomes, assuming that raisins are a normal good.
c. An increase in consumer incomes, assuming that raisins are an inferior good.
d. An increase in the price of grapes, which are an important input in the production of raisins.
e. A decrease in the price of prunes, which are a substitute for raisins.
f. A climate forecast, which suggests that *next* year will be a poor year for raisins. As a result of the forecast, people come to believe that raisin prices will be higher next year.
g. A decrease in the price of bran flakes, which are a complement of raisins.
h. An increase in the wages of workers at the raisin factory.

Price	Caps Demanded	Caps Supplied	Surplus or Shortage
$26/cap	70,000	130,000	
24	80,000	120,000	
22	90,000	110,000	
20	100,000	100,000	
18	110,000	90,000	
16	120,000	80,000	
14	130,000	70,000	

QP3-9. Each of the following changes can be expected to have an effect on the market for disposable diapers. Predict which curve will shift, and predict the direction of the shift in supply or demand.

a. A campaign by environmentalists, which causes parents to feel uncomfortable about using diapers that will eventually end up in a landfill.
b. An increase in the number of babies being born each year.
c. A new technology that allows producers to use fewer workers in making diapers.
d. A decrease in the price of pulp. (Pulp is used in the production of disposable diapers.)

QP3-10. Each of the following changes can be expected to have an effect on the market for newly built houses. Predict which curve will shift, and predict the direction of the shift in supply or demand.

a. The price of lumber (an input in the production of new houses) goes down.
b. There is a decrease in interest rates. (You may assume that most people borrow most of the money that is necessary to buy new homes.)

c. There is a decrease in the number of new households being formed.
d. New regulations on land development lead to a reduction in the amount of land available for new home construction.

QP3-11. The supply schedule and demand schedule for Pittsburgh Pirate baseball caps are given above.

a. Fill in the blanks. If you subtract the number of caps demanded from the number of caps supplied, a positive number will correspond to a surplus, and a negative number will correspond to a shortage.
b. What is the equilibrium price? What is the equilibrium quantity?

QP3-12. In the previous problem, we could express the supply schedule by an equation: $Q_s = 5000P$, where Q_s is the quantity supplied and P is the price in dollars. The demand schedule can be expressed as $Q_d = 200,000 - 5000P$, where Q_d is the quantity demanded. Equilibrium can also be expressed by an equation: $Q_s = Q_d$.

a. Substitute the equation for Q_s and the equation for Q_d into the equilibrium equation. Solve the equation to find the equilibrium price.

b. Now, take the equilibrium price that you found in (a), and substitute it into the equation for Q_d. Solve for the equilibrium quantity demanded.

c. Now, take the equilibrium price that you found in (a), and substitute it into the equation for Q_s. Solve for the equilibrium quantity supplied. Your answer should match the answer you found in (b).

d. If the price is $16 per cap, how many people will have unsatisfied demand for caps? (In other words, at a price of $16 per cap, what is the size of the shortage?)

Chapter 4

Applications of Supply and Demand

ECONOMICS AND YOU:
THE ECONOMICS OF FINDING A PARKING SPACE

At age 32, Jeanette Cogan has returned to her studies at a college in the southeastern United States. Once a year, she pays $50 to buy a parking sticker, which allows her to park her car in the college's parking lots for the next 12 months. However, Jeanette's sticker doesn't allow her to park in the lots that are closest to the center of the campus. And unless she arrives very early in the morning, some of the other lots are already full. She often has to drive around for several minutes before finding a parking space, and she still has to settle for a space that's far from her classes. As she lugs her books from the distant parking lot to her classroom, Jeanette thinks to herself that there must be a better way.

There may indeed be a better way to allocate parking spaces at Jeanette's campus, and it has to do with the pricing structure used by the college. In the previous chapter, we saw that the forces of supply and demand in the marketplace will usually move quickly to establish equilibrium. In other words, markets usually do a good job of eliminating shortages or surpluses. However, the parking situation at Jeanette's college is one of chronic shortages. Day after day, the quantity of good parking spaces demanded is greater than the

quantity supplied. This suggests that the college's pricing structure may be preventing the parking lots from achieving equilibrium. In this chapter, we will develop an understanding of how chronic parking shortages can occur, and of what might be done about them.

In this chapter, you will learn a great deal about how markets work:

- We will begin by looking at what happens to the equilibrium price and quantity, when something causes the demand curve or the supply curve to shift.

- Then, we will look at what happens when a market is not able to achieve equilibrium, because of a law or for some other reason.

After reading this chapter, you will know how markets respond to changes in supply or demand. You will also have an understanding of the public-policy issues that arise when prices aren't allowed to find their equilibrium level. In Chapter 3, we saw that markets have an exceptionally strong tendency to move toward equilibrium. Because the invisible hand is so strong, there will usually be serious consequences if a government tries to keep a market away from its equilibrium price and quantity.

We begin our study of applications of the supply-demand framework in the next section. We will look closely at examples in which something changes, causing a shift in the supply curve or the demand curve.

SHIFTS IN THE DEMAND CURVE

When a market is in equilibrium, the buyers are satisfied, and the sellers are also satisfied. At the equilibrium, there are no surpluses to push the price down, and no shortages to push the price up. Thus, as long as the supply curve and the demand curve stay the same, there will be no reason for the equilibrium price or quantity to change. But what if something causes one of the curves to shift? In that case, the supply and demand curves will intersect each other at a new point, and the market will have a new equilibrium price and quantity.

We begin by looking at shifts in the demand curve. Supply-curve shifts will come later in the chapter.

An Increase in Demand: The Demand Curve Shifts to the Right

In the previous chapter, we discussed the market for red-delicious apples. We'll continue with the apple example here, although this chapter also contains examples from several other markets. Before trying to understand the effects of a shift in the demand curve for apples, it's best to figure out the *original* equilibrium price and quantity, *before* the shift takes place. The original situation is shown in Figure 4.1. The original supply curve for red-delicious apples is S, and the original demand curve is D_{old}. We find the equilibrium by looking for the intersection of the supply curve and the demand curve. The original equilibrium price of red-delicious apples is P_{old}, and the original equilibrium quantity is Q_{old}.

Now that we have established the original equilibrium in the apple market, let's consider what will happen if the demand curve shifts. What would happen if medical researchers were to discover that cancer is completely prevented by eating red-delicious apples? After hearing this dramatic news, millions of people would want to eat more of these apples. People would stand shoulder to shoulder in the produce sections of grocery stores, eagerly shopping for red-delicious apples. At any given price, the quantity of apples demanded would be greater than it had been before. In other words, there would be an increase in demand. This increase in demand is represented by a rightward shift in the demand curve, as shown in Figure 4.1. Because of the news about the health effects of red-delicious apples, the market demand curve will shift from D_{old} to D_{new}.

After the shift, P_{old} can't continue to be the equilibrium price, and Q_{old} can't continue to be the equilibrium quantity. If P_{old} were still the price, some consumers would not be able to find the apples they want to buy. In other words, if P_{old} were still the price, there would be a shortage of red-delicious apples. The amount of the shortage would be (Q_d–Q_{old}). In this situation, some consumers will offer to pay a higher price. Therefore, the shortage will create pressure for the price to rise. The price will continue to rise until the apple shortage is eliminated, and the market reaches a new equilibrium. At the new equilibrium, quantity supplied will again be equal to quantity demanded. Graphically, the new equilibrium is given by the intersection of the original supply curve, S, with the new demand curve, D_{new}. In Figure 4.1, the new equilibrium price of red-delicious apples is P_{new}, which is *greater* than

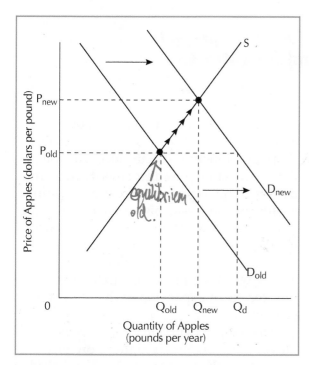

The figure shows a graph with "Price of Apples (dollars per pound)" on the vertical axis and "Quantity of Apples (pounds per year)" on the horizontal axis. The supply curve S slopes upward. Demand curves D_{old} and D_{new} slope downward, with D_{new} shifted to the right. Dashed lines mark P_{new} and P_{old} on the vertical axis and Q_{old}, Q_{new}, and Q_d on the horizontal axis. Handwritten annotation reads "equilibrium old." with an arrow pointing to the original equilibrium point.

Figure 4.1 The Effects of an Increase in the Demand for Red-Delicious Apples

The original demand curve for red-delicious apples is D_{old}, and the original supply curve is S. The original equilibrium is determined by the intersection of these curves. The original equilibrium price of red-delicious apples is P_{old}, and the original equilibrium quantity is Q_{old}. If buyers get new information about the health benefits of eating red-delicious apples, there would be an increase in the demand for the apples. In other words, the demand curve would shift to the right, to D_{new}. If P_{old} were to remain the price, there would be a shortage of ($Q_d - Q_{old}$). Thus, the old equilibrium cannot be sustained. The apple market will move to a new equilibrium, in which the price is P_{new} and the quantity is Q_{new}. As a result of the increase in demand, there is an increase in both the equilibrium price and the equilibrium quantity.

P_{old}. The new equilibrium quantity is Q_{new}, which is *greater* than Q_{old}.

Thus, when the demand curve shifts to the right, the equilibrium price will increase, and the equilibrium quantity will also rise. This will occur for *any* rightward shift of the demand curve in *any* market, as long as the supply curve slopes upward as we move from left to right (that is, as long as the sellers obey the Law of Supply). When the demand curve shifts to the right, the equilibrium point slides upward and to the right along the existing supply curve. This leads to a higher equilibrium price and a higher equilibrium quantity.

In this example, the news about the effect of apples on health leads to an increase in demand, which is represented by a rightward shift in the demand curve for red-delicious apples. Many other changes could also lead to an increase in demand. In other words, many other changes could also lead to a rightward shift in the demand curve. One such change is a decrease in the price of a complement. Let's say that red-delicious apples and cheddar cheese are complements. In that case, if the price of cheddar cheese were to fall, the demand curve for red-delicious apples would shift to the right. An increase in the price of a substitute for apples would also cause an increase in demand for apples. For example, let's assume that pears are a substitute for apples. Then if the price of pears were to rise, the demand curve for apples would shift to the right. Also, if red-delicious apples are a normal good, an increase in the incomes of consumers would shift the demand curve for apples to the right. In each of these cases, the increase in demand would cause increases in both the equilibrium price and quantity, as shown in Figure 4.1.

We have concentrated on rightward shifts in the demand curve for red-delicious apples, but similar influences could increase the demand for any good. In general, the demand curve for any good could be shifted to the right by

- certain changes in tastes and preferences, such that a good or service becomes "more popular", or

- a decrease in the price of a complement, or

- an increase in the price of a substitute, or

- an increase in incomes (if the good is a normal good), or

Real Economics for Real People 4.1: AIDS and the Demand for Latex Gloves

By the middle of the 1980s, the American public was becoming aware of the health hazard posed by Acquired Immune Deficiency Syndrome (AIDS). In August, 1987, the Centers for Disease Control in Atlanta urged health-care workers "to treat blood and other body fluids from all patients as potentially infective."

Prior to the AIDS advisory, some doctors and nurses did not wear gloves when examining patients. The AIDS advisory convinced many health-care professionals that the benefits of wearing examination gloves were greater than they had previously thought. In other words, the AIDS advisory led to a change in "tastes" or "preferences" regarding examination gloves. Examination gloves became more "popular". In economic terms, the announcement led to dramatic increases in the demand for latex examination gloves and surgical gloves, on the part of dental hygienists, doctors, and other health-care professionals. Many surgeons began to wear two pairs of gloves at a time. Over a six-month period, St. Mary's Hospital in Richmond, Virginia, doubled its orders for gloves, to 80,000 gloves per month. UCLA Medical Center in Los Angeles increased its orders by 60% in a year.

The increases in demand led to increases in price, as well as increases in quantity. Prices of latex gloves rose by as much as 40% in some cases.

The increase in demand for gloves was exceptionally fast. As a result, temporary shortages sometimes occurred, even though there were large price increases. Faced with possible shortages of latex gloves, some health-care professionals began to buy more vinyl gloves, even though these are of lower quality than latex gloves. In addition, some medical personnel are allergic to latex gloves, which are made from natural rubber. This led to an expansion of the market for synthetic gloves.

Since supplies of domestically produced gloves were extremely tight, more buyers began to look overseas. In 1987 and 1988, there were big increases in imports of gloves from Taiwan, China, Thailand, and Malaysia.

All of these changes occurred because the fear of AIDS caused an increase in demand for goods that could help protect against infection, such as latex gloves. In terms of the supply-demand diagram, this means that the demand curve for latex gloves shifted to the right. As with any increase in demand, this led to an increase in the equilibrium price, and an increase in the equilibrium quantity.

- a decrease in incomes (if the good is an inferior good), or
- a belief that future prices or future incomes will be higher than previously expected, or
- an increase in the number of buyers.

If demand increases, for any reason, the equilibrium price and quantity will both increase.

Real Economics for Real People 4.1 deals with another example of a rightward shift in a demand curve. Then we will move on to learn about what happens when the demand curve shifts to the left.

A Decrease in Demand: The Demand Curve Shifts to the Left

In much of the United States, the spring and summer of 1997 were unusually cloudy and cool. When the weather is cool and wet, most people don't like to engage in outdoor activities. Thus, the cool weather caused big decreases in the demand for swimming pools, swimming-pool chemicals, patio furniture, sunglasses, pleasure boats, mountain bikes, and many other goods.

We can use the tools of supply and demand to analyze the effects of the cool, cloudy weather on the market for sunscreen. Once again, we start by looking for the original situation, which occurs before there is any shift in either the supply curve or the demand curve. This original situation is shown in Figure 4.2. The original supply curve for sunscreen is S, and the original demand curve is D_{old}. The intersection of D_{old} and S gives us the original equilibrium price and quantity of sunscreen, which are P_{old} and Q_{old}.

Now, the summer of 1997 arrives, bringing temperatures that are cooler than had been anticipated. The weather means that, at any given price, consumers aren't willing to buy as much sunscreen as they had been willing to buy before. In a sense, poor weather changes people's tastes for sunscreen, and makes sunscreen less "popular". In other words, the strange weather causes the demand for sunscreen to decrease, so that the demand curve shifts to the left. This is shown in Figure 4.2 as a shift from D_{old} to D_{new}.

In Figure 4.2, as in the other figures in this chapter, the shift from D_{old} to D_{new} is a parallel shift. The shifts are drawn in this way to make them easy to read. However, shifts don't *have* to be parallel.

After the shift of the demand curve, P_{old} can't be the equilibrium price of sunscreen any more, and Q_{old} can't continue to be the equilibrium quantity. If P_{old} were still the price, there would be a surplus of ($Q_{old} - Q_d$). As a result of the surplus, there will be pressure for the price to fall. The price will continue to fall

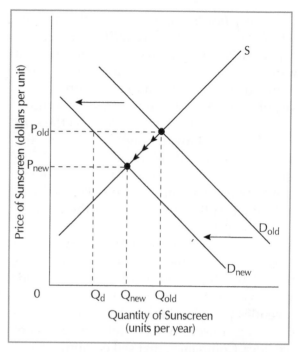

Figure 4.2 The Effects of a Decrease in the Demand for Sunscreen

The original demand curve for sunscreen is D_{old}, and the original supply curve is S. The original equilibrium price and quantity are determined by the intersection of these curves. The original equilibrium price of sunscreen is P_{old}, and the original equilibrium quantity is Q_{old}. Then, buyers experience unusually cool and cloudy summer weather, and this decreases the demand for sunscreen. The demand curve shifts to the left, to D_{new}. If P_{old} were to remain the price, there would be a surplus of ($Q_{old} - Q_d$). Thus, the old equilibrium cannot be sustained. The market for sunscreen will move to a new equilibrium, in which the price is P_{new} and the quantity is Q_{new}. As a result of the decrease in demand, there is a decrease in both the equilibrium price and the equilibrium quantity.

until the sunscreen market reaches a new equilibrium. When the market reaches its new equilibrium, quantity supplied will be equal to quantity demanded, which means that the surplus will be gone. The new equilibrium in the market for sunscreen is given by the intersection of the new demand curve, D_{new}, with the original supply curve, S. The new equilibrium price is P_{new}, which is *lower* than P_{old}. The new equilibrium quantity is Q_{new}, which is *lower* than Q_{old}.

Thus when the demand curve shifts to the left, the equilibrium price will decrease, and the equilibrium quantity will also fall. This will happen for *any* leftward shift in the demand curve in *any* market, as long as the supply curve slopes upward as we move from left to right (that is, as long as the sellers obey the Law of Supply). When the demand curve shifts to the left, the equilibrium point slides downward and to the left along the existing supply curve. This reduces both the equilibrium price and the equilibrium quantity.

The revenue received by sellers of sunscreen is equal to the price of sunscreen, multiplied by the quantity of sunscreen sold. When both the price and quantity fall, revenues for sellers have to fall. Thus the suppliers of sunscreen were hurt by the cool weather. Companies that sell equipment and chemicals for swimming pools also suffered, and so did the sellers of ice cream.

Of course, cool weather isn't the only thing that could reduce the demand for sunscreen. If sunscreen is a normal good, then a decrease in incomes would also lead to a leftward shift in the demand curve for sunscreen.

An increase in the price of a complementary good would have a similar effect. For example, let's assume that swimsuits are a complement of sunscreen. If the price of swimsuits were to increase, the demand for sunscreen would decrease.

A decrease in the price of a substitute for sunscreen would also cause the demand curve for sunscreen to shift to the left. For example, let's assume that cable-television services are a substitute for sunscreen. (If you're watching a lot of TV, you are probably staying indoors, so that you won't be using sunscreen.) If the price of cable-TV services were to fall, then the demand curve for sunscreen would shift to the left. As a result of any of these decreases in demand, the equilibrium price of sunscreen would fall, and so would the equilibrium quantity.

Similar influences could decrease the demand for any good. In general, the demand curve for any good could be shifted to the left by

- certain changes in tastes and preferences, such that a good or service becomes "less popular", or

- an increase in the price of a complement, or

- a decrease in the price of a substitute, or

- a decrease in incomes (if the good is a normal good), or

- an increase in incomes (if the good is an inferior good), or

- a belief that future prices or future incomes will be lower than previously expected, or

- a decrease in the number of buyers.

If any demand curve shifts to the left, for any reason, the equilibrium price and quantity will both decrease.

In this section, we've concentrated on shifts in the demand curve: When demand increases (so that the demand curve shifts to the right), the equilibrium price and quantity will both rise; when demand decreases (so that the demand curve shifts to the left), the equilibrium price and quantity will both fall. Later in this chapter, we'll look at what happens when a supply curve shifts.

Reality Check: Interim Review Questions

IR4-1. There is an increase in the demand for peanuts. In other words, the demand curve for peanuts shifts to the right. What will happen to the equilibrium price and quantity of peanuts?

IR4-2. Silk socks and cotton socks are substitutes. There is a decrease in the price of silk socks. As a result, the demand for cotton socks decreases; that is, the demand curve for cotton socks shifts to the left. What will happen to the equilibrium price and quantity of cotton socks?

USING THE TOOLS OF SUPPLY AND DEMAND TO ANALYZE THE EFFECTS OF SEPTEMBER 11

The Immediate Effects of September 11 on the Gasoline Market. On the morning of September 11, 2001, terrorists from Egypt and Saudi Arabia hijacked four commercial airliners. Two crashed into the World Trade Center towers in New York City, one crashed into the Pentagon Building, and one crashed in a field in rural Pennsylvania. Nearly 3000 people died.

As of this writing (nearly 15 years after September 11), there haven't been any more terrorist incidents of this magnitude. However, on the afternoon of September 11, people didn't know what to expect. Many were fearful that the disasters at the World Trade Center and the Pentagon were just the beginning of a long series of attacks. This created a sense of panic among many people.

In the panicky atmosphere of the afternoon of September 11, many people were afraid there would be an interruption in the supply of gasoline. Long lines formed at gasoline stations, as people rushed to fill up their tanks.

We can analyze the effects of this "panic buying", using the tools of supply and demand. We begin by showing the original equilibrium, before the terrorist attacks. Then we analyze the shift to the new equilibrium.

This analysis is shown in Figure 4.3. The supply curve is S. The supply curve in Figure 4.3 does obey the Law of Supply, but it is very steep. This represents the fact that there were severe limits on the amount of additional gasoline that could be brought to market between the morning and afternoon of September 11. Later in this book, we will analyze the reasons why some demand and supply curves are flat, while others are steep, and we will develop a vocabulary to describe curves with different shapes.

The demand curve at 8 a.m. on September 11 is D_{am}. The original equilibrium is given by the intersection of S and D_{am}. In some parts of the

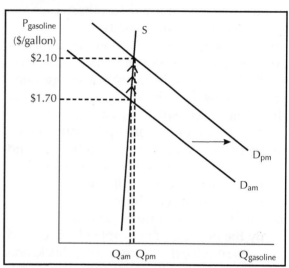

Figure 4.3   The Effects of the September 11 Terrorist Attacks on the Price of Gasoline

The supply curve is S. On the morning of September 11, 2001, the demand curve is D_{am}, and the equilibrium price is given by the intersection of S and D_{am}, which was about $1.70 per gallon in some parts of the country. The events of September 11 led to a temporary surge of panic buying, which is represented by a rightward shift in the demand curve, to D_{pm}. The new equilibrium price, given by the intersection of S and D_{pm}, is higher than the equilibrium price of a few hours before.

country, the equilibrium price was around $1.70 per gallon on the morning of September 11.

After the news of the terrorist attacks, some motorists began to feel panicked, and they rushed out to fill up their gasoline tanks. Panic buying can be represented graphically as a rightward shift in the demand curve: At any price, the quantity of gasoline demanded by motorists had increased. The demand curve at 2 p.m. on September 11 is D_{pm}.

After the demand curve shifted to the right, the old equilibrium price could not be sustained. If the price had stayed at $1.70 per gallon, there would have been excess demand (that is, a shortage). Thus, as a result of the rightward shift in the demand curve, there is pressure for the price to rise.

The new equilibrium is given by the intersection of the new demand curve, D_{pm}, with the supply curve, S. The new equilibrium quantity will be higher than it would otherwise have been. In Figure 4.3, the quantity is shown rising from Q_{am} to Q_{pm}. And the new equilibrium price will also be higher than it otherwise would have been. In many places, gasoline prices rose by 40 or 50 cents per gallon on the afternoon of September 11, 2001. In some isolated cases, the price went up by much more. As long as the supply curve and the demand curve have their usual shapes, a rightward shift in the demand curve will always lead to an increase in the equilibrium price, and an increase in the equilibrium quantity.

By the next day, the people of the United States were still experiencing grief, shock, and horror, but much of the panic was gone. Gradually, people became accustomed to the idea that life would go on. As a result, panic buying of gasoline all but disappeared.

As a result of the end of panic buying, the demand curve returned to something quite close to its original position. By the afternoon of September 12 and the morning of September 13, prices in many places had returned to about the levels that had existed on the morning of September 11.

The Effects of September 11 on the Market for Passenger Air Travel. Very soon after the terrorist attacks, all commercial airline traffic was grounded. Travelers were stranded for several days, until the system was declared secure enough for flights to begin again. However, even after the flight ban was lifted, the passenger airlines were not the same as they had been before.

Because of the terrorist attacks, many potential air travelers felt a fear of flying. We can analyze this by using supply-demand diagrams. As usual, we begin with the original situation, before the terrorist attacks. Then we see how fear of flying leads to a shift in the demand curve for passenger air travel, and we analyze the new equilibrium.

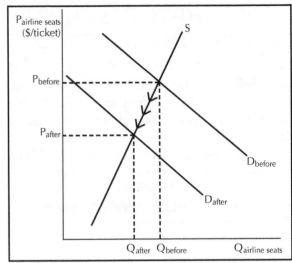

Figure 4.4   The Effects of the September 11 Terrorist Attacks on the Market for Passenger Air Travel

The supply curve is S. Before the September 11 attacks, the demand curve was D_{before}, and the equilibrium price and quantity were P_{before} and Q_{before}. The terrorist attacks lead to a leftward shift in the demand curve for air travel, to D_{after}. This leads to a reduction in the equilibrium price, and a reduction in the equilibrium quantity.

This analysis is shown in Figure 4.4. The supply curve is S. The original demand curve is D_{before}. The original equilibrium is given by the intersection of S and D_{before}. The equilibrium quantity of passenger seats sold is Q_{before}, and the original equilibrium price is P_{before}.

The equilibrium described in the previous paragraph was disturbed by the events of September 11. Suddenly, many people were much more afraid to fly than they would have been, if the terrorist attacks had not occurred. This can be represented as a leftward shift in the demand curve for air travel: At any price, the quantity of passenger airline seats demanded was smaller than it had been before.

The new demand curve is D_{after}. As a result of the shift to the new demand curve, the original equilibrium cannot be sustained. If the old equilibrium price had remained in place, there would have been large surpluses of unsold seats. As a result, there was strong pressure for the price to fall.

The new equilibrium is given by the intersection of the supply curve with the new demand curve, D_{after}. The new equilibrium price is P_{after}, and the new equilibrium quantity is Q_{after}. In the months after September 11, passenger airlines were offering tickets at deep discounts. Even with these large decreases in price, many passenger aircraft were only half full.

SHIFTS IN THE SUPPLY CURVE

When there is a change in demand, the equilibrium price and quantity will both move in the *same* direction. That is, when the demand curve shifts, either the equilibrium price and equilibrium quantity will both rise, or they will both fall. However, we will see that a supply-curve shift will cause the equilibrium price and quantity to move in *opposite* directions. In other words, when supply changes, either the equilibrium price will rise and the equilibrium quantity will fall, or the equilibrium price will fall and the equilibrium quantity will rise.

A Decrease in Supply: The Supply Curve Shifts to the Left

Let's return to our example of the market for red-delicious apples, and consider what would happen if the supply curve were to shift to the left. As usual, we begin by finding the *original* equilibrium price and quantity, which would exist before any shifts occur. The original situation is shown in Figure 4.5. The original supply curve for red-delicious apples is S_{old}, and the original demand curve is D. The intersection of these two curves gives us the original equilibrium price of red-delicious apples, P_{old}, and the original equilibrium quantity, Q_{old}.

The supply curve for apples could be shifted to the left as a result of a variety of influences. One such influence would be an event that disrupts supply, such as a drought in apple-growing regions. We can think of this as a deterioration of the technology of producing apples. At any given price, the drought means that the quantity of red-delicious apples

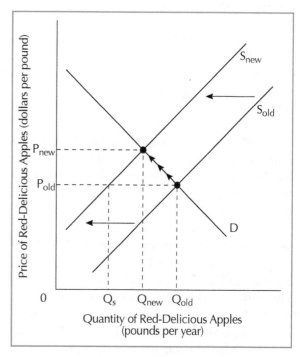

Figure 4.5 The Effects of a Decrease in the Supply of Red-Delicious Apples

The original demand curve for red-delicious apples is D, and the original supply curve is S_{old}. The intersection of these curves gives us the original equilibrium price of red-delicious apples, P_{old}, and the original equilibrium quantity, Q_{old}. Then, a drought in the apple-growing regions decreases the supply of red-delicious apples. The supply curve shifts to the left, to S_{new}. If P_{old} were to remain the price, there would be a shortage of $(Q_{old} - Q_s)$. The apple market will move to a new equilibrium, in which the price is P_{new} and the quantity is Q_{new}. As a result of the decrease in supply, the equilibrium price increases and the equilibrium quantity decreases.

supplied would be less than it had been before. Another way to think of the shift in the supply curve is that the drought makes it more costly to produce apples. The price that's necessary to get sellers to supply apples is higher than it had been before, because of the increased need for irrigation and the increased possibility of diseases in the apple trees. This decrease in supply is represented in Figure 4.5 by a leftward shift in the supply curve for red-delicious apples, from S_{old} to S_{new}.

After the supply-curve shift, P_{old} can no longer be the equilibrium price, and Q_{old} can't remain the equilibrium quantity. If P_{old} were still the price, there would be a shortage of $(Q_{old} - Q_s)$. The shortage will lead to upward pressure on the price of red-delicious apples. The price will continue to rise until the apple market reaches a new equilibrium. When the market reaches its new equilibrium, quantity supplied will be equal to quantity demanded, which means that the shortage will be over. The new equilibrium will be given by the intersection of the new supply curve, S_{new}, and the original demand curve, D. The new equilibrium quantity will be Q_{new}, which is *smaller* than Q_{old}. The new equilibrium price of red-delicious apples will be P_{new}, which is *larger* than P_{old}.

Thus, when the supply curve shifts to the left, the equilibrium price will increase, but the equilibrium quantity will fall. This will happen for *any* leftward shift of the supply curve in *any* market, as long as the demand curve slopes downward from left to right (that is, as long as buyers obey the Law of Demand). When the supply curve shifts to the left, the equilibrium point slides upward and to the left along the existing demand curve. This causes the equilibrium price to rise and the equilibrium quantity to fall.

There are many examples of how a disruption of production can cause a leftward shift in the supply curve. For instance, vegetable crops in Florida were damaged by an unexpectedly hard freeze in January of 1997. We would expect prices to rise as a result of

the leftward shift in supply, and that is exactly what happened. The price of cucumbers rose quickly from $8 per bushel to $25 per bushel. A similar story occurred in June, 1994, when coffee trees in Brazil were damaged by freezing temperatures. As a result of the freeze, coffee prices rose by 26 percent in one day.

Here is another example of a disruption in supply: In early June, 2000, Michigan drivers were paying about $1.70 or $1.75 per gallon of gasoline. Then, a gasoline pipeline ruptured near Jackson, Michigan. Before the rupture could be fixed, about 75,000 gallons of gasoline had spilled into the Grand River. The pipeline had to be closed for repairs. Previously, about seven million gallons had flowed through the pipeline every day. After the pipeline rupture, that source of supply was no longer available. For the next few weeks, gasoline had to be hauled over long distances by truck, rather than pumped through the pipeline. In a sense, there was a deterioration in the technology of supplying gasoline. This disruption of supply can be viewed as a leftward shift of the supply curve for gasoline. Because of the pipeline rupture, it had become fundamentally more expensive to get gasoline to service stations. For a few days, the price of gasoline was above $2.20 per gallon.

However, when the pipeline was fixed, it was once again possible to send gasoline through the pipeline. The supply curve for gasoline shifted back to the right. As a result, the price fell back to the range in which it had been before the pipeline disaster.

Other changes can also lead to a leftward shift in the supply curve. Suppose that the United States government imposes a new set of regulations governing the use of pesticides, and that these regulations increase costs in the apple-growing industry. This would effectively shift the supply curve to the left. It would cause a decrease in the equilibrium quantity, and an increase in the equilibrium price paid by consumers, as shown in Figure 4.5.

An increase in the price of an input will also cause a decrease in supply. When an input becomes more expensive, there is an increase in the price that is necessary to get sellers to bring a given quantity to market. For example, if the price of steel were to rise, the supply curve for automobiles would shift to the left, since steel is an input into the production of automobiles. This leftward shift in the supply curve would lead to an increase in the equilibrium price of automobiles, and a decrease in the equilibrium quantity.

Earlier, you read about the effects of a ruptured gasoline pipeline. The ruptured pipeline caused the supply curve for gasoline to shift to the left. As a result, the price of gasoline increased. The same sort of thing happens when there is an increase in the price of oil. Oil is a very important input in the production of gasoline. The price of oil increased dramatically in the summer of 2008. As a result, it became fundamentally more expensive to produce gasoline. This can be viewed as a leftward shift in the supply curve for gasoline. As a result, the equilibrium price of gasoline increased. In only a year, from July 2007 to July 2008, the price of crude oil doubled, reaching a peak of well over $140 per barrel. As a result, gasoline prices rose from about $3 per gallon to more than $4 per gallon. However, those historically high levels of gasoline prices did not sustain themselves because conditions changed again. The weakening world economy resulted in decreased demand for crude oil in the last few months of 2008. The price of oil dropped by more than two-thirds, and the price of gasoline fell back to less than $2 per gallon.

In recent years, oil-producing firms have increasingly adopted a new technology called hydraulic fracturing, or "fracking". Fracking, which is especially important in North Dakota and Texas, allows producers to reach underground oil deposits that were previously thought to be out of reach. As a result, the amount of oil produced in the United States increased by several million barrels per day.

As a result of this increase in supply, the price of oil plummeted in 2014 and 2015. Predictably, cheaper oil led to large reductions in the price of gasoline.

You have now read about several influences that could cause supply to decrease. The supply curve for a good could be shifted to the left by

- an increase in the price of an input, or
- the imposition of a regulation that increases costs, or
- a disruption in production, such as might be caused by bad weather in agricultural regions, or
- any kind of deterioration in technology.

If supply decreases, for any reason, the equilibrium price will increase and the equilibrium quantity will decrease.

Next, we will learn about what happens when supply increases, so that the supply curve shifts to the right.

An Increase in Supply: The Supply Curve Shifts to the Right

Many families would like to recycle their bottles, cans, and newspapers, to reduce the amount of solid waste that gets buried in landfill. However, recycling is difficult for people who live far away from a recycling center. In an effort to make it easier to recycle, many towns and cities established programs of curbside recycling in the late 1980s and early 1990s. In effect, the curbside recycling programs improved the technology of recycling. These programs made it cheaper and easier for people to recycle. Families responded by recycling huge amounts of material.

Most people who recycle do not get any money in return. However, after the city governments collect materials from recycling programs, they sell them.

At any price, the quantity of recycled material that is supplied will be higher, after curbside recycling programs are in place. In the language of supply and demand, the expansion of curbside recycling programs causes rightward shifts in the supply curves for recycled newsprint, scrap paper, tin, glass, and so on. In other words, curbside recycling programs lead to an increase in the supply of these materials.

We can study the effects of expanded curbside recycling on the market for scrap paper, using the tools of supply and demand. As usual, we begin by finding the original equilibrium, before any shifts take place. As shown in Figure 4.6, the original demand curve for scrap paper is D, and the original supply curve is S_{old}. In order to find the original equilibrium, we go to the intersection of D and S_{old}. This tells us that the original equilibrium price of scrap paper is P_{old}, and the original equilibrium quantity is Q_{old}.

Now, because of the increased availability of curbside recycling programs, there is an increase in the supply of scrap paper. This increase in supply is shown in Figure 4.6 as a shift in the supply curve for scrap paper, from S_{old} to S_{new}.

After the shift in the supply curve, P_{old} and Q_{old} can no longer be the equilibrium price and quantity of scrap paper. If P_{old} were still the price of scrap paper, there would be a surplus of $(Q_s - Q_{old})$. The surplus will create pressure for the price to fall. The price of scrap paper will continue to fall until the scrap-paper market reaches a new equilibrium. When the market reaches its new equilibrium, quantity supplied will be equal to quantity demanded, which means that the surplus will be gone. The new equilibrium will be given by the intersection of the new supply curve, S_{new}, and the original demand curve, D. The new equilibrium price of scrap paper will be P_{new}, which is *smaller* than P_{old}. The new equilibrium quantity will be Q_{new}, which is *larger* than Q_{old}.

Thus, when the supply curve shifts to the right, the equilibrium price will decrease, but

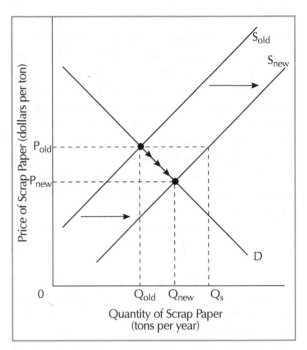

Figure 4.6 The Effects of an Increase in the Supply of Scrap Paper

The original demand curve for scrap paper is D, and the original supply curve is S_{old}. The intersection of these curves gives us the original equilibrium price of scrap paper, P_{old}, and the original equilibrium quantity, Q_{old}. Then communities institute curbside recycling programs, which make it easier to recycle. This increases the supply of scrap paper. The supply curve shifts to the right, to S_{new}. If P_{old} were to remain the price, there would be a surplus of $(Q_s - Q_{old})$. The market for scrap paper will move to a new equilibrium, in which the price is P_{new} and the quantity is Q_{new}. As a result of the increase in supply, the equilibrium price goes down, but the equilibrium quantity rises.

the equilibrium quantity will increase. This will happen for *any* rightward shift of the supply curve in *any* market, as long as the demand curve slopes downward from left to right (that is, as long as buyers obey the Law of Demand). When the supply curve shifts to the right, the equilibrium point slides downward and to the right along the existing demand curve. As a result, the equilibrium quantity rises and the equilibrium price falls.

The increase in curbside recycling caused major reductions in the prices of recyclable materials. Scrap paper sold for $120 per ton in 1988, but the price fell to $30 per ton by 1993. The price of recycled glass went down from $160 per ton to $90 per ton.

Many local governments have encouraged recycling, to cut down on the expense of burying garbage in landfill. However, the success of the recycling programs has caused new problems. When the amount of recycling increased, it became necessary to dispose of a tremendous amount of recycled material. As a result, governments have tried to find new ways to use recycled materials. In other words, they are trying to push the *demand curve* for recycled materials to the right. For example, some governments use recycled paper for letterheads, forms, and envelopes, and in copying machines, and they are encouraging private businesses to do the same.

A supply curve for a good could be shifted to the right by a variety of changes, including

- a decrease in the price of an input, or

- relaxation in government regulations, so that it becomes less costly to produce, or

- an improvement in the conditions of production, such as might be caused by unusually good weather in agricultural regions, or

- any improvement in technology.

If supply increases for any reason, the equilibrium price will fall and the equilibrium quantity will rise.

Technological improvements are associated with rightward shifts in supply curves. We discuss another example of a technological improvement in *Real Economics for Real People 4.2*.

Reality Check: Interim Review Questions

IR4-3. Because of technological improvements, there is an increase in the supply of electric pianos. In other words, the supply curve for electric pianos shifts to the right. What will happen to the equilibrium price and quantity of electric pianos?

IR4-4. Electricity is used in the production of aluminum. There is an increase in the price of electricity. As a result, the supply of aluminum decreases. In other words, the supply curve for aluminum shifts to the left. What will happen to the equilibrium price and quantity of aluminum?

Real Economics for Real People 4.2:
Changing Technology and the Price of Personal Computers

In April, 1982, the first issue of *PC Magazine* advertised the new IBM Personal Computer. For $1600, you could buy a machine with 256 kilobytes of memory, no hard disk drive, and a one-color monitor.

Because of inflation, the $1600 that you spent in 1982 would be equivalent to more than $3500 in 2016. What kind of computer could you buy in 2016 for that amount of money? In fact, you could get a fabulous computer for much less. But if you wanted to spend more than $3000 in 2016, you could get a workstation with a 17-inch monitor (in color, of course). It would have millions of times as much memory as the 1982 PC, and it would process information millions of times as fast. It would have an internal drive capable of storing a trillion bytes of information, whereas the 1982 computer had none. The 2016 version would have a built-in DVD drive, which did not exist in 1982. Finally, the 2016 version would come loaded with all sorts of software that was not available in 1982.

Technological change is the explanation for these phenomenal developments. In the last quarter of a century, the design of personal computers has been improved repeatedly. These improvements can be seen as increases in the supply of personal computers and computer accessories. In other words, the supply curves have shifted to the right. At any given price, the computer makers are now willing and able to produce more (and better) computers. If we combine a rightward shift in the supply curve with a demand curve that slopes downward and to the right, we get increases in quantity and decreases in price. That is exactly what we have observed in the computer industry.

The personal-computer hard drive is one of the best examples of the effects of technological change. As mentioned above, when the IBM PC was first introduced, it didn't even have a hard drive as standard equipment. However, by 1983, Corvus Systems was offering a 20-megabyte hard drive for $3495. In 2016, a one-terabyte (1,000,000-megabyte) hard drive could be bought for about $50.

Thus, in 33 years, the price per megabyte went down from ($3495/20 megabytes) = $174.75 per megabyte, to ($50/1,000,000 megabytes) = about $0.00005 per megabyte. Price fell by a factor of ($174.75/$0.00005), which is about 3.5 million! Even this doesn't quite give the full indication of the real price decrease, since inflation pushed up the overall price level by about 120 percent during that period. If we were to correct for inflation, the price per megabyte has fallen by a factor of about eight million.

Today's hard drives are far superior to the hard drives of 1983, in every way. They're faster, more reliable, more durable, lighter, and more compact. All of these changes are the result of technological improvements. Technological improvements push supply curves to the right. These increases in supply lead to decreases in price and increases in quantity.

Demand, Supply, and The Housing Bubble 房地产泡沫

We have now developed a basic understanding of shifts in the demand curve and shifts in the supply curve. We can use these tools to analyze the changes in the housing market in the United States in recent years.

We have seen that expectations about future prices can affect the demand curve. If people believe that prices will be higher in the future, they will increase their demand today. If they believe that prices will be lower in the future, they will decrease their demand today. Sometimes, these expectations about future prices can cause big problems for the economy. A classic example occurred in recent years in the U.S. housing market. In 2003 and 2004, home prices began to go up. Press reports included stories of people who had bought a house, and then sold it only a few months later for a huge profit. In some cases, it was possible to make hundreds of thousands of dollars in only a short time, by "flipping" houses.

In this environment, more and more people began to expect that prices would continue to go up. "If I buy now, I'll make a big profit. If I wait much longer, prices may get so high that they will be out of my reach." Thus, the expectation of higher *future* prices led to an increase in *today's* demand. And when demand increased, the price did indeed go up. Thus, for a while, these expectations were self-fulfilling: The expectation of higher prices led to increased demand, and the increased demand led to higher prices.

Most home buyers want to live in the home they purchase. However, as prices escalated, increasing numbers of people began to buy houses for investment purposes. These "speculators" were only interested in making quick profits. As the speculators added their demand to the demand of ordinary home buyers, prices continued to rise.

Banks and other lenders added fuel to the fire. Lenders started giving home loans to people who really did not have enough income to afford the house they were buying. For a few years, the American housing market saw "NINJA" mortgages. NINJA stands for "no income, no job or assets". For some of the folks who took out these loans, the only hope was that prices would continue to increase. If prices kept going up, these borrowers could refinance their mortgage every few years. However, if prices didn't keep going up, these people would be in serious financial trouble.

Prices increased dramatically for a few years, but prices simply could not race upward forever. As prices skyrocketed, many potential buyers found themselves priced out of the market. Also, some people looked at the astronomical prices, and began to doubt that prices could continue to rise. Thus, the demand curve stopped shifting to the right, and the price increases came to a halt.

Once prices stopped rising, the speculators began to drop out of the market. As a result, the demand curve began to shift to the left. Also, some homeowners found that they could no longer make their loan payments. If a homeowner defaults on a loan, then the bank takes over the house, in a "foreclosure proceeding". The bank then tries to sell the house. However, as more and more banks tried to sell empty houses, the supply curve for homes began to shift to the right.

Thus, demand began to shrink, and supply began to grow. By 2007, home prices were falling rapidly in many parts of the country. As a result, the expectations game began to reverse itself. Only a few years earlier, people were desperate to buy houses, as home prices soared. By 2007 and 2008, people saw falling prices, and expected the prices to keep falling. As a result, demand continued to shrink.

In some parts of the country, home prices lost 30 percent, or even more, and it took years for the housing market to bottom out. Finally, by 2012 and 2013, the market had stabilized in most parts of the United States. However, in many cases, home prices remained well below their 2006 levels.

The process that we have described here is called a "speculative bubble". On the way up, expectations of increasing prices became self-fulfilling. However, once the bubble burst, the expectations reversed themselves. Expec-tations of *higher* prices can be self-fulfilling (for a time), but expectations of *lower* prices can also be self-fulfilling.

Fortunately, most markets do not experience speculative bubbles, or experience them only very rarely. That's good news; the bursting of the housing-market bubble led to the deepest economic recession since the 1930s.

PRICE CONTROLS

In Chapter 3, we saw that market forces normally work to eliminate shortages and surpluses very quickly. Also, in all of the examples given so far in this chapter, we have assumed that the market will find its new equilibrium. However, in some situations, markets are unable to achieve equilibrium. We will look at some of these situations now.

Sometimes, a government will pass a *price-control law*, which makes it illegal to buy and sell at some prices. If a price-control law is enforced, it may prevent the market from finding equilibrium. As a result, shortages or surpluses may stay around for a long time. There are two basic types of price-control law. Some laws establish a *price floor*, which is a *minimum* price that must be paid. In other words, a price floor makes it illegal to buy and sell at *less* than a certain price. On the other hand, a *price ceiling* sets a *maximum* legal price: A price ceiling makes it illegal to buy and sell at *more* than a certain price.

In this section, we'll consider each of these types of price control, beginning with price floors. Later in the chapter, we'll discuss other situations in which markets can't easily get to equilibrium.

Price Floors

A price floor is a minimum legal price. In the United States, both price floors and price ceilings are fairly rare. Thus we are not able to point to a large number of examples. (That's probably a good thing. As we shall see, price floors and price ceilings can lead to some serious problems.)

Agriculture is one sector of the economy that has had some price floors. However, even in agriculture, the laws have changed many times, and the laws contain many complicated details that are beyond the scope of this book. Here we will present a simplified version of the way in which price floors once worked in the market for sugar.

Effects of the Sugar Price Floor. In the United States, the legally-mandated minimum price of raw cane sugar was 18 cents per pound for many years. In the rest of the world, the price of sugar rises and falls from time to time, depending on the conditions of supply and demand. However, the price in the rest of the world has most often been far below the price in the United States. On occasion, the world price has been as low as five cents per pound.

It's possible that the equilibrium price of sugar might actually be *above* the price floor. In this case, the price floor would have no effect. If the equilibrium price were higher than the price floor, then consumers and producers would voluntarily obey the law, simply by buying and selling at the equilibrium price. A different situation occurs when the equilibrium price is *below* the price floor, which has usually been the case in the sugar market. Figure 4.7 shows what will happen in a case like this. As

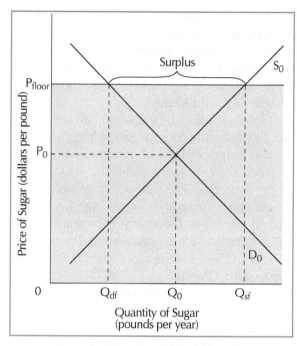

Figure 4.7 The Effects of a Price Floor in the Sugar Market

The supply curve in the sugar market is S_0, and the demand curve is D_0. This means that the equilibrium price of sugar is P_0, and the equilibrium quantity is Q_0. However, the United States government imposes a price floor on sugar, at P_{floor}. This means that all of the prices in the shaded region are illegal. Since the equilibrium price, P_0, is now illegal, the sugar market cannot reach equilibrium. If the price floor is enforced, the quantity supplied will be Q_{sf}, and the quantity demanded will be Q_{df}. The sugar market will have a surplus of $(Q_{sf} - Q_{df})$.

usual, we begin by finding the original equilibrium price and quantity. The demand curve is D_0, and the supply curve is S_0. The intersection of these two curves tells us that the equilibrium price is P_0, and the equilibrium quantity is Q_0. But with the price floor at P_{floor}, the prices in the shaded area are illegal! Most importantly, the price-floor law means that the equilibrium price of P_0 is unlawful.

If the equilibrium price is against the law, and if the price-floor law is enforced, then it will be impossible for the market to find its equilibrium. This will force the market into a *disequilibrium* situation, in which the quan-

tity supplied is different from the quantity demanded. When the price is P_{floor}, the quantity supplied is Q_{sf}, but the quantity demanded is Q_{df}. Thus, the price-floor law causes a surplus of $(Q_{sf} - Q_{df})$.

Because a surplus is created, you might predict that we would have more consumption than we had before the price-control law was imposed. However, the amount actually consumed is Q_{df}. Buyers can't be forced to buy more than an amount that is on their demand curves. Consequently, *the price floor reduces the amount of sugar that is actually consumed by consumers. Here, the consumption of sugar goes down from Q_0 to Q_{df}.*

If there were no price-control law, the market would quickly drive the price down to its equilibrium level, P_0. When the price floor is in effect, however, surpluses could pile up indefinitely, and this causes a problem. We would soon have miles and miles of warehouses full of surplus sugar. Thus, our next task is to think about what to do with the surpluses.

How to Deal with the Surpluses Caused By Price Floors. Governments create the potential for surpluses by imposing price-floor laws. This leads to political pressure for the same governments to do something to prevent the surpluses from building up. For example, price floors on dairy products have led to surpluses, and the government has responded by buying tons of surplus cheese, and storing it in warehouses.

In the case of sugar, the U.S. government has used a system of ***import quotas*** to control the surpluses. An import quota is a restriction on the quantity that can be imported from another country. Because of these sugar import quotas, the amount of sugar imported from Caribbean and Latin American countries, such as Jamaica, was much less than it would otherwise have been.

Figure 4.8 shows the effect of the import quotas on the sugar market. If there were no import quotas, the supply curve would be S_0, and the price in the United States would be

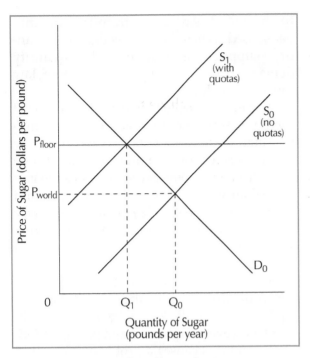

**Figure 4.8 The Effects of a System
of Import Quotas on the Sugar Market**

In the absence of import quotas, the supply curve in the sugar market in the United States is S_0, and the demand curve is D_0. This means that the equilibrium price of sugar is P_{world}, and the equilibrium quantity is Q_0. However, the United States government imposes a price floor on sugar, at P_{floor}. To keep the price above its equilibrium level without creating surpluses, the government imposes an import-quota law. This restricts the quantity of sugar that can be brought into the country from abroad, and it pushes the supply curve of sugar to the left, to S_1. In this case, the reduction in supply is so great that the price is driven all the way up to P_{floor}.

the same as the price in the rest of the world, P_{world}. The import quotas reduce the quantity of sugar that can be supplied in the United States. In Figure 4.8, because of the import quotas, the supply curve of sugar in the United States is driven leftward, to S_1. In the figure, S_1 is far enough to the left that the price of sugar goes all the way up to P_{floor}. In this case, the import quotas eliminate the surpluses that would otherwise occur.

If the import quotas were removed, sugar would be imported into the United States in

much greater amounts. This would drive the price of sugar in the U.S. down to P_{world}. In short, the import quotas raise the price at which sugar is sold in the United States, and they reduce the quantity of sugar that is bought and sold in the U.S.

One side effect of the sugar laws is that it can be profitable to go to great lengths to get around the import quota. When the difference between the U.S. price and the world price is large enough, the following sequence of events has occurred: (1) Sugar from Jamaica is sold to buyers in Germany. (There's a quota on sugar sent from Jamaica to the United States, but there is no quota on sugar sent from Jamaica to Germany.) (2) In Germany, the sugar is put into pancake mixes, iced-tea mixes, and other such products. (3) The mixes are sold to buyers in the United States. (There is no quota on imports of pancake mix from Germany into the U.S.) (4) Once the pancake mixes are in the United States, producers extract the sugar from the mix, and throw the rest of the mix away. (5) After two trips across the Atlantic Ocean, the sugar can still be sold for a profit, because the price of sugar is so much higher in the United States than in the rest of the world!

Winners and Losers from the Sugar Price Floor. The sugar price floor may have cost American consumers as much as $3 billion per year. It also had side effects. Domestically, the high price of sugar can make it very profitable to grow sugar beets. This raises the price of the land that can be used for growing sugar beets. Of course, the land that can be used for growing sugar beets can also be used to grow other crops, especially grains. This puts a financial squeeze on the grain farmers: They have to pay higher prices for land, but they don't receive as much government help as is received by the sugar-beet farmers. This has caused conflicts in Minnesota and North Dakota, where sugar-beet farmers are pitted against grain farmers.

The price floor also hurts sugar growers in the rest of the world, because it reduces their ability to sell in the United States. In addition, sugar is an important input in the production of candy, baked goods, and processed foods. Since the price of sugar is above its equilibrium level, the supply curves for candy and related goods are farther to the left than they would otherwise be. Therefore, the prices of candy and other goods are higher than they would be if there were no quotas on sugar. This hurts the consumers of candy and baked goods.

So far, we have discussed a number of problems and distortions caused by the sugar price floor. However, if *everyone* were harmed by the price floor, we would not expect that it would continue to receive support in Congress. In fact, some people do benefit from the sugar price floor. The main winners are the farmers who grow sugar cane and sugar beets. The high price of sugar also stimulates demand for corn syrup, artificial sweeteners, and other substitutes for sugar. Thus the sugar price floor also provides benefits for corn farmers, corn processers, and the producers of artificial sweeteners.

So, it's true that some groups do benefit from the price-floor law. However, these groups are small in number. Even the most optimistic assessment would say that the sugar price floor gives benefits for a few million Americans, out of a population of more than 320 million. How does a law stay on the books when the number of people harmed by the law is so much greater than the number of people who are helped? The reason is that the benefits are highly concentrated and visible, whereas the costs are dispersed and hard to see. Sugar-cane growers have the potential to gain huge sums of money every year from the price supports. The growers organize themselves politically, and give generously to political campaigns. On the other hand, each individual family loses only a relatively small amount every year, so that consumers haven't been well-organized in opposing the price controls.

In summary, a price floor can lead to three possible outcomes:

- If the price floor is below the equilibrium price, it has no effect.
- If the floor is above the equilibrium price but is not enforced by the government, it has no effect.
- If the price floor is above the equilibrium price and is enforced, it will lead to surpluses. To avoid having surpluses pile up, the government will often take some additional steps, such as instituting a sugar quota. Of course, the problem of surpluses could also be solved by repealing the price floor.

Minimum-wage laws are another form of price floor. These laws establish a minimum price in the labor market. If the minimum wage is below the equilibrium wage, there will be no effect. However, if the minimum wage is above the equilibrium wage, there can be surpluses in the form of unemployed workers. We will discuss minimum wages in Chapter 13.

Price Ceilings

A price *floor* sets a legal *minimum* price. We have seen that price floors can lead to surpluses. On the other hand, a price *ceiling* sets a legal *maximum* price. In many ways, price ceilings are a mirror image of price floors: Whereas price floors can lead to surpluses, price ceilings can lead to shortages.

Rent Controls. **Rent-control laws** are a type of price ceiling. Rent controls on apartment rentals are in effect in New York City, Washington, D.C., and about 200 other cities in the United States.

As usual, we begin the analysis by finding the equilibrium price and quantity. In Figure 4.9, the supply curve of rental apartments is S, and the demand curve is D. Therefore, the equilibrium rental price is P_0, and the equilibrium quantity is Q_0. If the price ceiling

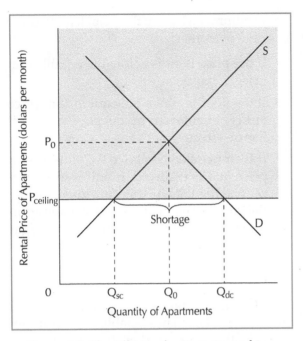

Figure 4.9 The Effects of a Rent-Control Law

The supply curve of rental apartments is S, the demand curve is D, the equilibrium price is P_0, and the equilibrium quantity of apartments rented is Q_0. However, the local government imposes a rent-control law, under which it is illegal to rent apartments for more than $P_{ceiling}$. If the law is enforced, the quantity demanded will be Q_{dc}, but the quantity supplied will only be Q_{sc}. As a result of the rent-control law, there is a shortage of $(Q_{dc} - Q_{sc})$.

is above the equilibrium price, it will have no effect, because the equilibrium price will still be legal. Therefore, we will concentrate on the more interesting (and more problematic) case, in which there is a price ceiling at $P_{ceiling}$, which is below the equilibrium price. When this price ceiling is in place, all prices in the shaded area (including the equilibrium price) are illegal. At this price, the equilibrium price P_0 is illegal. If the law is enforced, the market will not be able to find its way to the equilibrium. As a result, the quantity demanded is Q_{dc}, and the quantity supplied is Q_{sc}. The quantity demanded is greater than the quantity supplied, so we have a shortage of $(Q_{dc} - Q_{sc})$. The quantity of rental housing that is actually consumed goes down from Q_0 to Q_{sc}.

As a result of the rent-control law, there is a decrease in the total amount of rental housing actually consumed.

We have now seen that price floors and price ceilings are actually very similar in some important ways. If the equilibrium price is legal (either because a price floor is below the equilibrium price or because a price ceiling is above the equilibrium price), the price control will not have any effect on the market. If the price control is such that the equilibrium price is against the law, and if the law is enforced, either a price floor or a price ceiling will cause a reduction in the quantity that is actually bought and sold.

In most cases, one of the first effects of rent-control laws is that the quality of housing deteriorates. If landlords are prevented from charging a rent that covers their costs adequately, they may respond by reducing maintenance and postponing repairs. Many properties are eventually abandoned. In New York City, the local government has spent billions of dollars to buy abandoned properties. This is ironic, since the properties would not have been abandoned at all, if it weren't for the government's rent-control policy.

Rent-control laws can lead to some surprising uses of resources. For example, in Santa Monica, California, a young professional was renting a rent-controlled apartment near the ocean, at a price far below its equilibrium price. When she got a new job on the East Coast, she decided to keep her California apartment, since she was able to rent it for such a low rate. She could then use the rent-controlled apartment for a couple of weeks per year, when she was back in California on vacation. Thus, due to the rent-control law, a valuable apartment was empty for 50 or 51 weeks of the year.

As shortages appear in a rent-controlled city, some people may become homeless, but most will probably look for housing in nearby cities that don't have rent controls. This means that the demand curve for housing in the non-controlled cities will shift to the right. As a

Real Economics for Real People 4.3:
Food Price Controls and Starvation in China

In the mid-1950s, the communist government in China forced millions of small farmers to become part of large communes. In most of the communes, *food was given away free of charge.* When food is being given away for free, there's no incentive to use it wisely. Tremendous amounts of food were wasted. In many parts of China, food supplies were exhausted before the harvest could be collected in 1959, even though the 1958 harvest had been a good one.

The three years from 1959 to 1961 are known as the Great Famine. In terms of the number of people who starved to death, it was the worst famine in the history of the world. It is estimated that at least 20 million people died from the famine, and the death toll may have been as high as 30 million. In addition, there was a dramatic decline in the birth rate, since so many women suffered from malnutrition. It's estimated that there were about 30 million fewer births during this period than there would have been without the food crisis.

The Great Famine was one of history's worst tragedies, but it is not actually very surprising. The Chinese authorities set the price of food at zero. From our analysis of price controls, we know that a price ceiling below the equilibrium price will cause shortages. Certainly, a price of zero is below the equilibrium price of food, so it's not surprising that China suffered food shortages.

The price ceiling on food wasn't the only factor that contributed to the Great Famine. For example, when food began to run out, the government underestimated the size of the problem. If the authorities had allowed the market to work, the scarcity of food would have sent prices soaring. This might have helped to alert the government to the true dimensions of the problem. However, since prices were controlled, the government relied on crop forecasts, which turned out to be highly inaccurate. This reminds us that market prices are extremely good at conveying information.

Even when the food shortages became severe, it might have been possible to reduce the suffering by importing more food, but this did not happen. In fact, China continued to export food, and the Chinese government rejected an offer of food aid from the International Red Cross.

Weather conditions were not at their best during the years of the Great Famine, but they weren't extremely bad, either. When the famine ended in 1962, it was because of a change in government policies, rather than a change in the weather. The worst famine in history was primarily man-made, and the price ceiling on food played an important role in the disaster.

result, the equilibrium rental price of housing will rise in the cities without rent control. For example, the rent controls in New York City lead to increases in the price of rental housing in Fort Lee, New Jersey, and other nearby communities.

Fortunately, price ceilings aren't used very widely in the United States, but there are a few other examples. In the 1970s, price ceilings on gasoline led to severe shortages. Service stations often had to turn customers away because their supplies were sold out. Moreover, drivers began to form long lines because they were afraid of running out of gas. (When there's a shortage, it's important to be first in line.) About a billion gallons of gasoline were wasted, as cars sat in long lines with their engines idling.

Another example of the problems of price ceilings occurred in California in the spring of 2001. The California legislature had approved a badly flawed plan of deregulation in the electricity market. They allowed the whole-sale price of electricity to be determined by the market, but they maintained a price ceiling on the retail price of electricity. For a while, this worked OK, because the equilibrium retail price was below the price ceiling. However, when a variety of conditions caused the equilibrium price to rise, the price ceiling took effect. The state's largest retail electricity companies found themselves in the position of having to provide electricity at a lower price than the price at which they could buy it. This led to some blackouts, and it led to the bankruptcy of one large company.

Price ceilings are more common in social-ist countries, and in the poor countries of Africa and Asia. In some cases, the price ceil-ings can have devastating effects, as described in *Real Economics for Real People 4.3* on page 99.

Black Markets. When a price ceiling is below the equilibrium price, we see shortages, where the demands of buyers are not satisfied. Some buyers would be willing to pay more than the ceiling price, if only they could find someone who is willing to sell. In a situation like this, **black markets** may develop. A black market involves illegal sales, for the purpose of getting around a price control.

If the government enforces the price ceilings actively, black-market sales will have to occur in secret. The supply curves of sellers on the black market will be pushed to the left, since sellers will be afraid of being thrown in jail. This may raise the black-market price to a level that is higher than the equilibrium price. Since black-market sales are illegal, buyers will be uncertain about the quality of the goods they are buying: It's hard for a seller to maintain a reputation for quality merchandise when the buying and sell-ing take place in darkened doorways.

Summary of the Effects of Price Controls

We have seen that price floors can lead to sur-pluses, while price ceilings can lead to short-ages and black markets. We summarize some of these effects in Table 4.1.

Reality Check: Interim Review Questions

IR4-5. Assume that the equilibrium price of pencils is 10 cents each. What would happen to the price at which pencils are sold if the government were to impose a price floor, stating that it is illegal to sell pencils for less than 5 cents each? How would the price floor affect the quantity of pencils bought and sold? What would happen to the price and quantity if the price floor were at 20 cents per pencil?

IR4-6. Assume that the equilibrium price of pajamas is $20 per pair. What would hap-pen to the price at which pajamas are sold if the government were to impose a price ceiling, stating that it is illegal to sell pajamas for more than $30 per pair? How would the price ceiling affect the quantity of pajamas bought and sold? What would happen to the price and quantity if the price ceiling were at $10 per pair?

Table 4.1 Summary of Effects of the Price Controls

Type of Price Control	Relationship to Equilibrium Price	Effects
1. Price Floor (Legal minimum, such as sugar price support)	Below equilibrium	No Effect
2. Price Floor	Above equilibrium	Surpluses; Quantity actually consumed will decrease; Illegal sales may occur
3. Price Ceiling (Legal maximum, such as rent-control law)	Above equilibrium	No Effect
4. Price Ceiling	Below equilibrium	Shortages; Quantity actually consumed will decrease; Black markets may develop

PRICES THAT AREN'T SET AT THEIR EQUILIBRIUM LEVEL

A price control is a deliberate attempt to outlaw some prices. Consequently, the shortages and surpluses that are brought about by price controls are the result of deliberate policy decisions. On the other hand, shortages and surpluses are common in some other markets, even though these markets don't have price ceilings or price floors in the usual sense. We will take a look at some of these markets now. If a price isn't at its equilibrium level, the market will be out of equilibrium, regardless of whether the disequilibrium is caused by an explicit price-control law, or by something else.

Concert Pricing

Peppermint Sponge is a rock group. The band is giving a concert in a basketball arena, and exactly 12,000 tickets are available. Panel (a) of Figure 4.10 shows that the supply curve is a vertical line, S, at a quantity of 12,000. The demand curve is D. The equilibrium quantity is 12,000, and the equilibrium price is $50 per ticket. In other words, if the concert by Peppermint Sponge is in equilibrium, the people who go to the concert will pay a price of $50, and the arena will be full.

However, if the tickets are printed up several months ahead of time, the concert promoters may not know for certain whether the equilibrium price is $50 per ticket. If the promoters set the price at only $35 per ticket, the quantity demanded will be 18,000. There will be a shortage of (18,000 − 12,000) = 6000 tickets, even though the concert promoters did not set out intentionally to create a shortage.

Since there is unsatisfied demand for tickets to the concert, it would not be surprising if a black market were to arise. When there is a black market for tickets to a concert or sporting event, the sellers in the black market are often called "scalpers". Ticket "scalping" is restricted by law in many states, and in most cities with professional sports franchises. Some of the laws set a maximum re-sale price for tickets. Others make it illegal to sell near the site of the event. Still other laws require sellers to obtain a costly license. However, it's reasonable to ask whether scalpers are really doing a bad thing. After all, they serve the valuable function of moving the market closer to equilibrium. The scalpers help to allocate tickets to those who are willing to pay the most for tickets.

We can draw a parallel between "scalpers" and those who participate in black markets. Both groups are often vilified, but both provide a useful service. In the Soviet Union, price controls on food led to black markets. Governments officials loved to give speeches criticizing the black-market folks. But is it really so bad to break the law, when the law makes food illegal?

Panel (b) of Figure 4.10 shows a different possibility for the concert by Peppermint Sponge. Again, let's say that the equilibrium price is $50. This time, however, we assume that the promoters set the price at $65 per ticket. This time, there will be a surplus; that is, some of the tickets will not be sold. In Figure 4.10(b), the amount of the surplus is (12,000 − 6000) = 6000 tickets.

As the date of the concert draws near, the concert promoters will see that they have chosen a price that's higher than the equilibrium price. On the day of the performance, they

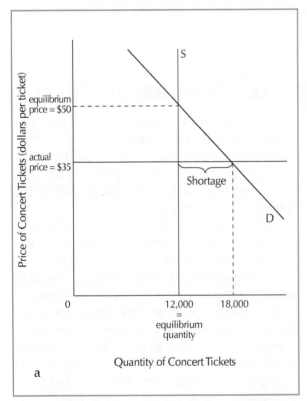

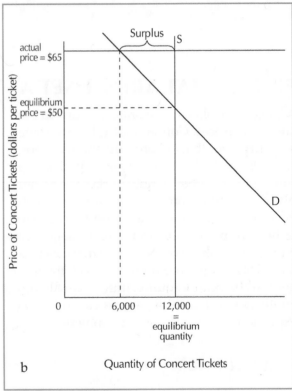

Figure 4.10 What Happens When the Price of Concert Tickets Cannot Easily Be Adjusted to its Equilibrium Level

In both panel (a) and panel (b), the supply of concert tickets is fixed at S, which says that the equilibrium quantity of tickets bought and sold is 12,000. Also, the demand curve for concert tickets is D in both panels (a) and (b), so that the equilibrium price is $50 per ticket in each case. In panel (a), the concert promoters set the price at $35. If this price can't be adjusted, the quantity demanded will be 18,000 tickets, and there will be a shortage of (18,000 − 12,000) = 6000 tickets. In this situation, we might expect "scalpers" to try to re-sell tickets. In panel (b), the concert promoters set the price at $65. If this price can't be adjusted, the quantity demanded will be 6000 tickets, which means that there will be a surplus of (12,000 − 6000) = 6000 tickets. In this situation, the concert promoters might cut prices for the unsold tickets, shortly before the concert.

may offer to sell the unsold tickets at a discount. After all, the sellers will make more money if they can sell the remaining tickets at a reduced price, instead of not selling them at all. Many concert halls and theaters have a system of selling tickets at a reduced price if some tickets remain unsold on the day of the performance. Similarly, if a commercial airline is committed to offering a particular flight, it will make more money by flying a full aircraft, rather than flying with empty seats. If airline tickets are still unsold within a few days of the flight, the airlines and ticket brokers may try to sell reduced-price tickets.

In short, tickets for rock concerts, Broadway plays, and similar events are often sold far in advance, so sellers must decide on ticket prices long before the event actually occurs. This means that it's relatively difficult to adjust prices in these markets, so that shortages or surpluses can occur.

Illegal Drugs and Other Illegal Activities

The market for cocaine doesn't have a price ceiling in the usual sense. Instead, it's illegal to buy and sell cocaine. Thus for all practical purposes, it's as if the market for cocaine has a price ceiling, at a price of zero. Not surprisingly, there is a shortage of cocaine, and a huge black market.

Similar things can be said about the market for babies for adoption. Once again, there is not a price ceiling, as such. However, it's illegal to buy and sell babies. Effectively, this means that the market for babies has a price ceiling of zero. It's no surprise, therefore, that there is a shortage of babies in the adoption market. Families who wish to go through an agency to adopt a baby must often spend five years or more on waiting lists. It is extremely rare to see outright purchases of babies, but it is now common for families who seek a private adoption to pay some of the expenses of the natural mother during her pregnancy.

These payments can amount to several thousand dollars. Payments to lawyers and other intermediaries often run to tens of thousands of dollars. In effect, there is an indirect black market.

We can think of the market for organs for transplant in a similar way. It's illegal to buy and sell livers, kidneys, or other organs. As we might expect, there is a shortage: Thousands of people die while waiting for a transplant. It might be possible to solve this problem by allowing payments to the estates of people who donate their organs when they die. In this way, the supply of transplantable organs could be increased, and the shortage could be relieved.

In this chapter, we have studied several examples of price ceilings. These include the price ceilings on food in China, as well as rent controls, and price ceilings on gasoline. Now, we have seen that we can think about the markets for cocaine, babies, and organs for transplant in a similar way. However, there is a crucial difference between these two sets of markets: The restrictions on the markets for drugs, babies, and human organs are based largely on *ethical* concerns, rather than narrowly economic concerns.

The case against price ceilings in the market for gasoline is extremely strong. However, it's more difficult to build a convincing case against restrictions on selling cocaine or babies, because of ethical concerns about such sales. Of course, there may be benefits from removing the restrictions on the markets for cocaine and babies. If cocaine were legalized, there might be a reduction in drug-related violence. If adoptive parents were allowed to pay for children, it would probably help those children who would otherwise be harmed by long waits for a home. On the other hand, reasonable people can reach the ethical judgment that buying and selling drugs and babies is morally wrong. If so, society may have an interest in restricting such buying and selling, even though it will lead to shortages.

Thus economic analysis can be an important tool for thinking about policy problems, but it shouldn't be viewed as the *only* tool.

To solve society's most difficult problems, we need to rely on our moral compass, as well as on the tools of supply and demand.

ECONOMICS AND YOU: HOW TO FIX THE SHORTAGE OF PARKING SPACES

We began this chapter with a discussion of the parking problem that can be found on many college campuses. At Jeanette's college, students have to pay a *fixed* fee to get a parking sticker. The amount of the fee does not depend on how heavily the student uses the parking lots: Students aren't required to pay anything at the time when they actually park their cars. Jeanette has to pay a parking fee of $50 per year, regardless of whether she uses the college parking lots for one hour per year, or for 1000 hours. Effectively, this means that the price of each additional hour of parking in the college lots is zero.

At two o'clock in the morning, a price of zero may not lead to shortages of parking spaces. However, at the times of peak usage during the day, a price of zero may not be high enough to achieve equilibrium. In other words, if the price is zero, we should not be surprised to see shortages, where the quantity of parking spaces demanded is greater than the quantity supplied. As a result, people will have to waste time and gasoline, looking for a parking space. If the price were at its equilibrium level, the parking lots would be just about full, but it wouldn't be necessary to wait a long time to find a spot.

One solution is to charge a positive price for parking (as is done at private parking garages). The price that would achieve equilibrium would be higher during the peak times of day, and it would be higher for the parking lots that are more centrally located. If people are faced with a schedule of prices, they can make sensible decisions about where to park. For instance, if Jeanette has plenty of time, she may be willing to pay a low price for a space in a far-away parking lot. However, if she is rushing to get to an interview for an on-campus job, she will probably be willing to pay something extra to find a parking space that's close to her destination. In this way, prices could be used to allocate parking spaces to those who need them most.

Shortages will occur whenever a price is below its equilibrium level, and surpluses will occur whenever a price is above its equilibrium level. In this chapter, we have learned about several situations in which markets aren't allowed to find their equilibrium prices. In most cases, it would probably be much better to let prices go to their equilibrium level. This would eliminate the shortages or surpluses. When markets are allowed to work properly, prices usually do a very effective job of allocating resources. The beauty of the price system is that its "invisible hand" matches buyers and sellers in a quick and efficient way. It does so without needing a vast government bureaucracy, and without forcing people to waste a lot of time waiting in line.

Chapter Summary

1. When demand increases, the demand curve shifts to the right. This leads to a new equilibrium, in which both the equilibrium price and the equilibrium quantity are higher than they were before the shift. If demand decreases, so that the demand curve shifts to the left, we get the opposite effects: Both the equilibrium price and the equilibrium quantity are lower than they were before the shift.

2. When supply increases, the supply curve shifts to the right. This leads to a new equilibrium, in which the equilibrium price is lower and the equilibrium quantity is higher than before the shift. If supply decreases, the supply curve shifts to the left, and we get a higher equilibrium price and a lower equilibrium quantity than before.

3. A price floor is a legal minimum price. (Examples include the price supports for sugar and milk, and the minimum-wage laws.) If the floor is not enforced, or if it is below the equilibrium price, it will have no effect. If the floor is above the equilibrium price, it will lead to surpluses. To deal with the surpluses, governments often pass additional laws, designed to buy up the surpluses or to decrease supply.

4. A price ceiling is a legal maximum price. (Examples include gasoline price controls and rent controls.) If the ceiling is not enforced, or if it is above the equilibrium price, it will have no effect. If the ceiling is below the equilibrium price, it will lead to shortages. Black markets often arise in response to the shortages.

Key Terms

Price-Control Law

Price Floor

Price Ceiling

Disequilibrium

Import Quota

Rent-Control Law

Black Market

Questions and Problems

QP4-1. The equilibrium price for a video rental differs from one part of the country to another, and from one part of the week to another. Nevertheless, it is common to see rental prices of $2 or $3. Suppose that the government passes a price-ceiling law, so that it is illegal to rent video for more than 25 cents. What do you expect would happen as a result? Would your answer change if the ceiling were set at $6? If so, how?

QP4-2. For each of the following changes, what will happen to the equilibrium price of boards cut from wood? What will happen to the equilibrium quantity?

a. An increase in incomes. (You may assume that wooden boards are a normal good.)
b. A decrease in the price of brick, which is a substitute for wooden boards.
c. A drought in the Pacific Northwest, which makes trees more susceptible to disease and insects.
d. A technological innovation which allows sawmills to cut trees into boards more quickly, and with less labor.

QP4-3. Explain why the price will go up when the demand curve shifts to the right. Explain why the price will go down when the supply curve shifts to the right.

QP4-4. For each of the following changes, what will happen to the equilibrium price of cotton sweaters? What will happen to the equilibrium quantity?

a. Good growing conditions lead to a record cotton crop, and this leads to lower prices for cotton, which is an important input in the production of cotton sweaters.

b. An increase in the price of wool sweaters, which are a substitute for cotton sweaters.

c. Large numbers of people decide they don't like the feel of cotton, and that they want to increase their use of polyester.

d. An improvement in technology, which allows textile mills to produce cotton sweaters more rapidly than before.

QP4-5. In the early 1990s, some studies indicated that red wine could reduce the risk of heart disease. As a result of this news, what do you expect would happen to the equilibrium price and quantity of red wine?

QP4-6. The equilibrium price of a particular type of dress shirt is $30. A price ceiling is passed into law, so that the legal maximum price is $40. Do you expect that this will lead to black-market activity? Would your answer change if the price ceiling were set at $20? If so, how?

QP4-7. A highly prized type of mineral water comes from a spring in the Alps. There is nothing that producers can do to speed up the flow of water. As a result, the supply of this water is completely unresponsive to price. No matter what happens to price, the quantity supplied per day is always the same. If a price floor is enforced above the equilibrium price for this type of water, what will happen to the quantity that is actually bought and sold? What about the case of a price ceiling below the equilibrium price? (Hint: In answering this question, it may be especially useful to draw a supply-demand diagram for yourself.)

QP4-8. Explain why shortages arise when the government enforces a price ceiling below the equilibrium price. Explain why surpluses arise when the government enforces a price floor above the equilibrium price.

QP4-9. The Transplant Act of 1984 makes it a felony to buy and sell body organs (such as livers and kidneys) for transplant. It is illegal to offer any financial compensation to the families of organ donors. Do you expect that this would lead to shortages or surpluses, or do you think the market for transplant organs will be in equilibrium?

QP4-10. For each of the following changes, what will happen to the equilibrium price of music compact discs (CDs)?

a. A change in tastes, such that many more music lovers prefer to attend live performances, instead of listening to recorded music.

b. An increase in the price of the plastic components that are used in manufacturing CDs.

c. A technological improvement that allows manufacturers to produce more CDs without increasing the number of workers.

d. An increase in income. (You may assume that CDs are normal goods.)

QP4-11. In the table on the following page, we have the demand schedule and supply schedule for imports from Belgium of a particular type of cut-glass vase.

a. What are the equilibrium price and quantity?

b. The government sets a price floor at $70. Will there be any effect? If so, will there be a shortage or a surplus? What will be the amount of the shortage or surplus?

c. How do your answers to (b) change if the price floor is set at $30?

d. The government sets a price ceiling at $80. Will there be any effect? If so, will there be a shortage or a surplus? What will be the amount of the shortage or surplus?

e. How do your answers to (d) change if the price ceiling is set at $20?

Table for Question QP4-11

Price	Quantity of Vases Demanded per week	Quantity of Vases Supplied per week
$100	0	100
90	10	90
80	20	80
70	30	70
60	40	60
50	50	50
40	60	40
30	70	30
20	80	20
10	90	10
0	100	0

QP4-12. The demand curve for a type of mountain bike is given by $Q_d = 100,000 - 250P$, where P is the price of the bike. The supply curve is given by $Q_s = 250P$. At the equilibrium price, the quantity demanded and the quantity supplied are equal, so that $Q_d = Q_s$.

a. Substitute the equation for the demand curve and the equation for the supply curve into the equation for equilibrium, and solve for the equilibrium price.

b. Once you have solved for the equilibrium price, substitute it into either the supply equation or the demand equation, to get the equilibrium quantity.

c. Senator Puffinstuff says that mountain bikes are too expensive, and he suggests that a price ceiling be instituted in the market for mountain bikes. If the price ceiling is set at $500, what will be the effect on the market? What quantity will be demanded? What quantity will be supplied? Will there be a surplus? Will there be a shortage? If there will be either a surplus or a shortage, how great will it be (that is, what will be the difference between quantity demanded and quantity supplied)?

d. If the price ceiling is set at $100, what will be the effect on the market? What quantity will be demanded? What quantity will be supplied? Will there be a surplus? Will there be a shortage? If there will be either a surplus or a shortage, how great will it be (that is, what will be the difference between quantity demanded and quantity supplied)?

Chapter 5

International Trade

ECONOMICS AND YOU:
IS THERE A GIANT SUCKING SOUND?

In 1992, the Texas billionaire Ross Perot ran for President of the United States. His opponents were the incumbent Republican President, George Bush, and Bill Clinton, the Democratic Party candidate, who won the election. Both Bush and Clinton were generally supportive of free international trade. In particular, both Bush and Clinton were in favor of the North American Free Trade Agreement (NAFTA), which would reduce barriers to international trade between Canada, Mexico, and the United States.

But Perot opposed NAFTA. He said that reduced barriers to trade with Mexico would create a "giant sucking sound", as American industries re-located to Mexico. Some of his campaign literature suggested that Americans might lose six *million* jobs.

No serious economist believed Perot's numbers. If the United States was to lose six million jobs as a result of NAFTA, the following things would have been necessary: (1) First, the Mexican economy would have had to double in size overnight. (2) Second, all of the growth of the Mexican economy would have had to be in the form of exports to the United States. (3) Third, there would have had to be no increase in exports from the United States to Mexico,

even though U.S. exports of machinery and equipment had been a very important source of Mexico's economic growth in the past.

The ultimate test of Perot's prediction would come from looking at what actually happened to employment in the United States. In 1992, when Perot made his prediction about the giant sucking sound, about 118 million Americans had jobs. NAFTA was enacted the following year. By 2000, the number of American jobs had risen to about 136 million. Whereas Perot predicted that there would be a huge Depression, the 1990s were actually the scene of one of the most remarkable economic expansions in history. Of course, international trade was not the only source of growth in the American economy, or in the economy of the rest of the world. However, there is no doubt that international trade was an important part of the economic expansion.

However, just because Perot's rhetoric was overblown, it does *not* follow that international trade doesn't create any problems. Exports from China to the United States have grown dramatically in the 21st century, reaching $500 billion in 2015. As a result, competition from China put major pressure on the American manufacturing sector. One study by prominent economists showed that import competition from China may be responsible for one-fifth of the decline in U.S. manufacturing employment.

Of course, import competition is not the only challenge for the American manufacturing sector. Technological innovations have been especially rapid in some parts of manufacturing in the last few decades. Fifty years ago, many automobile workers performed simple, repetitive tasks, over and over again. Today, many of those tasks have been taken over by computer-driven robots. As a result, employment in the auto industry would have shrunk substantially, with or without international trade.

In earlier chapters, we emphasized that technological change plays a crucial role in raising the standard of living. This is a good thing in the long run, but it creates difficult transitions in the short run. It's painful for a worker to lose his or her job, even if the job loss is due to a technological improvement that improves the overall standard of living. Job losses from import competition are no less painful.

Even though import competition is only one part of a much bigger story, criticism of international trade returned in a big way in the 2016 presidential campaign. Sharp attacks against trade were leveled by Vermont Senator Bernie Sanders in the Democratic Party, and by New York businessman and television celebrity Donald Trump in the Republican Party. However, it should be emphasized that these attacks focus only on one aspect of international trade, namely, the challenge of import competition. Trump, Sanders, and other critics of international trade typically ignore the fact that millions of American jobs depend on *exports* to other countries. They also ignore the benefits to American consumers from low-priced imports.

The consensus among economists is still that the benefits of international trade outweigh the costs by a wide margin. The answer to import competition is to do more to help the workers and companies that have been adversely affected by imports, rather than to erect huge barriers to trade.

SOME FACTS ABOUT INTERNATIONAL TRADE

When people in a country *sell* goods or services to people in another country, we say that the selling country has made an *export*. When people in a country *buy* goods or services from people in another country, we say that the buying country has made an *import*. Every transaction that is an export for one country is also an import for some other country.

In 2015, the United States exported about $2.25 trillion. This was about 12.6 percent of gross domestic product (GDP). Gross domestic product is the total value of all of the goods and services produced in the country. In the same year, imports into the United States were about $2.78 trillion, or about 15.5 percent of GDP.

Figure 5.1 shows that, over time, international trade has accounted for an increasing fraction of GDP for the United States. In most years in the 1950s and 1960s, exports accounted for about five percent of GDP, and imports were at about the same level. In the 1970s, exports and imports grew to around eight to ten percent of GDP. In the early 1980s, exports fell back slightly, and imports continued to grow as a percentage of GDP. As a result, the United States experienced unusually large trade deficits. A *trade deficit* occurs when imports are greater than exports. A *trade surplus* occurs when exports are greater than imports. In 1986 and 1987, the trade deficit was about three percent of GDP. However, exports surged in the late 1980s, and continued to grow rapidly in the 1990s. Imports grew, too, so that trade deficits continued, but they were not as

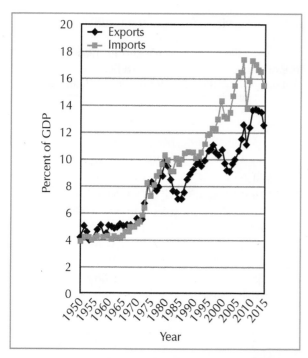

Figure 5.1 United States Exports and Imports as Percent of Gross Domestic Product, 1950–2015

large as they had been in the middle 1980s. The trade deficits widened again in the first decade of the 21st century. Both imports and exports fell sharply in 2008, as a result of the financial crisis, but rebounded after the recession. Since the recession, the overall trade deficit has stayed around three percent of GDP.

Thus, if we look at the last 60 years, we see a period in which international trade was growing more rapidly than purely domestic transactions. As a result, we can say that international trade was a major "engine of growth" for the United States. (The same is true for many other countries, as well. Overall, international trade has been an engine of growth for the entire world economy.)

Figure 5.1 presents the time trend of the *overall* level of exports and imports, for goods and services combined. Table 5.1 gives a *country-by-country* breakdown of exports and imports, for 2015. In this table, the coun-

tries are listed in order of the amounts of U.S. exports.

Table 5.1 reveals a number of things. First of all, trade is very dispersed. Although some countries clearly have more trade with the United States than do other countries, it is not as if one or two countries were dominating the picture completely. If we add imports and exports together, Canada has the largest total volume of trade with the United States. Our other nearest neighbor, Mexico, has the second-largest amount of U.S. exports and the third-largest amount of U.S. imports. It is probably not surprising that nearby countries play a big role in U.S. international trade, since the costs of transporting goods are lower for short distances. However, there is also considerable trade with countries that are much farther away. Second, the table shows that many of our biggest trading partners are other affluent countries, such as Australia, Belgium, Canada, France, Germany, Italy, Japan, the Netherlands, and the United Kingdom. A lot of our trade is with other rich countries, because that's where a lot of the money is. Third, China stands out in Table 5.1. The U.S. exports a very substantial amount (about one percent of U.S. GDP) to China, so that U.S. exports to China are surpassed only by U.S. exports to Canada and Mexico. However, imports from China are much larger than imports from any other country. As a result, the U.S. trade deficit with China is much larger than the trade deficit with any other country. In 2015, the trade deficit with China was more than four times as large as the second-largest deficit, with Germany. Fourth, although the United States has an overall trade deficit, it does not have a deficit with every country. As shown in Table 5.1, the U.S. had substantial surpluses in 2015 with Australia, Argentina, Belgium, Brazil, the Netherlands, Singapore, and the United Kingdom.

One of the most interesting features of Table 5.1 is that the United States has large

Table 5.1 United States Exports and Imports of Goods and Services, for Selected Countries, 2015*

Country	Exports from U.S. (in Billions of Dollars)	Imports to U.S. (in Billions of Dollars)	Trade Surplus (Positive) or Trade Deficit (Negative) (in Billions of Dollars)
Canada	$338.4	$332.9	$5.4
Mexico	267.3	324.6	−57.3
China	162.2	500.3	−338.0
United Kingdom	119.3	109.7	9.6
Japan	107.2	164.0	−56.8
Middle East[a]	101.5	79.9	21.6
Germany	78.2	156.9	−78.7
South Korea	66.8	83.6	−16.8
Brazil	59.4	34.8	24.6
Netherlands	56.8	27.4	29.4
France	49.5	65.2	−15.8
Australia	43.0	18.1	24.8
Singapore	42.9	25.2	17.8
Africa[b]	41.6	34.3	7.4
Belgium	40.1	25.4	14.7
Taiwan	39.0	48.8	−9.9
India	38.9	68.7	−29.7
Italy	23.9	55.9	−32.0
Argentina	16.5	6.0	10.5
Venezuela	14.4	16.5	−2.1

* Surpluses or deficits may not agree exactly with export and import levels, because of rounding.
[a] Includes Iran, Iraq, Israel, Saudi Arabia, United Arab Emirates, and 10 other countries.
[b] Includes more than 50 countries.

Source: U.S. Department of Commerce, Bureau of Economic Analysis.

surpluses with some countries, and very large deficits with some other countries. We are not even close to "bilateral trade balance", which is a situation in which the exports to each country are exactly equal to the imports to that country. In *Real Economics for Real People 5.1*, we explore the question of whether trade balance is a good thing. I urge you to read it. On the issue of international trade, there is a lot of emotional talk, much of which is misinformed. It's important to have a balanced perspective.

Reality Check: Interim Review Questions

IR5-1. Over the last few decades, have exports and imports become more important, or less important, as a fraction of gross domestic product?

IR5-2. In what regions of the world are the most important trading partners of the United States located?

If you listen to some commentators and politicians, it would be easy to think that there is nothing worse than a trade deficit. The idea is a fairly simplistic one. Exports are "good", because they create American jobs. Imports are "bad", because they create jobs for people in other countries. If exports are "good", and imports are "bad", then it must be that trade surpluses are good, and trade deficits are bad.

This sort of thinking can be very misleading. First of all, it is important to remember that the United States has been running substantial trade deficits in many years in which the unemployment rate has been low. Clearly, it is simplistic to think that trade deficits inevitably lead to unemployment. The Great Recession of 2007–09 was caused by factors such as a drop in home prices and a poorly regulated financial system, rather than by imports.

Second, although employment considerations are worth worrying about, they are not the only important thing. Consumption is also important. Americans import goods from other countries because they find that those goods provide a good level of satisfaction for the dollar. Part of the trade deficit is caused by imports of coffee from Brazil, wooden bowls from Thailand, radios from South Korea, and cheese from Denmark. It is very difficult to argue that consumers in the United States would be better off if we were to cut off these imports.

Part of the trade deficit is caused by imports of oil. In recent years, the United States has been importing about 9 or 10 million barrels per day. (We get the oil from all over the world, but our four biggest suppliers are Canada, Mexico, Saudi Arabia, and Venezuela.) We could "solve" a part of the trade deficit by prohibiting imports of oil, but would that make us better off? Instead of making us better off, a prohibition on oil imports would just make us cold in the winter, because it would be difficult to find enough energy to heat our homes. In recent years, hydraulic fracturing (or "fracking") technologies have caused large increases in production of oil and natural gas in the United States. This has reduced, but not eliminated, America's dependence on oil imports. The long-term solution to our energy problems will involve greater energy efficiency and conservation, as well as development of solar power and other alternative energy sources. Merely banning oil imports won't solve the problems.

A third important point is that there is no way for the world as a whole to run a trade surplus. By definition, one country's surplus is another country's deficit. This means that the world as a whole has a trade balance of exactly zero: For the world as a whole, total imports have to be exactly equal to total exports. Thus, there is no way for all countries to reduce deficits (or increase surpluses) simultaneously. If lots of countries were to try to increase their surpluses (or reduce their deficits) at the same time, the results could be disastrous. In the 1930s, a number of countries increased their barriers against imports, in the false belief that this would increase employment at home. This led to a downward spiral, as economic activity decreased around the globe. The Great Depression of the 1930s had many causes, and trade restrictions weren't the most important one. But trade restrictions certainly contributed to the Great Depression.

When a country runs an overall trade deficit, as the United States is doing now, the country is consuming more than it produces. In other words, the country is borrowing. If we really want to address the trade deficit, the best way to do it would be to save more. This has more to do with policies toward taxes, government spending, Social Security and pensions than with trade policies.

In thinking about trade deficits, it is useful to make an analogy between a country and a household. Most households have at least one worker. The workers earn money by working for an employer. Thus, we could say that most households have a big "trade surplus" with their employers. On the other hand, households spend money in all sorts of places, including the grocery store, the hardware store, the gasoline station, and so on. We could say that most households have "trade deficits" with all of these retailers.

In the aggregate, it would be good if the sum of the household's "trade surpluses" with employers is about as big as the sum of all of the "trade deficits" with the various retailers. If the household's "deficits" are extremely large in comparison with its "surpluses", then the household will go deeply into debt. It's not a big problem if the household runs a more moderate aggregate deficit: Households borrow all the time, and most do so without bad consequences.

Similarly, it would be good if the sum of a country's trade surpluses with some countries were roughly as big as the sum of its trade deficits with other countries. If the overall trade deficits are too large, the coun-

try will fall deeply into debt. But it's not a big problem if a country runs a modest aggregate deficit. It happens all the time, without severe repercussions. The key question is whether the trade deficits of the last few years are large enough to do harm. The answer is that the deficits may well be harmful, especially if they do not shrink in the next few years. However, if we desire to reduce the deficits, the solution is to get our consumption spending binge under control, rather than to erect artificial barriers to trade.

It's *especially* important to avoid worrying too much about trade deficits with any one country. As shown in Table 5.1, we run surpluses with some countries, and deficits with others. This is very common. Even when the United States has had an overall trade balance of zero, with total exports equal to total imports, we have always run deficits with some countries and surpluses with other countries. Once again, we can reinforce our ideas by using an analogy with the household. It simply would not make sense for a household to try to have bilateral trade balance with the grocery store, the clothing store, the book store, and so on. And it would be extremely counterproductive for a country to try to have exact bilateral trade balance with every other country.

Too often, international trade is characterized as a "win-lose" proposition. In fact, trade is most often a "win-win". In the next section, we will continue to develop our ideas about how trade can be beneficial for all.

COMPARATIVE ADVANTAGE REVISITED

In Chapter 2, we introduced the idea of comparative advantage. We showed that it would be beneficial for people and countries to specialize in the activities in which they have comparative advantage, and then to trade

with each other. In Figure 2.5, we illustrated the case for trade between Kenny, who has comparative advantage in the production of fish, and Stan, who has comparative advantage in the production of coconuts.

绝对优势：在某种商品的生产上，一个国家所耗费的劳动成本绝对低于自己的贸易伙伴国，在劳动生产上占绝对优势

But some readers might object to that example in Chapter 2. Not only did Kenny have *comparative* advantage in the production of fish, but he also had *absolute* advantage in fish production. Not only did Stan have *comparative* advantage in the production of coconuts, but he also had *absolute* advantage in coconut production.

Some readers might say that the example in Chapter 2 was too easy. Some might ask what would happen in a case in which one side has absolute advantage in *all* activities. In this section, however, we will show that it is still possible to enjoy gains from trade, even when one side has absolute advantage in every activity. This is not merely a sterile academic exercise. It has relevance to many of the most important debates in the international economy today. Often, the most heated opposition to free trade comes in the form of opposition to free trade with relatively poor countries, most notably Mexico and China. Although the debate is not usually carried on using the language that we have developed in this book, we could still characterize the opponents of trade with Mexico or China as saying something like this: "Workers from poorer countries are less productive than workers in the United States. Therefore, there is nothing to be gained from trading with these countries."

But that statement is simply not true. Even though American workers may have *absolute* advantage in every activity, when compared with workers in Mexico or China, it is impossible for American workers to have *comparative* advantage in every activity.

We'll illustrate this idea with another example from a desert island. Once again, there are two commodities, fish and coconuts. This time, the two workers are Alex and Zeke. Alex isn't as quick or clever as Zeke, and Zeke has absolute advantage, both in catching fish *and* in gathering coconuts.

The production-possibilities frontiers for Alex and Zeke are shown in Figure 5.2. If Alex devotes all of his energies and resources to fishing, he can catch 15 fish per month. If he devotes all of his energies and resources to gathering coconuts, Alex can gather 5 coconuts per month. Between those two endpoints, Alex's production-possibilities frontier is a straight line.

If Zeke devotes all of *his* energies and resources to fishing, he can catch 16 fish per month. If Zeke devotes all of his energies and resources to gathering coconuts, he can gather 16 coconuts per month. Between these two endpoints, Zeke's production-possibilities frontier is also a straight line.

Zeke has *absolute* advantage in both activities. However, in order to determine *comparative* advantage, we must calculate the opportunity costs for each man. Let's begin by calculating opportunity cost for Alex. Alex can produce either 15 fish or 5 coconuts. Therefore, for Alex, the opportunity cost of 5 coconuts is 15 fish. We can write this as an equation, as follows:

$$5C = 15F \text{ (for Alex)},$$

where C stands for coconuts and F stands for fish. If we divide both sides of this equation by 5, we can find the opportunity cost of *one* coconut for Alex:

$$(5/5)C = 1C = (15/5)F = 3F \text{ (for Alex)}.$$

We now know that, for Alex, the opportunity cost of one coconut is three fish.

Next, let's calculate the opportunity cost for Zeke. Zeke can produce either 16 fish or 16 coconuts. This can be expressed in equation form, as follows:

$$16C = 16F \text{ (for Zeke)}.$$

If we divide both sides of this equation by 16, we find that, for Zeke, the opportunity cost of one coconut is one fish.

To recap, the opportunity cost of one coconut is three fish for Alex, whereas the opportunity cost of one coconut is only one fish for Zeke. Therefore, Zeke has comparative advantage in coconut production, because

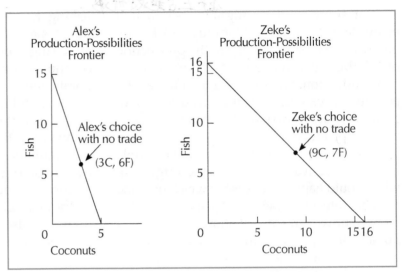

Figure 5.2 The Production-Possibilities Frontiers for Alex and Zeke, in the Absence of Trade

Zeke has *absolute* advantage in the production of both fish and coconuts. However, Alex has *comparative* advantage in the production of fish, while Zeke has comparative advantage in coconuts.

利用比较优势，每种商品的总产量都增加了

the opportunity cost of a coconut is lower for Zeke than it is for Alex. In other words, coconuts are "cheap" for Zeke. On the other hand, Alex has comparative advantage in fish production. Thus, even though Zeke has *absolute* advantage in both activities, Alex does have *comparative* advantage in the production of fish.

To illustrate the gains from trade, we have to figure out what each of these gentlemen would do, in the absence of trade. It is possible to develop an elaborate mathematical structure, to specify the consumer's preferences. But doing that would take us off on a distant tangent. So, for now, we will simply make assumptions about the consumption choices of Alex and Zeke. If the two men do not trade, Alex will have to consume one of the combinations of outputs that is given by his production-possibilities frontier. Let's assume that Alex would choose to consume three coconuts and six fish. (This point is indeed on Alex's production-possibilities frontier, as shown in Figure 5.2.)

Let's assume that, if there is no trade, Zeke will choose to consume nine coconuts and seven fish. (This point is on Zeke's production-possibilities frontier, as shown in Figure 5.2.)

So, if there were no trade, Alex would consume three coconuts and six fish, while Zeke would consume nine coconuts and seven fish. This means that the total production of this two-person society is (6 + 7) = 13 fish, and (3 + 9) = 12 coconuts.

Sooner or later, one of these guys is going to get an idea. What if Alex specializes in fish production (which is his comparative advantage), while Zeke specializes in coconut production (which is his comparative advantage)? Alex will then catch 15 fish, while Zeke will gather 16 coconuts. Note that *total production of each commodity has gone up, as a result of exploiting comparative advantage! The two men used to have a total of 13 fish, and they now have 15 fish. In addition, they used to have a total of 12 coconuts, and they now have a total of 16 coconuts.* This increase in total production is the thing that allows the two men to make themselves better off, by specializing and trading.

After they specialize, Alex and Zeke will have to figure out how to trade with each other. In effect, they will have to determine the price at which they can buy and sell coconuts and fish. In a more advanced course, it would be possible to spell out the process of price determination in more detail. Here, however, we will

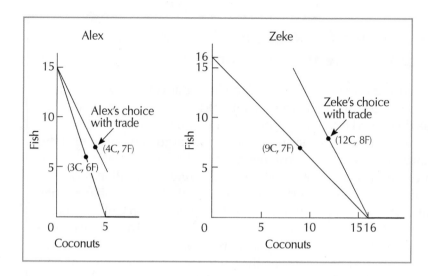

Figure 5.3 The Gains from Specialization and Trade

Alex has comparative advantage in the production of fish, and Zeke has comparative advantage in the production of coconuts. If each of them specializes in the activity in which he has comparative advantage, the total amount of production will increase. We assume that, after specializing, they trade with each other at the rate of two fish for one coconut. Trading in this manner allows each of the men to increase his consumption of both goods.

Table 5.2 The Gains from Trade for Alex and Zeke

	Alex's Consumption			Zeke's Consumption	
	No Trade	With Trade		No Trade	With Trade
Coconuts	3	4	Coconuts	9	12
Fish	6	7	Fish	7	8

just make an arbitrary assumption about the price of fish in terms of coconuts. In the absence of trade, Alex's production-possibilities frontier told him that he could trade *three* fish for one coconut. In the absence of trade, Zeke's production-possibilities frontier told him that he could trade *one* fish for one coconut. Let's assume they trade at a rate between three-to-one and one-to-one. Let's assume they trade at a rate of *two* fish for one coconut.

In Figure 5.3, we trace out the consumption possibilities available to each man, given that they trade at a rate of two fish for one coconut. These "consumption-possibilities frontiers" are farther out than the individual production-possibilities frontiers. This tells us that the two

men should be able to increase their consumption by specialization and trade, even though Zeke has *absolute* advantage in each activity.

The exact consumption choices will depend on the preferences of the two men. One possibility would be for Alex to trade eight of his 15 fish to Zeke. Since the rate at which they trade is two fish for one coconut, Alex will get four coconuts in return for the eight fish he gives up. As a result, Alex ends up with four coconuts and (15 − 8) = seven fish. Zeke ends up with eight fish and (16 − 4) = 12 coconuts.

Table 5.2 makes a "before-and-after" comparison for each of the two men. We see that, as a result of specialization and trade, Alex increases

Real Economics for Real People 5.2:
Trade, the Environment, and Human Rights

In November, 1999, the World Trade Organization tried to hold a meeting in Seattle, Washington. The meeting was disrupted by a series of protests. Some of the protestors were merely engaged in vandalism, and they trashed a large portion of downtown Seattle. However, other protestors were more peaceful. They brought forth a wide variety of complaints about free trade. Many of the same arguments were repeated a few months later, in protests in Washington, D.C., at the meetings of the International Monetary Fund and the World Bank. Some of the protestors suggested that international trade is harming human rights and the environment. Most of the criticism was aimed at international trade with poorer countries, since many of the poorer countries do not have especially good records on environment or human rights.

The question is whether a reduction in international trade is likely to lead to any improvement in human rights or the environment. Of course, unless one is able to read the future in a crystal ball, it is not possible to make any absolutely certain predictions. However, there are good reasons to think that cutting off trade with poor countries will *not* cause them to improve their records on human rights or the environment.

First of all, it is important to remember that trade barriers are viewed as unfriendly, hostile actions. If the United States were to impose trade restrictions on some other country because the other country has a poor human-rights record, it is possible that the other country would say "Oh, yes, USA, you are so right! We have been bad, but now that you have imposed trade restrictions on us, we will mend our ways!" However, it seems more likely that the other country will respond angrily, and say "None of your business."

Cuba is an important example of the problems of using trade restrictions in an attempt to punish other countries. The United States has now had an embargo in place against the Castro regime in Cuba for more than 50 years, and yet the Castro regime is still in power. It certainly appears that the embargo has strengthened Castro's grip on Cuban society. The embargo has given Fidel and Raul Castro the opportunity to blame their country's problems on the United States. If there were no embargo, it would be more difficult for the Castros to deflect the blame from their own mismanagement of the Cuban economy. Moreover, if there had been no embargo, it would have been much easier for private businesses to thrive in Cuba. This could have created an economically powerful middle class, which might have been much more successful in pushing for changes in policies.

Another problem with using trade restrictions to punish other countries is that people in glass houses should not necessarily be throwing stones. If the United States had a spotless record on human rights and the environment, it might make more sense for us to lecture others on the errors of their ways. However, American society is far from perfect. Even though the situation is not as bad as it once was, it is well known that racial minorities have often been treated very badly in the United States. (In Chapters 13 and 15, we will look at the gap between the races in earnings and income.) And, even though some improvements have been made, the United States is still a very big polluter. (We will study the economics of the environment in Chapter 17.) So, when the United States lectures other countries on their human-rights records, or their environmental records, it is hard to avoid the conclusion that we are being a little bit hypocritical.

In many countries, capital punishment is prohibited. This is not the place to debate the merits of the death penalty, but it is fair to say that many Europeans consider it barbaric that there are executions in the United States. What would happen if the Europeans were to use trade restrictions, as a means of convincing us that we should stop capital punishment? Most likely, the trade restrictions would reduce the rate of economic growth, and they would reduce the choices available to consumers, but it is not clear that the laws on capital punishment would be changed.

As mentioned above, the United States creates a lot of pollution. And yet, our environmental record is significantly better than it was before environmental laws were passed in the 1960s and 1970s. Why were those laws passed then? There are many reasons, of course, but one reason is that the United States had reached a level of economic development at which many Americans felt comfortable about turning their attention to environmental improvements. When people are very poor, they tend to worry much more about where their next meal is coming from, than about the environment. As the United States became more and more affluent, it was possible for environmental concerns to reach the top of the list. (In other words, environmental quality is a normal good.) It's no surprise that the richest countries are the ones with the strictest environmental laws. Therefore, there is reason to believe that other countries will improve their environmental records as their levels of income rise. One way to help their incomes to rise is to allow them to benefit from participation in the world economy, through international trade. Thus, if we punish poor countries with trade restrictions, we will help to keep them poor, and this may actually slow down their progress toward a cleaner environment.

Politics and economics on the world stage are very complicated. It is impossible to prove a mathematical theorem that trade restrictions will always fail to achieve their intended goals. Nevertheless, it is hoped that this discussion has made clear that the case for trade restrictions is a difficult one to make. Even though the people who call for trade restrictions are often very well-meaning, economic analysis helps us to see that trade restrictions can have serious adverse consequences.

his consumption by one coconut and one fish. Zeke increases his consumption by three coconuts and one fish. Each man is better off.

Some readers might object that this example was rigged. Well, of course it was rigged. As with so many other examples and problems in this book, the details have been chosen so that the numbers come out nicely. In this case, the numbers were chosen so that we didn't have to deal with any cumbersome fractions. Nevertheless, it is still true that this example tells us a lot. Even though the details have been streamlined and simplified, the underlying ideas can be applied in an extremely wide variety of real-world situations. American workers have *absolute* advantage over Mexican workers in virtually every activity. But we can't possibly have *comparative* advantage in every activity. Therefore, the United States exports machinery and equipment and computers to Mexico, and imports petroleum, fruits and vegetables, and textiles.

In *Real Economics for Real People 5.2,* we take a look at another set of issues associated with trade with low-income countries.

Reality Check: Interim Review Question

IR5-3. Is there any hope that a high-income country (such as the United States) can gain anything from trading with a low-income country (such as China)?

BARRIERS TO INTERNATIONAL TRADE

In Chapter 2, and again in this chapter, we have emphasized the idea that trade is mutually beneficial. If people specialize in the activities in which they have comparative advantage, and then trade with each other, everyone can be made better off. In spite of this, nearly all countries engage in at least some restrictions on international trade. Later in this chapter, we will discuss why this might occur. For now, however, our goal is to analyze the economic effects of the barriers to trade.

There are all sorts of barriers to international trade. Customs officials can put many obstacles in the way of firms that want to engage in international trade. Some countries require excessive amounts of paperwork, or impose complicated regulations. In this chapter, however, we will focus our attention on three types of barrier to free trade:

- *Tariffs* are taxes on imports,

- *Import Quotas* are restrictions on the quantity of a good that can be sold from one country to another. Import quotas are administered by the importing country.

- *Voluntary Export Restraints* (VERs) are also restrictions on the quantity of a good that can be sold from one country to another, except that VERs are administered by the exporting country.

The Economic Effects of a Tariff

To understand the effects of a tariff, we need to begin by looking at the equilibrium that would exist in the absence of any tariff. Then we introduce a tariff, and see how the market is affected.

Let's consider the exports of computer chips from the United States to France. Figure 5.4 shows the supply and demand curves in the market for sales of U.S. computer chips to France. The import-demand curve in Figure 5.4, D, represents the behavior of the French who

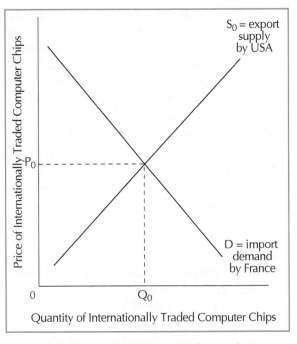

Figure 5.4 Equilibrium in the Market for Exports of Computer Chips from the United States to France

The behavior of sellers in the United States is represented by the export-supply curve, S_0. The behavior of buyers in France is represented by the import-demand curve, D. The equilibrium quantity of exports from the United States to France is Q_0, and the equilibrium price is P_0.

would like to import computer chips from the United States. The demand curve slopes downward as we move from left to right, because of the Law of Demand. The export-supply curve in Figure 5.4, S_0, represents the behavior of Americans who would like to export computer chips to France. The supply curve slopes upward as we move from left to right, because of the Law of Supply.

The equilibrium quantity of computer-chip sales from the U.S. to France is determined by the intersection of the export-supply curve and the import-demand curve. The equilibrium quantity is Q_0, and the equilibrium price is P_0. (Note that Americans carry on their transactions in dollars, while the French carry on their transactions in Euros. Thus, at some point, it will be necessary to have a conversion between dollars and Euros. However, to keep this example as simple as possible, we don't distinguish between dollars and Euros. This example is written as if both the buyers and the sellers were using the same currency. Still, you might want to keep in mind the fact that a currency conversion will be needed.)

Now, what will happen if the French government imposes a tariff on imports of computer chips from the United States? As a result of the tariff, the price paid by French buyers of U.S. computer chips will be greater than the price received by U.S. sellers. The difference between the buyers' price and the sellers' price is the per-unit amount of tariff. For example, if the net-of-tariff price received by the American sellers is $1 per unit, and if the tariff is $1 per unit, then the gross-of-tariff price paid by the French buyers is $(1 + 1) = $2 per unit. When we say "net-of-tariff price", it is the same as saying "the price without the tariff". When we say "gross-of-tariff price", it is the same as saying "the price including the tariff".

We represent the tariff as creating a shift in the supply curve. However, this supply-curve shift is different from any other shift that we have seen so far. In Chapter 4, when something caused a shift in one of the curves, the old curve no longer existed. In our model of the tariff, on the other hand, the old net-of-tariff supply curve is still there, and it still plays a role.

Figure 5.5 shows two supply curves in the market for sales of computer chips from the U.S. to France. The lower supply curve is the same as S_0 from Figure 5.4. In other words, the lower supply curve in Figure 5.5 is the same as the supply curve that existed when there was no tariff. In Figure 5.5, we refer to this old supply curve as S_{net}, to indicate that it represents the relationship between the _net-of-tariff_ price and the quantity supplied. S_{net} is the supply curve as perceived by the sellers, who are the American exporters of computer

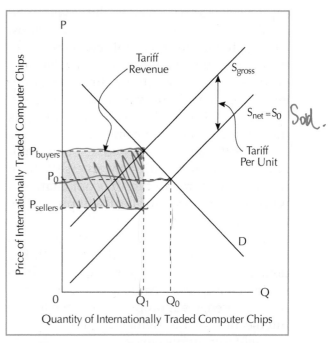

Figure 5.5 The Effects of a Tariff on Imports of Computer Chips from the United States into France

S_{net} is the supply curve that existed in the absence of the tariff. S_{net} represents the behavior of sellers, because sellers are interested in the net-of-tariff price. S_{gross} is the supply curve perceived by the buyers, because it includes all taxes. (S_{gross} is "gross of tariffs".) The new equilibrium is given by the intersection between D, the demand curve, and S_{gross}, the tariff-inclusive supply curve. The equilibrium quantity is reduced from Q_0 to Q_1 by the tariff. The price paid by buyers in the importing country rises to P_{buyers}, and the price received by sellers in the exporting country falls to $P_{sellers}$. The tariff revenue for the French government is represented by the area of the rectangle, $(P_{buyers} - P_{sellers}) \times Q_1$.

chips. Ultimately, the sellers are only concerned with the price that they will receive, _excluding_ any tariffs, so S_{net} is the supply curve that is relevant from the point of view of the exporters.

Figure 5.5 also shows a second, higher supply curve, S_{gross}. This is called S_{gross} to indicate that it represents the relationship between the gross-of-tariff price, or tariff-inclusive price, and the quantity supplied. S_{gross} is the supply curve as perceived by the buyers, who are the French importers of computer chips. Ultimately, the buyers are only concerned with the price they will have to pay, *including* any tariffs, so S_{gross} is the supply curve that is relevant from the point of view of the importers. The vertical distance between S_{gross} and S_{net} is the amount of tariff per computer chip.

After the tariff is imposed, the new equilibrium is determined by the intersection of the demand curve (which has not changed) with the new, gross-of-tariff supply curve, S_{gross}. The new supply curve is the one that is relevant from the buyers' point of view, because the new curve includes the tariff. The demand curve represents the buyers' behavior. In looking for the equilibrium after the tariff is imposed, it's appropriate to search for the intersection of the demand curve and the *gross-of-tariff* supply curve.

The new equilibrium quantity is Q_1, which is lower than Q_0. One of the effects of the tariff is to reduce the quantity of goods that are sold from one country to another.

The tariff also has an effect on prices. In fact, as a result of the tariff, there are now *two* prices. The price paid by the buyers is P_{buyers}, while the price received by the sellers is $P_{sellers}$. The difference between the two prices is the tariff per unit. Thus, in addition to reducing the quantity of international sales, the tariff will also raise prices for consumers in the importing country, and it will reduce the prices received by the sellers in the exporting country.

If we know Q_1 (the quantity bought and sold after the tariff is imposed), and if we know the amount of tariff per unit, we can figure out the amount of tariff revenue that is raised. The tariff revenue is collected by the government of the importing country. In this case, the tariff revenue is collected by the French government. The tariff revenue is equal to the amount of tariff per unit, multiplied by the number of units that are bought and sold. The number of units bought and sold is Q_1, and the amount of tariff per unit is $(P_{buyers} - P_{sellers})$. Thus, the French government's tariff revenue is $(P_{buyers} - P_{sellers}) \times (Q_1)$.

In Figure 5.5, this tariff revenue is represented by the area of a rectangle. The base of the rectangle is the quantity that is bought and sold after the tariff is imposed, Q_1. The height of the rectangle is the amount of tariff per unit, $P_{buyers} - P_{sellers}$.

In summary, the tariff will raise the prices paid by buyers in the importing country, and it will reduce quantities. Who wins and who loses as a result of the tariff? The biggest losers are the consumers in the importing country (in this case, the French buyers of computer chips). They face higher prices, and they end up buying a smaller quantity. The producers in the exporting country (in this case, the American sellers of computer chips) are also worse off as a result of the tariff. They sell fewer units, and they receive a lower net-of-tariff price per unit.

Of course, if *everyone* were made worse off by the tariff, it would be very difficult to understand why the tariff would exist. But two groups gain as a result of the tariff. One of these is the government of the importing country, which gets tariff revenue. The others who gain are the producers in the importing country. (In this case, French producers of computer chips are made better off.) Without having to work harder or produce a better product, the sellers in the importing country are able to sell for a higher price than before. The tariff makes it more difficult for foreign firms to compete, so that some of the sales may be diverted from the foreign producers (in this case, the American producers of computer chips) to the producers in the importing country. As a result, the producers in the importing country often have a lot to gain from tariffs. These companies often lobby very hard for tariffs (or for other trade barriers), and they often give big contributions to political campaigns, in the hope of influencing public officials.

Import Quotas

A tariff raises the *price* of imports. This causes a reduction in the quantity of imports, as the buyers move upward and to the left along their demand curves. The exact amount of the quantity reduction depends on the shape of the demand curve for the imported goods.

Another way to reduce imports is to clamp down directly on the quantity of imports. A direct control on the quantity of imports can occur as a result of an import quota, which is a sort of quantity ceiling. Let's return to the example of U.S. sales of computer chips to France. In Figure 5.5, we have seen what would happen if a *tariff* were imposed in that market. Figure 5.6 shows what would happen if an *import quota* were imposed, instead of a tariff.

Figure 5.6 has S_0 and D, which are the same as the net-of-tariff supply curve and the demand curve in Figures 5.4 and 5.5. As before, the original equilibrium (before any policy to restrict imports) is determined by the intersection of S_0 and D. The original equilibrium price is P_0, and the original equilibrium quantity is Q_0.

Now, the French government decides to impose a quota on imports of computer chips from the United States. In Figure 5.6, Q_{quota} is the level at which the quota is set. For example, a quota law might specify that only 10,000 computer chips can be imported during the year, and that, once that limit is reached, any attempt to import more will be punished by fines or jail time. If Q_{quota} were higher than Q_0, the quota would have no effect. (We can draw an analogy between a quota and a price ceiling. In Chapter 4, we saw that a price ceiling will have no effect if it is above the equilibrium *price*. Here, a quota will have no effect if it is above the equilibrium *quantity*. Thus you can think of a quota as a quantity ceiling.) The more interesting (and more problematic) case is the case in which the quota is *below* the equilibrium quantity. This case is illustrated in Figure 5.6. If the quota is below the equilibrium

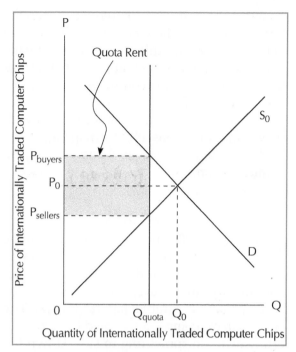

Figure 5.6 The Effects of a Quota on Imports of Computer Chips into France from the United States

Another way of restricting imports is to control the quantity of imports directly, through a quota. In this case, the quota is set at Q_{quota}. The price paid by the buyers will increase, and the price received by the sellers will decrease. The difference will be pocketed by the holder of the import license.

quantity, and if the authorities enforce the quota, then the quota will have an effect.

With the quota at Q_{quota}, the demand curve tells us that the buyers in the importing country are willing to pay a higher price than P_0. In this case, they will pay P_{buyers}.

In Figure 5.5, we saw that the government of the importing country gets revenue from a tariff. The tariff revenue is associated with the fact that the tariff drives a wedge between the price paid by buyers and the price received by sellers. Something very similar happens in the case of an import quota. After the quota is imposed, there is a gap between the buyers' price and the sellers' price. The biggest difference between the tariff and the quota has to do with who grabs the difference between the buyers' price and the sellers' price. In the case of the import quota, this money is taken by the person or organization that is given a license to import. In many countries, the import licenses are given to the dictator, or the dictator's brother-in-law, or to other people with powerful connections. As shown in Figure 5.6, the benefit to the holder of the import license is called a *quota rent*. 配額租金.

Voluntary Export Restraints

In the early 1980s, the American automobile industry was in bad shape. At that time, it was widely perceived that the quality of compact and midsize American cars was inferior to the quality of comparable Japanese cars. The American car companies wanted the U.S. government to do something to slow down the flow of imports from Japan. We have seen that a tariff or a quota would have accomplished this purpose. However, what occurred was a set of "voluntary export restraints" or VERs. (In fact, it is a bit misleading to use the word "voluntary" to describe these restraints. If the Japanese had not "voluntarily" imposed a system of export restraints, it is likely that the U.S. government would have imposed an import quota.)

The effects of the VER are shown in Figure 5.7. This figure should look very familiar. It is virtually identical to Figure 5.6, which showed the effects of an import quota. The only important difference between an import quota and a VER is that the exporters get to receive the full buyers' price with a VER, while the holder of the import license is the one to benefit from an import quota. In Figure 5.7, "$P_{supply\ curve}$" is the minimum price that exporters would have needed, in order to bring forth Q_{VER} to the market. But instead of receiving only $P_{supply\ curve}$, the exporters actually receive P_{buyers}. Thus, the exporters gain an amount that is analogous to the tariff revenue or the quota rent. In the case of the VERs on

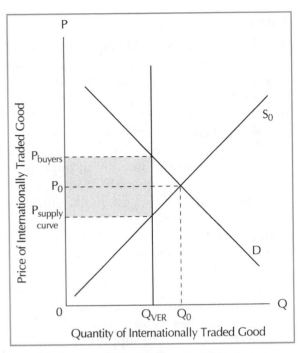

Figure 5.7 The Effects of a Voluntary Export Restraint

A voluntary export restraint (VER) is an explicit restriction on quantity. Thus it is similar to an import quota. The difference is that a quota generates an advantage for the person (or persons) who holds the import license. A VER generates an advantage for the exporters.

exports of Japanese automobiles to the United States, the Japanese auto companies received higher profits.

Comparison of the Different Ways of Restricting Trade

We have studied three ways of restricting international trade: tariffs, import quotas, and voluntary export restraints. In many ways, these mechanisms are very similar to each other. First of all, each hurts the consumers in the importing country. These consumers are forced to pay higher prices, and they consume a reduced quantity.

Second, each of these mechanisms gives an advantage to the producers in the importing country. These producers are able to charge higher prices. They don't have to compete as vigorously as they would have, if the trade restrictions were not in place. Therefore, it is not surprising that the producers in the importing country are almost always at the heart of efforts to restrict trade.

The big differences among the three mechanisms for restricting trade have to do with who gets the pot of money, represented by the rectangle $(P_{buyers} - P_{sellers}) \times Q_1$ in Figure 5.5, or by the Quota Rent in Figure 5.6. In the case of a tariff, the money goes to the government of the importing country. In the case of an import quota, the money goes to the holder of the import license. (If the government of the importing country were to auction the import license to the highest bidder, then the government would share in the pot of money, and the ultimate effect of the quota would be even more similar to the ultimate effect of the tariff. However, the auction method is rarely used.) In the case of a VER, the money goes to the producers in the exporting country.

Because of the damage done to the consumers in the importing country, each of these restrictions on trade would be considered skeptically by economists. However, if the political pressure to impose trade restrictions becomes overwhelming, so that some sort of trade restriction is unavoidable, then there may be an argument in favor of a VER. The reason is that the VER is the only one of the three mechanisms that provides any benefit to the exporting country. Consequently, the exporting country is probably less likely to retaliate against a VER than against some other sort of trade restriction. This is important, because one of the biggest potential dangers of trade restrictions is that they might lead to a vicious cycle of one restriction after another, as politicians in each country scramble to look tough by retaliating against the other country. If the restrictions were to escalate into a full-scale "trade war", with a major increase in barriers to trade, it could be catastrophic for the entire world.

Reality Check:
Interim Review Questions

IR5-4. What happens when an import quota is imposed at a level that is higher than the equilibrium quantity?

IR5-5. What are the similarities between a tariff, an import quota, and a voluntary export restraint? What are the differences?

ECONOMICS AND YOU:
DON'T BE AFRAID OF A SUCKING SOUND

Economists disagree about many things, but international trade is one thing about which virtually all economists are agreed. The arguments in favor of free trade are so compelling that economists are virtually unanimous in their view that relatively free trade is a good thing in most situations. This is not to say that there should be no restrictions on trade. Every country has a legitimate right to inspect entering cargo, to make sure that illegal goods are not being smuggled into the country.

Even though we have said that free trade is a good idea in most situations, it is still true that there are some situations in which free trade is not appropriate. For example, national-security concerns may make it sensible to restrict trade in some commodities. There are good reasons to have strict restrictions on trade in nuclear warheads and intercontinental ballistic missiles. And there are good reasons to have strict laws regarding human trafficking, as well as international trade in toxic substances.

It is also possible to argue against free trade when an industry is just getting started in a country. This is the *infant-industry argument*.

According to the infant-industry argument, it may be beneficial to give trade protection to a domestic industry during the first few years of its existence. This will give the domestic industry the opportunity to get on its feet, and not be run out of business by foreign firms that are already well established. However, if the infant-industry argument makes any sense at all, it would require that the trade restrictions must be removed soon after the domestic industry establishes itself.

Over the long run, international trade has helped to provide a higher standard of living. However, in the short run at least, some people are harmed by trade. What do we do about people who lose their job as a result of competition from imports? Some would answer that question by saying that we should ban imports, or impose high tariffs. However, if we do that, we would give up all of the benefits of trade that have been described in this chapter.

A better solution would be to allow international trade, but to reach out to help those who are adversely affected. Assistance to those who are hurt by international trade could take many forms. These include temporary financial assistance through unemployment insurance and other programs, as well as job training to help prepare for different jobs.

In a way, those who lose their jobs because of international trade are similar to those who lose their jobs because of technological improvements. At one time, many thousands of Americans earned a living as telephone switchboard operators. But when electronic switching technologies were developed, nearly all of the switchboard operators lost their jobs. Similarly, there was a time when many thousands of Americans earned a living as elevator operators. However, almost all of them lost their jobs when push-button elevators were developed.

Most of us would agree that it would not be good policy to outlaw electronic telephone switching, in order to "save jobs". And most of us would also agree that it would not be good policy to outlaw push-button elevators,

in order to "save jobs". The best solution is to allow technological improvements, but to provide assistance to help the displaced workers to cope with the transition. In most cases, the same argument holds for international trade.

We will close this chapter by thinking about how the United States became such a prosperous country. Certainly, one reason is that we have an abundance of natural resources: good harbors, navigable rivers, a temperate climate, fertile soil, and a wealth of minerals below ground. Another reason is that Americans tend to place a lot of value on education and hard work. But one other reason is that the United States has been dedicated to free trade from the very beginning.

The war for independence from Great Britain, from 1775 to 1783, was fought by 13 loosely federated colonies. Immediately after the 13 colonies achieved their independence, they continued to have only loose connections. Under the Articles of Confederation, the authority of the central government was very limited, and the 13 States were free to levy tariffs. Tariffs could be applied to goods traveling from New York to Massachusetts, or from Maryland to Pennsylvania, or from North Carolina to Virginia, or from Georgia to South Carolina.

When the Constitutional Convention met at Philadelphia in 1787, the Founding Fathers recognized that this system was harming the economies of all 13 States. The Constitution prohibited the States from interfering with interstate commerce. The new nation abolished its internal tariffs. Eventually, the United States of America became the world's largest free-trade area. As much as anything else, this dedication to free trade explains the nation's prosperity. In recent years, Americans have heard a lot of heated rhetoric against trade with other countries. Fortunately, no one has seriously taken these arguments to their logical conclusion by suggesting that Michigan should cut off trade with Ohio, or that Florida should cut off trade with New York, or that California and Texas should cease to trade with each other.

Chapter Summary

1. During the last several decades, both exports and imports have increased dramatically. In the early 1960s, exports accounted for about 5 percent of gross domestic product in the United States, and imports were of about the same size. By the early years of the 21st century, both exports and imports accounted for substantially more than 10 percent of gross domestic product. This pattern has been repeated in countries around the globe. Thus international trade has been an important engine for economic growth.

2. When exports are greater than imports, we say that a country has a trade surplus. When imports are greater than exports, we say that a country has a trade deficit. In recent years, the United States has run trade deficits. Modest trade deficits are not a cause for concern. However, if a country sustains large trade deficits for a long period of time, it may run up a very large external debt, which can cause problems.

3. Even if a country's overall level of imports were the same as its overall level of exports, it would still probably have deficits with some of its trading partners, and surpluses with some others. There is no reason to desire to have bilateral trade balance with every country.

4. It is beneficial for countries to specialize in the activities in which they have comparative advantage, and then to engage in international trade. This is even true in the case in which one country has absolute advantage in all activities.

5. A tariff is a tax on imports. An import quota is an explicit restriction on the quantity of imports. A voluntary export restraint is a quantity restriction, similar to an import quota. The difference is that an import quota is organized and administered by the importing country, whereas a voluntary export restraint is organized and administered by the exporters.

6. Tariffs, quotas, and voluntary export restraints all lead to higher prices for consumers in the importing country. They all reduce the quantity of imports. They all reduce the competition faced by producers in the importing country, so that those producers will usually increase their profits. However, a tariff collects revenue for the government of the importing country, while an import quota provides quota rents to the holder of the import license, and a voluntary export restraint boosts the profits of the exporting companies.

7. All of these interferences with international trade have adverse side effects, and economists are generally reluctant to recommend any of them. However, if the political pressure to interfere with trade is overwhelming, then a VER might be preferred to a tariff or quota. This is because a VER gives extra profits to the producers in the exporting country. As a result, a VER is less likely to lead to retaliation.

Key Terms

Export

Import

Trade Deficit

Trade Surplus

Tariff

Import Quota

Voluntary Export Restraint

Quota Rent

Infant-Industry Argument

Questions and Problems

QP5-1. The export supply curve for brupkas is given by $Q_s = 2P$. The import demand curve for brupkas is given by $Q_d = 100-2P$.

a. What is the equilibrium price of internationally traded brupkas?
b. What is the equilibrium quantity of internationally traded brupkas?
c. Now, the government of the importing country imposes a tariff of $10 per brupka. The old, net-of-tariff export supply curve, which is perceived by the exporters, stays the same as it was before: $Q_s = 2P$. It turns out that the new, gross-of-tariff export supply curve, which is perceived by the importers, is given by $Q_s = -20 + 2P$. What is the new equilibrium price of brupkas, gross of tariff (that is, including the tariff)?
d. What is the new equilibrium quantity of brupkas?
e. What is the new equilibrium price of brupkas, net of tariff (that is, *not* including the tariff)? You can find the answer to this question in one of two ways. You can take the quantity (from (d)) and substitute it into the net-of-tariff supply curve. Or, you can take the gross-of-tariff price (from (c)) and subtract from it the tariff of 10.
f. How much revenue is raised by the tariff?

QP5-2. Assume that the export-supply curve for brupkas (net of tariff) and the import-demand curve for brupkas are the same as in the previous question. However, this time there is no tariff. Instead, the government imposes a quota, such that only 40 brupkas can be imported into the country. Assume that the quota is enforced.

a. What price will be paid by buyers in the importing country? (Insert the quantity of 40 into the demand curve.)
b. What price will be received by sellers in the exporting country? (Insert the quantity of 40 into the supply curve.)
c. If the quota were set at 60 brupkas, what price would be paid by the buyers? What price would be received by the sellers? What quantity would be bought and sold?
d. If the quota were set at 20 brupkas, what price would be paid by the buyers? What price would be received by the sellers? What quantity would be bought and sold?

QP5-3. If a government decides that it must restrict imports from another country, is there any reason to prefer a tariff, or a quota, or a VER?

QP5-4. U.S. exports to Mexico are much higher than U.S. exports to any other low-income country. Why?

QP5-5. Evaluate the following statement: Exports are good, because exports create jobs in the domestic economy. Imports are bad, because imports create jobs somewhere else. Therefore, a trade surplus is better than a trade deficit. Therefore, the best outcome for the world as a whole is for every country to have a trade surplus.

Chapter 6

Elasticity of Demand and Supply

需求和焦给弹性.

ECONOMICS AND YOU: IF YOU *REALLY* WANT TO GO TO A PARTICULAR COLLEGE, YOU MAY HAVE TO PAY MORE

Ryan Flynn has always dreamed of going to Pastoria College, which has an attractive campus and good business programs. By his senior year in high school, Ryan has decided that Pastoria College is his top choice, and he applies for admission on an "early-admission" basis.

Unfortunately, Ryan's decision to apply for early admission may cost him several thousand dollars. Pastoria's Admissions and Awards Committee knows that early-admission applicants are especially enthusiastic about Pastoria. Because of this, the Committee believes that early-admission applicants are very likely to attend, even if they receive less financial aid than other students. Therefore, the Committee has secretly decided to offer less financial aid to early-admission applicants. If the College can get students like Ryan to attend, without giving them much financial aid, it will have more money left over for other purposes.

In recent years, more and more colleges have adopted this type of policy. In fact, it has been estimated that 60 percent of American colleges are adjusting their financial-aid offers, to offer more aid to those students who are most sensitive to price. In other words, if a stu-

dent is likely to go somewhere else unless he or she gets a good deal, a college will offer more financial aid. But if a student is likely to attend, even if the price is higher, that student will get less financial aid. The college is saying, "Why should we offer more financial aid to applicants like Ryan, since they will probably come here anyway?"

In Chapter 3, we learned that demand curves slope downward as we move from left to right across the diagram. In some cases, that's all we need to know about demand curves. However, in cases such as this example of college financial-aid policies, it's important to know *how rapidly* the demand curve slopes downward. An economist would say that Ryan's demand curve for attending Pastoria is *relatively unresponsive* to changes in price. Even if the price were to increase substantially, Ryan would still attend Pastoria. On the other hand, Stacey is less certain that she wants to attend Pastoria, but she might be convinced to come if she is offered a good financial-aid package. An economist would say that Stacey's demand curve for attending Pastoria is *relatively more responsive* to changes in price.

In this chapter, you will learn about how to measure the responsiveness of demand and supply. You will learn:

- how to calculate the *elasticity*, which is the economist's way of measuring the degree of responsiveness,

- how sellers (such as colleges, airlines, and others) can use information about the elasticity of demand to increase their revenues, and

- which factors have an effect on the elasticity of demand or supply.

PRICE ELASTICITY OF DEMAND

In Chapter 4, we saw that a drought in the apple-growing regions will cause the supply curve of apples to shift to the left. This will lead to an increase in the equilibrium price of apples, and a decrease in the equilibrium quantity of apples bought and sold.

In Figure 6.1, we show two examples of a leftward shift in the supply curve for apples.

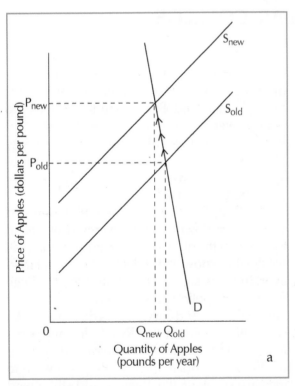

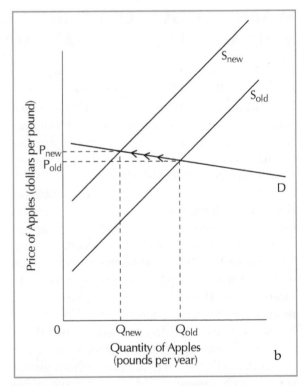

Figure 6.1 The Effect of a Supply Shift Depends on the Shape of the Demand Curve

Panel (a) and panel (b) both have the same original supply curve, S_{old}, and the same new supply curve, S_{new}. Both panels also have the same original equilibrium quantity of apples, Q_{old}, and the same original equilibrium price of apples, P_{old}. However, in the demand curve in panel (a), quantity demanded is very unresponsive to changes in price, while quantity demanded is very responsive to changes in price in panel (b). Because of the difference between the two demand curves, the supply shift has very different effects in the two panels. In panel (a), where quantity demanded is unresponsive, the supply shift leads to a relatively large increase in equilibrium price, and a relatively small decrease in equilibrium quantity. In panel (b), where quantity demanded is responsive, the supply shift leads to a relatively small increase in equilibrium price, and a relatively large decrease in equilibrium quantity.

The two panels of Figure 6.1 have the same original supply curve, S_{old}, and the same new supply curve, S_{new}. They both have the same original equilibrium price, P_{old}, and the same original equilibrium quantity, Q_{old}. The only difference between the two diagrams is in the shape of their demand curves.

In the demand curve shown in panel (a) of Figure 6.1, the quantity demanded is very unresponsive to changes in price. Even when the price increases by a large amount, there isn't much of a decrease in the quantity of apples demanded. Effectively, the buyers in panel (a) of Figure 6.1 are saying "We've gotta have our apples!" In this case, the supply-curve shift leads to a relatively large increase in the equilibrium price, and a relatively small decrease in the equilibrium quantity. The buyers are willing to pay substantially more, and they end up doing just that.

On the other hand, the buyers represented by the demand curve in panel (b) of Figure 6.1 are very responsive to changes in price. When the price increases, even by a small amount, there is a relatively large decrease in quantity demanded. The buyers in panel (b) are saying "If you raise the price on us, we'll spend our money on something else." In this case, the shift in the supply curve leads to a relatively small increase in the equilibrium price, along with a relatively large decrease in the equilibrium quantity. The buyers aren't willing to accept a very large price increase, and indeed, they don't end up paying a lot more.

Slope Is Not a Good Measure of Responsiveness

By comparing the two panels of Figure 6.1, you can see that the responsiveness of quantity demanded to changes in price is crucial for understanding the outcomes in the market. In this chapter, one of our most important goals is to develop a precise method for measuring responsiveness.

At first, it might seem sensible to measure the responsiveness of demand by calculating the slope of the demand curve. Unfortunately, this causes problems. For example, gasoline is sold by the gallon in the United States, but it's sold by the liter in Canada. If we were to draw a Canadian demand curve for gasoline and an American demand curve for gasoline, the slopes would differ by about a factor of four (since there are almost four liters in a gallon), even if the responses of consumers were *exactly* the same in the two countries. Here is a related problem: How do we compare the demand for chewing gum (which is measured in packs) with the demand for apples (which is measured in pounds or bushels)?

The problem is that *slope depends on the units of measurement.* Instead of using slope, we would like to use a measure that is unit-free. Economists use a unit-free measure of responsiveness called elasticity. Elasticity doesn't depend on the units of measurement, because it compares *percentage* changes or *proportional* changes, instead of absolute changes.

The Definition of Elasticity

Most of this chapter is concerned with the elasticities of supply and demand, since these are so important for our study of economics. However, the elasticity concept can be applied in many situations, some of which don't sound like economic examples. In every case, *elasticity is defined as the percentage change in one variable, divided by the percentage change in another variable.* For example, medical researchers collected information on the cholesterol levels of a sample of people. Over a period of many years, the researchers observed whether the people had heart attacks. They concluded that a 10-percent increase in cholesterol level is associated with a 20-percent increase in the chance of having a heart attack. The elasticity of heart attacks with respect to the cholesterol level is the percentage change in the chance of a heart attack, divided by the percentage change in cholesterol level. This is (20% / 10%) = 2. Thus, the elasticity of heart attacks with respect to cholesterol level is 2. Since the elasticity is based on percentage changes, the units in which we measure cholesterol are irrelevant.

Here's another example of an elasticity: An economics professor took attendance at every class, so that he was able to calculate the effect of class attendance on exam scores. He found that a ten-percent increase in attendance was associated with a 15-percent increase in exam scores. The elasticity of exam scores with respect to class attendance is the percentage change in exam scores, divided by the percentage change in class attendance. This is (15% / 10%) = 1.5.

You've now seen that the elasticity concept can be used in all sorts of situations. Next, it's time to look at elasticities of demand and supply.

We define the *price elasticity of demand* for jogging shorts as:

$$\text{elasticity} = \frac{\text{percentage change in quantity of jogging shorts demanded}}{\text{percentage change in price of jogging shorts}}.$$

This is also called the *own-price elasticity of demand*. The phrase *"own-price"* indicates that we are looking at the change in the quantity demanded for a good, caused by a change in its *own* price. (Later in this chapter, we'll look at the change in demand for one good, caused by a change in the price of a *different* good.)

In this chapter, we will sometimes use the phrase "price elasticity of demand", and we'll sometimes use the phrase "own-price elasticity of demand". Both phrases have the same meaning.

Another way to define the price elasticity of demand is to use proportional changes, instead of percentage changes:

$$\text{elasticity} = \frac{\dfrac{\Delta Q_d}{Q_d}}{\dfrac{\Delta P}{P}}.$$

where ΔQ_d is the change in quantity demanded, Q_d is the reference level of quantity demanded, ΔP is the change in price, and P is the reference level of price. In this equation, $(\Delta Q_d / Q_d)$ is the proportional change in quantity demanded, and $(\Delta P / P)$ is the proportional change in price.

In summary, we have two ways of calculating the own-price elasticity of demand. We can divide the *percentage* change in quantity demanded by the *percentage* change in price, or we can divide the *proportional* change in quantity demanded by the *proportional* change in price. Either way, we will get the same answer, since a percentage is equal to a proportion multiplied by 100.

Let's say the price of jogging shorts goes down from $13 per pair to $11 per pair. The change in price, ΔP, is ($13 – $11), or $2 per pair. As a result of the price change, the quantity demanded increases from 70,000 pairs of shorts per week to 90,000 pairs per week. The change in quantity demanded, ΔQ_d, is (90,000 – 70,000), or 20,000 pairs per week.

The elasticity formula has four parts: ΔQ_d, ΔP, Q_d, and P. We have now calculated ΔP and ΔQ_d. However, to complete the elasticity calculation, we need to decide what to use for the reference level of price, P, and the reference level of quantity demanded, Q_d. Do we use 70,000 pairs of jogging shorts for the reference level of quantity demanded, or do we use 90,000, or some number in between? And do we use $13 for the reference level of price, or $11, or something else? The elasticity will change somewhat, depending on the values we use for the reference level of price and the reference level of quantity demanded.

Calculating Elasticity

Economists make a standard assumption in calculating the elasticity. The standard assumption is to use the *midpoint* between the beginning quantity demanded and the ending quantity demanded as our reference level of quantity demanded. In other words, the reference level of quantity demanded is the *average* of the beginning quantity demanded and the ending quantity demanded. Similarly, we use the midpoint between the beginning price and the ending price as our reference level of price. The midpoint, or average, can be calculated by adding the two numbers together and dividing by two. The midpoint between $11 and $13 is ($11 + $13) / 2 = $12. The midpoint between 70,000 and 90,000, or the average of 70,000 and 90,000 is (70,000 + 90,000) / 2 = 80,000.

One advantage of using the midpoint is that it allows us to get the same answer for an increase or a decrease in price or quantity. If we were to use the starting point, we would get a different percentage change, depending on whether we move from $11 to $13 or from $13 to $11. By using the midpoint, we find the same percentage change, regardless of whether the price is going up or down.

Before we actually calculate the own-price elasticity of demand, we need to establish one more rule. Along any demand curve, as long as the Law of Demand is obeyed, the price and the quantity demanded will move in opposite directions; that is, if the change in price is greater than zero, the change in quantity demanded will be less than zero, and *vice versa*. However, to simplify the calculation of the price elasticity of demand, economists traditionally *drop the minus sign*. In other words, we use the absolute value. This means that the own-price elasticity of demand is never less than zero.

We now have three rules for calculating the price elasticity of demand:

- We use percentage changes, or proportional changes.

- We use the midpoint between the beginning quantity demanded and the ending quantity demanded as our reference level of the quantity demanded. We use the midpoint between the beginning price and the ending price as our reference level of price.

- We drop the minus sign, so that the elasticity is never a negative number.

With these three rules in mind, the next step is to calculate an elasticity.

Let's calculate the own-price elasticity of demand for the example described above, where the price of a pair of jogging shorts goes down from $13 per pair to $11 per pair. As a result of this price change, the quantity demanded goes up from 70,000 pairs per week to 90,000 pairs per week. Here is the elasticity calculation:

$$\text{elasticity} = \frac{\frac{\Delta Q_d}{Q_d}}{\frac{\Delta P}{P}}$$

$$= \frac{\frac{(90{,}000 - 70{,}000)}{\text{midpoint between 70,000 and 90,000}}}{\frac{(\$13 - \$11)}{\text{midpoint between \$11 and \$13}}}$$

$$= \frac{\frac{20{,}000}{80{,}000}}{\frac{\$2}{\$12}}$$

$$= (2/8) / (2/12).$$

We now have a fraction divided by another fraction. The easiest way to finish the calculation is to multiply the fraction in the numerator (2/8) by the reciprocal of the fraction in the denominator. The fraction in the denominator is (2/12), the reciprocal of which is (12/2). Multiplying (2/8) by (12/2) gives us (24/16), which is 1.5. In this case, the price elasticity of demand for jogging shorts is 1.5.

Note that, in solving for the value of the elasticity, we reduced (20,000/80,000) to (2/8). This is perfectly acceptable. As mentioned above, the elasticity is a unit-free measure of responsiveness. Thus it does not make any difference whether we measure the number of jogging shorts in pairs, or in tens of pairs, or hundreds of pairs, or thousands of pairs. What matters is the *relative* change in price and quantity demanded, rather than the *absolute* change.

Figure 6.2 contains a demand schedule for jogging shorts, as well as the corresponding demand curve. The demand schedule and demand curve include prices of $13 and $11, and quantities demanded of 70,000 and 90,000, which we used above, plus some other combinations of price and quantity demanded. In the example of Figure 6.2, the demand curve is a straight line: Every time the price increases by $2 per pair, the quantity demanded goes down by 20,000 pairs.

Next, let's calculate the elasticity of demand along a different part of the demand curve, where price falls from $11 to $9, and quantity demanded rises from 90,000 pairs to 110,000 pairs. The basic formula is the same, but the numbers are different.

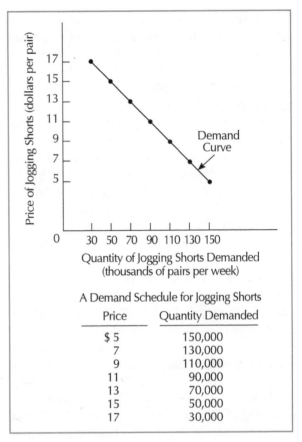

A Demand Schedule for Jogging Shorts

Price	Quantity Demanded
$ 5	150,000
7	130,000
9	110,000
11	90,000
13	70,000
15	50,000
17	30,000

Figure 6.2 A Demand Schedule for Jogging Shorts, and the Corresponding Demand Curve

Table for Figure 6.2 Calculating Total Revenue and the Price Elasticity of Demand from a Demand Schedule for Jogging Shorts

Price (P)	Quantity Demanded (Q_d)	Total Revenue (P)x(Q_d)	Price Elasticity of Demand
$ 5	150,000	$750,000	
			0.4286
$ 7	130,000	$910,000	
			0.6666
$ 9	110,000	$990,000	
			1.0
$11	90,000	$990,000	
			1.5
$13	70,000	$910,000	
			2.3333
$15	50,000	$750,000	
			4.0
$17	30,000	$510,000	

– 134 –

$$\text{elasticity} = \frac{\dfrac{\Delta Q_d}{Q_d}}{\dfrac{\Delta P}{P}}$$

$$= \frac{\dfrac{(110{,}000 - 90{,}000)}{\text{midpoint between } 90{,}000 \text{ and } 110{,}000}}{\dfrac{(\$11 - \$9)}{\text{midpoint between } \$9 \text{ and } \$11}}$$

$$= \frac{\dfrac{20{,}000}{100{,}000}}{\dfrac{\$2}{\$10}}$$

$$= (2/10) / (2/10) = 1.0.$$

In this case, the price elasticity of demand for jogging shorts is 1.0.

These two examples show that the price elasticity of demand can take on different values. In fact, as we move along a straight-line demand curve, such as the one in Figure 6.2, there is a regular pattern to the changes in elasticity. *As we move downward and to the right along a straight-line demand curve, the price elasticity of demand becomes smaller. As we move upward and to the left, the elasticity increases.*

Here is a way to think about how the elasticity changes as we move along a straight-line demand curve. In the upper-left corner of the demand curve, the price is high and the quantity demanded is low. Thus, in the upper-left corner of the demand curve, the *proportional* change in price is small and the *proportional* change in quantity demanded is large. If we divide a large proportional change in quantity demanded by a small proportional change in price, we get a large elasticity in the upper-left corner of the demand curve. Following the same kind of reasoning, we find that the own-price elasticity of demand is small in the lower-right corner of a straight-line demand curve.

We've now seen the basics of how to calculate the elasticity. This is an important step, but it's only a beginning. The real purpose of this chapter is to learn how to *apply* the elasticity concept. We'll see several applications in this chapter, and many more later in the book. The own-price elasticity of demand is one of the most useful concepts in all of economics.

Reality Check: Interim Review Questions

IR6-1. There is an increase in the price of red-delicious apples, from $1.35 per pound to $1.65 per pound. As a result, there is a decrease in the quantity demanded, from 4200 million pounds per year to 3800 million pounds per year. What is the own-price elasticity of demand for red-delicious apples?

IR6-2. There is a 10-percent increase in the price of renting the most popular movies from the video store. The price elasticity of demand for videos is 0.5, and price is the *only* thing that has changed. What will happen to the quantity of videos demanded?

ELASTICITY AND TOTAL REVENUE 总收入

Over the years, economists have calculated the own-price elasticity of demand for thousands of markets. They have found that it's useful to distinguish between demand curves with a price elasticity greater than one, and those with an elasticity equal to one, and those with an elasticity less than one.

- When the own-price elasticity is greater than one, we say that demand is *elastic.* Recall that the elasticity is equal to the percentage change in quantity demanded, divided by the percentage change in price. Thus if the elasticity is greater than one, it must be true that the percentage change in quantity demanded is larger than the percentage change in price. When demand is elastic, quantity demanded is relatively responsive to changes in price. The term "elastic" reminds us of things that respond a lot when a force is applied to them, such as a very stretchy fabric or a rubber band.

- When the elasticity is equal to one, demand is *unit elastic*. In this case, the percentage change in quantity demanded is exactly equal to the percentage change in price.

- Demand is *inelastic* when the elasticity is less than one. In this case, the percentage change in price is larger than the percentage change in quantity demanded. Later in this chapter, the discussion around Figure 6.5, talks about the elasticity of demand for gasoline. The demand for gasoline is "unresponsive" or "inelastic". Now we have given a precise definition to "inelastic"—the demand for a good is inelastic when the percentage change in quantity demanded is smaller than the percentage change in price.

We'll look at each of these cases in turn, with special emphasis on the relationship between elasticity and total revenue.

The *total revenue* that a business firm gets from selling a product is the amount of money the firm receives from its sales. When there are no taxes, the total revenue received by the sellers in a market is exactly the same as the total expenditure by the buyers. Business firms want to know what will happen to their total revenue if they raise prices, and what will happen if they cut prices. If you're a financial analyst for a firm, and you can figure out a way to increase total revenue, you will be very popular with your boss. In this section, you will learn how the relationship between price and total revenue depends on the own-price elasticity of demand.

Price, Quantity, and Total Revenue

The total revenue received by a business firm is equal to the price multiplied by the number of units sold:

Total Revenue = TR = (P)(Q).

Let's calculate total revenue for some of the points on the demand schedule that we used earlier. In our first example, the price of jogging shorts decreases from $13 per pair to $11 per pair. As a result, the quantity demanded increases from 70,000 pairs per week to 90,000 pairs per week. Before the change, total revenue is ($13/pair)(70,000 pairs) = $910,000. After the change, total revenue is ($11/pair)(90,000 pairs) = $990,000. Price went down, but total revenue went up! Even though each pair of shorts is sold for a lower price, the increase in quantity demanded is large enough that there is also an increase in total revenue!

Elastic Demand. There are two offsetting influences on total revenue. Taken by itself, the decrease in price would *decrease* total revenue. However, the drop in price also leads to an increase in quantity demanded. Taken by itself, this increase in quantity demanded would *increase* total revenue. The reason that total revenue goes up in this example is that the effect of quantity demanded is *relatively* stronger than the effect of price.

Here's another way to say the same thing: When the price went down, total revenue went up, because the proportional change in quantity demanded was greater than the proportional change in price. But remember that the own-price elasticity of demand is equal to the proportional change in quantity demanded, divided by the proportional change

Elastic Demand: $\boxed{\Delta D > \Delta P} \rightarrow \boxed{\text{elasticity} > 1} \rightarrow \boxed{\begin{array}{l}\text{total revenue} \uparrow \text{ if Price} \downarrow. \\ \text{total revenue} \downarrow \text{ if Price} \uparrow.\end{array}}$

Unit Elastic: $\boxed{\Delta D = \Delta P} \rightarrow \boxed{\text{elasticity} = 1} \rightarrow \boxed{\text{total revenue will not affect by price}}$

in price! Thus, the price elasticity of demand tells us what we need to know, to assess what will happen to total revenue.

When the proportional change in quantity demanded is greater than the proportional change in price, the elasticity is greater than one, which means that demand is elastic. In this case, a decrease in price will lead to an increase in total revenue, and an increase in price will lead to a decrease in total revenue. This is because, when demand is elastic, the proportional change in quantity demanded is large enough to outweigh the proportional change in price.

A special case of elastic demand is the case where the demand curve is completely horizontal. In this case, we say that demand is **perfectly elastic**. In the limit, as the demand curve becomes very nearly horizontal, the elasticity tends toward infinity. This may seem like a strange case, because there aren't any examples where the *market* demand curve would be perfectly elastic. However, in some cases, the demand for the product of an *individual firm* may be perfectly elastic. For example, the demand for the Anderson Farm's apples may be perfectly elastic, even though the market demand for apples isn't perfectly elastic. We will discuss this possibility in detail in Chapter 9.

Real Economics for Real People 6.1, on p. 138, deals with the airline industry and its response to elastic demand.

Unit-Elastic Demand. Now, let's consider another example from Figure 6.2: The price of a pair of jogging shorts drops from $11 to $9, and the quantity demanded rises from 90,000 pairs to 110,000 pairs. We have already calculated that the elasticity for this change is 1.0. This means that the proportional change in quantity demanded is exactly the same as the proportional change in price. What happens to total revenue? At the price of $11 per pair, total revenue is ($11)(90,000) = $990,000. At the new price of $9 per pair,

total revenue is ($9)(110,000) = $990,000. Total revenue is unchanged!

When the proportional change in quantity demanded is equal to the proportional change in price, the own-price elasticity of demand is 1.0, which means that demand is unit elastic. In this case, a change in price will not have any effect on total revenue.

When demand is unit elastic, it doesn't matter whether the price goes up or down— total revenue will remain the same, because the proportional change in quantity demanded is exactly large enough to offset exactly the proportional change in price.

Inelastic Demand. Finally, let's consider one more example from Figure 6.2: When there is a decrease in the price of a pair of jogging shorts from $9 to $7, the quantity demanded increases from 110,000 pairs of shorts to 130,000 pairs. The elasticity is two-thirds, or 0.6667. (See if you can do the calculation.) The proportional change in quantity demanded is *smaller* than the proportional change in price. At the price of $9 per pair, total revenue is ($9)(110,000) = $990,000. At the new price of $7, total revenue is ($7)(130,000) = $910,000. In this case, total revenue goes *down* as a result of the decrease in price.

When the proportional change in quantity demanded is less than the proportional change in price, the own-price elasticity of demand is less than one, and demand is inelastic. In this case, an increase in price will lead to an increase in total revenue, and a decrease in price will lead to a decrease in total revenue. This is because, when demand is inelastic, the proportional change in price is large enough to outweigh the proportional change in quantity demanded.

We can use graphs to increase our understanding of the relationship between elasticity and total revenue. Total revenue is equal to price multiplied by quantity. Therefore, total revenue is shown graphically by the area of a rectangle. Quantity demanded is the base of the rectangle, and price is the height of the rectangle.

Inelastic: $\boxed{\Delta D < \Delta P} \rightarrow \boxed{\text{elasticity} < 1} \rightarrow \boxed{\text{total revenue} \uparrow \text{ if Price} \uparrow}$

– 137 –

Real Economics for Real People 6.1:
The Revenue Effects of Decreasing Airline Prices

Before 1977, passenger airline prices in the United States were set largely by government agencies. Most economists believe that these prices were higher than those that would have been set by the market. From 1977 to 1984, a process of "deregulation" occurred, so that government regulations were increasingly replaced by market forces. After adjusting for inflation, the average price per mile for passenger airlines decreased by more than 28 percent between 1976 and 1986.

As a result of the decreasing prices, consumers increased their air travel dramatically. For example, prices for air travel from New York City to Norfolk, Virginia, went down by 30 percent between 1980 and 1984, and the number of passengers rose by 264 percent! Over the same time period, airfares between El Paso and Phoenix declined by 41 percent, and the number of passengers increased by 178 percent. Demand was elastic in these cases, because the percentage change in quantity demanded was greater than the percentage change in price.

These are not just isolated examples of elastic demand for air travel. Over the years, economists have used statistical methods to estimate the elasticity of demand for airline travel. Most of the studies suggest that air travel demand is elastic with respect to price. One study for Canadian routes found that the own-price elasticity of demand was 2.7. A study for some markets in the United States found an elasticity of 2.1, and a study of California routes found elasticities ranging from 2.3 to 3.2.

Since the demand for air travel is elastic, the price decreases of the late 1970s and early 1980s should have increased revenue for the airlines. That is exactly what happened in most airline markets: Total revenue increased.

In spite of the increase in revenues, some airlines went out of business during the 1980s. Some of the failed airlines simply weren't managed very well. Even for well-managed airlines, the increase in revenues didn't necessarily lead to an increase in profits, because costs went up, too. In order to serve all of those extra customers, the airlines had to hire more baggage handlers, more flight attendants, and more pilots. Also, the price of aviation fuel went up substantially during the late 1970s and early 1980s. It was a turbulent time in the skies.

We will look at the airline industry again in Chapters 11 and 12.

In Panel (a) of Figure 6.3, we show an elastic demand curve. When the price is P_0, total revenue is the rectangle $0P_0AQ_0$. When the price is P_1, total revenue is the rectangle $0P_1BQ_1$. You can see that the second rectangle is larger than the first. When demand is elastic, quantity demanded changes relatively more than price, and a price decrease means that total revenue will rise.

In Panel (b) of Figure 6.3, we show an *inelastic* demand curve. When the price is P_2, total revenue is represented by the rectangle $0P_2CQ_2$. When the price is P_3, total revenue is the rectangle $0P_3DQ_3$. The second rectangle is smaller than the first. When demand is inelastic, the change in quantity demanded is relatively less than the change in price, and a price decrease means that total revenue will fall. On

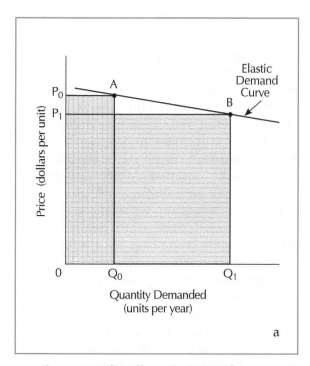

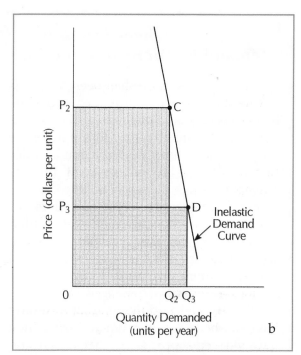

Figure 6.3 The Effect of a Price Change on Total Revenue Depends on the Elasticity of Demand

In panel (a), the original price is P_0, the original quantity demanded is Q_0, and the original total revenue is represented by the area of the rectangle, $0P_0AQ_0$. When price falls to P_1, there is a relatively large increase in quantity demanded, to Q_1. The new total revenue is the area of the rectangle, $0P_1BQ_1$. Demand is elastic, because the increase in quantity demanded is relatively larger than the decrease in price. Therefore, the new total revenue, $0P_1BQ_1$, is larger than the old total revenue, $0P_0AQ_0$. In panel (b), the original price is P_2, the original quantity demanded is Q_2, and the original total revenue is represented by the area of the rectangle, $0P_2CQ_2$. When price falls to P_3, there is a relatively small increase in quantity demanded, to Q_3. The new total revenue is the area of the rectangle, $0P_3DQ_3$. Demand is inelastic, because the increase in quantity demanded is relatively smaller than the decrease in price. Therefore, the new total revenue, $0P_3DQ_3$, is smaller than the old total revenue, $0P_2CQ_2$.

the other hand, when demand is inelastic, an increase in price will lead to an increase in total revenue.

Here is an example of the importance of inelastic demand: Some retailers use "everyday low prices", while others have advertised specials on a few items, with higher prices on other goods. A marketing research team compared stores using the two pricing strategies. They found that the stores featuring everyday low prices did get more sales. (We would expect this, because of the Law of Demand.) However, their profits were significantly lower. This suggests that the increases in quan-

tity were relatively small, when compared with the decreases in price. In other words, demand was inelastic for many of the goods that sold for lower prices. These calculations mean that these stores may want to re-think their pricing strategy.

A special case of inelastic demand is the case where quantity demanded does not change at all when price changes. The demand curve would be graphed as a vertical line. In this case, we say that demand is *perfectly inelastic*. The elasticity is zero. The demand for some goods might be perfectly inelastic, at least over some small ranges of price increases.

For many years, there has been a heated debate about how to reduce the use of marijuana, cocaine, and other drugs. For a long time, the dominant approach has involved what is called "supply interdiction". Under this approach, law-enforcement officers attempt to reduce the *supply* of drugs by capturing shipments and arresting dealers. An alternative approach might be called "demand control". Under this approach, we would increase our use of counseling and drug-treatment programs, in order to get drug users to reduce their *demand.*

Even though supply-interdiction efforts have not been completely successful, they have reduced supply somewhat. As a result, what has happened to total revenue from sales of marijuana? If the supply curve shifts to the left as a result of supply interdiction, the price will increase. The effect on total revenue will depend on the price elasticity of demand. Assuming that the demand for marijuana is inelastic, the increase in price will be relatively larger than the decrease in quantity demanded. This means that *successful supply interdiction will lead to increased total revenue for marijuana sellers.* Some individual sellers will lose their revenue if they get caught. However, if demand is inelastic,

the sellers who don't get caught will receive an increased amount of revenue, so that the overall amount of revenue will increase.

To many observers, it seems unfortunate that the reduced supply of marijuana will lead to higher revenues for marijuana sellers. This may be one reason why there has been more emphasis on demand control in recent years. If demand control is successful in pushing the demand curve for drugs to the left, the equilibrium price will fall, and the equilibrium quantity will also decrease. Therefore, total revenue *must* decrease, regardless of the elasticities.

Some estimates suggest that the demand for cocaine may be significantly more elastic than the demand for marijuana. If the demand for cocaine is unit-elastic, then a leftward shift in the supply curve will not change total revenues for cocaine sellers. Thus, the policy of supply interdiction may be more sensible for cocaine than for marijuana. However, it is still true that a policy of demand control would *definitely* reduce revenue for sellers. A leftward shift in the demand curve will *always* reduce total revenue, whereas the effect on total revenue of a leftward shift in the supply curve will depend on the elasticity of demand.

Ultimately, if prices rise far enough, demand simply cannot be perfectly inelastic, because buyers won't have enough money to purchase the amounts they were purchasing before. Thus, demand for some goods may be perfectly inelastic over some range of prices, but it cannot be perfectly inelastic for all price combinations. Even if the demand for heroin isn't *perfectly* inelastic, however, it is probably inelas-

tic. In *Real Economics for Real People 6.2*, we look at the markets for cocaine and marijuana.

We have now looked at elastic demand, unit-elastic demand, and inelastic demand. In each case, there is a unique relationship between the price elasticity of demand and the effect on total revenue of a change in price. These important relationships are summarized in Figure 6.4.

Price Elasticity	Name	Effect of Price Increase on Total Revenue	Effect of Price Decrease on Total Revenue	Graph
e=0	Perfectly Inelastic	P ↑ TR ↑	P ↓ TR ↓	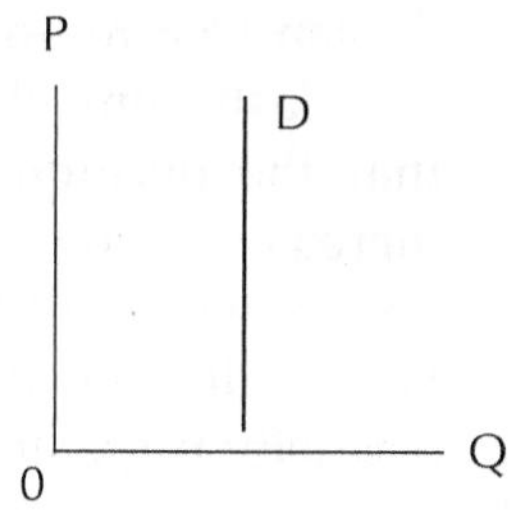
0<e<1	Inelastic but not Perfectly Inelastic	P ↑ TR ↑	P ↓ TR ↓	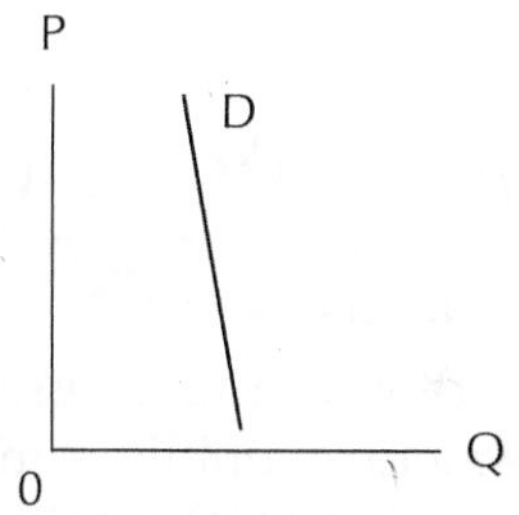
e=1	Unit Elastic	TR constant	TR constant	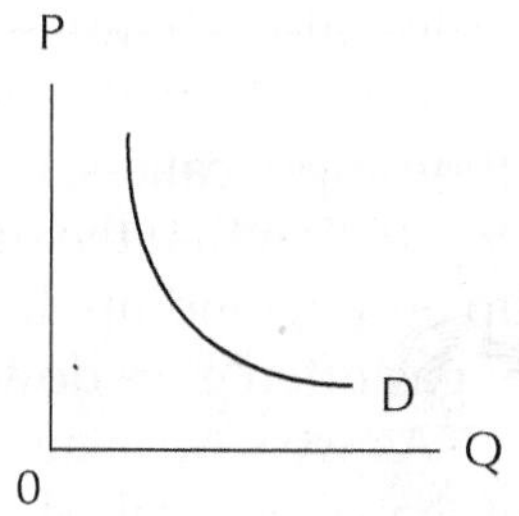
1<e<∞	Elastic but not Perfectly Elastic	P ↑ TR ↓	P ↓ TR ↑	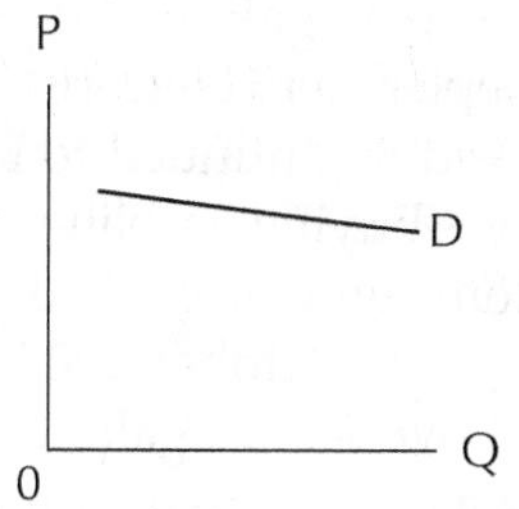
e=∞	Perfectly Elastic	Price does not change	Price does not change	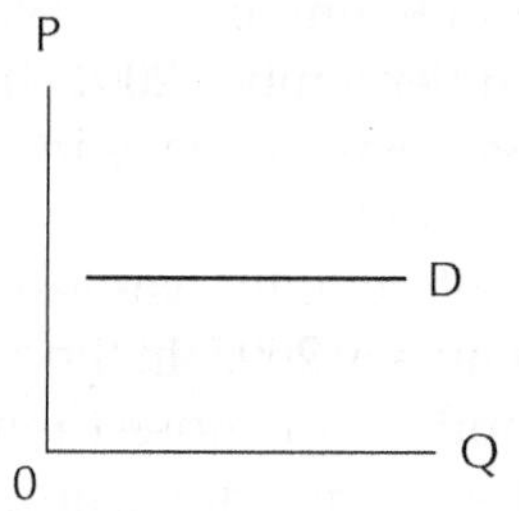

Figure 6.4 Summary of Relationships Between Price Elasticity and Total Revenue

IR6-3. Assume that the own-price elasticity of demand for red-delicious apples is 1.0. Is this elastic, unit elastic, or inelastic? Given that the elasticity is 1.0, if there is an increase in the price of red-delicious apples, what will happen to total revenue? How will your answer be different if the elasticity is greater than one?

IR6-4. The price of a USB flash drive falls by 10 percent. As a result of the decrease in price, there is a 7-percent increase in the quantity of USB flash drives demanded. What is the price elasticity of demand for USB flash drives? Is demand inelastic, unit elastic, or elastic? Will total revenue increase or decrease?

WHY DOES THE PRICE OF GASOLINE BOUNCE AROUND SO MUCH?

Very few things grab the attention of the American public as much as the price of gasoline. When the price of gasoline increases, radio call-in shows get lots of calls from upset motorists. If we listen to the statements of these angry callers, it would be easy to get the impression that the price of gasoline just goes up and up and up. In fact, however, the price of gas often goes down.

As we saw in an earlier chapter, the price of gasoline spiked upward to more than $2 per gallon for a few hours after the September 11 terrorist attacks, but then fell back. And it continued to fall. By December 2001, I was buying gasoline for less than $1.10 per gallon. Some places had prices below $1.00.

By October 2004, the price was back up above $2 per gallon, but two months later, it was back down around $1.70. (Thus, the price in December 2004 was the same as the price in September 2001. If we adjust for inflation, this was a *decrease* in the real price of gasoline.)

In July 2006, gasoline cost about $3.10 per gallon, but it was less than $2.00 per gallon by January 2007. In the summer of 2008, the price spiked to more than $4 per gallon. By the following winter, however, the price had fallen below $2 per gallon. In the spring of 2013, the price was around $3.80 per gallon. As of this writing, in the spring of 2016, the price is about $2.20 per gallon.

The most remarkable thing about the price of gasoline is that it bounces around so much. In other words, the price of gasoline is unusually *volatile*.

We can use the elasticities of supply and demand to get an idea about why the price of gasoline is so volatile. In the short run, the quantity of gasoline demanded is very unresponsive to changes in the price of gasoline. In other words, if we consider only a relatively short period of time for buyers to adjust, it is difficult for most people to reduce their gasoline purchases by very much. That's another way of saying that the short-run demand for gasoline is inelastic. When the price goes up, we complain, but we don't reduce our driving very much. (People may be able to respond more in the long run than in the short run. For example, motorists may buy more fuel-efficient vehicles. But the price fluctuations that get so much attention are caused primarily by short-run behavior.)

In the short run, the supply of gasoline is also unresponsive or inelastic. It is difficult to bring huge new quantities of gasoline to market quickly, even when the price of gasoline rises substantially. (In the long run, it may be possible to develop new oil fields, or to build new gasoline refineries. But once again, when we see the price of gasoline rising or falling from one day to the next, we are seeing the result of short-run interactions.)

So, the demand for gasoline is inelastic in the short run, and the supply of gasoline is also inelastic in the short run. This kind of situation is shown in Figure 6.5. In that figure, the original supply curve S_{old} is inelastic, and the demand curve D is also inelastic. The original equilibrium quantity is Q_{old}, and the original equilibrium price is P_{old}.

If there is no shift in either the demand curve or the supply curve, then the price will stay at P_{old}, and the quantity will stay at Q_{old}. But what will happen if there is a shift in one of the curves? If demand and supply are as inelastic as in Figure 6.5, then there is not much room for a change in the equilibrium quantity. Instead, any shift in either the demand curve or the supply curve will lead to a relatively large change in the equilibrium price, and a relatively small change in the equilibrium quantity.

Figure 6.5 shows a leftward shift in the supply curve of gasoline, from S_{old} to S_{new}. This could occur for a variety of reasons. For example, in the spring of 2007, several refineries were forced to reduce their output because of maintenance problems. This is a temporary deterioration in the technology of producing gasoline. We would represent this as a leftward shift in the supply curve. Alternatively, a leftward shift in the supply curve could be caused by an increase in the price of oil. That's what happened in the first half of 2008. Against the background of a very inelastic demand curve, a leftward shift in the supply curve must lead to a relatively large increase in the equilibrium price, and a relatively small decrease in the equilibrium quantity.

In Figure 6.5, the new equilibrium price is P_{new}, and the new equilibrium quantity is Q_{new}.

Figure 6.5 shows a leftward shift in the supply curve. If the supply curve had shifted to the right, we would have seen a *decrease* in the equilibrium price of gasoline, and an

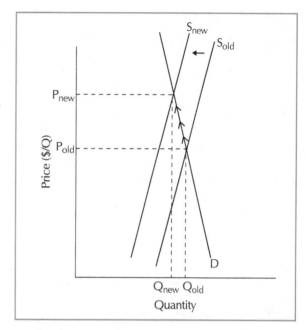

Figure 6.5 The Response of Equilibrium Price and Quantity to a Supply Shift When Demand Is Inelastic

The demand curve for gasoline is D, the original supply curve is S_{old}, and the original equilibrium price and quantity are P_{old} and Q_{old}. Production problems at refineries lead to a leftward shift in the supply curve for gasoline, to S_{new}. The new equilibrium price and quantity are P_{new} and Q_{new}. Because supply and demand are inelastic, the increase in price is relatively larger than the decrease in quantity.

increase in the equilibrium quantity. But we would still observe the same basic story: With an inelastic demand curve, a supply shift will lead to a relatively large change in the equilibrium price, and a relatively small change in the equilibrium quantity.

If the demand curve and supply curve were inelastic, like D and S_{old} in Figure 6.5, then a shift in the *demand* curve would also lead to a relatively large change in the equilibrium price, and a relatively small change in the equilibrium quantity. With inelastic demand and supply, there just isn't going to be much of a change in quantity. Therefore, most of the action will come in the form of relatively large changes in price.

FACTORS THAT INFLUENCE
THE PRICE ELASTICITY OF DEMAND

Economists have used statistical methods to estimate the price elasticity of demand for many goods. Table 6.1 contains some of these estimates. You can see that different goods have very different elasticities. In Table 6.1, the estimated own-price elasticity of demand for milk is 0.14. This is highly inelastic: If the price of milk were to increase by 10 percent, consumers would reduce their quantity demanded by only $(10)(0.14) = 1.4$ percent. On the other hand, a number of goods are approximately unit-elastic. For example, Table 6.1 indicates that the price elasticity of demand for furniture is estimated to be 1.01. Other goods are elastic. These include automobiles, for which the elasticity is estimated to be 1.35.

Table 6.1 Estimates of the Own-Price Elasticity of Demand for Selected Goods

Good	Elasticity	
Fresh tomatoes	4.60	
Fresh green peas	2.80	
Restaurant meals	1.63	Elastic
Automobiles	1.35	Demand
Cable television	1.20	
Furniture	1.01	
Movies	0.87	
Shoes	0.70	
Water	0.52	Inelastic
Toilet articles	0.44	Demand
Medical insurance	0.31	
Eggs	0.23	
Milk	0.14	

Sources: C.B. Blankart, "Towards an Economic Theory of Advice and its Application to the Deregulation Issue", *Kyklos*, 1981; G.E. Brandow, "Interrelations Among Demands for Farm Products and Implications for Control of Market Supply", Bulletin 680, Pennsylvania State University Agricultural Experiment Station, 1961; H.S. Foster, Jr., and B.R. Beattie, "Urban Residential Demand for Water in the United States", *Land Economics,* 1979; H.S. Houthakker and L.D. Taylor, *Consumer Demand in the United States: Analyses and Projections,* Harvard University Press, 1970.

We can identify a number of forces that cause demand to be elastic for some goods, but inelastic for others. These include

- the availability of substitutes,
- the importance of the good in the consumer's budget, and
- the amount of time during which consumers can adjust to the price change.

We'll discuss each of these in this section.

The Availability of Substitutes

Why is the demand for milk so inelastic? One reason is that parents believe there is no good substitute for milk for their children. Since milk provides so many important nutrients, many buyers feel they really must have it. In other words, families find it difficult to substitute away from milk when its price increases. If it's hard to find a good substitute for milk, then the quantity of milk that families buy will not change very much, even when the price changes. If a family is currently buying two gallons of milk per week, they won't suddenly drop to one gallon when the price goes up by a little bit. *Generally speaking, demand will be less elastic when it is hard to substitute away from the good whose price goes up, and more elastic when it is easy to substitute.*

It's important to understand that we have been referring to the *market* elasticity of demand for milk. This is different from the elasticity of demand for any *one brand* of milk. Consumers may find it difficult to substitute away from milk, in general, and yet they may find it very easy to substitute away from one particular brand of milk. If Golden Dairies raises the price of its milk, it may find that it faces a very elastic demand curve for *its* milk. People will substitute away from Golden Dairies milk, and buy Happy Cow milk instead.

While Table 6.1 indicates that the demand for milk is inelastic, it also indicates that the demand for restaurant meals is fairly elastic. If restaurants raise their prices, it's easy for most people to substitute away from restaurant meals, by eating more at home.

The Importance of the Good in the Consumer's Budget

If the price of toothpaste were to rise by 10 percent, many consumers would hardly notice the difference. However, if the price of a new car were to increase by 10 percent, it would mean an increase of $2000 or even more. Consumers would definitely notice this. If consumers pay close attention to the price of a good, their demand is likely to be relatively more elastic. *Other things equal, consumers will have more elastic demand for items that make up a larger portion of their budgets.*

Given the importance of items such as cars and houses, it isn't surprising that people shop around a great deal when they are about to buy these items. In fact, consumers try to get help in making decisions about these big purchases. This is why there are jobs for realtors and automobile salespersons.

Time for the Consumer to Adjust

In 1973 and 1979, and again in 1999–2000, and again in 2008, American consumers faced large increases in the prices of gasoline, heating oil, and other petroleum products. What happens to the quantity demanded, if the price of gasoline goes up by a large amount?

In the very short run, not much will happen. It may take days or weeks for workers to make carpooling arrangements. It will take even more time for people to trade in their old gas guzzlers for new, fuel-efficient cars. It will take months to acquire more buses, and years to build more mass-transit facilities.

The same is true for the demand for heating oil and natural gas. In the short run, it may be possible to turn down the thermostat a few degrees. It will take a much longer time for people to insulate their homes better, or to install newer, more efficient furnaces.

These examples suggest that *demand will be more elastic when consumers have a longer time to adjust to the change in price.* One study found that the short-run elasticity of demand for sports equipment is 0.88, while the long-run elasticity is 2.39. In other words, if there were a 10-percent decrease in sports-equipment prices, the quantity demanded would only increase by $(10)(0.88) = 8.8$ percent, at first. However, if consumers were given enough time to adjust, their quantity demanded would eventually increase by $(10)(2.39) = 23.9$ percent.

In the case of gasoline and oil, one estimate is that the short-run elasticity is 0.14, while the long-run elasticity is 0.48. This is important for policy. In Chapter 4, we discussed the gasoline price ceilings that were in effect during the 1970s. At that time, some people argued that the price controls would not lead to serious shortages, because they believed that demand was *extremely* inelastic. In fact, however, fairly serious shortages occurred almost immediately, with long lines of cars waiting to fill up with gasoline. In addition, we should expect the shortages to become even more severe over time, because demand is more elastic when we consider a longer period of time. Fortunately, the price ceilings were eventually removed, and this eliminated the shortages.

The long-run elasticity of demand for cigarettes is also much larger than the short-run elasticity. Among the people who smoke cigarettes, most began to smoke when they were in their teens or early twenties. In many cases, these folks thought they would smoke for a few years and then quit. However, at the end of a few years, they discovered that it was very hard to quit. Cigarettes contain nicotine, which is addictive.

Thus at any one time, most smokers have been smoking for a long time. Many of them have tried to quit, but have not yet been able to quit. These smokers have inelastic demand.

However, there are many young people who might begin to smoke at some time in the future, but who haven't begun yet. Since they haven't started smoking yet, they haven't yet become addicted to nicotine. Their demand is likely to be much more elastic.

What would happen if the price of cigarettes were to rise, either because of a shift in the supply curve, or because of an increase in cigarette taxes? At first, the reduction in quantity demanded might be very small, since current smokers have inelastic demand. Over time, however, the reduction in quantity demanded would become larger. Because of the higher price, fewer teenagers would begin smoking in the first place. Over time, there would be a steady increase in the number of people who responded to the price increase by not starting to smoke. Thus, over time, the response of quantity demanded would be more and more elastic.

Reality Check:
Interim Review Questions

IR6-5. In the eyes of many consumers of soft drinks, it's easy to substitute between Sprite, 7-Up, and Sierra Mist. If the price of Sprite were to increase substantially, while the prices of 7-Up and Sierra Mist stay the same, do you expect that the demand for Sprite would be elastic or inelastic?

IR6-6. Assume that the supply curve for eggs has exactly the same shape as the supply curve for red-delicious apples. However, the demand for red-delicious apples is more elastic than the demand for eggs. In addition, let's assume that the government institutes a price floor in both the egg market and the apple market. If the price floors are both 10 percent above the equilibrium price, which market will have a relatively larger surplus?

OTHER ELASTICITIES OF DEMAND

We have started with the own-price elasticity of demand, because it's the most important elasticity. However, the elasticity concept can also be used to describe other important relationships. In this section, we will look at the elasticity of demand with respect to income. We'll also look at the elasticity of demand for one good with respect to the price of another good, which is called the cross-price elasticity of demand.

It's important to understand one essential difference between the various elasticities of demand. The own-price elasticity of demand is concerned with *movements along an existing demand curve*, whereas the income elasticity of demand and the cross-price elasticity of demand are concerned with *shifts to different demand curves*.

Income Elasticity of Demand

The income elasticity of demand tells us how consumers change their demand for a given good when their incomes change.

The *income elasticity of demand*, e_I, is defined as:

$$e_I = \frac{\frac{\Delta Q}{Q}}{\frac{\Delta I}{I}} = \frac{\%\Delta Q}{\%\Delta I},$$

where Q is the quantity of some good, and I is income. The basic structure of the formula is identical to that of the price elasticity of demand. The only difference is that we have income in the denominator, instead of the price of the good.

In Chapter 3, we saw that most goods are *normal goods*, which means that the demand curve shifts to the right when incomes increase. In other words, if the change in income is greater than zero, the resulting change in demand will also be greater than zero for a normal good. This means that *the income elasticity of demand is greater than zero for a normal good.*

Certain poor-quality goods are *inferior goods*. If income goes up, the demand curve will shift to the left for an inferior good. Thus, when the change in income is *greater* than zero, the resulting change in demand will be *less* than zero for an inferior good. *The income elasticity of demand is less than zero for an inferior good.*

It's important to avoid one source of confusion about income elasticities of demand. When we calculate the own-price elasticity of demand, we drop the minus sign. This is an acceptable thing to do, because demand curves never slope upward as we move from left to right. Therefore, we can use the absolute value without causing a misunderstanding. However, when we deal with the income elasticity of demand, the minus signs have an important meaning. The income elasticity of demand is positive for a normal good, but negative for an inferior good. If we were to drop the minus sign, we wouldn't be able to tell the difference between the income elasticities for normal goods and inferior goods. Therefore, we *don't* drop the minus sign when calculating the income elasticity of demand.

In Table 6.2, we show some estimates of the income elasticity of demand for selected

Table 6.2 Estimates of the Income Elasticity of Demand for Selected Goods

Good	Income Elasticity	
Owner-occupied housing	1.49	
Books	1.44	
Restaurant meals	1.40	
Clothing	1.02	Normal
Gasoline and oil	0.48	Goods
Rental housing	0.43	
Butter	0.42	
Residential electricity	0.20	
Margarine	−0.20	Inferior
Flour	−0.36	Goods

Sources: H.S. Houthakker and L.D. Taylor, *Consumer Demand in the United States: Analyses and Projections,* Harvard University Press, 1970; L. Taylor and R. Halvorsen, "Energy Substitution in U.S. Manufacturing", *The Review of Economics and Statistics,* 1977; H. Wold and L. Jureen, *Demand Analysis,* Wiley, 1953.

goods. These estimates suggest that owner-occupied housing, rental housing, and butter are all normal goods, while margarine is an inferior good.

Cross-Price Elasticity of Demand

The own-price elasticity of demand tells us how the buyers of a good respond when the price of *that good* changes. The **cross-price elasticity of demand** tells us how the buyers of one good respond when the price of *some other good* changes. Here is the formula for the cross-price elasticity of demand for good X with respect to changes in the price of good Y, which we call e_{xy}:

$$e_{XY} = \frac{\dfrac{\Delta Q_X}{Q_X}}{\dfrac{\Delta P_Y}{P_Y}} = \frac{\%\Delta Q_X}{\%\Delta P_Y},$$

Once again, the basic structure of the elasticity formula is the same as we have seen before.

In Chapter 3, we discussed *substitutes.* Two goods are substitutes if an increase in the price of one good leads to an increase in demand for the other good. In other words, two goods are substitutes if an increase in the price of one good leads to a rightward shift in the demand curve for the other good. Similarly, two goods are substitutes if a decrease in the price of one good leads to a leftward shift in the demand curve for the other good. For example, cola drinks are substitutes for coffee, romaine lettuce is a substitute for green-leaf lettuce, and vacations in Europe are substitutes for vacations in the U.S. For any pair of substitutes, if there is an increase in the price of one good, there will also be an increase in the demand for the other good. In this case, the numerator and the denominator of the cross-price elasticity have the same sign. *The cross-price elasticity of demand is greater than zero for substitutes.*

Table 6.3 Estimates of the Cross-Price Elasticity of Demand for Selected Pairs of Goods

Good with Quantity Change	Good with Price Change	Cross-Price Elasticity	
Florida interior oranges	Florida Indian River oranges	1.56	
Margarine	Butter	0.81	Substitutes
Natural gas	Fuel oil	0.44	
Beef	Pork	0.28	
California oranges	Florida interior oranges	0.14	
Fruits	Sugar	−0.28	Complements
Cheese	Butter	−0.61	

Sources: M.B. Godwin, W.F. Chapman, Jr., and W.T. Hanley, *Competition Between Florida and California Valencia Oranges in the Fruit Market,* U.S. Department of Agriculture, Economic Research Service, Bulletin 704, 1965; R. Stone, The Measurement of Consumers' Expenditure and Behavior in the United Kingdom, 1920–1938, Cambridge University Press, 1954; L. Taylor and R. Halvorsen, "Energy Substitution in U.S. Manufacturing", *The Review of Economics and Statistics,* November, 1977; H. Wold and L. Jureen, *Demand Analysis,* Wiley, 1953.

Table 6.3 includes information on the cross-price elasticities between some pairs of goods. The table indicates that butter and margarine are substitutes. Other substitute pairs include natural gas and fuel oil, and beef and pork. We usually expect pairs of goods to be substitutes when consumers would like to use one or the other of the goods at any one time, but not both.

Two goods are independent in demand if a change in the price of one good has no effect on the demand for the other good. *If two goods are independent in demand, the cross-price elasticity of demand is zero.*

Two goods are *complements* if an increase in the price of one good leads to a decrease in demand for the other good. In other words, two goods are complements if an increase in the price of one good leads the demand curve for the other good to shift to the left. Similarly, two goods are complements if a decrease in the price of one good leads the demand curve for the other good to shift to the right. Automobiles and gasoline are complements, as are bread and butter. *The cross-price elasticity of demand is less than zero for complements.* Generally, we would expect to see complementary relationships when consumers would tend to use the two goods together.

Hot dogs and mustard are complements. If there is an increase in the price of hot dogs, it is as if the entire "hot-dog/mustard composite" had become more expensive. This will lead to a decrease in the demand for mustard. In other words, the demand curve for mustard will shift to the left as a result of an increase in the price of hot dogs.

If we were to drop the minus sign, we wouldn't be able to tell the difference between the cross-price elasticities for complements and substitutes. Therefore, we *don't* drop the minus sign when calculating the cross-price elasticity of demand.

Reality Check: Interim Review Questions

IR6-7. If incomes increase, the demand curve for sports cars will shift to the right. Does this mean that sports cars are normal or inferior? Is the income elasticity of demand for sports cars greater than zero or less than zero?

IR6-8. If there is an increase in the price of vacations in France, the demand curve for vacations in the United States will shift to the right. Does this mean that vacations in France and vacations in the United States are complements or substitutes? Is the cross-price elasticity of demand for vacations in the U.S. with respect to the price of vacations in France greater than zero or less than zero?

ELASTICITY OF SUPPLY

We have concentrated on demand elasticities so far. However, it's also important to measure the responsiveness of supply.

The *price elasticity of supply,* e_s*, is defined as:*

$$e_s = \frac{\frac{\Delta Q_s}{Q_s}}{\frac{\Delta P}{P}} = \frac{\%\Delta Q_s}{\%\Delta P},$$

where Q_s is the quantity supplied. Suppose there's an increase in the price of breath mints, from 45 cents per roll to 55 cents per roll. The change in price is $(55 - 45) = 10$ cents. The reference level of price is the midpoint between 45 cents and 55 cents, which is 50 cents. This means that the proportional price increase is $(10/50) = 0.2$. As a result of this price change, the quantity supplied increases from 16,000 to 24,000 rolls per day. This is a change of $(24{,}000 - 16{,}000) = 8000$ rolls per day. Therefore, the reference level of quantity supplied is the midpoint between 16,000 rolls per day and 24,000 rolls per day, which is 20,000 rolls per day. The proportional increase in quantity supplied is $(8000/20{,}000) = 0.4$. In order to calculate the elasticity of supply, we divide the proportional increase in quantity supplied by the proportional increase in price. This gives us $0.4/0.2 = 2$.

The Law of Supply tells us that quantity supplied will move in the same direction as price. *Since supply curves typically slope upward, the price elasticity of supply is typically greater than zero.* In some cases, however, the supply elasticity is exactly zero. Leonardo da Vinci's famous painting, "Mona Lisa", hangs in Louvre Museum in Paris. Leonardo died in 1519, and so he isn't expected to produce any more paintings. Thus, there is only one "Mona Lisa". The Louvre probably won't try to sell it. But if they do, no matter what price is offered, the quantity supplied will be exactly one. This would be represented graphically by a vertical line.

Real Economics for Real People 6.3 discusses the hotel industry, in which the elasticity of supply is very small over a short period of time.

Supply Elasticity and Adjustment Time

What would happen if fish prices in Boston were to increase during the late afternoon? By late in the day, New England's fishing boats would either have returned to port, or they would be committed to spending the night on the water. It wouldn't be possible to bring any additional fresh fish to market that day. This means that the change in quantity supplied is zero, so that the elasticity of supply is also zero. Thus, in the very short run, the supply elasticity may be zero. In order for the Law of Supply to hold, producers often need some time to respond to a change in price.

If the firms in the fishing industry believe that the price will stay higher, they might be able to increase the quantity supplied over a period of a few days or weeks. They might keep their boats at sea for longer periods. They might speed up the work on boats that need repairs, so as to get more boats into the water. Thus, if firms are given a certain amount of time, the elasticity of supply will be greater than zero.

But if we give the fishing firms even more time to adjust, they may be able to increase their catch a great deal. If the firms believe that the higher price will continue for a long time, they can build new boats. The conclusion is that the elasticity of supply will often be higher when firms have a longer time to adjust. In the very long run, the elasticity of supply may be very large.

This relationship between adjustment time and supply elasticity occurs in virtually every industry. For example, if oil prices go up in the afternoon, oil companies won't be able to increase the quantity supplied by evening. However, the oil producers will be able to increase supply within a few weeks, by running their existing wells harder. It will take months or years to increase production substantially by drilling new wells.

Supply Elasticity and the Specialization of Resources

Many industries have some special requirements. They require specialized workers, specialized machinery, and specialized equipment. For example, the grape-growing industry requires particular types of soil and climate. The land on which the best grapes can be grown is very limited in supply. Thus the elasticity of supply of the highest-quality grapes is likely to be small. The problem of specialized resources is even more severe in the entertainment and sports industries. There is only one Tiger Woods, only one Madonna, only one Mick Jagger. These artists can only give so many performances per year, regardless of how high the ticket prices go. The elasticity of supply of superstars is small. Generally speaking, the elasticity of supply will be smaller when the resources that are used in a particular industry are relatively more specialized and scarce.

In summary, all else equal, supply is more elastic:

- when sellers have a longer period of time over which to respond to changes in price, and

- when the resources employed in the production process are not especially scarce or specialized.

Reality Check:
Interim Review Questions

IR6-9. The price of bicycle helmets increases by 20 percent. As a result, there is a 10-percent increase in the quantity of bicycle helmets supplied. What is the elasticity of supply for bicycle helmets?

IR6-10. Explain why the elasticity of supply of red-delicious apples is likely to be much larger over a period of ten years than over a period of ten weeks.

ECONOMICS AND YOU:
IF YOU WANT TO PAY LESS, DON'T LET THEM KNOW THAT YOU REALLY WANT TO BUY

We began this chapter by noting that some colleges give less-generous packages of financial aid to early-admission applicants. These colleges believe that the early-admission applicants are less likely to respond to a higher price by going elsewhere. In other words, the colleges believe that these applicants have inelastic demand. The colleges know that they can increase their revenues if they charge higher prices to those with inelastic demand. As a result, many colleges try to identify the groups of students who are more inelastic. These students are offered less-generous financial aid, while the ones with elastic demand are given more attractive aid packages.

This suggests that if you want a good deal, you don't want to appear too eager. By applying for early admission, students give the impression that their demand is inelastic. A better strategy might be to apply for regular admission, so as to make it appear that you are thinking seriously about many different colleges.

There are many other examples in which buyers may be able to get a better deal if they appear to have elastic demand. For instance, a friend of mine was once planning an out-of-town trip. He called the reservation office of a hotel in his destination city. When he asked for the rate for a standard double room, he was told that it would be $152 plus tax. If he had asked the reservation agent to book the room right then, he would have revealed that he was willing to pay the full price of $152 plus tax. Instead, however, he asked whether any discounts were available. This indicated to the hotel that his demand was more elastic. Rather than lose his business, the hotel offered him a room for $105 plus tax. By indicating that he is sensitive to price, the traveler got the price reduced by nearly one-third. Of course, discounts aren't always available, but it doesn't hurt to ask.

Elasticity is especially important for the pricing strategies of business firms, which we will study in Chapters 9 through 11. Elasticity is also crucial for understanding the effects of taxes, as we shall see in Chapter 16. Elasticity is one of the most important concepts in economics, and we will continue to use it throughout this book.

Chapter Summary

1. Elasticity is the economist's measure of the responsiveness of demand or supply. Elasticity has the advantage of being unit-free, so it does not depend on the units in which quantity demanded, quantity supplied, and other variables are measured.

2. The price elasticity of demand, or own-price elasticity of demand, is defined as the percentage change in quantity demanded, divided by the percentage change in price. As with the other elasticities introduced in this chapter, we calculate the price elasticity of demand at the *midpoint* or average of the beginning and ending values of price, and the beginning and ending values of quantity demanded. We also take the *absolute value* of the own-price elasticity of demand, so that it will not be negative. All else equal, the price elasticity of demand will be larger: (a) if it is easier to substitute for the good, or (b) if the good makes up a larger fraction of the consumer's budget, or (c) if consumers have a longer period of time over which to adjust to the price change.

3. If the percentage change in quantity demanded is greater than the percentage change in price, the price elasticity of demand is greater than one, and demand is said to be elastic. If demand is elastic, a price increase will lead to a decrease in total revenue, and a price decrease will lead to an increase in total revenue.

4. If the percentage change in quantity demanded is the same as the percentage change in price, the price elasticity of demand is exactly 1.0, and demand is said to be unit elastic. In this case, price changes will not have any effect on total revenue.

5. If the percentage change in quantity demanded is less than the percentage change in price, the price elasticity of demand is less than one, and demand is said to be inelastic. In this case, a price increase will lead to higher total revenue, and a price decrease will lead to lower total revenue.

6. The income elasticity of demand is defined as the percentage change in quantity, divided by the percentage change in income. The income elasticity is greater than zero for normal goods, and less than zero for inferior goods.

7. The cross-price elasticity of demand is defined as the percentage change in the quantity of one good, divided by the percentage change in the price of some other good. The cross-price elasticity is greater than zero for substitutes, and less than zero for complements. The cross-price elasticity is zero for any pair of goods that are independent in demand.

8. The price elasticity of supply is defined as the percentage change in quantity supplied, divided by the percentage change in price. The Law of Supply tells us that the supply elasticity will typically be greater than zero. If a good (such as a rare painting by a painter who is now deceased) cannot be reproduced, the elasticity of supply is zero. This is a violation of the Law of Supply. Still, the Law of Supply holds in many cases. The supply elasticity will be larger when producers have a longer period of time over which to adjust to the price change. Also, if the resources necessary to produce a good are very scarce or highly specialized, the supply elasticity of that good may be fairly small.

Key Terms

Elasticity

Own-Price Elasticity of Demand

Elastic Demand

Unit-Elastic Demand

Inelastic Demand

Total Revenue

Perfectly Elastic Demand

Perfectly Inelastic Demand

Income Elasticity of Demand

Cross-Price Elasticity of Demand

Price Elasticity of Supply

Key Figure

The key figure for this chapter is Figure 6.4, which summarizes the different types of price elasticity of demand, and the relationships between price elasticity and the change in total revenue.

Questions and Problems

QP6-1. The price of lettuce goes up from $1.75 per head to $2.25 per head. As a result, the quantity of lettuce demanded goes down by 25 percent.

a. What is the price elasticity of demand for lettuce?
b. Is the demand for lettuce inelastic, unit-elastic, or elastic?
c. What will happen to total revenue for lettuce sellers?

QP6-2. Both coffee and tea contain caffeine. Many people like caffeine, but really don't care what drink gives them their caffeine. For people like this, would the cross-price elasticity of demand for coffee with respect to the price of tea be positive or negative?

QP6-3. Incomes increase. As a result, the demand for turnips goes down. On the basis of this information, what can we say about the income elasticity of demand for turnips? Are turnips a normal good or an inferior good?

QP6-4. A price ceiling is instituted on leather belts. The price ceiling is below the equilibrium price, so that it leads to shortages.

Let us assume that the supply elasticity is 0.5. Will the shortages be more severe if the own-price elasticity of demand is 0.5 or 0.8?

QP6-5. The price of a type of hand-held programmable calculator goes down from $55 to $45. As a result, the quantity demanded rises from 1000 units per week to 1500 units per week.

a. What is the own-price elasticity of demand for this type of calculator?
b. Is the demand for this type of calculator unit-elastic, elastic, or inelastic?
c. What is the change in total revenue for sellers of this type of calculator, as a result of this change?

QP6-6. Ace Computer Equipment Company raises the price on its printer cables by 20 percent. All other companies in the area keep their prices unchanged. As a result, the quantity demanded for Ace printer cables goes down by 80 percent.

a. What is the own-price elasticity of demand for cables from Ace?
b. Is the demand for Ace's cables elastic, unit-elastic, or inelastic?
c. If *all* companies were to raise their prices by 20 percent, do you think the *market* elasticity of demand would be different from the elasticity facing Ace? If so, how would the market elasticity be different from the elasticity for an individual firm?

QP6-7. Real income in Winesburg, Ohio, goes up from $80 million to $120 million. As a result, there is a 10-percent increase in the quantity of bread demanded.

a. What is the income elasticity of demand for bread?
b. Is bread a normal good or an inferior good in Winesburg, Ohio?

QP6-8. The cross-price elasticity of demand for automobiles with respect to the price of gasoline is –0.2. The cross-price elasticity of demand for chicken with respect to the price of fish is 0.7. The cross-price elasticity of demand for oranges with respect to the price of notebook paper is zero.

a. Which of these pairs of goods shows a substitute relationship?
b. Which of these pairs shows a complement relationship?
c. Which of these pairs is independent in demand?

QP6-9. A price floor is instituted for sunflower seeds. The price floor is above the equilibrium price, so that a surplus occurs. Assume that the price elasticity of demand for sunflower seeds is 1.0. Will the surpluses be greater if the price elasticity of supply is 0.6 or 1.3?

QP6-10. The own-price elasticity of demand for raisins is 0.8. An industry analyst suggests that the price will go up by 50 percent next year.

a. Is the demand for raisins elastic, unit-elastic, or inelastic?
b. What will be the percentage change in the quantity of raisins demanded?
c. Will total revenues for raisin sellers go up or down as a result of the price change and the resulting change in quantity demanded?

QP6-11. The price elasticity of demand for computer spreadsheet programs is 1.5. We observe that the quantity demanded increases by 30 percent. Assume that the change in quantity demanded was caused by a change in price.

a. What must have happened to the price of the spreadsheets?
b. Is the demand for spreadsheet programs elastic, unit-elastic, or inelastic?
c. What will have happened to total revenue for spreadsheet sellers as a result of the decrease in price and the associated increase in quantity demanded?

QP6-12. List and briefly discuss the factors that have an influence on the own-price elasticity of demand.

QP6-13. For each of the following sets of assumptions, state what will happen to total revenue.

a. Demand is inelastic; price rises.
b. Demand is elastic; price rises.
c. Demand is unit elastic; price rises.
d. Demand is elastic; price falls.
e. Demand is unit elastic; price falls.
f. Demand is inelastic; price falls.

Chapter 7

Consumer Choice

ECONOMICS AND YOU: WHY ARE BASEBALL CARDS WORTH MORE THAN WATER?

Very few people can survive more than a few days without a drink of water. And yet, in spite of the extreme importance of water, most Americans pay very little for water. Residential water is often sold for much less than a penny per gallon.

In 2007, a collector paid $2.8 million for a baseball card from 1909 featuring Honus Wagner, the Pittsburgh Pirates' shortstop. In 2013, two collectors paid more than $3.1 million for a five-cent coin—a "Liberty Head nickel" minted in 1913. In 2006, an art collector paid $140 *million* for a painting by Jackson Pollock.

Water is essential for life, while even the most die-hard baseball fan would probably not suggest that baseball cards are necessary for survival. Why would people pay so little for water and so much for baseball cards, nickels, and paintings?

The answer has to do with the demand behavior of consumers. We have already talked about demand curves, in Chapters 3 and 4. Now is the time to study the subject in more depth. The purpose of this chapter is to develop our ideas about consumer behavior more fully. In this chapter, you will learn:

- how to measure consumer satisfaction,

- how the consumer makes choices about how much to spend on various items, and

- how to measure the extent of the consumer's gains or losses that occur as a result of changes in price.

By the end of this chapter, you will have a clearer understanding of why consumers behave as they do. Among other things, you will learn why baseball cards sell for more than water.

THE RELATIONSHIP BETWEEN MARGINAL QUANTITIES AND TOTAL QUANTITIES

We have one other thing to take care of, before we develop our ideas about consumer behavior. To understand the economic theory of the consumer (as well as many other ideas presented later in this book), it is important to understand the relationships between *marginal* quantities, *total* quantities, and *average* quantities. It's easiest to illustrate these relationships with examples. In this section, we will look at an example that involves marginal and total quantities. Then, in Chapter 8, we'll consider average quantities.

In this section, we'll use an example that involves the distances traveled by a truck driver. However, this does *not* mean that the relationships between marginal quantities and total quantities can *only* be applied to the distances traveled by truck drivers. In fact, the concepts of marginal and total can be applied in one situation after another, and they always have the same relationship to each other.

Joe Andrews is a driver for a moving and storage company. His current assignment is to drive the Leone family's household goods from Portland, Maine, to their new home in Texarkana, Texas. Here is Joe's route:

- On the first day, Joe drives through New Hampshire and Massachusetts, and ends up in Syracuse, New York. On this day, he drives *400 miles*. (He might have gone farther, but he had to wait for the final items to be loaded onto the truck.)

- On day 2, Joe drives past Erie, Pennsylvania, and Cleveland, Ohio, and ends up near Cincinnati, Ohio. He covers *600 miles* on this day.

- On the third day, Joe drives past Louisville, Kentucky, and Nashville, Tennessee, and ends up near Memphis, Tennessee. On this day, he travels *500 miles*.

- On day 4, Joe drives across Arkansas. Early in the afternoon, he delivers his cargo in Texarkana. On this day, he drives *300 miles*.

The distances traveled on each day are listed in the second column of Table 7.1.

Marginal Quantities

In the next several chapters, you will learn about concepts like "marginal cost" and "marginal revenue". The details differ, but they are all defined in fairly similar ways. Whenever we use the word *marginal*, we refer to the value associated with *one additional unit*. In our example of the distances traveled by Joe's truck, the marginal distance is the distance traveled on the most recent day. When we consider the first day of Joe's journey, the "marginal distance traveled" is 400 miles. When we consider the second day, the marginal distance traveled is 600 miles. And so on.

Day	Marginal Distance Traveled (Additional Distance This Day)	Total Distance Traveled (Total Distance for All Days So Far)
1	400 miles	400 miles
2	600 miles	1000 miles (= 400 + 600)
3	500 miles	1500 miles (= 400 + 600 + 500)
4	300 miles	1800 miles (= 400 + 600 + 500 + 300)

Table 7.1 Marginal and Total Distances Traveled in a Journey from Portland, Maine, to Texarkana, Texas

Total Quantities

If we start at the beginning of Joe's trip, and add together the marginal distances traveled each day, we can calculate the *total* distance traveled. If we consider only the first day, the total distance traveled is 400 miles. If we consider the first two days, the total distance traveled is equal to the marginal distance traveled on the first day (400 miles) plus the marginal distance traveled on the second day (600 miles), for a total of 1000 miles. Then, if we consider the first three days, the total distance becomes 400 miles + 600 miles + 500 miles = 1500 miles. Thus, *we get the total distance by adding the marginal distances.* Finally, if we consider all four days of the journey, the total distance is equal to the sum of the marginal distances traveled on each of the four days, which is 1800 miles. The total distances, as of the end of each day on the trip, are shown in the third column of Table 7.1.

In the chapters to come, you will learn how to use concepts like "total cost" and "total revenue". Again, the details differ, but the definitions really have a lot in common. We always find a *total* value by adding all of the relevant *marginal* values.

Notice the connection between our definitions of total distance and marginal distance: *Marginal* distance is the additional distance traveled in one additional day, and *total* distance is calculated by adding all of the marginal distances together. Thus, *marginal distance is the change in total distance when we travel for one additional day.*

In summary, *marginal* is associated with one additional unit, regardless of whether we are talking about marginal distance traveled, or marginal cost, or marginal revenue. *Total* is calculated by adding up the marginals. Thus, we calculate total distance traveled by adding the marginal distances, and we calculate total revenue by adding the marginal revenues, and so on.

So far, we have defined the relationships between total distance and marginal distance in words. We can also define them in equa-tions. When we say that marginal distance is the change in total distance, we could write

$$MD = \Delta TD / \Delta \text{ Number of Days,}$$

where MD is marginal distance, TD is total distance, and Δ (the Greek letter delta) is our symbol for change. Also, when we say that total distance is the sum of the marginal distances, we could write

$$TD = \Sigma \, MD,$$

where Σ (the Greek letter sigma) is our symbol for summation.

Graphs of Marginal and Total Quantities

So far, we have defined marginal and total, and we've given a numerical example. It's also useful to represent these ideas in a graph. In later chapters, we will have many graphs of marginal and total quantities. Figure 7.1 illustrates these concepts, using the numbers from our example of Joe's trip from Maine to Texas.

In Figure 7.1, when we consider only the first two days of the journey, the total distance traveled is 1000 miles. When we include a third day, the total distance increases to 1500 miles. In other words, when we move from considering the first two days to considering the first three days, total distance increases by 500 miles. This is because Joe drove 500 miles on the third day of his trip.

We can calculate the slope of the total-distance graph in Figure 7.1. Remember that the slope of a line is the change in the variable on the vertical axis, divided by the change in the variable on the horizontal axis. In this case, the slope of the total-distance graph is equal to the change in the total distance traveled, divided by the change in the number of days. The slope of the total-distance graph will change, depending on which day we are considering. If we calculate the slope of the total-distance graph for the third day, we get (500 additional miles / one additional day) = 500 additional

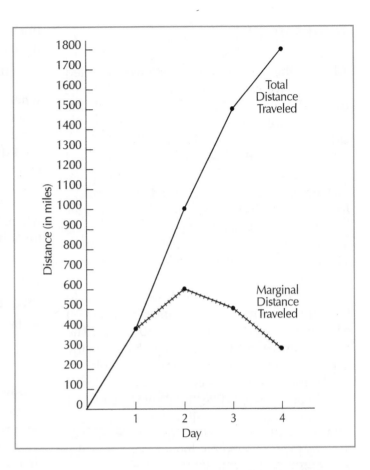

Figure 7.1 Graph of Marginal and Total Distances Traveled on a Journey from Maine to Texas

The marginal distance traveled on the first day is 400 miles. Therefore, the total distance traveled by the end of the first day is 400 miles. The marginal distance on the second day is 600 miles, so that the total distance by the end of the second day is (400 + 600) = 1000 miles. The marginal and total distances are connected in a similar manner for the third and fourth days. You can always find the total distance traveled, by adding up the marginal distances. Graphically, the marginal distance traveled is the slope of the total-distance curve.

miles per day. If we calculate the slope of the total-distance graph for the fourth day, we get (300 additional miles / one additional day) = 300 additional miles per day.

Now, take a look at the graph of *marginal* distances in Figure 7.1. When we consider the third day of the trip, the marginal distance traveled is 500 miles. But we just showed that, when we consider the third day, the change in total distance is also 500 miles. *Graphically, the marginal distance is the slope of the total-distance curve.* This is not a coincidence. This kind of relationship occurs for all sorts of marginal and total quantities. In later chapters, for example, we will see that the slope of a total-revenue curve is marginal revenue, and the slope of a total-cost curve is marginal cost. *The marginal value of a variable is the slope of the graph of the total value of that variable.*

In Figure 7.1, when we move from Day 1 to Day 2, the total-distance curve gets steeper (i.e.,

its slope increases). Then when we move to Day 3 and Day 4, the slope of the total-distance curve decreases. This is because marginal distance is the slope of the total-distance curve, and marginal distance increases from Day 1 to Day 2, but then decreases on Days 3 and 4.

Reality Check: Interim Review Questions

IR7-1. The Miami Dolphins football team has the ball. They make a marginal gain of six yards on their first play, followed by marginal gains of four yards on the second play, and 11 yards on the third play. What is the total gain from the first two plays? What is the total gain from the first three plays?

IR7-2. A financial analyst draws a "total-revenue curve" for a corporation. What would we call the slope of the total-revenue curve?

UNDERSTANDING CONSUMER BEHAVIOR

We have already studied consumer demand, in Chapters 3 and 4. However, we did not go into very much depth. Now is the time to get a more complete understanding. The main purpose of this chapter is to develop a framework and a vocabulary for thinking about how consumers make decisions regarding how much to buy. In this section, we introduce some economic ideas that can help us to understand consumer behavior. As part of this effort, we will use the marginal and total concepts that were just introduced.

The Rational Consumer

Economists do *not* believe that consumer decisions are just accidents. Instead, economists believe that consumers behave with purpose. The economic theory of consumer behavior starts from the idea that *consumers are rational, which means that they do the best they can with what they have.*

Is this a good assumption? Are people really rational? After all, people make little mistakes all the time, and people sometimes make really big mistakes. If you have studied abnormal psychology, or even if you have just watched the news, you have probably been exposed to plenty of stories about people who engage in self-defeating and self-destructive behaviors. Thus it is not true that every person behaves in a completely rational way at all times.

On the other hand, the vast majority of people do not behave randomly. People really do make thoughtful plans about spending, saving, education, careers, and many other aspects of life. People really do try to carry out those plans. This process may not be perfect, but it is pretty good in a lot of cases.

Thus while economists understand that people are not perfectly rational all the time, we still believe that the assumption of rationality is a decent starting point. People may not be completely rational all the time, but they are close enough to rational that we will stick

with the assumption of rationality. However, we won't have a complete understanding of consumer behavior until we have an idea of the *exact way* in which consumers are rational. To do that, we have to be precise about the benefits that consumers get when they consume goods and services.

In the 19th century, economists developed a concept called *utility*, to describe the psychological satisfaction that consumers get from consuming goods and services. Sometimes, economists also use other words, such as "happiness" or "satisfaction", to describe the consumer's benefit from consuming. However, utility is the word that is used most commonly, and we will use it here.

In the early days, it was believed that utility could be measured precisely. Economists began to say that one unit of psychological satisfaction is one "util". So, for example, we might say that Adam gets 3.4 utils from consuming a hamburger, and Stephanie gets 6.9 utils from watching the movie *Titanic* on video.

Unfortunately, there's a problem with this approach, because it is extremely difficult to measure psychological satisfaction so precisely. Therefore, in this book, we will use another approach. We simply measure utility in dollars of willingness to pay. Under this approach, it doesn't matter how much happiness Courtney gets from buying a wristwatch. The only thing that matters is the *amount of money she is willing to pay* for the wristwatch.

Marginal Utility and Total Utility, Measured in Dollars

Jason O'Donnell has a summer job with a roofing company. It's one of the hottest, sweatiest jobs around. At the end of one very steamy day, Jason sees some neighborhood children selling plastic cups of lemonade. Jason now has a decision to make: Should he buy any lemonade? If so, how many cups should he buy?

In part, Jason's decision will depend on how much each cup of lemonade is worth to him. We define Jason's *marginal utility* of lemonade consumption as the maximum amount of money he would be willing and able to pay, to receive one additional cup of lemonade.

Jason decides he would be willing to pay as much as $1.25 for his first cup of lemonade. Thus, his marginal utility from the first cup is $1.25. A second cup would taste good, too, but it wouldn't quite match the first one. He decides he would be willing to pay up to an additional $1.00 for a second cup. According to our definition, this means that his marginal utility for the second cup is $1.00.

Jason decides he would be willing to pay an additional $0.75 for a third cup, so that the marginal utility of a third cup is $0.75. We have put these marginal utilities in Table 7.2, along with some others.

Note that the first line of Table 7.2 is for the case in which Jason doesn't drink any lemonade. It's possible to define *total* utility in this situation. The total utility is zero, because Jason would not be willing to pay anything, if he were to get nothing in return. However, for the case in which no lemonade is consumed, we have not put a number in the column for *marginal* utility. Since Jason's marginal utility is the amount he would be willing to pay for one *additional* cup of lemonade, it isn't possible to define marginal utility until the first cup is consumed.

You should also notice that this example only has *positive* marginal utilities. That is, all of the numbers in Table 7.2 are greater than zero. However, you can imagine that marginal utility could eventually be negative. If Jason had already drunk 10 cups of lemonade in the space of a few minutes, one more cup of lemonade might actually make him worse off. His marginal utility from the 11th cup of lemonade would be less than zero. Whereas Jason is willing to pay for the first few cups of lemonade, someone would have to pay Jason in order to get him to take the 11th cup.

If Jason is willing to pay as much as $1.25 for the first cup of lemonade, plus as much as another $1.00 for the second cup, it follows that the maximum total amount he is willing to pay for two cups would be $1.25 + $1.00 = $2.25. If he's willing to pay as much as another $0.75 for a third cup, then his total willingness to pay for all three cups is $1.25 + $1.00 + $0.75 = $3.00. We define Jason's *total utility* from a given number of cups of lemonade as the maximum total amount that he is willing and able to pay to receive them all. *Total utility is the sum of the marginal utilities.* The total utilities are also shown in Table 7.2. This is just another example of the relationship between marginal quantities and total quantities, which we developed earlier in this chapter with our example of a trip from Maine to Texas.

The Law of Diminishing Marginal Utility

In Figure 7.2, we graph Jason's marginal utility and total utility from consuming lemonade. In other words, Figure 7.2 is a graph of the information contained in Table 7.2. The total-utility curve is increasing, but at a decreasing rate. This is because marginal utility is the slope of the total-utility curve, and marginal utility is decreasing. In this example, Jason does become better off each time he drinks an additional cup of lemonade (up to the fifth cup, at least). But he becomes better off by less and less with each additional cup. This is not just because of something unusual about lemon-

Table 7.2 Jason's Marginal Utility and Total Utility from Additional Cups of Lemonade

Cup	Marginal Utility	Total Utility
0	—	$0.00
1	$1.25	1.25
2	1.00	2.25
3	0.75	3.00
4	0.50	3.50
5	0.25	3.75

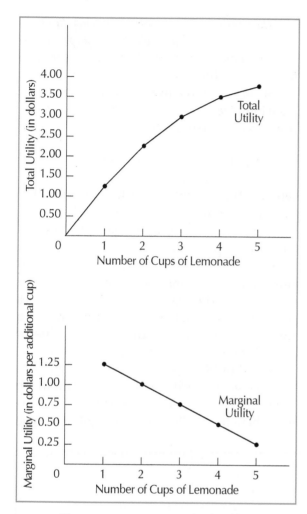

**Figure 7.2 Jason's Marginal Utility
and Total Utility from Cups of Lemonade**

We are measuring utility in dollars. Jason is willing and able to pay as much as $1.25 for the first cup of lemonade, so his marginal utility is $1.25 for the first cup. His marginal utility declines to $1.00 for the second cup, $0.75 for the third, $0.50 for the fourth, and $0.25 for the fifth. Thus Jason obeys the Law of Diminishing Marginal Utility. His total utility is calculated by adding up the marginal utilities. Thus Jason's total utility from the first two cups of lemonade is $(1.25 + 1.00) = $2.25. His total utility from the first four cups is $(1.25 + 1.00 + 0.75 + 0.50) = $3.50. Marginal utility is the slope of the total-utility curve. Since marginal utility is decreasing, the slope of the total-utility curve is decreasing. In other words, when marginal utility is positive but declining, total utility will increase at a decreasing rate.

ade. In fact, this relationship occurs so often that economists refer to the *Law of Diminishing Marginal Utility*: *For virtually every consumer good, the amount of additional utility provided by consuming one additional unit of the good will eventually go down, as the consumer increases his or her level of consumption.* The first hot dog at a picnic is really great, but the second is only OK. For most people, the marginal utility of the fifth hot dog would be small, or even negative.

In this example, Jason's marginal utility decreases by $0.25, every time he drinks one additional cup of lemonade. This means that the marginal-utility curve in Figure 7.2 is a straight line. However, it's important to understand that marginal-utility curves do not *have* to be straight lines. They can curve in a variety of ways, and still obey the Law of Diminishing Marginal Utility. The important thing is that the marginal-utility curve should eventually slope downward as we move from left to right.

The Consumer's Equilibrium: Marginal Utility Meets Price

So far, we have described the *benefits* that Jason gets from drinking lemonade, but we have said nothing about the *costs*. However, if Jason is to make an intelligent decision, he has to consider *both* the benefits and the costs. If the children operating the lemonade stand were to charge $1000 for a cup, Jason would be foolish to buy one. In fact, if the price is set at *any* level above $1.25 per cup, Jason will decide not to buy any lemonade from the children, because he is not willing to pay any more than $1.25 for the first cup. If the children were to charge $2.00 per cup, Jason would not buy from them.

What if the price of a cup of lemonade were $0.50 (that is, 50 cents)? Jason's first cup gives him utility of $1.25, and this means that it will make sense for him to buy at least one cup, if it only costs 50 cents. Any time you can pay $0.50 to get $1.25 worth of satisfaction, you should do it. In fact, Jason should buy a second cup and a third cup, as well. The second cup provides $1.00 of utility, and the third cup provides $0.75 of utility, but each of them costs only $0.50. Finally, Jason should buy a fourth cup, for which the marginal utility of $0.50 is exactly equal to the price. However, if he were to buy a fifth cup, he would have to pay 50 cents more, but the fifth cup would only generate 25 cents worth of satisfaction. Therefore, after Jason buys his fourth cup of lemonade, he shouldn't buy any more.

We can now state the **consumer decision rule**: *Consumers should continue to buy products as long as marginal utility is equal to or greater than price. For the last unit purchased, marginal utility will be equal to price.* When the consumer buys the quantity at which marginal utility equals price, we say that **consumer equilibrium** has been reached. When the consumer is in equilibrium, he or she is making the best possible decision. Therefore, when the consumer is in equilibrium, there is no reason to change behavior by consuming more or less.

The consumer is in equilibrium when he or she consumes the quantity at which the marginal utility from consuming the last unit of a good is equal to the price of the good.

So far, we have expressed the consumer decision rule in words. We can say the same thing in an equation:

$$MU = P,$$

where MU is marginal utility, and P is the price of the good.

The consumer decision rule (which is also called the optimal purchase role) is the first of many similar rules that we will develop in this book. Again and again, we will see that people should engage in economic activities until the value of what they get from one extra unit of the activity is equal to the value of what they have to give up. In other words, people should engage in economic activities until *marginal benefit equals marginal cost*. In the case of the consumer's decision rule, the marginal benefit is called "marginal utility". The

Figure 7.3 The Consumer's Equilibrium

Jason's marginal utility is the maximum amount that he would be *willing and able* to pay for an additional cup of lemonade. The price is the amount that he is actually *required* to pay. If his marginal utility is equal to or greater than the price, he should buy. If his marginal utility is less than the price, he should not buy. When the price is $0.50, Jason's marginal utility is greater than price for the first three cups of lemonade, and his marginal utility is equal to price for the fourth cup of lemonade. Thus, when the price is $0.50, Jason's equilibrium decision is to buy four cups of lemonade.

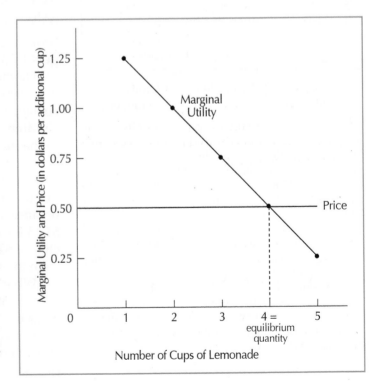

marginal cost of consuming a good is the price of the good.

The Graph of the Consumer's Decision. We graph Jason's decision in Figure 7.3. The price is graphed as a horizontal line. This is because Jason pays the same price (50 cents per cup) for every cup he buys. In fact, most consumers face constant prices for most of the goods they buy. In other words, *consumers usually take prices as given.* This is because, in most markets, each individual consumer only accounts for a small fraction of the demand. When you go to the supermarket to buy a loaf of bread, you are only one of thousands of buyers. If the individual consumer is small relative to the market, he or she won't have much bargaining power. Therefore, the individual will just have to take the going market price as given. The consumer faces the same price for the first unit, and the second, and the third, and the hundredth. The graph of this kind of price relationship is drawn as a horizontal line. (Later, we will consider the case in which buyers are large relative to the market. In that case, they will not necessarily take the price as given. If a buyer is a powerful player in the market, he or she may be able to exploit that power by manipulating the price.)

We have said that the consumer equilibrium occurs at the quantity at which marginal utility is equal to price. Graphically, Jason's consumer equilibrium is found at the place where the marginal-utility curve crosses the price line. In Figure 7.3, with a price of 50 cents per cup, the equilibrium quantity of lemonade is four cups.

The Individual's Demand Curve

We have illustrated Jason's decision rule by looking at the case in which a cup of lemonade costs 50 cents. What would happen if the price of a cup were to increase to $1.00? When facing a different price, Jason would still want to obey the consumer decision rule, or optimal purchase rule. This means that he would still want to con-

sume the quantity at which marginal utility is equal to price. But just because he follows the same *rule* in every case, it does not follow that he would choose the same *quantity* in every case. If the price were to increase to $1.00 per cup, Jason would respond by buying only two cups. This is because when the price is $1.00 per cup, marginal utility equals price for the *second* cup. If the price of a cup of lemonade were to rise to $1.25, Jason would only buy one cup, because marginal utility would equal price for the *first* cup.

Every time we have considered a price, we have found the quantity demanded by consulting the marginal-utility curve. But remember that a demand curve is a graph of the relationship between price and quantity demanded. By changing the price and observing the changes in Jason's quantity demanded, we can derive his *individual demand curve.* The demand curve is shown in Figure 7.4. *The individual demand curve is the same as the marginal utility curve!*

The individual demand curve in Figure 7.4 slopes downward as we move from left to right. In other words, the demand curve in Figure 7.4 obeys the Law of Demand. We introduced the Law of Demand in Chapter 3, but we did not go into much detail about it. Now we have used a set of assumptions and calculations to *derive* a demand curve that obeys the Law of Demand. We assume that the consumer is rational, which means that he or she wants to do as well as possible. We also assume that the individual consumer has no control over price. We also assume that marginal utility is diminishing. Following from those assumptions, we found that the demand curve is exactly the same as the marginal-utility curve. Since the marginal-utility curve slopes downward, the demand curve also slopes downward.

In Chapter 3, we saw that market demand curves can be derived by adding the individual demand curves. If Jason is one of 20 people who are interested in buying lemonade in this neighborhood, we would add all

Figure 7.4 The Marginal-Utility Curve and the Individual Demand Curve

Jason's marginal utility from the first cup of lemonade is $1.25. Therefore, if the price were $1.25, he would choose to buy one cup. His marginal utility from the second cup is $1.00, so that he would choose to buy two cups if the price were $1.00. His marginal utility from the third cup is $0.75, so that, if the price were $0.75, he would choose to buy three cups. If we follow this same reasoning, we see that Jason will increase his quantity demanded to four cups if the price is $0.50, and his quantity demanded will be five cups if the price is $0.25. Thus every point on the marginal-utility curve represents the quantity that would be demanded at a particular price. In other words, the marginal-utility curve is the individual's demand curve.

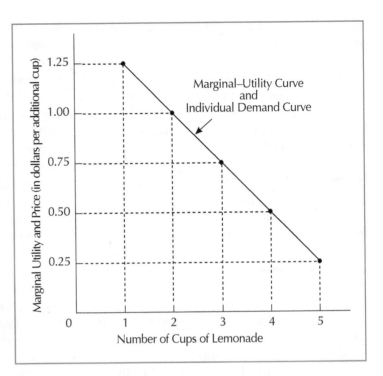

Real Economics for Real People 7.1:
Marginal Utility and the Demand for Keeping Warm

In his book, *Here Is Your War*, the American journalist Ernie Pyle tells a story that we can understand in terms of marginal utility. Americans armies fought in North Africa during the Second World War, in 1942 and 1943. Although temperatures in the North African deserts are warm during the day, it can become bitterly cold at night. One day, Pyle met a soldier who had an old-fashioned kerosene stove. Pyle offered him $50 for it, even though it would only have cost about $3 in the United States. The soldier "didn't hesitate a second. He just said 'No, sir,' and that was the end of that... (W)ithout the stove he would have been miserable."

For Ernie Pyle, the marginal utility of that kerosene stove was at least $50. (It's pos-sible that he may have been willing to pay even more. All we know for sure is that he was willing to pay *at least* $50.) For the soldier, the marginal utility of that kerosene stove was certainly *more than* $50, because he refused an offer to give up the stove in exchange for $50. The marginal utility of a stove in the Tunisian desert was dramati-cally higher than the marginal utility of the same stove back home. When the soldier and the journalist moved from America to Tunisia, their marginal-utility curves were shifted. Since the individual demand curve is identical to the marginal-utility curve, this means that the individual demand curves shifted to the right.

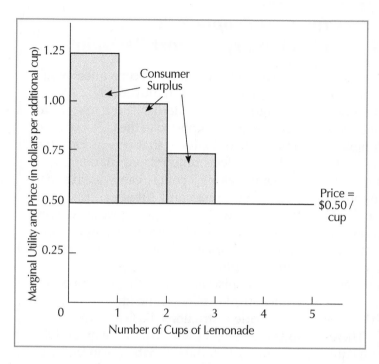

Jason's marginal utility from the first cup of lemonade is $1.25. However, if the price is only $0.50, then $0.50 is all he has to pay. Therefore, his consumer surplus from the first cup of lemonade is $(1.25–0.50) = $0.75. His marginal utility from the second cup of lemonade is $1.00. Using the same kind of reasoning, we can calculate his consumer surplus from the second cup of lemonade, which is $(1.00–0.50) = $0.50. Similarly, his consumer surplus from the third cup of lemonade is $(0.75–0.50) = $0.25. Jason actually consumes a fourth cup of lemonade, but he doesn't get any additional consumer surplus from the fourth cup, because marginal utility is exactly equal to price for the fourth cup. If we add together the consumer surpluses from the first three cups, we find that Jason's total consumer surplus is $(0.75 + 0.50 + 0.25) = $1.50.

of their individual demand curves together to get the market demand curve.

In Chapters 3 and 4, we looked at shifts in demand curves. In *Real Economics for Real People 7.1*, we take another look at demand-curve shifts, using the concept of marginal utility.

Consumer Surplus

Our example of Jason the lemonade drinker has an important implication. Let's say that the price of lemonade is 50 cents per cup. Jason is *willing and able to* pay $1.25 for the first cup, but he only *has* to pay 50 cents. He's then *willing* to pay $1.00 for the second cup, but, once again, he only *has* to pay 50 cents. He gets a bargain! This bargain is called consumer surplus. *Consumer surplus is the number of dollars by which total willingness to pay exceeds the total amount actually paid.* We can also say that consumer surplus is the difference between total utility and the total amount paid by the consumer. In other words, consumer surplus is the difference between total utility and total expenditure.

Jason's consumer surplus is represented by the shaded area in Figure 7.5. His consumer surplus is $(1.25 – 0.50) = $0.75 for the first cup of lemonade, plus $(1.00 – 0.50) = $0.50 for the second cup, plus $(0.75 – 0.50) = $0.25 for third cup. For the fourth cup, Jason is willing to pay exactly 50 cents, and he must pay exactly 50 cents. Thus, the fourth cup doesn't generate any additional consumer surplus. Jason's total consumer surplus is $0.75 + $0.50 + $0.25 + $0.00 = $1.50. *Graphically, consumer surplus is represented by the area between the demand curve and the horizontal line that represents the price.*

Consumer Surplus and the Consumer Decision Rule. We can use the concept of consumer surplus to gain a better understanding of the consumer decision rule. Remember that the consumer decision rule says that consumers should continue to buy products as long as marginal utility is equal to or greater than price. In Jason's case, the consumer decision rule dictates that he should buy four cups of

In the 1970s and early 1980s, American automobile manufacturers lost a great deal of market share to their Japanese competitors. As we saw in Chapter 5, the American firms responded by putting pressure on Congress, asking for restrictions on Japanese exports. The United States government threatened to put tariffs or quotas on Japanese exports, unless the Japanese restricted those exports themselves. As a result, the Japanese began a policy of "voluntary export restraints", or VERs.

Figure 7.6 shows what happened as a result of the VERs. The supply curve of Japanese cars exported to the United States was S, and the demand curve was D. Therefore, the equilibrium price was P^*, the equilibrium quantity was Q^*, and consumer surplus was represented by the area ABC. However, the export restriction set Q_{VER} as the maximum number of Japanese cars that could be sent to the United States. Because of this, the Japanese firms were able to charge a higher price. The new price was P_{VER}, instead of P^*. American consumers were forced to move upward and to the left, along their demand curve for Japanese cars. As a result of the VERs, consumer surplus fell to ADE. Consumer surplus decreased for two reasons: (1) fewer units were bought, and (2) for those items that were still bought, the price was higher than it had been before. The lost consumer surplus was (ABC – ADE), which is the area EDBC. This lost consumer surplus is the maximum amount that consumers would pay to have the VER removed.

Figure 7.6 only looks at the market for Japanese autos exported to the U.S., but economists also believe that the VERs had spillover effects onto related markets: With higher prices for Japanese cars sold in America, the European and American manufacturers could charge higher prices, as well. This means that buyers of European and American cars also lost some of their consumer surplus.

Economists have used the concept of consumer surplus to get some idea of the losses from trade restrictions. Basically, the idea is to try to estimate the size of the area EDBC in Figure 7.6. Some estimates are in the vicinity of $10 billion per year. This could translate into a cost of about $250,000 per year, for every American job "saved". The auto industry is not the only one in which international trade has been restricted. The U.S. government also restricts trade in a wide variety of other industries, including steel, textiles, and shoes. In each of these industries, the losses to consumers are much greater than the gains for American workers.

Trade restrictions are only one of several government policies that raise prices. For example, in Chapter 4, we looked at price supports for sugar. The costs of these policies can also be measured by calculating the lost consumer surplus.

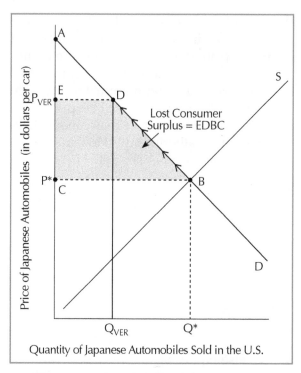

Figure 7.6 The Loss of Consumer Surplus as a Result of a Trade Restriction

The supply curve of Japanese automobiles exported to the United States is S, and the demand curve is D. As a result, the equilibrium quantity is Q*, and the equilibrium price is P*. Consumer surplus is the area between the demand curve and the price line. When the price is P* and the quantity is Q*, consumer surplus is represented by the area of the triangle, ABC. When a "voluntary export restraint" is instituted, there is a limit on the number of Japanese automobiles that can be purchased in the U.S. Consumer surplus decreases, for two reasons. First, the quantity is reduced. Second, the price is higher, so there is less consumer surplus from the units that are purchased. The new consumer surplus is the area of the smaller triangle, ADE. Therefore, the lost consumer surplus is (ABC – ADE), or the area EDBC. This loss of consumer surplus is a measure of the amount by which consumers have been made worse off by the trade restriction. This lost consumer surplus is the maximum amount that consumers would pay to have the VER removed.

lemonade when the price is 50 cents per cup. This gives him $1.50 of consumer surplus.

What if Jason were *not* to follow the consumer decision rule? For example, what if he were to buy only one cup of lemonade? The answer can be found in Figure 7.5. If Jason were to buy only one cup, his consumer surplus would be only $0.75. If he makes the correct decision, Jason would have $1.50 of consumer surplus. By stopping at only one cup of lemonade, Jason would give up $(1.50 − 0.75) = $ 0.75 of consumer surplus. That would be a mistake. If he were to buy two cups of lemonade, his consumer surplus would be $0.75 from the first cup, plus $0.50 from the second cup, for a total consumer surplus of $1.25. Once again, Jason's consumer surplus is less than the consumer surplus he would have from following the consumer decision rule.

On the other hand, what if Jason had bought five cups of lemonade? The fifth cup generates marginal utility of only $0.25, but it costs $0.50. Therefore, the additional consumer surplus from the fifth cup is −$0.25. If Jason were to buy a fifth cup of lemonade, his total consumer surplus would actually *decrease* by 25 cents. If Jason were to follow the consumer decision rule by buying four cups of lemonade, his consumer surplus would be $1.50. However, if he were to violate the consumer decision rule by buying five cups, his consumer surplus would fall to $1.25.

Jason maximizes his consumer surplus by following the consumer decision rule! There is no way for him to get more consumer surplus than he gets by following the consumer decision rule. In fact, this gives us another way to think about the consumer decision rule: If you want to maximize your consumer surplus, the way to do it is to keep buying as long as marginal utility is equal to or greater than price.

In *Real Economics for Real People 7.2*, we show how consumer surplus can be used to measure the true cost of a government policy that leads to higher prices.

IR7-3. Vicky is considering whether to buy a scarf. Her marginal utility from the first scarf is $10, and the scarf costs $15. Should she buy?

IR7-4. For Derek, the marginal utility of the first grapefruit is $1. If Derek obeys the Law of Diminishing Marginal Utility, will the marginal utility of the second grapefruit be greater than or less than $1?

IR7-5. Catherine's marginal utility from the first movie in a month is $10, her marginal utility from the second movie in a month is $8, her marginal utility from the third movie is $6, and her marginal utility from the fourth movie is $4. The price of a movie ticket is $6. How many movie tickets should Catherine buy? How much consumer surplus does she get?

MORE APPLICATIONS OF THE THEORY OF CONSUMER BEHAVIOR

We have now introduced some ways of thinking about consumer behavior. In fact, these ideas have proven to be very useful for many different applications. We've already seen some applications, such as the use of consumer surplus to measure the loss from restrictions on international trade. Some additional applications are discussed in this section.

The Value of Time

In domestic travel, people often have the choice of flying, driving, or riding a bus. Over short distances, the time advantage of air travel is very small, so travelers usually choose to take ground transportation. However, as the distance traveled becomes greater and greater, travelers can save more and more time by taking an airplane. Even though the airfare from Houston to St. Louis is higher than the price of a bus ticket, many people decide to fly, in order to save time. Time is money. People who place a higher value on their time will be willing to pay more money to save time.

All else equal, people may be willing to pay more to get a meal quickly, especially if they are in a hurry. Taco Bell, McDonald's, and other companies are not just selling food; they're selling *fast* food. In addition, many people want their food to be just as fast at home as it is in restaurants. In recent years, ready-to-eat preparations and microwave cuisines have been one of the most rapidly growing parts of the food industry.

Wage rates have a very important effect on the value of time. As wage rates increase, time becomes more valuable. In the 1940s, 1950s, and 1960s, wage rates rose for just about all American workers. Since then, wage rates have risen rapidly for those with a college education, but much less rapidly (if at all) for those who only have a high-school diploma. Still, overall, wage rates are higher than they used to be for large numbers of American workers. As a result, there are lots of people whose time is very valuable. Because of this, it's not surprising that an increasing number of business firms are focused on meeting the needs of customers who are in a hurry. You can get around the golf course more quickly if you use a golf cart than if you walk, and you can mow your lawn more quickly if you use a riding mower than if you use a push mower. For some people, time is valuable enough that they will pay extra for golf carts and riding mowers.

In this section, we have mentioned a few markets that are affected by the value of time. You can probably think of many more. In *Real Economics for Real People 7.3*, we consider another topic that has to do with consumer behavior: the value of saving a life.

Reality Check: Interim Review Question

IR7-6. Mr. A is a highly paid accountant, and Mr. B is a janitor. Each of them lives in Sacramento, and each needs to travel to Los Angeles. Which of the two is more likely to travel by air, and which is more likely to travel by bus? Why?

Real Economics for Real People 7.3: The Value of Saving a Life

We can think of any number of projects that would help to make life safer, by reducing the chance of injury or death. We could hire more police to patrol the streets and to enforce the speed limit. We could do more to clean up toxic waste. We could install more smoke detectors and fire alarms in homes and office buildings. However, each of these projects is costly. In order to know whether to undertake a particular project, we need to compare the costs with the benefits.

But how do we measure the benefits of saving a life? For some people, it's immoral even to ask the question. After all, how can we put a dollar value on a human life? The economist would answer that life is very precious indeed, but it isn't *infinitely* so. First of all, we know that people don't really *behave* as if life were infinitely valuable. It's safer to drive at moderate speeds, but lots of people drive very fast. This indicates that these drivers are willing to take some risks, in order to get to their destinations more quickly. In addition, some people are willing to work at jobs that are unhealthy, or even dangerous, if the wage rates are attractive enough.

If life were infinitely valuable, then *every* safety project should be undertaken, because *any* improvement in safety would yield an infinite benefit. But our resources are scarce, and we need to set priorities by choosing the most valuable safety projects and discarding the least valuable ones. Therefore, it's important to try to measure the value of saving a life.

Let's say that we could design a safety project that saves one life per year. If the project were to cost only $1, then you would probably agree that the project is a good one. If you agree, then you are saying that the value of saving one life per year is greater than $1. However, if the project were to cost $1,000,000,000,000 per year (that's $1 *trillion*), you would probably agree that society would actually be worse off if the project

---

were carried out. If you agree, then you are saying that the value of saving one life per year is less than $1 trillion.

Economists have attempted to estimate the dollar value of a life saved. One way to do this is to compare the wages of workers in dangerous jobs with the wages of workers in safe jobs. Some people are willing to work for a lower wage rate, in order to work at a safer job. In measuring the tradeoff between risk and wage rates, we are measuring the amount that workers are willing to pay for safety.

To get a meaningful estimate of the value of saving a life, we have to measure the relationship between wage rates and the risk of death, *while holding everything else constant*. The other things that should be held constant would include the education, age, and experience of workers, as well as other factors. Fortunately, modern statistical techniques allow us to control for these other factors. The estimates vary, but they tend to give us numbers in the ballpark of several million dollars per life saved. With an esti-

mate like this, we can judge which safety projects are worthwhile, and which are not.

Many safety projects have been shown to be very beneficial, in that their marginal benefits are greater than their marginal costs. For example, the steering-column protection equipment installed in cars has been estimated to cost only about $100,000 per life saved. Since the estimates of the value of saving a life are all much higher than $100,000, steering-column protection is a bargain. A variety of regulations to reduce fires in automobiles are also very effective at saving lives.

However, some safety projects have been estimated to save only a very few lives, at very high cost. For example, it has been estimated that the cost of regulations to reduce arsenic in the workplace is more than $90 million per life saved. Even if we assume that the value of a life saved is $10 million, the arsenic regulations are bad for society. If the marginal costs of a safety project are high enough, then society would be better off if the project were *not* undertaken.

HOUSEHOLD EXPENDITURE: WHERE DOES THE MONEY GO?

So far in this chapter, we have developed some ideas about consumer behavior, and we have applied those ideas to some interesting cases, such as the value of time and the value of saving a life. However, we haven't discussed the amounts of money that consumers actually spend on different goods and services. Table 7.3 shows the amounts that were spent by U.S. consumers on different commodities in 2014.

From looking at Table 7.3, you may get an idea of the immense size and diversity of the U.S. economy. First of all, in 2014, American

consumers spent about $11.866 *trillion* (that is, about $11,866 billion). Another thing to notice from Table 7.3 is how little is spent on items that are absolute necessities. In the U.S. economy of the 19th century, most expenditure was on the basics of food, clothing, and shelter. The same is true for the poorest countries today. However, in the United States in 2014, much less than half of the total was spent on food, clothing, housing, and household operation. Moreover, it's important to remember that even these categories include many items that

Table 7.3 Categories of Personal Consumption Expenditure in the United States, 2014

Category	Expenditure (in Billions of Dollars)	Percentage of Total Expenditure
Food and Beverages	**$1,510.3**	**12.7%**
Food and beverages for home consumption	886.5	7.5
Food in restaurants, hotels, bars, schools	623.8	5.3
Clothing and Footwear: Garments, Cleaning, Repair	**$385.7**	**3.3%**
Housing, Utilities, and Fuels	**$2,170.9**	**18.3%**
Housing	1,824.8	15.4
Household utilities and fuels	346.1	2.9
Furnishings, Household Equipment, and Maintenance	**$481.6**	**4.1%**
Health	**$2,446.9**	**20.6%**
Doctors and dentists	565.1	4.8
Hospital and nursing-home services	1,079.3	9.1
Pharmaceuticals	423.5	3.6
Transportation	**$1,167.5**	**9.8%**
New motor vehicles	265.5	2.2
Motor, vehicle fuel and oil	372.8	3.1
Motor-vehicle maintenance and repair	177.4	1.5
Communication	**$287.2**	**2.4%**
Telecommunication services	164.1	1.4
Internet access	96.0	0.8
Recreation	**$1,040.7**	**8.8%**
Computers, audio, and video	306.6	2.6
Magazines, newspapers, and books	107.6	0.9
Gambling	123.3	1.0
Pets	92.8	0.8
Education	**$277.0**	**2.3%**
Accommodation at Hotels, Motels, Clubs, Schools	**$109.2**	**0.9%**
Financial Services and Insurance	**$882.7**	**7.4%**
Other Goods and Services	**$799.3**	**6.7%**
Cosmetics, toiletries, personal-care services	247.6	2.1
Legal services	98.1	0.8
Accounting and business services	31.5	0.3
Foreign Travel and Other Expenditures Abroad	**$146.5**	**1.2%**
Nonprofit Institutions Serving Households	**$322.3**	**2.7%**
TOTAL	**$11,865.9**	**100.0%**

NOTE: Percentages of sub-categories may not add to percentages of categories, because of rounding and because some sub-categories are not included in this table. Category totals do not add to aggregate total, because aggregate total is net of expenditures in the United States by nonresidents.

Source: U.S. Department of Commerce, Bureau of Economic Analysis, National Income and Product Accounts, Table 2.5.5: http://222.bea.gov.

can't really be called necessities, such as restaurant meals, alcoholic beverages, designer clothing, luxury homes, and vacation homes.

The United States has more people than any other country except China and India. In addition, average incomes in the U.S. are among the highest in the world. As a result, Americans spend remarkable amounts of money. In 2014, Americans spent about $96 billion on Internet access, which is about the same as the value of *everything* that was produced in Sri Lanka or Cuba or the Dominican Republic in that year. In about half of the countries in the world, the value of *everything* produced in a year is less than the amount Americans spend on their pets.

In the last generation, medical care has been one of the fastest-growing parts of the economy. By 2014, medical care accounted for nearly $2.5 trillion, which is more than 20 percent of personal consumption expenditure. Other services have also grown very rapidly. For example, Americans spent $883 billion on financial services and insurance, which is about 7.4 percent of personal consumption expenditure. In addition, about $98 billion (or 0.8 percent of the total) were spent on legal services.

All of these expenditures were the result of the decisions of individual consumers. In this chapter, we have shown how utility maximization can be used to explain the behavior of consumers. The numbers shown in Table 7.3 give an overview of the millions of decisions that are made by consumers every day, in an effort to maximize their utility.

ECONOMICS AND YOU: RESOLVING THE PARADOX OF BASEBALL CARDS AND WATER

At the beginning of this chapter, we raised a paradox. Why do consumers pay so little for water, which is necessary for survival, and so much for some baseball cards and paintings? Actually, this is not a new dilemma. The Scottish economist Adam Smith wondered about it more than 200 years ago. There weren't any baseball cards in Smith's time, but there were diamonds. Smith was puzzled about why diamonds could be sold for prices that were so much higher than the price of water. This puzzle has come to be called the *Diamond-Water Paradox*.

We can resolve the paradox with the use of our ideas about marginal utility. It is true that we need water to survive. The marginal utility of the first cup of water that you consume in a given day is very great, because you might die if you don't have a little bit of water.

However, the marginal utility of the next cup is a little less, and the marginal utility of the third cup is even less than that.

Only a tiny fraction of the water we use is absolutely necessary for survival. We use water to keep our lawns green, and to keep our cars clean. We use water in swimming pools, and we use it to take showers. If all of these uses of water were eliminated, nobody would die of thirst. Even though the *total* utility of water is very great, the *marginal* utility is really quite small. Water is so plentiful that the marginal utility of the last gallon of water is tiny.

By contrast, rare coins, rare baseball cards, diamonds, and Picasso paintings are in short supply, and they have great *marginal* value, at least for some people. If diamonds were as plentiful as water, the price of a diamond would be much lower than it is today.

Chapter Summary

1. The marginal value for any variable is the value of one additional unit of the variable. A marginal value can also be defined as the change in the total value. A marginal value is the slope of the graph of a total value. A total value is equal to the sum of all of the marginal values.

2. Marginal utility is the maximum amount that a consumer is willing and able to pay (measured in dollars) to have one additional unit of some good. The Law of Diminishing Marginal Utility states that marginal utility will decrease, as more and more units of a good are consumed.

3. When marginal utility is defined in dollars, the consumer should buy additional units of a good, as long as marginal utility is equal to or greater than the price that must be paid for an additional unit. The consumer's equilibrium involves buying a good until its marginal utility is equal to its price.

4. If the price changes, the consumer equilibrium will change. If we change the price repeatedly, we see that the marginal-utility curve is the consumer's individual demand curve. Because of the Law of Diminishing Marginal Utility, the individual demand curve will slope downward as we move from left to right.

5. Except for the last unit consumed, the consumer's marginal utility will be greater than the price. Consumer surplus is the difference between the total number of dollars that the consumer is willing to pay and the total number of dollars actually paid. Graphically, consumer surplus is the area under the demand curve but above the price line.

6. When a price increases, consumers are harmed. When a price decreases, consumers are helped. The change in consumer surplus is our measure of the benefit to consumers from a price decrease, and the harm to consumers from a price increase.

7. The "Diamond-Water Paradox" refers to the fact that water commands a much lower price than diamonds, in spite of the fact that water is essential for life. This paradox is resolved when we understand that the *marginal* utility that most people get from water is small, even though the *total* utility is very great.

Key Terms

Rational

Utility

Marginal Utility

Total Utility

Law of Diminishing Marginal Utility

Consumer Decision Rule, or Optimal Purchase Rule

Consumer Equilibrium

Individual Demand Curve

Consumer Surplus

Diamond-Water Paradox

Questions and Problems

QP7-1. Explain the Law of Diminishing Marginal Utility. Can you think of any goods for which the Law might not hold?

QP7-2. Stu Incinerator is a basketball player. In the first game of the season, he scores 20 points. In the next games, he scores 24, 15, 19, and 26 points.

a. Construct a table showing Stu's marginal points for each game, and his total points for all games up to and including that game.
b. Graphically, what is the relationship between marginal points and total points?

QP7-3. Police officers have higher rates of death and injury on the job than do file clerks. *All else equal*, what effect do you expect this will have on the relative wage rates of police officers and file clerks?

QP7-4. Convenience stores, such as 7-Eleven and Stop 'n' Shop, typically allow consumers to make quick purchases. However, they usually charge higher prices than other stores charge. Explain why buyers would be willing to pay higher prices at convenience stores.

QP7-5. To answer this question, use the information from the chart below.

a. Assuming that the price of a movie ticket is $6, calculate Betsy's consumer surplus.
b. How does consumer surplus change if the price increases to $9?

Movie	Marginal Utility
1	$15
2	9
3	6
4	4
5	2
6	1

QP7-6. If you travel with an airline, you can get from Chicago to San Francisco in less than four hours. The airfare will probably be several hundred dollars, with the exact price depending on when you fly, and how far in advance you book your flight. You can also get from Chicago to San Francisco by bus. It will cost less money, but it will take several days. Explain who would be more likely to take the bus, and who would be more likely to fly.

QP7-7. The daily market demand curve for kazoos in Kokomo is given by $Q_d = 10 - P$, where Q_d is the quantity demanded and P is the price. The supply curve is perfectly horizontal, and is given by P = $1. This means that sellers will sell as many units as buyers want to buy, as long as the price is $1.

a. Substitute the expression for supply (P = $1) into the expression for demand, and solve for Q_d. This is the equilibrium quantity.
b. Calculate consumer surplus.

QP7-8. Assume that the demand curve from question (QP7-7) is unchanged. However, the government levies a tax on kazoos, such that the supply relationship is changed to P = $2.

a. Substitute the new expression for supply (P = $2) into the expression for demand, and solve for the new equilibrium quantity.
b. Calculate the consumer surplus that consumers will have under the new equilibrium.
c. How much consumer surplus is lost as a result of the tax?

Chapter 8

Production and Cost

ECONOMICS AND YOU: IF YOU'VE ALREADY PAID FOR A MEAL, DO YOU HAVE TO EAT IT?

Allison and Zachary go to Pat's Pasta Palace for spaghetti and meatballs every Wednesday night, because Wednesday is all-you-can-eat night. After they pay $10 at the door, Allison and Zachary can have as many helpings as they want.

Unfortunately, on this particular Wednesday, the chef is out sick. The spaghetti is overcooked, the sauce is watery, and the meatballs are hard and gritty, with a taste of sawdust. Zachary says "This food is horrible, but I guess I should pig out anyway, to get my money's worth." Allison asks him whether he's hungry. He says "Not really. I ate a big lunch." She says "I'm not really hungry, either. As for getting my money's worth, I kissed my ten dollars goodbye when I paid at the door. It doesn't make sense to eat this food unless I like it, and I don't."

If Allison and Zachary are to make the right decision, they will need to think carefully about the *true cost* of eating tonight's spaghetti at Pat's Pasta Palace. In this chapter, you will learn more about how to think about costs, in a variety of situations. You have already learned about the idea of opportunity cost, in Chapter 2 and Chapter 5. Here, we will focus

on costs in much greater detail. Before this chapter is over, you will have a framework for thinking about the dilemma facing Allison and Zachary at Pat's Pasta Palace, and you will also learn a great deal more. In fact, most of this chapter is concerned with the costs that business firms have to pay when they produce goods and services. These cost concepts are important, in and of themselves. In addition, they provide the foundation for our understanding of how firms make their production decisions. We will take a close look at the firm's decision-making processes in Chapters 9, 10, and 11.

Some students find the material in this chapter to be harder than most other parts of a course in microeconomics. If this stuff is difficult for you, here is a word of advice: The best strategy is to take it one step at a time. Don't try to learn the entire chapter in one big gulp. Instead, concentrate on one concept at a time, and don't move on to the next concept until you have mastered the current one. It's true that this chapter has a lot of pieces. However, if you take the pieces one at a time, you can learn them all.

THE RELATIONSHIPS AMONG MARGINAL, AVERAGE, AND TOTAL QUANTITIES

We introduced marginal and total relationships in Chapter 7, by looking at the distances traveled on a trip from Maine to Texas. In that example, the marginal distance is the number of additional miles traveled in one additional day. The total distance is the total number of miles traveled, on *all* of the days up to some point in the journey. Thus, we can calculate the total distance by adding the marginal distances. Graphically, the marginal distance is the slope of the total-distance curve. The marginal distances and total distances for the trip from Maine to Texas are shown in Table 8.1, which is adapted from Table 7.1.

Now that we have information on marginal distance and total distance, our next step is to define the *average* distance. The average distance is the average number of miles traveled *per day*, for a group of days. *The average distance per day is defined as the total distance divided by the number of days traveled.* (The word "per" refers to dividing one quantity by another. Thus, for example, miles per gallon is calculated by dividing the number of miles traveled by the number of gallons that were burned in the process.) Table 8.1 shows that, at the end of the first day of the journey, the total distance is 400 miles. Therefore, the average

distance per day at the end of the first day is (400 miles) / (1 day) = 400 miles per day. When we include the second day of travel, the total distance increases to 1000 miles, while the number of days increases to two. Therefore, the average distance increases to (1000 miles) / (2 days) = 500 miles per day.

When we include the third day, the average distance is (1500 miles) / (3 days) = 500 miles per day. Finally, when we include the fourth day, the average distance is (1800 miles) / (4 days) = 450 miles per day. The average distance at the end of each day in the trip is shown in the fourth column of Table 8.1.

Later in this chapter, and in the chapters to come, we will look at several other concepts involving averages, such as average cost and average revenue. Every one of these average concepts is defined in a way that is similar to the definition of average distance that we have just used. In each case, the average is calculated by dividing a total quantity by the number of units that have occurred so far. For example, average revenue is the firm's sales revenue per unit sold. To calculate average revenue for the business firm, we start with the total revenue for all units sold, and divide by the number of units sold. If the firm's total

Table 8.1 Marginal, Total, and Average Distances Traveled in a Journey from Maine to Texas

Day	Marginal Distance = Additional Mileage on This Day	Total Distance = Total Mileage for All Days So Far	Average Distance = Total Distance / Number of Days	Comment
1	400	400	400	
2	600	1000	500	Marginal > Average => Average increases
3	500	1500	500	Marginal = Average => Average is unchanged
4	300	1800	450	Marginal < Average => Average decreases

revenue is $10 million, and if the firm sells one million units, then average revenue is ($10 million)/(1 million units) = $10 per unit.

The Relationship between Marginal and Average Quantities

Let's look at some of the relationships between marginal distances and average distances, beginning with the information in the first row of Table 8.1. On the first day of the trip, the marginal distance traveled is 400 miles, and the average distance is also 400 miles. If we only consider the first day of the trip, the average distance traveled must be equal to the marginal distance traveled.

Now, let's compare the first and second lines of Table 8.1. On the second day, the marginal distance traveled is 600 miles. This is *more* than the average distance at the end of the first day, which was only 400 miles. As a result, there is an *increase* in the average distance traveled per day, from 400 miles per day to 500 miles per day. When the marginal distance is greater than the average distance from the earlier days, the average distance must increase.

Next, compare the second and third rows of Table 8.1. On the third day of the trip, the marginal distance traveled is 500 miles. This is *exactly equal* to the average distance at the end of the previous day. As a result, the average distance *stays the same*. Since the average distance per day was already 500 miles per day, and the distance traveled on the third day was also 500 miles per day, the average had to remain unchanged. When the marginal distance is equal to the average distance from the earlier days, the average distance stays the same.

Finally, compare the third and fourth rows of Table 8.1. At the end of the third day, the average distance traveled was 500 miles per day, while the marginal distance for the fourth day is only 300 miles. Therefore, the marginal distance for the fourth day is *less* than the average distance for the previous three days. As a result, the average distance *decreases*, from 500 miles per day to 450 miles per day. When the marginal distance is less than the average distance from the earlier days, the average distance must decrease.

These relationships aren't just the result of coincidence. In fact, we will see these same relationships again and again:

- *When the marginal is <u>more</u> than the average for the preceding units, the average will <u>increase</u>.*

- *When the marginal is <u>equal</u> to the average for the preceding units, the average will <u>stay the same</u>.*

- *When the marginal is <u>less</u> than the average for the preceding units, the average will <u>decrease</u>.*

Now, to reinforce your understanding, let's consider another example. We measure the heights of five people in a room. We then add the heights of the five people, and divide by five. This gives us the average height for these five people. Let's say that this average is 5 feet, 8 inches. Next, we bring a sixth person into the room. At this point, this sixth person can be considered the *marginal* person.

If the marginal person is 6 feet, 2 inches tall, what will happen to the average height? The marginal person is *taller* than average, so the average height would *increase*. (In fact, the average height would increase to 5 feet, 9 inches.) On the other hand, if the sixth person is exactly 5 feet, 8 inches tall, then the marginal person is *just as tall* as the average. In this case, the average height would *stay the same*. Finally, what if the sixth person is only 5 feet, 2 inches tall? In this case, the marginal person is *shorter* than average, so the average height would *decrease*. (In fact, the average height would drop to 5 feet, 7 inches.)

In summary: When marginal exceeds average, the average rises. When marginal is equal to average, the average is unchanged. When marginal is less than average, the average falls. These relationships can also be written as follows:

Marginal > Average => Average ↑

**Marginal = Average => Average is
unchanged**

Marginal < Average => Average ↓

These relationships will keep coming up. Later in this chapter, we will revisit these relationships when we look at marginal cost and average cost. In later chapters, we will see the same relationships between marginal revenue and average revenue.

A Graph of Marginal and Average Distance

Figure 8.1 is a graph of the information in Table 8.1, showing the marginal and average distances from our example of a journey from Maine to Texas. This figure illustrates the points we were just making. On the second day of the trip, the marginal distance traveled is greater than the average distance for the previous day, and the average-distance curve is pulled upward. In other words, when we go from Day 1 to Day 2 on the horizontal axis of Figure 8.1, the value on the average-distance curve increases on the vertical axis. On the third day, the marginal distance is equal to the average distance, and the average distance remains the same. Therefore, the graph of average distance is a flat line as we move from Day 2 to Day 3. Finally, on the fourth day, the marginal distance is less than the average distance, and the average-distance curve is pulled downward: The graph of the average-distance curve slopes downward as we move from Day 3 to Day 4.

Reality Check:
Interim Review Questions

IR8-1. A basketball team is averaging 68 points per game. How will this average be changed if the team scores 75 points in its next game? (In other words, if the team scores 75 points in its next game, will the

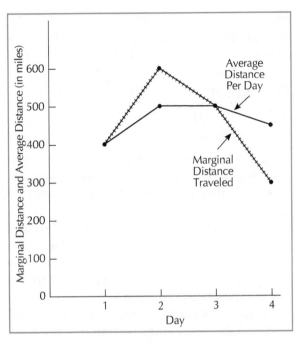

Figure 8.1 Marginal and Average Distances on a Trip from Maine to Texas

The marginal distance traveled on the first day of the journey is 400 miles. Therefore, at the end of the first day, the average distance is also 400 miles. On the second day, the marginal distance is 600 miles. Because the marginal distance is larger than the average distance, the average distance increases. At the end of the second day, the average distance is 500 miles. The marginal distance on the third day is 500 miles, which is exactly equal to the average distance from the previous days. Therefore, the average distance stays the same. On the final day, the marginal distance of 300 miles is less than the average distance. Therefore, the average distance decreases.

average increase, or decrease, or stay the same?) What if instead the team scores 68 points in its next game? What if instead the team scores only 59 points in its next game?

IR8-2. Hot Stuff Corporation has produced 10,000 smoke detectors so far this year. On average, the cost of production has been $20 per detector. If the marginal cost of producing the 10,001st smoke detector were $22, would the average cost go up, or go down, or stay the same? What if the marginal cost of the 10,001st smoke detector were $20? What if it were $19?

PRODUCTION: THE RELATIONSHIP BETWEEN INPUTS AND OUTPUTS

In Chapter 7, we took a close look at the decisions of consumers. We found that consumers make their choices by comparing the price of a good with the marginal utility of consuming the good. In other words, consumers compare the marginal benefit of consuming (which is their marginal utility) with the marginal cost of consuming (which is the price of the good).

Firms also compare marginal benefits and marginal costs. The firm's marginal benefits are the additional revenues it gets from selling more of its product. These marginal benefits are called "marginal revenues." The firm's marginal costs are the additional costs of producing more of its product. These marginal costs are just called "marginal costs." We will get to the revenue side of the picture in Chapter 9. In this chapter, we focus on costs.

If a business firm wants to have something to sell, it must produce some good or service. The goods and services that the firm produces are called *outputs*. To produce these outputs, the firm must use *inputs*. For example, in the case of a barber shop, the outputs are haircuts. The inputs are the barbers, the shop, the scissors and combs, electricity for the lights and electric trimmers, and so on.

Variable Inputs and Fixed Inputs

We separate inputs into two broad categories—variable inputs and fixed inputs. *Variable inputs* are inputs whose quantity can be varied during the time period under consideration. *Fixed inputs* are those for which quantity *cannot* be changed during the time period under consideration. An example will help us to understand these definitions.

Let's consider a small Midwestern firm that makes apple cider. The firm is called Cider Space. If the firm wants to hire more workers, it will usually take only a few days or a few weeks to find new workers who are willing to work in the cider mill. If we are thinking about the firm's production choices over the next year, then labor will be considered a *variable* input, because one year is the time period under consideration, and the amount of labor can be changed in less than one year. If we're thinking about the firm's production choices over the next year, *any* input that can be altered in less than one year is a variable input.

Labor is certainly an important input in the production of cider at Cider Space. Another important input is the mill itself, which consists of a building with an office, machinery for shredding and squeezing apples, and other equipment. Cider Space has a two-year lease on the mill. Therefore, if we are considering the firm's production choices over the next year, the cider mill itself would be considered a *fixed* input. If we're thinking about the firm's production choices over the next year, *any* input that can't be altered in less than one year is a fixed input.

The distinction between variable inputs and fixed inputs will depend on the length of time that we are thinking about. If we consider the production choices for a firm like Cider Space over the next *ten* years, then every input would be considered a variable input.

In the example that we have just given, labor was considered a variable input. In many cases, workers and materials are variable inputs. The number of workers and the amount of materials can usually be changed in a fairly short period of time. However, workers and materials aren't variable inputs in every case. For example, some workers (such as professional athletes) are hired according to long-term contracts. If we are considering a time horizon of one year, and if a professional baseball player has three more years remaining on his contract, he would *not* be considered a variable input.

Buildings and capital equipment are often fixed inputs. This is because, in many cases, buildings and capital equipment cannot easily be varied in a short period of time. However, buildings and capital equipment aren't fixed inputs in every case. For example, it's sometimes possible to rent a bulldozer, or some other piece of heavy machinery, for as little as half a day. In this case, the bulldozer would be considered a variable input, as long as we are thinking of the firm's production choices over a period of more than half a day.

The Short Run and The Long Run

In the discussion of variable inputs and fixed inputs, the "time period under consideration" played an important role. The distinction between the short run and the long run is related to the time period under consideration. The *short run* is defined as a period of time over which at least one input is fixed. In the *long run*, all inputs are variable.

The length of time that is necessary to take us to the long run will vary from one production process to the next. In heavy industries, such as chemicals, steel, and automobiles, it may take years to design and construct a new factory. In these industries, the long run might be two years, five years, or even ten years. For the child operating a lemonade stand, the long run may be only a few minutes. For many businesses, the long run will be between these extremes, at a few months or a year.

For most of this chapter, we will study production and cost in the short run. Toward the end of the chapter, we'll consider the long run, in which *all* inputs are variable.

THE SHORT-RUN COSTS OF PRODUCTION

So far, we've talked about the relationship between inputs and outputs. That's fine, as far as it goes. But a business firm like Cider Space is interested in more than the number of gallons of cider it can produce. The firm is ultimately interested in the number of *dollars* that it must spend for its inputs. In this section, we show how the firm can begin with information on the productivity of its inputs, and end up with information on the dollar amount of its costs.

Total Fixed Cost and Average Fixed Cost

Fixed costs are the costs of fixed inputs. *Total fixed cost* is the total of all of the payments to fixed inputs. By definition, fixed costs are fixed. They are unchanging. Fixed costs are incurred regardless of the level of output. Thus when the quantity of output changes, total fixed cost (TFC) does not change. Let's say that

the total fixed cost for Cider Space is $100 per day. That means that TFC is $100 if the quantity of output is zero, and $100 if the quantity of output is one gallon, and $100 if the quantity of output is 100 gallons, and so on.

Total fixed cost is shown in the middle column of Table 8.2. It's about as simple as it can be: Every entry in the middle column of Table 8.2 is the same. The graph of total fixed cost is simply a horizontal line, as shown in Panel (a) of Figure 8.2.

Average fixed cost (AFC), or fixed cost per unit, is calculated by dividing total fixed cost by the quantity of output. Average fixed cost is given by

$$AFC = TFC / Q,$$

where Q is the quantity of output. If we take a constant (like TFC) and divide it by a number that keeps increasing (like Q), we get a ratio that keeps decreasing. For example, if Cider Space were to produce only one gallon

Table 8.2 Total Fixed Cost and Average Fixed Cost for Cider Space

Total Product = Quantity of Output (Q) (in gallons per day)	Total Fixed Cost (TFC, in dollars)	Average Fixed Cost (AFC, in dollars per gallon)
0	$100	—
1	$100	$100.00
2	$100	$ 50.00
3	$100	$ 33.33
4	$100	$ 25.00
5	$100	$ 20.00
6	$100	$ 16.67
7	$100	$ 14.29
8	$100	$ 12.50
9	$100	$ 11.11
10	$100	$ 10.00
.	.	.
.	.	.
20	$100	$ 5.00
30	$100	$ 3.33
40	$100	$ 2.50
50	$100	$ 2.00
60	$100	$ 1.67
70	$100	$ 1.43
80	$100	$ 1.25
90	$100	$ 1.11
100	$100	$ 1.00
.	.	.
.	.	.
200	$100	$ 0.50
300	$100	$ 0.33
400	$100	$ 0.25
500	$100	$ 0.20
600	$100	$ 0.17
700	$100	$ 0.14
800	$100	$ 0.13
900	$100	$ 0.11
1000	$100	$ 0.10

of apple cider per day, average fixed cost would be ($100/1 gallon) = $100 per gallon. If production were to increase to two gallons per day, AFC would be ($100/2 gallons) = $50 per gallon.

The right-hand column of Table 8.2 shows the values of AFC, for a wide range of values of the quantity of output. Average fixed cost decreases rapidly, but it never quite gets to zero. (In other words, AFC approaches zero asymptotically.)

In Table 8.2, when Q = 0, we have a value of $100 for TFC, but we do not include a value for AFC. That's because, if we were to try to calculate average fixed cost when Q = 0, we would be dividing by zero. Thus it doesn't make any sense to try to define AFC until we have at least one unit.

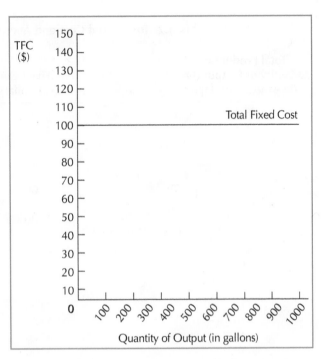

Figure 8.2 Panel (a)
Total Fixed Cost for Cider Space (in dollars)

Fixed costs do not change when the quantity of output changes. Therefore, the graph of total fixed cost (TFC) is a horizontal line.

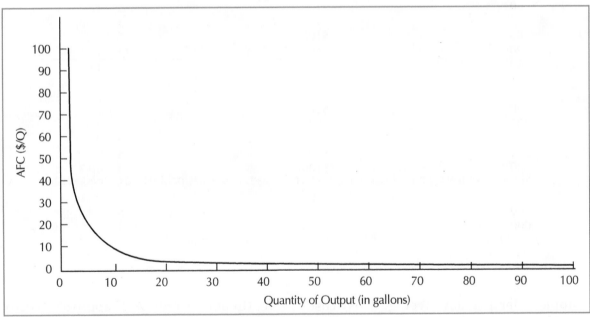

Figure 8.2 Panel (b)
Average Fixed Costs for Cider Space (in dollars per gallon)

Average fixed cost (AFC), or fixed cost per unit, is equal to total fixed cost divided by the quantity of output. When we divide total fixed cost (which is constant) by quantity, the result gets smaller when quantity gets larger. Thus when we graph the relationship between AFC and the quantity of output, we have a line that slopes downward as we move from left to right. As the quantity of output becomes large, AFC approaches zero.

Panel (b) of Figure 8.2 shows average fixed cost for this example. On the horizontal axis of Panel (b), we only consider quantities up to 100 gallons. We could go farther, but it is already clear that average fixed cost is getting close to zero.

Total Variable Cost, Average Variable Cost, and Marginal Cost

In Table 8.2, we saw the *fixed* costs for Cider Space. Table 8.3 shows the *variable* costs. *Variable costs* are the costs of the variable inputs. In our example, the only fixed cost for Cider Space is the amount that has to be spent on the lease for the cider mill. The variable costs include the wages paid to the workers who operate the machinery, as well as the cost of the electricity that is necessary to keep the mill running, and the cost of the apples themselves. *Total variable cost* is the total of all of the payments to variable inputs.

If the firm does not produce any output, it isn't necessary to incur any variable costs. Thus in the first row of Table 8.3, total variable cost (TVC) takes on a value of zero.

Whereas total fixed cost does not change when the quantity of output changes, total variable cost *does* change. In order to produce more output, it is always necessary to incur additional variable costs. Thus as we move down the column, TVC is always increasing.

The total variable cost of the first 100 gallons of cider is $110. Then, when output increases by another 100 gallons, to a total of 200 gallons, TVC increases to $200. For the first 100 gallons, TVC increased by $110, but for the second 100 gallons, TVC only increased by $(200 − 110) = $90. Thus over this range of output, TVC is increasing at a *decreasing* rate. However, after that, TVC increases at an *increasing* rate. This can be seen graphically in Panel (a) of Figure 8.3. At first, the TVC curve increases at a decreasing rate (i.e., it gets less steep as we move from left to right). However, for most of the graph, the TVC curve is increasing at an increasing rate (i.e., it gets steeper as we move from left to right).

Marginal Cost. Total variable cost is a very useful concept, but marginal cost is the most important cost concept of all. *Marginal cost* is

Table 8.3 Total Variable Cost, Average Variable Cost, and Marginal Cost for Cider Space

Total Product = Quantity of Output (Q) (in gallons per day)	Total Variable Cost (TVC, in dollars)	Average Variable Cost (AVC, in dollars per gallon)	Marginal Cost (MC, in dollars per gallon)
0	$ 0	—	—
100	$ 110	$1.10	$1.10
200	$ 200	$1.00	$0.90
300	$ 300	$1.00	$1.00
400	$ 420	$1.05	$1.20
500	$ 550	$1.10	$1.30
600	$ 700	$1.17	$1.50
700	$ 880	$1.26	$1.80
800	$1080	$1.35	$2.00
900	$1300	$1.44	$2.20
1000	$1550	$1.55	$2.50

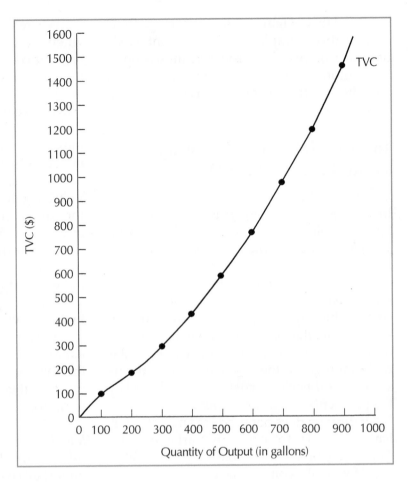

Figure 8.3 Panel (a) Total Variable Cost for Cider Space (in dollars)

Total variable cost (TVC) must increase whenever there is an increase in the quantity of output. Thus the TVC curve must always slope upward as we move from left to right. In the particular case shown here, at low quantities, TVC increases at a decreasing rate. However, at larger quantities, TVC increases at an increasing rate.

the additional cost that is necessary to produce one additional unit of output. It is defined as

Marginal Cost =

$$\frac{\text{Change in Total Variable Cost}}{\text{Change in Quantity of Output}} = \frac{\Delta TVC}{\Delta Q}$$

Looking at the first two rows of Table 8.3, we see that when the quantity of output increases from zero to 100 gallons, total variable cost increases from zero to $110. Thus the change in total variable cost, ΔTVC, is $(110 – 0) = $110, and the change in output, ΔQ, is (100 – 0) = 100. If we divide ΔTVC by ΔQ, we see that the marginal cost of the first 100 gallons of cider is $110/100 = $1.10 per additional gallon.

If we compare the second and third rows of Table 8.3, and follow the same procedures, we

see that ΔTVC is $(200 – 110) = $90, and ΔQ is (200 – 100) = 100. If we once again divide ΔTVC by ΔQ, we see that the marginal cost of the next 100 gallons of cider is $90/100 = $0.90 per additional gallon. Following the same method for the rest of Table 8.3, we see that marginal cost begins to increase when output is increased from 200 gallons to 300 gallons. After that, marginal cost continues to increase, eventually reaching $2.50 per additional gallon.

In Panel (a) of Figure 8.3, total variable cost is on the vertical axis, and the quantity of output is on the horizontal axis. Remember that the slope of a line is the change in the value of the variable on the vertical axis, divided by the change in the value of the variable on the horizontal axis. Thus *marginal cost is the slope of the total variable cost curve!*

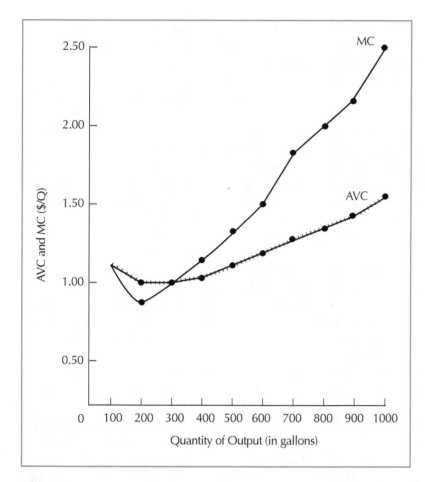

**Figure 8.3 Panel (b)
Average Variable Cost and
Marginal Cost for Cider Space
(in dollars per gallon)**

In the case of Cider Space, the TVC curve begins by increasing at a decreasing rate. However, at larger quantities, the TVC curve increases at an increasing rate. Since marginal cost (MC) is the slope of the TVC curve, this means that the MC curve slopes downward before sloping upward. When MC is less than average variable cost (AVC), AVC will decrease. When MC is equal to AVC, AVC will stay the same. When MC is greater than AVC, AVC will increase. Thus the AVC curve reaches its minimum point at the quantity at which MC = AVC.

In Table 8.3 and in Panel (a) of Figure 8.3, we saw that TVC increased at a decreasing rate at relatively low quantities of output, and then increased at an increasing rate at higher quantities. Since marginal cost is the slope of the TVC curve, it follows that marginal cost is decreasing at first, and then increasing. This can be seen in Panel (b) of Figure 8.3. At first, the MC curve slopes downward as we move from left to right across the diagram. Soon, however, the MC curve begins to slope upward, and it continues to slope upward as the quantity of output grows higher and higher.

Average Variable Cost. We have now taken a look at total variable cost and marginal cost. There is one more cost concept that has to do with variable costs, and that is average variable cost.

Earlier, we saw that average fixed cost is equal to total fixed cost divided by the number of units of output. The definition of average variable cost (AVC) is very similar. *Average variable cost*, or variable cost per unit, is equal to total variable cost divided by the number of units of output. Thus average variable cost is given by

AVC = TVC / Q.

In Chapter 7, we learned about some relationships between marginal values and average values. When marginal is greater than average, average will increase. When marginal is less than average, average will fall. When marginal is equal to average, average will stay the same. These relationships of marginal and average will hold for marginal *anything* and average *anything*. Thus these relationships also hold for marginal cost and average variable cost.

In the second row of Table 8.3, we see that MC and AVC are both equal to $1.10 for the first 100 gallons of cider. For the next 100 gallons, marginal cost is only $0.90. Thus marginal cost is less than the average variable cost of the previous units. Based on what we know about the relationships between marginal values and average values, we expect that average variable cost will fall, and that is exactly what happens: For the second 100 gallons of cider, AVC decreases from $1.10 per gallon to $1.00 per gallon.

The marginal cost of the third 100 gallons of cider is $1.00. This is the same as the average variable cost of the previous units. Thus we expect that AVC will stay the same, and indeed it does! For the third 100 gallons of cider, average variable cost stays unchanged at $1.00 per gallon. Thus *AVC is minimized at the quantity at which AVC is equal to MC.*

Beginning with the fourth 100 gallons of cider, and continuing through the rest of Table 8.3, marginal cost is greater than average variable cost. As a result, average variable cost is pulled upward.

Why Would the Variable Cost Curves Be Shaped Like This? Every production process has its own unique characteristics. However, many processes have variable cost curves that look approximately like the ones we have seen in Figures 8.2 and 8.3. At a low level of output, the cider mill would only have one worker. He or she would have to run back and forth from one task to another. This would not be very efficient.

At a somewhat higher level of output, Cider Space might hire a second worker. The two workers would be able to divide the tasks in a way that would increase efficiency. If that occurs, marginal cost would fall, which means

that the total-cost curve would increase at a decreasing rate, as we have seen in Figures 8.2 and 8.3.

Eventually, however, all production processes will begin to bump up against the constraint imposed by the presence of a fixed input. In the case of Cider Space, the fixed input is the cider mill itself. The mill has only one machine, and it has only a limited amount of floor space. If we add more and more people, the workers will begin to bump into each other, and it will become increasingly difficult to coordinate them. Tempers will flare. Fistfights will erupt. If we add more and more apples, the machinery will need to be cleaned more often, and it may break down. These inefficiencies mean that marginal cost will increase, which is the same as saying that the total-variable-cost curve will get steeper.

The Law of Diminishing Marginal Product. Lots of production processes have the character that we have just seen. For example, consider the productivity of fertilizer in a cotton field. To focus on the productivity of fertilizer, we hold constant the size of the field, the quality of the soil, the climate, and so on. As we add a small amount of fertilizer, the field will become more productive. However, as we add more and more fertilizer to the same plot of ground, the additional increases in output that we can squeeze out of the field will get smaller and smaller. Eventually, if we were to add more and more fertilizer, we could burn the soil so much that output would decrease.

This happens in so many cases that economists refer to the "Law" of Diminishing Marginal Product. The *Law of Diminishing Marginal Product* states that, if we increase variable inputs (while holding the fixed inputs constant), the additional output that we can get from the variable inputs will decrease, which means that marginal cost will increase. The Law of Diminishing Marginal Product is sometimes also called the Law of Diminishing Marginal Returns, or the Law of Diminishing Returns.

Total Cost and Average Total Cost

We showed total *fixed* cost in Table 8.2 and Figure 8.2(a). We showed total *variable* cost in Table 8.3 and Figure 8.3(a). Now it's time to put them together. **Total cost** (TC) is the sum of total fixed cost and total variable cost:

TC = TFC + TVC

Table 8.4 combines some of the information from Tables 8.2 and 8.3, so that we can see TFC, TVC, and TC side by side. Since TC is the sum of TFC and TVC, it has to be true that the *change* in TC is the sum of the *changes* in TFC and TVC:

ΔTC = ΔTFC + ΔTVC

However, we have already seen that total fixed cost does not change, which means that ΔTFC is equal to zero. It follows that

ΔTC = ΔTVC.

In other words, since TFC does not change as the quantity of output changes, TVC is the only thing that will lead to changes in TC. This means that when we draw TVC and TC on the same graph, the two curves are parallel. This is shown in Figure 8.4.

Earlier, we saw that marginal cost is the change in total variable cost, divided by the change in the quantity of output. But now we have seen that the change in total variable cost is exactly equal to the change in total cost. Thus we can also say that marginal cost is the change in total cost, divided by the change in the quantity of output:

$$\text{Marginal Cost} = \frac{\Delta \text{TVC}}{\Delta Q} = \frac{\Delta \text{TC}}{\Delta Q}$$

Average Total Cost. We have seen that average *fixed* cost is equal to total fixed cost divided by the quantity of output. We have also seen that average *variable* cost is equal to total variable cost divided by the quantity of output. Average total cost is calculated in exactly the same way: **Average total cost** (ATC) is equal to total cost divided by the quantity of output:

ATC = TC / Q

It turns out that there is also another way to calculate ATC. We have seen that TC = TFC + TVC. If we divide both sides of this equation by the quantity of output, we find that TC/Q = TFC/Q + TVC/Q, which is another way of saying that average total cost is the

Table 8.4 Total Fixed Cost, Total Variable Cost, and Total Cost for Cider Space

Total Product = Quantity of Output (Q) (in gallons per day)	Total Fixed Cost (TFC, in dollars)	Total Variable Cost (TVC, in dollars)	Total Cost (TC, in dollars)
0	$100	$ 0	$ 100
100	$100	$ 110	$ 210
200	$100	$ 200	$ 300
300	$100	$ 300	$ 400
400	$100	$ 420	$ 520
500	$100	$ 550	$ 650
600	$100	$ 700	$ 800
700	$100	$ 880	$ 980
800	$100	$1080	$1180
900	$100	$1300	$1400
1000	$100	$1550	$1650

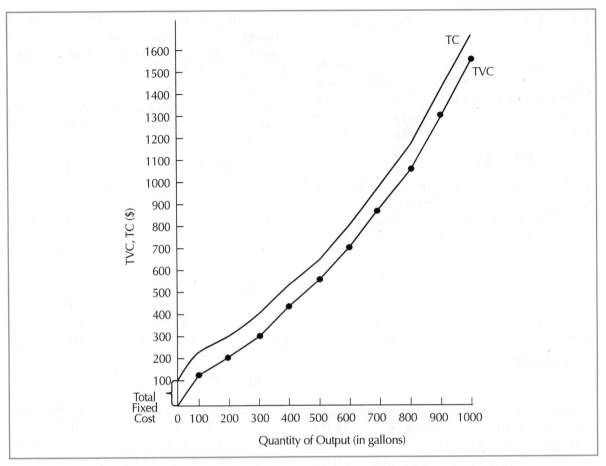

Figure 8.4 Total Variable Cost and Total Cost for Cider Space (in dollars)

Total cost (TC) is equal to total fixed cost (TFC) plus total variable cost (TVC). Since TFC is a constant, the vertical distance between the TVC curve and the TC curve is always the same. In other words, the TC curve is parallel to the TVC curve.

sum of average fixed cost and average variable cost:

ATC = AFC + AVC

These two ways of thinking about average total cost are both equally good. We can get ATC by dividing total cost by the quantity of output, or we can get ATC by adding AFC and AVC together. If we do the math correctly, we will get the same answer, either way.

We now have enough information to combine marginal cost and average total cost. We have already seen average fixed cost in Table 8.2, and we have already seen average variable cost

in Table 8.3. We put them together in Table 8.5. Table 8.5 shows AFC and AVC side by side. The next column is ATC. Looking at the numbers in these columns, we can see that ATC is indeed the sum of AFC and AVC (except for small differences due to rounding).

Earlier, we saw that average *variable* cost reaches its minimum value at the quantity at which AVC = MC. In Table 8.5, we see that the same is true for the relationship between average *total* cost and marginal cost: ATC reaches its minimum value at the quantity at which ATC = MC.

A few paragraphs ago, we saw that ATC = AFC + AVC. If we subtract AVC from both sides

Table 8.5 Average Costs and Marginal Cost for Cider Space

Total Product = Quantity of Output (Q) (in gallons)	Average Fixed Cost (AFC, in $ per gallon)	Average Variable Cost (AVC, in $ per gallon)	Average Total Cost (ATC, in $ per gallon)	Marginal Cost (MC, in $ per gallon)
0	—	—	—	—
100	$1.00	$1.10	$2.10	$1.10
200	$0.50	$1.00	$1.50	$0.90
300	$0.33	$1.00	$1.33	$1.00
400	$0.25	$1.05	$1.30	$1.20
500	$0.20	$1.10	$1.30	$1.30
600	$0.17	$1.17	$1.33	$1.50
700	$0.14	$1.26	$1.40	$1.80
800	$0.13	$1.35	$1.48	$2.00
900	$0.11	$1.44	$1.55	$2.20
1000	$0.10	$1.55	$1.65	$2.50

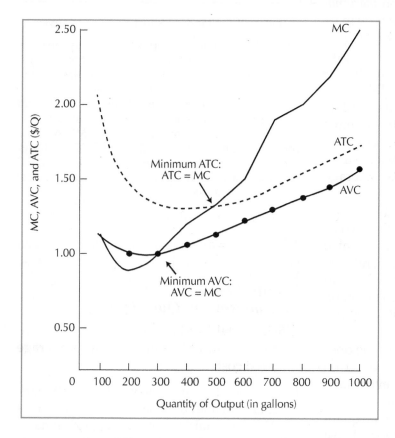

Figure 8.5 Marginal Cost, Average Variable Cost, and Average Total Cost for Cider Space (in dollars per gallon)

Average total cost (ATC) is equal to average fixed cost (AFC) plus average variable cost (AVC): ATC = AFC + AVC. If we subtract AVC from both sides of this equation, we see that AFC = ATC − AVC. Thus the vertical distance between the ATC curve and the AVC curve is AFC. Since AFC is always decreasing as we move to a larger quantity, the vertical distance between the ATC curve and the AVC curve gets smaller as we move from left to right. The AVC curve reaches its minimum point at the quantity at which MC = AVC, and the ATC curve reaches its minimum point at the quantity at which MC = ATC.

of this equation, we have ATC − AVC = AFC. Thus the difference between average total cost and average variable cost is average fixed cost. This can be seen in Figure 8.5, which is a graph of the information in Table 8.5. Since ATC − AVC = AFC, the vertical distance between the ATC curve and the AVC curve is average fixed cost.

At a relatively low level of output, the vertical distance between ATC and AVC is relatively large, because AFC is relatively large. However, as the quantity of output increases, AFC gets smaller and smaller. As a result, the vertical distance between the ATC curve and the AVC curve gets smaller and smaller, as we move from left to right across Figure 8.5.

When a business firm is deciding how much to produce, it will continually ask: "If we produce one more unit, can we increase our profit?" If the answer is "no" then the firm will ask: "If we produce one *less* unit, would that increase our profit?" By thinking in this way, the firm will find the level of output at which profit is maximized. Therefore, the firm will always want to concentrate on *marginal* costs and *marginal* revenues. This is why marginal costs are the most important of all.

In the most recent few pages, we have presented a large number of terms and definitions. These are summarized in Table 8.6. Until now, almost all of our discussion has been in terms of a specific example. We have emphasized a specific case, in an effort to show that the cost curves are not just abstract ideas. The curves for marginal cost, average variable cost, and average total cost are representations of very real ideas, and it is possible to calculate the real values of these costs for real business firms. However, we also want to make clear that these are general concepts. The concepts can be applied far beyond the particular example given here. Therefore, Figure 8.6 shows a set of "standard" short-run cost curves.

These curves are not identical to the ones for Cider Space, but they share some common features. The marginal-cost curve eventually slopes upward. The average-variable-cost curve reaches its minimum point at the quantity where AVC = MC. The average-total-cost curve reaches its minimum point at the quantity where ATC = MC. Finally, the vertical distance between ATC and AVC is shrinking as quantity increases. This is because the

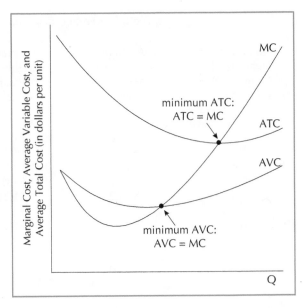

Figure 8.6 Standard Short-Run Cost Curves

It is unlikely that any two firms have exactly the same cost curves. However, many firms have short-run cost curves that look somewhat like these. Notice that the minimum point of the average-variable-cost curve (the AVC curve) is at the quantity where AVC = MC, and the minimum point of the average-total-cost curve (the ATC curve) is at the quantity where ATC = MC. Also, the vertical distance between ATC and AVC is always decreasing. This is because the difference between ATC and AVC is average fixed cost, and average fixed cost is always decreasing.

ATC – AVC = average fixed cost (AFC), which is decreasing as the level of output increases.

Reality Check: Interim Review Questions

IR8-3. If total fixed cost is $10 and the quantity of output is 5 units, what is average fixed cost?

IR8-4. When the quantity of output is 10 units, total variable cost is $100. When quantity is 11 units, total variable cost is $105. What is the marginal cost of the 11th unit of output?

IR8-5. When the quantity of output is zero, total cost is $10,000. What is total fixed cost?

Table 8.6 Summary of Terms and Definitions on Production and Cost

Term	Abbreviation (if any)	Definition	Equation (if any)
Variable input		An input whose quantity can be varied during the time period under consideration.	
Fixed input		An input whose quantity *cannot* be varied during the time period under consideration.	
Short Run		Period of time during which at least one input is fixed.	
Long Run		Period of time during which all inputs are variable.	
Total Variable Cost	TVC	Total spending by the firm for variable inputs.	
Total Fixed Cost	TFC	Total spending by the firm for fixed inputs. TFC does not change as output changes.	
Total Cost	TC	Total spending by the firm for both fixed and variable inputs.	$TC = TFC + TVC$
Average Variable Cost	AVC	Total variable cost per unit of output (equals total variable cost divided by the number of units of output).	$AVC = TVC / Q$
Average Fixed Cost	AFC	Total fixed cost per unit of output (equals total fixed cost divided by the number of units of output).	$AFC = TFC / Q$
Average Total Cost	ATC	Total cost per unit of output. Also, sum of average fixed cost and average variable cost.	$ATC = TC / Q$ and $ATC = AVC + AFC$
Marginal Cost	MC	Change in total cost as a result of producing one additional unit of output. Also, change in total variable cost as a result of producing one additional unit of output.	$MC = \dfrac{\Delta TC}{\Delta Q}$ $= \dfrac{\Delta TVC}{\Delta Q}$

THE LONG-RUN COSTS OF PRODUCTION

In the short run, at least one input is fixed. In the long run, all inputs are variable. In our example of Cider Space, we have thus far looked only at the short run.

Let's say that Cider Space has a two-year lease on its building and equipment. This means that the long run is two years for Cider Space. When that lease is up, the firm must decide whether to continue in the same building, with the same equipment. If not, it must decide how big its next cider mill should be. If Cider Space chooses a larger building, then it will have a different set of short-run average-total-cost curves and marginal-cost curves.

In fact, the firm will potentially have a very large number of short-run average-total-cost curves and marginal-cost curves. Each of these corresponds to a particular size of cider mill. In Figure 8.7, we see a whole family of short-run average-total-cost curves, labeled SRAC, and a whole family of short-run marginal-cost curves, labeled SRMC. Right now, the firm uses a fairly small mill. In Figure 8.7, these are marked "$SRMC_{now}$" and "$SRAC_{now}$".

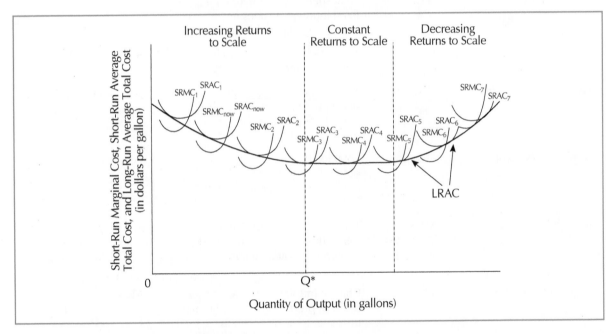

Figure 8.7 Long-Run Average Total Cost for Cider Space

In the long run, *all* inputs are variable. This graph shows several pairs of short-run marginal-cost curves (SRMC) and short-run average-total-cost curves (SRAC), each corresponding to a different size of plant. The long-run average-total-cost curve (LRAC) connects the SRAC curves. At relatively low levels of output, the firm experiences increasing returns to scale, which means that there are decreases in long-run average total cost. Eventually, the firm reaches a level of output at which it is no longer possible to have increasing returns to scale. This level of output is called minimum efficient scale, and it is shown as Q*. As the level of output increases beyond Q*, the firm experiences constant returns to scale. In this region, the LRAC curve is a horizontal line. Finally, at even higher levels of output, the firm experiences decreasing returns to scale, which is represented by the portion of the LRAC curve that slopes upward as we move from left to right across the diagram.

From Figure 8.7, you can see that the firm would have lower short-run costs if it were to use a somewhat larger mill. Eventually, however, we might get to a mill that is so large that it becomes hard to manage. If so, the short-run costs associated with a very large mill would be higher than the short-run costs associated with a somewhat smaller mill. This is shown in Figure 8.7, where the short-run costs are eventually higher for a larger scale of operations.

Underneath all of the short-run average-total-cost curves in Figure 8.7, we have drawn the long-run average-total-cost curve, which is labeled LRAC. We see that the current size of cider mill does *not* give Cider Space the lowest possible costs. The least-cost cider mill is about twice the size of the current cider mill. This implies that, when its current lease is up, Cider Space should think very seriously about expanding.

Returns to Scale

In constructing the *short-run* cost curves, we hold constant the size of the mill. In constructing the *long-run* cost curves, we allow *all* inputs to change. When we allow *all* inputs to change, we observe *returns to scale*. In measuring returns to scale, we increase all inputs by the same proportion, and see what happens to the quantity of output.

Increasing Returns to Scale. We have *increasing returns to scale* or *economies of scale* when the percentage increase in output is *greater* than the percentage increase in inputs. Under increasing returns to scale, if we double the amounts of all inputs, total product will *more* than double. More generally, if we have increasing return to scale, an increase of X% in all inputs will lead to an increase of more than X% in output.

When a firm is experiencing increasing returns to scale, what will happen to its costs? To answer this question, let's assume that the firm is small relative to all of the markets in which it buys inputs. If this is the case, then the firm will take input prices as given. If every unit of an input is paid the same as any other unit, then doubling all inputs will double the firm's costs. Under increasing returns to scale, when all inputs are increased by the same proportion, output increases by an even greater proportion. Thus, *under increasing returns to scale, when costs double, outputs more than double. This means that long-run average total cost will decrease.* Increasing returns to scale are observed in the left-hand portion of Figure 8.7, where the long-run average-total-cost curve slopes downward from left to right.

Constant Returns to Scale. We have *constant returns to scale* when the percentage change in output is *the same* as the percentage change in all inputs. For example, under constant returns to scale, if we double all inputs, the level of output will double. More generally, under constant returns to scale, an increase of X% in all inputs will lead to an increase in output of exactly X%. Thus under constant returns to scale, when costs double, outputs also double. This means that, if the firm is experiencing constant returns to scale, long-run average total cost will stay the same. In Figure 8.7, constant returns to scale are seen in the area where the LRAC curve is a horizontal line.

Decreasing Returns to Scale. We have *decreasing returns to scale* or *diseconomies of scale* when the percentage increase in output is *less* than the percentage increase in all inputs. In this case, if we double the amounts of all inputs, the output will *not* double. More generally, with decreasing returns to scale, an increase of X% in all inputs will lead to an increase in output of *less* than X%. Thus, under decreasing returns to scale, when costs double, outputs will not double. This means that, if the firm is experiencing decreasing returns to scale, long-run average total costs will increase. Decreasing returns to scale are seen in the right-hand portion of Figure 8.7, where the

LRAC curve slopes upward as we move from left to right across the diagram.

Firms sometimes encounter decreasing returns to scale when they have difficulty in managing and coordinating the activities of ever-increasing numbers of workers, buildings, machines, and so on. However, for some production processes, decreasing returns don't set in until the firm reaches a very high level of output. For example, studies of the automobile industry have shown that firms can grow to be multi-billion-dollar enterprises before they encounter decreasing returns to scale.

Many production processes have increasing returns to scale, at least up to a certain point. Beyond that point, it is common to have constant returns to scale over a fairly large range of sizes. In a case like this, we say that the firm reaches its *minimum efficient scale* when it no longer has increasing returns to scale. At output levels below the minimum efficient scale, the firm would be able to decrease its long-run average total cost by increasing the scale of its operations. In Figure 8.7, the firm's minimum efficient scale is Q*.

In *Real Economics for Real People 8.1*, we discuss returns to scale in the supermarket industry.

Reality Check: Interim Review Questions

IR8-6. The LRAC curve for Corporation X is a horizontal line. What does this imply about the returns to scale for Corporation X?

IR8-7. If Corporation Y were to increase all of its inputs by 20 percent, its output would increase by 30 percent. In this range of output, does Corporation Y have increasing returns to scale, constant returns to scale, or decreasing returns to scale? In this range of output, does Corporation Y's LRAC curve slope upward, or downward, or is it horizontal?

Returns to Scale and International Trade

The idea of scale economies is very important for our understanding of the effects of tariffs and other barriers to international trade. Many economists have attempted to measure the gains from removing trade barriers, using computer simulation models. Most of these models have assumed that production is characterized by constant returns to scale. However, some economists have suggested that scale economies play an important role. If there are trade barriers, a firm can survive, even when it is operating at less than the minimum efficient scale. In other words, with trade barriers, firms don't always take advantage of scale economies, and inefficiently small firms can stay in business. On the other hand, if the trade barriers were removed, the firms would be forced to take advantage of scale economies, in order to survive: With no trade protection, the firms would have to minimize their long-run average total cost, or they would go out of business.

Richard Harris, a Canadian economist, has done research using a computer simulation model that has scale economies. He shows that the gains from removing trade barriers for a country like Canada can be very large. A large portion of these gains comes about because Canadian firms become more efficient when trade barriers are removed. As the firms take advantage of scale economies, their long-run average total costs go down.

Sunk Costs

A *sunk cost* is an expenditure that has already been made in the past, and cannot be recovered. As a result, it should not have any influence on our decisions. We make decisions regarding the future, not the past.

Let's think about a firm that buys a new boiler in September, 1973, when the price of oil is low. Because oil is cheap at this time, there isn't much of an incentive to use tech-nologies that conserve oil. Therefore, the boiler's technology uses a lot of oil. Assume that the boiler is highly specialized, so that this firm can't sell it to some other firm.

One month after the boiler is installed, the Organization of Petroleum Exporting Coun-tries (OPEC) succeeds in raising the price of oil by 300 percent. The firm may *wish* that it hadn't bought the inefficient boiler, but the old boiler is a sunk cost. It has no alternative use, and its opportunity cost is zero. Therefore, it shouldn't have any influence on the firm's decisions. If the firm now wants to buy a more energy-efficient boiler, it should compare the cost of the *new* boiler with the projected savings in fuel costs. The amount that the firm paid for the *old* boiler is irrelevant. For better or worse, the past has already happened, and we can't change it. Therefore, whenever we make a decision, we are looking toward the future. Yesterday is gone, and we can't get it back.

In *Real Economics for Real People 8.2*, we take a look at another example involving sunk costs.

Another application of the idea of sunk cost arises in the debates over the B–2 Stealth bomber, the V-22 Osprey aircraft, and other weapons systems. Some have argued that these weapons systems are no longer needed, because the United States doesn't face a powerful military opponent, as it once did with the Soviet Union. Others say that the world is still a very dangerous place, so that the weapons systems are needed just as urgently as ever.

This isn't the place to give a final judgment about how much safety is provided by the B–2. This *is* the place to point out that one type of argument should not be made. These weapons systems have already cost many billions of dollars, but it makes no sense to say "We should continue these weapons systems because we have invested so much already." The money already spent is a sunk cost. All that matters at this point is whether the weapons will give benefits that justify the *additional* spending that is proposed *for the future.*

ECONOMICS AND YOU:
IF YOU'VE ALREADY PAID FOR IT,
YOU SHOULDN'T EAT IT UNLESS YOU WANT TO

At the beginning of this chapter, we considered the situation of Allison and Zachary, who paid $10 each for an all-you-can-eat spaghetti dinner, only to find that the food was very bad.

Our analysis of sunk costs can help us to understand this situation. Allison and Zachary probably *wish* they hadn't paid $10. But that money is a sunk cost. Zachary says that he wants to pig out, because he wants to get his "money's worth." But this doesn't make any economic sense. His money is gone, and no amount of indigestion caused by horrible pasta will get the money back.

After Zachary pays at the door, he doesn't have to pay any more money to get more food at Pat's Pasta Palace. In other words, the opportunity cost to Zachary of eating the pasta is zero. If the benefit of eating the spaghetti is greater than zero, he should eat. If not, then he should not eat. If he decides that he doesn't want to eat at Pat's Pasta Palace, he still has other alternatives. If he wants, he can go across the street to buy food at Samantha's. If the marginal benefit from eating at Samantha's is greater than the marginal cost, then Zachary will come out ahead.

It was Allison who said "As for getting my money's worth, I kissed my ten dollars goodbye when I paid at the door." Zachary would do well to listen to her. If he tries to get his "money's worth," all he is likely to get is indigestion.

Of course, sunk costs are not the only costs that we have considered in this chapter. We have made a distinction between fixed inputs and variable inputs, and between fixed costs and variable costs. We have shown how the business firm can calculate its total costs and average costs. Most important of all, we've shown how the business firm can calculate its marginal cost.

For many students, this information on production and costs is not very satisfying. In this chapter, we have said a lot about how to *define* costs, and how to *calculate* them, but we have only said a little about how to *use* this information. It's understandable if this is frustrating. However, you can rest assured that we *will* show how to use this information, especially in Chapters 9, 10, and 11. In those chapters, we will concentrate on how business firms actually behave. Usually, we assume that business firms want to maximize their profits. Profits are equal to the difference between total revenues and total costs. Thus, if we want to know something about profits, we have to know something about costs. Now that you have read this chapter, you have an understanding of costs. In the chapters to come, you will build on that understanding again and again.

Chapter Summary

1. In the short run, at least one input is fixed. The Law of Diminishing Marginal Product (or the The Law of Diminishing Returns) describes a production relationship that is often observed in the short run. The Law of Diminishing Marginal Product states that, if we increase one input repeatedly, while holding all other inputs constant, the amount of additional output will eventually decline.

2. Variable costs are the costs that the firm pays for its variable inputs. Fixed costs are the costs that the firm pays for its fixed inputs. The distinction between variable costs and fixed costs is only relevant in the short run. In the long run, all inputs are variable.

3. Marginal cost is the additional cost the firm has to pay when it produces one additional unit of output. By definition, marginal costs must be variable costs, since fixed costs are paid regardless of the level of production.

4. Short-run average-total-cost curves are often U-shaped. Average total cost decreases when the level of output is small, because average fixed cost goes down when quantity goes up. Eventually, however, average total cost may be pulled up by increasing marginal costs. At the quantity at which average total cost is minimized, average total cost is equal to marginal cost. Also, average variable cost is minimized at the quantity at which average variable cost is equal to marginal cost.

5. In the long run, all inputs are freely variable, so that the firm can adjust its entire scale of operations. We say that the firm has increasing returns to scale if, when all of its inputs are increased by the same proportion, output increases by a larger proportion. If the firm has increasing returns to scale, its long-run average-total-cost curve will slope downward as we move from left to right across the diagram. We have constant returns to scale if, when all inputs increase by a given proportion, output increases by that same proportion. If the firm has constant returns to scale, its long-run average-total-cost-curve is a horizontal line. If all inputs increase by the same proportion and output increases by a smaller proportion, we have decreasing returns to scale. In this case, the long-run average-total-cost curve will slope upward as we move from left to right.

Key Terms

Outputs

Inputs

Variable Inputs

Fixed Inputs

Short Run

Long Run

Fixed Costs

Total Fixed Cost

Average Fixed Cost

Variable Costs

Total Variable Cost

Marginal Cost

Average Variable Cost

Law of Diminishing Marginal Product

Law of Diminishing Returns

Total Cost

Average Total Cost

Returns to Scale

Increasing Returns to Scale

Economies of Scale

Constant Returns to Scale

Decreasing Returns to Scale

Diseconomies of Scale

Minimum Efficient Scale

Sunk Cost

Key Figures

The key figures for this chapter are Figures 8.5 and 8.6, which show sets of short-run cost curves.

Questions and Problems

QP8-1. Which of the following is a short-run decision? Which deals with the long run?

a. A mail-order catalog company hires six extra customer-service representatives.
b. A hardware store chain opens up a new store.
c. A corn farmer applies additional fertilizer to a cornfield.
d. A corn farmer cuts down some trees, to increase the size of the cornfield.

QP8-2. Fill in the blanks in the table below.

QP8-3. Explain the distinction between the following pairs of concepts:
a. Short run and long run.
b. Fixed costs and variable costs.

QP8-4. If marginal cost is greater than average total cost, is average total cost increasing, or decreasing, or constant? How would your answer change if marginal cost is equal to average total cost? What if marginal cost is less than average total cost?

QP8-5. During television broadcasts of professional football games, it is common to announce the attendance and the number of "no-shows" (people who purchased tickets but who did not come to the stadium). Explain why it might be rational for a season-ticket holder to be a no-show.

Quantity Of Output	TVC	ATC	TC	MC
0	0	—	20	—
1	10	_____	30	_____
2	_____	19	38	_____
3	28	_____	_____	10
4	_____	_____	60	12
5	56	15.2	76	_____
6	_____	16	_____	20

Chapter 9

Perfect Competition

ECONOMICS AND YOU:
CAN YOU MAKE A BUNDLE IN THE STOCK MARKET?

Frank Owens and Jenny Krueger work for a software-consulting firm. In their spare time, they like to "play the stock market". They read *Barron's,* the *Wall Street Journal,* and other financial publications, looking for hot ideas. Then, they buy the stocks of companies they think will do unusually well.

Over lunch one day, Frank says "I'm a smart guy. I think I can pick stocks that will do better than the market average for the next year." But Jenny isn't so sure. Frank didn't predict that his stocks would merely perform *as well as* the market average. He predicted that his stocks would do *better than average.* We'll see that it might not be very easy to do this, even for a smart guy like Frank.

The Dow Jones Industrial Average measures the performance of the stocks of 30 large companies that are listed on the New York Stock Exchange (NYSE). Stock markets, such as the NYSE, are examples of what we call "competitive" markets. It's relatively easy to

get involved in the stock market, and millions of investors do so. Because so many investors are competing against each other, it may be difficult to do much better than average.

Most of this chapter is devoted to a discussion of "perfectly competitive" markets. We'll develop the theory of the perfectly competitive firm, by working through an example of a company that produces apple cider. (This example was first introduced in Chapter 8.) At the end of the chapter, we will return to the case of the stock market.

At the beginning of Chapter 8, we said that many students find that chapter to be relatively difficult. The same is true for this chapter on perfect competition. Therefore, once again, it's important to go one step at a time: This chapter contains many details, but you should be able to learn the details if you work on them in a systematic way. You may need to go slowly, but don't worry. If you keep at it, you will master the material.

MARKET STRUCTURES

Not all markets are perfectly competitive. In fact, perfect competition is only one of four *market structures*. The term *"market structure"* refers to the way in which the firms in a market relate to each other, and to their customers. The four market structures are:

- perfect competition or pure competition,
- monopoly,
- monopolistic competition, and
- oligopoly.

In this section, we'll briefly describe the characteristics of the four market structures. Then, in the rest of the chapter, we will take a closer look at perfectly competitive firms and markets. We will consider monopoly, monopolistic competition, and oligopoly in later chapters.

Perfect Competition

In *perfect competition* or *pure competition*, the market has many firms, and each firm is small relative to the market. Some of the best examples of perfect competition are in agriculture. For instance, more than a million American farms grow grain. Perfect competition can also be found in some other parts of the economy. For example, the cotton-weaving industry has more than 200 firms, and the men's work-clothing industry has nearly 300. There are about 10,000 sawmills in the lumber industry. Stock exchanges, commodity markets, and foreign-exchange markets are also highly competitive, with thousands of sellers.

Another characteristic of perfectly competitive firms is that they produce a *standardized product*, or *homogeneous product*. For example, in the market for winter wheat, Farmer Olson's wheat is virtually identical to Farmer Johnson's wheat.

Since perfectly competitive firms are all small relative to the market, and since they produce homogeneous products, the individual firms are unable to control the prices of the goods they sell. If Farmer Olson were to raise his price above Farmer Johnson's price, Olson would lose all of his customers.

Changes in *market* supply or *market* demand will lead to changes in *market* price. However, in a perfectly competitive industry, the individual *firm* can't do anything to change the price.

In a perfectly competitive industry, it's relatively easy for new firms to start up. We say that perfectly competitive markets are characterized by *free entry* into the industry: If profits are high, new firms will enter the industry.

Perfectly competitive markets are also characterized by *free exit* from the industry: If firms are doing badly, some of them will go out of business.

Monopoly

Perfect competition is at one end of the spectrum of market structures. The opposite end of the spectrum is occupied by *monopoly*, in which there is only one firm in an industry. Some of the best examples of monopolies are in the utilities that provide electric power, or water and sewerage services, or natural gas. In many communities, these services are only provided by one company. Monopolies can also be found at football and baseball stadiums: At many of these places, food and beverages are provided by only one company. We have seen that a perfectly competitive firm has no control over price. But a monopoly may be able to control the price to a very large degree. Since the monopolist is the only firm in the market, it faces the entire market demand curve. Therefore, the monopolist can choose among different points on the demand curve.

If a monopoly is to be maintained over time, there must be some very significant *barriers to entry*, which keep new firms from entering the industry. (If there were no barriers to entry, new firms would quickly enter the market, and the monopoly wouldn't be a monopoly any more.) Sometimes, the barriers to entry have to do with the high cost of setting up a new company. Sometimes, the barriers are the result of legal restrictions, such as patents and exclusive franchise arrangements.

The monopolist's output must not have very close substitutes: If the output has close substitutes, the firm isn't really a monopoly. For example, the Coca-Cola company is the only producer of the drink known as "Coke", but this doesn't mean that this company is a monopolist. Many consumers view other soft drinks, such as Pepsi Cola and RC Cola, as close substitutes for Coca-Cola. Therefore, instead of saying that the Coca-Cola company is a monopolist in the market for "Coke", we would say that the Coca-Cola company is only one of several firms in the soft-drink market.

We will discuss monopoly in more detail in Chapter 10.

Monopolistic Competition

Perfect competition is at one extreme, and monopoly is at the other extreme. However, most industries fall *in between* the definitions of perfect competition and monopoly. There are two categories of "in-between" market structures. These are called *monopolistic competition* and *oligopoly*.

First, let's talk about monopolistic competition. Ice-cream stores and gasoline stations have some of the characteristics of perfect competition, but they are also different from perfectly competitive firms in one important way. The difference is that ice-cream stores and gasoline stations sell *differentiated products,* whereas perfectly competitive firms sell homogeneous, standardized products. We say that a market is characterized by *differentiated product* if there are noticeable differences in quality, or location, or service, among the goods produced by the various firms in the market.

For example, one gasoline station may be located right next to the freeway exit ramp, while another gasoline station might be harder to get to. As a result, the conveniently located station may be able to charge higher prices, without losing all of its customers. Also, one ice-cream store may have more flavors than another store, or it may have a nicer atmosphere. Because of these characteristics, it may be possible for one ice-cream store to charge higher prices, without losing all of its customers. In other words, some gasoline stations and ice-cream stores may be able to control their selling prices, at least to a small degree. These firms do not have as much control over price as a monopoly, but they have more control over price than a perfectly competitive firm. (Remember that perfectly competitive firms have *no* control over price.)

Ice-cream stores and gasoline stations are engaged in *monopolistic competition.* **Monopolistic competition** is similar to perfect competition, in that there are many firms in an industry, and each firm is relatively small, and it's easy to enter the industry or exit from it. The big difference is that monopolistically competitive firms have differentiated products.

Many of the best examples of monopolistic competition are in retailing, because differences in location and the quality of service can be extremely important to retail firms. Monopolistic competition applies to clothing stores and grocery stores, as well as to ice-cream stores and gasoline stations. We will discuss monopolistic competition in detail in Chapter 11.

Oligopoly

Perfect competition and monopolistic competition are both characterized by free entry and exit, and both have a relatively large number of firms. In many important industries, however, there are only a few firms. For example, the automobile industry is dominated by

Fiat Chrysler, Ford, General Motors, Honda, Nissan, Toyota, Volkswagen, and a few other large firms. The commercial-aircraft-manufacturing industry includes only two firms: Boeing and a European consortium called Airbus.

The automobile industry and the commercial-aircraft-manufacturing industry are examples of *oligopoly*. When a market has only a few firms, we say that it is an *oligopoly*. Many of the best examples of oligopoly are in manufacturing. The domestic passenger-airlines industry is an oligopoly, with many routes dominated by American, Delta, Southwest, and United. The breakfast-cereal industry is an oligopoly, dominated by General Foods, General Mills, Kellogg, Nabisco, Post, Quaker, and Ralston-Purina.

Whereas competitive industries are characterized by free entry, oligopolies usually have significant barriers to entry. In many cases, the entry barriers have to do with the high costs of setting up a new firm: In steel, automobiles, oil, and other oligopolistic industries, it is often necessary to invest billions of dollars to compete effectively. This means that it's difficult (but not necessarily impossible) for new firms to enter the industry.

The products of oligopolistic firms may be standardized (as in the case of some parts of the chemical industry), or they may be differentiated (as in the case of the automobile industry and the breakfast-cereal industry).

Because oligopolistic industries have relatively few firms, the firms are very much aware of each other. For example, when an automobile producer brings out a new model of car, engineers at the other car companies will take it apart, piece by piece. They analyze the car in the smallest detail, looking for technological improvements and ways to cut costs. The automobile firms are also very much aware of each other's TV commercials and other marketing strategies. In oligopolistic industries, firms are *interdependent*, so that strategy becomes important. We will discuss oligopolies and their strategies in Chapter 11.

Sometimes, the firms in an oligopolistic industry try to cooperate with each other. When oligopolistic firms cooperate with each other, we say they are engaged in *collusion*. If the firms can collude with each other, they may be able to maintain higher prices and higher profits. If the collusion is very effective, the oligopoly firms may be able to charge a price that is as high as the monopoly price. However, collusion is illegal in the United States. The laws don't necessarily eliminate collusion, but they probably mean that we have less collusion than we would otherwise have. We will discuss the laws against collusion in Chapter 12.

The characteristics of the four market structures are summarized in Table 9.1.

Reality Check: Interim Review Questions

IR9-1. Name the four types of market structure, and give an example of an industry of each type.

IR9-2. In a perfectly competitive market, do the firms have differentiated products? What about the firms in a monopolistically competitive market?

Table 9.1 Characteristics of the Different Market Structures

Market Structure	Number of Firms	Product Differentiation	Ability of Firms to Control Price	Barriers to Entry	Examples
Pure Competition or Perfect Competition	Many	None: Products Are Standardized	None	None	Agriculture, Sawmills, Some Financial Markets, Some Textiles
Monopolistic Competition	Many	Products Are Differentiated	Depends on Product Differentiation	None	Retailing, Some Manufacturing, Some Publishing
Oligopoly	Few	Can Be Either Standardized or Differentiated	Depends on Interaction Between Firms: Can Be Substantial if Firms Can Collude	Major Barriers	Steel, Automobiles, Breakfast Cereals, Oil, Aircraft Manufacture, Some Chemicals
Monopoly	One	Product Must Not Have Close Substitutes	Very Substantial	Barriers Must Be Very Strong	Electric Utilities, Some Pharmaceuticals

THE IDEAL OF PERFECT COMPETITION

Here again are the key characteristics of a perfectly competitive market:

- many firms, each of which is small relative to the market,

- output that is standardized, or homogeneous, and

- free entry and exit.

We now discuss these characteristics (and some others) in greater detail.

A Large Number of Firms, Each of Which Is Small Relative to the Market

The first characteristic is that perfectly competitive industries have a large number of firms, *each* of which is small relative to the market. If a firm is large relative to the market, it will be powerful enough to manipulate the price. Therefore, if a market is to be perfectly competitive, *every* firm in the market must be relatively small. If there were one huge firm and hundreds of tiny ones, we wouldn't have a perfectly competitive industry, because the one huge firm would be able to manipulate the price.

Standardized Product

Another important assumption is that perfectly competitive firms produce an output that is standardized, or homogeneous. What would happen if outputs *weren't* homogeneous? If different firms were to make significantly different products, we would observe two effects. First, if one firm's products are viewed as having higher quality, that firm might be able to raise its price, without losing all of its customers. Second, the firms might engage in non-price competition, such as advertising. When we observe a lot of advertising, as in the automobile industry and the beer industry, we know that we aren't dealing with perfectly competitive firms. If an industry were perfectly competitive, we would observe very little non-price competition, and every firm would charge the same price.

Price-Taking Firms

If a firm is small relative to the market, and if its product is the same as the product of the other firms, then the firm won't have any power to influence the price. It will just take the market price as given. A *price-taking firm* is one that accepts the market price. By assuming that firms are small and that they produce homogeneous products, we are assuming that perfectly competitive firms are price takers. It takes both small size and homogeneous products for a firm to be a price taker. If *either* of these conditions is absent, then the firm cannot be a price taker.

If a firm is able to control its price, we say that the firm has *market power*. However, a perfectly competitive, price-taking firm does not have any market power.

Freedom of Entry and Exit

We assume that there are no significant barriers to entry into a perfectly competitive industry. If there are high profits in a perfectly competitive industry, new firms will enter the industry.

Conversely, if the firms in an industry are doing badly, some firms will exit from the industry. Later in this chapter, we will investigate how bad it has to be for firms to think about going out of business, and we will see what happens when they do exit the industry.

Perfect Information

If a perfectly competitive market is to work properly, consumers must have accurate information about the market price. After all, if a consumer doesn't *know* the prices that are being charged by different firms, he or she might end up paying a price that is too high. We assume that consumers have all the information they need to make intelligent decisions.

In reality, people don't always have *perfect* information. However, in many cases, people are sufficiently well-informed that perfect information is an OK assumption. In fact, as time passes, more and more markets are characterized by perfect information (or at least nearly perfect information). As consumers make more use of toll-free telephone numbers, Internet shopping, and other services, they have more and more access to accurate information.

Reality Check:
Interim Review Question

IR9-3. A perfectly competitive firm has several characteristics. Which of these characteristics is/are an important reason why the firm is a price-taking firm?

DEMAND AND REVENUE FOR PERFECTLY COMPETITIVE FIRMS

In Chapter 8, we studied the production and cost relationships of Cider Space, a small manufacturer of apple cider. The market for apple cider is perfectly competitive: It's relatively easy to enter the industry, which has many firms. In this section, we will study the demand and revenue relationships for Cider Space. Later in this chapter, we'll put the cost information together with the revenue information. When we know about both costs and revenues, we can determine whether the firm will make a profit.

Perfectly Elastic Demand for the Output of the Price-Taking Firm

In a typical year, Cider Space produces about one-tenth of one percent of the apple cider that is sold in the Midwest. What will happen if Cider Space were to try to drive up the market price of cider, by reducing the quantity of its output? Since Cider Space only produces one-tenth of one percent of the market output, even a ten-percent reduction in the *firm's* quantity will mean that the *market* quantity will go down by only one-hundredth of 1%.

This means that Cider Space will have great difficulty in raising the market price. For all practical purposes, the firm must take the market price as given. Therefore, *the demand for the individual firm's output is perfectly elastic: The firm can sell as many units as it wants to sell, at the going market price.*

It's very important to keep this straight: *Even though the market demand may be relatively inelastic, the demand for the output of a perfectly competitive firm is perfectly elastic.* The individual perfectly competitive firm is a price taker, with no control over the market price. We will assume that *all* perfectly competitive firms are price takers.

The relationship between the market demand curve and the demand curve for the output of the individual perfectly competitive firm is shown in Figure 9.1. In panel (a) of the figure, we see the downward-sloping *market* demand curve, and the upward-sloping *market* supply curve. The intersection of these two curves gives us the market equilibrium price. The individual perfectly competitive firm observes the market equilibrium price,

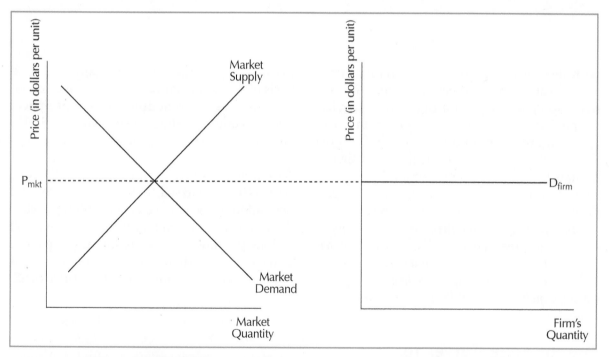

Figure 9.1 Panel (a)

The market demand curve is downward sloping. The market equilibrium price is determined by the intersection of the market demand curve and the market supply curve.

Figure 9.1 Panel (b)

The individual perfectly competitive firm takes the market price as given. Therefore, the demand curve for the output of the individual firm is a horizontal line, given by the market price.

Table 9.2 Revenue Information for Cider Space

Quantity of Apple Cider Produced (Gallons per Day)	Price of Apple Cider, in Dollars per Gallon	Marginal Revenue, in Dollars per Additional Gallon	Average Revenue, in Dollars per Gallon	Total Revenue, in Dollars
0	$2	—	—	$0
1	$2	$2	$2	$2
2	$2	$2	$2	$4
3	$2	$2	$2	$6
.	.	.	.	.
.				
.				
100	$2	$2	$2	$200
200	$2	$2	$2	$400
300	$2	$2	$2	$600
400	$2	$2	$2	$800
500	$2	$2	$2	$1000
600	$2	$2	$2	$1200
700	$2	$2	$2	$1400
800	$2	$2	$2	$1600
900	$2	$2	$2	$1800
1000	$2	$2	$2	$2000

with the knowledge that the individual firm can't do anything to affect the price. Thus the demand curve for the output of the individual perfectly competitive firm, shown in panel (b) of Figure 9.1, is a horizontal line given by the market price. The individual firm's demand curve is a horizontal line, even though the market demand curve slopes downward as we move from left to right.

In a perfectly competitive _industry_, *the market demand curve is downward sloping as we move from left to right, but the demand curve facing an individual perfectly competitive* _firm_ *is perfectly elastic, which means that the firm's demand curve is a horizontal line.*

The Revenue Curves for the Perfectly Competitive Firm

The market price is the *only* information that we need to know about the revenues of a perfectly competitive firm. Currently, the market

price of apple cider is $2 per gallon. On the basis of this information, we can construct the various revenue schedules for Cider Space. These revenue schedules are shown in Table 9.2, and the corresponding revenue curves are graphed in Figure 9.2.

Cider Space can sell as many gallons of cider as it wants to sell, at the market price of $2 per gallon. If the firm sells one gallon per day, the price is $2 per gallon. If the firm sells 100 gallons per day, the price is still $2 per gallon. Thus, the firm's demand curve in panel (a) of Figure 9.2 is a horizontal line at the price of $2.

Marginal Revenue. **Marginal revenue (MR) is the extra amount of money that the firm receives when it sells one more unit of output.** For managers of any company, marginal revenue is an extremely important piece of information. When Cider Space sells its first gallon of cider, it receives $2. When it sells its second one, it

Figure 9.2 Panel (a)
Marginal Revenue and Average Revenue for Cider Space

A perfectly competitive firm, such as Cider Space, can sell as many units as it wants to sell, at the market price. Because of this, the additional revenue that the firm gets from selling one more unit is always equal to the market price. This means that the firm's marginal-revenue curve and average-revenue curve are both horizontal lines.

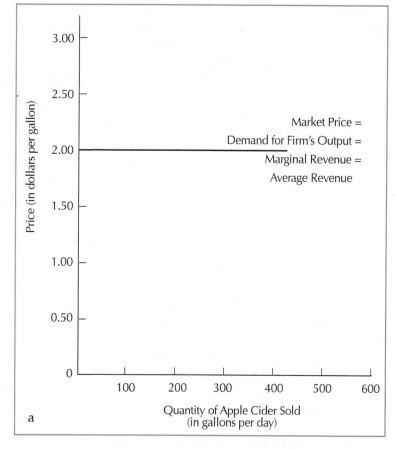

Market Price =
Demand for Firm's Output =
Marginal Revenue =
Average Revenue

Price (in dollars per gallon)

Quantity of Apple Cider Sold
(in gallons per day)

a

Figure 9.2 Panel (b)
Total Revenue for Cider Space

Total revenue is the total amount of money that a firm receives from selling a product. Total revenue is equal to price multiplied by quantity. A perfectly competitive firm can sell as many units as it wants to sell, at the market price. Therefore, the total-revenue curve is a straight line, whose slope is the market price.

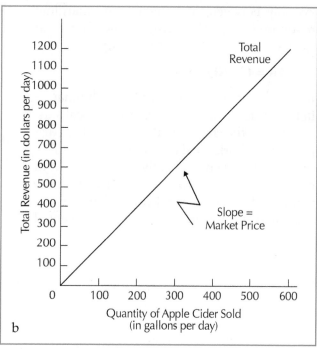

Total
Revenue

Total Revenue (in dollars per day)

Slope =
Market Price

Quantity of Apple Cider Sold
(in gallons per day)

b

gets another $2. When it sells its hundredth gallon of cider, the extra revenue is still $2. Thus, Cider Space's marginal revenue is $2 for each additional gallon of cider, regardless of how many gallons are produced by the firm. *For any perfectly competitive firm, marginal revenue is given by the market price.*

If we graph the marginal-revenue curve (as in panel (a) of Figure 9.2), we get a horizontal line at $2. For the perfectly competitive firm, the demand curve and the marginal-revenue curve are identical.

Total Revenue. **Total revenue** is the total number of dollars that the firm receives from all sales of its product. If Cider Space were to sell only one gallon of cider, its total revenue would be (1 gallon)x($2 per gallon) = $2. If two gallons were sold, total revenue would be (2)x($2) = $4. If the firm were to sell 100 gallons of cider, its total revenue would be (100)x($2) = $200. *We calculate total revenue by multiplying the price by the quantity:*

TR = (P)(Q).

Here is another way to express the relationship between total revenue and marginal revenue. Marginal revenue is the change in total revenue, divided by the change in output:

MR = (ΔTR) / (ΔQ).

Remember that the slope of a line is the change in the value of the variable on the vertical axis, divided by the change in the value of the variable on the horizontal axis. In panel (b) of Figure 9.2, total revenue is on the vertical axis, and quantity is on the horizontal axis. Thus the slope of the line in panel (b) of Figure 9.2 is equal to ΔTR/ΔQ. But this is marginal revenue!

The slope of the total-revenue curve is the marginal revenue.

Average Revenue. Finally, ***average revenue*** is the average number of *dollars per unit* that the firm receives. Average revenue is total revenue divided by the quantity sold:

AR = TR/Q.

Remember that total revenue is price multiplied by quantity. Therefore,

AR = (TR/Q) = ((PQ)/Q) = P.

In other words, *average revenue is equal to the price.* Average revenue could also be called "revenue per unit".

We also graph average revenue in panel (a) of Figure 9.2. Average revenue is identical to marginal revenue, and they are both identical to the demand curve for the perfectly competitive firm. For *any* perfectly competitive firm, average revenue and marginal revenue are given by the market price.

Reality Check: Interim Review Questions

IR9-4. A manufacturer of corn flakes knows that if it produces 1,000,000 boxes, it can sell them for a price of $3.50 each. However, if the firm wants to produce 100,000 additional boxes of corn flakes, the firm will have to cut its price to $3.40 per box. Is this a perfectly competitive firm?

IR9-5. For a perfectly competitive firm, what is the relationship between price, marginal revenue, and average revenue?

HOW THE PERFECTLY COMPETITIVE FIRM BEHAVES IN THE SHORT RUN

In Chapter 8, we described the cost curves of business firms. Here in Chapter 9, we have described the perfectly competitive firm's revenues. Next, we put the revenues and costs together. When we look at revenues and costs at the same time, we can understand the perfectly competitive firm's decision about how much to produce.

In the rest of this chapter, and in the next few chapters, we'll use the cost concepts from Chapter 8 very often. Again and again, we will use marginal cost, average variable cost, and average total cost. If you're not sure you understand the cost curves, this would be the best time to go back for a brief review of Chapter 8.

The Goal of Profit Maximization

To understand the behavior of the firm, we need to have some idea of what it is trying to accomplish. *We assume that firms maximize profit.* Profit is equal to the difference between total revenue and total cost:

Profit = TR – TC.

The assumption of profit maximization may not be completely correct all of the time. Some firms may be sloppy and wasteful. In addition, some firms may desire to increase their share of the market, and this may mean that they don't maximize their profits immediately. And yet, the assumption of profit maximization is probably pretty close to the truth. After all, firms that do maximize profits will be more likely to stay in business. Firms that consistently don't maximize profits will be more likely to be forced out of business.

Finding the Maximum Profit by Comparing Total Revenue and Total Cost

We have already seen the revenues of Cider Space, in Table 9.2 and Figure 9.2. Table 9.3 repeats some of the numbers from Table 9.2, and adds some additional information. You can tell that Cider Space is a perfectly competitive firm, because the price of apple cider is the same ($2 per gallon) for every possible level of output for the firm. When we multiply the price by the quantity, we get the firm's total revenue, which is shown in column (3) of Table 9.3.

The cost information for Cider Space was given in Tables 8.2, 8.3, 8.4, and 8.5. Some of those numbers are repeated here, in columns (4)–(7) of Table 9.3.

The firm's total costs are shown in column (7) of Table 9.3. These are equal to its total fixed costs (shown in column (6)) plus its total variable costs (shown in column (5)): TC = TFC + TVC.

We calculate the profits for Cider Space by subtracting total cost from total revenue: Profit = TR – TC. Profits are shown in column (8) of Table 9.3. When the firm produces only a small quantity of output, total cost is greater than total revenue. This means that the firm's profit is negative: Cider Space will suffer a loss if it produces only a small amount of apple cider.

However, if the firm were to increase its output, it would eventually earn a profit. As shown in column (8) of Table 9.3, profits continue to increase until the firm is producing 700 gallons of cider per day. At this quantity, profit is $420 per day. Profit remains at $420 when the firm increases output from 700 gallons per day to 800 gallons per day. If the firm

Table 9.3 Revenues, Costs, and Profits for Cider Space, When the Price Is $2 per Gallon

(1) Q Quantity of Apple Cider, in Gallons per Day	(2) P Price, in Dollars per Gallon = Marginal Revenue = Average Revenue	(3) TR Total Revenue, in Dollars (= PxQ)	(4) MC Marginal Cost, in Dollars per Additional Gallon	(5) TVC Total Variable Cost, in Dollars	(6) TFC Total Fixed Cost, in Dollars	(7) TC Total Cost, in Dollars (=TFC+TVC)	(8) Profit Profit, in Dollars (=TR–TC)
0	$2.00	$ 0	—	$ 0	$100	$ 100	–$100
100	$2.00	$ 200	$1.10	$ 110	$100	$ 210	–$ 10
200	$2.00	$ 400	$0.90	$ 200	$100	$ 300	$100
300	$2.00	$ 600	$1.00	$ 300	$100	$ 400	$200
400	$2.00	$ 800	$1.20	$ 420	$100	$ 520	$280
500	$2.00	$1000	$1.30	$ 550	$100	$ 650	$350
600	$2.00	$1200	$1.50	$ 700	$100	$ 800	$400
700	$2.00	$1400	$1.80	$ 880	$100	$ 980	$420
800	$2.00	$1600	$2.00	$1080	$100	$1180	$420
900	$2.00	$1800	$2.20	$1300	$100	$1400	$400
1000	$2.00	$2000	$2.50	$1550	$100	$1650	$350

were to increase its output beyond 800 gallons per day, profits would fall.

You may be bothered by the fact that there is not a *unique* profit-maximizing quantity. The maximum profit of $420 is earned when the firm produces 800 gallons per day, but the same level of profit is also earned when the firm produces 700 gallons per day. Will the firm produce 700 gallons or 800? We assume that Cider Space will go ahead and produce 800 gallons per day. We will discuss this in more detail below.

Graphical Analysis of Profit Maximization

Figure 9.3 contains some of the information from Table 9.3. The total-revenue curve is a straight line, as it should be for any price-taking firm. In Figure 9.3, *profit is the vertical distance between the total-revenue curve and the total-cost curve.* Profit is largest at the quantity where this vertical distance is greatest. Figure 9.3 shows that the vertical distance between the two curves is greatest when the quantity of output is 800 gallons of cider per day. This means that the profit-maximizing quantity is 800 gallons per day, which is the same answer that we got from looking at Table 9.3.

In Figure 9.3, the maximum profit occurs at the quantity where the slope of the total-revenue curve is equal to the slope of the total-cost curve. In other words, *at the profit-maximizing quantity, the total-revenue curve (TR) is parallel to the total-cost curve (TC).*

Let's think about this, by considering cases in which the TR curve and the TC curve are *not* parallel. For example, as quantity increases from 200 gallons to 300 gallons, the TR curve is steeper than the TC curve. That is, the vertical distance between the two curves is getting larger. Therefore, as output increases from 200 gallons per day to 300 gallons per day, profit is increasing. *If profit is increasing, the firm can't be at the maximum profit.* In this situation, the firm would increase its profit by producing more output.

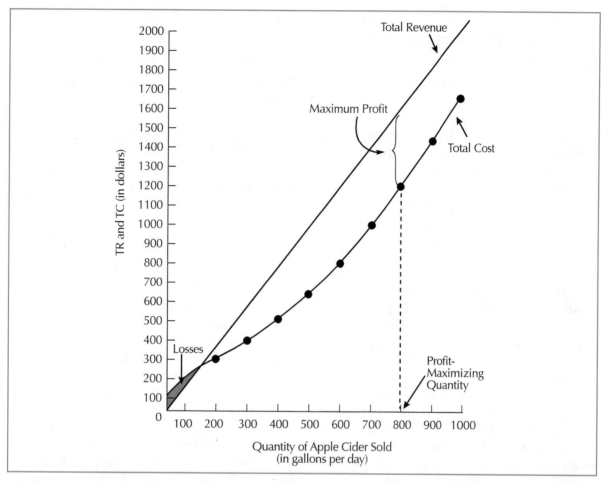

Figure 9.3 Total Revenue, Total Cost, and Profit for Cider Space

The firm's profit-maximizing quantity is found where the vertical distance between the total-revenue curve and the total-cost curve is greatest. This occurs at the quantity where the TR curve is parallel to the TC curve. In the case of Cider Space, the firm maximizes profit by producing 800 gallons of apple cider per day.

On the other hand, as quantity increases from 900 gallons per day to 1000 gallons per day, the TR curve is flatter than the TC curve: The slope of the TR curve is *less* than the slope of the TC curve, so that the vertical distance between the two curves is shrinking. Therefore, as output increases from 900 gallons per day to 1000 gallons per day, profit is falling. *If profit is falling, the firm can't be at the maximum profit*. In this case, the firm would increase its profit by reducing its output.

So, profit can't be maximized if the TR curve is steeper than the TC curve, and profit also can't be maximized if the TR curve is less steep than the TC curve. This leaves us with only one possibility: *If profit is to be maximized, the slope of the TR curve must be the same as the slope of the TC curve*. In Figure 9.3, the two curves have the same slope between the quantities of 700 gallons per day and 800 gallons per day, and this is the region in which profit is maximized.

Finding the Maximum Profit by Comparing Marginal Revenue and Marginal Cost

In the preceding section, we calculated profit by subtracting *total* cost from *total* revenue. We then studied the profit numbers to find the profit-maximizing level of output. This method is OK, but a different method is even better. Our second method uses *marginal* revenue and *marginal* cost.

Since Cider Space is a perfectly competitive firm, its marginal revenue is equal to the market price. Marginal revenue (MR) is $2 for each additional gallon of apple cider. But marginal cost (MC) is only $1.10 for the first 100 gallons produced. Therefore, MR is greater than MC for the first 100 gallons, so it makes sense for the firm to produce and sell those units. Whenever a firm can spend an extra $1.10 to get $2 of extra revenue, it should do so.

As Cider Space increases its output from 100 gallons per day to 200 gallons per day, and to 300 gallons, and to 400 gallons, MR continues to be greater than MC, so the firm should also produce and sell those units. *When MR is greater than MC, a firm should expand its output.*

As the firm increases its output from 700 gallons per day to 800 gallons per day, MR is exactly equal to MC. Even though profit doesn't change as Cider Space increases its output from 700 gallons to 800 gallons, we assume that the firm will go ahead and produce 800 gallons per day.

However, if Cider Space were to increase its output from 800 gallons per day to 900 gallons per day, MR would be $2 and MC would be $2.20. It doesn't make sense for the firm to produce apple cider for an additional cost of $2.20 per gallon, when the stuff can only be sold for $2 per gallon. Therefore, Cider Space won't produce any more than 800 gallons per day. *When MC is greater than MR, firms should not produce more.* Instead, they should reduce their output.

The Rule for Profit Maximization: Marginal Revenue Equals Marginal Cost

We can now state the rule by which the profit-maximizing, perfectly competitive firm chooses its quantity. We call it the *MR = MC Rule*:

If a perfectly competitive firm is to maximize its profit, it should produce the quantity at which marginal revenue is equal to marginal cost. In symbols, MR = MC. Since the perfectly competitive firm's marginal revenue is equal to its price (MR = P), it follows that MR = MC = P at the profit-maximizing quantity. *Thus, we can also say that, to maximize profit, the firm should produce the quantity at which price is equal to marginal cost. In symbols, P = MC.*

If there is no level of output at which price is exactly equal to marginal cost, we would state the rule as follows: The perfectly competitive firm will maximize profit by producing the highest quantity at which MR>MC.

This isn't the first time that we have seen a rule like this. Back in Chapter 7, which dealt with consumer behavior, we saw that the consumer maximizes consumer surplus by choosing to purchase and consume the quantity at which marginal utility is equal to price. This is really very similar to the MR=MC rule for the perfectly competitive firm. In each case, economic activity is expanded until *marginal benefit is equal to marginal cost.* For the consumer, the marginal benefit from consuming more of a good is called marginal utility, and the marginal cost is the price that must be paid to buy the good. For the perfectly competitive firm, the marginal benefit from producing and selling more of a good is called marginal revenue, and the marginal cost is just called marginal cost.

The MR = MC rule can also be shown graphically. Figure 9.4 shows the MR curve and MC curve for Cider Space. The MC curve looks like a bunch of stair steps, rather than a smooth line. The MC curve is the same as the

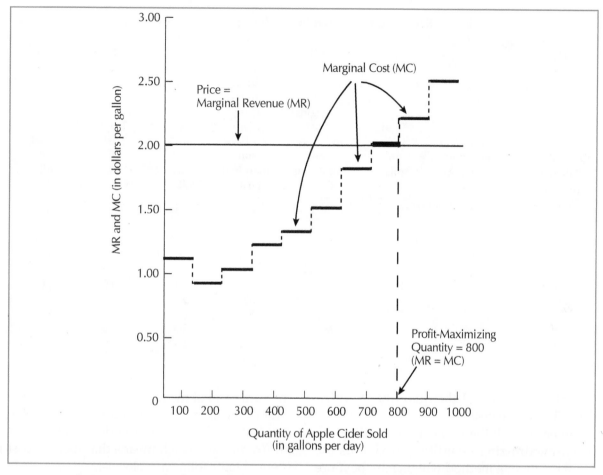

**Figure 9.4 Marginal Revenue, Marginal Cost, and the Profit-Maximizing Quantity
of Output for Cider Space**

Any firm that wants to maximize profit will produce and sell the quantity at which MR = MC. For a perfectly competitive firm like Cider Space, marginal revenue is the market price. Therefore, it is also true that the perfectly competitive firm will maximize profit by producing and selling the quantity at which P = MC.

MR curve between 700 gallons per day and 800 gallons per day, which is where profit is maximized.

We now have two ways of finding the profit-maximizing quantity for a perfectly competitive firm. (1) Profit is maximized where the vertical distance between the TR curve and the TC curve is greatest. This is the same as saying that profit is maximized by producing and selling the quantity at which TR is parallel to TC. (2) Profit is maximized where the MC curve crosses the MR curve.

These two statements are very closely related. Remember that marginal revenue is the slope of the total-revenue curve, and marginal cost is the slope of the total-cost curve. When we say that MR equals MC, this is *the same* as saying that the slopes of the TR and TC curves are equal. When the slopes of the two curves are equal, the vertical distance between them is greatest. In other words, the two ways of finding the profit-maximizing quantity will always get the same answer! If we find the quantity at which MR = MC, we

Table 9.4 Revenues, Costs, and Profits for American Gizmos, Inc.

(1) Q	(2) P	(3) TR	(4) MC	(5) TVC	(6) TFC	(7) TC	(8) Profit
Quantity of Gizmos per Day	Price, in Dollars per Gizmo = Marginal Revenue = Average Revenue	Total Revenue, in Dollars (= PxQ)	Marginal Cost, in Dollars per Additional Gizmo	Total Variable Cost, in Dollars (= sum of marginal costs)	Total Fixed Cost, in Dollars	Total Cost, in Dollars (=TFC+TVC)	Profit, in Dollars (=TR–TC)
0	$5	$ 0	—	$ 0	$0	$ 0	$ 0
1	$5	$ 5	$1	$ 1	$0	$ 1	$ 4
2	$5	$10	$2	$ 3	$0	$ 3	$ 7
3	$5	$15	$3	$ 6	$0	$ 6	$ 9
4	$5	$20	$4	$10	$0	$10	$10
5	$5	$25	$5	$15	$0	$15	$10
6	$5	$30	$6	$21	$0	$21	$ 9
7	$5	$35	$7	$28	$0	$28	$ 7
8	$5	$40	$8	$36	$0	$36	$ 4
9	$5	$45	$9	$45	$0	$45	$ 0

will also have found the quantity at which (TR – TC) is greatest.

Even though the two ways of finding the profit-maximizing quantity will give us the same result, one method will usually be more useful. It's often much easier to think in terms of *marginal* revenues and costs. If MR > MC, the firm ought to expand output; if MR < MC, the firm ought to cut back. If MR = MC, the firm is maximizing profit.

Another Example

Let's face it—This chapter presents a lot of material for you to digest. To help you to solidify your understanding, we'll now present another numerical example.

American Gizmos, Inc., is a perfectly competitive producer of gizmos. The firm's costs and revenues are shown in Table 9.4. The market price of a gizmo is $5. Therefore the firm's marginal revenue is $5, and its average revenue is also $5. The firm's marginal cost is $1 for the first gizmo, $2 for the second gizmo, $3 for the third gizmo, and so on. Total variable cost is

the sum of all of the marginal costs. Therefore, when three gizmos are produced, total variable cost is ($1+$2+$3) = $6. American Gizmos has no fixed costs, which means that its total cost is equal to its total variable cost.

American Gizmos should produce at least one gizmo, since the MR of the first gizmo is $5, while the MC is only $1. By similar reasoning, American Gizmos should also produce a second, third, and fourth gizmo. The MR of the fifth gizmo is $5, and the MC is also $5. Profit doesn't increase by adding the fifth gizmo, but profit doesn't decrease, either. We assume that the firm will go ahead and produce the fifth gizmo. However, the MC of the sixth gizmo is $6, which is greater than the MR of the sixth gizmo. Therefore, the firm should *not* produce the sixth gizmo. American Gizmos will maximize its profit by producing and selling five gizmos. As shown in column (8) of Table 9.4, the firm will earn a profit of $10.

By comparing MR and MC, we have seen that American Gizmos maximizes profit by producing five gizmos. This is shown in panel

(a) of Figure 9.5. We can also get the same answer by comparing *total* revenue with *total* cost, as shown in panel (b) of Figure 9.5. The vertical distance between the TR curve and the TC curve is greatest at a quantity of five gizmos, so that five gizmos is the profit-maximizing quantity.

The Firm's Profit: Further Graphical Analysis

When we compared total revenue and total cost in Figure 9.5(b), we could actually show the *amount* of profit, because profit is the vertical distance between the TR curve and the TC curve. Profit is measured in dollars, and Figure 9.5(b) has *dollars* on the vertical axis. However, in Figure 9.5(a), the vertical axis shows *dollars per unit*. So far, in Figure 9.5(a), we've only shown the profit-maximizing *quantity*; we haven't yet shown how much profit the firm makes. Fortunately, it only takes one more step for us to draw the amount of profit in a graph like Figure 9.5(a).

We have seen that profit is equal to total revenue minus total cost: Profit = TR–TC. If we divide both sides of this equation by quantity, we have the following:

Profit/Q = TR/Q – TC/Q.

In other words, profit per unit is equal to revenue per unit minus cost per unit.

Revenue per unit, which is also called average revenue, is total revenue divided by quantity. The average revenue is the price of the firm's output. *Cost per unit,* which is also called average total cost, is total cost divided by quantity. *Profit per unit,* which is also called average profit, is equal to (revenue per unit) minus (cost per unit). In other words,

**Average Profit =
Average Revenue – Average Total Cost.**

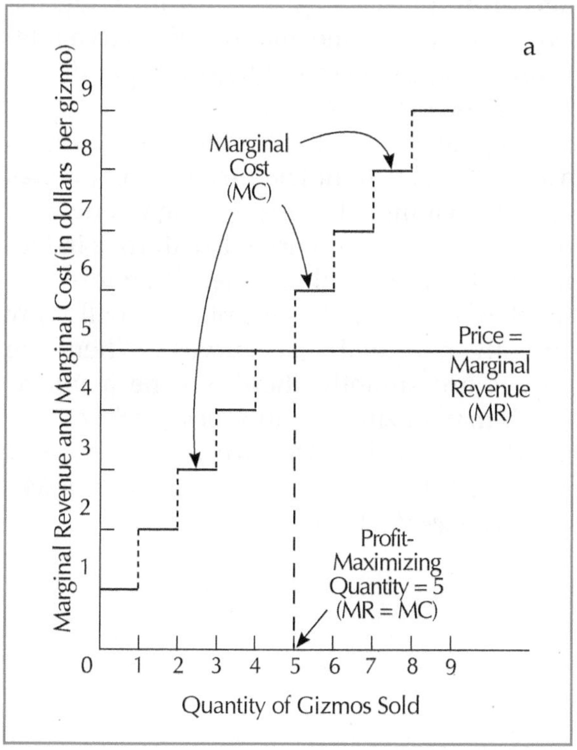

**Figure 9.5 Panel (a)
Marginal Revenue, Marginal Cost, and the Profit-Maximizing Quantity of Output for American Gizmos**

Any firm will maximize profit by choosing the quantity at which MR = MC. In the special case of a perfectly competitive firm, such as American Gizmos, marginal revenue is the price. Therefore, American Gizmos maximizes profit by producing and selling five gizmos: At this quantity, P = MR = MC.

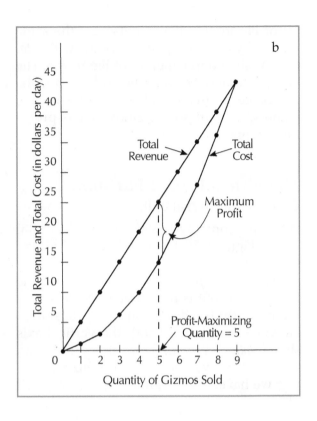

Figure 9.5 Panel (b)
Total Revenue, Total Cost, and Profit
for American Gizmos

The firm's profit-maximizing quantity is found where the vertical distance between the total-revenue curve and the total-cost curve is greatest. In the case of American Gizmos, the firm maximizes profit by producing and selling five gizmos per day.

Next, if we use the fact that average revenue is equal to price, we can say that

Average Profit = P – ATC.

Now, if we multiply average profit by quantity, we get back to total profit:

Profit = (Average Profit)x(Q) =
(P – ATC)x(Q).

We have already seen that the firm's profit-maximizing quantity is 5 gizmos per day. Table 9.4 shows that the firm's total cost is $15 when the quantity is 5 gizmos per day. Therefore, average total cost is ($15/5 gizmos), which is $3 per gizmo. If we take the price of $5 per gizmo, and subtract the average total cost of $3 per gizmo, we get an aver-

age profit of $2 per gizmo. Multiplying the average profit by the quantity gives us a total profit of ($2 per gizmo)x(5 gizmos per day) = $10 per day.

In Figure 9.5(a), the marginal-cost curve is a stair-step function: The curve makes a series of sudden jumps. There's nothing wrong with that, except that MC curves like the one in Figure 9.5(a) are cumbersome. Therefore, for much of the rest of this chapter, we will draw smooth marginal-cost curves. When the curves are smooth, there will be a *unique* profit-maximizing quantity. *In a graph in which the MR curve and the MC curve are smooth, profit is maximized at the unique quantity where the MR curve crosses the MC curve.*

ECONOMIC COSTS VS. ACCOUNTING COSTS

Economists and accountants define costs differently. The difference arises because economists emphasize the idea of opportunity cost, whereas accountants place less emphasis on opportunity cost.

When an accountant puts together a balance sheet for a firm, he or she will focus on the *explicit* costs of the firm. These are the direct, out-of-pocket costs, such as payments of wages, purchases of materials, and so on. If the firm has a check stub or an electronic record saying that it paid wages to a worker, the accountant will record the expense. *Accounting cost* is the sum of all of these explicit, out-of-pocket costs.

However, accounting costs don't necessarily include all of the relevant costs. To see this, consider the following example: Lyle Robinson owns an ice-cream store. He doesn't pay himself a salary, as such. Since no explicit payment is made, an accountant would not include Lyle's labor as a cost. From the economist's point of view, though, the time that Lyle spends working at the store is most definitely a cost. It is a cost because of the *opportunity cost* of working at the ice-cream store. If Lyle didn't work at the ice-cream store, he could earn money somewhere else.

Before he opened the ice-cream store, Lyle worked as a loan officer in a bank. If he wants to, he could go back to a job in the financial-services industry, at an annual salary of $40,000. Thus we would say that the opportunity cost of Lyle's time is $40,000 per year.

Let's say that Lyle's accountant tells him that the ice-cream store's revenues for the year are $200,000, and its out-of-pocket expenses are $150,000. Thus, the accountant would say that Lyle's profit is ($200,000 − $150,000) = $50,000. In other words,

**Accounting Profit =
Total Revenue −
Explicit, Accounting Costs**

However, this calculation gives a misleading impression, because it doesn't include all of the true economic costs. Economists say that *economic costs* are the payments that a firm must make, to attract resources away from other activities in which they might be used. Economic costs include the explicit, accounting costs, *and* they also include *implicit* costs, such as the opportunity cost of Lyle's time.

**Economic Costs =
Accounting Costs + Implicit Costs**

Economic profit is equal to total revenue minus all costs, regardless of whether they are explicit or implicit. In other words,

Economic Profit
= Total Revenue − Economic Cost
= Total Revenue − Accounting Costs − Implicit Costs
= Accounting Profit − Implicit Costs

Figure 9.6 is a graphical representation of the differences between economic costs and accounting costs.

In our example of Lyle, the owner of an ice-cream store, an economist would say that Lyle has to pay an implicit cost when he runs the ice-cream store. The implicit cost is the opportunity cost of his time, which is $40,000 per year. To find Lyle's true *economic* profit, we begin with the accounting profit, and then subtract the opportunity cost of Lyle's time. This gives an economic profit of ($50,000 − $40,000) = $10,000.

What if Lyle's accounting profit were only $40,000? In this case, his economic profit from the ice-cream store would be ($40,000 − $40,000) = zero. When you see that Lyle's economic profit is zero, you might think that it's bad news, but it really is not a problem. When Lyle is making an economic profit of zero in the ice-cream store, it means that he is doing just as well at the ice-cream store as he would have done in his alternative employment in a bank.

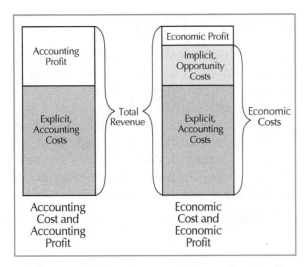

Figure 9.6 Accounting Cost, Accounting Profit, Economic Cost, and Economic Profit

Accounting cost includes only the explicit, out-of-pocket costs that are paid by the firm. Economic cost includes accounting cost, *plus* any implicit opportunity costs. These implicit opportunity costs include a "normal" rate of return on capital investment. Thus, economic cost is *greater* than accounting cost. Accounting profit is total revenue minus accounting cost, and economic profit is total revenue minus economic cost. Therefore, economic profit is *less* than accounting profit.

Thus there is no reason for Lyle to abandon the ice-cream store.

But what if Lyle's accounting profit were only $20,000? In this case, his economic profit from the ice-cream store would be ($20,000 – $40,000), or –$20,000. We have just seen that an economic profit of zero is OK, but this is a *negative* economic profit, and that is definitely a problem. When Lyle's economic profit from the ice-cream store is –$20,000, he could do a lot better by giving up the ice-cream store and getting a job with a bank.

Economic cost and economic profit provide extremely important information, because they are defined to include opportunity cost. Thus economic cost and economic profit give us a good guide to making

correct decisions. If the business firm is making a positive economic profit, it may be beneficial for the firm to expand. If the firm is making a zero economic profit, there is no incentive to change its actions. However, if the business firm is making negative economic profit, it should consider the possibility of going out of business. In this chapter, we will take a more detailed look at these concepts, including the decision to go out of business.

A "Normal" Rate of Return

In the case of Lyle Robinson, the owner of the ice-cream store, the difference between accounting cost and economic cost is the amount he could earn if he were to work in a bank. In this example, the relevant opportunity cost is the value of the *labor* provided by the owner of the firm. In other cases, the value of *capital* can be an important opportunity cost, as well.

Investors expect to earn a positive rate of return on their capital investments. Let's say that the "normal" rate of return on a capital investment is 10 percent per year. If this is the case, then a 10-percent rate of return is the opportunity cost of capital investment. Even though this "normal" rate of return is not an explicit, accounting cost, it certainly is an economic cost. After all, if a firm had not invested in its current line of business, it could have invested in some other line of business. The firm could earn a "normal" return by investing in a portfolio of stocks and bonds from many different companies. If the firm is earning less than the "normal" or "average" return, it must consider the possibility that it could do better by going out of business, and putting the money where it *does* earn a normal return.

What is a "normal" return on investment? In fact, what is "normal" may change from year to year. However, when you think of a normal return, you might think of a rate of return of 7 percent per year, or 10 percent, or 12 percent.

As a result of this way of thinking, economists say that the firm is making zero *economic* profits, even when it makes a normal return on its capital investment. Let's assume that a normal rate of return is 10 percent per year. Then, if the firm earns an accounting profit of 18 percent per year, it is making an economic profit of (18–10) = 8 percent per year. If the firm earns an accounting profit of only 10 percent per year, it is making zero economic profit because the firm's accounting profit is exactly equal to the normal rate of return. Still, if the firm is earning zero economic profit, it should stay in business, because it is doing as well as the market average. Only when the firm is earning a negative economic profit should it think about going out of business.

Reality Check:
Interim Review Questions

IR9-6. Is economic cost greater than, equal to, or less than accounting cost?

IR9-7. Is economic profit greater than, equal to, or less than accounting profit?

IR9-8. Joe's Burger Joint is earning an accounting profit of 6%. The normal rate of return on an investment in the burger industry is 12%. What is Joe's economic profit?

Profit and Loss for the Perfectly Competitive Firm

Panel (a) of Figure 9.7 shows the profit for a perfectly competitive firm that is mak-ing positive economic profit. *In a diagram like this, profit is the area of a rectangle. The base of the rectangle is the quantity sold by the firm, and the rectangle's height is the difference between price and average total cost.*

In Figure 9.7(a), we can tell that the firm is making positive profit, because P > ATC at the profit-maximizing quantity, Q*. (The profit-maximizing quantity is Q* because that is the quantity of which marginal revenue is equal to marginal cost.) If P = ATC at the profit-maximizing quantity, then the firm is making zero economic profit, as in Figure 9.7(b). In this case, there isn't any rectangle to represent profit, because profit is zero. Finally, when P < ATC at the quantity where MR = MC, the firm is suffering economic losses, as in panels (c) and (d) of Figure 9.7.

Reality Check:
Interim Review Questions

IR9-9. At its current level of output, a farm's marginal cost of producing hogs is less than the price of hogs. Should the firm expand output, or reduce output, or keep output the same?

IR9-10. Profit is maximized at the quantity where MR equals MC. Also, profit is maximized at the quantity where the TR curve is parallel to the TC curve. Explain why these two methods of finding the profit-maximizing quantity will lead us to the same answer.

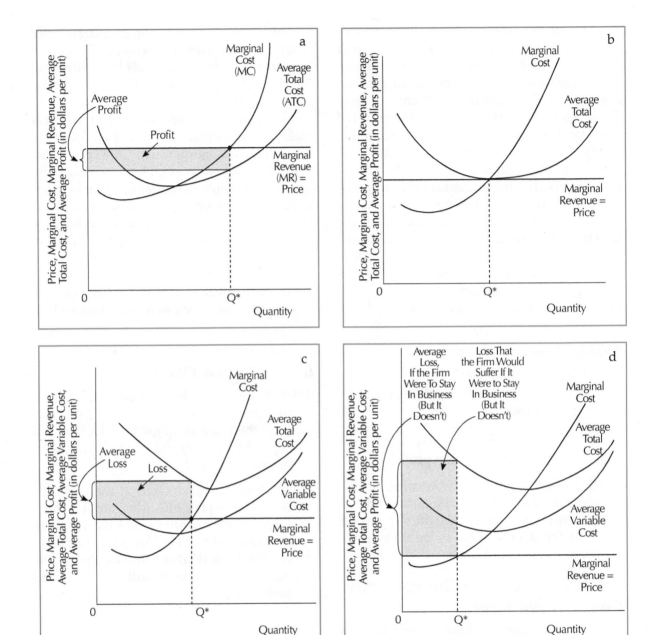

Figure 9.7 Revenues, Costs, and Profits, for Perfectly Competitive Firms

For any firm that maximizes profit by producing a positive amount, the profit-maximizing quantity is always found where MR = MC. If P > ATC at the profit-maximizing quantity (as in panel (a)), the firm is making positive economic profit. If P = ATC at the profit-maximizing quantity (as in panel (b)), the firm is making zero economic profit. If P < ATC at the profit-maximizing quantity (as in panels (c) and (d)), the firm is suffering economic losses. If the firm is suffering economic losses, it will stay in business if P > AVC (as in panel (c)). If P < AVC at the profit-maximizing quantity (as in panel (d)), the firm should shut down.

THE SUPPLY CURVE OF THE PERFECTLY COMPETITIVE FIRM

When the market price is $2 per gallon of cider, Cider Space maximizes its profit by producing 800 gallons per day. But what if the price were to rise to $2.20 per gallon? The firm would still want to maximize its profit, so it would still choose to produce the quantity at which P=MR=MC. The profit-maximizing quantity would rise to 900 gallons per day. If the price were to fall to $1.80 per gallon, quantity would decrease to 700 gallons per day. For each of these market prices, Cider Space will maximize its profit by producing the quantity at which P = MR = MC.

The Supply Curve and the Marginal-Cost Curve: A First Look

In the preceding paragraph, we have outlined the relationship between the market price and the quantity that Cider Space would supply. In other words, we've described how to construct the firm's supply schedule and supply curve! If the firm produces at all, it will find the quantity at which P=MC. Therefore, at first glance, it appears that the firm's supply curve is the same as its marginal-cost curve.

However, this description of the supply curve of a perfectly competitive firm isn't quite complete. The problem is that the firm may go out of business if the price is low enough. We turn to this problem in the next section.

The Short-Run Shut-Down Decision of the Perfectly Competitive Firm

Earlier in this chapter, we considered the case in which the price of apple cider is $2 per gallon. When the price is this high, Cider Space is able to earn a profit. However, if the price were to fall far enough, the firm would suffer economic losses. Let's assume that the price is low, and that Cider Space is losing money.

You might think that the firm would go out of business immediately if its economic profit is negative, but this isn't necessarily the case. If the firm shuts down, its total revenue will go to zero, but its total costs will still be greater than zero. This is because *the firm has to pay its total fixed costs, even if it produces nothing.* If the firm shuts down, it will have losses equal to its total fixed costs. On the other hand, if the firm stays in business, its losses are equal to the difference between total cost and total revenue:

Losses if Firm Stays in Business = TC – TR

Losses if Firm Shuts Down = TFC

Thus the firm's choice of whether to shut down depends on whether TFC is larger than (TC – TR). *If TFC < (TC – TR), the firm should quit producing,* because its losses from shutting down are smaller than its losses from staying in business.

Now, remember that total cost (TC) is equal to the sum of total variable cost (TVC) and total fixed cost (TFC): TC = TVC + TFC. If we substitute this into our earlier expression, we see that the firm should *shut down if TFC < (TFC + TVC – TR)*. Now, we subtract TFC from each side of the inequality. The firm should *quit producing if 0 < (TVC – TR)*. Finally, if we add TR to both sides of this inequality, we see that the firm should *shut down if TR < TVC*.

Now, we can describe the ***short-run shut-down decision*** for the perfectly competitive firm: *The firm should go out of business if total revenue is less than total variable cost. If we divide total revenue by the number of units of output, we get average revenue, which is equal to price. If we divide total variable cost by the number of units of output, we get average variable cost. Thus when we say that the firm should go out of business if* *total revenue is less than total variable cost, it's the same as saying that the firm should go out of business if average revenue (which is equal to price) is less than average variable cost.* If the price isn't even high enough for the firm to cover its *variable* costs, it's time to go out of business.

However, if price is equal to or greater than average variable cost, the firm should stay in business in the short run, even when it is suffering economic losses. Why would a firm stay in business, even if it is suffering losses? The reason is that its losses would be even worse if it were to shut down. However, this does not mean that such a firm will stay in business forever. The firm will face a long-run decision of whether to continue to produce. Consider a firm with a one-year lease on buildings and equipment. For this firm, the short run is one year. The firm's decision will depend on whether it believes that it can turn its losses into profits by next year. If demand increases, or if the firm can find a way to cut its costs, it should try again next year. If not, it would be best to go out of business when the lease is up.

Panels (c) and (d) of Figure 9.7, on p. 222, show two possibilities for firms that are suffering losses. Unlike panels (a) and (b), panels (c) and (d) include the average-variable-cost curve, because the shut-down decision depends on whether price is below average variable cost. In panel (c), price is greater than average variable cost, which means that the firm should stay in business. In panel (d), however, price is less than average variable cost. Thus if the firm's cost and revenue curves are like the ones shown in panel (d), the firm should shut down.

In the long run, the firm is free to choose any scale of operations, including an output of zero. So, just because a money-losing firm stays in business for the time being, it does not necessarily follow that it will stay in business indefinitely.

Notice that the shut-down decision only involves *variable* costs. In other words, *fixed* costs do not play any role in the choice about whether a firm should shut down. This is because, by their very nature, fixed costs cannot be avoided. The firm has to pay its fixed costs if it goes out of business, just as it has to pay its fixed costs if it does not go out of business. Since the fixed costs are there in either case, they cannot have any effect on the shut-down decision. When we make decisions, there is no need to pay any attention to the things over which we have no control.

In *Real Economics for Real People 9.1*, we discuss some of the changes that have occurred in American agriculture, as farms have decided to go out of business.

The Short-Run Supply Curve of the Perfectly Competitive Firm

We now can give a complete description of the perfectly competitive firm's **short-run supply curve**: *When price is greater than or equal to average variable cost, the supply curve is the marginal-cost curve. When price is less than average variable cost, the firm will shut down, and its quantity supplied will be zero.*

The perfectly competitive firm's short-run supply curve is shown in Figure 9.8. When the price is greater than or equal to average variable cost, the firm will produce a positive quantity. The firm will choose the quantity at which price is equal to marginal cost, which means that this portion of the supply curve is the same as the MC curve. However, when the price is less than average variable cost, the firm will stop producing. This is why a part of the firm's supply curve is on the vertical axis, because all points on the vertical axis have a quantity of zero.

Real Economics for Real People 9.1:
The Shrinkage of American Agriculture

In the last several decades, the agricultural sector has had enormous technological improvements. As a result, the supply curves for many agricultural commodities have shifted dramatically to the right. At the same time, the demand for most agricultural products is fairly inelastic. Thus, the prices of agricultural products have not kept pace with the prices of other goods. Therefore, it isn't surprising that many farms have decided to go out of business. In 1950, the United States had about 5.4 million farms. By 2010, there were only about 2.2 million farms. Some farms have found that prices aren't high enough to cover their average variable costs, and they have shut down in the short run. Other farms have been able to stay in business in the short run, but have decided to quit sooner or later.

On average, the farms that have survived are larger than the farms that existed at an earlier time. Still, the total number of cultivated acres in the United States has decreased.

This situation creates some difficult problems for the political system. Legislators from rural areas are understandably concerned about their shrinking populations. This probably provides at least a partial explanation for why American taxpayers have paid such massive subsidies to farmers. The subsidies can be seen as an attempt to slow down the painful process of adjustment in the agricultural sector. As a result of the hundreds of billions of dollars of subsidies, some farms have probably managed to stay in business, even though they would have gone out of business without the subsidies. Farm employment is probably somewhat higher than it would have been without the subsidies.

However, even with subsidies in the billions, many farms have concluded that they need to go out of business. When prices are too low to cover costs, millions of farmers have decided that it was time to stop.

Reality Check:
Interim Review Questions

IR9-11. Jones and Company is a perfectly competitive firm, which makes men's dress shirts. The market price is $20 per shirt. Average total cost is $24 per shirt, and average variable cost is $16 per shirt. Is the firm making profits or losses? If it is suffering losses, should it go out of business in the short run?

IR9-12. How would your answer to question IR9-11 change if you were told that average variable cost is $22 per shirt, while price is still $20 per shirt, and average total cost is still $24 per shirt?

Figure 9.8 The Short-Run Supply Curve for a Perfectly Competitive Firm

If price is greater than or equal to average variable cost (AVC), the firm will produce a positive quantity of output. If a positive quantity is produced, the quantity will be given by the marginal-cost curve (MC). This is why a portion of the perfectly competitive firm's supply curve is the same as a part of the MC curve. However, if price falls below AVC, the firm's best decision is to shut down. This means that the firm's output will be zero, so that a portion of the firm's supply curve is on the vertical axis.

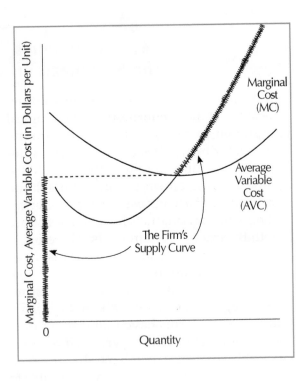

THE SHORT-RUN MARKET SUPPLY CURVE

We construct the short-run *market supply curve* in a perfectly competitive industry by adding together the supply curves for all of the individual firms. The market supply curve for winter wheat is the sum of the supply curves for all wheat farmers, and the market supply curve for work gloves is the sum of the supply curves for all glove manufacturers. If a perfectly competitive industry has 1000 firms, and if each firm is willing to produce five units when the price is $10 per unit, then the quantity supplied in the market is (1000 firms)x(5 units per firm) = 5000 units when the price is $10. Graphically, we add the supply curves of the individual firms horizontally to get the market supply curve.

This is basically the same procedure that we used in Chapter 3 and Chapter 7, where we formed the market *demand* curve, by adding together the individual demand curves for all of the consumers in the market.

CHANGES IN THE NUMBER OF FIRMS IN A PERFECTLY COMPETITIVE INDUSTRY

Modern industries are dynamic, with lots of changes over time. Sometimes new firms start up, and sometimes existing firms shut down. We need to take a closer look at why the number of firms might change, and we need to study what happens as a result.

Profits and Entry into the Industry

In one of our examples from earlier in this chapter, Cider Space was earning positive economic profit. But that profit can't be sustained for long, because it's easy for new firms to enter a perfectly competitive industry. If the existing firms are earning positive economic profits, new firms will want to get in on the action.

What will happen when new firms come into the industry? Since the market supply curve is the sum of the supply curves of the individual firms, *an increase in the number of firms will shift the industry supply curve to the right.* Like any rightward shift in the market supply curve, this will cause an increase in the market equilibrium quantity, and a decrease in the market equilibrium price.

This process is illustrated in Figure 9.9, for the market for ballpoint pens. Panel (a) of Figure 9.9 shows the situation faced by an individual firm, called Pen & Tell, while panel (b) shows the entire market. Let's say that the original market price for a particular type of pen is $0.80 per pen, and that this is high

enough that the firms can earn positive economic profit. The profit is indicated by the shaded rectangle in panel (a) of the figure. Pen & Tell produces Q_{f0}, and the market quantity is Q_{m0}. (Note that, in the two panels of Figure 9.9, the horizontal axes aren't drawn to the same scale.)

In response to the positive economic profit, new firms will enter the industry. This will shift the market supply curve for pens to the right, from S_{m0} to S_{m1}, as shown in panel (b) of Figure 9.9. The price will continue to drop until the economic profit has been eliminated. In the case shown, economic profit will fall to zero when the price drops to $0.70 per pen. The individual firm's quantity drops from Q_{f0} to Q_{f1}, and the market quantity increases from Q_{m0} to Q_{m1}. Pen & Tell and the other individual firms will actually produce slightly fewer pens in the long-run equilibrium than they

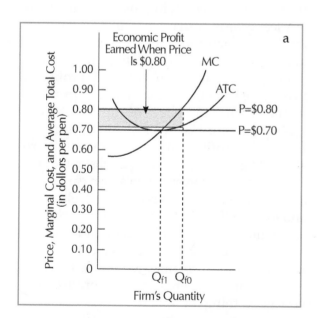
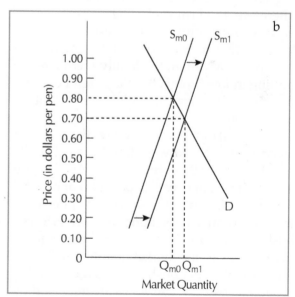

Figure 9.9 The Response of the Firm and the Market, When Positive Economic Profit Is Being Made

When the price of a pen is $0.80, positive economic profit is earned. For the individual firm, profit is the shaded region in panel (a). As a result of the profits, new firms enter the industry, which pushes the market supply curve to the right, from S_{m0} to S_{m1} in panel (b). This lowers the market price to $0.70. When the price is $0.70 per pen, panel (a) shows that the firm's profit-maximizing quantity is Q_{f1}. At this quantity, P = ATC, which means that the firm is earning zero economic profit. Entry into the industry has eliminated the economic profit.

did before the new firms entered. However, even though each individual *firm* produces less, there are enough new firms that the total *market* quantity will rise.

Losses and Exit from the Industry

We have just seen that economic *profit* will bring new firms into the industry, and that this will drive prices down. If the firms in an industry are suffering economic *losses*, the process runs in reverse.

Consider the Renkowski family farm, which is earning an *accounting* profit of $20,000 per year from its corn operation. Even though the farm is making an accounting profit, which means that its revenues are greater than its explicit, out-of-pocket costs, it is still doing very poorly. The Renkowski farm is making enough to cover its out-of-pocket costs, but it isn't making enough to cover its opportunity costs. Therefore, the firm is earning a negative *economic* profit. Its return on investment is very low, relative to what other investments are earning. In addition, the family members are putting in long hours, but they aren't earning the kind of money they might earn in other occupations.

Panel (a) of Figure 9.10 shows the situation faced by the Renkowski family farm, while panel (b) shows the entire market. (As in Figure 9.9, the horizontal axes of panel (a) and panel (b) aren't drawn to the same scale.) Let's say that the original market price for corn is $4 per bushel. The individual farm produces a quantity of Q_{f0}, and the market quantity is Q_{m0}. At the price of $4 per bushel, farms are suffering economic losses. These losses are indicated by the shaded rectangle in panel (a) of Figure 9.10.

After considering the prospects for the future, some of the farms will decide to go out of business. However, we assume that the Renkowskis decide to stay in business. This might happen, for example, if the Renkowskis are more optimistic about the future than are some other farming families. Another possibility is that different farms have slightly different cost curves, so that the price is below average variable cost for some farms, but not for the Renkowski farm.

When some farms go out of business, the market supply curve shifts to the left, as shown in panel (b) of Figure 9.10. The price will rise until the economic losses are gone. In the case shown, economic profit will rise to zero when the price increases to $5 per bushel. The firm's quantity goes up from Q_{f0} to Q_{f1}, and the market quantity decreases from Q_{m0} to Q_{m1}.

Because of free entry and exit, perfectly competitive industries will always be moving in the direction of zero economic profit. If firms are making positive economic profit, new firms will enter, and this will compete the profits away. If firms are experiencing losses, some firms will leave the industry. This will raise the price until the remaining firms can earn zero economic profit. It bears repeating that there is nothing wrong with zero economic profit. If a firm were earning zero *accounting* profit, it would be in bad shape. (A firm with zero accounting profit has a substantially negative economic profit. That is, a firm with zero accounting profit is suffering a substantial economic loss.) However, when a firm earns zero *economic* profit, the firm is doing as well as lots and lots of other firms. A firm that earns zero economic profit is earning enough to stay in business. In the next chapter, we will see that zero economic profits are not just "good enough". In fact, zero economic profits are a very good thing for society.

In *Real Economics for Real People 9.2*, we discuss a policy debate that has to do with the problems faced by workers when industries are shrinking.

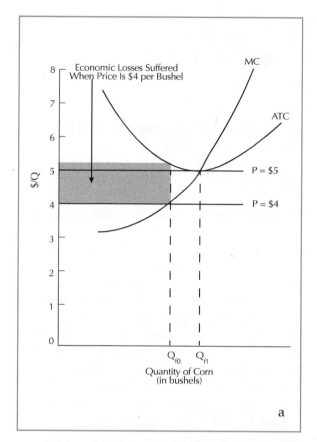
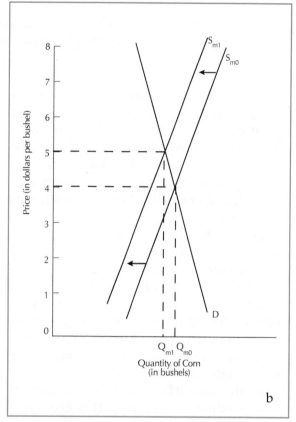

Figure 9.10 The Response of the Firm and the Market, When Economic Losses Are Being Made

When the price of a bushel of corn is $4, firms are suffering economic losses. For the individual firm, losses are represented by the shaded region in panel (a). As a result of the losses, some firms go out of business. This pushes the market supply curve to the left, from S_{m0} to S_{m1} in panel (b). This raises the market price to $5 per bushel. When the price is $5 per bushel, panel (a) shows that the firm's profit-maximizing quantity is Q_{f1}. At this quantity, P = ATC, so that the firm is earning zero economic profit. Exit from the industry has eliminated the economic losses.

Reality Check:
Interim Review Question

IR9-13. Currently, all of the firms in a perfectly competitive industry are earning positive economic profit. In response to these prof- its, what will happen in the future to (a) the number of firms in the industry, (b) the market price, and (c) the level of profit in the industry?

Real Economics for Real People 9.2:
Should Businesses Be Required to Give
Advance Notice of Layoffs?

Free entry is crucial to the operation of competitive industries, because it guarantees that positive economic profits will be competed away. Free exit is just as important, because free exit is the way in which losses are eliminated. If firms cannot leave an industry easily, they will know that they may be stuck in an unprofitable position for a long time. Therefore, firms may be less willing to get into the industry in the first place.

Freedom of exit is at the heart of an important debate in the past few decades. On one side of the debate are those who believe that business firms have a responsibility to notify their workers in advance, when they are planning layoffs or plant closings. On the other side are those who believe that firms should be able to leave an unprofitable industry quickly, so that economic activity can be carried on more efficiently.

In 1988, Congress passed the Worker Adjustment and Retraining Notification Act (WARN), despite the objections of President Reagan. This law requires employers with more than 100 employees to give at least 60 days' advance notice of plant closings or mass layoffs. (Some States and cities have stricter requirements, often including a 90-day notification period.) In addition to the exemption for firms with fewer than 100 employees, there are also exemptions for firms in special circumstances. Seasonal layoffs, which are common in agriculture and construction, are excluded from the law, as are layoffs caused by natural disasters. Also excluded are companies that are trying to find new financing in order to avoid bankruptcy. This is because an announcement of a plant closing or layoff might make it harder to obtain the financing.

Critics of the law say that it puts an unfair burden on the very businesses that are most in need of help. With the notification requirements, firms have the unpleasant choice of continuing to suffer losses for two more months, or paying workers up to two months' additional wages. Thus, the notification requirement for a single plant could push an entire firm into bankruptcy.

However, it appears that WARN hasn't caused too much dislocation so far. The many exclusions were designed to reduce the disruption that the law would cause for businesses. In fact, some firms have complied with the law, even though they were eligible to be excluded from its provisions. Nevertheless, mandatory notification laws will probably continue to be debated. Some proposals in Congress would extend the law to a six-month notification period, with four weeks of severance pay for each year of employment, health-care benefits for 18 months, and up to $10,000 in job-training benefits.

However, even these requirements look small when compared with some of the ones in Europe. In Italy, for a 45-year-old worker with 20 years of service who is currently earning $50,000 per year, a company must pay termination benefits of $130,000. In future debates, critics of these policies will surely point to the strict laws in Europe, where the number of jobs has increased much more slowly than in the United States.

THE EFFICIENCY OF PERFECT COMPETITION

Since only a few industries are perfectly competitive, it may seem strange that we study perfect competition before we study any other market structure. One reason for this is that perfectly competitive markets lead to some very good results. In the language of economists, perfect competition tends to lead to "efficient" outcomes.

Average Total Cost Is Minimized

We can demonstrate the efficiency of perfect competition in several ways. One aspect of efficiency is that *perfectly competitive firms will produce for the minimum cost per unit.* In other words, average total cost will be minimized under perfect competition.

To understand this, recall two things about perfectly competitive firms. First, they maximize profit, which means that they produce the quantity at which *price is equal to marginal cost.* Second, because of free entry and exit, perfectly competitive industries have a tendency to move toward zero economic profit. When profit is zero, *price equals average total cost.* Since P = MC *and* P = ATC, it follows that MC = ATC. But ATC reaches its minimum point at the quantity where MC = ATC. Therefore, if MC = ATC, it must be true that ATC is minimized!

You can see this graphically by taking another look at Figure 9.7(b), or Figure 9.9(a), or Figure 9.10(a). Since Figure 9.10(a) is the most recent of the three, we'll concentrate on it. When the price of corn is $5 per bushel, the Renkowski family farm produces Q_{f1}, and earns zero profit. Figure 9.10(a) shows that Q_{f1} is the quantity at which price, marginal cost, and average total cost are all equal. *The average-total-cost curve is at its minimum point!*

Cost minimization is a very desirable property of perfectly competitive markets. After all, if we don't minimize costs, we are being wasteful. This cost minimization comes about automatically, through the normal workings of the market.

Deadweight Loss Is Avoided

Figure 9.11 shows the supply and demand curves, in the perfectly competitive market for cotton sheets. As usual, the market equilibrium is given by the intersection of the supply curve and the demand curve, so that the perfectly competitive market quantity is Q*.

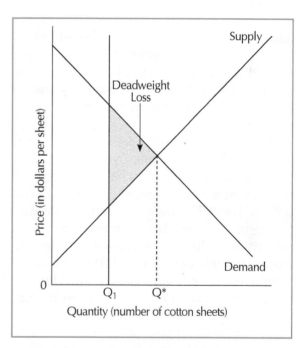

Figure 9.11 The Deadweight Loss When Quantity Is Reduced Below Its Perfectly Competitive Level

In a perfectly competitive market for cotton sheets, the equilibrium quantity is Q*. The demand curve represents the marginal benefit to society's consumers, and the supply curve represents the marginal cost to society's producers. For quantities of sheets between Q_1 and Q*, the marginal benefit is greater than the marginal cost. Therefore, if we only produce and consume Q_1, we will suffer a deadweight loss. The deadweight loss is the difference between marginal benefit and marginal cost, added over all of the units from Q_1 to Q*. In Figure 9.11, this is represented graphically by the area of the shaded triangle.

The marginal benefit from consumption of sheets is represented by the demand curve, and the marginal cost of production is represented by the supply curve. Since supply is equal to demand at the competitive equilibrium, a perfectly competitive market will produce the quantity that sets marginal benefit equal to marginal cost.

What would happen if society were to produce and consume some quantity other than Q^*? For example, what if the government were to institute a quota system, making it illegal for consumers to buy more than Q_1? (We saw an example of this kind of government restriction in Chapter 5, when we studied an import quota.) In Figure 9.11, when the quantity falls to Q_1, we give up consumption of all cotton sheets between Q_1 and Q^*. For each of these sheets, marginal benefit (given by the demand curve) is greater than marginal cost (given by the supply curve).

Q_1 is associated with a *deadweight loss*. Society is worse off consuming Q_1 than consuming Q^*. The *deadweight loss* is the difference between how well off we are at the perfectly competitive equilibrium quantity and how well off we are at some other quantity. Graphically, the deadweight loss is represented by the shaded triangle in Figure 9.11. We get a deadweight loss because we don't consume the cotton sheets between Q_1 and Q^*, even though

each of those sheets would give us more benefits than costs. The triangle of deadweight loss in Figure 9.11 is the sum of all of the losses that result from consuming Q_1, instead of Q^*.

For many people, it makes sense that we will suffer a deadweight loss if we reduce quantity *below* the perfectly competitive level. It may be a little more surprising that we also suffer a deadweight loss by increasing quantity *above* the perfectly competitive level. If we were to produce and consume more than Q^* in Figure 9.11, the marginal benefit of any additional sheets would be less than the marginal cost. In fact, *any* deviation from the perfectly competitive quantity will lead to a deadweight loss.

Again and again, we have seen that the way to maximize something is to choose the quantity at which marginal benefit is equal to marginal cost. Here, the best choice for society is to produce and consume the quantity at which marginal benefit equals marginal cost. Therefore, the best choice for society is the perfectly competitive equilibrium quantity, Q^*!

Reality Check:
Interim Review Question

IR9-14. Why does a deadweight loss occur when the market quantity is increased beyond the competitive equilibrium level?

ECONOMICS AND YOU: BEATING THE STOCK MARKET MAY BE HARDER THAN YOU THINK

At the beginning of this chapter, we told about Frank and Jenny, who were discussing whether it would be possible to beat the stock market. Certainly, *some* investors are able to pick stocks that do better than the market as a whole. If no one ever did better than average, the stock market would be pretty dull.

However, if Frank, or Jenny, or anyone else, is to beat the market *systematically*, it's

necessary to have special information or special ability. Getting special information is harder than you might think. If you see a stock-market analysis in the pages of the *Wall Street Journal*, you should remember that a few million other investors will see the same story on the same day. By the time a piece of information gets into the papers, it's probably too late to help you very much. Everybody else will be reacting to the same information. You may be able to earn a *good* rate of return on your investments, but it will be hard to do much *better* than the others.

If it's hard to obtain special information, it's even harder to bring special abilities to bear in the marketplace. Many billions of dollars change hands every day at the New York Stock Exchange. When that kind of money is involved, lots of very smart people will buy and sell in the market. You would have to be an extraordinary market analyst to be smarter than all of those other folks.

In fact, Wall Street occasionally produces some spectacular successes. One of the best-known is the Fidelity Magellan mutual fund. Investors who bought shares in Fidelity Magellan were hoping that the fund's managers would buy stocks that would outperform the market. And, for a while, that's exactly what Magellan's managers did! One popular way of charting a fund's performance is to compare its total return with the total return on the Standard and Poor's 500-stock index (S&P 500), which measures the performance of the stocks of 500 important companies. From 1977 to 1990, under the management of Peter Lynch, Fidelity Magellan had an average rate of return of 29.2 percent per year, compared with 15.8 percent per year for the S&P 500! Morris Smith served as fund manager from 1990 to 1992, and

he beat the market, too. Jeffrey Vinik took over in 1992, and he beat the S&P 500 by nearly nine percentage points in his first year.

By 1993, however, even Magellan was falling behind. Vinik resigned as fund manager in 1996, after three years of returns that were below those of the S&P 500. In 1997, Magellan closed its doors to new investors. Even though it is *sometimes* possible for a mutual fund to beat the market, *most* mutual funds aren't able to outperform the S&P 500.

The *Wall Street Journal* has sometimes held a contest, in which stock-market professionals pick certain stocks. The performance of those stocks over the next six months is compared with the performance of a group of stocks that are chosen by throwing darts at a dartboard. The professionals often beat the dart throwers, but they don't always do so.

This is the way it is with competitive markets, where information is freely available, and the individual players are all small relative to the market. Just as it's hard for one investor in the stock market to do better than average systematically, it's also hard for one wheat farmer to do better than the average wheat farmer systematically. It's also hard for one small textile firm to do better than the average small textile firm systematically. In a perfectly competitive market, you may do well, but it will be hard to do better than everybody else.

Chapter Summary

1. Economists distinguish among four types of market structure. These are perfect competition, monopoly, monopolistic competition, and oligopoly.

2. There are many firms in a perfectly competitive market, and each firm is small relative to the market. The firms produce standardized, or homogeneous, output. As a result of these two characteristics, the firms are price takers: They take the market price as given. Perfectly competitive markets are also characterized by free entry and exit, and by perfect information.

3. Since the perfectly competitive firm is a price taker, the demand for the firm's product is perfectly elastic. Even though the *market* demand curve slopes downward as we move from left to right, the demand curve facing the *individual firm* is a horizontal line. The height of the firm's demand curve is given by the market price.

4. Marginal revenue for the perfectly competitive firm is given by the market price, and average revenue is also given by the market price. Thus the individual firm's marginal-revenue curve and its average-revenue curve are both the same as the firm's demand curve.

5. If *any* firm (regardless of market structure) is to maximize profit, it will produce the quantity at which marginal revenue is equal to marginal cost. For a perfectly competitive firm, marginal revenue equals the price. Thus the perfectly competitive firm will maximize profit by producing the quantity at which price is equal to marginal cost.

6. Economists use the idea of opportunity cost. Thus economic cost is defined to include the "normal" return on a capital investment. Economic profit is defined to be net of this normal return. Economic cost is larger than accounting cost, so that economic profit is less than accounting profit.

7. The short-run supply curve for the perfectly competitive firm is the same as the firm's marginal-cost curve, as long as the price is at least as great as average variable cost. When price is less than average variable cost, the firm will shut down, and its quantity supplied will be zero.

8. The market supply curve is formed by horizontally adding the supply curves of the individual firms.

9. If positive economic profit is being earned in a perfectly competitive industry, new firms will enter. This will increase market supply, and will drive down the market price until the economic profits have been eliminated. If firms are suffering economic losses, some firms will leave the industry. This will increase the market price until firms are once again able to earn zero economic profit. The long-run tendency of a perfectly competitive industry is toward zero economic profit.

10. Perfect competition leads to some very attractive outcomes. First, in the long run, average total costs will be minimized. Second, at the perfectly competitive output, marginal benefit is equal to marginal cost. At any other level of output, there will be a deadweight loss.

Key Terms

Market Structure

Perfect Competition

Standardized or Homogeneous Product

Free Entry

Free Exit

Monopoly

Barriers to Entry

Differentiated Products

Monopolistic Competition

Oligopoly

Collusion

Price-Taking Firm

Market Power

Marginal Revenue

Total Revenue

Average Revenue

MR = MC Rule

Profit Maximization

Accounting Cost

Economic Cost

Economic Profit

Short-Run Shut-Down Decision

Short-Run Supply Curve

Market Supply Curve

Deadweight Loss

Key Figures

The key figures for this chapter are Figures 9.7(a), 9.7(b), 9.7(c), and 9.7(d), which show the profits for firms that are earning positive economic profit, or zero profit, or negative profit.

Questions and Problems

QP9-1. XYZ Corporation is currently producing 1000 units of output. The marginal cost of one additional unit is $10, and the marginal revenue is $12. Is the firm maximizing profit? If not, should it produce more or less?

QP9-2. The following table gives information on the costs of a perfectly competitive firm.

Quantity	Total Cost	Marginal Cost
0	20	—
1		5
2		3
3		5

a. When two units are produced, what is average variable cost?
b. When three units are produced, what is average total cost?
c. When two units are produced, what is average fixed cost?

QP9-3. List the characteristics of a perfectly competitive firm. What sets a perfectly competitive firm apart from a monopolistically competitive firm?

QP9-4. What type of market structure would apply most closely to each of the following firms?

a. Boeing Corporation, a producer of commercial aircraft.
b. A corn farm in Illinois.
c. A gasoline station on Interstate 80, in Auburn, California.
d. An electric power utility.

Quantity	Price	Marginal Revenue	Average Revenue	Total Revenue
1	$5	_____	_____	_____
2	5	_____	_____	_____
3	5	_____	_____	_____

QP9-5. Fill in the blanks in the table above.

QP9-6. Explain why a portion of a perfectly competitive firm's supply curve coincides with its marginal-cost curve. Why does the firm supply a quantity of zero when the price is less than average variable cost?

QP9-7. The perfectly competitive firm whose supply schedule is shown in the second table on this page is one of 1000 identical firms in its industry. Using this information, write down the market supply schedule for the entire industry.

QP9-8. A perfectly competitive market has 100 identical firms. The curves for one such firm are shown at the right. In the future, what would you expect to happen to the industry? Assuming that it stays in business, what would happen to the individual firm?

Price	Firm Supply	Industry Supply
$0	0	_____
1	5	_____
2	10	_____
3	15	_____

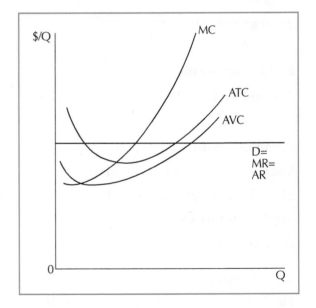

QP9-9. This question refers to the figure at the right. This figure shows the cost curves for another perfectly competitive firm, from another industry with many identical firms. What would we expect to happen to the industry? Assuming that it stays in business, what would happen to the individual firm?

QP9-10. Complete the table below. Assume that the firm is a perfect competitor. What is the profit-maximizing level of output for the firm? How much profit does it earn?

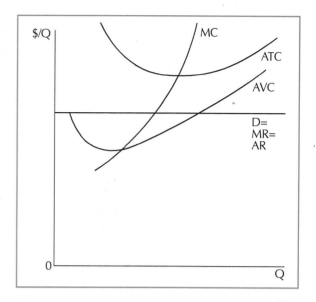

Quantity	Total Cost	Marginal Cost	Price	Marginal Revenue	Average Revenue	Total Revenue	Profit
0	$10	—	$10				
1		$6					
2		4					
3		5					
4		7					
5		10					
6		14					
7		19					
8		25					
9		32					

Chapter 10

Monopoly

ECONOMICS AND YOU: DIALING FOR DOLLARS IN THE TELEPHONE MARKETS

Tamika Chandler makes lots of telephone calls. She calls her parents in Chicago, one set of grandparents in Mississippi, and another set of grandparents in Tennessee. Now that she has graduated from college, Tamika also keeps in touch with her college roommates, who have moved to Los Angeles, Detroit, and Baltimore.

Because she is on the phone so much, Tamika keeps careful track of her phone bills. She used to subscribe with AT&T. But then she learned of a discount plan that allowed her to save money by subscribing with Verizon Wireless. As the phone companies have continued to compete with each other, Tamika has continued to find new ways to save.

The telephone market offers choices for consumers. It isn't a *perfectly* competitive market, like the ones that we discussed in Chapter 9, because the phone companies are large. Nevertheless, consumers do have choices. The phone companies are wary of charging prices that are too far out of line, because customers are free to switch to other carriers.

However, it hasn't always been this way in the telephone market. Only a few decades ago, the phone business was completely dominated by one company, American Telephone &

Telegraph. Thus there was a time when the phone market did not provide consumers with the benefits of competition. When there's only one seller in a market, we say that the firm is a *monopoly*. In this chapter, we'll see that monopolies usually don't behave nearly as well as perfectly competitive industries. If there aren't any other firms in the industry, the monopoly knows it can raise its prices and not lose its customers to other firms. As a result, monopolies tend to charge higher prices than competitive firms would charge.

If one firm has a very large share of the market, it may be able to act like a monopoly, even if there are some other firms. For example, Microsoft Corporation is not the only seller of personal computer operating systems, but it has such a dominant position that it is nearly a monopoly. The analysis in this chapter can be used to apply to "near monopolies" as well as to pure monopolies.

The United States Postal Service has a monopoly on the delivery of first-class mail. Most communities have only one cable-TV firm, and many parts of the country also have local monopolies in the markets for electric power, natural gas, and water. Many professional sports franchises are regional monopolies: If you're in the Denver area and you want to see a major-league baseball game in person, your only choice is to see one of the home games of the Colorado Rockies. If you go to Yosemite National Park in California, you will find that virtually *all* services are provided by a monopoly called Yosemite Concession Services Corporation. This firm provides hotel rooms, cabins, restaurants, snack stands, gasoline stations, bus services, grocery stores, gift shops, sports shops, vending machines, guided tours, horse stables, and other services.

In this chapter, we'll discuss monopoly. We begin by describing the characteristics of monopoly, and we then describe the way in which monopolies maximize their profits. Finally, we provide some comparisons between the behavior of monopolies and the behavior of competitive firms.

CHARACTERISTICS OF MONOPOLY

If an industry is to be a monopoly, it has to have several characteristics:

- The industry must have only *one firm*. (However, we will use the same set of ideas to analyze a "near monopoly", which may have more than one firm, but for which there is one *dominant* firm.)

- The firm must have *barriers to entry*, so potential competitors are unable to enter the industry.

- There must be *no close substitutes* for the firm's product.

Let's discuss these characteristics of monopoly in greater detail.

Only One Firm

Perfectly competitive firms are price takers, but monopolists are *price makers*: Because there is only one firm in the industry, the monopolist may be able to increase its profit by raising prices. Another way to say this is that the monopolist has a great deal of *market power*, whereas the perfectly competitive firm has no market power.

Monopolies have the greatest amount of market power that we can imagine, but they aren't the only firms with market power. In later chapters, we will talk about monopolistically competitive firms and oligopolistic firms. These firms also have some market power, although they don't have as much market power as monopolies have.

Some industries have one firm that controls the overwhelming majority of the market, even though it isn't literally the *only* firm. For example, Microsoft Corporation produces more than 90 percent of the operating systems for personal computers. Therefore, according to our definition, Microsoft isn't a true monopoly. However, Microsoft's position is so dominant that it can behave in about the same way that a true monopoly would behave. Firms like Microsoft could be called "near monopolies". In this chapter, we'll look at "near monopolies", as well as true monopolies.

Barriers to Entry

A monopoly can only maintain its monopoly status in the long run if it has some way to keep out competitors. In the next few paragraphs, we will discuss some of the many ways in which monopolists may be able to keep competitors from entering the market.

Legal Barriers. One way to keep out potential competitors is to have legal barriers to entry, such as patents and exclusive licenses. A *patent* gives an inventor a monopoly on his or her invention. Patents are extremely important for companies like Dupont, General Electric, and Xerox. These firms take great care to make sure that other firms don't threaten the patent monopoly by cheating on their patents. Patents are exceptionally important in the pharmaceutical industry. In *Real Economics for Real People 10.1*, we discuss patent monopoly in the pharmaceutical industry.

Another type of legal barrier to entry is the *exclusive franchise*. An exclusive franchise is a business arrangement under which only one firm is allowed to produce in a particular territory. For example, professional sports teams have monopoly power in their regional markets because they have exclusive franchises.

Also, the law sometimes gives monopoly power to government agencies. We've already mentioned the Postal Service monopoly. In many States, the State government gives itself a monopoly in liquor sales. Many States also give themselves monopolies in the market for lottery games. In Japan, a government agency runs monopolies on salt and tobacco. In the socialist economies of Cuba and North Korea, *many* industries are organized as government-run monopolies.

Natural Monopoly: Cost Advantages As Barriers to Entry

So far, we have spoken of *legal* barriers to entry. In virtually every case of legal barriers, competitors could enter the market successfully, *if* it were legal to do so. For example, when a patent expires, new firms usually enter the market quickly. Another example is that if the State of Pennsylvania were to stop giving itself a monopoly in the retail liquor business, many private liquor stores would probably open their doors in a very short time.

However, it is possible that in some cases, the barrier to entry has to do with a cost advantage for the monopolist. If a single firm can produce at a lower average total cost than any combination of two or three or more firms, we say that the firm is a *natural monopoly*.

Economists are often quite critical of legal barriers to entry. We expect that these barriers will lead to higher prices and less consumer satisfaction, relative to what would occur if the industry were competitive. But things aren't so clear-cut in the case of natural monopoly. If a natural monopoly were replaced by a group of competing firms, those firms would have higher costs. As a result, there's no guarantee that breaking up a natural monopoly will help consumers. We'll discuss natural monopoly in more detail, later in this chapter. In fact, however, natural monopoly is probably rare. Most monopolies rely on legal barriers, rather than on cost advantages.

No Close Substitutes for the Monopolist's Product

The first characteristic of a monopoly is that the market has only one firm or one dominant firm. The second is that there are barriers to entry. The third characteristic is that, *if a firm is to have monopoly power, there must not be any close substitutes for its product.* For example, Ford Motor Company is the world's only manufacturer of the Escape, but it isn't very useful to think of Ford as a monopolist. Instead, we think of Ford as competing in the minivan market with Toyota (which produces the Sienna), Fiat Chrysler (which produces the Dodge Caravan), and other companies. The Sienna and the Caravan aren't identical to the Escape, but they are reasonably close substitutes.

The "company store" is an example of a monopoly that can be maintained because it is difficult for consumers to buy substitute products. In some isolated rural areas, there is only a single grocery store. Such a store can sometimes charge monopoly prices, because it's very costly for consumers to get to other stores. In John Steinbeck's novel, *The Grapes of Wrath* (set in the 1930s), the Joad family find themselves trying to buy hamburger from such a store. The Joads complain that the prices are

Real Economics for Real People 10.1: Monopoly in the Pharmaceutical Markets

Article I, Section 8 of the United States Constitution allows Congress "to promote the progress of science and useful arts, by securing for limited times to authors and inventors the exclusive right to their respective writings and discoveries". By law, the company that owns a patent gets a monopoly for a period of 14 to 20 years. Other firms can't infringe on the patents without breaking the law. When a company acquires a patent, it gets monopoly power.

Even after a patent expires, however, it's still possible for the inventor to produce successfully. For example, the Bayer Company had the patent on aspirin. The patent expired in 1917, and many other companies rushed in to produce aspirin. But Bayer still produces aspirin to this day.

We can get a sense of the importance of patent monopoly by looking at what happens when a patent expires. When this happens, lower-cost "generic" products can often produce and sell for far less than the monopoly price.

For many years, Lipitor (the brand name for avortastatin calcium, a cholesterol medication) was the best-selling drug in the world. But the patent, held by the pharmaceutical giant Pfizer, Inc., expired in November 2011. In an effort to reduce its revenue losses, Pfizer undertook an aggressive marketing campaign. The campaign was only modestly successful—Pfizer's worldwide sales of Lipitor plunged from $9.6 billion in 2011 to $3.9 billion in 2012.

Lipitor is only one of several big-selling drugs to lose patent protection in 2011 and 2012. Others include Levaquin (an antibiotic produced by Johnson & Johnson), Plavix (a blood-clot inhibitor from Bristol-Myers/ Squibb), and Singulair (an asthma medica-

tion from Merck). In each case, the producer's revenues fell by billions as a result of competition from low-cost generic drugs.

It's probably too early to feel sorry for the pharmaceutical companies. Despite the loss of monopoly profits from Lipitor, Pfizer actually had a good year in 2012. They made solid profits from drugs that were still patented. For example, Lyrica (a drug to treat seizures and fibromyalgia) racked up more than $4 billion in sales in 2012.

Patent laws allow companies to make hefty monopoly profits. On the other hand, without the incentive provided by those profits, the companies might not have made the inventions in the first place.

How much incentive is enough? If the period of patent monopoly were shortened, would we still get valuable research, without having to pay so much for so long? It's hard to say for sure. However, as drug prices have increased, more and more Americans are thinking about public policies that would reduce the ability of pharmaceutical companies to exploit their monopoly power.

Daraprim is a drug that has been used for decades to treat a parasitic infection. In 2015, Daraprim was acquired by a start-up company run by a former hedge-fund manager. The new owners raised the price from $13.50 per tablet to $750 per tablet. Another company acquired Cycloserine, which is used to treat certain virulent forms of tuberculosis, and raised the price from $500 to $10,800. Other such price increases have also taken place.

These and other spectacular price increases did not have to do with patents. Instead, even without patent protection, these drugs conferred monopoly power because they are the only treatments for some rare diseases.

These cases have led to a renewed public discussion of monopoly power. It certainly seems that a case can be made for stricter government regulations on the prices of life-saving drugs. In Chapter 4, we saw that price ceilings can have adverse side effects, in the form of shortages. In the case of pharmaceuticals, however, the government is already involved in the market to a very large extent, through the Medicare and Medicaid programs. Effectively, the demand for Daraprim may be very inelastic, because these government programs are unlikely to allow people to die for lack of the drug. Thus the usual arguments against price controls do not appear to be very strong in this case.

one-third higher than at other locations. The store clerk admits that the prices are high. But he explains that the Joads would have to use a gallon of gasoline to reach another store, and they don't have enough money to buy a gallon of gasoline. Basically, the clerk is saying that the store can get away with charging monopoly prices, because it would cost a lot to go to another store. Therefore, from the Joads' point of view, the other stores aren't close substitutes for the company store.

In the 80 years since the time of *The Grapes of Wrath*, the American population has become more urbanized, more affluent, and more mobile. These days, for most Americans, it's inexpensive to choose among several different stores. The Internet has further reduced the cost of comparison shopping. Since most people can shop at a variety of stores and online outlets that are close substitutes for each other, it is less likely for any one store to exercise monopoly power. As a result, the situation faced by the Joads has (fortunately) become increasingly rare.

Occasionally, a large firm or a wealthy individual will attempt to buy so much of a resource that monopoly control is achieved. This is called "cornering the market". For example, in 1991, the Wall-Street firm of Salomon Brothers cornered the market in an auction of $12 billion of United States Treasury notes. In fact, the Treasury Department has rules that prohibit any individual firm from buying more than 35 percent of the notes at any particular auction. Nevertheless, Salomon Brothers violated the rules and acquired more than 85 percent of the notes sold on May 22, 1991. Other firms had accepted orders from customers, under the assumption that Salomon Brothers would *not* corner the market (that is, the other firms assumed that Salomon Brothers would not violate the rules). Since these other firms had promised to provide their customers with Treasury notes from that particular auction, there wasn't any available substitute. To meet their obligations to their customers, these other firms had to pay inflated prices to Salomon Brothers. The other firms suffered losses of more than $100 million. When news of the "squeeze" got out, a scandal erupted, and several Salomon Brothers executives were forced to resign.

The market for rough diamonds is another example of a monopoly that arises from control of resources for which there are few substitutes. In the eyes of many buyers, there are simply no close substitutes for diamonds: You don't give your fiancée a sapphire engagement ring; you give her the real thing. Because of the lack of substitutes, any firm that controls most of the world's diamonds will have a monopoly position, or at least a near-monopoly position. In fact, a substantial fraction of the world's diamonds was once controlled by the South

Real Economics for Real People 10.2:
Letters and Diamonds: How Monopoly Can Slip Away

A monopolist's product must not have close substitutes, and there must not be other sources of supply. If a substitute product appears, or if alternate sources of supply become available, the monopolist is in trouble.

One case in point is the United States Postal Service. The Constitution gives Congress the power to "establish post offices and post roads". This has usually been interpreted as meaning that the Postal Service should have a monopoly in the delivery of first-class mail.

The Postal Service has used its monopoly in an unusual way. Most monopolies would try to maximize their profit. However, for many years, the Postal Service had *losses*, which were covered with tax dollars. After the government subsidies were removed, the Postal Service was forced to become more efficient, but its profits were still fairly modest in most years. Instead of making high profits, the Postal Service has used its monopoly power to grant high wage rates for its workers. One study suggested that Postal-Service workers were paid 84 percent more than comparable workers in other mailrooms.

For years, the Service has faced competitors in practically every area except first-class mail. (For example, United Parcel Service, Federal Express, and other firms have taken over most of the market for small package delivery.) And now, the first-class mail monopoly is threatened, too. The threats come from overnight delivery services, electronic mail, text messages, and fax machines. From the point of view of many customers, these are close substitutes for first-class letters. As faxes, e-mail messages, and overnight delivery have become cheaper and more widely available, it has become harder and harder for the Postal Service to keep its customers. The challenge for the Postal Service is to continue to become more efficient, so that it can continue to guarantee service to every home in America, without suffering large losses. But this is a very difficult challenge. By 2013, the Postal Service was considering an end to Saturday delivery.

Another case of a threatened monopoly is in the diamond market. Strictly speaking, DeBeers Consolidated Mines is only a near monopoly, since it never controlled more than 80 percent of the world market in rough diamonds. However, this 80-percent share was large enough that DeBeers has been able to behave like a monopolist.

DeBeers can only keep its monopoly position if it maintains control over the vast majority of supplies. However, in the early 1990s, the diamond market began to be flooded by new supplies that weren't under the control of DeBeers. Most of the new supplies came from Angola and from the new nations of the former Soviet Union. These new supplies would tend to depress prices. In order to keep prices high, DeBeers bought more than $200 million of new diamonds in 1991 and 1992. Also, the firm negotiated agreements with Russian diamond producers, in an effort to keep control over as much of the market as possible.

By the 21st century, more and more countries and companies were refusing to channel everything through DeBeers. This led the company to change strategy. Instead of trying to control the entire industry, the firm focused on its own brand of diamonds, marketed in upscale retail stores around the world.

However, even though DeBeers has morphed into something very different from what it was a few decades ago, the firm is still very profitable—the firm's widely recognized brand name, nurtured over many decades, still gives it a great deal of market power.

Monopolies like DeBeers and the Postal Service are only secure if they are shielded by strong barriers to entry. If the barriers are leaky, competitive forces will challenge the monopolist again and again. That may not be a good thing for the monopolists, but it is a very good thing for consumers.

African firm of DeBeers Consolidated Mines. However, in *Real Economics for Real People 10.2,* we see that DeBeers's monopoly position was weakened by competitors.

Reality Check:
Interim Review Question

IR10-1. Bell's Brewery is the only producer of a tasty beverage called Bell's Oberon Ale. Would you say that Bell's Brewery is a monopolist?

THE DEMAND FOR THE OUTPUT OF A SINGLE-PRICE MONOPOLY

Slam Dunk State College is famous for its basketball teams, which play their home games in the Slam Dunk Coliseum. Like many other sports arenas, the Coliseum runs its food and beverage service as a monopoly. Fans aren't allowed to bring their own food or drinks into the Coliseum. If the fans get hungry and thirsty, they can only buy from Coliseum Enterprises, Inc. To understand the behavior of a monopolist, let's study the market for hot dogs at the Slam Dunk Coliseum.

Coliseum Enterprises is what we call a *single-price monopoly*, which means that the firm sells all of its hot dogs at the same price. This is because it's very hard for the firm to distinguish the customers who are willing to pay a lot of money for a hot dog from those who aren't willing to pay very much. (Near the end of this chapter, we'll discuss *price discrimination*, under which a firm will sell the same product to different customers at different prices. *If* a firm is able to distinguish

among its customers on the basis of how much they are willing to pay, the firm can increase its profit by engaging in price discrimination.)

The Monopoly Firm's Demand Curve

Since Coliseum Enterprises is a monopolist, *it faces the entire market demand curve for hot dogs at the Coliseum. The demand curve for the firm's output is the same as the market demand curve.*

Since the monopolist faces the entire market demand curve, the monopolist is in a position of considerable power. Much of the purpose of this chapter is to show how the monopolist uses that power to increase its profit. This is good for the monopolist, but bad for the society as a whole. However, this does not mean that monopolists are *infinitely* powerful. A monopoly firm may be able to charge a higher price than a competitive firm, but it can't charge a price that goes beyond the market demand curve.

Table 10.1 shows the demand schedule for the hot-dog monopoly at Slam Dunk Coliseum. To keep the numbers manageable, we show the demand schedule for hot dogs *per minute.*

If hot dogs were priced above $5.00 each, no one would be willing to buy. If the price were $5.00, the basketball fans would be willing to buy one hot dog per minute. When the price falls to $4.50, the quantity demanded would increase to two hot dogs per minute. In fact, every time the price falls by 50 cents, the quantity demanded increases by one hot dog per minute. Therefore, if we were to graph this demand schedule, the resulting demand curve would be a straight line. This can be seen in panel (a) of Figure 10.1. We use a straight-line demand curve because straight lines are very easy to draw. Also, as we shall see later in this chapter, a straight-line demand curve has some very useful properties. But that doesn't mean that every monopolist in the world faces a demand curve that is a straight line. We are certain that all monopolists face demand curves that slope downward and to the right, but those demand curves may or may not be straight lines.

The demand facing a monopolist is fundamentally different from the demand facing a perfectly competitive firm. As we saw in Chapter 9, the perfectly competitive firm can sell as many units as it wants to sell at the market price. On the other hand, *if a single-price monopolist wants to sell more output, it has to decrease the price on all units that it sells.*

Marginal Revenue, Total Revenue, and Average Revenue for the Single-Price Monopolist

In Chapter 9, we learned about marginal revenue, which is a very important concept for the business firm. Marginal revenue is the additional amount of money that the firm receives from selling one more unit of output. Marginal revenue is constant for the perfectly competitive firm, because the firm can sell as many units as it wants to sell at the market price. *For the monopolist, however, marginal revenue will decrease as quantity increases.* We can

Table 10.1 Demand, Total Revenue, and Marginal Revenue for Hot Dogs at Slam Dunk Coliseum

P Price (in Dollars per Hot Dog)	Q Quantity Demanded (Hot Dogs per Minute)	TR Total Revenue (= P x Q)	MR Marginal Revenue (= Change in TR/ Change in Q)
$5.50	0	$0	—
5.00	1	5	$5
4.50	2	9	4
4.00	3	12	3
3.50	4	14	2
3.00	5	15	1
2.50	6	15	0
2.00	7	14	−1
1.50	8	12	−2
1.00	9	9	−3
0.50	10	5	−4
0.00	11	0	−5

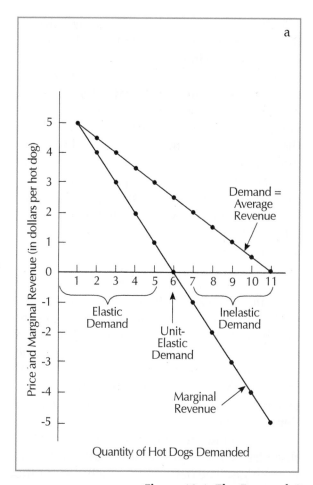

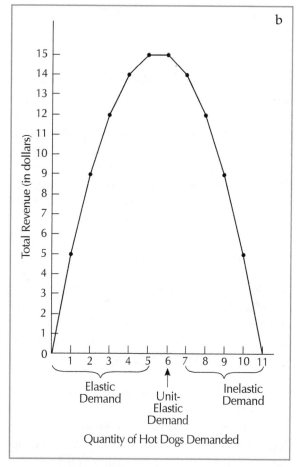

Figure 10.1 The Demand Curve, Marginal-Revenue Curve, and Total-Revenue Curve for Coliseum Enterprises, Inc.

Since Coliseum Enterprises is a monopolist, it faces the entire downward-sloping market demand curve for hot dogs. The demand curve is shown in panel (a). The demand curve could also be called the average-revenue curve.

The total-revenue curve shows the total sales revenue that the firm receives from all of its sales of hot dogs. The total-revenue curve is shown in panel (b). For a downward-sloping demand curve, the total-revenue curve will rise at first, and then fall.

The marginal-revenue curve shows the additional sales revenue that the firm receives, when it sells one additional hot dog. The marginal-revenue curve is shown in panel (a). For a downward-sloping demand curve, the marginal-revenue curve will always be below the demand curve. When the demand curve is a straight line, the marginal-revenue curve is also a straight line, and the marginal-revenue curve is exactly twice as steep as the demand curve. In other words, the slope of the marginal-revenue curve is twice as great as the slope of the demand curve.

Marginal revenue is the change in total revenue when one additional hot dog is sold. Thus, marginal revenue represents the slope of the total-revenue curve. When total revenue slopes upward, marginal revenue is positive. This occurs when demand is elastic. When the total-revenue curve reaches its peak, marginal revenue is zero. This occurs when demand is unit elastic. When total revenue slopes downward, marginal revenue is less than zero. This occurs when demand is inelastic.

see this by working through the example of hot dogs at Slam Dunk Coliseum.

Marginal Revenue and Total Revenue. Table 10.1 shows the demand schedule for hot dogs at Slam Dunk Coliseum, and it also shows total revenue and marginal revenue. We get total revenue by multiplying the price by the quantity. In symbols, TR = (P)x(Q). *Marginal revenue is the change in total revenue, when quantity increases by one unit. Equivalently, marginal revenue is the change in total revenue divided by the change in quantity.* In symbols, MR = ΔTR / ΔQ.

For the first hot dog sold at Slam Dunk Coliseum, the maximum price that consumers would be willing to pay is $5. Therefore, if one hot dog per minute were sold, total revenue per minute would be $5: TR = (P)x(Q) = ($5 per hot dog)x(1 hot dog) = $5. The marginal revenue for the first hot dog sold is also $5: When the number of hot dogs increases from zero to one, total revenue increases from $0 to $5, so that the marginal revenue for the first hot dog is $(5 − 0) = $5.

If Coliseum Enterprises were to sell two hot dogs per minute, the firm would have to drop the price to $4.50. Total revenue would now be ($4.50 per hot dog)x(2 hot dogs) = $9.00 per minute. Total revenue increases from $5 to $9 when the firm sells a second hot dog, so that the marginal revenue for the second hot dog is $(9 − 5) = $4. If Coliseum Enterprises were to sell a third hot dog, the price would have to fall to $4. Total revenue would be ($4)x(3) = $12, and marginal revenue would be $(12 − 9) = $3.

The information in Table 10.1 is graphed in Figure 10.1. Panel (a) of the figure shows the demand curve and marginal-revenue curve for the hot-dog monopoly. *When the demand curve is a straight line, as in this case, the marginal-revenue curve is also a straight line, and the marginal-revenue curve is exactly twice as steep as the demand curve.*

In order to show that the marginal-revenue curve is twice as steep as the demand curve, it is necessary to use calculus. If you haven't had calculus, please don't worry. You can skip the derivation, and you will still be able to get everything else in the chapter.

If the demand curve is a straight line, we can describe it using the formula for a straight line: P = a − bQ, where P is the price, a is the vertical intercept of the demand curve, -b is the slope of the demand curve, and Q is the quantity demanded. We know that total revenue is equal to price multiplied by quantity: TR = (P)x(Q). Thus if we multiply the equation for P times Q, we have total revenue: PQ = (a − bQ)Q = aQ − bQ². So, in this case, Total Revenue = aQ − bQ².

Now here is where the calculus comes in: Marginal revenue is the derivative of total revenue with respect to quantity. Thus MR = δTR/δQ = δ(aQ − bQ²)/ δQ = a − 2bQ. To sum up, the demand curve is P = a − bQ, and the marginal-revenue curve is MR = a − 2bQ. The two curves have the same vertical intercept, and the slope of the MR curve is exactly twice as large as the slope of the demand curve.

Once again, if you haven't had calculus, don't freak out. That's the only calculus in this entire book. The derivation is included for the benefit of those who have had calculus, but it is not meant to terrorize those who haven't.

Panel (b) of Figure 10.1 shows the total-revenue curve for the hot-dog monopoly. *Since marginal revenue is the change in total revenue when one additional unit is sold, the marginal-revenue curve is the slope of the total-revenue curve.* This relationship is similar to some other relationships that we have seen in earlier chapters. For example, in Chapter 8, we saw that marginal cost is the slope of the total-cost curve. In Chapter 7, we saw that marginal utility is the slope of the total-utility curve.

The slope of the total-revenue curve is positive when total revenue is increasing. This means that marginal revenue must be positive when the total-revenue curve slopes upward as we move from left to right across the diagram.

In this example, total revenue increases until the quantity reaches 5 hot dogs per minute. If Coliseum Enterprises were to sell five hot dogs per minute, it would charge $3 per hot dog, and total revenue would be (5 hot dogs)x($3 per hot dog) = $15. If the firm were to sell a sixth hot dog per minute, it would have to reduce the price from $3.00 to $2.50. Now, total revenue would be (6)x($2.50) = $15. The increase in quantity is exactly offset by the reduction in price, so that total revenue remains unchanged. Therefore, the marginal revenue of the sixth hot dog per minute is zero. When quantity increases from five to six, total revenue stays at its maximum value, and the slope of the total-revenue curve is zero.

If the quantity goes above six, total revenue actually decreases. When the total-revenue curve slopes downward from left to right, marginal revenue is negative.

Average Revenue. In Chapter 9, on perfect competition, we defined average revenue. Recall that the definition of average revenue is similar to the definitions of other averages that we have seen: *Average revenue* is total revenue divided by the number of units sold. In symbols, AR = TR/Q.

A few paragraphs ago, we saw that total revenue is the price multiplied by the number of units sold: TR = (P)x(Q). If we put the expression for AR together with the expression for TR, we have AR = TR/Q = (P)x(Q) / Q = P. For the single-price monopolist, *average revenue equals price.* (Average revenue is also equal to price for a perfectly competitive firm, because a perfectly competitive firm will also sell all units at the same price.)

Now, recall that a demand curve is a graph of the relationship between price and quantity demanded. Since average revenue is the price, *the average-revenue curve is identical to the demand curve for the firm's output.* In Figure 10.1(a), we see that the average-revenue curve (that is, the demand curve) slopes downward, and the marginal-revenue

curve slopes downward more steeply. This is yet another example of the relationships between marginal quantities and average quantities—When marginal revenue is less than average revenue, average revenue must be decreasing.

Total Revenue, Marginal Revenue, and the Elasticity of Demand

If you aren't clear about how to calculate and use the own-price elasticity of demand, this would be a good time to take another look at Chapter 6.

Here is a brief review of the relationship between price, quantity, total revenue, and the own-price elasticity of demand: Whenever we move downward and to the right along a demand curve, the quantity demanded increases and the price decreases. Since total revenue is price multiplied by quantity, we have two influences on total revenue that go in opposite directions. By itself, the decrease in price will tend to *decrease* total revenue. However, the increase in quantity will tend to *increase* total revenue. The net effect on total revenue will depend on whether the price decrease is stronger than, weaker than, or the same as the increase in quantity demanded.

If the percentage increase in quantity demanded is larger than the percentage decrease in price, we say that demand is *elastic.* When demand is elastic, total revenue will increase when quantity increases. In other words, when demand is elastic, a decrease in price will lead to a relatively large increase in quantity demanded, so that total revenue will actually rise.

If the percentage increase in quantity demanded is equal to the percentage decrease in price, we say that demand is *unit elastic.* When demand is unit elastic, total revenue will not change. This is because when demand is unit elastic, the decrease in price and the increase in quantity demanded are of the same relative size. Consequently, the two effects offset each other exactly.

Finally, if the percentage increase in quantity demanded is smaller than the percentage decrease in price, we say that demand is *inelastic*. When demand is inelastic, total revenue will decrease when quantity increases. This is because when demand is inelastic, even a relatively large decrease in price will only lead to a relatively small increase in quantity demanded. Therefore, a drop in price will lead to a drop in total revenue.

Now that we have reviewed the elasticity concepts, we can divide the total-revenue and marginal-revenue curves in Figure 10.1 into three regions, which are closely related to the own-price elasticity of demand.

- *Total revenue increases* as we move from a quantity of zero to a quantity of five, and this means that *marginal revenue is positive*. Since the increase in quantity is associated with an increase in total revenue, we know that *demand is elastic* in this region of the demand curve. This corresponds to the region on the left of Figure 10.1.

- *Total revenue is constant* as we move from Q=5 to Q=6, and this means that *marginal revenue is zero*. Since total revenue is unchanged, *demand is unit elastic* in this region of the demand curve.

- When quantity increases above six, *total revenue is declining*, and this means that *marginal revenue is negative*. Since the increase in quantity is associated with a decrease in total revenue, *demand is inelastic* in this region of the demand curve. This corresponds to the region on the right of Figure 10.1.

We've now looked at the monopolist's revenues. The next step is to combine this information on revenues with information on costs, so that we can study profit.

Reality Check: Interim Review Questions

IR10-2. Marginal revenue is a constant for a perfectly competitive firm. However, for a monopolist, marginal revenue decreases when sales increase. Explain why this is so.

IR10-3. Colossal Corporation is a monopolist. If the firm were to sell one more unit of output, its total revenue would increase. Is Colossal Corporation's marginal revenue greater than zero or less than zero? Is the firm facing elastic demand, inelastic demand, or unit-elastic demand?

THE PRICE AND QUANTITY DECISIONS OF THE SINGLE-PRICE MONOPOLIST

In Chapter 9, on perfect competition, we saw that there are two ways to think about how the firm chooses its profit-maximizing quantity: We can compare *total* revenue and *total* cost, or we can compare *marginal* revenue and *marginal* cost. We'll do the same here for monopolies. We begin by comparing total revenue and total cost. Later, we will compare marginal revenue and marginal cost.

The Monopolist's Profit-Maximizing Decisions: Comparing Total Revenue and Total Cost

In Table 10.2, we repeat the revenue information from Table 10.1, and we also add some information on costs. We want to concentrate on the most important things, so we will

Table 10.2 Revenues, Costs, and Profits for Hot Dogs at Slam Dunk Coliseum

P Price	Q Quantity Demanded	TR Total Revenue	MR Marginal Revenue	TC Total Cost	MC Marginal Cost	Profit (= Total Revenue Minus Total Cost)
$5.50	0	$0	—	$0	—	$0
5.00	1	5	$5	1	$1	4
4.50	2	9	4	2	1	7
4.00	3	12	3	3	1	9
3.50	4	14	2	4	1	10
3.00	5	15	1	5	1	10
2.50	6	15	0	6	1	9
2.00	7	14	−1	7	1	7
1.50	8	12	−2	8	1	4
1.00	9	9	−3	9	1	0
0.50	10	5	−4	10	1	−5
0.00	11	0	−5	11	1	−11

assume that Coliseum Enterprises has a simple cost structure. If one hot dog per minute is produced, total cost is $1. If two are produced, total cost is $2. If 47 hot dogs are produced, total cost is $47, and so on. In other words, the firm has no fixed costs, and its marginal costs are constant. For *each* additional hot dog, the marginal cost is $1.

Total variable cost is the sum of the marginal costs. Since there are no fixed costs, total cost is equal to total variable cost. Therefore, in this special example with no fixed costs, total cost is also the sum of the marginal costs.

Profit is total revenue minus total cost. When Coliseum Enterprises sells one hot dog per minute, total revenue is $5, total cost is $1, and profit is $(5 − 1) = $4. Since the first hot dog gives positive profit, the firm will sell at least one hot dog. If the firm were to sell a second hot dog, total revenue would increase to $9, total cost would increase to $2, and profit would rise to $(9 − 2) = $7. Since profit is higher with two hot dogs than with one, it makes sense for the firm to sell at least two hot dogs.

We can continue to think in this way until we find the quantity with the maximum profit. The maximum profit in this example is $10, at a quantity of 4 or 5 hot dogs per minute. As in Chapter 9 on perfect competition, we assume that the firm will produce the larger amount: Coliseum Enterprises will produce and sell five hot dogs per minute.

The information on total revenue and total cost, from Table 10.2, is graphed in panel (a) of Figure 10.2. The vertical distance between the total-revenue curve and the total-cost curve is the firm's profit. Thus, the firm will maximize its profit by producing the quantity at which the vertical distance between the TR curve and the TC curve is greatest. As we showed in Chapter 9, the vertical distance between two curves is maximized where the two curves are parallel. In other words, the distance between the curves is greatest when the slope of the total-revenue curve is the same as the slope of the total-cost curve. This occurs at a quantity of five hot dogs per minute, so that the profit-maximizing quantity is five hot dogs per minute.

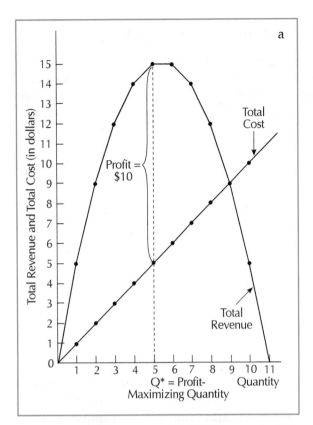
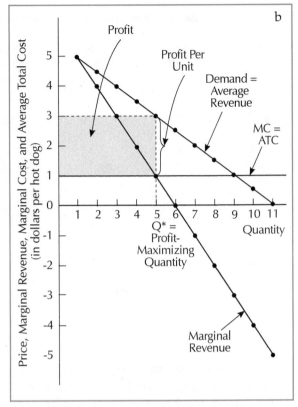

Figure 10.2 Finding the Level of Output and Profit for Coliseum Enterprises

In panel (a), profit is the vertical distance between the total-revenue curve and the total-cost curve. The profit-maximizing quantity of output is the quantity at which this vertical distance is the greatest. In this case, the profit-maximizing quantity of output is five. In other words, Coliseum Enterprises maximizes its profit by producing and selling five hot dogs per minute.

Panel (b) shows the marginal-revenue and marginal-cost curves. The profit-maximizing quantity is at the intersection of these curves. (Once again, the profit-maximizing quantity is five hot dogs per minute.) The firm's profit per unit is the difference between price and average total cost, at the profit-maximizing quantity. If we multiply profit per unit by the quantity, we get the firm's profit, which is the shaded area in panel (b).

The Monopolist's Profit-Maximizing Decisions: Comparing Marginal Revenue and Marginal Cost

In the preceding section, we studied the information on *total* revenue and *total* cost, from Table 10.2. That table also contains information on *marginal* revenue and *marginal* cost. In Chapter 9, we learned that *any firm will maximize profit by producing the quantity at which marginal revenue is equal to marginal cost.* From Table 10.2, we can see that MR = MC when Q = 5. At this quantity, both MR and MC are $1 per additional hot dog. The graph is found in panel (b) of Figure 10.2. There, we see that the MR curve intersects the MC curve at a quantity of 5. In any graph like the one in panel (b) of Figure 10.2, we find the profit-maximizing quantity by locating the quantity at which the MR curve crosses the MC curve.

We find the same profit-maximizing quantity, regardless of whether we look at *total* revenue and cost, or *marginal* revenue and cost. This makes a lot of sense, if we consider the close relationship between total quantities and marginal quantities. Marginal revenue is the slope of the total-revenue curve, and marginal cost is the slope of the total-cost curve. As a result, *when marginal cost is equal to marginal revenue, total cost will have the same slope as total revenue, and profit will be maximized.*

Using Graphs to Calculate Profit

How much profit does Coliseum Enterprises make? In Chapter 9, on perfect competition, we learned that *profit per unit is equal to price minus average total cost.* It would be valuable to use panel (b) of Figure 10.2 to show the firm's profit. If we are to do this, we need to identify the firm's price and its average total cost.

First, let's find the price. The profit-maximizing quantity is five hot dogs. At this quantity, how much are consumers willing to pay? The answer comes from the demand schedule, which is found on the left side of Table 10.2. When Q = 5, consumers are willing to pay $3 per hot dog, and this is the price the monopolist will charge. Even though the marginal cost of producing the fifth hot dog is only $1, the price will be $3. We can also see this by looking at panel (b) of Figure 10.2. If we go to the profit-maximizing quantity of 5, and then follow the dotted line up to the demand curve, we can see that the firm will charge a price of $3 per hot dog.

Next, let's find the average total cost for Coliseum Enterprises, Inc. The firm has no fixed costs, which means that average total cost and average variable cost will be the same in this example. Average variable cost is the average of all of the marginal costs. If the marginal cost for the first hot dog is $1, and the second hot dog also has marginal cost of $1,

then the average variable cost will be $1 when two hot dogs are produced. Since marginal cost stays constant at $1 for each additional hot dog, average *variable* cost will also stay constant at $1 per hot dog. With no fixed costs, average *total* cost in this example will also be $1 per hot dog.

We now know that Coliseum Enterprises will sell five hot dogs per minute at a price of $3 each, and that its average total cost is $1 per hot dog. Profit per hot dog is (P – ATC), or $(3 – 1), or $2. When we multiply the profit per hot dog by the number of hot dogs, we get the firm's profit. This is ($2 per hot dog)(5 hot dogs per minute) = $10 per minute.

The firm's profit is drawn in panel (b) of Figure 10.2. Profit per hot dog is the vertical distance between the price of $3 and the average total cost of $1. The number of hot dogs per minute is 5, which is shown on the horizontal axis. If we multiply profit per hot dog (on the vertical axis) by the number of hot dogs per minute (on the horizontal axis), we get a rectangle for the firm's profit per minute. This profit rectangle is the shaded area in panel (b) of Figure 10.2. The base of the rectangle is the quantity sold by the monopoly (5 hot dogs), and the height of the rectangle is the profit per unit ($2 per hot dog).

More Examples of Revenues, Costs, and Profits for Monopolies

Coliseum Enterprises has a simple cost structure. The firm has no fixed costs, and it has constant marginal costs. Figure 10.3 shows a somewhat more involved set of cost and revenue curves. The information in Figure 10.3 is for Monolithic Pharmaceutical Company, which has a patent on a drug called soma. The patent gives Monolithic a monopoly in the soma market. Monolithic has fixed costs, and it also has increasing marginal costs. We can tell that the firm has fixed costs by looking at panel (a) of Figure 10.3: Total cost is positive,

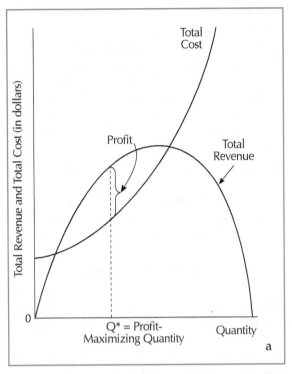

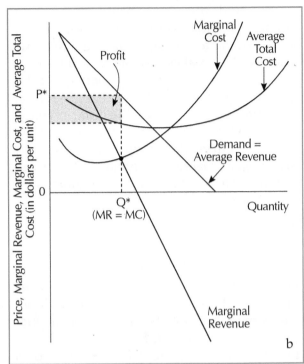

**Figure 10.3 Finding the Level of Output and Profit
for Monolithic Pharmaceutical Company**

In panel (a), profit is the vertical distance between the total-revenue curve and the total-cost curve. The profit-maximizing quantity of output is the quantity at which this vertical distance is greatest. In this case, the profit-maximizing quantity of output is Q*. In other words, Monolithic Pharmaceutical Company maximizes its profits by producing and selling Q* units of soma.

Panel (b) shows the firm's marginal-revenue and marginal-cost curves. The profit-maximizing quantity, Q*, is at the intersection of these curves. The corresponding price is P*, which we find by going up to the demand curve at the quantity of Q*. The firm's profit per unit is the difference between price and average total cost, at the profit-maximizing quantity. If we multiply profit per unit by the quantity, Q*, we get the firm's profit, which is the shaded area in panel (b).

even when output is zero. This graph also reveals that the firm has increasing marginal costs, because the slope of the total-cost curve becomes larger and larger as we move from left to right in the diagram.

Even though the details of Figure 10.3(a) are different from the details of Figure 10.2(a), the basic idea is still the same. Profit is the vertical distance between the total-revenue curve and the total-cost curve. Profit is maximized when the firm produces the quantity at which

the total-revenue curve is parallel to the total-cost curve. In Figure 10.3(a), the profit-maximizing quantity is Q*.

Panel (b) of Figure 10.3 has the *marginal* cost and revenue curves for Monolithic Pharmaceutical Company. Monolithic has a U-shaped average-total-cost curve (ATC), in contrast to the horizontal cost curves of our example of Coliseum Enterprises. As always, the ATC curve reaches its minimum when ATC = MC.

Figures 10.2(a) and 10.3(a) are basically similar, and this is also true for Figures 10.2(b) and 10.3(b). Here are some of the similarities between Figure 10.2(b) and Figure 10.3(b):

- The firm still finds its profit-maximizing quantity by looking for the quantity at which the MR curve intersects the MC curve.

- Once the profit-maximizing quantity is found, we still go up to the demand curve to find the price.

- Then, we determine profit per unit by subtracting average total cost from price.

- Once again, the profit is shown as a shaded rectangle. The base of the rectangle is the profit-maximizing quantity, while the height of the rectangle is the vertical distance between price and average total cost, evaluated at the profit-maximizing quantity. Monolithic Pharmaceutical Company makes a positive profit, just as Coliseum Enterprises did.

So far, we've only studied monopolies that are making positive economic profits. Monopolies often do make very large profits, but there's no guarantee that a monopoly will always earn profits. If costs are relatively high, and/or if demand is relatively low, the monopoly firm may not be able to make economic profits. Figure 10.4(a) shows the cost and revenue curves for a monopolist called Enormous Corporation. In this case, the monopoly is just breaking even, earning zero economic profit. Price and average total cost are equal at the profit-maximizing quantity, and this means that the firm has zero profit per unit. Finally, Figure 10.4(b) shows the cost and revenue curves for a monopoly called Gigantic Corporation, which is actually suffering economic losses: Price is *less* than average total cost. The shaded area in Figure 10.4(b) represents the firm's economic losses.

In Chapter 9, on perfect competition, we showed that the perfectly competitive firm will produce at minimum average total cost. However, Figures 10.3(b) and 10.4 show that this is not necessarily the case for the monopolist. It's *possible* that a monopoly might produce at minimum average total cost, but it would only be a coincidence. In general, we don't expect that monopolies will locate at the minimum points on their ATC curves.

The Monopolist Raises Price Until Demand Is Elastic

Figure 10.1 showed that the monopolist's demand curve can be divided into three regions: At relatively low quantities, demand is elastic, which means that marginal revenue is positive. At high quantities, demand is inelastic, so that marginal revenue is negative. In between, there will be a quantity at which demand is unit elastic, and marginal revenue is zero.

We've also seen that any monopolist will produce and sell the quantity at which MR = MC. Since marginal cost is always positive, and since marginal revenue is equal to marginal cost at the profit-maximizing quantity, it follows that *marginal revenue must be positive at the monopolist's profit-maximizing quantity.* Now, marginal revenue can only be positive if demand is elastic. This means that *demand must be elastic at the monopolist's profit-maximizing quantity. The monopolist will raise prices until demand becomes elastic.*

Here's another way to understand the ideas of the last paragraph: Business firms are always asking themselves whether they can make more profit by producing and selling one more unit. Producing one extra unit is always costly—marginal cost has to be positive. Therefore, the firm can't possibly be maximizing its profit unless marginal revenue is also positive. If marginal revenue were negative, then the firm could always do better by reducing its output. If marginal revenue were negative, reducing output would save costs *and* increase revenue. This is why the monopolist will never choose a quantity at which demand is inelastic. Instead, the monopolist

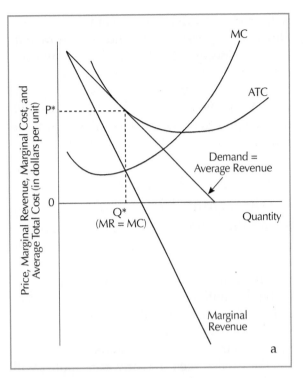

Figure 10.4 Panel (a)
Output and Profit For Enormous Corporation,
Which Earns Zero Economic Profit

Like any firm, Enormous Corporation will maximize profit by producing and selling the quantity at which marginal revenue is equal to marginal cost. In this case, the quantity is Q*, and the corresponding price is P*. Profit per unit is the difference between price and average total cost. In this case, at Q*, price is exactly equal to average total cost. Therefore, Enormous Corporation is making zero economic profit.

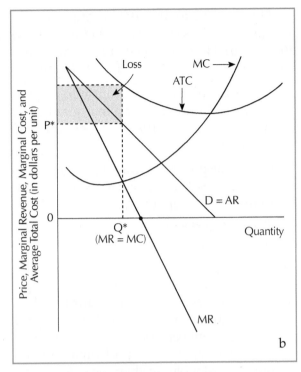

Figure 10.4 Panel (b)
Output and Profit For Gigantic Corporation,
Which Earns Negative Economic Profit

Like any firm, Gigantic Corporation will maximize profit by producing and selling the quantity at which marginal revenue is equal to marginal cost. In this case, the quantity is Q*, and the corresponding price is P*. Profit per unit is the difference between price and average total cost. In this case, at Q*, price is less than average total cost. Therefore, Gigantic Corporation is making negative economic profit. In other words, the firm is suffering losses. The losses are represented by the shaded area in the figure.

will always choose to raise prices until it finds itself in the elastic region of its demand curve.

The Monopolist Has No Supply Curve

A supply curve is a graph of the relationship between price and quantity supplied. For any price, a supply curve will identify the *unique* quantity that a firm will bring to market. But monopolists don't have any such unique rela-

tionship between price and quantity supplied, because the monopolist's behavior depends on the shape of the demand curve. Give a monopolist a different demand curve, and the firm will change to a different quantity supplied. Because of this, it doesn't make sense to talk of the monopolist's supply curve.

However, when we say that the monopoly does not have a unique, well-defined supply curve, it's not the same as saying that we can't analyze monopoly behavior. For example, if there is a change in the firm's marginal costs, we can trace out the effects on the firm's price, quantity, and profit. If a monopoly's entire marginal-cost curve shifts upward, the marginal-cost curve will intersect the marginal-revenue curve at a smaller quantity. Thus the monopolist will produce a smaller quantity, and sell for a higher price. On the other hand, if a monopoly's entire marginal-cost curve shifts downward, the MC curve will intersect the MR curve at a larger quantity. The monopolist will produce a larger quantity, which will be sold at a lower price. We are able to say quite a lot about how monopolies behave, even though we aren't able to identify a unique supply curve for a monopoly.

Reality Check: Interim Review Questions

IR10-4. A monopolist will produce the quantity at which marginal cost is equal to _____.

IR10-5. Does a monopoly firm have a unique, well-defined supply curve? Why, or why not?

IR10-6. Explain why the monopolist will produce a quantity at which demand is elastic.

ECONOMIC EVALUATION OF MONOPOLY

In Chapter 9, we studied the behavior of perfectly competitive firms. We've now studied the behavior of monopolies. It's time to combine our understanding of these two market structures, so we can learn how to measure the damage done by monopoly.

Let's return to the Slam Dunk Coliseum, where Coliseum Enterprises has a monopoly on the sale of hot dogs. Earlier in this chapter, we saw that this firm would maximize its profit by charging $3 per hot dog, and selling five hot dogs per minute. With average total costs of $1 per hot dog, the firm would make a profit of $2 on every hot dog sold. This information was shown in Figure 10.2(b), part of which is reproduced here as part of Figure 10.5. In this figure, $P_m = \$3$ is the monopolist's price, and $Q_m = 5$ is the monopolist's quantity. The firm's profit per minute is ($2 per hot dog)x(5 hot dogs per minute), for a total profit of $10 per minute. The monopoly profit is represented by the rectangle DEFC, in Figure 10.5.

What would happen if Coliseum Enterprises were to lose its exclusive franchise? What if anyone could come in and start selling hot dogs competitively? When we discussed perfect competition in the previous chapter, we learned that the perfectly competitive firm's supply curve is its marginal-cost curve. In this example, the marginal-cost curve is a horizontal line at $1 per hot dog. Therefore, if hot dogs were sold competitively, each competitive firm's supply curve would be a horizontal line at $1, and the market supply curve would also be a horizontal line at $1. This supply curve intersects the demand curve at a quantity of 9 hot dogs per minute. In Figure 10.5, $P_c = \$1$ is the competitive price, and $Q_c = 9$ is the competitive quantity. If competition were allowed, economic profit would be zero. With competition, the price would be $1, average total cost would also be $1, and all of the firms would just break even. In other words, by earning zero economic profit, the firms would make enough money to stay in business, but they would not make any "supernormal" profits.

It's clear that *producers are better off under monopoly*: The monopolist makes positive economic profit, whereas there aren't any economic profits with perfect competition. On the other hand, *consumers are worse off under monopoly*. They pay higher prices, and they buy a lower quantity.

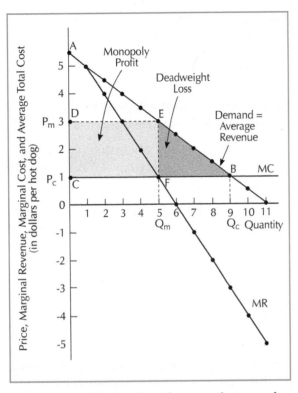

Figure 10.5 The Deadweight Loss of Monopoly

If the hot-dog market is run as a monopoly, the profit-maximizing quantity is Q_m, and the corresponding price is P_m. (In this case, Q_m is five hot dogs per minute, and P_m is $3 per hot dog.) If the market is organized according to perfect competition, the market equilibrium quantity is Q_c, and the corresponding price is P_c. (In this case, Q_c is nine hot dogs per minute, and P_c is $1 per hot dog.) With perfect competition, the firms earn zero economic profit. With monopoly, the firm earns a positive economic profit of DEFC. For the units between Q_m and Q_c, the marginal benefit of consumption is greater than the marginal cost of production. Therefore, society is worse off when we consume Q_m units, instead of Q_c units. The loss from consuming only Q_m units is called the deadweight loss of monopoly. The deadweight loss is represented by the triangle, EBF.

In fact, *the consumer's losses are greater than the monopolist's gains.* In other words, *society as a whole is made worse off by monopoly.* We can see this by looking at Figure 10.5. The marginal benefit of hot-dog consumption is represented by the demand curve, and the marginal cost of hot-dog production is represented by the marginal-cost curve. For every unit between Q_m, the monopoly quantity, and Q_c, the competitive quantity, marginal benefit is greater than marginal cost. Therefore, society should produce and consume Q_c. If we produce and consume Q_m instead of Q_c, society suffers a loss. The loss is the sum of the differences between marginal benefit and marginal cost, for all units from Q_m to Q_c. The loss, which is represented by the triangle EBF in Figure 10.5, is called the *deadweight loss* of monopoly. The *deadweight loss* of monopoly is the amount by which society is worse off, as a result of having monopoly instead of competition. The base of the deadweight-loss triangle is $(9–5) = 4$. The height of the triangle is $(3–1) = 2$. Thus, the area of the triangle is $(0.5)(4)(\$2) = \$4$. The deadweight loss is $4 per minute. This is fairly large, when we consider that the total cost of production is only ($1 per hot dog)(5 hot dogs per minute) = $5 per minute.

There is another way to look at the deadweight loss. With competition, producers have zero economic profit. With monopoly, the producers' economic profit is shown by the rectangle DEFC in Figure 10.5. Thus producers are better off with monopoly than with competition. However, consumers are worse off as a result of monopoly. With competition, consumer surplus is represented by area of the triangle ABC. As a result of monopolization, consumer surplus decreases to the area of the triangle AED. Thus the reduction in consumer surplus is the difference between those two triangles, which is the area of the trapezoid DEBC. This is the amount by which consumers are harmed by monopoly.

In summary, producers benefit from monopoly, to the tune of the rectangle DEFC, but consumers are harmed by monopoly, in the amount of the trapezoid DEBC. The consumers' loss is bigger than the producers' gain! The difference between the two is represented by the area of the triangle, EBF. This is the deadweight loss of monopoly, which is the loss to the entire society as a result of monopoly.

The losses caused by monopoly can be large. Some economists have estimated that the transfer to monopolists, in terms of higher profits, might be between 2 percent and 3 percent of gross domestic product. The deadweight loss of monopoly might be of similar size. In other words, the deadweight loss of monopoly in the United States might be as large as a few hundred billion dollars per year.

Using this example, we've identified four effects of monopoly:

- The monopolist charges higher prices than perfect competitors would charge.

- Because of the higher prices under monopoly, a lower quantity is bought and sold under monopoly than under competition.

- The monopolist makes economic profit in the long run, whereas perfectly competitive firms will only earn a normal return. That is, competitive firms will earn zero economic profit in the long run.

- Monopoly causes a deadweight loss.

In the next few sections, we'll look at some other possible effects of monopolies.

Do Monopolies Keep Their Costs under Control?

In the previous section, we analyzed the differences between competition and monopoly, *assuming that the cost curves were the same in the two cases*. But monopolies might also be wasteful, in the sense that they don't produce the greatest possible output with their resources. It takes hard work to control costs, and to use the latest technologies. If your firm is a secure monopoly, you'll be tempted to take leisurely coffee breaks and long lunches.

The workers of the monopoly firm probably don't have as much incentive to work hard as they would if they worked for a competitive firm, and the managers don't have as much incentive to adopt the latest and most efficient techniques. This lack of incentives can lead to wasted resources. This type of waste is sometimes called *X-inefficiency*.

Many studies have shown that X-inefficiency can be important. For example, some electric-power utilities are monopolies, while others are not. One study showed that the power companies that faced competition had unit costs that were about 11 percent lower than the monopolies' costs. Another example is the British glass-bottle industry, which had a price-fixing agreement that allowed the firms to share in monopoly profits. When this agreement broke down, the firms had to learn how to compete. They introduced modern equipment, and output per worker went up by nearly 100 percent!

We have now seen that *monopolies cause three distinct types of inefficiency*. The deadweight loss occurs because the monopolist charges prices above marginal cost. The second type of inefficiency comes from the fact that the monopoly doesn't usually produce at the minimum point of its average total cost curve. Finally, the monopoly may be guilty of X-inefficiency.

Reality Check: Interim Review Question

IR10-7. When compared with the situation under perfect competition, will consumers be better off or worse off under monopoly?

CAN WE SAY ANYTHING GOOD ABOUT MONOPOLY?

So far, we've seen that monopolies tend to raise prices and reduce quantities. Monopolies generate deadweight losses, and they tend to be less efficient than competitive firms. It's not a pretty picture. In this section, we'll consider whether there are any situations in which monopolies may not be so bad.

Natural Monopoly

In our example of the hot-dog market at the Slam Dunk Coliseum, we assumed that average total cost was constant. In other words, the average-total-cost curve was drawn as a horizontal line. In a situation like this, monopolies wouldn't have any cost advantage over competitive firms. But what if average total cost were decreasing over the entire range of output? Figure 10.6 shows the cost curves for a firm of this type. From earlier chapters, we know that marginal cost will be less than average total cost, if average total cost is decreasing. In Figure 10.6, ATC always slopes downward to the right, and MC is always below ATC.

An industry is a natural monopoly if a single firm could produce at lower average total cost than could any combination of two or more smaller firms. If the ATC curve is always downward-sloping, the ATC of a larger firm is always lower than the ATC of a smaller firm. Therefore, if the ATC is always downward-sloping, the industry is a natural monopoly. Because of this cost advantage for the natural-monopoly firm, it can produce at a lower cost per unit than any combination of competitive firms would (assuming that the firm uses its resources as efficiently as it can).

Still, if the natural monopoly is left to its own devices, it will charge prices that are greater than its marginal costs. There is no guarantee that a natural monopoly will charge lower prices than competitive firms would have charged. This presents a tough problem

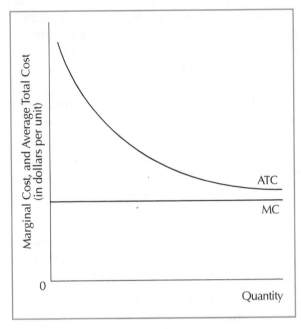

Figure 10.6 The Cost Curves for a Natural Monopoly

In a natural monopoly, the average-total-cost curve is decreasing throughout the entire range of output. This means that the natural monopoly can produce at a lower average cost than any combination of two or more smaller firms. Since ATC is always decreasing, the marginal-cost curve must always be below the ATC curve.

for public policy. On the one hand, if it avoids X-inefficiency, the natural monopoly can produce at lower cost. On the other hand, it won't necessarily pass those lower costs on to consumers in the form of lower prices. Because of this problem, many governments have chosen to regulate the industries that were believed to be natural monopolies. In Chapter 12, we will discuss the regulation of natural monopolies in greater detail.

However, some industries that have traditionally been treated as natural monopolies may not really *be* natural monopolies. The most important such case is the industry that generates and transmits electric power. For most of the 20th century, governments gave regional monopolies to the electric-power utilities. However, in the 1980s, many small, independent power plants began to generate electricity at costs that were *lower* than those of the monopoly utilities. If small firms can produce at lower cost than large firms, then the industry cannot be a natural monopoly. It now appears that the electric-power industry may not have been a natural monopoly at all. The industry was monopolized, but the source of the monopoly may have been government restrictions, rather than cost advantages.

Partly as a result of this evidence, the Energy Policy Act of 1992 brought greater competition to electric-power transmission, by forcing utilities to transmit the electricity of other companies on their transmission lines. Several state governments have encouraged competition by requiring the old monopolies to sell off some of their plants. Unfortunately, California botched its reforms of the electricity market very badly. As mentioned in Chapter 4, the faulty plan led to blackouts. This may have had the side effect of reducing enthusiasm for reform across the nation, even if it is possible to reform the electricity market much more wisely.

In theory, natural monopolies have the potential to perform better than the industry could do if it were organized competitively. However, as a practical matter, it appears that very few industries actually fit the definition of a natural monopoly.

Innovation

We've already seen that patents give temporary monopoly power. This means that firms that invent new products will be rewarded with monopoly profits, at least for a while. We don't know for sure what would have happened if the promise of monopoly profits had not been there. But it's possible that the firms work harder on their research efforts because they believe they will earn monopoly profits as a result. If this is the case, then patent monopoly may be socially useful.

Quite apart from patent monopoly, some economists emphasize that large-scale firms have advantages in research and development. More than a century ago, Thomas Edison created some of his inventions in a small laboratory, with very little help. Gradually, however, Edison's operation became larger and larger. Today, research is often carried out in big laboratories, with large teams of scientists. Small firms will be at a big disadvantage in carrying out this kind of research.

The economist Joseph Schumpeter is best-known for advocating the idea that economic progress requires large-scale organizations. In his book, *Capitalism, Socialism, and Democracy*, Schumpeter says that large-scale establishments have "come to be the most powerful engine of (economic progress) . . . In this respect, perfect competition is not only impossible but inferior, and has no title to being set up as a model of ideal efficiency."

Schumpeter's ideas do have some merit. Many innovations are developed by large-scale organizations, some of which are monopolies or near-monopolies. For example, a century ago, John D. Rockefeller's Standard Oil Company had a near-monopoly in refining and distributing petroleum products. Standard Oil improved the pipeline system, and the price of kerosene actually decreased.

However, it's important not to carry Schumpeter's ideas too far. Many innovations are still developed by small teams of inventors. Also, in many cases, monopolies have not been very good innovators. For example, for most of the 20th century, the American Telephone and Telegraph Company (AT&T) had a monopoly in producing telephone equipment. AT&T took a long time to implement several important technological improvements. The firm was slow to replace live operators with dial telephones in the 1940s, and slow to introduce electronic switching in the 1960s. The designs for telephone receivers were improved greatly in the 1970s, with automatic redialing, memory dialing, and so on. But this only occurred *after* the Federal Communications Commission ordered AT&T to let its customers use non-AT&T equipment.

Why are some monopolies good at introducing new techniques, while others aren't so good? The answer may lie in the fact that some monopolies feel safer than others. AT&T was protected from competition by laws and regulations, and this may have contributed to a feeling of complacency. On the other hand, Microsoft Corporation has not depended on legal barriers to entry. Instead, Microsoft has achieved its strong position by other means. Some of Microsoft's success has been due to very aggressive business tactics, some of which may be illegal. On the other hand, it is also true that Microsoft has developed many useful products. Microsoft's executives probably realize that their near-monopoly could be eroded quickly if they don't continue to innovate.

If a monopoly is protected by airtight barriers to entry, it will be tempted to slack off and take it easy. Larger firms do have some advantages in research and development, but it's important that the firm not feel too safe and comfortable.

Summary

On balance, we aren't left with a very good impression of monopolies. Some monopolies may be able to achieve technological break-throughs, but not all have done so. Natural monopolies may have a cost advantage, but it appears that natural monopolies are rare in reality. In most cases, monopolies lead to high prices, reduced output, and inefficiency.

Reality Check: Interim Review Question

IR10-8. Describe the shape of the average-total-cost curve for a natural monopoly.

PRICE DISCRIMINATION

Until now, we have been discussing "single-price monopolies", which sell to all of their customers at the same price. But lots of firms charge different prices to different customers, for the same service. Many movie theaters allow children to pay less than adults. Many restaurants give discounts to Senior Citizens. When different customers of the same firm are charged different prices for the same good or service (even though the costs of production are the same), we say the firm is practicing *price discrimination.*

Store coupons are another example of price discrimination. If you go to your local grocery store without a coupon, you might pay $3.39 for a box of Raisin Nut Bran. But if you have a "75 cents off" coupon, you only have to pay $(3.39 − 0.75) = $2.64 for the identical item. Some customers get coupons from the Sunday newspaper, or from online sources. If they have a coupon, they get to buy the cereal for a lower price. Other customers, who don't have a coupon when they go to the store, end up paying a higher price for an identical product.

Most colleges and universities practice price discrimination by offering financial aid to some (but not all) students. Doctors, lawyers, social workers, and other professionals often practice price discrimination by using a "sliding fee scale", which means that they charge higher prices to higher-income clients.

The passenger-airlines industry is well known for practicing price discrimination. Most airlines offer lower fares to passengers who stay at their destination over a Saturday night. Sometimes, lower fares are only available to those who book their tickets well in advance. Sometimes, the passenger has to stay for at least a week or two to qualify for the lower fare.

Since we believe that firms desire to maximize profit, it must be that firms engage in price discrimination because they believe that doing so will increase their profit. The basic idea is that *the firm may be able to increase its profit if it can somehow charge a higher price to those who are willing to pay more, and a lower price to those who aren't willing to pay as much.*

Shortly, we'll say more about exactly how the price-discriminating firm can increase its profit. For now, however, let's list the conditions that have to exist, if a firm is to engage in successful price discrimination. (We say that a scheme of price discrimination is "successful" if it helps the firm to increase profit. Of course, this is not necessarily good for consumers.)

Conditions Necessary for Price Discrimination

In principle, *all* firms would like to price discriminate, because doing so would increase their profit. But many firms find it impossible to practice price discrimination successfully. If a firm is to increase its profit through price discrimination, several conditions must be met.

- The firm must have some market power.
- The firm must be able to estimate which customers are willing to pay more.
- It must be difficult or impossible for customers to re-sell to other customers.

Let's think about these three conditions in more detail.

Market Power. Remember the characteristics of perfectly competitive firms: They're small relative to the market, and their outputs are homogeneous, or standardized. Because of these characteristics, perfectly competitive firms are *price takers*. If one competitor tries to sell her corn crop at a higher price than the market price, she will lose all of her customers. Since perfect competitors are price takers, *perfectly competitive firms cannot practice price discrimination.*

Some price-discriminating firms are monopolies. For example, many electric-power monopolies charge different prices to different customers. However, some price-discriminating firms aren't monopolies. Thus, even though monopolies are the main focus of this chapter, our discussion of price discrimination doesn't apply only to monopolies. Price discrimination can also be practiced by oligopolistic and monopolistically competitive firms, which are discussed in the next chapter. The key thing is that *price discrimination can only succeed if the firm has some market power.* Either the firm must have a differentiated product, or it must be large relative to the market, or both.

In each of the examples of price discrimination given above, the firms do indeed have market power. Store coupons are issued by the breakfast-cereal manufacturers, such as General Mills and Kellogg. These firms are large relative to the market, and they also have some market power because their products are differentiated. Passenger airlines also have market power.

The Firm Must Be Able to Estimate Which Customers Are Willing to Pay More. The idea of price discrimination is to charge higher prices to those customers who are willing to pay more. Therefore, the sellers need to have some way of determining who is willing to pay more, and who isn't. In the case of store coupons for breakfast cereal, the customer has to go to the trouble of finding the coupon and carrying it to the store. If you collect coupons, you have revealed that lower prices are important to you. In other words, coupon cutters reveal that they are relatively sensitive to price differences. If you don't go to the trouble of clipping the coupon, you have revealed that you don't care as much about getting a lower price, which means that you are relatively insensitive to price differences.

Passenger airlines distinguish their customers on the basis of the details of their travel plans. Generally speaking, the airlines have found that business travelers are willing to pay more than vacationers. This is why lower prices are often charged to customers who are willing to stay over a Saturday night. Since business travelers are especially eager to get home for the weekend, they don't like to stay over Saturday night, even if they could save money by doing so. Similarly, some airlines charge less for a longer stay. If you stay at the same destination for two weeks, you're probably a vacationer. Also, in some cases, cheap fares are only available to those who book their reservations a week or more in advance. Travelers who make their reservations at the last minute have to pay higher prices. Most often, these travelers either have an emergency, or they are too disorganized to make their reservations in advance. In either case, those who book at the last minute are likely to be willing to pay more.

Ideally, breakfast-cereal manufacturers and passenger airlines would like to distinguish among their customers *perfectly*. The makers of Cheerios would like to identify those consumers who are willing to pay *exactly* $4.73, for example, and charge them exactly that much. If a firm were able to charge the exact maximum that each customer is willing to pay, we would say that the firm is engaged in *perfect price discrimination*. Cereal coupon schemes don't go this far—they are a very imperfect way of distinguishing among customers. (In fact, it is probably impossible for any price-discrimination scheme to go all the way to perfect price discrimination.) Nevertheless, coupon schemes do help the cereal firms to identify their high-paying and low-paying customers.

In many cases, it's very hard for firms to tell which of their customers are willing to pay more. For example, hardware stores can't easily judge high-paying customers from low-paying customers. Consequently, most hardware stores charge *all* of their customers the same price for the same item. In other words, there is no price discrimination at most hardware stores: You pay more for a circular saw than for a screwdriver, but everyone who buys a particular kind of circular saw pays the *same* price.

It Must Be Difficult or Impossible for Customers to Re-sell the Product. If it were possible for customers to buy large quantities of discounted merchandise, and then re-sell them, the whole purpose of the price-discrimination scheme would be defeated. One example of an attempt to avoid re-selling is that movie theaters only sell one ticket per customer. Consequently, even if a child gets a discount price, he or she won't be able to re-sell movie tickets in large quantities.

Sometimes, however, buyers are able to do a substantial amount of re-selling. A supermarket in Udine, Italy, started to offer a 20-percent discount to Senior Citizens in 1995. At first, the store's managers thought the plan was a success. However, they discovered that teams of grandmothers were loading up carts of groceries, carrying them out of the store, and re-selling to younger folks. The younger shoppers saved money, the older shoppers made a small fortune, and the store discovered that it wasn't increasing its profit as much as it had hoped. Soon, the Italian supermarket quit offering the Senior Citizen discount. If a price-discriminating firm learns that customers are doing lots of re-selling, the firm will try to find a way to stop the re-selling. If the firm is unable to prevent re-selling, it may have to stop its attempt at price discrimination.

The Role of Demand Elasticities in Price Discrimination

If a firm could engage in perfect price discrimination, it would have the potential to make enormous profits. Of course, in most cases, firms can't distinguish among their customers perfectly. But there is still plenty of room for increasing profit, even when a firm can't tell its customers apart perfectly.

For example, let's consider the airlines. They certainly can't read the minds of all of their customers. Still, they manage to discriminate on the basis of certain characteristics that are rough indicators of willingness to pay. If you arrange your flight months in advance, and if you plan a two-week stay, then the airlines can guess that you are probably a vacation traveler. As such, you are probably sensitive to price. In other words, your demand is probably relatively *elastic*.

On the other hand, what if you were to call an airline on a Monday, and say that you need to fly on Tuesday and be back by Wednesday? In this case, the airline will guess that you are a business traveler, so that you are less sensitive to price. In other words, your demand is probably relatively *inelastic*.

The trick is to *charge higher prices to customers who have relatively inelastic demands, and charge lower prices to those who have relatively elastic demands.* When price is increased for those with inelastic demand, total revenue goes up. Similarly, when price is decreased for those with elastic demand, total revenue goes

up. All of the price-discrimination schemes listed earlier in this section have the same character: They find ways to charge higher prices to those with less elastic demand.

When firms give a discount to Senior Citizens, they would like their customers to believe they do it out of the goodness of their hearts. However, we now see that price discrimination is more accurately viewed as a method of trying to increase profit. Firms may indeed respect their elders, but all we know for sure is that they believe Senior Citizens have relatively elastic demand. If the firms were really motivated by charity, rather than by profit, they would give the same low prices to *all* of their customers, and not just to Senior Citizens.

Reality Check: Interim Review Questions

IR10-9. Do perfectly competitive firms engage in price discrimination? Why, or why not?

IR10-10. Explain why price-discriminating firms charge higher prices to customers with relatively inelastic demand.

ECONOMICS AND YOU: COMPETITION, MONOPOLY, AND THE FUTURE OF TELECOMMUNICATIONS

We began this chapter with a discussion of Tamika Chandler, who can choose among several different suppliers of long-distance telephone services. We end this chapter by returning to our discussion of the telecommunications industry. This industry has a long history of monopoly, but competition has increased during the last few decades. The increases in competition have resulted from new technologies, as well as from changes in government policy.

Alexander Graham Bell invented the telephone in 1876. When he received a patent, it gave the Bell Telephone Company a monopoly in the telephone business. Even after the tele-

phone patent expired in 1894, the Bell System maintained a monopoly in virtually all phases of telephone service for most of the next century. Bell monopolized equipment manufacturing and long-distance phone service, and it also monopolized many local telephone markets through its local operating companies.

Bell's monopoly position began to erode in the late 1960s and early 1970s. The Federal Communications Commission (FCC) allowed a new company, MCI, to begin to compete in long-distance service. The FCC also allowed telephone subscribers to use non-Bell equipment. This allowed new firms to introduce new technologies, such as microwave transmission, fiber-optic transmission, and cellular telephones. Many of the new inventions weakened the Bell monopoly.

In 1974, the U.S. government sued under the antitrust laws. (The antitrust laws are designed to combat monopoly. We'll discuss these laws in detail in Chapter 12.) This monumental court case was settled in 1982, in a way that led to the break-up of the Bell System. The local operating companies were reorganized into seven regional holding companies, which were nicknamed the "Baby Bells". These companies were separated from the long-distance company, American Telephone and Telegraph (AT&T).

After the mid–1980s, long-distance telephone service became increasingly competitive. MCI, Sprint, and a host of smaller firms offered discount prices. This forced AT&T, the former long-distance monopoly, to lower its prices as well.

However, local phone service presented a dramatically different picture. Each of the Baby Bells maintained a near-monopoly in its own region. The United States now had seven regional monopolies in local telephone service, instead of one nationwide monopoly. Customers were still forced to pay monopoly prices.

This situation led Congress to pass the Telecommunications Act of 1996. The idea was for the Baby Bells to get involved in long-distance service, and for the long-distance companies to get involved in local service. This would lead to a competitive free-for-all, resulting in lower prices and better services for telephone users.

Unfortunately, the initial response of the Baby Bells was to fight against competition, by making it difficult for long-distance companies to hook up customers for local service. The Baby Bells appeared to be more interested in preserving their local monopolies than in competing in the long-distance market.

In fact, much of the energy of these telephone giants went into merging with each other, rather than competing. Bell Atlantic paid $26 billion to take over Nynex in 1997. In the same year, SBC Communications bought Pacific Telesis for $17 billion, creating a local-service monopoly in California, Texas, and other States. SBC also gobbled up Ameritech, and became the dominant provider of local phone service in the Great Lakes region. Much of the competitive pressure has been from smaller start-up companies, rather than from the Baby Bells themselves.

Once again, however, freewheeling new companies came to the rescue of the consumer, with help from new technologies. In the 1990s and into the 21st century, cellular phones were shaking up the market, and blurring the once-important distinction between local and long-distance service. Voice-over-Internet Systems gave even more choice to the consumer. At this point, it's hard to predict the future in the rapidly evolving telecommunications market. However, as of this writing, it's possible to be optimistic that the old days of monopoly are gone.

Chapter Summary

1. There is only one firm in a monopolized market. Some markets have one dominant firm, with a very large share of the market, even though they literally have more than one firm. We can use the analytical tools of this chapter to analyze these "near monopolies", just as we would analyze a pure monopoly. If the firm is to remain a monopoly, it must be protected by barriers to entry. In addition, there must not be any close substitutes for the product of the monopolist.

2. Monopolists are sometimes protected from competition by legal barriers to entry, such as patents or exclusive franchise arrangements. In the case of a natural monopoly, the barrier to entry is the firm's cost advantage.

3. Whereas the perfectly competitive firm has a horizontal demand curve for its product, the monopoly firm faces the entire market demand curve, which slopes downward as we move from left to right across the diagram.

4. The marginal revenue of the monopolist is the amount of extra sales revenue that it receives, when it sells one extra unit of output. The monopolist's marginal-revenue curve slopes downward as we move from left to right across the diagram. In the case of a straight-line demand curve, the marginal-revenue curve is also a straight line, and it is twice as steep as the demand curve. When marginal revenue is positive, demand is elastic. When marginal revenue is zero, demand is unit elastic. When marginal revenue is negative, demand is inelastic.

5. The monopolist maximizes profit by producing and selling the quantity at which marginal revenue is equal to marginal cost. The firm sells at the price given by the demand curve. Thus the monopolist charges a price that is greater than marginal cost, whereas the perfectly competitive firm's price is equal to marginal cost.

6. The price chosen by the monopolist will depend on the shapes of the demand and marginal-revenue curves. There is no unique relationship between quantity and price. Therefore, the monopoly firm does not have a unique supply curve.

7. Compared with a perfectly competitive industry, a monopolized industry will charge a higher price, sell a lower quantity, and make larger economic profit. Because of the higher price and lower quantity, consumers will be worse off when the industry is monopolized than when it is perfectly competitive. The consumer's loss is larger than the monopolist's profit. As a result, society as a whole is worse off. The loss due to monopoly is called the deadweight loss of monopoly.

8. Monopolists may be able to survive, even if they do not control their costs. If they are wasteful, they create "X-inefficiency".

9. A price-discriminating firm is one that sells the same product at different prices to different customers, even though there are no differences in costs. To increase profits by engaging in price discrimination, a firm must have some ability to control the price, and it must have some way of distinguishing customers on the basis of willingness to pay, and it must be able to prevent its product from being re-sold. If these conditions are met, the firm will increase its profit by selling at higher prices to those with relatively inelastic demands, and selling at lower prices to those with relatively elastic demands.

Key Terms

Monopoly

Price Makers

Market Power

Patent

Exclusive Franchise

Natural Monopoly

Single-Price Monopoly

Deadweight Loss

X-Inefficiency

Price Discrimination

Perfect Price Discrimination

Key Figures

The key figures for this chapter are Figures 10.3(a) and 10.3(b), which show how to find the profit-maximizing quantity for a monopoly.

Questions and Problems

QP10-1. Different monopolies are protected by different barriers to entry. Name as many barriers to entry as you can. Which of these barriers to entry (if any) makes society better off?

QP10-2. What is the difference between the demand curve facing a perfectly competitive firm and the demand curve facing a monopoly firm? What is the difference between the marginal-revenue curve facing a perfectly competitive firm and the marginal-revenue curve facing a monopoly firm? Why are the curves different?

QP10-3. AAAA Corporation has a monopoly in the production of gizmos. Financial analysts calculate that the elasticity of demand for AAAA's gizmos is 0.4, which means that the demand is inelastic. What does this imply about the marginal revenue of selling one additional gizmo? How would your answer change if the demand for gizmos were unit elastic? What if the demand for gizmos were elastic?

QP10-4. In the previous question, it was stated that AAAA Corporation (a monopoly firm) faces a demand curve with an elasticity of 0.4. Is the firm maximizing its profit? If the firm is not maximizing profit, and if it desires to maximize profit, how would it change its level of output?

Price	Quantity Demanded	Total Revenue	Marginal Revenue	Marginal Cost	Total Cost	Profit
$10	0					
9	1					
8	2					
7	3					
6	4					
5	5					
4	6					
3	7					
2	8					
1	9					
0	10					

QP10-5. A demand schedule in the market for zolotkas is on the previous page:

a. Assume that the firm does *not* practice price discrimination. Fill in the columns for total revenue and marginal revenue.
b. Assume that marginal cost is a constant: At any quantity, MC = $3 per additional unit. Also, assume that there are no fixed costs. Fill in the columns for marginal cost and total cost.
c. What is the firm's profit-maximizing quantity of output? What price does the firm charge? How much profit does the firm make?
d. Verify that we get the same profit-maximizing quantity, regardless of whether we compare *total* revenue and cost, or *marginal* revenue and cost.
e. Now, assume that the firm has fixed costs of $15, but that all of the other information on costs and revenues stays the same. How does this affect your answers about the firm's profit-maximizing quantity of output, price, and profit?

QP10-6. Return to the demand schedule of the previous question. Now, however, assume that the firm is able to practice perfect price discrimination. In other words, it can charge $9 to the first customer, $8 to the second customer, $7 to the third customer, and so on.

a. Now, re-calculate total revenue and marginal revenue.
b. Assuming that the firm has no fixed costs, what is its profit-maximizing quantity of output? What is its price? How much profit does it earn?
c. Assume that the firm has fixed costs of $15. How does this affect your answers about the firm's profit-maximizing quantity of output, price, and profit?
d. What are the differences between the single-price monopoly of the previous question, and the price-discriminating monopoly of this question? Who is better off with price discrimination, and who is better off with the single-price monopoly?

QP10-7. Once again, return to the demand schedule from question (QP10-5). This time, however, assume that the industry is perfectly competitive.

a. If the marginal cost of production is $3 for any firm, and if every firm has zero fixed costs, what are the market equilibrium price and quantity?
b. Compare this price and quantity with the price and quantity that would occur with a single-price monopolist (as in question QP10-5).
c. Next, compare this equilibrium price and quantity with the various prices and the quantity that would occur with a perfectly price-discriminating monopolist (as in question QP10-6).

QP10-8. It is observed that a firm is making a very large positive economic profit. Does this imply that the firm must be a monopoly?

QP10-9. John Q. Monopolist inherits a monopoly firm from his parents. He knows that a monopolist has market power. On this basis, he decides it is best for the firm to charge the highest possible price that can be charged, without driving the quantity demanded all the way down to zero. Comment on this strategy.

QP10-10. A movie theater charges $3 for all seats for its shows at 4 p.m. The theater charges $6 for all seats for its shows at 8 p.m. Is this price discrimination? Why or why not?

QP10-11. A hardware store is having a "buy one, get the second one for half price" sale on screwdrivers. This means that all customers must pay $10 for the first screwdriver, but, if they want a second screwdriver, the price will only be $5 more. Is this price discrimination? Why or why not?

Chapter 11

Monopolistic Competition and Oligopoly

ECONOMICS AND YOU: FROSTED FLAKES AND COUNT CHOCULA; CHIPS AHOY AND OREOS

When you walk past the breakfast cereals in your grocery store, what do you see? There are Frosted Flakes and Cinnamon Toast Crunch, Grape Nuts and Mueslix, Shredded Wheat, Frosted Mini-Wheats, and Frosted Wheat Bites. This certainly *isn't* a perfectly competitive world, where one farmer's wheat is identical to another farmer's wheat. This is a world of *product differentiation*, in which the different firms in an industry make products that are noticeably different.

If you look closely, you'll also see that there are only a few firms in the breakfast-cereal market. The market certainly isn't a monopoly, but it is dominated by a few giants: Kellogg, General Foods, General Mills, Post, Ralston, Quaker, and Nabisco have the lion's share of the market. Once again, this is not the perfectly competitive world, because perfect competition involves hundreds or thousands of small firms. Instead, this is a world of competition among the few.

In short, the breakfast-cereal industry is different from the perfectly competitive ideal in two important ways: (1) the products are differentiated, and (2) there are only a few firms.

In fact, *most* American industries have at least one of these two characteristics. The automobile industry has differentiated products, and most of the world's production is generated by a few firms. The steel industry has some goods that are homogeneous, as well as some specialty products that are differentiated. However, the steel industry *is* dominated by a relatively small number of firms.

Each industry is unique, and no simple model can hope to tell us everything we want to know about every industry. And yet, certain basic patterns do emerge. Economists have found it convenient to classify industries into four broad categories, based on the way in which the firms interact with each other in a given industry. These four categories are called *market structures*.

We've already studied two market structures—perfect competition and monopoly. The third market structure is *monopolistic competition*. When we study monopolistic competition, we are concerned with the effects of product differentiation. The final market structure is *oligopoly*. When we study oligopoly, there's more emphasis on the interactions among a small number of firms.

If we consider monopolistically competitive industries and oligopolies together, we sometimes speak of industries that are characterized by *imperfect competition*.

Before we begin to study the *theories* of imperfect competition, we need to know more about the *facts*. In the next section, we will take a look at the sizes of the biggest business firms. After that, we develop some ways of thinking about monopolistic competition, and we begin the study of oligopoly.

GIANTS OF THE ECONOMY

Table 11.1 shows some information on the largest corporations in the world in 2015. There are many ways to measure the size of a company; Table 11.1 shows the 20 companies with the largest sales revenues. In a world that produces nearly 100 million barrels of oil per day, it may not be surprising that eight of these 20 companies are engaged in production and refining of petroleum. A lot of that oil is made into gasoline for automobiles, and five of the 20 companies are in the auto business.

It's also interesting to note that Microsoft Corporation is not on the list. In fact, Microsoft's sales were only about $87 billion in 2015, which put it in 58th place. Google came in 80th, with $66 billion of revenue.

Table 11.1 The 20 Largest Corporations in the World, 2015

Ranking	Company	Headquarters	Sector	2015 Sales Revenues (in Billions of Dollars)
1.	Walmart	Bentonville, Arkansas	Retailing	$485.7
2.	Sinopec Group	Beijing, China	Energy	446.8
3.	Royal Dutch Shell	The Hague, Netherlands	Energy	431.3
4.	China National Petroleum	Beijing, China	Energy	428.6
5.	Exxon Mobil	Irving, Texas	Energy	382.6
6.	BP	London, United Kingdom	Energy	358.7
7.	State Grid	Beijing, China	Utilities	339.4
8.	Volkswagen	Wolfsburg, Germany	Automotive	268.6
9.	Toyota Motor	Toyota, Japan	Automotive	247.7
10.	Glencore	Baar, Switzerland	Mining	221.1
11.	Chevron	San Ramon, California	Energy	191.8
12.	Samsung Electronics	Suwon, South Korea	Electronics	188.5
13.	Apple	Cupertino, California	Computers	182.8
14.	Phillips 66	Houston, Texas	Energy	161.2
15.	Daimler	Stuttgart, Germany	Automotive	157.0
16.	General Motors	Detroit, Michigan	Automotive	155.9
17.	General Electric	Fairfield, Connecticut	Diversified	148.6
18.	Ford Motor	Dearborn, Michigan	Automotive	144.1
19.	Petrobras	Rio de Janeiro, Brazil	Energy	143.4
20.	CVS Caremark	Woonsocket, Rhode Island	Drugstores	139.4

Source: *Fortune* magazine.

CHARACTERISTICS OF MONOPOLISTIC COMPETITION

The theory of monopolistic competition was developed in the 1930s, by Edward Chamberlin (an American) and Joan Robinson (an Englishwoman). We can identify several characteristics that monopolistically competitive industries have in common. These include

- a large number of producers,
- easy entry and exit,
- product differentiation, and
- frequent use of non-price competition.

Let's look at each of these features in turn.

Many Firms

In an earlier chapter, we saw that a perfectly competitive industry has many firms. The same is true for an industry with monopolistic competition. Some of the best examples of monopolistic competition are in retailing. Most Americans can easily go to dozens of different gasoline stations, or fast-food restaurants, or clothing outlets.

Easy Entry and Exit

Another of our assumptions regarding perfect competition was that it is easy for firms to enter the industry when positive economic profits are being earned, and easy for firms to exit when losses are being suffered. In this way, a perfectly competitive industry will be driven toward zero economic profit.

Free entry and exit also apply to monopolistically competitive industries. This means that these industries will also tend toward zero economic profit in the long run. Once again, some of the best examples are in retailing. It's often possible to set up a new burger franchise for an investment of thousands of dollars, instead of millions. Think about opening an ice-cream store, compared with starting up a new company to manufacture commercial aircraft. Entry is relatively easy in the retail ice-cream business (which we think of as

monopolistically competitive). But entry is extremely costly in the aircraft industry (which we think of as oligopolistic).

Product Differentiation

So far, we've seen that monopolistic competition shares some of the characteristics of perfect competition. But perfectly competitive firms produce homogeneous, standardized products, whereas monopolistically competitive firms produce differentiated products.

Product differentiation can come in many forms. Firms often differentiate themselves on the basis of location, or product quality, or service.

Location. If one gasoline station is located right next to the freeway exit ramp, it will be easy to drive in and fill up quickly. Even if another gas station is located only a few blocks away, it may not be so convenient. Consumers take location into consideration, and so they will have greater demand for gasoline from the conveniently located station. This is why we sometimes see one station charging, say, $2.39 for a gallon of regular unleaded gas, while a station a block away only charges $2.37. Some people are willing to pay a little extra, to save time and trouble. (In other words, some people will conclude that the opportunity cost of buying gasoline is lower at the conveniently located station, even if the price per gallon is higher.) The amount of the price difference will depend on the degree of difference in convenience.

The same is true in many other monopolistically competitive industries. Some people find it more convenient to buy eyeglasses and frames from a store in a shopping mall, rather than from some other store. Therefore, the mall stores may be able to charge higher prices than other stores.

Product Quality and Service. Most shopping malls have literally dozens of stores that sell clothing. Some have lots of selection; others have less. Some have friendly, courteous

Real Economics for Real People 11.1: Let the Buyer Beware of Product Differentiation

Product differentiation is often a good thing. For example, the automobile market offers station wagons, minivans, and pickups for those who want to haul around a lot of people or a lot of goods. But the market also offers subcompacts for those who don't need as much space. Some people prefer muscled sports cars, while others prefer conservative sedans, and the market caters to both tastes.

The market for cough-and-cold medicines is highly differentiated. There are syrups, tablets, gels, and nasal sprays. Some medicines treat flu symptoms; others don't. Some give 12-hour relief; some work for only four or six hours. Once again, it's probably beneficial to have different products for different needs.

However, some of the differentiation in the cough-and-cold market may not be worth very much to the consumer. On a recent trip to the local pharmacy, we found three liquid cough-and-cold medicines with *identical* active ingredients. The adult dose for each medicine includes exactly 30 milligrams of the *same* cough suppressant, and exactly 60 milligrams of the *same* decongestant. Thus, the only product differentiation involves brand name, the taste of the syrup, the color of the package, and so on.

All of these medicines were sold in four-ounce bottles. One sold for $5.69 per bottle, one for $4.99, and the other for $4.49. Thus, if we compare the $5.69 bottle with the $4.49 bottle, there is a price gap of nearly 27 percent. But the price differences don't end there. The ingredients of the $4.99 bottle were more heavily diluted by the syrup. Even though all of the bottles have the same number of *ounces*, they don't all have the same amount of active *ingredients*. Consequently, if we were to adjust the price of the $4.99 bottle, to make it comparable with the other two, the "true" price of the $4.99 bottle would jump to $6.65. If we compare this with the $4.49 bottle, there is a price gap of more than 48 percent. The brand that sold for $4.49 in a four-ounce bottle also offered an eight-ounce bottle, for $7.49. If we compare the price per unit of medicine between this "giant economy size" and the most expensive brand, there is a price difference of more than 77 percent!

It may be that some customers really make a wise decision when they buy the more expensive brands. (Maybe they have doubts about whether the less-expensive brands are really of equal quality.) But it's also possible that some customers would have come to a different decision, if they had read the labels carefully.

In a world of homogeneous products, there isn't much reason to shop around. However, many of our expenditures are devoted to differentiated products. In this type of environment, it pays to shop wisely.

salespeople; others don't. Some have jackets that are made of finest linen and fully lined; others have unlined polyester. For all of these reasons, shoppers perceive that the different clothing stores are *not* perfect substitutes for each other. If you want the highest quality, you'll have to pay more. If you don't need such high quality, you may be able to save a lot.

Many other industries have differences in quality. Some restaurants have starched white tablecloths; others offer an ordinary atmosphere. Some photo developers offer one-hour service; others don't. In all of these cases, consumers will have different demand for the products of the different firms, depending on the perceived differences in quality.

New! Improved! Bigger! Better! Faster!

Every day, Americans are bombarded with advertisements from websites, billboards, TVs, radios, newspapers, and magazines. Is all of this advertising good for society, or is it merely a big con game, in which gullible consumers are suckered into buying worthless junk? There are different answers for different types of advertising.

At one extreme, some advertising is simply false. The Federal Trade Commission and various State agencies are involved with policing this kind of advertising. Much "image" advertising isn't exactly false, but it doesn't provide much valuable information, either.

At the other extreme, even the most competitive firms will usually want their name, address, and telephone number in the Yellow Pages, so that customers can find them. It's hard to object to this kind of informational advertising. A similar example is advertising for new products. Consumers can't benefit from a product unless they know it exists. Advertising of new products can be beneficial to society.

Advertising can also provide valuable information on prices, and this can help to make industries more competitive. Imagine a world in which gasoline stations did *not* have large signs advertising prices. This would make it more difficult for customers to choose the stations with lower prices. Therefore, we would expect that prices would be higher if there were no advertising. In fact, studies by economists have shown that price advertising has big benefits for consumers, in industries such as gasoline, toys, drugs, and eyeglasses. The prices for eyeglasses were much higher in States that banned advertising than in States that permitted advertising.

Since advertising can lead to lower prices, many professional groups have resisted advertising. At one time, advertising was banned by associations of doctors, dentists, and lawyers. (They argued that advertising was "unprofessional", although their opposition to advertising was almost certainly based on the effect on prices.) Supreme Court decisions have removed the bans on advertising. There is reason to believe that consumers are better off as a result.

Advertising. In a perfectly competitive industry, it's understood that firms produce homogeneous, standardized outputs. As a result, Farmer Jones doesn't have much reason to put up a billboard advertising his wheat. But under monopolistic competition, buyers recognize that the products are not the same. As a result, firms may decide to engage in *advertising*. When a firm advertises its products, it tries to affect the shape and location of its demand curve. Effective advertising can push the firm's demand curve outward. Effective advertising can also make the firm's demand curve more inelastic. If it is successful, the firm will be able to sell a larger quantity, or sell at a higher price, or both.

Advertising is one form of *non-price competition*. Firms still do use price as a competitive weapon, but the buyers' perceptions of product differences will also have an important effect. Many monopolistically competitive firms try to shape those consumer perceptions through advertising.

Real Economics for Real People 11.1 shows that some product differentiation is more imaginary than real, and *Real Economics for Real People 11.2* discusses the advantages and disadvantages of advertising.

PRICES AND OUTPUTS
WITH MONOPOLISTIC COMPETITION

Now that we have discussed the *characteristics* of monopolistically competitive firms, it's time to analyze their *behavior,* as they interact with each other in the marketplace.

The Firm's Demand Curve

When we discussed *perfect* competition, we learned that the individual firm's demand curve was given by the market price. Since all perfectly competitive firms face the same market price, it has to be true that all perfectly competitive firms face the same demand curve. The reason for this is that perfectly competitive firms all produce the same homogeneous output.

However, because of product differentiation, *each monopolistically competitive firm faces its own, unique demand curve.*

Jean's Jeans is a monopolistically competitive firm, selling blue jeans and other clothing items. Jean's has a convenient location, free parking, and a reputation for friendly service. Even though there are plenty of other clothing stores in the area, Jean's good reputation means that the store can raise its price somewhat, without losing all of its customers.

In other words, *the demand curve for a monopolistically competitive firm is downward sloping.* This is shown in Figure 11.1, where the demand curve for Jean's Jeans slopes downward as we move from left to right across the diagram. Our analysis of monopolistic competition will be very similar to our analysis of monopoly, since monopolists also face a downward-sloping demand curve. As we saw in the chapter on monopoly, a downward-sloping demand curve means that the marginal-revenue curve (MR) is also downward sloping. As shown in Figure 11.1, the downward-sloping MR curve for Jean's Jeans is always below the demand curve. In fact, as shown in Figure 11.1, when the demand curve is a straight line, the MR curve is also a straight line, and the

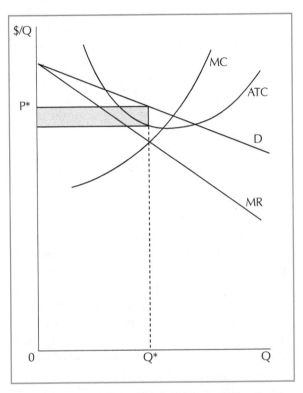

Figure 11.1 Short-Run Profit Maximization for Jean's Jeans

The monopolistically competitive firm maximizes profit by choosing to produce and sell the quantity at which marginal revenue (MR) is equal to marginal cost (MC). This gives a quantity of Q*, and a price of P*. Profit per unit is P* minus average total cost (ATC). Total profit for the firm is given by the shaded area.

slope of the MR curve is exactly twice as great as the slope of the demand curve.

However, even though monopolistic competitors and monopolists both face downward-sloping demand curves, they aren't identical. The reason for this is that the monopolist doesn't have any rivals. On the other hand, the monopolistic competitor has lots of rivals, so that a monopolistic competitor like Jean's Jeans will only have a limited ability to raise its price. If it raises its price very much, the monopolistically competitive firm will lose lots of customers. Therefore, even though the demand curve for Jean's Jeans slopes downward, it is fairly flat.

Profit Maximization in the Short Run

We always assume that firms want to maximize their profit. Like *any* profit-maximizing firm, Jean's Jeans will *choose to produce and sell the quantity at which marginal revenue is equal to marginal cost.* This quantity is given by Q^* in Figure 11.1. When we go from Q^* up to the demand curve, we find that Jean's will sell at a price of P^*.

In earlier chapters, we learned that economic profit per unit is equal to price minus average total cost (ATC). In Figure 11.1, when the quantity is Q^*, price is greater than ATC. This means that Jean's Jeans is earning positive economic profit. (If price had been less than ATC, Jean's would have had economic losses.) The amount of profit is represented by the area of the shaded rectangle in Figure 11.1.

The Long Run: Zero Economic Profit

Figure 11.1 represents a *monopolistically competitive firm* in the short run, but it is basically the same as the short-run profit picture for a *monopolist*. However, that's the end of the story for a monopolist, since the monopoly firm has no rivals. But remember that there are no barriers to entry in monopolistic competition. If Jean's Jeans and the other existing firms were earning economic profit (as in Figure 11.1), there would be an incentive for new firms to enter the market.

When new firms enter the retail clothing market, there will be an effect on the demand curve facing Jean's Jeans. At any given price, the quantity that Jean's can sell will be smaller than it was before. This means that the demand curve and MR curve for Jean's will

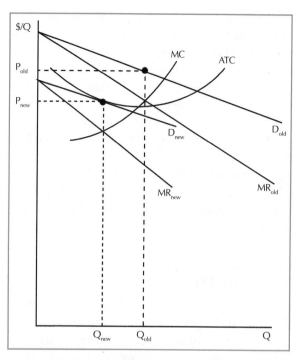

Figure 11.2 Long-Run Profit Maximization for Jean's Jeans

If the existing monopolistically competitive firms are making positive economic profit, new firms will enter the industry. This will shift the demand curve and marginal-revenue curve for an existing firm from D_{old} and MR_{old} to D_{new} and MR_{new}. The new profit-maximizing price and quantity will be P_{new} and Q_{new}. Price equals average total cost, which means that economic profit is now zero because of the increased competition from new firms.

shift to the left, as shown in Figure 11.2. The original demand curve is D_{old}, and its marginal-revenue curve is MR_{old}. In this case, the firm's profit-maximizing quantity is Q_{old}, and the price is P_{old}. As a result of the entry of new firms, there is a leftward shift in the demand curve for Jean's Jeans. The new demand curve is D_{new}, and the new marginal revenue curve is MR_{new}. The new equilibrium price and quantity are P_{new} and Q_{new}. Because of the entry of new firms, the prices charged by the existing firms will fall.

Entry into the industry will continue for as long as there is any incentive for new firms to enter the market. In other words, this process will continue until the firms in the market are making zero economic profit. *The long-run tendency of a monopolistically competitive industry is toward zero economic profit.*

Profit per unit is equal to price minus ATC. If the firm has zero economic profit, then price must be equal to ATC. In Figure 11.2, Jean's is earning zero economic profit, since the ATC curve is just touching the demand curve at a quantity of Q_{new} and a price of P_{new}.

"Excess Capacity" and the Value of Differentiated Products

If the ATC curve for Jean's Jeans is tangent to the demand curve, it has to be true that the ATC curve is downward-sloping (since the firm's demand curve slopes downward). This means that *the monopolistically competitive firm does not minimize its average total costs.* If the firm were to minimize its costs per unit, it would have to increase its output to a larger quantity than Q_{new}.

Over the years, monopolistically competitive firms have been criticized because they don't minimize costs. It has been said that these firms have *excess capacity*, since they could reduce their average total costs by expanding. Another way to state the criticism is this: Monopolistically competitive industries have too many firms, each of which is too small.

However, many economists have concluded that "excess capacity" is not really a very strong criticism of monopolistic competition. First of all, excess capacity may just not be a very big deal. Even though average total costs aren't minimized, they may be *close* to their minimum values. Remember that the demand curve facing the firm will usually be fairly flat. (Product differentiation may give the firm a little bit of market power, but it doesn't usually give a tremendous amount of market power.) If the firm's demand curve is fairly flat, then the ATC curve will probably be close to its minimum point, as in Figure 11.2. In other words, the difference between the firm's *actual* ATC and its *minimum* ATC may be very small.

Second, even though the firms may not minimize their costs, they *do* produce a wide variety of products. If you can even imagine a world of no product differentiation, it would be a very boring place. Every ice-cream store would sell only vanilla. There would be exactly one style of shirt, one style of pants, and one style of shoes. Every radio station would have the same format. If "excess capacity" is the price we have to pay for product differentiation, it may well be worthwhile.

Reality Check: Interim Review Questions

IR11-1. In what ways are a monopolistically competitive firm similar to a perfectly competitive firm? In what ways are a monopolistically competitive firm similar to a monopoly?

IR11-2. The firms in a monopolistically competitive industry are suffering economic losses. What will happen to the number of firms in the industry? What will happen to the prices charged by firms?

IR11-3. Explain why the firms in a monopolistically competitive industry do not minimize average total cost in the long run (after entry or exit have driven economic profit to zero).

CHARACTERISTICS OF OLIGOPOLY

We have now completed our discussion of monopolistic competition. Our next goal is to learn about oligopoly, which is the other "in-between" market structure. Earlier in this chapter, we saw that monopolistically competitive firms have free entry and exit, a large number of sellers, product differentiation, and non-price competition. The features of oligopoly are rather different. In particular, oligopolistic industries are characterized by

- a small number of firms,
- barriers to entry in many cases (although clearly the barriers to entry may not be as strong as in monopoly), and
- strategic interdependence among firms.

Let's take a look at these features in turn.

Few Firms

Oligopoly refers to an industry in which there are only a few sellers. (One special case of oligopoly is *duopoly*, in which there are exactly two sellers.) For example, household laundry equipment is dominated by Maytag, Whirlpool, and a few other brands. Other oligopolistic industries include automobile tires, cigarettes, greeting cards, malt beverages, and telephone apparatus.

Barriers to Entry

Perfect competition and monopolistic competition are similar, in that they both have free entry and exit. But oligopoly is more like monopoly, in that there are usually significant barriers to entry into the industry.

Size as a Barrier to Entry. Oligopolistic firms are often very large. Sometimes the large scale of operations can be a barrier to entry. The investment needed to start a new firm in most oligopolistic industries runs to many millions of dollars, and it can even run into the billions. If you want to set up a new firm to make automobiles, you would have to hire thousands of engineers and technicians. It would take years before you could roll out a car that could compete in the market.

Reputation and Experience. Most oligopolistic firms have had years of experience with their customers. Their salespeople have detailed knowledge of the customers' needs, and this knowledge can be extremely effective in competing with rival firms. Even if a new firm could make automobiles that are better than those currently produced by Toyota, Ford, and the other firms in the industry, the new firm would have to convince a skeptical group of buyers. The relationships between the existing firms and their customers can be an important barrier to entry.

Interdependence

In perfect competition, the firms are very passive. Each firm is so small that it can't do anything to affect the market price. The firms are more active under monopolistic competition. Since the firms have differentiated products, they have some market power. They will try to exploit that market power, in an effort to increase their profits.

With oligopoly, the firms have even more market power. Oligopolistic industries have only a few firms, and this means that the firms are very much aware of each other. If one firm changes its price, the other firms have to decide whether they will change their prices in a similar way. If one firm starts a campaign of research and development, or brings out a new product, the other firms must decide how to respond. Thus oligopolies have an element of strategic interdependence that is mostly missing from perfectly competitive or monopolistically competitive industries.

Since oligopolistic industries have barriers to entry, they may be able to make economic profits for a very long time. However, the amount of profit will depend on whether the firms engage in *collusion*. When we say that firms collude, we mean that they cooperate with each other. If the firms cooperate by promising not to cut prices, they may be able to make the kind of profits that a monopoly firm would make. On the other hand, if each firm cuts prices in an attempt to gain a larger market share, prices may fall to the levels that we would expect for competitive firms.

Advertising by Oligopolists. Earlier in this chapter, we said that advertising and other forms of non-price competition are common features of monopolistic competition. Some important oligopolistic industries do *not* engage in much advertising or other non-price competition. (The crude-oil industry is a good example.) However, many of the most important oligopolies have a lot of product differentiation, and they tend to do a lot of advertising.

The heaviest advertiser in the nation is the consumer-products company, Procter & Gamble. In 2014, Procter & Gamble spent over $4.6 billion on advertising. AT&T spent about $3.3 billion, and both Comcast and General Motors spent about $3 billion. Thus, the amount spent on *advertising* by each of these firms is greater than the *entire* output of Liberia, Central African Republic, Belize, or any of several other countries.

In Table 11.2, we list some more of the firms that did the most advertising in 2014. The list is a who's-who of oligopolistic firms.

Table 11.2 The 20 Largest Advertisers in the United States in 2014

Ranking	Company	Industry	Advertising Spending in 2014 (in Billions of Dollars)
1.	Procter & Gamble	Home products, personal care	$4.61
2.	AT&T	Telecommunications	3.27
3.	General Motors	Automotive	3.12
4.	Comcast	Cable television	3.03
5.	Verizon Communications	Telecommunications	2.53
6.	Ford Motor	Automotive	2.47
7.	American Express	Financial services	2.36
8.	Fiat Chrysler	Automotive	2.25
9.	L'Oréal	Cosmetics	2.16
10.	Walt Disney	Entertainment	2.11
11.	Toyota Motor	Automotive	2.09
12.	Johnson & Johnson	Personal care	1.97
13.	Walmart	Retailing	1.94
14.	JP Morgan Chase	Financial services	1.90
15.	Samsung Electronics	Electronics	1.83
16.	Time Warner	Media communications	1.70
17.	Pfizer	Pharmaceuticals	1.67
18.	Target	Retailing	1.65
19.	Macy's	Retailing	1.60
20.	Bank of America	Financial services	1.58

Source: *Advertising Age,* July 13, 2015.

Table 11.3 Characteristics of Monopolistic Competition and Oligopoly

Monopolistic Competition	Oligopoly
1. Many Firms	1. Few Firms
2. Free Entry and Exit	2. Barriers to Entry
3. Product Differentiation	3. Products May Be Differentiated or Homogeneous
4. Advertising and Other Non-Price Competition	4. May or May Not Have Non-Price Competition
	5. Strategic Interdependence

We summarize the features of imperfectly competitive firms in Table 11.3.

Reality Check:
Interim Review Question

IR11-4. An industry has 75 firms. Is this industry an oligopoly? Why or why not?

STRATEGIC INTERDEPENDENCE

Now that we have outlined the *characteristics* of oligopoly, it's time to learn more about the *behavior* of oligopolistic firms. We start by looking at a couple of important aspects of oligopolistic interdependence. Then, we use the tools of "game theory" to think about collusion. Third, we'll talk about whether an industry that appears to be oligopolistic might actually be fairly competitive, because of the *threat* of entry by new firms.

Adam Smith, the great 18th-century Scottish economist, once wrote, "people of the same trade seldom meet together, even for merriment and diversion, but the conversation ends in a conspiracy against the public, or in some contrivance to raise prices." In other words, firms are often tempted to collude with each other.

The firms in an oligopolistic industry may be able to form a *cartel*, which is an agreement that sets the industry price. The ultimate goal of every cartel is to act as a *shared monopoly*, which means that the cartel firms would charge the same price that would be charged by a monopolist. This will maximize the profits of the industry as a whole.

If the cartel members desire to charge the monopoly *price*, they will have to restrict output to the monopoly *quantity*. Consequently, cartel agreements usually try to restrict quantity, by specifying the amount that can be produced by each firm.

However, if a cartel is successful in charging the monopoly price, some of the firms may be tempted to cheat on the cartel. If one firm can secretly lower its price, it can increase its own profits at the expense of the other cartel members. If enough firms do enough cheating, the price will fall and fall. If the cartel breaks down completely, the price will eventually fall all the way to the competitive price.

Thus, every cartel faces a difficult dilemma: *Once a firm is a member of a cartel, it has an incentive to cheat, but cheating can destroy the cartel.* This is good news for consumers, but bad news for the cartel members.

Game Theory

In the last few decades, economists and other social scientists have developed a framework, called *game theory,* for thinking about a wide variety of situations. *Game theory* is the study of how people and organizations interact with each other in strategic situations. A game-theoretic analysis involves identifying the "players" in the game, and the rules of the game. Then, the analysis will specify the *payoffs* that accompany various outcomes. On the basis of the rules and the payoffs, each player will develop a set of *strategies* that determine how they will play the game.

These game-theoretic ideas can be illustrated by thinking about a game of poker. Each player in a poker game knows the rules of the game: In poker, two pair beats one pair, three of a kind beats two pair, and so on. At the end of each hand, the player with the best hand wins all of the money that has been bet. After the cards are dealt, each player assesses the strength of his or her own hand. Each player will make some guesses about whether his or her cards are likely to beat the cards held by the other players. On that basis, each player must develop a strategy. The player can fold (that is, quit the game) or continue to bet. As the play develops, other players will discard old cards, draw new cards, and bet. Based on these actions, each player may revise his or her strategy.

Poker is a *zero-sum game.* In a game of poker, the amount lost by some players is exactly equal to the amount won by the winner. However, some games are *non-zero-sum games,* because the sum of the gains and losses can be positive or negative.

The Prisoner's Dilemma. One famous non-zero-sum game is the *Prisoner's Dilemma.* The standard story of the Prisoner's Dilemma goes something like this: Sneaky Sam and Harry the Heist are arrested during the commission of a burglary. The evidence against them is overwhelming. There are eyewitnesses, and Harry and Sam are caught with burglary tools. The police and prosecutors have no doubt that they will get a conviction on the charge of breaking and entering.

However, the police and the prosecutors suspect that these two men may also be the culprits in a whole series of other crimes. But the evidence in the other crimes is not so clear-cut, and it won't be possible to get a conviction for the other crimes, unless one or both of the men makes a confession.

The police and prosecutors keep the two men in separate jail cells. In this way, the prisoners won't be able to communicate with each other. In separate discussions with Sam and Harry, the authorities emphasize that they want the men to confess. To each of the prisoners, they say "If you confess to all of these crimes, and the other guy doesn't confess, we'll let you go free, and he will be sent to prison for 20 years. If you both confess, you will each get a sentence of five years in prison. If you don't confess, but the other guy does confess, he will go free and you will be sent to prison for 20 years. If neither of you confesses, we still have enough evidence to convict you of this one burglary, and both of you will be sent to prison for 2 years."

In other words, the authorities describe a "payoff matrix" to each of the men. The payoff matrix tells what will happen, depending on whether the men confess. The payoff matrix is shown in Figure 11.3.

Let's consider Sneaky Sam's decision about whether to confess. It's possible for him to subdivide this decision into two parts. The first part has to do with the situation in which Harry confesses. The second part has to do with the situation in which Harry *does not* confess.

If Harry confesses, Sam can confess and get a sentence of five years, or he can not confess and get a sentence of 20 years. Not surprisingly, Sam wants to get the lightest possible sentence. Therefore, if Harry confesses, Sam's choice will be to confess.

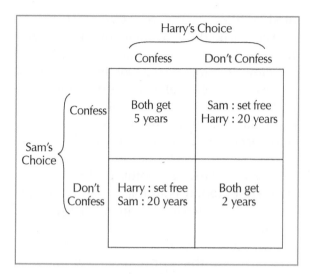

| | | Harry's Choice | |
		Confess	Don't Confess
Sam's Choice	Confess	Both get 5 years	Sam : set free Harry : 20 years
	Don't Confess	Harry : set free Sam : 20 years	Both get 2 years

Figure 11.3 The Payoff Matrix in the Classic Prisoner's Dilemma

If both prisoners confess, they will each get a five-year prison sentence. If neither confesses, they will each receive a two-year prison sentence. If one confesses and the other does not, the one who confesses will be set free, while the one who does not confess will receive a 20-year sentence. This structure of payoffs will give each man an incentive to confess, regardless of what the other man does.

If Harry does not confess, Sam can confess and go free, or he can not confess and get a sentence of two years. Therefore, if Harry doesn't confess, Sam's choice will be to confess.

This is the remarkable result of the Prisoner's Dilemma: Regardless of whether Harry confesses, Sam's best choice will be to confess. In another prison cell, Harry faces the identical problem. If Sam confesses, Harry's best choice is to confess. If Sam doesn't confess, it is still in Harry's interest to confess.

Because of the payoff matrix presented by the police and the prosecutors, each of the prisoners has an incentive to confess. It doesn't matter whether they are actually guilty of the other crimes. Their own selfish interest will lead each of them to confess. As a result, each of them will confess, and they will both get five years in prison. This is *not* the optimal choice for the two men as a group. As a group, they

would be better off if they could agree not to confess. In this case, they would each be sentenced to two years in prison, instead of five years. This is why the Prisoner's Dilemma is a non-zero-sum game: Harry and Sam *both* lose as a result of their inability to cooperate.

This is an unusual result, and a very interesting one. If the two men could cooperate, and agree not to confess, they would each have to spend only two years in prison. However, it is in the selfish interest of each man to confess, which means they will each have to spend five years in prison. Their inability to cooperate has made them worse off. (Clearly, the Prisoner's Dilemma is very different from the "Invisible Hand". The idea of the Invisible Hand, introduced much earlier in this book, is that there will be good outcomes for society as a whole, even though everyone is pursuing his or her own interest. The Invisible Hand arises in a competitive situation, with lots of buyers and sellers interacting with each other. The Prisoner's Dilemma, by contrast, involves the strategic interaction of only two players.)

Application of the Prisoner's Dilemma to Oligopoly. At this point, you may be wondering what this Prisoner's Dilemma stuff is doing in a chapter on monopolistic competition and oligopoly. The answer is that the idea of the Prisoner's Dilemma can be applied to a wide variety of problems, including the problem facing a group of oligopolists who are trying to act as a cartel. We will consider the simplest version of this problem, in which there is a duopoly (an oligopoly with only two firms). The two firms are Colossal Corporation and Immense Industries. The payoff matrix for the two firms is shown in Figure 11.4.

If both of the firms cooperate with the cartel agreement, they will act as a shared monopoly. They will cut back on output and raise prices, and each firm will make $30 million in (economic) profit. If both of the firms cheat on the cartel agreement by secretly increasing sales, they will produce the same

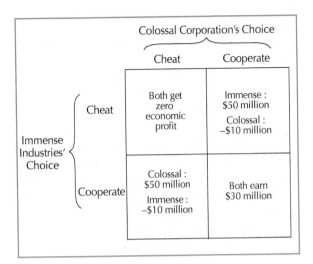

Figure 11.4 The Payoff Matrix for Duopoly Firms

If both firms cheat on the cartel agreement, they will each earn zero (economic) profit. If neither firm cheats, each will earn economic profit of $30 million. If one cheats and the other does not cheat, the firm that cheats will earn economic profit of $50 million, while the firm that cooperates with the agreement will suffer losses of $10 million. This structure of payoffs will give each firm an incentive to cheat on the cartel agreement, regardless of what the other firm does.

output that would be produced if the industry were perfectly competitive, and each of the firms will earn zero economic profit. On the other hand, if one firm cooperates with the agreement, and the other cheats, the cheating firm will increase its share of the market, at the expense of the other firm. The cheating firm will make $50 million in economic profit, and the cooperating firm will suffer economic losses of $10 million.

Let's analyze the decision facing Immense Industries. We begin by looking at the payoffs for Immense Industries when Colossal Corporation cheats on the agreement. If Colossal cheats, then Immense can also cheat, in which case Immense will earn zero economic profit. The other possibility is that Immense can cooperate with the agreement, and lose $10 million. Of course, earning zero economic profit is better than suffering economic losses

of $10 million. Therefore, if Colossal Corporation cheats on the agreement, Immense Industries will be better off if it also cheats.

Now, let's look at the payoffs for Immense Industries when Colossal Corporation cooperates with the cartel agreement. If Colossal cooperates and Immense cheats, Immense will make economic profit of $50 million. If Colossal cooperates and Immense also cooperates, Immense will earn economic profit of $30 million. Here, too, it is in the selfish interest of Immense Industries to cheat on the cartel agreement.

In summary, if Colossal Corporation cheats, it is in the selfish interest of Immense Industries to cheat. If Colossal Corporation cooperates with the cartel agreement, it is still in the selfish interest of Immense Industries to cheat. Regardless of what Colossal Corporation does, it is in the interest of Immense Industries to cheat. Therefore, Immense Industries will cheat. Since Colossal Corporation faces the same payoff matrix, it will also cheat on the agreement. The result is that both firms will cheat, and each will earn zero economic profit.

Earlier, in the example of Sam and Harry, we saw that each man would confess, even though the two of them would be better off if they could somehow agree not to confess. Our application of the Prisoner's Dilemma to oligopoly is similar. Each firm will cheat on the cartel agreement, even though the two firms would be better off if they could somehow agree not to cheat. (However, even though the *firms* would be better off if the cartel holds together, the *consumers* would be worse off.)

Of course, the payoff matrix shown in Figure 11.4 is not the only possible payoff matrix. It is possible to change the payoffs in such a way that the oligopoly firms would *not* be driven to a result like this. The outcome will depend on a variety of factors, including the cost curves of the two firms. The point of this example is not to say that *all* duopolies will always find themselves in a Prisoner's Dilemma. Instead, the idea here is to show that outcomes like the Prisoner's Dilemma *can* occur in an oligopoly.

Mechanisms for Tacit Collusion. If oligopoly firms could cooperate with each other, they might be able to increase their profits greatly. With so much money on the line, it's no surprise that oligopolists are always looking for ways to cooperate. In the next few paragraphs, we will discuss some of the methods of cooperation.

In the United States, collusion is illegal. The laws against collusion are known as the "antitrust laws", and we will discuss them in detail in the next chapter. If American firms are to avoid getting caught by the government, they must engage in *secret* or *tacit* collusion. Over the years, firms have used a number of imaginative schemes in their efforts to collude. Here are a few examples. (We'll study collusion some more in the next chapter.)

Basing-Point Pricing. In the 1920s, American steel manufacturers developed a price-fixing scheme called "Pittsburgh Plus". All producers agreed that the price of steel in, say, Nashville, Tennessee, would be equal to the price at a steel mill in Pittsburgh, plus the charge for shipping the steel from Pittsburgh to Nashville. *All* producers used this formula, regardless of whether their mills were in Pittsburgh, or Birmingham, Alabama, or Gary, Indiana.

The Pittsburgh-Plus pricing scheme is an example of *basing-point pricing*. Basing-point pricing is an attempt to allow the cartel members to collude on prices, by reducing the number of prices that must be agreed upon. The Pittsburgh-Plus system was finally stopped because of an antitrust order in 1924. In the meantime, however, this scheme made it easier for the steel companies to collude, since they only needed to agree on the price at Pittsburgh. If they hadn't used such a scheme, then the manufacturers would have been able to quote different prices to customers in different locations. This would have made it necessary for the firms to agree on

thousands of prices, instead of just one. Without Pittsburgh Plus, it would have been much more difficult to collude.

The Great Electrical Equipment Conspiracy. One of the most elaborate price-fixing schemes in history involved the manufacturers of turbine generators, transformers, and other electrical equipment, during the 1950s. General Electric, Westinghouse, and Allis-Chalmers were the biggest players in the industry, but at least 29 companies were involved.

These firms used different price-fixing schemes for different products. The most imaginative scheme had to do with the prices of high-voltage switchgear. This was known as the "phases of the moon" scheme. The firms first decided on their market shares. Then, to achieve those market shares, they arranged for each firm to be the low bidder on a specified number of contracts. The firms would rotate into the low-bidding position for two-week periods, according to the phases of the moon. This gave the *appearance* of competition, even though it was the result of collusion.

Ultimately, however, the collusion couldn't be sustained. In some cases, firms cheated on the agreement, causing it to break down into a price-cutting war. In addition, the government found out about the conspiracy. (After all, if no one had ever found out about it, we wouldn't be writing about it here!) Seven executives went to jail, and the companies eventually had to pay fines and damages of about $400 million.

Collusion in the Airline Industry. Some airlines share the same computerized reservation systems. This may allow them to signal information to each other about their pricing intentions. By sending information in this way, the airlines may be able to collude to raise prices.

A great many industries have stories of price-fixing agreements. Although most cartels eventually break down, it may be possible for oligopoly firms to earn hefty profits for

Real Economics for Real People 11.3:
The Rise, Fall, and Rise of OPEC, the World's Most Famous Cartel

Few industries have had a more profound effect on the modern economy than the petroleum industry. Industries, automobiles, and homes all require energy, which often comes from petroleum products. In recent years, the U.S. economy has consumed about 20 million barrels of oil *per day*. (A substantial fraction of this oil is imported.)

Unfortunately, the oil industry has a long history of collusive behavior. Right after the Second World War, the world market was dominated by the "Seven Sisters": British Petroleum, Chevron, Exxon, Gulf, Mobil, Royal Dutch/Shell, and Texaco. Through a series of joint ventures, they developed the huge oil fields in Iran, Kuwait, and Saudi Arabia. Because of these joint ventures, the companies were reluctant to compete aggressively with each other.

Thus, the oil industry of the 1940s and 1950s was a cozy, profitable oligopoly. But high profits will always be an incentive for other producers to enter the market. In 1954, several smaller, independent oil companies got a foothold in Iran. By 1960, the Seven Sisters were losing their grip on the world market, and prices began to fall.

However, falling prices meant falling tax revenues for the host countries. In an effort to halt the price cuts, the Organization of Petroleum Exporting Countries (OPEC) was formed in 1960.

OPEC didn't have much influence at first. By the early 1970s, however, the oil-producing countries became more aggressive. Algeria, Iraq, and Libya all nationalized their oil fields. The Seven Sisters' oligopoly had been effectively replaced by an oligopoly of Middle-Eastern governments. Finally, in 1973, OPEC made big cuts in the supply

of crude oil. Prices soared from about $3 per barrel to about $10 per barrel. In 1979, further reductions in supply sent prices soaring to more than $30 per barrel. (These prices may seem low by today's standards, but it's important to remember that there has been considerable inflation since the 1970s. A price of $30 in 1979 would be equivalent to more than $80 today.).

But OPEC, like most cartels, couldn't ride high forever. The high prices encouraged conservation, in the form of more fuel-efficient cars, homes, and industrial processes. The high prices also made it profitable for non-OPEC producers to increase their exploration and drilling for oil. These activities take a long time, but large quantities of oil eventually began to flow in from Alaska, Mexico, Norway, and other oil fields. OPEC controlled about 55% of the world's crude-oil production in 1973, but only about 30% by 1985.

In addition, many OPEC members were cheating on the cartel by exceeding their production quotas. This led to disagreements within the cartel. In an effort to keep prices up in the early 1980s, Saudi Arabia decreased its production by several million barrels per day. Finally, Saudi Arabia got tired of trying to carry the entire cartel, and it increased production in late 1985. This was probably an attempt to punish the countries that had been cheating. Prices soon tumbled, briefly falling as low as $6 per barrel. For most of the 1980s and 1990s, after adjusting for inflation, prices were lower than they had been in 1974.

It has happened again and again, in oil and many other industries: Cartels are often able to raise prices for a time, but they eventually lose control over the market, and prices go back down. However, it would probably be a bad idea for oil-importing countries (such as the United States) to get too complacent. The relatively low prices discouraged energy conservation, and the low prices also led to a reduction in exploration by the non-OPEC countries. When Mexico and Norway began to cooperate with OPEC in 1998, the oil-producing countries succeeded in reducing production for the first time in more than a decade. World output went down by about 5 million barrels per day, and the price of oil surged from $10 per barrel to more than $30 per barrel.

In recent years, the price of oil has bounced around considerably. The recession of 2001, combined with the shock of the ter-rorist attacks on September 11 of that year, reduced demand for petroleum. As a result, prices fell. As the world economy strengthened, however, demand increased again. In the summer of 2008, oil prices briefly soared to more than $140 per barrel. However, as mentioned in an earlier chapter, hydraulic fracturing (or "fracking") led to a very large increase in oil production in the United States. This increase in supply helped to send prices back down. In 2015, the price fell below $30 per barrel before rebounding somewhat. What does the future hold? It's hard to predict. But it's likely that some of these ups and downs will continue, as the market forces described here continue to play themselves out.

a long time. Price fixing is more difficult in the United States than in many other countries, because of the antitrust laws. Still, we will probably continue to see attempts to fix prices, for as long as the human imagination can dream up collusive schemes.

Real Economics for Real People 11.3 discusses the most famous cartel of all.

Reality Check: Interim Review Questions

IR11-5. In earlier chapters, we emphasized the fact that trade can make everyone better off. In the language of game theory, is trade a zero-sum game, or a non-zero-sum game?

IR11-6. Can game theory be used to understand a perfectly competitive industry? Why or why not?

IR11-7. What is a shared monopoly?

IR11-8. Company A and Company B are the two firms in a duopoly. When you go to the store, you notice that Company A's products are on sale for one week. Then, the sale on Company A's products ends, and Company B's products go on sale for one week. The pattern continues, with the firms having sales on alternate weeks. Could this be a scheme for tacit collusion? If so, is it likely to be effective?

ECONOMICS AND YOU: WHAT'S THE FUTURE OF COMPETITION?

Competition is bad for profits, but good for consumers and good for the economy as a whole. That's why nearly all economists are sympathetic to competition, and that's why it is a good thing that competition is flourishing in many sectors of the economy.

In the previous chapter, we discussed the transformation of telecommunications from a monopoly to a sector that provides more choices to consumers. The former monopoly, AT&T, must now compete with Verizon, Sprint, and other companies. The ride-sharing service, Uber, has reduced the cost of transportation for millions of travelers. In the next chapter, we will discuss improvements in competition in railroads, trucking, and commercial airlines. In addition, the Internet has allowed consumers to shop more effectively for bargains. All of these developments are good for consumers.

One of the most successful discount-store chains is Walmart, which grew from a single store in Arkansas until it became the largest retailer in the world. Affiliated with Walmart are the Sam's Club stores, which are one of a number of deep-discounting warehouse stores. For a modest annual fee, the members of Sam's Club, Price Club, and other clubs get to roam down aisle after aisle of heavily discounted merchandise.

Despite these pieces of good news, there are plenty of reasons to be concerned about the state of competition. Despite the end of the AT&T monopoly, subsequent mergers have left the telecommunications sector with much less competition than it might have had. Mergers have also reduced competition in pharmaceuticals, chemicals, commercial airlines, and other industries. Between 1997 and 2012, most industries experienced an increase in the share of revenue received by the biggest firms. Meanwhile, the rate of entry of new firms has decreased since the 1970s. With fewer new firms coming in, many existing firms have less reason to be concerned about competition.

Thus the overall picture for competition is mixed, with some bright spots but plenty of reasons for concern. If competition decreases substantially, consumers will be harmed. That is why economists and others have worked over the years to fashion a set of public policies to restrain monopoly and promote competition. We will discuss some of those policies in the next chapter.

Chapter Summary

1. A monopolistically competitive industry has a large number of firms, which have free entry into and exit from the industry. These firms sell products that are differentiated on the basis of location and/or product quality and service. This product differentiation can lead to the frequent use of advertising and other forms of non-price competition.

2. Because of product differentiation, the monopolistically competitive firm faces a downward-sloping demand curve (unlike the flat demand curve of the perfectly competitive firm). The firm maximizes its profit by choosing the quantity at which marginal revenue is equal to marginal cost.

3. If firms in a monopolistically competitive industry are earning positive economic profit, then new firms will enter. If the existing firms have economic losses, some of them will exit the industry. Thus, the long-run tendency in a monopolistically competitive industry is toward zero economic profit.

4. In the long run, monopolistically competitive firms will not minimize their average total costs: If the individual firms were to produce more, their average costs would decline. This is called "excess capacity". However, on the positive side, it must be remembered that monopolistic competition does provide the benefits of variety as a result of product differentiation.

5. Oligopolistic industries have relatively few firms, and they have barriers to entry. When we study oligopoly, the emphasis is on the strategic interdependence among the firms.

6. Oligopolies often attempt to establish cartels, for the purpose of raising prices and profits. If a cartel is successful, the total profits of the cartel members will be maximized (that is, the firms will make monopoly profits). However, the individual members of the cartel will often have an incentive to cheat, by secretly reducing prices. As a result, cartels tend to break down.

7. The incentive for oligopoly firms to cheat on a cartel agreement can be studied using the Prisoner's Dilemma, which is a type of non-zero-sum game.

Key Terms

Product Differentiation

Market Structure

Monopolistic Competition

Oligopoly

Imperfect Competition

Advertising

Non-Price Competition

Excess Capacity

Duopoly

Strategic Interdependence

Collusion

Cartel

Shared Monopoly

Game Theory

Payoff

Strategy

Zero-Sum Game

Non-Zero-Sum Game

Prisoner's Dilemma

Basing-Point Pricing

Questions and Problems

QP11-1. In alphabetical order, the four market structures are monopolistic competition, monopoly, oligopoly, and perfect competition. Rank them from most competitive to least competitive.

QP11-2. Compare the elasticity of demand for a monopolistically competitive firm's product with the elasticity of demand for a perfect competitor. Compare both of these with the elasticity of demand for a monopolist.

QP11-3. For the nation as a whole, the airlines industry has several large firms, but it does not have a single dominant firm. However, if we focus on specific cities, we see that Delta dominates the flights into and out of Detroit and Minneapolis, American dominates Dallas-Ft. Worth, and so on. In your opinion, should we focus our attention on concentration at the national level, or should we focus on local markets?

QP11-4. Assume that a perfectly competitive firm has a U-shaped average-total-cost curve. Graph the long-run price and quantity for this firm (after entry or exit have led to zero economic profit). Now, assume that a monopolistically competitive firm has exactly the same average-total-cost curve. Graph this firm's long-run price and quantity. Compare the long-run prices and quantities for the two market structures.

QP11-5. The cola industry is dominated by Coca-Cola and Pepsi. Together, these firms control about 90% of the production of cola drinks in the United States. One could imagine an alternative scenario, under which Coke and Pepsi lost market share to low-priced store brands. Discuss the advantages and disadvantages of these two situations.

QP11-6. The steel industry was once characterized by "price leadership". U.S. Steel (now USX Corp.) would announce a change in prices. Within a matter of days, virtually all of the other firms would follow. Could this pattern of price leadership be explained as a mechanism of tacit collusion?

Chapter 12

Market Power, Regulation, and Antitrust

ECONOMICS AND YOU:
A DAY IN THE REGULATED LIFE

Alan Altobelli is a travelling salesman. He wakes up in a hotel room in Altoona, Pennsylvania, and makes a few phone calls over a telephone system that is regulated by the Federal Communications Commission (FCC). He also watches television programs that are regulated by the FCC. The TV runs on electricity, which is regulated by Pennsylvania authorities and by the Federal Energy Regulatory Commission (FERC).

Alan's allergy medicine is approved by the Food and Drug Administration (FDA). Many of the items on his breakfast plate have been inspected by the U.S. Department of Agriculture (USDA). After breakfast, he drives to a factory to meet his client for the day. The workers at the factory have a contract that conforms to the regulations of the National Labor Relations Board (NLRB). The emissions from the factory smokestack are regulated by the Environmental Protection Agency (EPA). The factory uses safety procedures that are mandated by the Occupational Safety and Health Administration (OSHA).

At day's end, Alan drives to the airport, and buys toys for his daughter and son at the gift shop. The toys are manufactured according to the standards of the Consumer Product Safety Commission (CPSC). Finally, Alan flies home on a flight regulated by the Federal Aviation Administration (FAA).

FCC, FERC, FDA, USDA, NLRB, EPA, OSHA, CPSC, FAA: All day long, our economic lives are regulated by government agencies. In this chapter, we will look at some of the government rules, and we'll study their effects on the private economy. As is so often the case in this introductory book, we will not be able to cover all of the regulations in detail. We focus on three areas of government involvement in the economy.

First, we study an area that is usually called economic regulation, or industrial regulation. *Economic regulation* includes the regulation and deregulation of prices, entry, and quantities, in industries such as utilities, airlines, and trucking. Second, we look at some aspects of social regulation, including rules for health and safety. Finally, we consider the *antitrust laws*, under which it is possible for the government to break a large firm into smaller pieces in an attempt to overcome the problems of monopoly.

Our discussion of government involvement in the economy will not end with this chapter. In Chapter 13, we discuss minimum-wage laws and other aspects of government involvement in the labor market. In Chapter 16, we discuss the effects of the taxes that are used to finance government operations. In Chapter 17, we discuss government efforts to regulate air pollution, water pollution, garbage disposal, and similar problems. Before we move on to look at regulations, it's worthwhile to keep regulation in perspective. Government regulations are important to the modern U.S. economy, just like they are important in all other modern economies. And it's also true that government regulation is more important than it was 50 years ago. Nevertheless, government regulation is not at the heart of the U.S. economy. A huge percentage of the economic decisions made in the United States are made by private households and private companies. Government regulations may serve as the background for these decisions, but the private households and private companies are still at center stage.

REGULATION OF PRICES AND QUANTITIES

In this section, we will talk about several types of regulation, including:

- Price regulations

- Requirements that firms provide certain services

- Restrictions on entry into an industry

Price regulation is one of the most widespread types of regulation of business. We've already studied some price controls (such as rent controls, agricultural price supports, and so on) in earlier chapters. In this chapter, we'll study price regulation of the utility firms that provide electricity, natural gas, or water, as well as price regulation of airlines, trucking companies, and other industries.

In many cases, governments require the regulated firms to provide certain types of service. For example, airlines were once required to serve many smaller communities, even if the service was unprofitable. This amounts to a restriction on *exit* from the industry. Governments also regulate industries by putting restrictions on *entry*. For instance, many cities put severe limits on entry into the taxicab industry.

Are these regulations good or bad? The answer will depend on the nature of the industry. If the industry has the potential to be competitive, then this type of regulation has the potential to do more harm than good. After all, competition tends to deliver good outcomes, *without* any government interference. However, if the industry is a natural monopoly, government regulation may be better for society. We begin by looking at the regulation of natural monopolies.

Regulation of Natural Monopolies

In Chapter 10, we learned that an industry is a natural monopoly if a single firm can always produce at lower average total cost than any combination of two or more smaller firms. Another way to say this is that an industry is a natural monopoly if the average-total-cost curve is downward sloping, throughout the entire relevant range of output.

Economists have long thought that electric-power utilities are among the best examples of natural monopoly. In the discussion that follows, we will *assume* that Gigantic Power Company is a natural monopoly. (However, as suggested in Chapter 10, some new evidence suggests that electric power utilities might have the potential to be competitive. We'll discuss this evidence at the end of this section.)

The cost curves for Gigantic Power Company are shown in Figure 12.1. Since the average-total-cost curve is always decreasing

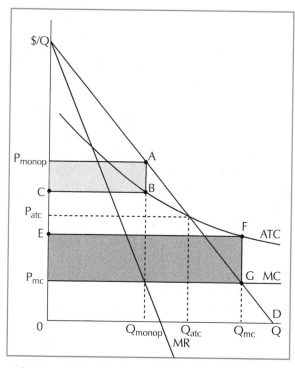

Figure 12.1 Prices, Quantities, and Profits of a Natural Monopoly, Under Different Regulations

If the natural monopolist is allowed to maximize profits without any regulation, the price will be P_{monop}, the quantity will be Q_{monop}, and economic profits will be the rectangle $P_{monop}ABC$. If a regulatory agency forces the firm to price according to marginal cost, the price will be P_{mc}, and the quantity will be Q_{mc}. The firm will have economic losses, which will be the rectangle $P_{mc}EFG$. If the regulator gets the firm to price according to average total cost, the price will be P_{atc}, the quantity will be Q_{atc}, and economic profits will be zero.

as we move from left to right in the diagram, we have a natural monopoly: when ATC is always decreasing, one large firm can always produce at a lower per-unit cost than some combination of two or more firms. If average total cost (ATC) is always decreasing as we move to higher outputs, then marginal cost (MC) must always be below average total cost. Therefore, in Figure 12.1, MC < ATC.

Since Gigantic Power is a monopoly, it faces the downward-sloping market demand curve. The marginal-revenue curve (MR) slopes downward even more steeply than the demand

curve (D). These curves are also drawn in Figure 12.1. In fact, in Figure 12.1, we have drawn a straight-line demand curve. In this case, the MR curve is also a straight line, and its slope is exactly twice as large as the slope of the demand curve.

There are many possible combinations of price and quantity. We will discuss three of these possibilities:

- Monopoly profit maximization
- Marginal-cost pricing
- Average-cost pricing

Monopoly Profit Maximization. What will happen if we just let Gigantic Power maximize its profit, without any interference from government? The intersection of the MR curve and the MC curve determines the monopolist's profit-maximizing level of output. This gives a quantity of Q_{monop}. At this quantity, the demand curve tells the firm that it can charge a price of P_{monop}. Gigantic Power's economic profit is shown by the rectangle, $P_{monop}ABC$.

If the government doesn't intervene, that is the end of the story. But monopoly profit maximization has some very undesirable features. Consumers pay high prices and consume low quantities, while the monopolist gets a big profit. Moreover, as we saw in Chapter 10, monopoly profit maximization leads to deadweight loss. Thus, unregulated monopoly is both economically inefficient and politically unpopular. Consequently, governments often decide to intervene in the monopolized markets.

Marginal-Cost Pricing for the Natural Monopoly. If the government decides to intervene, what should it do? The economist's instinct is to say that price should be set equal to marginal cost. If the government forces Gigantic Power to use marginal-cost pricing, we will get a price of P_{mc}, and a quantity of Q_{mc}. From the point of view of the consumer, this is a lot better than allowing the monopoly to maximize its profit. The consumer can buy more units because the price is much lower. Consumer surplus will be much larger.

Unfortunately, there's a problem with requiring a natural monopoly to set P=MC. Marginal cost is below average total cost for the natural monopolist. If price is equal to marginal cost, and if marginal cost is less than average total cost, then price must be less than average total cost. Since profit per unit is the difference between price and average total cost, the firm will suffer economic losses. In Figure 12.1, the losses are shown by the rectangle, EFGP$_{mc}$.

If Gigantic Power is required to have losses year after year, it will go out of business. The firm won't keep producing unless the government covers the losses. This will probably involve raising taxes on some other parts of the economy. As we shall see in Chapter 16, taxes lead to inefficiencies of their own. (And taxes aren't very popular politically, either.) Thus, marginal-cost pricing is not a magical solution to the problem of natural monopoly.

Average-Cost Pricing for the Natural Monopoly. So far, we've shown that monopoly profit maximization has its problems, and that marginal-cost pricing has *its* problems, too. There is one other alternative, although it has difficulties of its own. If the government requires Gigantic Power to set P=ATC, then we get a price of P$_{atc}$, and a quantity of Q$_{atc}$. Since profit per unit is the difference between price and average total cost, the firm will earn zero economic profit.

In theory, average-cost pricing is very attractive. It gives consumers a better deal than they would get from monopoly profit maximization. It also avoids the problem of economic losses that would occur under marginal-cost pricing. In practice, however, average-cost pricing creates difficulties. The trouble is that other firms aren't there to *force* the firm to earn zero economic profit. Instead, the government tries to *guarantee* a price that

will lead to zero economic profit. In other words, the government tries to guarantee a normal rate of return for the firm. (Average-cost pricing is sometimes called guaranteed-rate-of-return regulation.)

Practical Problems in Regulation. As a practical matter, setting a price that will guarantee a normal rate of return is very tricky. In order to know what price to set, *the regulatory agency needs very detailed information on the firm's costs.* But the firm itself provides most of those cost data. The firm has an incentive to use clever accounting techniques to make its costs appear to be higher than they really are. The firm will also have very little incentive to keep its costs tightly under control.

A second problem is that *the regulators may come to identify more with the firm than with the consumers.* It's easy to see how this might happen. The people at the regulatory agency work very closely with the people at the regulated firm. It's only natural for friendships to form. As a result, the regulatory commission may be "co-opted" or "captured" by the firm that it is supposed to regulate. The regulators may be tempted to allow prices that are higher than those that would lead to zero economic profit.

A third problem is that *the rate-setting process is very slow.* If economic conditions change, the prices the firm are allowed to charge may not keep pace. This problem is called *regulatory lag.* If the firm installs new, cost-reducing technologies, it can make higher profits until the regulatory commission forces it to lower its rates. But if inflation is unexpectedly rapid, the firm's profits may be depressed until the commission allows higher rates to be charged.

We've now seen that natural monopolies create problems, no matter how we try to regulate them. Before we turn to a different subject, however, we should ask whether electric-power utilities are really natural monopolies at all. If they aren't really natural monopolies, then it can be argued that we would do best to let them compete.

Is There a Competitive Future for the Electric-Power Industry?

In the late 1970s and early 1980s, some factories began to build their own power plants. In many cases, these small power plants had lower costs than the bigger plants of the utilities. This suggests that the utilities may *not* truly be natural monopolies. However, these independent power plants couldn't sell to far-away customers, because the big utilities owned almost all of the high-voltage transmission lines. In other words, monopoly in the *transmission* of electric power helped to prop up monopoly in the *generation* of power.

But everything changed as a result of a new federal law passed in 1992. The Energy Policy Act required utilities to transmit other companies' electricity on their power lines. This allows low-cost producers to compete for customers. As a result, big industrial customers and some city governments have insisted on rate cuts from their electricity suppliers. Now that local utilities are no longer protected from competition, the industry is beset by mergers.

In *Real Economics for Real People 12.1*, we discuss some other problems that can arise in regulated industries.

Real Economics for Real People 12.1: How Cable TV Rates Went Up, When Regulators Tried to Make Them Go Down

After several years of unregulated price increases in the cable-television industry, Congress passed the Cable Act of 1992. The law, which was passed over President George H. W. Bush's veto, set prices for "basic cable" packages that were lower for most customers. However, the law left all sorts of loopholes:

- The law set *minimum* rates. Although these rates represented price reductions for many cable customers, they meant price *increases* for some others. In Connecticut, Continental Cablevision *raised* rates to the new minimum.

- Time Warner's cable operation in Milwaukee didn't change its price for "basic" cable, but it did remove four channels from the "basic" package. Customers who wanted to receive these four channels (including the Discovery Channel) would have to pay an additional $2.20 per month. Since most of the law relates only to basic cable packages, the cable companies have an incentive to remove channels from basic cable, and add them to other, unregulated categories of service.

- In Los Angeles, before the law was passed, Century Communications Corp.'s cheapest rate was $16.30, for which buyers received a package of 23 channels. After the law, the cheapest rate rose to $24.67, for 31 channels. According to the rules of the 1992 Cable Act, the cable companies have an incentive to change the number of channels, so that higher rates can be charged.

In short, regulation is almost never an easy task. If the regulated industry sells a wide variety of products, the regulator's job gets even tougher.

IR12-1. A natural monopolist is required to use marginal-cost pricing. Will its economic profit be positive, negative, or zero?

IR12-2. For a natural monopoly, rank (1) monopoly profit maximization, (2) average-cost pricing, and (3) marginal-cost pricing, according to the prices that will be charged.

IR12-3. For a natural monopoly, rank (1) monopoly profit maximization, (2) average-cost pricing, and (3) marginal-cost pricing, according to the quantities that will be produced.

REGULATION AND DEREGULATION
IN POTENTIALLY COMPETITIVE INDUSTRIES

There may be practical problems in regulating monopolies, but at least there's a good reason to try to regulate them: If a monopoly is left to its own devices, it will usually reduce its output and charge high prices. However, American government agencies have often regulated the prices of industries that aren't monopolies by any stretch of the imagination. Our next step is to study the regulation of competitive industries.

Federal Regulation of Railroads and Trucking

When the Interstate Commerce Commission (ICC) was organized in 1887, the railroad industry was the first to be regulated. The railroad industry wasn't the most competitive, but it also wasn't a monopoly. Under ICC regulation, the existing railroads were protected from competition. If a railroad wanted to enter a new market and charge a lower price, it now had to get the ICC's permission.

As a result of the ICC, railroad competition was stifled, and high prices tended to provide comfortable profits. By the 1930s, however, the railroads were facing competition from unregulated truckers. But instead of allowing trucks and railroads to compete, the ICC extended its regulations to the trucking industry. As a result, it became much harder for trucking firms to cut prices.

By the 1970s, the ICC's policy of high prices was under attack. Economists led the charge, saying that competition would deliver better results for consumers. The Federal government engaged in *deregulation* of trucking and railroads in the late 1970s and early 1980s, by removing some of the rules that had restricted competition.

Deregulation allowed trucking and railroad firms to compete by charging lower prices. The gains to consumers from trucking deregulation have been estimated at $30 billion *per year*, and the gains from railroad deregulation have been estimated at $15 billion *per year*.

State Regulation of Trucking and Railroads

One problem with the first wave of transportation deregulation is that it only applied to *interstate* trips. But some States continued to regulate the trips that occurred completely within their borders. This meant that prices for *intrastate* trips were often much higher than prices for trips that did not cross State lines.

For example, a company in Beaumont, Texas, paid $297 to ship fire hydrants to Texarkana, Arkansas. Since the trip crossed a State line, it was not regulated by Texas authorities. However, if the company had wanted to ship a fire hydrant to Texarkana, *Texas* (which is right next to Texarkana, Arkansas), it would have to pay a regulated price of $603.

As a result of regulation by the States, many shipping firms went far out of their way to cross State lines. Instead of going straight from Grand Rapids, Michigan, to Detroit, Michigan, one company would send shipments through South Bend, Indiana. In this way, it created two unregulated interstate trips, instead of one regulated intrastate trip. Similarly, a Virginia company would ship through Landover, Maryland, to avoid Virginia's regulators.

Finally, in 1994, Congress overrode the regulations of the States, to allow competition in trucking *within* States.

Regulation and Deregulation in the Airline Industry

The 1930s brought an explosion of price and quantity regulation by the Federal government, as shown in Table 12.1.

One of the agencies that opened its doors in the 1930s was the Civil Aeronautics Board (CAB). The CAB set maximum and minimum airline fares, and it controlled entry and exit in airline markets. Between 1938 and 1978, the CAB received dozens of applications from new firms that wanted to enter the industry. The CAB turned down every single application. The effect of the CAB's airline regulation was similar to the effect of railroad and trucking regulation by the ICC. Where airline fares were regulated by the CAB, they tended to be higher than they would have been with competition.

Recall that most States continued to regulate trucking, even after the Federal government had deregulated. As a result, in the 1980s, trucking prices were often much higher for *intrastate* trips than for interstate trips. For many years, the airline industry had exactly the opposite arrangement, because CAB regulation only applied to interstate flights. The prices of *intrastate* airline trips were generally not regulated. Therefore, intrastate flights were often much cheaper than interstate flights of similar distance. One study of airfares in 1972 showed that, for flights of about 350 miles, interstate fares averaged about 93 percent higher than intrastate fares within the state of California.

As a result of CAB regulation of interstate flights, the airlines weren't able to compete on the basis of price. So they competed on the basis of service, by offering more flights, fancier meals, more flight attendants,

Table 12.1 Some Federal Agencies Involved in Economic Regulation

Agency	Area of Interest
Interstate Commerce Commission (1887)	Railroads, trucks, and water carriers. Also had responsibility for telephone service from 1910–1934, and for oil pipelines from 1906–1977.
Federal Communications Commission (1934)	Telephones, television broadcasting, radio broadcasting, and cable television.
Securities and Exchange Commission (1934)	Stocks, bonds, and other securities.
Federal Power Commission (1935, renamed Federal Energy Regulatory Commission in 1977)	Electricity and natural gas. After 1977, inherited responsibility for oil pipelines.
Civil Aeronautics Board (1938, disbanded in 1983)	Airlines.

and so forth. But these arrangements were very costly.

By the mid–1970s, there was growing political pressure for deregulation of the airlines. Congress passed a deregulation law in 1978. New firms entered the industry, and the existing firms re-organized their fare and route structures.

One major *unanticipated* consequence of deregulation was that the airlines developed *hub-and-spoke route systems*. Under this system, the airlines sent more traffic through their "hubs". Delta established a hub in Atlanta, Northwest in Minneapolis, USAir in Pittsburgh, United in Chicago, Continental in Houston. By concentrating traffic at the hubs, the airlines were able to use larger, more efficient aircraft. In this way, the airlines were able to offer more frequent flights over many routes, at the same time that they lowered their prices!

The move to hub-and-spoke systems was not predicted beforehand. This reveals an important point: We can't always predict what will happen as a result of deregulation. By unleashing the forces of competition, deregulation gives incentives for creativity and innovation.

Not all airline customers are better off than they were before deregulation, however. Before deregulation, the CAB established fares that were generally *above* cost for flights of over 400 miles, but *below* cost for shorter flights. In this way, passengers on longer flights were forced to subsidize passengers on shorter flights. When deregulation came, this type of *cross-subsidization* was no longer required. Thus, prices increased for some passengers.

However, it appears that airline passengers as a group were made much better off as a result of deregulation. One study for 1977 suggests that airline regulation cost consumers nearly $10 billion per year.

In *Real Economics for Real People 12.2*, we discuss some problems that have occurred in other regulated industries.

The Politics and Economics of Regulation

We've talked about economic regulation of utilities, railroads, trucking firms, airlines, taxicabs, and cosmetologists. Economic regulations often seem to be helpful only to a relatively small group. For society as a whole, some of these regulations lead to losses of many billions of dollars per year.

How can we explain regulations that, on balance, make society worse off? We can get a few answers by learning about the "economic theory of regulation", which was developed by George Stigler and other economists. The economic theory of regulation starts by recognizing that the power to coerce is the most fundamental resource of government. An interest group (such as the taxicab owners) can make itself better off, if it can get the government to use its coercive powers in a particular way (such as by restricting entry into the taxicab industry).

How does an interest group get the government to do its bidding? The economic theory of regulation stresses that legislators want to maximize their political support. Entry restrictions in the taxicab industry do make consumers worse off, but the loss to any individual consumer is probably small, and it's probably difficult to organize the consumers into a powerful lobbying group. On the other hand, each existing taxicab firm has a very large stake in the outcome. Because the number of firms is relatively small, it won't be

Real Economics for Real People 12.2:
Cabs and Cornrows: The Effects of Licensing Regulation

If you want to operate a taxicab legally in New York City, you have to have a medallion. The city government issues about 12,000 medallions. There are fewer medallions now than there were in 1937, even though the city's economy has grown a lot since then. By controlling the number of medallions, the city effectively controls entry into the industry. The city also regulates the fares that can be charged.

If you want to enter the industry, you have to pay the market price for a medallion, which is as much as $400,000. This indicates that the regulated fares are high enough to generate substantial economic profits. (Otherwise, no one would be willing to pay that kind of money to get into the industry.)

The story is similar in many other cities. Baltimore, Boston, Chicago, and San Francisco all restrict entry into the taxicab industry, using systems similar to the one in New York. San Francisco has about the same population as Washington, D.C., but San Francisco restricts entry into the industry, while the nation's capital does not. The difference is dramatic: In 1983, there were only 711 cabs in San Francisco, compared with 8600 in Washington, D.C.

The main winners from taxicab regulation are the existing firms, which get economic profits. The chief losers are the consumers. Restricting the number of taxicabs causes special problems for people who are elderly, or disabled, or who don't own cars. A Transportation Department study estimated that taxicab restrictions cost consumers nearly $800 million per year.

Another group hurt by taxicab regulations are those who would like to earn a living by driving a cab, but are prevented from doing so. It's estimated that removing the restrictions would create 38,000 jobs in the taxi industry.

Driving a cab isn't the only profession with restrictions on entry. Dozens of professions require some sort of licensing or certification. In many States, you need a license to practice as a barber, beautician, or cosmetologist. For instance, Washington, D.C., has a Board of Cosmetology, which regulates hair salons. The members of the Board are all owners of existing salons. In order to get a license, it's necessary to pay $5000 and take a nine-month course of study. The beautician exam involves hairstyles that were popular in the 1930s, but nothing on braiding, which is more popular today.

Usually, regulators say that licensing regulations protect the public, by ensuring that professionals are adequately trained. This makes the most sense for doctors and other professionals who are doing complicated work that affects public safety. However, entry restrictions also serve to increase the profits of the existing firms, by eliminating potential competitors. It seems likely that the Cosmetology Board does more to support the profits of the existing firms than to protect the public. The owner of a new company challenged the regulations, saying "We're not talking about gene splicing or test-tube babies or something complicated here. We're talking about hair-braiding."

very hard for the firms to organize to pressure the government.

When we view regulations in this way, we see that they are likely to be most helpful to small, easily organized interest groups, especially if those groups feel very strongly. Regulations are likely to hurt large, diffuse groups whose desires aren't very strong. According to the economic theory, regulations *may* be socially beneficial, but there is no reason to believe they will always be good for the nation as a whole. A regulation may be approved, even if it hurts a lot of people, and only helps a few.

Reality Check: Interim Review Questions

IR12-4. What is cross-subsidization?

IR12-5. It is commonly believed that businesses dislike regulation. However, in some cases, businesses may actually prefer regulation. Under what circumstances would you expect a business to desire to be regulated?

SOCIAL REGULATION

Before 1970, the Food and Drug Administration (FDA) was the only agency involved in "social regulation" of health and safety. But several new regulatory agencies were founded in the early 1970s. These include the Occupational Safety and Health Administration (OSHA), which deals with health and safety in the workplace, and the Consumer Product Safety Commission (CPSC), which regulates products like household appliances and children's toys.

Another agency of social regulation is the Environmental Protection Agency (EPA), which is mainly concerned with industrial pollution. We will deal with pollution and the EPA in Chapter 17. Table 12.2 summarizes information about some of the Federal social-regulation agencies.

OSHA and Regulation of Health and Safety on the Job

In the United States in 1930, there were 15.4 work-related accidental deaths for every 100,000 workers. By 1940, the number of accidental deaths on the job had dropped to 12.9 per 100,000 population. The work-related accidental death rate continued to fall, to 10.2 in 1950, 7.7 in 1960, 6.8 in 1970, 5.8 in 1980, 4.0 in 1990, and 3.5 in 2011.

Most of this decrease in job-related accidental deaths occurred *before* OSHA was estab-

Table 12.2 Some Federal Agencies Involved in Social Regulation

Agency	Area of Interest
Food and Drug Administration (1906)	Food, drugs, medical devices, and cosmetics.
Occupational Safety and Health Administration (1971)	Health and safety in the workplace.
Environmental Protection Agency (1971)	Air and water pollution, toxic waste.
Consumer Product Safety Commission (1972)	Safety of toys, appliances, and other products used in the home.

lished in 1971. Most statistical studies indicate that OSHA has only had a small effect on death rates. This leaves us with two questions: First, why did on-the-job safety improve even without government regulation? Second, why didn't OSHA have a bigger effect?

The Market for Job Safety. Let's assume you understand that there is a greater chance of getting injured on one job than on other jobs, and let's also say that you're able to choose among a variety of different jobs. Then, the only way an employer can get you to take the riskier job is by offering a higher wage rate. This gives employers an incentive to improve safety on the job, even without government regulation: An employer that maintains a safer workplace will not have to pay as much in wages as an employer with a dangerous workplace, all else equal.

The market incentives for a safer workplace have grown stronger over the years. During the 20th century, labor markets have become more competitive than they were before, so workers have more opportunities to avoid dangerous jobs. Also, the American population has become much more affluent over the last couple of generations. When incomes go up, it appears that the "demand for safety" goes up as well. So it really isn't very surprising that the accidental death rate on the job was reduced by more than half from 1930 to 1970.

The Successes and Failures of OSHA. The preceding paragraphs suggest that the market will often provide on-the-job safety, even if there is no regulation. However, the market will only work well if workers are well informed about the risks. This means that one of the most important functions for an agency like OSHA is to provide information.

In fact, providing information has been the key to some of OSHA's greatest successes. Chemical companies must now put labels on containers of some kinds of chemicals, and workers are trained in handling certain chemicals.

Unfortunately, OSHA has also been beset by problems. The problems include:

- frivolous, nitpicking regulations,
- regulations that don't give firms much flexibility,
- regulations that are extremely costly to comply with, and
- an enforcement effort that is too small to have much effect.

In the early days of OSHA, the agency issued over 4000 industry standards. Many of these, such as the standards for portable toilets for cowboys, were viewed as being silly. In one case, an employer was cited by OSHA for not giving life jackets to the workers who were building a bridge, even though the riverbed below the bridge was dry. In order to improve OSHA's credibility, the Carter Administration eliminated or modified nearly 1000 of the regulations in 1978.

Another problem is that OSHA regulations are often written in a very rigid way. For example, the OSHA regulation for handrails has specific requirements for height, spacing of posts, thickness, and clearance from the wall. An alternative approach would be for OSHA to specify performance standards, and to let firms achieve the standards in the way they see fit. OSHA has moved very gradually to allow greater flexibility. In 1984, the agency issued standards for controlling the build-up of dust within grain elevators, and it gave employers considerable flexibility in how to reach the standards.

On many occasions in this book, we have stressed the importance of thinking in terms of the *marginal* benefits and *marginal* costs of an economic action. If we were to design OSHA's regulations in the best possible way, we would want to achieve a balance between the marginal benefits and marginal costs of each regulation. But the legislation that created OSHA doesn't say anything about taking costs into account.

The basic approach has been that firms are supposed to comply with the regulations if it's at all possible, regardless of cost. As a result, some OSHA regulations would certainly not survive, if they were subjected to a serious analysis of costs and benefits. For instance, it has been estimated that the OSHA arsenic standard costs as much as $90 million per life saved.

It appears that OSHA is more aware of cost considerations than it once was. Nevertheless, we are unlikely to get a fully sensible set of regulations unless Congress changes the law, so that cost concerns can be taken into account directly.

Finally, one reason that OSHA has only had a very modest effect is that its enforcement effort is so small. In any given year, inspectors only visit the workplaces of about 3 million workers, out of a workforce of more than 100 million. The average inspection leads to fines of only about $100. Over the years, OSHA has secured only 12 convictions. This just isn't big enough to give employers a strong financial incentive to improve safety.

What does the future hold? If OSHA were to strengthen its enforcement efforts, while at the same time taking the costs of compliance into account, we could hope for further improvements in workplace safety. Of course, experience suggests that some improvements would be likely, regardless of what is happening at OSHA.

Product Safety Regulation

Since early in the 20th century, the Food and Drug Administration has regulated food products, drugs, medical devices, and cosmetics. More recently, the Consumer Product Safety Commission has regulated toys and other products.

Seat Belts, Safety Caps, and the Role of Human Behavior. In trying to understand the effects of any product-safety regulation, it's important to remember that human behavior plays an important role. If a toy has sharp edges, parents may take special precautions to reduce the chance of an accident. If the toy is made safer, parents may be less careful. The ultimate effect on the number of accidents will depend on *both* the inherent safety of the toy and on the extent to which people take care.

Automobile safety regulations are one important example of this. If the roads are wet and slippery, most people will slow down. This tells us that people adjust their behavior to the conditions they perceive. Studies have shown that, when seat belts were made mandatory, the average driving speed increased. As a result, the actual improvement in safety was not as great as it would have been if people had continued to drive at the same speeds.

On balance, automobile safety regulations have helped to reduce injuries and deaths. It's possible that the increased safety has been so great that it would justify the additional cost, which can run to a few thousand dollars per car. However, it isn't always the case that safety regulations improve safety. "Child-resistant" caps on medicine containers are difficult to open, even for many adults. Some families respond to this by leaving the caps off. There is some evidence that the number of poisonings may have actually *increased* since the introduction of the child-resistant cap.

The examples of seat belts and safety caps tell us that safety is not just a matter of technology. It's also a matter of behavior. If future safety efforts are to be more successful, they will need to involve teaching people to act in a safe way, in addition to merely concentrating on safety technology.

Uncertainty and the Regulation of Medical Treatments. Finally, it's important to keep in mind that the scientific evidence about safety is often uncertain. This uncertainty causes big problems for the Food and Drug Administration (FDA), which is heavily involved in regulating drugs and medical devices.

One example of the problem is the controversy over silicone breast implants, which are widely used by women who have had a mastectomy. In the 1980s and early 1990s, there were several highly publicized cases of women who developed medical problems after implant surgery. One of the most serious of these problems was a skin-hardening disease called scleroderma. The question is whether the breast implants caused the diseases, or whether the diseases would have happened anyway. This is a difficult question to answer, since any large population will have at least a few people who develop diseases.

In the early 1990s, the FDA came down on the side of those who said that the silicone implants were responsible for the diseases. As a result, the implant manufacturers put together a fund of $4.3 billion to settle lawsuits. (About $1 billion of this total would go to trial attorneys.) The manufacturers also dropped out of the business.

However, in June, 1994, a study published in the *New England Journal of Medicine* found "no association between breast implants and the connective-tissue diseases and other disorders. . . ". In other words, these medical researchers suggested that the FDA had made the wrong decision, because the silicone implants didn't really cause the problems they were accused of causing.

An agency like the FDA can make two very different kinds of mistake. First, it can disapprove products that are really beneficial.

(The previous paragraph suggests that this may have happened in the case of breast implants.) Second, the agency can approve products that are harmful. Mothers who took the drug thalidomide during pregnancy gave birth to terribly deformed children, despite the fact that thalidomide had been approved by the FDA. These "thalidomide babies" are a strong reminder of the dangers of this second type of mistake.

Ultimately, the FDA would like to avoid both types of mistake. This is a very hard task, however, since the scientific evidence is often uncertain. The consensus seems to be that the FDA is more afraid of approving a harmful drug than of failing to approve a helpful one. Thus the FDA usually takes a very conservative approach. New drugs and devices are subjected to a very long and exacting approval process.

This cautious approach is understandable, given the politics of the situation. The FDA probably has more to lose by approving a bad drug or device, than by failing to approve a good one. Those who are hurt by a bad drug or device are likely to be highly vocal and organized. Those who are hurt by the absence of a device that has never been approved are less likely to pressure the FDA. (One exception to this is the well-organized campaign for the FDA to move faster in approving drugs that might help AIDS patients.)

Reality Check: Interim Review Question

IR12-6. Let's say that an occupational safety regulation is expected to save one life per year. If the annual cost of this regulation were $1 million, do you think it would be beneficial to adopt the regulation? What if the cost were $10 million? $100 million? $1 billion? $1 trillion?

ANTITRUST IN ACTION

Government regulation of business is a worldwide phenomenon. Nearly every nation regulates businesses, and the regulations found in many other countries are similar to those found in the United States. Now, we move to consider the antitrust laws, which are an American invention that has been pursued further in the United States than anywhere else.

Monopoly was very common in England in the early 17th century. By 1621, there were 700 monopolies. In the words of the English historian Christopher Hill, a man lived

"in a house built with monopoly bricks, with windows of . . . monopoly glass; heated by monopoly coal (in Ireland monopoly timber), burning in a grate made of monopoly iron . . . He washed himself in monopoly soap, his clothes in monopoly starch. He dressed in monopoly lace, monopoly linen, monopoly leather . . . His clothes were held up by monopoly belts, monopoly buttons, monopoly pins. They were dyed with monopoly dyes. He ate monopoly butter, monopoly currants, monopoly red herrings, monopoly salmon . . . His food was seasoned with monopoly salt, monopoly pepper, monopoly vinegar . . . He wrote with monopoly pens, on monopoly writing paper; read (through monopoly spectacles, by the light of monopoly candles) monopoly printed books."

These monopolies enriched a very small slice of the population. Ordinary Englishmen saw hundreds of industries in which they could build a successful business, if only the monopolies could be broken. Eventually, from the 1620s to the 1690s, the English middle class became powerful enough to get Parliament to repeal most of the monopolies. This contributed to the rapid growth of the English economy in the next few centuries.

These English anti-monopoly sentiments were carried across the Atlantic Ocean to America. Outside of patents, the United States government has never granted many business monopolies. But monopolies can arise in a variety of ways, even without explicit support from the government.

In the 1870s and 1880s, giant monopolistic organizations called "trusts" came to dominate many American industries, including petroleum, tobacco, sugar, meatpacking, and coal. The business practices of trusts caused a great deal of resentment. The public outcry led to the passage of the first antitrust law, the Sherman Antitrust Act of 1890.

The Sherman Act of 1890

The original antitrust law was named for Senator John Sherman of Ohio. Section 1 of the *Sherman Act* prohibits "(e)very contract, combination . . . or conspiracy, in restraint of trade. . . ". This makes it illegal for competing companies to collude to fix prices. Section 2 of the Sherman Act prohibits monopoly or attempting to monopolize. Under the Sherman Act, the Justice Department could bring lawsuits aimed at eliminating price fixing or monopoly, and private citizens could also bring lawsuits.

The enforcement of the Sherman Act got off to a very slow start. In fact, the period from 1890 to 1904 is sometimes called the "merger-to-monopoly wave", because dozens of fairly competitive industries were transformed into monopolies or near-monopolies. During this period, giants such as United States Steel, General Electric, DuPont, Eastman Kodak, American Tobacco, and International Paper came to dominate important markets.

Even when the Sherman Act was used, the effect was often small. For example, a cartel was formed by six manufacturers of cast-iron pipe in 1895, and this arrangement was declared illegal by an Appeals Court. To avoid the court ruling, the firms simply merged to form a new company, which controlled three-quarters of the national market. Despite the Sherman Act, the merged firm was allowed to exist.

Finally, in the *Northern Securities Case* of 1904, the Supreme Court used the Sherman Act to rule that two railroads (Northern Pacific and Great Northern) could not merge. In the *Standard Oil Case* of 1911, the Supreme Court broke John D. Rockefeller's Standard Oil Trust into 33 separate companies. (These included the forerunners of such firms as Exxon, Mobil, Socal, and Sohio. Ironically, the two largest pieces, Exxon and Mobil, merged with each other in 1999.) A few weeks after the *Standard Oil* decision, the Supreme Court decided the *American Tobacco Case*, by breaking James B. Duke's Tobacco Trust into 16 smaller companies.

The Clayton Antitrust Act of 1914

Even though the Sherman Act had been used successfully on a few occasions, there was still a feeling that the antitrust laws needed to be strengthened. As a result, Congress passed the *Clayton Act* in 1914. The Clayton Act prohibits some specific practices that we have discussed in earlier chapters, including:

- Price discrimination, when it is not justified on the basis of cost differences.

- Mergers achieved through the acquisition of stock, when the merger reduces competition substantially. (It is important to recognize that many mergers may be perfectly legal.)

A *conglomerate merger* is a merger between two firms in unrelated industries. For example, if a manufacturer of computer equipment merges with a maker of sports equipment, it would be a conglomerate merger. Conglomerate mergers are not much of a concern, because they are unlikely to reduce competition in any important way. It is unlikely that conglomerate mergers would be challenged under the antitrust laws. A *vertical merger* is a merger between a firm and one of its suppliers. For example, a vertical merger would occur if an automobile company were to merge with a maker of tires. Vertical mergers have some potential to reduce competition, but they are still not the most dangerous type of merger. A *horizontal merger* is a merger between two firms that are competing with each other directly in the same industry. It is much more likely that the Clayton Act would be used to challenge a horizontal merger than a vertical merger or a conglomerate merger. Even a horizontal merger is not necessarily a cause for alarm. The damage to competition that occurs as a result of a horizontal merger will depend on the size of the two firms. If both of the firms are small relative to the market, then the degree of competition of the industry would not be greatly affected. However, if the combined firm would be large relative to the market, then competition might be reduced significantly by the merger.

The Clayton Act also prohibits these other practices:

- *Tying arrangements*, under which a seller uses its market power in one market to gain market power in a related market. These arrangements are called "tying arrangements" or "tied sales" because the seller tries to tie one market to another. Eastman Kodak once had a near monopoly in the market for photographic film. They used a variety of schemes to extend their market power to cameras and film developing. These practices were declared a violation of the antitrust laws, and Kodak had to pay a multi-million dollar settlement to a smaller company.

  Tying arrangements were at the center of the antitrust case against Microsoft Corporation, which we will discuss later in this chapter. Recently, the antitrust authorities of the European Union accused Google of using illegal tying arrangements, by requiring manufacturers of smartphones to pre-load Google applications onto Android phones.

- *Exclusive dealing arrangements*, under which a dealer agrees to buy all of its supplies from one supplier. For example, Standard Oil Company of California had an exclusive dealing arrangement with several thousand retail gas stations, until this was declared illegal by the Supreme Court.

- *Interlocking directorates*, under which the same person would sit on the Board of Directors of several competing companies.

One other important piece of antitrust law was passed in the same year as the Clayton Act. The *Federal Trade Commission Act* of 1914 created a new agency for dealing with antitrust issues. (Previously, the U.S. Department of Justice had been the only agency involved with antitrust.)

Two sections of the Clayton Act were later amended in a major way. The price-discrimination section was changed drastically by the *Robinson-Patman Act* of 1936. This law was designed to protect small businesses from competition from large discount chains. The Robinson-Patman Act made it illegal for large food chains to pay less than small stores for produce, even when the chains could reduce costs by acting as their own wholesalers. Although many of the antitrust laws are generally believed to be beneficial, the Robinson-Patman Act is not. Most of the antitrust laws encourage competition, but Robinson-Patman discourages it. Fortunately for consumers, the Robinson-Patman Act hasn't been enforced very strictly in recent years.

The anti-merger provisions of the Clayton Act had one big loophole. Although the Act made it illegal to acquire *stock*, it still allowed firms to merge by acquiring *physical assets*. This loophole was plugged by the *Celler-Kefauver Act* of 1950.

Table 12.3 has a summary of the major antitrust laws.

Exemptions from the Antitrust Laws

Some activities have been specifically exempted from the antitrust laws. By far the most important exemption applies to labor unions. Without an exemption, much union organizing activity would violate the antitrust laws. Agricultural cooperatives are also exempt from the antitrust laws.

Since 1922, major-league baseball has been given an exemption from the antitrust laws. As a result, major-league baseball is a cartel, and it is perfectly legal. Entry into the cartel is strictly controlled by the existing firms. New firms (called expansion franchises) are sometimes allowed to enter the industry, but only if they receive the approval of the existing firms. Consequently, when entry does occur, it usually happens in such a way as to maintain the regional monopolies of the existing firms.

Changing Interpretations of the Antitrust Laws

The passage of a law by Congress is only the beginning. The ultimate effect of any law will depend on how it is enforced, and how it is interpreted by the courts. We have already seen that the Sherman Act did not have much effect for more than a decade after its passage. Beginning in 1904, however, there was a period of more aggressive enforcement. This roller coaster continued for most of the 20th century: Periods of strict interpretation of the antitrust laws have alternated with periods of looser enforcement.

U.S. Steel and the Rule of Reason. In 1920, the Supreme Court issued a landmark ruling in the *U.S. Steel Case*. The Court refused to rule against U.S. Steel because they said that the firm had not acted badly. The Court thus stated the *Rule of Reason*—a firm would not be found guilty unless it had behaved in an

Table 12.3 Antitrust Laws in the United States

Law	Important Provisions of the Law
Sherman Act (1890)	Prohibits combinations or conspiracies in restraint of trade. This has been used to outlaw price-fixing conspiracies. Prohibits monopoly, or the attempt to monopolize.
Clayton Act (1914)	Prohibits price discrimination, if the discrimination is not based on cost differences. Prohibits mergers achieved through acquisition of stock, if the merger is deemed to reduce competition significantly. Prohibits "tying arrangements", which force a buyer to buy a second product from the same seller. Prohibits "exclusive-dealing arrangements", which force a dealer to buy all of its supplies from one seller. Prohibits "interlocking directorates", under which the same person sits on the Board of Directors of two or more competing companies.
Federal Trade Commission Act (1914)	Forms a new agency to enforce the antitrust laws. The FTC has been especially interested in deceptive business practices.
Robinson-Patman Act (1936)	Changes price-discrimination provisions of the Clayton Act, by prohibiting large retailers from selling at lower prices, even when the different prices arise from lower costs.
Celler-Kefauver Act (1950)	Strengthens anti-merger provisions of Clayton Act by prohibiting mergers through acquisition of physical assets, if the merger is deemed to reduce competition significantly.

unreasonable way. In other words, it wasn't illegal for U.S. Steel merely to be a big company. In fact, U.S. Steel (which is now called USX Corporation) had already been losing market share. Its share of the American market had dropped to 52 percent by 1915.

The End of the Rule of Reason. In the *ALCOA Case* of 1945, the Rule of Reason was dramatically reversed. ALCOA (the Aluminum Company of America) had actually performed very well. Aluminum prices had *fallen* on several occasions. Nevertheless, it was ruled that ALCOA had violated the antitrust laws, merely by having a dominant position in the aluminum market. As a result, government-owned aluminum plants were sold to create two new competing firms, Reynolds Aluminum and Kaiser Aluminum.

The *ALCOA* case ushered in a quarter century of aggressive antitrust decisions. The Supreme Court stopped some mergers in the 1960s, even though the firms had relatively small market shares. Thus it is not clear whether the mergers would have led to much of a reduction in competition. Today's Supreme Court probably would have allowed these mergers.

Antitrust Law Since 1970. By the early 1970s, the Supreme Court was becoming more moderate, by showing an increased willingness to approve mergers. In 1984, the Justice Department issued new, more lenient guidelines for its antitrust actions.

Whereas antitrust enforcement may have been too strict from the 1940s to the 1960s, it may have become too lenient after that. In the more permissive atmosphere, a great deal of merger activity has occurred in the last few decades. In the energy field, Getty joined Texaco, Gulf joined Chevron, and Chevron joined Texaco. In the skies, Northwest joined Republic, USAir joined Piedmont, Northwest joined

Table 12.4 Some Important Mergers

Year	Industry	Purchaser	Acquired Company	Name of New Company	Price
1998	financial	Travelers	Citicorp	Citigroup	$ 73 billion
1999	telecommunications	AT&T	TCI	AT&T	$ 70 billion
1999	energy	Exxon	Mobil	Exxon Mobil	$ 85 billion
2000	telecommunications	SBC Comm.	Ameritech	SBC	$ 70 billion
2000	pharmaceuticals	Pfizer	Warner Lambert	Pfizer	$ 90 billion
2001	pharmaceuticals	GlaxoWellcome	SmithKline Beecham	GlaxoSmithKline	$ 79 billion
2001	media	AOL	Time Warner	AOL Time Warner	$164 billion
2002	telecommunications	Bell Atlantic	GTE	Verizon	$ 71 billion
2002	telecommunications	Comcast	AT&T Broadband	Comcast	$ 72 billion
2006	telecommunications	AT&T	BellSouth	AT&T	$ 89 billion
2008	beer	InBev	Anheuser-Busch	AB InBev	$ 52 billion
2015	computers	Dell	EMC	Dell	$ 67 billion
2015	cigarettes	Reynolds	Lorillard	Reynolds	$ 27 billion

Delta, and Continental joined United. But many of these mergers are small compared to the blockbuster mergers listed in Table 12.4.

Even when the government tried to use the antitrust laws, it was sometimes unsuccessful. In the *IBM Case*, the government charged International Business Machines Corp. with a number of anti-competitive practices. Over a 13-year period, the case generated $200 million in legal costs and a trial transcript of more than 100,000 pages. However, the Justice Department dropped the case in 1982. In the same year, the Federal Trade Commission lost a breakfast-cereal case against Kellogg, General Mills, and General Foods.

In spite of the more permissive antitrust atmosphere of the last few decades, a few important cases were decided by *consent decrees*, which are negotiated settlements between the government and a company. The *Xerox Case* ended in 1975 with a consent decree, under which Xerox Corp. agreed to license its photocopying patents to its competitors.

One of the most famous antitrust cases of recent years is the *AT&T Case*, which was decided by a consent decree in 1982. The decree, which went into effect in 1984, required American Telephone & Telegraph Co. to divest itself of its local telephone operating companies. AT&T still had a very prominent position in *long-distance* service, but *local* service fell to the "Baby Bells": Ameritech, Bell Atlantic, Bell South, Nynex, Pacific Telesis, Southwestern Bell, and USWest.

In 1998, the agribusiness giant Archer Daniels Midland (ADM) was found guilty of price-fixing in the market for lysine. Fines of $100 million were imposed.

One important recent case is the *Microsoft Case*. In 1999, Federal District Court Judge Thomas Penfield Jackson issued a "finding of fact", in which he found that Microsoft Corporation had violated the antitrust laws. Specifically, it was found that Microsoft had aggressively used its near-monopoly position in the market for personal-computer operating

Table 12.5 Some Important Antitrust Cases

Case	Result
Northern Securities (1904)	First major Supreme Court decision involving Sherman Act; Northern Pacific and Great Northern railroads not allowed to merge.
Standard Oil Co. (1911)	Oil trust violates Sherman Act, and is broken into 33 pieces.
American Tobacco Co. (1911)	Tobacco trust violates Sherman Act, and is broken into 16 pieces.
U.S. Steel Co. (1920)	Dominant firm in the industry is *not* guilty. Mere size is not sufficient for a guilty verdict. Decision is a strong statement of the "Rule of Reason".
ALCOA (1945)	Dominant firm *is* guilty, merely because of its size. Decision marks the end of the "Rule of Reason".
Xerox (1975)	Xerox Corp. ordered to license its patents to its competitors, and change its pricing policies.
IBM (1982)	Case dropped by Justice Department, after 13 years of prosecution.
AT&T (1982)	American Telephone & Telegraph agrees to divest itself of its local operating companies.
Microsoft (1999–2001)	A court ruling to break up Microsoft was thrown out, and the company remained intact.

systems as a means of creating market power in other markets, such as the market for internet-browsing software. In April, 2000, the Justice Department recommended that Microsoft be divided into two pieces, one for its operating-system software, and one for its other software. Later, Judge Jackson issued a ruling to break up Microsoft along these lines. However, in 2001, an Appeals Court threw out Judge Jackson's order, and ruled that the case would be given to another judge. The administration of George W. Bush was not enthusiastic about the case, and the case against Microsoft ended with only minor actions against the company.

A summary of some of the most important antitrust cases is shown in Table 12.5.

Merger Mania, Antitrust Pushback

The year 2015 saw a record amount of merger activity, partly because low interest rates made it relatively easy for companies to finance takeovers. One estimate put the total of all of the mergers at more than $3 *trillion*.

In one prominent deal, the computer maker Dell acquired the network-storage company EMC for $67 billion. In another, the cigarette giant Reynolds acquired Lorillard for $27 billion. This merger would leave two behemoths, Altria and Reynolds, with about three-fourths of the market.

In another blockbuster merger, Anheuser-Busch InBev is acquiring SAB Miller for more than $100 million. (Anheuser-Busch InBev was the product of a $52 billion merger only seven years earlier.) As of this writing, it appears that the beer merger is likely to go through, despite protests from craft brewers. In order to satisfy the concerns of antitrust authorities in the U.S. and Europe, AB InBev and SAB Miller sold some of their brands to competitors. Nevertheless, there is little doubt that the new company will pose threats to competition.

However, at the same time, antitrust authorities have become increasingly aggressive. A proposed merger of the food-industry giants Sysco and U.S. Foods was cancelled as a result of an antitrust decision. A proposed merger between Staples and Office Depot was cancelled for the same reason. In the oilfield-services industry, pressure from American and European antitrust regulators caused Halliburton to cancel a deal to acquire Baker Hughes.

Thus we see a mixed picture, with many mergers being carried out, while some mergers have been blocked by antitrust concerns. It is difficult to know what the ultimate degree of competitiveness will be. The welfare of consumers hangs in the balance.

Evaluation of Antitrust

In this section, we have seen some of the ups and downs in the history of antitrust. Certainly this history is imperfect. Not every feature of the law makes sense, and the law has been enforced unevenly over time. Still, we can ask whether the United States economy is better off, as a whole, than it would have been if there were no antitrust laws. Most economists would probably say "Yes".

Without the antitrust laws, we would almost certainly have much less competition in petroleum, tobacco, telecommunications, and many other industries. The antitrust laws have

---

Real Economics for Real People 12.3: Financial Aid and the Antitrust Laws

The *official* price for a year's stay at an elite private college can be $50,000 or more. But many students don't have to pay the full price, because they receive financial-aid packages. By offering price discounts in the form of financial aid, the colleges are engaged in price discrimination.

In an attempt to limit the cost of financial aid, a group of 22 private colleges and universities in the northeast entered into a cartel agreement. Beginning in the 1950s, these colleges would meet every year to compare notes on the financial-aid packages offered to students. The goal was for each student's "family contribution" (or net price) to be the same at every school. In this way, the colleges could avoid getting into a "bidding war" for the most promising students.

In 1991, the Justice Department brought an antitrust suit against Massachusetts Institute of Technology (MIT) and the eight Ivy-League colleges (Brown, Columbia, Cornell, Dartmouth, Harvard, Pennsylvania, Prince-

ton, and Yale). The Ivy-League colleges agreed to stop their price-fixing meetings, but MIT defended itself. MIT argued that the cartel led to better opportunities for needy students. In 1993, an Appeals Court issued a ruling favorable to MIT, saying that the arrangement "promoted equality of access to higher education and economic and cultural diversity." The Justice Department soon dropped the case.

The return to price fixing will have many effects. Some students will end up paying lower prices (that is, they will receive more financial aid). Since the existing financial-aid systems are based on financial need, lower-income students will tend to do better (on average) when the present system is preserved. However, some students will end up paying higher prices (that is, they'll get less financial aid). For any particular student, the effects of price-fixing will depend on the details of his or her own situation.

been used to stop price fixing in industries such as those producing steel, electrical equipment, pharmaceuticals, and folding boxes. The antitrust laws have also been used to strike down "tying" practices in a variety of industries, including the movie-distribution industry. On the whole, antitrust law probably means more choices and lower prices for consumers.

Reality Check:
Interim Review Questions

IR12-7. What is the common feature of the *Standard Oil, American Tobacco,* and *ALCOA* cases?

IR12-8. How is the Robinson-Patman Act different from the other antitrust laws?

ECONOMICS AND YOU: REGULATION, ANTITRUST, AND TELEPHONE SERVICE

What do the recent changes in telecommunications mean for the consumer? Overall, deregulation has led to big price reductions. But deregulation also means that consumers must make choices that they did not have to make when AT&T held a monopoly. The savvy consumer will do much better than the one who doesn't shop for the best deal.

If your *business* makes a large volume of calls, it may make sense to shop around a lot, remembering that the market doesn't only include AT&T, Sprint, and Verizon. In fact, there are several hundred smaller companies. Most of these deal with niches in the business market.

If you're just trying to save on your *home* phone bill, you can probably concentrate your attention on the firms mentioned above, and possibly a few other companies. If you are a cell-phone user, you will want to pay attention to T-Mobile and Alltel. Still, it makes sense to be a smart shopper. The most important

thing to do is to get on some kind of discount plan. If you're paying the basic rate with no discounts, you could be losing big money.

You can start by calling the customer-service line at your current telephone carrier. The representative can use a computer to bring up your bills for the last few months. He or she can quickly calculate which plan would be cheapest for you. (This can be seen as a form of price discrimination. If you don't go to the trouble of calling the customer-service line, you reveal that your demand is inelastic, and you get stuck with the basic rate. If you do make the call, you can often get a lower rate.)

If you become dissatisfied with your carrier, you can always change to another. If you *are* satisfied with your current carrier, and another company sends you a check in an effort to get you to switch, you can call your own company and ask them to match it. They may be willing to bargain with you to keep your business.

Chapter Summary

1. If a natural monopoly is allowed to maximize profit without government regulation, it will charge a high price and sell a low quantity. Prices would be substantially lower if the government were to require the natural monopoly to charge according to marginal cost. However, marginal-cost pricing would cause the firm to have economic losses.

2. Most States have chosen an intermediate strategy of allowing natural monopolists to charge prices according to average total cost. This is sometimes called "guaranteed-rate-of-return regulation". If this is done correctly, the firm will have zero economic profit. However, average-cost pricing may reduce the firm's incentives to innovate or to cut costs aggressively.

3. The electric-power utility industry has been regulated heavily on the grounds that it is a natural monopoly. But recent evidence suggests that the industry may actually have the potential to be competitive.

4. Governments have also regulated many industries that have the potential to be very competitive. These include railroads, trucking, and airlines. During the 1970s and 1980s, these industries were substantially deregulated. This process of deregulation is generally viewed as a success. By allowing greater competition, the deregulation brought lower prices in many cases. Another example of anti-competitive regulation is licensing regulations, which make it excessively difficult to enter many professions.

5. The economic theory of regulation studies the way in which interest groups attempt to make themselves better off, by getting the government to use its coercive powers to their advantage. According to this theory, regulations are likely to help small, easily organized groups that have strong interests. Regulations are likely to hurt poorly organized groups whose interests are not strong.

6. "Social regulations" dealing with health and safety issues increased substantially in the 1970s, with the formation of the Occupational Safety and Health Administration and the Consumer Product Safety Commission. Even without government regulation, firms have an incentive to provide safe workplaces, because they would have to pay higher wages to get workers to work in unsafe conditions. Also, when new safety technologies are introduced, people may respond by reducing the amount of effort they devote to safety. For example, people tend to drive faster when wearing seat belts. This may reduce the ultimate effectiveness of the safety regulations. One of the most difficult problems facing the social-regulatory agencies is that the scientific evidence on health and safety questions is often inconclusive.

7. The American experience with antitrust laws began in 1890 with the Sherman Act. This law prohibited conspiracies in restraint of trade, as well as monopolization and the attempt to monopolize. After an initial period of lax enforcement, the Sherman Act was used to break up the Standard Oil Trust and the American Tobacco Trust in 1911.

8. The antitrust laws were strengthened in 1914 with the creation of the Federal Trade Commission, and with the Clayton Act. The Clayton Act prohibits tying arrangements, exclusive dealing arrangements, interlocking directorates, certain types of price discrimination, and certain mergers. The price-discrimination provisions of the Clayton Act were greatly weakened by the Robinson-Patman Act of 1936. The anti-merger provisions of the Clayton Act were strengthened by the Celler-Kefauver Act of 1950.

9. Some activities are exempt from the antitrust laws. These include labor unions, agricultural cooperatives, and major-league baseball.

10. In 1920, the Supreme Court stated the "Rule of Reason", under which only "unreasonable" activities were illegal. However, the Rule of Reason came to an end in 1945 with the *ALCOA* case. ALCOA was found guilty of violating the antitrust laws, merely because of its size. This trend toward very strict antitrust enforcement continued until the 1970s.

11. In the last few decades, antitrust policy has not been as strict as it was in the middle of the 20th century. The government finally dropped its antitrust suit against IBM, it lost its suit against the breakfast-cereal manufacturers, and it never tried to stop many of the big mergers of the 1980s and 1990s. However, Xerox Corp. was forced to license its patents to its competitors, and AT&T was forced to divest itself of its local telephone operating companies. In 1999, a Federal judge found that Microsoft Corporation had violated the antitrust laws, but the ruling was overturned.

Key Terms

Economic Regulation

Antitrust Laws

Marginal-Cost Pricing

Average-Cost Pricing

Guaranteed-Rate-of-Return Regulation

Regulatory Lag

Deregulation

Hub-and-Spoke Route Systems

Cross-Subsidization

Sherman Act

Northern Securities Case

Standard Oil Case

American Tobacco Case

Clayton Act

Conglomerate Merger

Vertical Merger

Horizontal Merger

Tying Arrangements

Exclusive Dealing Arrangements

Interlocking Directorates

Federal Trade Commission Act

Robinson-Patman Act

Celler-Kefauver Act

U.S. Steel Case

Rule of Reason

ALCOA Case

IBM Case

Consent Decrees

Xerox Case

AT&T Case

Microsoft Case

Questions and Problems

QP12-1. Describe the economic theory of regulation. Can you use the theory to understand why trucking was regulated during the 1930s, and then deregulated during the 1970s and 1980s?

QP12-2. What is the "Rule of Reason"? Discuss the landmark antitrust cases that marked the beginning and end of the Rule of Reason. Do you think the Rule of Reason is a good interpretation of the antitrust laws, or would you prefer a more rigid interpretation? Why?

QP12-3. Describe the most important features of the Sherman Act and the Clayton Act.

QP12-4. Suppose that you are the head of the Antitrust Division of the Justice Department. Which of the following cases would you prosecute very aggressively? Which would you consider prosecuting, but only if the Department's resources permit? Which would you definitely not prosecute?

a. A merger between two adjacent soybean farms, each of which has 160 acres planted.
b. A merger between United Airlines and American Airlines.
c. A merger between a manufacturer of potato chips and a chain of auto parts stores.
d. A takeover of 10,000 gasoline stations by Exxon Mobil.

Would you change any of your answers if the firms in question said that they would reap large economies of scale by merging?

QP12-5. Here is a further list of cases. To which of these would you assign the highest priority, which would get lower priority, and which would you not prosecute at all?

a. The simultaneous election of the same person to the Boards of Directors of Fiat Chrysler, Ford, and General Motors.
b. A contract requiring that anyone who buys an automobile from a dealer must also get all of their repair and maintenance work done at the dealership.
c. Meetings between the financial-aid committees at several colleges, designed to coordinate their financial-aid offers to students.
d. A charge by small retailers that Walmart is competing unfairly by offering lower prices.

QP12-6. Discuss the similarities and differences between the *Standard Oil* case, the *Xerox* case, and the *AT&T* case.

QP12-7. For which of the following professions would you require very strict licensing regulations? For which would you require minimal licensing? In which cases would you allow completely unregulated entry into the profession?

a. Heart surgeon.
b. Dental hygienist.
c. Barber.
d. Newspaper delivery person.
e. Social worker.
f. Automobile assembly-line worker.

QP12-8. The railroad industry was largely in favor of regulation in the 1880s. However, by the 1950s, they were at least partly in favor of deregulation. What changes might have brought this about?

QP12-9. "If a firm is extremely successful, it will drive its competitors out of business. As a result, the firm will become a monopoly. Thus, the ultimate measure of success for any firm is its ability to become a monopoly. However, the antitrust laws penalize this behavior. Therefore, the antitrust laws are fundamentally inefficient." Comment on this statement.

QP12-10. Sometimes, a member of a regulatory commission will resign, and accept a job with a company in the industry that he or she had formerly regulated. What effect, if any, will this have on the regulatory relationship? Should this practice be allowed?

QP12-11. People who suffer from epileptic seizures are usually given prescription medicines, in an effort to control the seizures. A number of medications have been on the market for many years, but every medication has some side effects. In 1993, the FDA approved a new anti-seizure drug, called felbamate, for use in the United States. Before felbamate was put on the market, it was tested on 1000 subjects, and no severe side effects were found. Within a few months, felbamate was being used by 100,000 people. In the summer of 1994, however, it was discovered that 10 people taking felbamate had developed a rare form of anemia, and two of these had died. The FDA did not pull the drug off the market, but it did issue a strong warning. The FDA suggested that felbamate users should consult with their doctors, and consider switching to another medication.

a. Given that several other medications were already on the market, should the FDA have considered approval for felbamate under any circumstances?
b. Should the FDA have insisted on a larger pre-market test? Remember that testing is costly, so that more testing will ultimately be reflected in higher prices. What will determine the optimal size of a test?
c. After it was discovered that felbamate has a severe side effect in about one case out of 10,000, what course of action do you think the FDA should have pursued? Under what circumstances should the FDA issue an outright ban, instead of a warning?

Chapter 13

Labor Markets

ECONOMICS AND YOU: WHO MAKES BIG BUCKS?

In 2014, about 83 million American men had a job, and so did about 75 million women. For most of these people, the lion's share of their income is from wages and salaries.

Wages and salaries are much higher for some people than for others. On average, computer workers make about four times as much as food-preparation workers. The average worker in private industry earns more than $20 per hour, plus benefits, but some workers work for the minimum wage. (The federal minimum wage has been $7.25 since 2009.) At the other end of the spectrum, the actor Will Smith typically charges $20 million for appearing in a movie. Baseball star Alex Rodriguez makes more than $25 million per year.

In this chapter, we'll learn where these wage differences come from. The answers usually have to do with the workings of supply and demand in the marketplace. We will see how wage differences are caused by the interaction of the supply of labor and the demand for labor.

THE DEMAND FOR FACTORS OF PRODUCTION

Until now, most of the examples in this book have been taken from *goods markets*, which are also called *product markets*. We've talked about the markets for computers and corn and chemicals, for automobiles and steel. These are all *outputs*.

But what about *inputs*? What about the *resources* that are used to produce the computers and corn and chemicals? In order to get an ear of corn to your picnic table, it takes work by a farmer, and it takes farm machinery, farmland, fertilizer, and pesticides. It takes other inputs as well, such as gasoline or electricity to run the machinery. It's necessary to use a wide variety of inputs in the production of virtually any good. Let's look at these inputs more closely.

Labor

The most important input is the work that people do. Without people, there would be no economy at all. Economists use the word *labor* to refer to the work done by workers. The importance of labor is reflected by the fact that, in many countries, payments to workers account for two-thirds or three-fourths of national income. In this chapter, we will study labor markets in detail.

Capital

No matter how many workers are available, or how hard they work, they won't be very productive if they have to work with their bare hands. The machinery, equipment, structures, and vehicles that people work with are called *capital*. All of these types of capital have two characteristics in common. First, they are man-made goods. Second, they are long-lived, in the sense that they are not immediately used up in the production process. The carpenter's hammer is a piece of capital, and so is the rail-road car that brings cattle to market, and so is the warehouse used by a mail-order clothing company. In recent years, business computers have been among the fastest-growing types of capital. We'll discuss capital markets in more detail in the next chapter.

Other Inputs

Land is another important input in many production processes, especially in agriculture and real estate. Most production processes use *energy* from oil, coal, natural gas, electricity, solar, wind, and other sources. Finally, many production processes involve *materials*, such as bricks, wood, plastics, and steel.

Labor, capital, land, energy, and materials: We use the term *factors of production* to refer to these inputs. The purpose of this chapter is to begin thinking about the markets in which factors of production are bought and sold. These markets are called *factor markets* or *input markets*. We start by looking at factor demand, for *any* kind of factor of production. Then for the rest of this chapter, we focus on labor markets. We look at labor supply, and then we put demand and supply together to learn about equilibrium in labor markets.

THE DEMAND FOR A FACTOR OF PRODUCTION

In Chapter 7, we learned that the demand for *goods* arises from the fact that the consumer gets utility from consuming those goods. In goods markets, the good is an end in itself.

The demand for factors of production is somewhat different. Consider a construction firm that hires a worker, or rents a bulldozer, or buys a truckload of dirt. The firm does *not* buy these things because it wants to consume them. Instead, the construction firm hires a worker because that worker can help to produce outputs (such as apartment houses or office buildings), which the firm can then sell.

Thus, the factor of production is *not* an end in itself. Rather, it is a means to the end of making revenue for the firm. This is why we say that the demand for factors of production is a *derived demand*. The demand for factors is *derived* from the demand for goods.

The Firm's Revenue from Using Factor Inputs

What would be the benefit to the firm, if it were to hire one additional worker? First, the worker would produce additional output. A worker in a bicycle factory will help to produce more bicycles, and a worker in an oil field will help to produce more oil. However, firms aren't in business to make bicycles or oil; they're in business to make *money*. The ultimate benefit to the firm from hiring one additional worker is that the firm can increase its revenue, by selling the extra output that is made by the extra worker.

We define the *marginal revenue product* of labor as the additional revenue the firm gets when it hires one additional worker, and then sells the extra output that is made by that extra worker. The marginal revenue product of capital is defined in a similar way: The marginal revenue product of capital is the extra revenue the firm makes when it employs one more machine, and then sells the additional output. The marginal revenue products of land, energy, and materials are all defined similarly.

In the next few paragraphs, we will analyze marginal revenue product in more detail.

Marginal (Physical) Product. The definition of marginal revenue product has two distinct parts: (1) the extra output produced, and (2) the additional revenue that comes from selling that output. The extra output that is produced by an extra unit of input is called the *marginal product*, or *marginal (physical) product,* of the factor of production. (We insert the word "physical", to make clear that we are talking about the actual output, rather than about dol-

lar amounts. But note that "physical" does not necessarily mean that we are only talking about goods that take up space. Many workers produce services.) In the case of a worker in a bicycle factory, her marginal (physical) product is the number of extra bicycles produced as a result of hiring her. In the case of a worker in an oil field, marginal (physical) product is the number of extra barrels of oil.

The first few columns of Table 13.1 give some information on the productivity of the workers in a garment factory. The factory is operated by a small firm called Blair's Blouses. As we add more workers, we get more blouses, as can be seen by looking down the "Total (Physical) Product" column.

However, as Blair's Blouses adds more and more workers, there is a decrease in the number of extra blouses that can be produced by adding one extra worker. This can be seen by looking at the "Total (Physical) Product" (TPP) column of Table 13.1. We use Q (for quantity of output) to represent Total Product. For example, as we go from one worker to two workers,

Table 13.1 Product of Labor and Marginal Revenue Product of Labor
For Blair's Blouses (We Assume the Firm Is a Perfect Competitor
in Its Output Market, and That the Price of a Blouse Is $30/Blouse)

Number of Workers	Q: Total (Physical) Product (in Blouses per Day)	MP: Marginal (Physical) Product of Labor (in Extra Blouses (per Extra Worker)	MRP: Marginal Revenue Product (in Extra Dollars per Extra Worker) = MP x (Price of Blouses)
0	0	—	—
1	25	25	$750
2	40	15	450
3	52	12	360
4	62	10	300
5	70	8	240
6	75	5	150
7	78	3	90
8	80	2	60
9	81	1	30

Q increases from 25 blouses to 40 blouses, for an increase of (40 – 25) = 15 blouses. However, when we go from two workers to three workers, Q goes from 40 blouses to 52 blouses, for an increase of only (52 – 40) = 12 blouses.

The same information is conveyed by the "Marginal (Physical) Product" column. This is because marginal (physical) product is the change in total (physical) product, divided by the change in the number of workers.

In Table 13.1, the marginal (physical) product of garment workers decreases when we add more workers. Therefore, the example of Table 13.1 obeys the "law of diminishing marginal product" or "law of diminishing returns," which we introduced in Chapter 8. Figure 13.1 is a graph of the information on marginal physical product and total physical product, from Table 13.1. The marginal (physical) product curve in Figure 13.1 slopes downward as we move from left to right.

Marginal Revenue. The second part of the definition of marginal revenue product is the additional revenue the firm gets, when it sells the additional output. This extra revenue is the firm's ***marginal revenue***.

As we saw in earlier chapters, the firm's marginal revenue depends on the market structure of its *output* market. For example, let's assume that Blair's Blouses is very small, compared to the world garment market. Therefore, the firm behaves like a perfect competitor, and takes the price as given. *For a firm that is perfectly competitive in its output market, marginal revenue is the market price.*

If we assume that the price of a blouse is $30, then the marginal revenue for Blair's Blouses is $30 for the first blouse, $30 for the second blouse, and $30 for each subsequent blouse. This means that a graph of marginal revenue for this perfect competitor is a horizontal line, as shown in panel (a) of Figure 13.2.

However, some companies are large enough that they may have some market power. *For a firm that is <u>not</u> a perfect competitor*

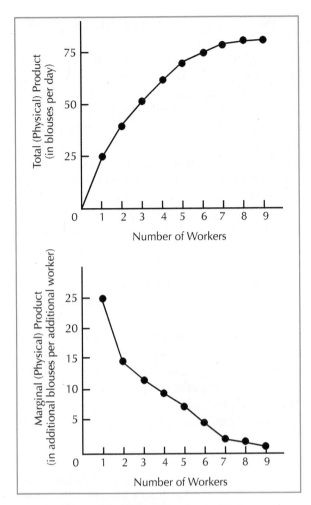

Figure 13.1 Total Product of Labor and Marginal Product of Labor for Blair's Blouses

As this garment firm adds more workers, it increases its output. However, the output increases at a decreasing rate. This can be seen in two ways. First, the slope of the total (physical) product curve becomes smaller as we move to the right (that is, the slope becomes smaller when we add more workers). Second, the marginal (physical) product curve decreases as we move from left to right.

in its output market, the marginal-revenue curve slopes downward, as in panel (b) of Figure 13.2.

Marginal Revenue Product. As we said above, marginal revenue product is the additional revenue the firm gets when it hires one additional unit of a factor of production, and then

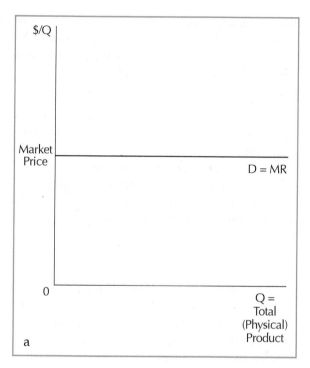

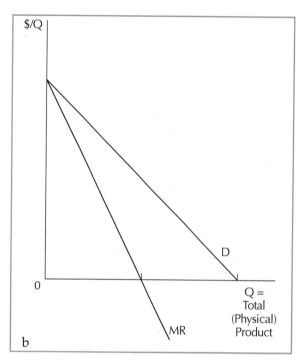

Figure 13.2 Panel (a)
Marginal Revenue for a Firm That Is
a Perfect Competitor in Its Output Market

We assume that the perfectly competitive firm is small relative to the market, and that it does not produce a differentiated product, so that it cannot have any effect on the
price. Therefore, the firm takes the market price as given.
The firm's demand curve is a horizontal line, and the firm's
marginal-revenue curve coincides with the demand curve.

Figure 13.2 Panel (b)
Marginal Revenue for a Firm That Has
Market Power in Its Output Market

For a firm with market power in its output market, the
demand curve slopes downward as we move from left to
right across the diagram. Since the firm must cut its price
in order to sell one more unit of output, its marginal revenue is declining. For a straight-line demand curve, the
marginal-revenue curve will be twice as steep as the
demand curve.

sells the extra output made by that factor. In
other words, marginal revenue product (MRP) is
equal to marginal (physical) product (MP), multiplied by marginal revenue (MR):

MRP = (MP) x (MR), *for any firm.*

In the special case of a firm that is perfectly
competitive in its output market, MR is the
same as price. Therefore,

MRP = (MP)x(P), *for a firm that is perfectly
competitive in its output market.*

To calculate the MRP for Blair's Blouses, we
multiply MP (which decreases) by MR (which
is constant and equal to price for this firm,

since it is a perfect competitor in its output
market). The result is shown in the final column of Table 13.1, and is graphed in Figure
13.3 on p. 322. The MRP curve slopes downward as we move from left to right.

We have assumed that Blair's Blouses is a
perfect competitor in its output market, and
we've seen that it has a downward-sloping MRP
curve. What about the MRP curve for a firm
that has some market power in its output
market, so that it *isn't* a perfect competitor?
We still use the same formula: MRP = (MP) x
(MR). The MP curve still slopes downward and
to the right, because of the law of diminishing
marginal product. And, for a firm with market

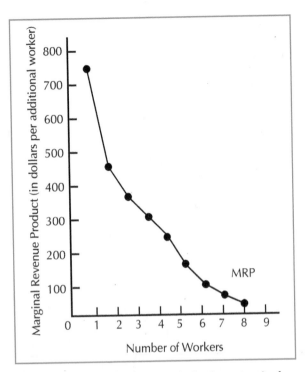

Figure 13.3 The Downward-Sloping Marginal-Revenue-Product Curve for Blair's Blouses

The marginal-revenue-product curve for Blair's Blouses Drillers is found by multiplying marginal (physical) product by marginal revenue. The result is a curve that slopes downward as we move from left to right.

power, the MR curve *also* slopes downward and to the right. If we combine a downward-sloping MP curve with a downward-sloping MR curve, we get a downward-sloping MRP curve.

Thus, *the marginal-revenue-product curve can be expected to slope downward as we move from left to right, regardless of the market structure in the firm's output market.*

The Firm's Demand Curve for Factors of Production

In an earlier chapter, we saw that the consumer makes purchase decisions by comparing marginal utility and price. In another earlier chapter, we saw that the business firm makes output decisions by comparing marginal revenue and marginal cost. In each of these cases,

the decision was based on a comparison of some type of *marginal benefit* with some type of *marginal cost*. The same basic principle also applies for the firm's input decisions.

Marginal Factor Expense. If Blair's Blouses were to hire one additional worker, the *marginal benefit* to the firm is the marginal revenue product of that worker. The *marginal cost* of hiring one more worker is the extra money the firm has to spend, to get one more worker to work for the firm. This extra money is called the *marginal factor expense* of labor. (The marginal factor expense of capital, or of any other input, is defined in a similar way.)

Let's assume that Blair's Blouses is small relative to the overall market for garment workers. This means that the firm won't be able to affect the market wage rate. In other words, Blair's Blouses is a perfect competitor in this labor market, and it takes the market wage rate as given.

The market wage rate is $150 per day, so that the additional cost of the first worker hired by Blair's Blouses is $150 per day. The extra cost of the second worker is also $150 per day, as is the extra cost of the third, or the fourth, or the hundredth worker. *For a firm that is a perfect competitor in the market for a factor of production, marginal factor expense is equal to the price of the input.*

Thus for a perfect competitor, the marginal factor expense of labor is the wage rate, the marginal factor expense of a bulldozer is the rental price of the bulldozer, the marginal factor expense of land is the rental price of land, and so on.

The Optimal Hiring Decision. Later in this chapter, we'll talk about the case of a firm that is *not* a competitor in an input market. For now, however, let's focus on the competitive firm and its input hiring decision. Table 13.2 shows the marginal revenue product of labor (MRP) for Blair's Blouses, and it also shows the firm's marginal factor expense of

Table 13.2 The Optimal Decision of How Many Workers to Hire for Blair's Blouses

Number of Workers	Marginal Revenue Product (MRP)	Marginal Factor Expense (MFE)	Result	
0	—	—	—	
1	$750	$150	MRP > MFE	(Hire)
2	450	150	MRP > MFE	(Hire)
3	360	150	MRP > MFE	(Hire)
4	300	150	MRP > MFE	(Hire)
5	240	150	MRP > MFE	(Hire)
6	150	150	MRP = MFE	(Hire)
7	90	150	MRP < MFE	(Don't Hire)
8	60	150	MRP < MFE	(Don't Hire)
9	30	150	MRP< MFE	(Don't Hire)

labor (MFE). For the first worker, MRP is $750 per day, and MFE is $150. Since the marginal benefit is far greater than the marginal cost, it follows that the firm should definitely hire at least one worker.

What about a second worker? Here, the MRP is $450 per day, and the MFE is still $150, so the second worker should be hired, too. We repeat this reasoning for as long as MRP is equal to or greater than MFE. For Blair's Blouses, the best decision is to hire six workers.

The information in Table 13.2 is graphed in Figure 13.4. For a firm that is a perfect competitor in an input market, the marginal-factor-expense curve is a horizontal line. *The optimal input hiring decision is shown by the intersection of the MRP curve and the MFE curve. In the case of a firm that is a perfect competitor in its input market, the optimal hiring decision comes at the intersection of the MRP curve and the horizontal line that represents the input price.*

The Individual Firm's Demand Curve. When the wage rate is $150 per day, Blair's Blouses should hire six workers, because the sixth worker is the one whose MRP is $150 per day. What would happen if the market wage rate

were to rise to $240 per day? The optimal decision still involves setting MRP equal to the wage rate, but now this comes at a quantity of five workers. On the other hand, if the market wage rate were to fall to $90 per day, Blair's Blouses should hire seven workers.

In every case, the firm's decision is described by a point on its MRP curve. This tells us that, *for the firm that is a competitor in a market for a factor input, the firm's factor-demand curve is given by the marginal-revenue-product curve.* The MRP curve slopes downward, which means that the firm's factor-demand curve is downward sloping as we move from left to right.

Market Demand for Factors of Production

In Chapter 3 we saw that, to get the market demand curve for some good or service, we add up the demand curves of the individual consumers horizontally. We do the same thing to get the market demand curve for a factor of production. To get the market demand curve, we add up the demand curves of the individual firms horizontally.

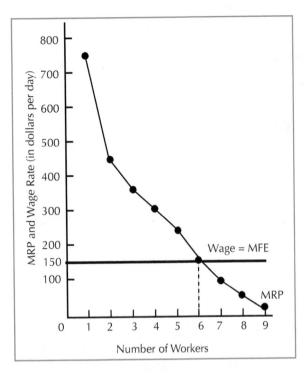

Figure 13.4 The Optimal Hiring Decision for Blair's Blouses

The marginal benefit from hiring one additional worker is given by the marginal-revenue-product curve (MRP). The marginal cost from hiring one additional worker is given by the marginal-factor-expense curve. Blair's Blouses is a perfect competitor in the labor market, so its marginal-factor-expense curve (MFE) is a horizontal line, equal to the market wage rate. The firm's best choice involves hiring the number of workers at which marginal revenue product is equal to marginal factor expense. In this graph, the firm chooses the quantity of labor at which the marginal-revenue-product curve intersects the marginal-factor-expense curve.

This model of demand for labor, based on marginal revenue product, is a good starting point. It predicts that, all else equal, workers will have higher wages if they are more productive and if they produce something that can be sold for a high price. Those predictions are broadly consistent with the facts—more productive workers are paid more, on aver-

age. However, it should be emphasized that the model based on marginal revenue product is only a starting point. It cannot account for many important features of real-world labor markets.

For one thing, marginal revenue product is often difficult to measure. This is especially true in organizations where work is done in groups or teams. In a group setting, it is often difficult or impossible to distinguish the marginal contribution of one worker from the marginal contributions of the other workers.

Many nonprofit organizations, including churches, synagogues, and mosques, don't actually produce and sell a "product". Thus the model based on marginal revenue product is clearly incomplete in the nonprofit setting.

Finally, the model based on marginal revenue product makes the most sense in *competitive* labor markets. If either the employer or the employee has market power, the wage rate is likely to be different from marginal revenue product, even in cases where marginal revenue product can be measured precisely. Later in this chapter, we will look at some labor markets in which the buyer or seller has market power.

In *Real Economics for Real People 13.1*, we discuss the effects of technological changes on employment.

Reality Check: Interim Review Questions

IR13-1. Does the marginal-revenue-product curve slope upward or downward as we go from left to right?

IR13-2. In a competitive labor market, what is the relationship between the marginal-revenue-product curve for labor and the firm's demand curve for labor?

IR13-3. Name the five main categories of factors of production.

One of the oldest concerns of workers is that they will lose their jobs, as a result of the introduction of machinery. Indeed, many workers *have* lost their jobs as a result of technological changes. People who wove cloth by hand were replaced by power looms. People who picked cotton and threshed wheat by hand were replaced by farm machinery.

Today, there is much concern that workers will be replaced by computers. This is a legitimate concern, but we need to keep it in perspective. The last few decades have seen tremendous technological changes in the computer field. If these changes were disastrous for the employment of workers, we would expect that the unemployment rate would have risen over time. But the unemployment rate was lower in 2000 than it had been since 1970. The unemployment rate increased during the recessions of 2001 and 2008–09, but there is general agreement that these recessions were not caused by the introduction of computer technology. Some workers *have* lost their jobs to computers, but others have found jobs in the computer industry, as programmers, software developers, maintenance technicians, and so on.

Moreover, people tend to have *better* jobs, as a result of technological improve-ments. Imagine a world in which we had decided to "protect jobs", by outlawing tech-nological changes. Since we would not have had any improvements in agricultural tech-niques, most people would have to be employed in backbreaking agricultural jobs, in order for society to feed itself.

For society as a whole, technological improvements are the key to a rising stan-dard of living, especially in the long run. However, in the short run, many workers face difficult problems of transition. These problems are greatest for those who have few skills. Several economic studies suggest that capital tends to be a *complement* for highly skilled labor, but a *substitute* for less-skilled labor. This means that new tech-nologies will tend to help skilled workers, while they may not help the unskilled.

The real wage rates of less-skilled Amer-ican workers have been fairly stagnant since the 1970s. The problem is especially severe for those who don't have a high-school diploma. One of the greatest challenges for economic policy is to find ways to reap the benefits of technological improvements, while still protecting those workers who have the fewest skills. We will return to this issue later in this chapter, and in Chap-ters 15 and 16.

LABOR SUPPLY

Labor is the most important of the factor inputs. In most countries, something like two-thirds or three-quarters of national income is paid to workers in the form of wages, salaries, and benefits. If we want to understand the workings of a modern economy, we have to understand both labor demand and labor sup-ply. In the previous section, we looked at the *demand curve* for labor. Now, we turn to the *sup-ply curve* for labor. In the section after that, we'll put them together, so that we can analyze equi-librium in the labor market.

Utility Maximization

In an earlier chapter, we studied the consumer's demand for goods and services. You have a certain amount of money, and you have to decide how much to spend on housing, how much to spend on food, and so on. We suggested that when people make these choices, their goal is to maximize utility, subject to the constraint that consumers are not allowed to spend beyond their budgets. This is the same as saying that the consumer's goal is to maximize consumer surplus. The way to maximize utility is to consume the quantity at which marginal utility is equal to price for bananas, and for blue jeans, and for every other good.

We think about labor supply in a similar way. In this case, however, we aren't considering a choice between bananas and blue jeans. Instead, we think of the labor-supply decision as coming from a choice between *labor* and *leisure*. In our model of labor supply, a fixed amount of time is allocated between working in the labor market (which we call labor) and doing other things (which we call leisure).

People like leisure. It's fun to spend a week at Disney World, or to watch your favorite TV program, or to take a walk in the park. For better or worse, however, there's only a fixed amount of time. Also, the main way in which most people get more money is by giving up leisure, to work in the labor market. If we were to devote all of our time to leisure, most of us would have very little money to spend. Thus we face a tradeoff: More leisure means less money to spend, and *vice versa*. As usual, we end up with a requirement that the marginal something must be equal to the marginal something else. In this case, you would maximize utility by choosing amounts of labor and leisure, such that *the marginal utility of an extra hour of leisure is equal to the marginal utility of the consumption goods that could be bought if you were to work an extra hour.*

The Income Effect: Non-Labor Income

We've just described the condition that is necessary for the consumer to maximize utility from leisure and consumption. This is fine, but our ultimate goal is more ambitious: We want to say something about how labor supply will change when wage rates change. This will give us the information we need to draw labor-supply curves.

We start by asking what would happen when the consumer has a change in his or her *non-labor income*, which includes transfer payments (such as Social-Security benefits), as well as interest income, dividend income, lottery winnings, and gifts and inheritances. It's easiest to see the effect of non-labor income by thinking about an extreme case. If a long-lost aunt were to leave you a billion dollars, would you work more or less? The answer would vary from person to person, but most people would probably choose to work less. Many would leave the labor market completely. It's possible to buy all sorts of consumer goods with the billion-dollar inheritance, without having to work in the labor market. Usually, people will reduce their labor supply when they have more non-labor income. This is called the *income effect on labor supply*.

Of course, most people who have non-labor income don't have a billion dollars of it. However, it doesn't take a lot of non-labor income to generate an income effect. There will be at least *some* income effect, even with modest amounts of non-labor income.

Another way to say this is that *leisure is a normal good*: When people get more non-labor income, they tend to take more leisure, which means they work less.

The Income Effect of a Change in the Wage Rate

We have just seen that a change in non-labor income could lead to a change in the amount of labor supplied. A change in the wage rate could also have an effect on the quantity of labor supplied. However, the effect of a wage-rate change is more complicated than the effect of a change in non-labor income. A change in the wage rate has **two** distinct effects on labor supply. One of these effects is similar to that of non-labor income, but the other is not.

One effect of an increase in wage rates is that you would suddenly be "richer". With a higher wage rate, you would face some new opportunities that weren't there before. For instance, you could now buy the same consumption goods as before, while working less. You might say to yourself, "I can take more time off, and still put food on the table, so I'll work less."

The income effect of an *increase* in the wage rate is that people tend to take more leisure, and therefore to *work less.* The income effect of a *decrease* in the wage rate is that people tend to reduce their leisure, which means they *work more.* You might say to yourself, "Unless I can bring in more money to offset the drop in my wage rate, I won't be able to pay my bills. So I have to work more."

The Substitution Effect of a Change in the Wage Rate

If the income effect were the only thing going on, the story would end with the previous paragraph. However, a change in the wage rate also leads to another important effect, which we call the *substitution effect on labor supply.* To understand the substitution effect, we need to think some more about the role played by the wage rate. When you take one extra hour of leisure, you give up the extra consumption goods that you could have bought if you had worked that hour instead. The amount of extra consumption that can be bought, as a result of working one more hour, is given by the wage rate. In other words, *we can think of the wage rate as the opportunity cost of leisure, or the price of leisure.* If your wage rate were to rise, leisure would be more expensive. (And, if your wage rate were to fall, leisure would be less expensive.) When your wage rate rises, you might

say to yourself, "Think of all the stuff I could buy if I earn wages like these! I can't pass up that kind of money, so I'll work more." On the other hand, if your wage rate were to fall, you might say to yourself, "If that's all I will get paid for working, why should I even bother? I'll work less."

Throughout this book, we have seen that people tend to change their behavior when prices change. They tend to substitute away from items that become more expensive, and they tend to substitute toward items that become less expensive. The *substitution effect* of an *increase* in the wage rate is that people tend to substitute away from leisure, because an increase in the wage rate means that leisure has become more expensive. This means that they *work more.* The substitution effect of a *decrease* in the wage rate is that people tend to substitute toward leisure, which means they *work less.*

The Overall Effect of a Change in the Wage Rate

In the last few paragraphs, we've described both the income effect and the substitution effect of a wage-rate change. Here is a summary:

- For a wage *increase,* the substitution effect says that work should increase, while the income effect says that work should decrease.

- For a wage *decrease,* the substitution effect says that work should fall, while the income effect says that work should rise.

The overall effect of a wage-rate change will be a combination of the substitution effect and the income effect. If the substitution effect is stronger, then higher wages will bring about more labor supply. However, if the income effect is stronger, higher wages will lead to *less* labor supply. It could go either way. One possibility is that the income effect would be larger than the substitution effect. This possibility is graphed in panel (a) of Figure 13.5. When the income effect is larger than the substitution effect, we have a *backward-bending labor-supply*

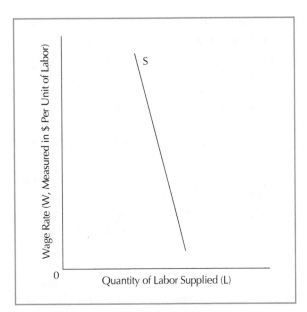

Figure 13.5 Panel (a)
A Backward-Bending
Labor-Supply Curve

If the income effect is greater than the substitution effect, the labor-supply curve will be backward bending. In this case, the labor-supply elasticity is negative.

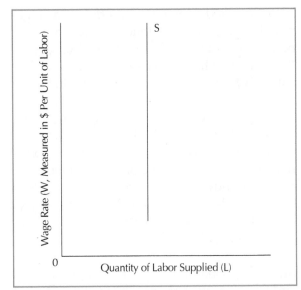

Figure 13.5 Panel (b)
A Perfectly Inelastic Labor-Supply Curve

Statistical studies suggest that the labor supply of married men is fairly inelastic. If the income effect and the substitution effect cancel each other out exactly, the labor-supply curve will be perfectly inelastic, as shown here. In this case, the labor-supply elasticity is zero.

curve. This is the only time in this entire book when we have a supply curve that slopes downward as we move from left to right across the graph. Even though it is an unusual case, it is not an impossible one: Some studies have suggested that some workers may actually have a backward-bending labor-supply curve.

Economists have conducted many studies of labor supply, to find out more about the sizes of the income effects and substitution effects. Usually, the goal of these studies is to get an estimate for the *elasticity of labor supply with respect to the wage rate* (or just the "labor-supply elasticity", for short.) This elasticity is defined as follows:

Labor-Supply Elasticity =
(% Change in Quantity of Labor Supplied)/
(% Change in Wage Rate).

The topic is still controversial, but there seems to be a consensus along the following lines:

- For married men, aged 25–54, labor supply is *very inelastic.* Most of these men desire to be in the labor force on a full-time basis, usually working between 35 and 45 hours per week. A man in this group might say to himself, "If the wage rate goes up, that's fine. I'll work 40 hours per week. If the wage rate goes down, that's too bad, but I'll still work 40 hours per week." In other words, the income effect and the substitution effect approximately balance each other out.

For married men, many studies have found a labor-supply elasticity between –0.1 and +0.1. If the labor-supply elasticity is less than zero, we have a backward-bending labor-

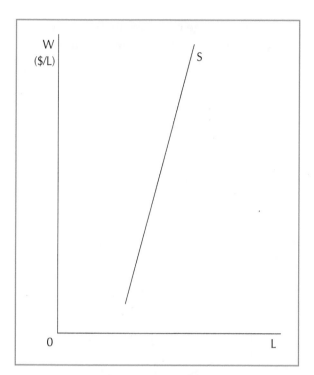

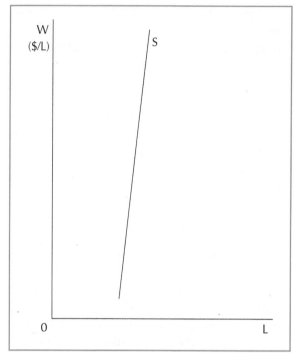

Figure 13.5 Panel (c)
An Upward-Sloping Labor-Supply Curve

For married women, most studies suggest that the substitution effect is greater than the income effect, so that the labor-supply curve slopes upward as we move from left to right. In this case, the labor-supply elasticity is greater than zero.

Figure 13.5 Panel (d)
A Slightly Upward-Sloping Labor
Supply Curve, Representative
of the Overall American Labor Market

If we take the weighted average of the labor-supply responses of all groups of workers, we get a labor-supply curve that slopes upward slightly, perhaps with an elasticity of 0.1 or 0.2.

supply curve. If the elasticity is greater than zero, we have an upward-sloping curve. Many of the estimated elasticities are right around zero, which would mean that labor supply is perfectly inelastic for this group of workers.

We show a perfectly inelastic labor-supply curve in panel (b) of Figure 13.5.

- For married women, labor supply is probably somewhat more elastic than it is for married men. The labor-supply elasticity for women might be about +0.2 or +0.4, although this is a controversial subject among economists. Some studies have found higher values for the female labor-supply elasticity. For positive elasticities

like these, the labor-supply curve is upward sloping, as shown in panel (c) of Figure 13.5.

If we put men and women together, we can find the overall labor-supply elasticity for the entire economy. This overall elasticity may be around +0.1 or +0.2. In other words, *for the labor force as a whole, the substitution effect is slightly more important than the income effect.* If the overall elasticity is +0.1, it means that a 10-percent *decrease* in wage rates would lead to a one-percent *decrease* in the quantity of labor supplied. A 20-percent *increase* in wage rates would lead to a two-percent *increase* in the quantity of labor supplied.

Panel (d) of Figure 13.5 shows a labor-supply curve with a very modest upward slope, which is probably representative of the American labor force as a whole.

Reality Check:
Interim Review Questions

IR13-4. If the wage rate were to *increase,* would the substitution effect lead toward an increase or decrease in labor supply?

IR13-5. If the wage rate were to *decrease,* would the income effect lead toward an increase or decrease in labor supply?

EQUILIBRIUM IN COMPETITIVE LABOR MARKETS

We began this chapter by looking at the demand for factors of production. Next, we studied labor supply. Now it's time to put them together. In Figure 13.6, D_{old} is a market demand curve, and S is a market supply curve, in the market for oil-field workers. The supply curve is more inelastic than the demand curve. The market equilibrium is given by the intersection of the supply curve and demand curve. Thus, the equilibrium wage rate is W_{old} and the equilibrium amount of labor is L_{old}.

Shifts in the
Labor-Demand Curve

A competitive firm's demand curve for an input is the marginal-revenue-product curve, which comes from the marginal-product curve and the output price. As a result, factor-demand curves are shifted when there are changes in marginal productivity or in output prices. Let's look at these in turn.

Changes in Output Prices. In 1986 and again in 2015, there was a major drop in the world-wide price of oil. Because of this, the marginal revenue product of oil-field workers was suddenly lower than it had been before. Therefore, the demand curve for oil-field workers shifted from D_{old} to D_{new}, as shown in Figure 13.6. The equilibrium wage fell to W_{new}.

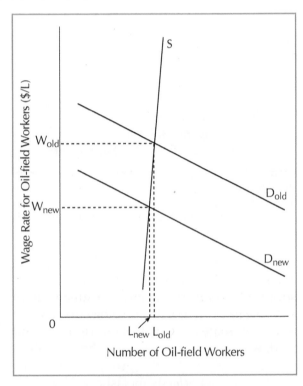

Figure 13.6 The Effect of a Decrease in the Price of Oil on the Market for Oil-Field Workers

At first, the demand curve for oil-field workers is D_{old}, and the supply curve is S. The market equilibrium wage rate is W_{old}, and the equilibrium quantity of labor is L_{old}. Then a decrease in the price of oil leads to a leftward shift in the demand curve, from D_{old} to D_{new}. The new equilibrium wage rate is W_{new}, and the new equilibrium amount of labor is L_{new}.

Whenever an output price falls, we would expect a reduction in the demand for the workers who produce that output. This will lead to lower wage rates. On the other hand, if an output price increases, the labor-demand curve will shift to the right, and wages will rise. In fact, this occurred in the oil industry during the 1970s and early 1980s, as rising oil prices increased the demand for oil-field workers.

Changes in Productivity. Educated people have more skills than those who are un-educated. Those with more education and training are able to solve problems and do other things that they could not have done, if they had not had the additional education and training. In other words, the educated ones have higher productivity. We have seen that the demand for labor comes from the marginal revenue product, and that marginal revenue product depends on productivity. Thus when you get an education, you are pushing the demand curve for your labor to the right, which will lead to an increase in your equilibrium wage rate, all else equal. This is one big reason why wage rates are higher in the United States, Canada, western Europe, and Japan than in the rest of the world: The workers in these countries tend to be more highly educated, and therefore more productive. We will discuss the relationship between education and wages in more detail, later in this chapter.

Immigration and the Supply of Labor

The United States of America is a nation of immigrants. Just about everyone here either came from somewhere else, or is descended from people who came from somewhere else. Until the mid–1800s, most of the immigrants came from Great Britain (voluntarily) or from Africa (in chains). In the middle of the 19th century came waves of immigrants from Ger-

many and Ireland. In the late 19th and early 20th centuries came still more immigrants, from Italy, Greece, Poland, Russia, and other countries. From 1901 to 1910, a nation of about 80 million people absorbed nearly nine million immigrants. That's an influx of more than 10 percent of the population in only 10 years!

The immigration laws were made more strict in the 1920s. As a result, immigrants came at a slower rate from the 1920s to the 1960s. However, the immigration laws were loosened again in 1965. Since then, the immigration rate has been higher than it was in the 1950s, but still much less than it was in the early 1900s. In addition, the mix of immigrants has changed: Until 1965, most immigrants came from Europe, but the largest numbers of immigrants in recent years have come from Latin America and East Asia.

Over the years, there has been a lot of tension between newcomers and those who were already here. The tensions have often had to do with differences in culture, language, or religion. However, the tensions have also had to do with economic issues. The most important of these issues is the fear that immigrants will reduce the wages of natives.

Has immigration hurt those who were already here? We can begin to think about this question by using supply-demand analysis. The entrance of new immigrants causes the market supply curve for labor to shift to the right. As shown in Figure 13.7, the rightward shift in the labor-supply curve leads to a decrease in the equilibrium wage rate.

It's important to remember, however, that workers are not all the same. Thus immigration will have more of an effect in some labor markets than in others, and some native workers will be affected by immigration more than others will. In fact, large numbers of immigrants in the last few decades have been less educated than most of the native population. Consequently, we would expect that recent immigrants would have more of an effect on less-skilled Americans than on those of greater

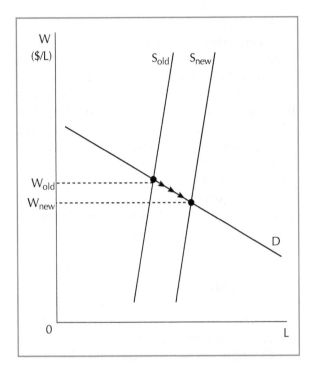

Figure 13.7 The Effect of Immigration on the Labor Market

At first, the demand curve for labor in a particular labor market is D, and the supply curve is S_{old}. The market equilibrium wage rate is W_{old}. Immigration leads to a rightward shift in the supply curve, from S_{old} to S_{new}. The new equilibrium wage rate is W_{new}.

skill. This appears to be the case. There is little evidence that immigration has hurt highly skilled American workers, but one study suggests that the wages of Americans without a high-school education have dropped by as much as five percent, as a result of the influx of relatively poorly educated immigrants.

Still, it's not correct to see the less-skilled immigrants as a heavy weight, dragging down the economy. They provide valuable services (often doing work that native-born Americans are reluctant to do), and they pay taxes. Many of the immigrants own their own homes and businesses. Also, while many of the immigrants are unskilled, some are very highly skilled. During the 1980s, 1.5 million college-educated immigrants arrived in the United States, many with degrees in medicine or engineering. At American universities, nearly half of the new Ph.D.s in the sciences and engineering are foreign-born, and many of these people stay on to contribute strongly to the U.S. economy.

As is so often the case in economics, an overall assessment of immigration would have to consider the pluses and the minuses. The immigrants do contribute to the economy. At the same time, it is true that they may hurt the labor-market chances of less-skilled native-born Americans. Earlier in this chapter, we mentioned that less-skilled Americans may lose their jobs to computers. Here, we are making a similar statement about the effect of immigration. Most of the economy stands to gain from immigration, just as most of the economy stands to gain from computers. But some will be hurt, especially those with the fewest skills. Unquestionably, these are hard times for American workers with little education, skill, or training. One of the most important economic trends of the past 25 years has been the declining status of less-skilled workers. We will continue to study this trend in Chapter 15, which deals with poverty and income distribution.

Education, Experience, and Wages

Why do people go to college? One big reason is that they believe they will earn more money if they have a college education. The facts are pretty powerful: For men working full time in the United States in 2014, the average labor-market earnings for those with less than a high-school education were about $37,100 per year. Those with a high-school diploma earned an average of about $48,400 per year, those with a bachelor's degree averaged about $86,100, and those with a professional degree averaged about $172,700 per year. Clearly, *education* has a strong effect on earnings in the labor market.

Experience also has an important effect. As in the previous paragraph, let's focus on those who are full-time workers. For men with a bachelor's degree, aged 18–24, the average earnings in 2014 were about $33,500. The average earnings then rose to about $60,500 for the 25–34 age group, and to about $87,300 for those aged 35–44. At the peak of their careers, male college graduates aged 45–54 were earning about $94,800 per year.

Human Capital. It really isn't very surprising that people make more money when they have more education and experience. After all, the demand for workers will be greater when their marginal revenue products are higher. Since workers with more education and experience tend to be more productive, it follows that the demand for these workers will be relatively greater.

Different people have widely different amounts of education. In 2014, about 158 million Americans earned money in the labor market. Of these, about 13.6 million did not have a high-school diploma, and about 42.5 million had a high-school diploma but no college education. About 30.5 million had some college, but no degree. About 16.5 million had an Associate degree. About 35.3 million had a Bachelor's degree only, and about 19.9 million had an advanced degree.

We would like to understand why some people get a lot of education, while others don't get very much. In order to do so, we need a theory of investment. The relationships among education, experience, and earnings can be explained by the theory of *human-capital investment*. When we make a human-capital investment, we *invest in ourselves,* in the hope that the human capital will pay off in higher labor-market earnings in the future. Human-capital investments can take many forms, but education and on-the-job training are certainly among the most important. Human-capital investments have much in common with other investments, such as investments in factories or delivery vans or warehouses. Whenever we make *any* investment, we reduce our *current* consumption, with the idea of having an increased flow of *future* consumption.

Educational Choices. Sophia is thinking of going to college. To decide whether this is a good human-capital investment, she needs to compare the *benefits* and *costs* of the investment. After graduation, Sophia should be able to earn a higher wage or salary. The higher wages are one of the *benefits* of a college education. (The benefits also include the intellectual satisfaction that goes with an education, as well as a wide variety of other valuable experiences. In other words, college students learn a lot more than marketable skills.)

For Sophia, as for anyone else, there are two main *costs* of a college education:

- The explicit, out-of-pocket costs, including tuition, fees, and books, and

- The *foregone earnings* associated with going to college. Sophia's foregone earnings are the extra dollars she would have earned during the years she was considering going to college, *if* she had decided not to go to college.

For many students, foregone earnings are greater than the explicit costs of college, as we saw in Chapter 2.

Figure 13.8 illustrates the decision that Sophia faces, when she decides whether to go to college. A college education will be a wise investment if the value of the benefits (area "B", for benefits, in Figure 13.8) is greater than the value of the costs (area "C", for costs, in the figure).

Figure 13.8 gives us an idea of who will be most likely to go to college:

- Most college students will be young, because young people have a longer period over which to reap the benefits of an education.

- All else equal, college attendance will increase if there is an increase in the difference in earnings between college graduates and high-school graduates.

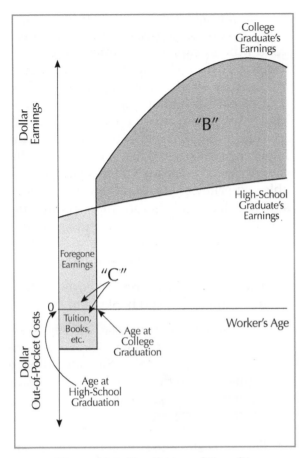

Figure 13.8 The Costs and Benefits of Sophia's College Education

If she goes to college, Sophia will have to pay some out-of-pocket costs for tuition, books, and so on. She will also bear another cost in the form of foregone earnings. Together, these costs are "C". However, she will gain benefits of "B", in the form of higher earnings after she gets her degree. If the value of B is greater than the value of C, it will make sense for Sophia to go to college.

- All else equal, college attendance will increase if tuition costs go down.

- All else equal, people who place greater value on the future are more likely to go to college. In other words, people who find it hard to plan for the future are less likely to go to college.

- Finally, all else equal, those with certain abilities will be more likely to go to col-

lege. People who have the intellectual capacity to get the most out of a college education will receive the greatest benefit from going to college. (If a person of limited intelligence were to go to college, his or her productivity might not be increased by very much.)

Experience and Training. We have seen that those with more education tend to earn more. In addition, earnings grow as workers acquire more experience. This can also be explained in terms of human capital. As people work, they learn more about how to cooperate with others in their organization, and they continue to learn more of the technical details of their business. As a result, people acquire human capital when they get work experience, even if their formal schooling has come to an end.

In fact, experience in the labor market causes a sharper increase in earnings for those who have more education, especially in the early years of a career. The theory of human capital provides a good explanation for this as well. People who are faster learners can get more out of a college education. As a result, fast learners are more likely to go to college. But the fast learners are also the ones who can be expected to learn the most on the job! Also, the jobs held by college graduates are likely to provide more and better opportunities for learning on the job. College graduates are more likely to be engaged in complex tasks, for which experience on the job can lead to large improvements in productivity.

Figure 13.9 represents the relationships in a graph. This figure shows that men with higher levels of education have higher earnings in the labor market. (There is a similar pattern for women.) Figure 13.9 also shows that workers tend to increase their earnings as they get older, although the rate of growth eventually gets very small.

Before we go on, we need to mention a few other things about Figure 13.9. The data shown in the figure are not for hourly wage rates. They

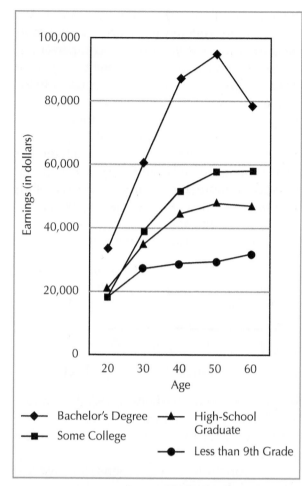

Figure 13.9 Average Labor-Market Earnings of Male Full-Time Year-Round Workers in the United States, 2014, by Age and Education

are for annual *earnings*, which are equal to the total number of dollars that a person makes in the labor market in a year. Earnings are equal to the wage rate multiplied by the number of hours worked. However, for the workers included in Figure 13.9, there is not a whole lot of variation in the number of hours worked. This graph is for full-time, year-round workers. Thus, this graph of *earnings* is similar to what we would see in a graph of *wages*.

It is also important to mention that Figure 13.9 shows the *average* level of earnings for groups with different levels of education and experience. This does not mean that every worker with more education makes more than every worker with less education, or that every worker with more experience makes more than every worker with less experience. For example, LeBron James of the Cleveland Cavaliers went directly to the National Basketball Association without attending college, but he earns a great deal more than many workers who have a college education.

Eventually, when workers get old enough, the graphs of earnings flatten out, and they even turn downward in some cases. This is partly because, for most workers, most of the opportunities for enhancing skills occur during the first few decades of the career. Thus while many workers increase their productivity when they are in their twenties, thirties, and forties, the rate of productivity increase slows down a great deal when the workers get to their fifties.

Compensating Wage Differentials

We have seen that differences in education and experience can lead to wide differences in wage rates. However, some wage differences aren't easily explained by the theory of human capital. For example, people who work the evening shift or the night shift tend to get wages that are about 3 percent higher than those of comparable day-shift workers. Since the skills required for these jobs are the same during the day or night, we can't use the theory of human capital to explain the differences. In this section, we'll develop a way of thinking about wage differences such as these.

Job Characteristics. If all jobs were identical, then every job would pay the same wage rate. But each job has many characteristics, and the characteristics of different jobs tend to be very different. For example:

- Most office jobs are safe, but the job of a police officer or firefighter can be very dangerous.

- Some jobs have a lot of flexibility, whereas an assembly-line job has a very rigid work schedule.

Let's compare two jobs that are identical in every way, except that one is clean and comfortable, while the other is dirty and unpleasant. If the two jobs were to offer the same wage rate, few workers (if any) would be willing to take the dirty job. In other words, all else equal, the supply curve for the unpleasant job will be further to the left than the supply curve for the pleasant job. Therefore, the two jobs won't have the same equilibrium wage rate. We can only reach an equilibrium if the dirty job has a higher wage rate.

Let's say that the market equilibrium involves a wage rate of $11 per hour for the dirty job, and $10 per hour for the clean job. We say that the $1 difference in wage rates is a *compensating wage differential*. A compensating wage differential is the extra wage that must be paid, all else equal, to attract workers to an unpleasant job. We would say that the higher wage rate is necessary to compensate the worker for the unpleasantness of the job.

We began this section with the statement that evening and night-shift workers earn about 3 percent more than comparable day-shift workers. In other words, the compensating wage differential associated with evening and night-shift work is about 3 percent.

The Importance of the "Ceteris Paribus" Assumption. All else equal, a job with unpleasant characteristics will have to pay a higher wage

---

Real Economics for Real People 13.2:
The Effects of Dangerous Working Conditions on Wage Rates

Some jobs are safe; others are dangerous. For example, in logging camps, there is about one death every year for every 1000 workers. If our theory of compensating wage differentials is correct, then a higher likelihood of fatal injury should be associated with a higher wage rate (all else equal).

Economists have done many studies of compensating wage differentials for jobs that have a risk of death. Some of these studies suggest big wage differentials, while others find that the differentials are more modest. But virtually all of the studies find that the wage differentials are in the expected direction: It's necessary to pay higher wages to attract workers to more dangerous jobs.

The estimates of compensating differentials suggest that a firm must pay *each* worker an extra wage of from $35 to $500 more per year, to compensate for an extra annual risk of one death per 10,000 workers. This implies that a plant with 10,000 employees could save between $350,000 and $5,000,000 per year in wages, if it were to improve safety by enough to save one life per year.

We conclude that compensating wage differentials serve some very valuable functions for society:

- Compensating differentials give an incentive for workers to take on tasks that are valuable to society, even though they are unpleasant or dangerous.

- Because of compensating differentials, employers have an incentive to improve safety on the job.

Of course, some jobs are inherently dangerous. No matter how much we spend on safety programs, there will still be some deaths on the job. But compensating differentials help to improve the situation, by giving employers a financial incentive to improve working conditions.

rate, in order to attract workers. It's very important to emphasize the assumption of "all else equal", or "*ceteris paribus*". Our theory of compensating wage differentials *does not* say that everyone with an unpleasant job will get a higher wage than anyone with a nice job. In fact, many of the lowest-paying jobs are boring, dangerous, or dirty. For example, most jobs in poultry-processing plants are fairly unpleasant, but the wage rates are not much more than the minimum wage, because these jobs don't require much skill.

Still, compensating wage differentials can be seen in the wage rates paid in many jobs, including the wages of different workers at poultry-processing plants. The toughest job of all is that of a "live hanger", who shackles the live chickens as they come into the plant, at a rate of 25 or more per minute. The live hangers are pecked and scratched, and they often develop rashes from contact with the birds. But they earn a few dollars per day more than the other workers in poultry-processing plants.

In *Real Economics for Real People 13.2*, we discuss the compensating wage differentials associated with different degrees of safety on the job.

Reality Check:
Interim Review Questions

IR13-6. Before her award-winning performance in the film "Boys Don't Cry", the actress Hilary Swank earned fairly ordinary wages. Afterward, analysts in the entertainment industry expected that she would get $2 million per movie. In analyzing this change in wage rates, would you say that there was a shift in the demand curve or the supply curve? For the curve that shifted, was there a shift to the right or to the left?

IR13-7. Does immigration cause a shift in the demand curve for labor, or the supply curve? In which direction does the curve shift?

IR13-8. Because of compensating wage-rate differentials, do you expect that pleasant jobs will have wage rates that are higher or lower than the wage rates for jobs that are unpleasant but otherwise comparable?

WAGE DIFFERENTIALS BY RACE AND GENDER

So far, we've seen that people tend to earn higher wages if they have more skill, or if they work in unpleasant jobs. But these influences don't necessarily explain all of the variation in wages. Historically, people of different racial, ethnic, and gender backgrounds have had very different levels of earnings.

Differences by Sex

On average, the earnings of women have long been lower than those of men. Back in 1890, on average, the earnings of American women were *less than half* of those of men (for full-time, year-round workers). In the 1960s and early 1970s, this ratio stayed in the range from 56 percent to 60 percent, although the gap closed substantially in the 1980s.

Reasons for the Gender Wage Gap. One reason for the earnings gap between women and men is that many women leave the labor force during their childbearing years. As a result, these women don't get as much labor-market experience as men do. When they return to work, their job skills have often deteriorated.

The theory of human capital says that people are more likely to invest in themselves, if they expect to reap the benefits of those investments over a long period of time. If women expect to be out of the labor force for several years, they may not make the same kind of human-capital investments that men would make. If a woman expects to leave the labor force to raise children, she might not get as much education and on-the-job training as otherwise.

There are other reasons for the gap between men's and women's earnings, as well. First, women don't work as much overtime as men do, and they don't tend to choose occupations that offer high pay but demand long hours. Second, many women are crowded into low-paying occupations that have typically been dominated by females (such as cosmetologists, nurses' aides, and child-care workers). This phenomenon is called *occupational segregation*. Finally, at least some of the wage gap is probably due to outright discrimination, although there is some evidence that the amount of discrimination may be decreasing.

The Recent Increase in the Relative Earnings of Women. In the late 1970s, the gap between women's and men's earnings began to shrink. From 1976 to 1990, the earnings gap fell by about one percentage point per year.

Figure 13.10 shows the changes in women's earnings as a percentage of men's earnings from 1967 to 2014. In Figure 13.10, the comparison is between the median female worker and the median male worker. (The worker with median earnings is the one for whom half of the workers have higher earnings, and half of the workers have lower earnings.) For example, Figure 13.10 shows that, for full-time year-round workers in 2014, the median female worker earned about 78 percent as much as the median male worker. This was an all-time high.

One reason for the decrease in the gap between women's earnings and men's earnings is that women increased their labor-market experience dramatically. Women's participation in the labor force increased over a period of several decades. Also, occupational segregation decreased substantially. And, as

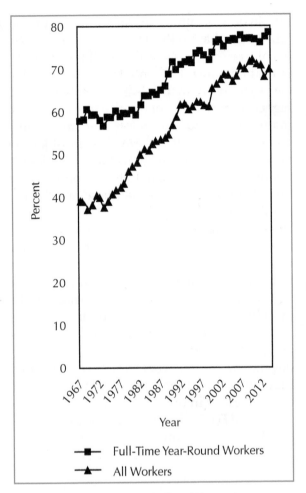

Figure 13.10 Median Women's Labor-Market Earnings as Percent of Median Men's Earnings in the United States, 1967–2014

we shall see, women's educational attainment increased more rapidly than men's, and labor-market discrimination against women probably decreased.

The Gender Earnings Gap for Full-Time and Part-Time Workers. Figure 13.10 shows the relationship between women's earnings and men's earnings for two groups of workers. One graph line refers to those who work full-time, year-round. The other graph line refers to all workers, including those who only work part-time and those who only work for a part of the year. The graph line for all workers is lower than the graph line for full-time, year-round workers. This means that the gap between women and men is larger when we consider all workers than when we only consider those who work full-time year-round. For instance, for all workers, the median female worker earned about 70 percent as much as the median male worker in 2014. This is substantially lower than the 78-percent figure for full-time, year-round workers.

The reason for this difference is that women are more likely than men to engage in part-time work. It is not surprising that part-time workers earn less, on average, than those who work full-time, year-round. Therefore, when we include the part-time workers, women's earnings fall more than men's earnings.

However, Figure 13.10 also shows that the difference between the gap for all workers and the gap for full-time, year-round workers has been shrinking over time. This is because, over the last few decades, a higher and higher percentage of working women have been working full time.

Prospects for Women's Earnings in the Future. In the last several decades, women have greatly increased their human capital. They have done this by getting more education, and also by staying in the labor force for longer periods of time, so that they are getting more experience. Education and experience are the two most important factors in the decrease of the earnings gap between women and men.

There is every reason to believe that these trends will continue in the future. One very important trend is the long-term increase in the number of women who are getting a college degree. Figure 13.11 shows that, until the early 1980s, more men than women were getting a Bachelor's degree. However, in the last quarter century, the number of men getting a college degree has increased much more slowly than number of women getting a college degree. In

2011, more than 980,000 women received a Bachelor's degree in the United States, compared to only about 734,000 men.

Thus, as time goes on, the number of college-educated women is continuing to increase, relative to the number of college-educated men. Unless this trend reverses suddenly (and there is no reason to believe it will), the female labor force will continue to have increasing amounts of human capital. It isn't possible to predict the future with certainty. However, if present trends continue, there is a very good chance that the gender earnings gap will continue to decrease.

Several factors explain the surge in women's earnings. As we have seen, women are getting more education. Also, the rate of return to education has increased. As a result,

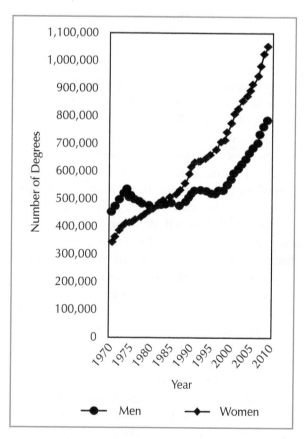

Figure 13.11 Bachelor's Degrees Conferred in the United States, by Sex, 1970–2014

women were increasing their education at exactly the time that the pay-off to an education was increasing. The period since about 1980 has been relatively better for white-collar workers, and not very good for blue-collar workers. The widening gap between white-collar and blue-collar workers has applied to men as well as to women, but it has helped women relatively, since they aren't in blue-collar jobs as much as men are.

Also, women (especially younger women) are staying in the labor market longer. This means that these women have more reason to get on-the-job training, and their employers also have a greater incentive to invest in them. As a result, the rate of return to experience for women has increased.

How Much of the Gap Is Due to Discrimination? Even after these increases, women's average earnings are still about one-fourth less than men's. Some of this difference is due to the fact that men and women still have different levels of education and experience. (In other words, the gap in human capital is smaller than it used to be, but it still isn't zero.) Another part of the difference is still due to occupational segregation.

If we control for differences in human capital and occupation, the gender wage gap is probably no more than 10 percent, and may be smaller than that. Some of the remaining gap is probably due to discrimination. But discrimination is very hard to measure. After all, if we were to ask an employer whether he is discriminating against his female employees, by paying them a lower wage than men who do comparable work, the employer will certainly say "no", regardless of whether "no" is a truthful answer.

Thus when economists try to assess the extent of labor-market discrimination, they usually have to rely on indirect methods. However, at least one study produced direct evidence of discrimination. Only a few decades ago, major symphony orchestras were either all-male, or nearly so. At that time, when a musician would audition for a spot in an orchestra, he or she would be in full view of the conductor who would be making the hiring decision. Thus the prospective employer could tell whether the potential employee was a man or a woman. Some women pointed out that this system had the potential for discrimination.

As a result, orchestras began to hold auditions in which the musician played from behind a screen. This led to a substantial increase in the number of women who were accepted for membership in orchestras. Most economists would agree that this case provides clear evidence that discrimination was taking place, and it also points to at least one case where discrimination has clearly reduced.

The laws against discrimination were strengthened in 2009, when President Obama signed the Ledbetter Fair Pay Act. This law was named after Lilly Ledbetter, who was receiving a lower salary than men with less experience who were doing the same job. She sued her employer, Goodyear Tire and Rubber. However, the U.S. Supreme Court decided that she was not legally eligible to sue. The Ledbetter Fair Pay Act clarified the law, and made it easier for victims of discrimination to bring lawsuits.

It's difficult to say how much of the gender wage gap is due to discrimination, and how much is due to other factors that are hard for researchers to observe. However, it should be noted that the amount of the wage gap that can't be explained is smaller than it used to be. This does not *prove* that discrimination is shrinking, but it is *consistent* with the idea that discrimination is getting smaller over time.

Differences by Race

A century ago, on average, blacks earned less than half of what was earned by whites. However, from the 1930s to the 1970s, there was a tremendous migration of African Americans from the South to the North and West. This was one of the forces that caused the earnings gap between blacks and whites to shrink. The black/white gap in educational attainment also shrank, and this played an important role in reducing the earnings gap. But the earnings gap has not changed as much since the 1970s.

Figure 13.12 shows the earnings gap between blacks and whites in the last few decades. The figure shows the trends separately for men and women, and we begin our discussion with men. In 1967, for full-time, year-round workers, the median black male earned about 65 percent as much as the median white male. By 1983, black men's earnings had increased to about 72 percent of white men's earnings. By 2014, the number was about 80 percent. Thus, the earnings of black men have increased relative to the earnings of white men in the last three or four decades, although the increases have been slow and uneven.

Throughout the period shown in Figure 13.12, the ratio of black women's earnings to white women's earnings has been larger than the ratio of black men's earnings to white men's earnings. In 1967, for full-time, year-round workers, the median black female earned about 75 percent as much as the median white female. (This compares to only about 65 percent for males.) By the mid-1970s, the median black woman had nearly caught up with the median white woman. Since then, however, black women have lost some ground relative to their white counterparts. By 2014, the median black woman was earning about 83 percent as much as the median white woman. Thus, as shown in Figure 13.12, the difference between the black/white earnings gap for men and the black/white earnings gap for women has shrunk very substantially since the 1970s.

We've seen that a part of the earnings difference between men and women is explained by differences in human capital. The same is true of black-white differentials. Black men

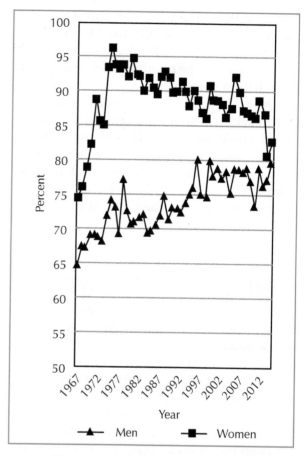

Figure 13.12 Median Labor-Market Earnings for Blacks as Percent of Median Earnings for Whites, for Full-Time Year-Round Workers in the United States, 1967–2014

still tend to have less education and experience than white men, and this probably explains a portion of the gap. Some studies suggest that other factors (such as union membership and region of residence) may explain another part of the gap.

This still leaves us with a substantial earnings gap, however: Even after controlling for everything that they can measure, economists still find that black men probably earn no more than about 90 percent as much as comparable white men. It is difficult to say how much of the remaining gap is due to outright discrimination. It may be that the entire gap is due to discrimination. However, some of it may be due to factors that are very hard to measure, such as the quality of schooling. (It's relatively easy to measure the *quantity* of schooling, but much harder to measure *quality*.)

On average, Hispanics earn even less than blacks. In 2014, among full-time, year-round workers, the median Hispanic man earned about 68 percent as much as the median white man, and the median Hispanic woman earned about 75 percent as much as the median white woman. Not surprisingly, a part of this gap is explained by differences in language skills. In other words, a Hispanic man who is fluent in English will tend to earn considerably more than a Hispanic man who isn't fluent. Differences in schooling also play an important role.

Reality Check: Interim Review Question

IR13-9. In the last 30 years, what has happened to the ratio of women's earnings to men's earnings? What has happened to the ratio of earnings for black men to the earnings of white men?

MINIMUM-WAGE LAWS

Some states began to pass minimum-wage laws as early as 1912, but these laws were struck down by the Supreme Court. The first federal minimum wage wasn't established until 1938, when the Fair Labor Standards Act set the minimum wage at 25 cents per hour.

Table 13.3 gives additional history of the federal minimum wage. The federal minimum has been increased 22 times since it began in 1938. Thus, on average, the minimum wage has been increased about once every three years and five months.

The numbers in Table 13.3 are "nominal" minimum-wage rates. In other words, they have not been adjusted for inflation. We can get a better sense of the changes over time by using a price index to adjust for inflation. Figure 13.13 is based on an adjustment with the Gross Domestic Product deflator, a price index developed by the U.S. Department of Commerce. Figure 13.13 converts the minimum wages from past years into 2014 dollars. The graph shows a "sawtooth" pattern over time. When Congress passes an increase in the minimum wage, the graph suddenly jumps up. However, since the minimum wage is usually not changed every year, its real value is eroded over time by inflation, until the next increase.

In real, inflation-adjusted terms, the minimum wage reached its highest value in 1968, at about $8.56 in 2014 dollars. Some have argued for increasing the minimum wage again. Another possibility would be to index the minimum wage with respect to inflation, so that the real value of the minimum wage would not be eroded over time. Whether this would make a good policy depends on the size of the employment losses associated with the minimum wage. We now turn our attention to the economic effects of the minimum wage.

Economic Effects of Minimum-Wage Laws

In Chapter 4, we saw that price controls may have an effect, or they may not. First of all, these laws won't do anything unless they are enforced. The minimum-wage law in the United States is probably obeyed most of the time, but violations do happen. Moreover, a small part of the labor force is not covered by the law.

Second, the minimum-wage law will only have a direct effect if it is above the equilibrium wage in a particular labor market. The law doesn't affect the wages of doctors, engineers, and accountants, because they earn far

Table 13.3.   History of the Federal Minimum Wage in the United States

Effective Date	Minimum Hourly Wage
October 24, 1938	$0.25
October 24, 1939	0.30
October 24, 1945	0.40
January 25, 1950	0.75
March 1, 1956	1.00
September 3, 1961	1.15
September 3, 1963	1.25
February 1, 1967	1.40
February 1, 1968	1.60
May 1, 1974	2.00
January 1, 1975	2.10
January 1, 1976	2.30
January 1, 1978	2.65
January 1, 1979	2.90
January 1, 1980	3.10
January 1, 1981	3.35
April 1, 1990	3.80
April 1, 1991	4.25
October 1, 1996	4.75
September 1, 1997	5.15
July 24, 2007	5.85
July 24, 2008	6.55
July 24, 2009	7.25

Source: U.S. Department of Labor, Employment Standards Admission. Wage and Hour Division, http://www.dol.gov/esa/minwage/chart.htm

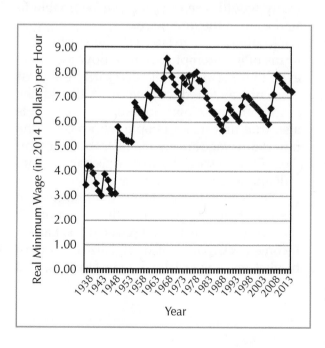

Figure 13.13   Real (Inflation-Adjusted) Minimum Wage in the United States, 1938–2014 (in 2014 Dollars)

more than the minimum wage, even without any law.

If the minimum wage has any effect at all, it will be in markets for low-skilled labor. These are the markets that might have equilibrium wages below the legal minimum. The minimum wage shown in Figure 13.14 has an effect, because it is above the equilibrium wage. The equilibrium amount of labor hired is L^*, and the equilibrium wage rate is W^*. However, employers have to pay W_{min}. More workers are willing to work at this wage rate, so the quantity supplied is L_{sm}. But employers have a downward-sloping demand curve for workers, so the quantity demanded is only L_{dm}.

The minimum-wage law causes a surplus of workers, which we call unemployment. The amount of unemployment caused by the minimum wage is ($L_{sm} - L_{dm}$). The amount of job loss will depend on the elasticity of demand for labor. There is controversy in the literature about the value of the labor-demand elasticity. The consensus is probably that the elasticity is less than one. This would mean that the gains to those who keep their jobs are relatively larger than the losses to those who lose their jobs. Thus, the total earnings of the affected group of workers would increase. The job losses are likely to be greatest for teenagers.

In the 2016 campaign for the Democratic Party's nomination for President, Vermont Senator Bernie Sanders proposed raising the minimum wage to $15 nationwide. As of this writing, it seems unlikely that such a large increase will be enacted. However, if it were to be enacted, it would more than double the existing federal minimum wage. That would be the largest increase in history. It is difficult to know how large the job losses would be in that case, because all of the statistical evidence on the shape of the labor-demand curve comes from rather small changes in wages. We have very little evidence about what would happen in response to such a large wage increase.

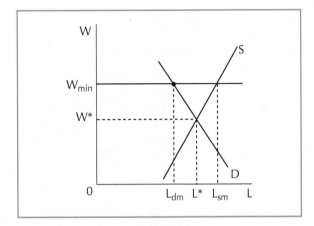

Figure 13.14 The Effects of a Minimum Wage Above the Equilibrium Wage

The supply curve is S, and the demand curve is D. The equilibrium wage rate is W^*, and the equilibrium amount of employment is L^*. If the government enforces a minimum-wage law at W_{min}, the quantity of labor supplied will be L_{sm}, and the quantity of labor demanded will be L_{dm}. This surplus of labor results in unemployment.

Some low-wage workers would certainly keep their jobs, and their earnings would increase by a lot. But it's very hard to predict how many would lose their jobs, or be unable to find a job in the first place.

Minimum-wage laws are often justified in terms of an attempt to reduce poverty. However, these laws are not necessarily the most efficient way to reduce poverty. Although the minimum-wage laws do reduce poverty, it is also true that many people who receive the minimum wage are not members of poor families. This is especially true of teenagers from affluent families.

The bottom line is that the minimum-wage laws do help the poor, but they are not the most effective way to fight poverty. The Earned Income Tax Credit, which subsidizes the labor-market earnings of low-wage families, is a more effective way to reduce poverty.

LABOR UNIONS

In many labor markets, individual workers reach individual agreements with their employers. However, in some markets, the workers are organized into *labor unions*, which negotiate with employers about wages, fringe benefits, and working conditions. Many labor unions are also active in political lobbying.

We begin our discussion with a brief outline of the history of the union movement in the United States.

In colonial times, members of the same craft (such as carpenters, shoemakers, printers, and so on) began to organize into guilds. By the late 1700s, many of these organizations had begun to operate as *craft unions*. A *craft union* is an organization representing members of the same skilled trade.

The American Federation of Labor

After the Civil War, there were several attempts to bring members of different craft unions into a single organization. The most long-lasting of these groups was the *American Federation of Labor* (AFL), founded in 1886. For nearly 40 years, the AFL was led by Samuel Gompers (who had started out as a cigar maker). Gompers concentrated on improving wages and working conditions.

The National Labor Relations Act

The centerpiece of federal labor law is the *National Labor Relations Act* (NLRA) of 1935, which is also known as the *Wagner Act*, for Senator Robert Wagner of New York. The NLRA outlawed several unfair labor practices by employers. For example, the Wagner Act made it illegal for an employer to prohibit workers from joining a union, or to refuse to join in *collective bargaining* with a union. The Wagner Act established the National Labor Relations Board, which is responsible for making sure that employers comply with the law.

The Taft-Hartley Act

In 1947, Congress passed the Labor-Management Relations Act, better known as the *Taft-Hartley Act*. Whereas the Wagner Act prohibits some labor practices of *employers*, the Taft-Hartley Act prohibits some labor practices of *unions*.

The Taft-Hartley Act allows the President to order strikers back to work for an 80-day "cooling-off" period, if it is found that a strike "imperils the national health or safety". It also outlaws the *closed shop*, under which union membership is a requirement for being hired. The Act also allows the individual States to pass *"right-to-work laws"*, which outlaw the *union shop*. A union shop allows employers to hire non-union employees, but requires that they join the union within a specified period of time. Some 24 States have passed right-to-work laws.

Advocates of right-to-work laws suggest that these laws will lead to employment gains. There is some evidence that this may occur in some cases. However, in recent years, only about one out of every eight or nine American workers is a union member. Thus, the advantages claimed by those who are in favor of right-to-work laws are likely to be small, because unions are already relatively weak. Also, it should be remembered that the way in which right-to-work laws may increase employment is by reducing the ability of unions to raise wages. Therefore, even if a right-to-work law succeeds in increasing employment, the resulting jobs may have relatively low wages.

Indeed, per-capita income in the right-to-work states is lower than in the rest of the United States, to the tune of more than $6000 per year. This does not mean that per-capita income would suddenly drop by $6000 if a state were to adopt a right-to-work law. However, it does suggest that right-to-work laws are not necessarily associated with greater prosperity. Earlier in this chapter, we saw that education has a very strong effect on incomes. Thus it is probably not surprising that the most affluent states are those with the highest levels of educational attainment. Most of the more affluent states are *not* right-to-work states.

Taft-Hartley also outlaws sympathy strikes. A *sympathy strike* occurs when one union goes on strike, to show its support for another union that is already on strike.

The AFL-CIO

From the very beginning, the American Federation of Labor had been a federation of craft unions, whose members were skilled tradespersons. However, much of the growth of unions in the early part of the 20th century involved *industrial unions*, which tend to serve semi-skilled workers. The goal of an industrial union is to represent all of the workers in an industry, regardless of their specific trade. Examples of industrial unions are the United Mine Workers and the United Steel Workers.

Craft unions and industrial unions had a great deal of conflict in the 1930s. Several industrial unions were driven out of the AFL, and they formed the *Congress of Industrial Organizations (CIO)* in 1938. Finally, the two organizations merged in 1955, to form the AFL-CIO.

Changes in Union Membership

The Wagner Act greatly improved the climate for union organizing. Union membership in the United States grew from about 3 million in 1934 to more than 14 million in 1944.

For most of the period since the Second World War, however, unions have represented a smaller and smaller portion of the labor force. Unions had about 14.6 million members in 2014. This is about the same number that they had in 1947, even though

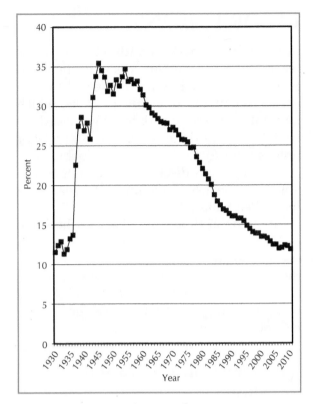

Figure 13.15   Union Members as Percentage of U.S. Workers, 1930–2014

the labor force increased tremendously during that time. Figure 13.15 shows the trend in the percentage of workers who are union members.

The decline in union membership is even more pronounced among unions in the private sector. By 2014, only about 6.6 percent of private-sector workers were members of unions, compared with about 35.7 percent of public-sector workers.

In recent years, only about 11 percent of American workers have been union members. Still, it would be wrong to say that American unions are unimportant or irrelevant. After all, when we say that one out of every nine workers is a union member, we are talking about more than 14 *million* workers. In addition, unions may have powerful effects on *nonunion* labor markets.

The Economic Effects of Labor Unions

When asked what unions want, Samuel Gompers of the American Federation of Labor said "More!" However, economists would ask "More of what?" After all, labor unions are complicated organizations, serving social and political functions, as well as economic ones. Even when we concentrate on the economic effects, we can see that it's possible for unions to influence labor markets in many ways.

The economic goals of most unions could include the following:

- Increasing wages;

- Increasing fringe benefits, such as pensions or health insurance;

- Improving working conditions;

- Increasing employment.

Unfortunately for the union, there are tradeoffs among these goals. If the union is successful in raising wages or fringe benefits, it will raise the firm's cost of labor. This will cause the firm to hire fewer workers. In most cases, it appears that unions *do not* maximize employment: They are usually willing to accept some decreases in employment, in return for increased wages.

Figure 13.16 shows some of the effects of a union on wages and employment. At first, the supply and demand curves are S_{0u} and D_{0u} in the union sector, and S_{0n} and D_{0n} in the non-union sector. If there are no unions or other distortions between the two sectors, an equilibrium will require that comparable workers will receive the same wage rate in either sector. Therefore, the wage rate is W_0 in *both* sectors. The level of employment is L_{0u} in the union sector and L_{0n} in the non-union sector.

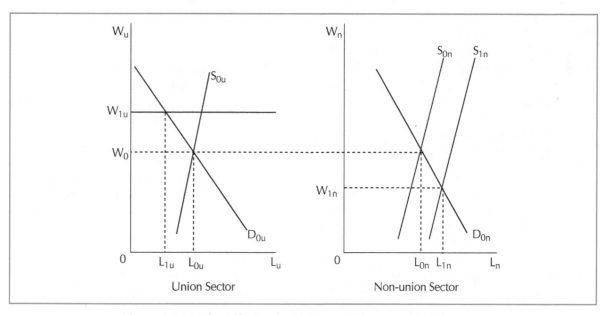

Figure 13.16 The Effects of a Union on Wages and Employment in the Union Sector and in the Non-Union Sector

Without a union, the wage rate is W_0 in each sector. The equilibrium levels of employment are L_{0u} in the union sector and L_{0n} in the non-union sector. When the union raises its wage rate to W_{1u}, the level of unionized employment falls to L_{1u}. Some of the workers who lose their union jobs will seek work in the non-union sector. As a result, the non-union wage rate falls to W_{1n}, and non-union employment increases to L_{1n}. This is the union spillover effect.

Now, suppose that the union succeeds in raising the wage rate for union workers from W_0 to W_{1u}. As a result, we move upward and to the left along the labor-demand curve in the union sector. Some workers will lose their jobs in the union sector: The new level of unionized employment is given by L_{1u}.

Eventually, some of the workers who lose their union jobs will start to look for work in the non-union sector. This means that the labor-supply curve in the non-union sector will shift to the right, to S_{1n}. *Because of the increased supply of labor in the non-union sector, the non-union wage rate will fall to W_{1n}.*

The Union Wage Gap. We would like to know the size of the wage differential between union and non-union workers (while holding constant any other influences on wages). This wage differential is sometimes called the *union wage gap.*

According to Figure 13.16, the wage gains in the union sector can lead to wage losses in the non-union sector, as displaced workers are forced to seek non-union jobs. This is called the *union spillover effect.* However, there is another effect that works in the opposite direction. Some non-union employers may be willing to pay higher wages, if they believe that this will keep their workers from organizing into a union. This is called the *union threat effect.* However, it appears that the union threat effect is not as large as the spillover effect, because we do observe that union members earn more than their non-union counterparts, all else equal. The consensus among economists seems to be that, when we put these two effects together, the true wage gap in the United States is between 10 percent and 15 percent. In other words, if we hold constant the other influences on wage rates, a unionized worker will make 10 to 15 percent more than a comparable non-union worker.

How Do Unions Deal with Job Losses?

Figure 13.16 shows that some unionized jobs are lost when a labor union raises the wage rate above its equilibrium level. Some workers will get to keep their union jobs, but others will lose theirs, or have trouble finding a union job in the first place. There has to be some system for deciding who gets to keep the union jobs. In other words, there must be a system of *job rationing.*

Many job-rationing schemes have been used over the years. One very popular scheme has been the "seniority system". When layoffs occur, a seniority system preserves the jobs of those who have been on the job for the longest time.

In an effort to limit the job losses, unions also try to affect the labor-demand curves that they face. The union can reduce job losses if it can *make the demand curve for union labor more inelastic.* Job losses can also be limited if the union can *push the demand curve for union labor to the right.*

Here are some of the tactics that unions have used, to increase the demand for their own labor, and/or decrease the demand for competing non-union labor:

- *Unions typically support increases in the minimum wage.* If the government enforces a relatively high minimum wage, it will be hard for employers to substitute low-wage workers for higher-paid union workers.

- *Unions encourage people to buy union-made products.* For example, union-sponsored TV commercials urge shoppers to "look for the union label".

MONOPSONY IN LABOR MARKETS

In earlier chapters, we studied market power on the *seller's* side of the market. Monopolists and oligopolists can use their market power to raise their profits. Here we will look at market power on the *buyer's* side of the market. A *monopsony* exists when there is only one buyer in a market. *Oligopsony* refers to markets with only a few buyers.

Back in Chapter 7, we discussed the behavior of buyers in output markets. To simplify the analysis, we assumed that the individual consumer was small relative to the market, and thus could not affect prices. However, some buyers in output markets do have market power. For example, if you were a clothing buyer for Walmart Stores, you would be able to place very large orders, and this would give you the power to negotiate about price.

Some of the best examples of monopsony and oligopsony occur in labor markets, which is why we study them here. For example, in isolated Appalachian communities, a coal-mining firm may be the only large employer in town. If a firm is to exercise monopsony power, the workers must find it difficult to move in search of better job opportunities. The coal miners might be immobile because they're reluctant to leave their home region, or because they are unaware of opportunities elsewhere, or because they have relatively few skills. Fortunately, improved transportation and communication mean that most workers are not completely at the mercy of oligopsonistic or monopsonistic employers.

Professional sports provides other examples of labor markets with monopsony or oligopsony power. Before the 1970s, major-league baseball players were effectively tied to only one team. The players weren't allowed to sell their services to the highest bidder. Obviously, this gave the teams tremendous bargaining power in determining player salaries. More recently, players have acquired much greater freedom, as a result of "free-agency" rules. As a result, the salaries of professional athletes are dramatically higher than they were a few decades ago.

Next, we will learn about the theory of decision-making for monopsony firms.

Marginal Factor Expense for the Monopsonist

In a perfectly competitive labor market, the individual firm is too small to manipulate the wage rate. Therefore, the firm takes the market wage as given. In a monopsonistic labor market, however, the firm is a "wage maker". The firm faces the entire *market* labor-supply curve, and this has important effects on its hiring behavior.

Let's assume that the market labor-supply curve slopes upward. In other words, the only way to get more workers to supply their labor is to raise the wage rate. *If the monopsony firm wants to hire one additional worker, it has to pay all of its workers a higher wage rate.*

Table 13.4 shows the labor-supply schedule that faces Big Brother, Inc., which is the only employer in its town. If the wage rate is less than $6 per hour, nobody will show up for work. At a wage rate of $6, one worker will come to work for Big Brother. If we multiply the number of workers (one) by the wage rate ($6), we get *total factor expense*, which is $6 in this case. The firm's total factor expense is the total amount it spends on a particular factor of production.

The *marginal factor expense* is the *extra* amount of money the firm has to pay, to employ one additional unit of a factor of production. In the case of labor, the marginal factor expense is the extra amount of money the firm has to pay, to get one additional worker to come to work. Marginal factor expense is defined as the change in total factor expense, divided by the change in the quantity of labor:

Marginal Factor Expense =
(Δ Total Factor Expense) / (Δ Labor).

Table 13.4 The Labor-Supply Schedule and Marginal Factor Expense, for Big Brother, Inc.

Number of Workers (L)	Wage Rate (W)	Total Factor Expense (TFE) = (W)(L)	Marginal Factor Expense (ΔTFE/ΔL)
0	$5.50	$0	—
1	6.00	6	$6
2	6.50	13	7
3	7.00	21	8
4	7.50	30	9
5	8.00	40	10

In the example of Table 13.4, marginal factor expense is $6 for the first worker hired. If Big Brother, Inc., wants to hire a second worker, it has to raise the wage from $6.00 to $6.50. It's important to remember that the increase in the wage rate will apply to *all* workers—not only will the second worker get the higher wage, but the first worker will also get a wage increase. When we multiply the number of workers (two) by the wage rate ($6.50), we find that total factor expense has risen to $13. To get *marginal* factor expense, we then subtract $6 (which was the total expense when there was only one worker) from $13 (which is the total expense when there are two workers). The result is that the marginal factor expense of the second worker is $(13 – 6) = $7.

In this example, when the firm hires a second worker, the wage rate increases by 50 cents per hour, but marginal factor expense increases by $1. This trend continues in the rest of Table 13.4. Whenever Big Brother wants to hire one additional worker, it is necessary to raise the wage rate by 50 cents, but marginal factor expense increases by $1.00.

The labor-supply schedule of Table 13.4 is graphed as a labor-supply curve (called S) in Figure 13.17, and the marginal-factor-expense curve is shown as MFE. In this case, with a straight-line labor-supply curve, the slope of the marginal-factor-expense curve is exactly twice as great as the slope of the labor-supply curve. (This may remind you of the relation-ship between demand and marginal revenue for the monopolist. When the monopolist's demand curve is a straight line, the marginal-revenue curve is twice as steep as the demand curve.)

The Monopsonist's Hiring Decision

In the last several chapters, we've studied several of the problems facing economic decision-makers. The utility-maximizing consumer buys the quantity at which marginal utility is equal to the price of the good. The profit-maximizing firm produces the quantity at which marginal revenue is equal to marginal cost. *In each of these problems, the solution involves choosing the quantity at which some kind of marginal benefit is equal to some kind of marginal cost.*

The case of the monopsonist is no different. For the monopsonist, the marginal benefit of hiring one additional worker is the marginal revenue product. The marginal cost of hiring one extra worker is the marginal factor expense. Thus *the monopsony firm should hire the number of workers at which marginal revenue product (MRP) is equal to marginal factor expense (MFE).* In Figure 13.17, the intersection of the MRP curve and the MFE curve tells us that Big Brother, Inc., should hire L_{mon}, which means that three workers will be hired.

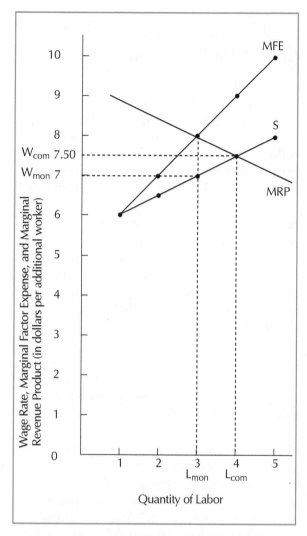

Figure 13.17 The Labor-Supply Curve and Marginal-Factor-Expense Curve for Big Brother, Inc., and the Firm's Hiring Decision

Big Brother, Inc., is a monopsonist. The labor-supply curve facing the firm is S, its marginal-factor-expense curve is MFE, and its marginal-revenue-product curve is MRP. The firm's best choice is to hire L_{mon} workers, because this is the quantity of labor at which MRP = MFE. The firm then pays a wage rate of W_{mon}, given by the labor-supply curve. Note that the wage is less than the worker's marginal revenue product. If the firm were a perfect competitor in the labor market, it would pay a wage of W_{com}, and the wage would be equal to the marginal revenue product of labor.

The labor-supply curve shows the relationship between the wage rate and the number of workers who are willing to supply their labor. Therefore, the supply curve tells us that Big Brother will pay a wage rate of W_{mon}. In this case, the wage rate is $7 per hour.

Figure 13.17 also shows the outcomes that would have occurred if this labor market had been competitive. In the competitive case, equilibrium would be given by the intersection of the supply curve and the MRP curve. This would have led to the hiring of four workers, each of whom would have received a wage of $7.50 per hour. Thus, relative to the case of competition, monopsony leads to a lower level of employment *and* a lower wage rate.

Figure 13.17 shows us that *the monopsonist's workers are paid less than their marginal revenue product.* This is sometimes called *monopsonistic exploitation.* The monopsonist's market power allows it to "exploit" the workers, by paying them less than their MRP.

We can continue the analogy between the labor-market monopsonist and the product-market monopolist. The monopolist uses its market power to exploit the buyers, by charging a price that is greater than marginal cost. The labor-market monopsonist uses its market power to exploit the workers, by paying a wage rate that is less than the workers' marginal revenue product.

In *Real Economics for Real People* 13.3, we discuss the wages paid to college athletes. These wages are affected by the fact that the employers (colleges and universities) have a lot of market power.

Real Economics for Real People 13.3:
Should College Basketball Players Be Paid a Salary?

In April of 2010, the CBS television network announced an agreement with the National Collegiate Athletic Association (NCAA). Under the agreement, CBS has the right to broadcast the NCAA men's basketball tournament for 14 years. CBS paid $10.8 *billion* for this privilege. (That's $10,800,000,000.)

CBS was willing to pay such an astronomical sum of money because tens of millions of people are eager to watch the college basketball players when they perform in March and April of every year. In other words, the basketball players' product has great value. The amount paid by CBS works out to more than $900,000 *per year*, for *every* player on *every* team.

In a competitive labor market, the workers who produce very valuable products would receive high wages and salaries. This is what we mean when we say that a competitive labor market pays each worker according to his or her marginal revenue product. However, this clearly doesn't happen for the young men who play in the NCAA basketball tournament. They do get paid a small amount for their services, in the form of tuition waivers. But the free tuition is only a small fraction of the marginal revenue product of the players. Since the basketball players aren't paid their marginal revenue products, we can conclude that they

are victims of exploitation. (The same is true for those who play other revenue-producing sports, especially football.)

By joining together in the NCAA, the colleges have effectively created a buyer's cartel. We can call it a case of collusive oligopsony. One of the most remarkable things about this arrangement is that it receives so much public support. Quite often, colleges are caught and punished when they secretly try to reduce the exploitation (and win games) by paying their worker-athletes more than the maximum amount allowed by the NCAA. When this happens, the press is full of talk of scandal. The public support for monopsonistic exploitation is a great public-relations triumph for the colleges and the NCAA. (Certainly, we would not expect press reports to praise an employer for exploiting pipefitters or dishwashers.)

If we view the situation from the perspective of the athletes, the NCAA may not seem so virtuous. If it's proper for workers to be paid according to the value they provide for their employers, then it's hard to argue that college athletes should not be paid more. However, it seems unlikely that the current system will be changed any time soon.

Reality Check:
Interim Review Questions

IR13-10. What does the union spillover effect do to the wages paid by non-union firms? What does the union threat effect do to the wages paid by non-union firms?

IR13-11. For a monopsonistic firm that faces an upward-sloping labor-supply curve, is the marginal-factor-expense curve above or below the labor-supply curve?

IR13-12. What is monopsonistic exploitation?

ECONOMICS AND YOU:
SOME WORKERS GET BIG BUCKS, AND SOME DON'T

Again and again in this book, we have seen that prices are higher when there is a lot of demand, or when supply is relatively small.

The wage rate is the price at which a worker is hired. If you want a higher wage rate, you need to be working in a labor market where demand is strong, or in a labor market where there is a relatively short supply of the kind of skill that you have to offer, or both.

Of course, one way to do that is to have unique and highly desirable talents. (If you have very unusual talents, then the supply of your skills is small. If those talents are highly desirable, there will be a lot of demand.) For example, if you are seven feet tall and can move with strength and speed and grace, you may be able to make a lot of money in the National Basketball Association. If you are extremely attractive physically, you may be able to make a lot of money as a fashion model.

But very few people have the body to be a champion athlete, and very few are gor-geous enough to appear on the cover of *Cosmopolitan*. For more ordinary people, the best prescription for high wages is to acquire human capital. People with a lot of human capital are able to earn higher wages, because of both labor supply and labor demand. It takes time and effort to acquire a lot of human capital. Since not everyone will go to the trouble to get a lot of education and experience, it follows that those who *do* get education and experience will have skills that are somewhat special, and somewhat limited in supply. In addition, education and experience make us more productive, which means that there will be more demand for our skills. So, here's the secret: Stay in school, and concentrate on your studies. Then, when you get a job, work hard, and make the most of your experience. More than any other things, education and experience are the pathway to earning more money.

Chapter Summary

1. The factors of production include labor, capital, land, energy, and materials. The demand for these factors of production, or inputs, is derived from the demand for the goods they produce.

2. The marginal revenue product of a factor of production is the extra money the firm makes when it hires one additional unit of a factor input, and then sells the additional output created by that additional input. In other words, the marginal revenue product equals the marginal (physical) product, multiplied by the marginal revenue. The marginal-revenue-product curve for a factor of production slopes downward as we move from left to right.

3. The marginal factor expense of a factor of production is the extra money the firm has to pay to hire one additional unit of the factor. If the firm is a competitor in its input market, marginal factor expense will be the price of the input.

4. For the firm that is a competitor in its input market, the demand curve for a factor of production is the marginal-revenue-product curve.

5. The market demand curve for a factor of production is found by adding horizontally the demand curves of the individual firms.

6. A change in the wage rate has two effects on labor supply. The substitution effect leads to an increase in the quantity of labor supplied when the wage rate increases. The income effect goes in the opposite direction: The income effect of an increase in the wage rate will lead to a reduction in the quantity of labor supplied. For men, the income effect and substitution effect approximately cancel each other out, so that the labor-supply elasticity is close to zero. For women, the substitution effect

appears to be relatively stronger, so that the labor-supply elasticity may be something like 0.2 or 0.4.

7. If the price of the output increases, or if productivity increases, then the demand curve for a factor of production will shift to the right. This will tend to increase factor prices. If the demand curve were to shift to the left, factor prices would fall.

8. The theory of human capital says that people will invest in education or on-the-job training, if the value of the benefits is greater than the value of the costs. In fact, labor-market earnings are substantially higher for those with more education and experience.

9. A compensating wage differential is the extra wage rate that must be paid (all else equal), to attract a worker to a job that is unpleasant. All else equal, higher wage rates are paid to workers who hold dangerous jobs, night jobs, and jobs with other unpleasant characteristics.

10. As recently as the mid–1970s, women's earnings were only about 55 percent of men's earnings in the United States. Since then, the gap has narrowed, and the earnings ratio now stands at about 78 percent, for full-time year-round workers. This is explained primarily by the fact that women are now getting more education and experience and are not subject to as much occupational segregation. Part of the remaining gap is probably the result of discrimination.

11. Among full-time year-round workers, the median black male earns about 80 percent as much as the median white male in the United States. This gap has shrunk by only a small amount since the 1970s. The gap is smaller for women: Black females earn about 83 percent as much as white females. Hispanics earn even less than blacks. With both of these groups, differ-

ences in human capital explain a large portion of the earnings differences. For Hispanics, part of the difference is also explained by lack of proficiency in English. It's likely that the remaining gaps are partly the result of unmeasured influences, and partly the result of discrimination.

12. If a minimum-wage law is below the equilibrium wage, it will have no effect. However, if the minimum wage is above the equilibrium wage, and if the law is enforced, it will lead to a surplus of labor, in the form of unemployment.

13. The American labor-union movement had some of its greatest successes in the 1930s and 1940s, after the National Labor Relations Act made it easier for unions to organize. At the peak, in the early 1950s, about one-third of workers were union members. However, since the 1950s, there has been a decline in the proportion of workers who are union members. By 2014, only about one-ninth of the work force was in unions. In the last few decades, the main source of union growth has been public-employee unions.

14. Unions typically attempt to increase wage rates, relative to the wages that would have prevailed in the absence of the union. If the union is successful in raising wages, the unionized firms may reduce their employment. If the displaced union workers go to work for non-union firms, the wages at the non-union firms will be reduced. In an attempt to limit the job losses, unions try to reduce the elasticity of demand for their labor, or they try to shift the labor-demand curve to the right.

15. A monopsony occurs when there is only one buyer in a market. If there are only a few buyers, the market is an oligopsony. Monopsony or oligopsony can lead to market power on the buyers' side of the market. A monopsonist in a labor market will choose to hire workers up to the point at which marginal revenue product is equal to marginal factor expense.

16. A monopsonist or oligopsonist will pay workers less than their marginal revenue product. This is called "monopsonistic exploitation".

Key Terms

Labor

Capital

Land

Energy

Materials

Factors of Production

Factor Markets, Input Markets

Derived Demand

Marginal Revenue Product

Marginal (Physical) Product

Marginal Revenue

Marginal Factor Expense

Leisure

Non-Labor Income

Income Effect

Substitution Effect (in Labor Supply)

Upward-Sloping Labor-Supply Curve

Backward-Bending Labor-Supply Curve

Elasticity of Labor Supply with Respect to the Wage Rate

Human Capital Investment

Foregone Earnings

Compensating Wage Differentials

Occupational Segregation

Minimum-Wage Laws

Labor Unions

Craft Unions

American Federation of Labor

National Labor Relations Act

Collective Bargaining

Taft-Hartley Act

Closed Shop

Right-to-Work Laws

Union Shop

Sympathy Strike

Congress of Industrial Organizations

Union Wage Gap

Union Spillover Effect

Union Threat Effect

Monopsony

Oligopsony

Total Factor Expense

Marginal Factor Expense

Monopsonistic Exploitation

Questions and Problems

QP13-1. Explain how the marginal-revenue-product curve for a perfectly competitive firm is different from the marginal-revenue-product curve for a firm that is a monopolist in its output market. What is the direction of the slope of these marginal-revenue-product curves?

QP13-2. Explain the difference between the income effect on labor supply and the substitution effect on labor supply. If the income effect is stronger than the substitution effect, what kind of labor-supply curve will we have? If the income effect and the substitution effect are of equal strength, what will be the shape of the labor-supply curve?

QP13-3. What factors of production are involved in producing an automobile?

QP13-4. Spain's Placido Domingo is one of the most popular opera singers in the world. His splendid voice and vibrant personality combine to make him instantly recognizable all over the world. Joe Dokes flips hamburgers at the Shazam Burger restaurant in Anytown, U.S.A. For which of these workers do you believe that the labor-demand curve would be more elastic? Why?

QP13-5. The "Mariel boatlift" brought more than 100,000 Cubans to the United States in 1980. More of these people ended up in the Miami metropolitan area than in any other part of the country. What do you expect would be the effect on the equilibrium wage rate for less-skilled workers in the Miami area? What would be the effect on the equilibrium quantity of labor in the Miami area? How would your answer change if you were to learn of a recent study, which indicates that the immigration from Cuba was coupled with a substantial reduction in the number of people moving from other parts of the United States to the Miami area? What effects would you expect for other labor markets in the United States?

QP13-6. The marginal (physical) product of labor for firm A is given by $MPP_L = 10 - L$. Like all of the firms in the market, firm A is a perfect competitor in both its output and input markets. The price of firm A's output is $10 per unit. Draw the firm's marginal-revenue-product curve.

QP13-7. Sam, who studied through four years of college and five years of graduate school, earns $39,000 per year as an Assistant Professor of Classics. Zelda, who has only a high-school diploma, earns $50,000 per year by repairing telephone wires. How can this be? How can someone with only a high-school education be paid more than someone with an advanced degree? You should be able to come up with at least three or four influences that could help to explain this earnings comparison.

QP13-8. The International Pencil Sharpener Workers Union (IPSWU) succeeds in raising the wage rate for its workers above the rate that would have occurred otherwise. However, this leads to substantial layoffs for IPSWU members. Eventually, many of these workers seek work elsewhere. What will happen in the labor markets where these displaced workers end up?

QP13-9. In a competitive labor market, the labor-supply curve facing the individual firm is the same as the firm's marginal-factor-expense curve. However, in a monopsonized labor market, the marginal-factor-expense curve is higher than the labor-supply curve. Explain why this is the case.

QP13-10. Should college football players be paid a salary? Why, or why not?

Chapter 14

Capital Markets

ECONOMICS AND YOU: WHO WANTS TO BE A BILLIONAIRE?

In Chapter 13, we discussed the market for labor, which is the most important factor of production. In this chapter, we'll discuss the market for capital, which is also a very important factor of production. Capital includes the machinery and equipment, computers, office buildings, warehouses, factories, delivery vans, railroad cars, and other such man-made stuff that is used in the production process. One important aspect of capital assets is that they are long-lived. A unit of capital, such as a business computer or a drop forge, is not used up immediately. Some capital assets last for a few years; others last for decades.

The analysis in this chapter will be shaped by one very big difference between labor markets and capital markets. The Thirteenth Amendment to the United States Constitution, ratified in 1865, makes slavery illegal. (As documented in Douglas Blackmon's book, *Slavery by Another Name*, white southerners quickly established a convict-labor system that was very, very much like slavery, despite the Thirteenth Amendment. But that system had died out by the time of the Second World War. Even today, there are isolated cases of involuntary servitude, but the overwhelming majority of employer-employee relationships are volun-

tary.) This means that all legal labor relationships, and almost all actual labor relationships, are in the nature of rental contracts, rather than ownership contracts. However, it is possible to own machines. Our discussion of capital markets has to reflect the fact that capital ownership involves long-term decisions. Thus, the most important part of this chapter will consider how to compare dollar values that occur at different times.

Much of the nation's capital stock is owned by corporations and other businesses. These businesses, in turn, are owned by people. The people who invest their money in businesses would not do so, unless they expected to earn a return on their investments. The return on a capital investment can come in many forms. If you buy a bond, you will receive *interest payments*. If you buy a share of stock in a corporation, you may receive *dividends*. If the price of the stock goes up, then you will also receive a *capital gain,* which is the difference between the current price of a share of stock and the price at which the share was purchased. If you buy a piece of real estate, you will receive *rents*.

When we talk about dividends and capital gains, we are talking about a type of income that is not very large for the average household. Relative to labor income, capital ownership tends to be much more highly concentrated in the hands of a few. When we say that Microsoft Corporation's Bill Gates is the richest person in the world, we aren't referring to his salary. We're referring to the value of his holdings of Microsoft stock. The richest people in the world are all owners of very substantial amounts of capital wealth.

So, if you want to be a billionaire, don't expect to get there on the basis of your salary alone. The really rich folks own capital.

THE SUPPLY OF LOANABLE FUNDS

The stock of capital is fixed at any one moment, since it takes time to produce new capital. In other words, the supply of capital cannot change in the very short run. In the very short run, the supply of capital is perfectly inelastic with respect to prices.

However, over time, it's possible to build new buildings and install new machines. Thus, when we discuss the supply of capital, we often focus on the supply of *new* capital, which we call **capital investment**.

Where do businesses get the money for new capital investments? There are a variety of sources, but one of the most important is the **market for loanable funds**. Private households save, and entrust their money to financial institutions, such as banks, insurance companies, and so on. The financial institutions then make loans to businesses.

In every market, there is a price that will achieve equilibrium. In the labor market, the key price was the wage rate. In the market for loanable funds, the key price is the interest rate. Thus, if we were to draw a supply curve for loanable funds, we would graph the relationship between the interest rate and the amount of loanable funds that are put aside by savers.

In Chapter 13, we saw that a change in the wage rate leads to an income effect on labor supply, as well as a substitution effect on labor supply. We have a similar story when we consider the effect of a change in the interest rate on the savings decisions of households. Once again, there is an income effect and a substitution effect. When the interest rate rises, today's consumption becomes relatively more expensive, and future consumption becomes relatively cheaper. The substitution effect of an increase in the interest rate will lead people to substitute away from today's consumption, which means that they will save more.

However, an increase in the interest rate also makes us "richer", in that it is possible to consume more in the present *and* more in the

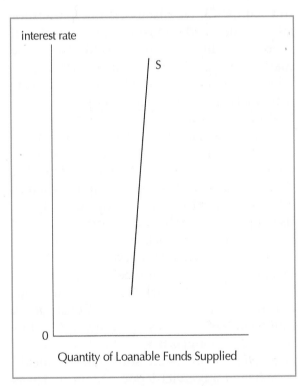

Figure 14.1 The Supply of Loanable Funds

When interest rates change, the substitution effect on savings goes in one direction, while the income effect goes in the opposite direction. Overall, the substitution effect is probably slightly stronger than the income effect. This means that the savings supply curve will slope upward as we move from left to right.

future. The income effect of an increase in the interest rate leads people to save less.

Once again, the income effect and the substitution effect go in opposite directions. The subject is highly controversial among economists, but the consensus seems to be that the income effect and the substitution effect approximately cancel each other out. The elasticity of saving with respect to the interest rate may be positive, but it is probably not much greater than zero. For example, the savings elasticity might take on a value of 0.2 or even 0.4, but it is unlikely that it is higher than that.

In Figure 14.1, we show a fairly inelastic supply curve for savings.

Reality Check: Interim Review Questions

IR14-1. If the interest rate increases, will the substitution effect cause saving to increase or decrease?

IR14-2. If the interest rate decreases, will the income effect cause saving to increase or decrease?

PRESENT DISCOUNTED VALUE AND THE DEMAND FOR LOANABLE FUNDS

As we pointed out in the previous section, it is possible to rent certain types of capital. However, it is also possible to own capital. If you are thinking about buying a piece of capital, you have to be thinking about the entire flow of returns you will receive, over the entire life of the asset. This makes it necessary to compare dollar values that are received at different times. Economists and financial analysts use a concept called *present discounted value* to facilitate comparison of dollar amounts in different time periods.

Present Discounted Value

If you receive one dollar today, it is worth exactly one dollar today. However, if you receive one dollar today, it is worth *more* than one dollar a year from now. This is because you can take the dollar and put it in a savings account, or in a money-market fund, or in government bonds, and it will earn interest.

Therefore, if i is the interest rate:

$1 today = $1(1 + i) in one year.

For example, if the interest rate is 6%, or 0.06, then $1 today has the same value as $1.06 in one year.

If we turn this around, we can see that, if you receive one dollar in a year, it is worth *less* than one dollar today. If we divide both sides of the above equation by $(1 + i)$, we have:

$(1/(1+$i$)) today = $1 in one year.

For example, if the interest rate is 6%, or 0.06, then $1 received in one year will have the same value as $1/(1 + i), or $(1/(1.06)) today, which is about 94.3 cents. If the interest rate is 10% or 0.10, then $1 received in one year will have the same value as $(1/(1.10)) today, which is about 90.9 cents.

Economists use the phrase "present discounted value" to refer to calculations such as those in the preceding equation. The *present discounted value* of a future payment is the maximum amount that a person should be willing to pay *today*, in order to receive that payment in the *future*. For example, the present discounted value of $1, received in one year, is $(1/(1+$i$)).

Now, what if you put $1 in the bank, and leave it in your account for *two* years? At the end of one year, the $1 has grown to $(1 + i). During the second year, you earn interest on the original principal of $1, *and you also earn interest on the accumulated interest.* Thus, at the end of two years, $1 doesn't just grow to $(1 + 2i)$. Instead it grows to $\$1(1+i)^2$, which is $\$(1+2i+i^2)$. For example, if the interest rate is 6%, or 0.06, $1 today will grow in two years to $\$1(1.06)^2$ or $1.1236. If the interest rate is 10%, or 0.1, $1 today will grow in two years to $\$1(1.1)^2$ or $1.21. If you put $1 in your bank account today, and if you then leave the money in the bank without withdrawing any of the interest or principal for three years, the $1 will grow to $\$1(1+i)^3$. In general, if you put $1 in your account today, and leave it in the account for N years, the $1 will grow to $\$1(1+i)^N$.

In all of the formulas shown in the last few paragraphs, we have assumed that the interest rate stays the same over time. If the interest rate were to change from one year to the next, we would have a somewhat more complicated formula. For example, let's say that the interest rate is i_1 in the first year, and i_2 in the second year. In this case, if you put $1 in the bank today and leave it for two years, the $1 will grow to $\$1(1 + i_1)(1 + i_2)$. Other complications include taxes and uncertainty about the future. However, all of these complications are beyond the scope of this book.

The Miracle of Compound Interest and the Rule of 72

Because you earn interest on the accumulated interest, as well as on the principal, the value of an investment can grow with surprising speed. This is the "miracle of compound interest". If you invest $1 today, and let it accumulate at an interest rate of 6%, you will have $2 in a little less than 12 years. In other words, at an interest rate of 6%, you would double your money in about 12 years. At an interest rate of 10%, it only takes a little more than 7 years to double your money. (Not surprisingly, the time necessary to double your money is less when the interest rate is greater.) Table 14.1 gives the amount of time it takes to double your money, for different values of the interest rate.

Notice that, if we multiply the interest rate (in percentage points) by the number of years it takes to double your money, we always get a number close to 72. For example, for an interest rate of 5%, it takes a little more than 14 years to double your money. If we multiply 5 by 14, we get 70. At an interest rate of 8%, it takes about 9 years to double your money, and if we multiply 8 by 9, we get 72. At an interest rate of 12%, it takes a little more than 6 years to double your money, and if we multiply 12 by 6, we get 72. This is *the Rule of 72*: over a fairly wide range of interest rates, the number of years to double your money is approximately equal to 72 divided by the interest rate (where the interest rate is expressed in percentage points).

The General Formula for Present Discounted Value

Earlier in this section, we introduced the concept of present discounted value, and applied it in the case of a payment that is to be received one year in the future. Next, we showed how compounding can lead an investment to grow over a period of many years. Now we put the two parts together. The present discounted value of $1, received in two years, is $\$(1/(1+i)^2)$. More generally, if we use PDV for present discounted value, the PDV of $1, received in N years, is $\$(1/(1+i)^N)$.

Table 14.1 The Rule of 72	
Interest Rate	Approximate Amount of Time to Double Your Money
4%	17 years, 8 months
5%	14 years, 2 months
6%	11 years, 11 months
7%	10 years, 3 months
8%	9 years, 0 months
9%	8 years, 0 months
10%	7 years, 3 months
11%	6 years, 8 months
12%	6 years, 1 month

Real Economics for Real People 14.1:
How Much Do You Really Win, When You Win the Lottery?

In January, 2016, the largest lottery jackpot in history was awarded in the Powerball drawing. The jackpot was announced at $1.586 billion. But was the jackpot really worth that much? The winners were given the option of receiving the money over a period of 30 years, or receiving an immediate payment of substantially less than $1 billion. This indicates that the administrators of the lottery have a clear understanding of the concept of present discounted value.

Most states now have lotteries, and these lotteries typically pay out their prizes over a period of many years. The most common pay-out period is 20 years. Let's say you win the lottery, and the State government says your prize is $20 million. This is a bit misleading. In fact, what they mean is that they will pay you $1 million per year in each of 20 years. That is very different from paying the entire $20 million right now. If the entire $20 million were paid right now, its PDV would be exactly $20 million. (Payments that happen right now do not have to be discounted.) However, when the actual payment is $1 million per year for 20 years, the PDV will be much lower.

Let's calculate the PDV of a stream of 20 payments of $1 million each, where the first one happens right now, the second one happens in one year, the third one happens in two years, and so on, and the final payment happens 19 years from now. The PDV of the first payment is exactly $1 million. Since the first payment occurs now, its PDV is always $1 million, regardless of the interest rate.

The PDV of the second payment is ($1 million/$(1 + i)$). If the rate at which we discount the future is 8 percent, or 0.08, then the PDV of the second payment is ($1 million/1.08), which is about $925,926. The PDV of the third payment is ($1 million/$(1 + i)^2$), because it occurs two years into the future. If the discount rate is 8 percent, or 0.08, then the PDV of the third payment is ($1 million/$(1.08)^2$), which is about $857,339. The PDV of the twentieth and final payment is ($1 million/$(1 + i)^{19}$), because it occurs 19 years into the future. If the discount rate is 8 percent, or 0.08, then the PDV of the final payment is ($1 million/$(1.08)^{19}$), which is about $231,712.

To get the present discounted value of the entire stream of 20 payments, we add together each of the pieces. The PDV of the entire stream is

$$(\$1 \text{ million}) + (\$1 \text{ million}/(1 + i)) + (\$1 \text{ million}/(1 + i)^2) + \ldots + (\$1 \text{ million}/(1 + i)^{19}).$$

If the discount rate is 8%, this PDV is about $10,603,599. If the discount rate is 10%, this PDV is about $9,364,920. On the other hand, if the discount rate is lower, the present discounted value of this stream of payments will be higher. If the discount rate is 5%, the PDV is about $13,085,321. If the discount rate is 2%, the PDV is about $16,678,462.

If you win the lottery, the authorities will say that you have won $20 million. However, you may only have won about half of that in present discounted value. If you win a stream of 20 annual payments of $1 million each, and you offer to sell this to a bank in return for a single up-front payment, they will only be willing to pay a fraction of $20 million.

Many companies are in the business of paying an amount of money up front, in return for the right to a series of future payments. You may have seen the advertisements: "You need your money NOW, and we can help you get it!!!" These companies are not charities; their goal is to make a profit. They make a profit by offering an implicit interest rate that is not as favorable as the rate of return they can make on their investments. If you win the lottery, or a structured settlement in a lawsuit, you may be approached by one of these companies. It's a good idea to treat their offers with a healthy degree of skepticism. Don't make one of these deals unless you know the implied discount rate.

A more general expression of the formula is this: **The PDV of $X, received in N years, is $(X/(1 + i)^N).** Thus, if the discount rate is 8%, or 0.08, the PDV of $1000, to be received in 5 years, is $(1000/(1.08)^5), which is about $680.58.

If the discount rate is relatively high, and/or if the number of years is large, then the PDV of a sum of money to be received in the future can be surprisingly small. For example, if the discount rate is 8%, or 0.08, then the present discounted value of one dollar, to be paid or received in 10 years, is $(1/(1.08)^{10}), which is only about 46.3 cents. If the discount rate is 10%, then the PDV of one dollar that is to be paid or received in 10 years is $(1/(1.1)^{10}), which is only about 38.6 cents. If the discount rate is 10%, then the PDV of one dollar received in 20 years is $(1/(1.1)^{20}), which is about 14.9 cents.

The Rule of 72 can help in making some PDV calculations. We have seen that, if the interest rate is 8%, it takes about nine years to double your money. Therefore, we can say that, if the interest rate is 8%, $1 today is about equal to $2 nine years from now: $1 today = $2 in nine years. If we divide both sides of that equation by 2, we find that $0.50 today = $1 in nine years. In other words, if the interest rate is 8%, the present discounted value of one dollar that is to be paid or received in nine years is about $0.50 = 50 cents.

If we follow the same logic for another nine years, we can see the following: If the discount rate is 8%, $1 today is about equal to $4 in 18 years. In other words, $1 today = $4 in 18 years. If we divide both sides of that equation by 4, we find that $0.25 today = $1 in 18 years. Therefore, if the discount rate is 8%, the present discounted value of one dollar that is to be paid or received in 18 years is about $0.25 = 25 cents.

In *Real Economics for Real People 14.1*, we use the concept of present discounted value to think about the value of payments under the lottery.

Using Present Discounted Value to Make Investment Decisions

We can apply the concept of present discounted value to firms that are deciding whether to make an investment, such as building a new chemical factory. For most investments, the costs come at the beginning of the life of the project, and the revenues come later. In the case of a new chemical factory, it might take a year or more before the factory is ready to produce chemicals. During this time, the firm incurs costs, but does not receive any revenues. Only after the factory is built will the firm be able to earn any revenues from the factory.

If the costs happen at the very beginning of the project, they will not have to be discounted. However, if the revenues don't come until several years later, they will indeed have to be discounted.

It is beneficial for a firm to undertake an investment project if the present discounted value of the revenues is equal to or greater than the present discounted value of the costs. Another way to say this is that it is beneficial for the firm to undertake the investment project if the project has net present discounted value that is equal to or greater than zero. We define the *net present discounted value* as

> **Net PDV =**
> **PDV (Revenues) – PDV (Costs)**

We define today's revenues as R_0. Similarly, we define revenues that are to be received in one year as R_1, and we define revenues to be received in two years as R_2, and so on. We define today's costs as C_0, and we define costs to be incurred in one year as C_1, and so on. Then, the *net present discounted value* is represented by

> **Net PDV = $(R_0 - C_0) + (R_1 - C_1)/(1+i)$**
> **$+ (R_2 - C_2)/((1+i)^2) + (R_3 - C_3)/((1+i)^3)$**
> **$+ \ldots$**

Let's consider a project for which all costs come immediately, and all revenues come in exactly one year. For example, what if the project costs $1000, and the revenues (all of which come one year later) are $1100? The net PDV of this project is

> $(\$1100/(1 + i)) - \$1000.$

Note that the costs are *not* discounted, because they happen today, while the revenues *are* discounted, because they happen in the future.

If the discount rate is 7%, or 0.07, then the net PDV of the above project will be ($1100/1.07) – $1000, which is equal to about $28.04. In a case like this, in which the net PDV is positive, it is in the firm's interest to undertake the project. The value of the firm will be larger if it does the project than if it does not.

If the discount rate is 10%, or 0.1, then the net PDV of the above project will be ($1100/1.1) – $1000, which is equal to exactly zero. In a case like this, the firm doesn't get a big surplus from the project, but it still breaks even, and it would be acceptable for the firm to undertake the project.

However, if the discount rate takes on any value that is greater than 10%, the net PDV of this project will be negative. In this case, the value of the firm will actually be smaller if it undertakes the project. Firms should not proceed with projects that have negative net PDV.

An Example

Let's say that your company is considering four separate projects. The cost of each of the four projects is exactly $1000. In each case, the cost is incurred today. Since the cost happens today, it doesn't have to be discounted, because it is already in today's dollars. Whereas all of the projects have exactly the same cost, they have different revenues. In every case, however, the revenues are to be received one year from now. Since the revenues happen one year from now, they *do* have to be discounted. Table 14.2 shows

Table 14.2 An Example of the Relationship Between the Discount Rate and the Number of Investment Projects Undertaken

Project Number	Cost Today	Revenue in One Year	Net Present Discounted Value (rounded to the nearest dollar) for Interest Rate of:			
			4%	7%	10%	13%
1	$1000	$1150	$106	$75	$45	$18
2	$1000	$1120	$77	$47	$18	–$9
3	$1000	$1090	$48	$19	–$9	–$35
4	$1000	$1060	$19	–$9	–$36	–$62

the net present discounted values for each of the four projects, under different assumptions about the interest rate that should be used to discount the future.

Table 14.2 shows that, if the interest rate used to discount the future is only four percent, each of the four projects has positive net present discounted value. Consequently, at an interest rate of four percent, all four projects will be undertaken. If the interest rate used to discount the future is seven percent, three of the projects still have positive net present discounted value, but one of them now has negative net PDV. Therefore, at a discount rate of seven percent, only three of the projects will be undertaken. When the discount rate rises to 10 percent, only two projects will be undertaken. Finally, at a discount rate of 13 percent, only one of the projects will be undertaken.

These results are graphed in Figure 14.2. In this figure, the interest rate used to discount the future is on the vertical axis, and the number of projects undertaken is on the horizontal axis. The figure displays an inverse relationship between the interest rate and the number of projects undertaken. This is a graph of the demand for loanable funds. Like most demand curves, it slopes downward as we go from left to right.

This example is an extremely simple one. It has not dealt with taxes, and it does not include any uncertainty. Moreover, it is clearly unrealistic to assume that the projects last for exactly one year. Some of you may learn about more complicated situations when you take courses in finance, or financial economics. Nevertheless, even a very simple example like this one can illustrate some important ideas. First, all else equal, more projects will be undertaken if the interest rate used to discount the future is lower.

Second, all else equal, a project is more likely to be undertaken if its revenues come sooner, rather than later. If the revenues arrive in one year, they will only be discounted once.

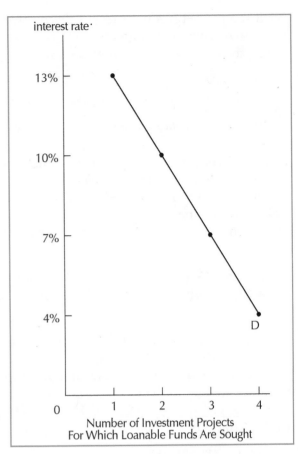

Figure 14.2 The Demand for Loanable Funds

When the interest rate used to discount the future is four percent, four projects will be undertaken by the firm. When the interest rate rises to seven percent, only three projects will be undertaken. At a discount rate of 10 percent, two projects are undertaken. At a discount rate of 13 percent, only one project is approved. The result is a downward-sloping demand curve for loanable funds.

If they arrive in ten years, they must be discounted ten times. This is why construction contracts often have clauses that provide bonuses for early completion of the project, and penalties for delays. Time is money.

Reality Check:
Interim Review Questions

IR14-3. What is the present discounted value of $100, to be paid or received one year from now, if the discount rate is 5%? What if the discount rate is 10%? What if it is 20%?

IR14-4. What is the present discounted value of $100, to be received *ten* years from now, if the discount rate is 5%? What if the discount rate is 10%? What if it is 20%?

IR14-5. You are given the opportunity to invest $100 in a capital investment project. You are certain that the revenues, to be received in one year, are $110. If the interest rate used to discount the future is 5%, should the project be undertaken? Would your answer change if the revenues of $110 were to be received in three years?

CAPITAL-MARKET EQUILIBRIUM

Figure 14.1 showed us a supply curve for loanable funds. The curve is upward sloping (although fairly steep). And now we have seen Figure 14.2, which has a downward-sloping demand curve for loanable funds.

By now, you can probably guess what we are going to do next. We are going to put the supply curve together with the demand curve to find equilibrium in the market for loanable funds. This is shown in Figure 14.3. In this figure, the interaction of supply and demand determines the equilibrium interest rate. The equilibrium interest rate is i^*, and the equilibrium quantity of loans is I^*.

Of course, this description of equilibrium in the credit markets has been greatly simplified, in an effort to concentrate on the basics. In fact, at any one time, there will be a whole family of equilibrium interest rates, depending on the characteristics of the loans. All else equal, if there is uncertainty about whether the loan will be repaid on time, the equilibrium interest rate will have to be higher to compensate the leader for the risk. Taxes on interest income can also have important effects on credit-market equilibrium. Moreover, equilibrium interest rates are affected by expectations of future inflation. And finally, interest rates are affected by the policies of the U.S. Treasury Department and the Federal Reserve.

All of these influences on interest rates are interesting and important, but the details are

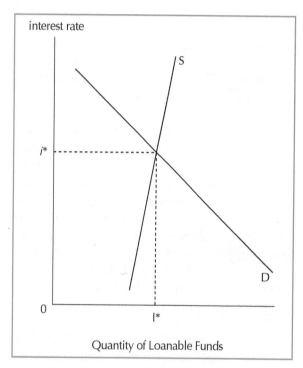

Figure 14.3 Equilibrium in the Market for Loanable Funds

As in any market, the equilibrium price and quantity are determined by the intersection of the supply curve and the demand curve. In the case of the market for loanable funds, the supply curve, S, and the demand curve, D, determine the equilibrium quantity of investment, I^*, and the equilibrium interest rate, i^*.

beyond the scope of this book. You can learn more about these topics if you take courses in macroeconomics, finance, and money and banking.

Usury Laws

Most State governments have *usury laws*, which place a ceiling on the interest rates that can be charged. The effects of these laws are similar to the effects of the other price ceilings that we studied in Chapter 4. If the usury ceiling is above the equilibrium interest rate, then the usury law will not have any effect. For example, if the ceiling is at an interest rate of 20% and the equilibrium interest rate is 7%, then the equilibrium is perfectly legal. Therefore, the usury law will not have any effect. However, if the usury ceiling is below the equilibrium interest rate, the equilibrium rate will be illegal. For example, if the usury ceiling is at an interest rate of 20% and the equilibrium interest rate is 25%, then the equilibrium is against the law. If the law is enforced, it will not be possible for the market to find an equilibrium.

Figure 14.4 shows what will happen if the usury law is enforced at a rate below the equilibrium rate. With the interest-rate ceiling below the equilibrium interest rate, the quantity of loanable funds demanded will be greater than it had been at the equilibrium interest rate, and the quantity of loanable funds supplied will be less. As a result, there will be a shortage of credit: The quantity of loanable funds demanded will be greater than the quantity supplied.

When there is a shortage of credit, there will not be enough funds to provide loans for all of the people or firms that want to borrow money at the prevailing interest rate. In ordinary times, with no usury ceiling, the market does an excellent job of allocating credit. However, the usury ceiling weakens the market's ability to serve as a rationing device. The usury law will make it necessary for other devices to be used to ration credit. Some financial institutions may simply issue loans on a first-come, first-served basis, until their funds run out. Others may allocate loans on the basis of racial prejudices, or on the basis of personal connections, or according to any of a number of other schemes.

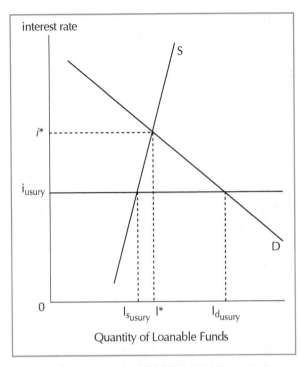

Figure 14.4 The Effects of a Usury Ceiling

The equilibrium interest rate is i^*, and the equilibrium quantity of investment is I^*. An interest-rate ceiling is enforced at i_{usury}. As a result, the quantity of loanable funds demanded increases to $I_{d_{usury}}$, and the quantity of loanable funds supplied decreases to $I_{s_{usury}}$. Therefore, there is a shortage of credit. The amount of the shortage is ($I_{d_{usury}} - I_{s_{usury}}$). Only $I_{s_{usury}}$ loans will be made, because the suppliers of loanable funds cannot be forced off their supply curve.

Fortunately, usury ceilings in the United States are often set at fairly high levels, such as 18 percent or 25 percent. These are high enough that equilibrium interest rates for most loans are usually well below the usury ceilings. As a result, usury laws have not caused any major credit shortages since the late 1970s and early 1980s, during a time of high inflation.

A lender won't want to lend money at 6% interest if the inflation rate is 10%, because the interest payments won't even keep up with the rising prices. Thus if the inflation rate is expected to be 10%, equilibrium interest rates will be pushed above 10%. The higher the inflation rate, the higher the equilibrium interest rates will be. In the late 1970s and early 1980s, double-digit inflation meant that equilibrium interest rates rose to 15%, 20%, or even more.

However, usury laws are often specified in nominal terms. In other words, the usury ceiling is defined as a particular number of percentage points, and there is no adjustment for inflation. Thus in some cases in the late 1970s and early 1980s, equilibrium interest rates did run into the usury limits, even though the real, inflation-adjusted interest rates were not unusually high. This problem can be avoided by allowing the usury ceiling to float up or down in response to economic conditions, as is done in some states.

Although usury laws can lead to credit shortages, it does not necessarily follow that all usury laws are a bad public-policy idea. "Loan sharks" operate in the shadows of the credit markets, often charging astronomical interest rates. These lenders, who are often involved with organized crime, take advantage of vulnerable borrowers. Also, large fees are sometimes hidden in the fine print of loan contracts, and these fees can effectively translate into extremely high interest rates.

Economists don't want usury ceilings to be so low that they interfere with the normal workings of the legitimate credit markets, but there is definitely a place for laws to protect consumers from predatory lending practices.

The Stock Market

When economists use the word "investment", they are often referring to physical investments, such as factory buildings, warehouses, computers, machinery, and the like. However, in popular usage, "investment" often refers to *financial investment*, such as a share of stock, or a bond, or a savings account. Financial investments are issued by banks, corporations, and other institutions.

If you own one of these financial instruments, it usually gives you a claim on some of the income that is produced by the real assets that are owned by the issuing company. For example, those who invest in bonds or savings accounts will usually receive interest payments. Those who invest in stocks will often receive dividends.

In this section, we will discuss the market for stocks, which are a financial investment issued by corporations. The owner of a share of stock is a part owner of the corporation that issued the stock. For example, if Sanjay owns one share of stock in XYZ Corporation, and if there are one million shares of stock in XYZ Corporation, then Sanjay owns one-millionth of the company.

People would not buy stocks unless they thought they could get something of value for their purchase. Some people buy stocks because they expect to receive dividends from the corporation issuing the stock. However, because of tax considerations, some corporations do not pay dividends. The other reason to buy a share of stock is because of the hope that the price of the stock will go up. When there is an increase in a share price, we say that the owner of the share of stock has experienced a capital gain. Let's say that Sanjay buys a share of XYZ Corporation for $10. A year later, if the price of XYZ stock has increased to $20 per share, Sanjay could sell his share and make a capital gain of $(20 − 10) = $10.

A Good Investment for the Long Haul

Regardless of whether the return comes in the form of dividends, or capital gains, or both, stocks can be a very attractive investment. Of course, buying a stock is not a sure thing. Stock prices can go down, just as they go up. On a few occasions, the stock market has suffered a "crash", in which the market loses a large portion of its value in a relatively short period of time. (The most famous of these crashes occurred in October 1929, and in October 1987. The market recovered quickly from the Crash of '87, but the Crash of '29 was the beginning of several years of bad performance by stocks. The year 2008 was also a very bad one for stock prices.) However, over the years, stocks have been a very good investment on average. Over the long haul, stocks usually provide a higher rate of return than many other investments.

At any one moment, investing in the stock market can be risky. If you had bought stock just before the 1987 Crash, and sold soon thereafter, you might have lost a bundle. However, as we have emphasized, stocks have tended to make a very good investment for the long haul. This is why many financial advisers urge their clients not to try to "time the market". Unless you are very comfortable with risk, it would probably be best to buy stocks for the long haul. Buy stocks with the expectation of holding onto them for years, rather than for weeks. If you try to time the market by making clever purchases and sales at just the right instant, you run the risk of losing your shirt.

The Importance of Diversification

In the preceding paragraph, we suggested that stocks can be a very good investment, *on average*. That is not the same as saying that every individual stock is a good investment. Some stocks do very well, while others perform poorly. The problem is that it is not always easy to tell which stocks are the good ones. Even very savvy investors can sometimes make a mistake, and choose a stock that loses a lot of value.

Thus, if you only own stock in one company, you might get lucky and pick a stock that is a big winner. But the danger of "putting all your eggs in one basket" is that you might not be so lucky. If you only own stock in one company, and if that particular stock performs poorly, you could suffer a large loss. For example, some employees of Enron Corporation had their entire life savings in Enron stock.

When the company collapsed in 2001, these people lost everything. This is why many financial advisers suggest that their clients hold a *diversified portfolio* of stocks. If your stock portfolio is diversified, you own a little bit of a large number of stocks. This is a way of spreading your risk.

One way to diversify is to invest in *mutual funds*. A mutual fund owns shares in many different companies. Thus, if you buy a share of a mutual fund, you are effectively buying a little bit of ownership in dozens, or even hundreds, of companies.

Based on the insights of the last few paragraphs, many financial advisers suggest that investors acquire a diversified portfolio, and that they stick with it for the long haul.

Stock Averages

If you own a diversified portfolio, you could check regularly on the price of each of the companies you own, or you could check on the performance of your mutual funds. However, people often want to get a sense of how the overall market is doing. Stock averages help people to assess the overall performance of the stock market.

The most famous stock average is the Dow Jones Industrial Average (known by its initials, DJIA, or just as "The Dow"). When the Dow was established in 1896, it included 12 companies. The list was expanded to 20 companies in 1916, and to 30 in 1928. It has had 30 companies ever since, although the exact companies have changed over time. General Electric is the only company that has been part of the Dow since the beginning. In fact, many of the companies that are part of the Dow today did not even exist when the Dow first started. The latest change in the composition of the Dow occurred in 2015. Table 14.3 shows the companies that are in the DJIA today, as well as the companies that were in the DJIA in 1928, when it was first expanded to 30 companies. Table 14.3 gives an indication of some of the

Table 14.3 Companies in the Dow Jones Industrial Average, 1928 and 2015

October 1, 1928–January 8, 1929	March 18, 2015–present
Allied Chemical	3M
American Can	American Express
American Smelting	Apple
American Sugar	Boeing
American Tobacco	Caterpillar
Atlantic Refining	Chevron
Bethlehem Steel	Cisco Systems
Chrysler	Coca Cola
General Electric	DuPont
General Motors	Exxon Mobil
General Railway Signal	General Electric
Goodrich	Goldman Sachs
International Harvester	Home Depot
International Nickel	Intel
Mack Truck	IBM
Nash Motors	Johnson & Johnson
North American	JP Morgan Chase
Paramount Publix	McDonald's
Postum	Merck
Radio Corporation of America	Microsoft
Sears Roebuck	Nike
Standard Oil of New Jersey	Pfizer
Texas Company	Procter & Gamble
Texas Gulf Sulphur	Travelers
Union Carbide	United Health Group
U.S. Steel	United Technologies
Victor Talking Machine	Verizon Communication
Westinghouse Electric	Visa
Woolworth	Walmart Stores
Wright Aeronautical	Walt Disney

structural changes that have taken place in the American economy in the last 85 years. Perhaps the biggest change is that the 1928 index did not have any computer companies, for the simple reason that computers did not exist in 1928. The 2015 index includes Cisco Systems, Intel, IBM, and Microsoft, all of which are involved with computer hardware and software.

Why Do Stock Prices Bounce Around So Much?

If you have ever listened to financial reports on television or radio, you know that stock prices can change from minute to minute, and even from second to second. Stock prices change with unusual frequency. There are several reasons for this.

First, stock markets are very competitive. There are lots of buyers and lots of sellers. It is very difficult to fix prices.

Second, stocks are traded on exchanges that are linked electronically with buyers and sellers. Thus, the players in the market have instant access to information about what is happening. Orders to buy or sell can be carried out extremely rapidly. It's almost as if the stock market can change at the speed of light.

There is one other reason why stock prices jump around quickly, and we can understand it with the use of a supply-demand diagram. At any moment, each company has a fixed number of shares of stock. Companies do issue new shares occasionally, but this doesn't happen on a regular basis. In fact, when a company does issue new stock, the resulting increase in supply will tend to drive share prices down. This is frowned upon by the owners of the shares of stock that existed previously, since they suffer capital losses.

Thus, at any one time, the supply for the stock of a particular company is perfectly inelastic. This is shown in Figure 14.5, where the supply curve for shares of XYZ Corporation stock is shown as a vertical line.

The demand for a company's shares of stock comes from investors' expectations of the financial returns that will be received in the future. For any investor, all else equal, a particular stock will be more attractive if it is selling at a low price. Also, some investors may be more optimistic than others. For both of these reasons, the demand curve for shares of XYZ Corporation, D_{old}, is downward sloping, as in Figure 14.5.

At a given moment, the equilibrium price of a stock will be determined by the intersection of the supply curve and the demand curve. In the case shown in Figure 14.5, this would be at a price of $10 per share. The equilibrium quantity is determined by the supply curve alone, since the supply of shares is perfectly inelastic.

In this book, we have studied lots of shifts in demand curves. In the usual case, in which the supply curve is upward-sloping, a shift in the demand curve will lead to *both* a change in the equilibrium price and a change in the equilibrium quantity. If the supply curve slopes upward, then it must be possible for the equilibrium quantity to change. In a sense, the quantity response provides a "cushion" to the price response. When there is a quantity response, the price response is not as large as

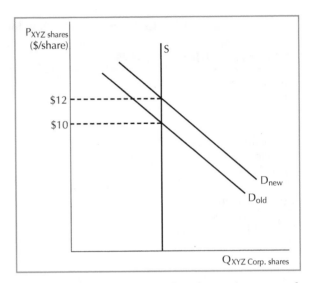

Figure 14.5   The Effects of a Change in Demand for a Stock When the Supply Curve Is Perfectly Inelastic

The vertical supply curve indicates that the supply of the stock is perfectly inelastic. Thus the equilibrium quantity is determined by the supply curve alone. When the demand curve shifts to the right, from D_{old} to D_{new}, the only effect is an increase in the equilibrium price.

it would have to be, if there were no quantity response.

However, in the case we are studying here, the supply curve of stock is perfectly inelastic. It isn't possible to have a quantity response. Thus there is nothing to cushion the change in price. When there is a shift in the demand curve for a stock, the only thing that can change is the equilibrium price. If the demand curve were to shift from D_{old} to D_{new}, the entire effect of the demand shift has to be absorbed by a change in price. In the case shown in Figure 14.5, a rightward shift in the demand curve for XYZ Corporation stock leads to an increase in the price of XYZ shares. The price goes up from $10 to $12. If the supply curve had been upward sloping, and if the exact same demand shift had occurred, the increase in price would not have been so large.

Stock-Market Bubbles

The stock market performed exceptionally well in the 1990s. There are many ways to measure the performance of the stock market, but the best-known is to look at changes in the Dow Jones Industrial Average. Until February 1995, the DJIA had never been above 4000. By November of that year, it was over 5000. The DJIA reached 6000 in October 1996, 8000 in July 1997, and 10,000 in March 1999. Early in the year 2000, the DJIA soared above 11,700.

And then the market came crashing down. By the fall of 2002, the DJIA fell briefly below 7300. Some other stock market indexes did even worse. What happened? Of course, it is possible that something fundamental happened to the economy, so that the rapid rise and rapid fall of the stock market would make perfect sense. However, the changes in the stock market (in each direction) were *very* large, and it appears that something else was going on.

Recall that the demand for a share of stock is based on *expectations* about the future returns. As the stock market began to surge forward in the early and middle 1990s, some people began to *expect* that the price increases would continue. If you come to expect that prices will be going up in the future, then it makes more sense to buy now. (If you buy now, and if the price goes up, then you can sell later and make a profit.) In other words, a belief in higher prices *in the future* will lead to an increase in demand *today*.

When people act on the expectation of increasing prices, they will put more money into the stock market. This increase in the demand for stocks will push stock prices upward. As a result, the expectation of increasing prices will be reinforced. The cycle becomes self-sustaining: People think stock prices are going up, so they put more money into stocks, so the prices go up, so they think prices will continue to go up, so they put even more money into stocks, and so on.

But the upward cycle cannot continue forever. Eventually, prices will get further and further out of line. At some point, an increasing number of investors will come to believe that the high prices don't fit with realistic projections of company profits. Those investors will reduce their demand for stocks, and this will put downward pressure on stock prices. And then the self-fulfilling cycle can happen again, except this time it goes in reverse. People think stock prices are going down, so they put less money into stocks, so the prices go down, so they think prices will continue to go down, so they put even less money into stocks, and so on.

When stock prices rise because of a frenzy of expectations of rising prices, and then fall because of expectations of falling prices, we say that the stock market is experiencing a *speculative bubble*. Unfortunately, history has many examples of speculative bubbles. They can be especially damaging for some investors. Some investors wait until late in the surge before they buy stocks. Then, after the bubble begins to burst, they panic and sell their stocks. That's a formula for losing money.

When the time came for the stock-market bubble of the 1990s to burst, investors lost trillions of dollars of value. This probably contributed to the recession of 2001. If there is any good news about the bubble, it is that it could have been worse. The Japanese stock market experienced an even larger bubble in the 1980s. The losses from the bursting of the Japanese bubble were relatively larger than those associated with the bursting of the bubble in U.S. stock markets. The woes of the stock market in Japan contributed to a very long period of economic stagnation in Japan.

ECONOMICS AND YOU: THE DARK SIDE OF FINANCE

Financial markets, like any kind of market, work best when both buyers and sellers have accurate information about what is being bought and sold. Unfortunately, the history of financial markets suggests that they can often be manipulated. This can sometimes make a lot of money for the manipulator, but the outcomes can be very bad for society.

In an earlier chapter, we discussed the bubble in the housing market in the first decade of the 21st century. The housing bubble was pumped up by "mortgage-backed securities." Each of these securities consisted of a small part of each of a large number of home mortgages. By itself, that's not a bad idea. However, lots of mortgages were being made for homebuyers with bad credit. The banks that made these mortgage loans knew that they could immediately sell them to hungry investors in the market for mortgage-backed securities. Thus in many cases, the mortgage-backed securities turned out to be toxic, even though the investors who bought the securities believed they were buying safe assets.

This is a classic case of "asymmetric information": The sellers of mortgage-backed securities knew that they were selling garbage, but the buyers did not. Eventually, when enough bad loans had been made, the housing bubble burst. Home prices fell sharply, many homebuyers defaulted on their mortgage loans, and many of the mortgage-backed securities were revealed to be worthless.

Financial institutions that were deeply involved with mortgage-backed securities found themselves in big trouble. One such institution was the Wall-Street firm, Lehman Brothers. The collapse of Lehman Brothers on September 15, 2008, triggered a major financial crisis, and led to the deepest downturn of the American economy since the Great Depression of the 1930s.

One reason why these financial institutions engaged in such practices is that they believed themselves to be "too big to fail". In other words, they believed (with some justification) that the government would not allow them to fail, because if they failed, there would be a risk that the entire financial system would collapse. Indeed, the Treasury Department and the Federal Reserve had to bail out some financial institutions, and they had to pump huge amounts of money into the system to keep it afloat. This has led to the argument that the biggest banks should be broken up into smaller pieces.

Congress passed a law in 2010 that did tighten up some regulations, although it is not clear that these rules will be strong enough to head off another crisis. The banking sector is even more concentrated today than it was before the crisis. However, the banks did have to pay financial penalties as a result of their role in the mortgage bubble. The fines totaled about $110 billion.

Unfortunately, the mess in the market for mortgage-backed securities is not the only example of a serious malfunctions in the financial markets. Another example is the case of Bernie Madoff, who ran what is believed to be the biggest Ponzi scheme in history. A Ponzi scheme, named after an early-20th-century con artist named Charles Ponzi, uses money from new investors to pay high returns to earlier investors. Madoff was able to keep the scheme going for years, through a system of falsifying records. Lax oversight by regulators at the Securities and Exchange Commission also helped Madoff to keep going. He was finally arrested, and sentenced in 2009 to 150 years in prison. The total losses associated with Madoff's scheme may exceed $10 billion.

"Insider trading" is another problem that arises periodically in the financial markets. If someone can get a piece of information before other investors, the one with the inside information may be able to reap big profits. One important recent case involved a hedge-fund manager named Raj Rajaratnam, who was convicted in 2011 on 14 counts of conspiracy and securities fraud. He is currently serving an 11-year prison sentence.

The problems described here are certainly not the only problems in the financial-services sector. On the other hand, it's important not to give the impression that all bankers are corrupt. Many, many of the people who work in financial services are completely honest and law-abiding. But the list of problems is enough to suggest that the potential for fraud is unusually large in the financial-services sector, and that a strong regulatory system is necessary.

Chapter Summary

1. In the short run, the supply of capital is fixed. Over time, however, the supply of capital can increase as a result of new capital investment. Many capital investments are financed in the market for loanable funds.

2. The substitution effect of an interest rate increase leads to a higher amount of saving. The income effect of an interest rate increase leads to a lower amount of saving. Overall, the income effect and the substitution effect probably come close to canceling each other out, so that the supply of loanable funds is probably fairly inelastic with respect to the interest rate.

3. The present discounted value of a future payment is the maximum amount that a person should be willing to pay today, for the privilege of receiving that payment in the future. In particular, if the interest rate used to discount the future is i, a payment of \$X, to be made N years in the future, will have present discounted value of $\$X/(1+i)^N$.

4. The Rule of 72 states that, over a fairly wide range of interest rates, the number of years to double your money is approximately equal to 72 divided by the interest rate, where the interest rate is expressed in percentage points.

5. The net present discounted value of a capital-investment project is equal to the present discounted value of the revenues from the project, minus the present discounted value of the costs of the project. If the net present discounted value of a project is zero or positive, it is in the firm's interest to undertake the project. However, if the net present discounted value of a project is negative, the firm should not undertake the project.

6. Typically, the costs of an investment project will occur early in the life of the project, whereas the revenues will not occur until later. As a result, a given project is more likely to be approved if the interest rate used to discount the future is lower. On this basis, we can derive a downward-sloping demand curve for loanable funds. Also, a project is more likely to be approved if the revenues come earlier rather than later.

7. Equilibrium in the market for loanable funds (that is, equilibrium in the credit market) is determined by the intersection of the supply curve (which depends on the behavior of savers) and the demand curve (which depends on the decisions of business firms).

8. A usury law is an interest-rate ceiling. If the usury ceiling is above the equilibrium interest rate, the law will not have any effect. However, if the usury ceiling is below the equilibrium interest rate, there will be a shortage of credit.

9. Asset markets, such as the stock market, can sometimes be plagued by speculative bubbles. If stock prices go up (for any reason), some investors may come to believe that prices will continue to rise. The expectation of higher prices in the future leads to an increase in demand today. This leads to further price increases. As a result, the expectations of higher prices can be self-reinforcing for a while. Eventually, however, prices will become so high that the speculative bubble is burst. If prices start to fall, it is possible that investors may come to believe that prices will continue to fall. If so, they will reduce their demand, which will lead to further price decreases. Unfortunately, history is replete with speculative bubbles; the most recent major bubble in the stock market was in the late 1990s and early 2000s.

Key Terms

Interest Payments

Dividends

Capital Gains

Rents

Capital Investment

Market for Loanable Funds

Present Discounted Value

The Rule of 72

Net Present Discounted Value

Usury Law

Financial Investment

Diversified Portfolio

Mutual Funds

Speculative Bubble

Questions and Problems

QP14-1. Ms. Zylks will receive a series of payments from the estate of her great aunt. Each of the three installments is to be $10,000. The first arrives today, the second arrives one year from now, and the third arrives two years from now. The interest rate used to discount the future is 8%. Calculate the present discounted value of this stream of cash flows.

QP14-2. XYZ Corporation is considering whether to undertake a new capital investment project. Analysts at XYZ have determined that the project will cost $300 million, and that it will generate revenues of $330 million, exactly one year after the costs are incurred. What is the present discounted value of the project if a discount rate of 8% is used? What about 10%? 12%? Under what conditions should XYZ undertake the project?

QP14-3. The supply curve for cement-mixer trucks is given by $Q_s = 0.1P$. The demand curve is given by $Q_d = 100 - 0.1P$. What are the equilibrium price and quantity of cement-mixer trucks?

QP14-4. The equilibrium interest rate is 6%. A usury ceiling is established at 20%. What effect, if any, will this usury law have on the market? How would your answer change if the usury ceiling were set at 5%?

QP14-5. The interest rate is 6%. At this rate, approximately how many years will it take to double one's money? How would your answer change if the interest rate were 10%?

Chapter 15

Income Distribution and Poverty

ECONOMICS AND YOU: WILL THE POOR ALWAYS BE WITH US?

At the very beginning of this book, we saw that any economic system must make three fundamental decisions. The economy must decide *what* gets produced, *how* it gets produced, and *for whom* it gets produced. Since then, we have concentrated mostly on "what" and "how", and we've seen that a private-market economy can deliver goods and services in a very efficient manner, especially if the business firms are not monopolies.

But what about the "for-whom" decision? Who gets the goods? Unfortunately, there's no guarantee that a private-market economy will lead to an income distribution that people consider fair or desirable. The market economy could generate a highly unequal distribution of income. A relatively small number of people might live in great luxury, while many people subsist in relative poverty. This might be an *efficient* economy, but many people would say that it isn't a *good* one. In fact, most countries use government policies in an effort to reduce poverty and inequality.

In this chapter, we take a look at the distribution of income and the problem of poverty. Why talk about income distribution now? The reason is that labor and capital are the main sources of income for most people, and we have just finished studying labor markets and capital markets. Thus, it is only now that we have the tools to study income distribution in a serious way.

Regardless of whether we study income distribution at the beginning or end of the book, it is a very important topic. Throughout most of human history, most people have struggled to survive. However, as a result of the tremendous economic growth of the last century, it is now possible to imagine a world without poverty. In this chapter, we will take a look at some of the policies that have been used in the "war on poverty", in an attempt to get a clearer understanding of the way toward a poverty-free world.

SOME FACTS ABOUT THE DISTRIBUTION OF INCOME

Table 15.1 describes the income distribution in the United States. For each year shown, the population is divided into five groups, each of which has 20 percent of the households.

(These 20-percent groups are called "quintiles".) More than 51 percent of all income was received by the highest-income group in 2014. The lowest-income group also had 20 percent of the households (just like the top group), but these poorer households received only a little more than three percent of all income.

The Disequalization of the Late Twentieth Century

Table 15.1 shows that the distribution of income has become *more unequal* since the mid–1970s. In 1975, the lowest-income 80 percent of the population received 56.4 percent of all income. By 2014, this group's share had shrunk to 48.8 percent of income. Over the same period, the share of the top 20 percent of the population went up from 43.6 percent of all income to 51.2 percent. In other words, from 1975 to 2014, the American economy changed in such a way that 7.6 percent of all income got shifted away from the bottom 80 percent of the population to the top quintile.

This may not seem like a big change. However, 7.6 percent of the total income of all households amounts to more than $1 trillion

every year. If the distribution of income had remained the same after 1975, the top 20 percent would have received more than $1 trillion *less* in 2014, and the bottom 80 percent would have received more than $1 trillion per year *more*. That's a lot of money.

Table 15.1 provides a good starting point for understanding the changes over time in the income distribution in the United States. Figure 15.1 shows some of the same trends, but it provides a much longer historical perspective. Figure 15.1 shows the shares of income received by each quintile of families, going all the way back to 1929. Figure 15.1 has one line for each of the five quintiles. The top line shows the percentage of income received by the highest-income quintile. The bottom line shows the percentage of income received by the quintile with the lowest incomes.

The right side of Figure 15.1 shows the large increase in inequality that has occurred in the United States since the 1970s. The share of income received by the top 20 percent of families has increased from just more than 40 percent to about 49 percent. The income shares of the four lower quintiles have all decreased. (Note that the data in Figure 15.1

Table 15.1 Shares of Aggregate Income Received by Each 20 Percent of Households in the United States, for Selected Years from 1967 to 2014

| | Percent of Aggregate Income Received by: | | | | |
Year	Lowest 20 Percent	2nd-Lowest 20 Percent	Middle 20 Percent	2nd-Highest 20 Percent	Highest 20 Percent
1967	4.0	10.8	17.3	24.2	43.6
1970	4.1	10.8	17.4	24.5	43.3
1975	4.3	10.4	17.0	24.7	43.6
1980	4.2	10.2	16.8	24.7	44.1
1985	3.9	9.8	16.2	24.4	45.6
1990	3.8	9.6	15.9	24.0	46.6
1995	3.7	9.1	15.2	23.3	48.7
2000	3.6	8.9	14.8	23.0	49.8
2005	3.4	8.6	14.6	23.0	50.4
2010	3.3	8.5	14.6	23.4	50.3
2014	3.1	8.2	14.3	23.2	51.2

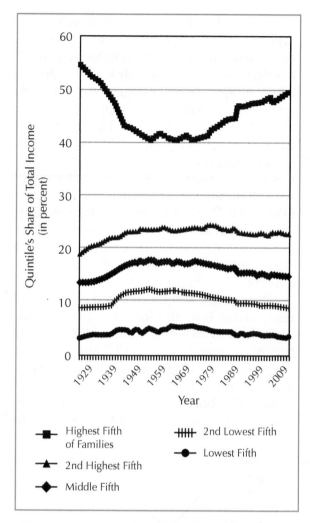

Figure 15.1   Quintile Shares for Family Income in the United States, 1929–2014

Chart legend:
- Highest Fifth of Families
- 2nd Highest Fifth
- Middle Fifth
- 2nd Lowest Fifth
- Lowest Fifth

Y-axis: Quintile's Share of Total Income (in percent)
X-axis: Year

The Equalization of the Early Twentieth Century

The disequalization of the 1970s, 1980s, and 1990s is a very important change in the U.S. distribution of income. However, Figure 15.1 shows that the recent disequalization is not the only change. In fact, an equally dramatic change in the U.S. distribution of income came much earlier. Figure 15.1 shows that the distribution of income became much more equal from 1929 to about 1953.

In 1929, the highest-income quintile of families in the United States received more than 54 percent of the income. By 1953, the top quintile's share had fallen to less than 41 percent. That is an enormous change. In the space of just a quarter century, the top quintile's share decreased by more than 13 percentage points. If we translate into today's economy, that would be equivalent to moving well over one and one-half *trillion* dollars per year from the top quintile to the bottom four quintiles.

Each of the bottom four quintiles gained relatively during the 1930s and 1940s. From 1929 to 1953, the share of the poorest quintile of families went up from 3.5 percent of income to 4.7 percent. The share of the second-lowest quintile went up from 9 percent to 12.5 percent. The middle quintile increased its share from 13.8 percent to 18 percent. The second-highest quintile increased its share from 19.3 percent to 23.9 percent.

Of course, the economy is very complex, and many factors contributed to this huge equalization. However, economists believe that the educational system played a very important role in causing the equalization.

The Effects of Increased Education

In 1910, only about 11 percent of students who were old enough to graduate from high school were actually graduating from high school. Many did not even get to high school at all,

are for *families*, which only include related people who are living together. Table 15.1 has data for *households*, which include families as well as people who live alone or with unrelated roommates. Thus, the numbers in Figure 15.1 are slightly different from the numbers in Table 15.1. However, the overall picture is very similar. Most discussions of the income distribution are based on data for households. The reason for using families in Figure 15.1 is that data for families go further back in time.)

but dropped out after the fourth or sixth or eighth grade. However, in the early part of the twentieth century, state legislatures around the United States passed laws that helped to increase the rate of high-school graduation.

Many states passed compulsory-attendance laws, requiring that students had to stay in school until a certain age, such as 15 or 16. The states also required local school districts to provide for high-school education. If a local district did not have a high school of its own, it was required to pay to send students to the nearest district with a high school. (This process was greatly assisted by the invention of the school bus, which made it possible to transport children to high school from remote rural areas.) High schools also updated their curricula to adjust to the needs of an expanded population.

As a result of these and other changes, the rate of high-school graduation had increased to 60 percent by 1940. By 1960, the high-school graduation rate had increased to about 80 percent, which is about where it still stands today.

Today, almost everyone gets a high-school diploma, and a large fraction of the population goes on to college. Thus in today's world, it would be natural to think of "high-skill labor" as applying to college-educated workers, and "low-skill labor" as applying to those without a college education. However, as we have seen, a century ago, those with a high-school education were elite. Thus for the purposes of this analysis of the early 20th century, we will divide the labor force into two parts. One part is "high-skill labor", which includes those with at least a high-school diploma. The other part of the labor force is "low-skill labor", which includes those who do not have a high-school diploma.

We can use supply-demand diagrams to understand how the increase in education could lead to an equalization of the distribution of income. In Figure 15.2, we draw two supply-demand diagrams side-by-side. On the left side of the figure, we have a market for "low-skill labor" (i.e., those without a high-school diploma). On the right side is the mar-

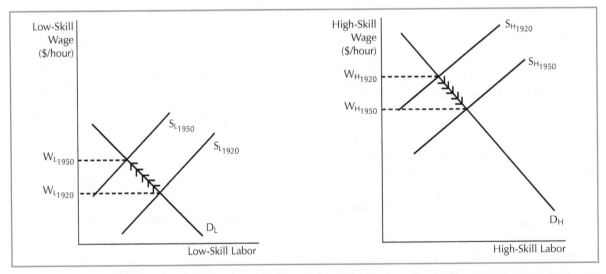

Figure 15.2   The Effects of the Increase in Education on Wages for Low-Skill and High-Skill Workers

As a result of the increase in educational opportunities in the United States in the early 20th century, there was a decrease in the supply of low-skilled workers, as well as an increase in the supply of high-skilled workers. As a result, the equilibrium wage rate for low-skilled workers rose relative to the equilibrium wage rate for high-skilled workers. This contributed to a major equalization of the income distribution.

ket for "high-skill labor" (i.e., those with a high-school diploma or more).

The initial situation in Figure 15.2 represents the labor markets in 1920. On the left side of the diagram, the demand curve for low-skill labor is D_L. The supply curve of low-skill labor in 1920 is S_{L1920}. From the intersection of the curves D_L and S_{L1920}, we see that the equilibrium wage rate for low-skill workers in 1920 was W_{L1920}.

Between 1920 and 1950, as a result of the large increase in the number of workers with a high-school education, the supply curve for low-skill workers shifted to the left, to S_{L1950}. By 1950, fewer people were competing for low-skill jobs. As a result, the equilibrium wage rate for low-skill workers rose to W_{L1950}.

The right side of Figure 15.2 represents the market for high-skill labor, by which we mean the labor of those who have at least a high-school education. The demand curve for high-skill labor is D_H. (The demand curve for high-skill labor, D_H, is farther to the right than the demand curve for low-skill labor, D_L, to indicate that high-skill workers are more productive.) The supply curve of high-skill labor in 1920 is S_{H1920}. The intersection of these two curves tells us that the equilibrium wage rate for high-skill workers in 1920 was W_{H1920}.

Between 1920 and 1950, there was a rightward shift in the supply curve for high-skill workers, from S_{H1920} to S_{H1950}. As a result of this shift, there was a decrease in the equilibrium wage rate for high-skill workers, from W_{H1920} to W_{H1950}.

All else equal, because of the increase in the number of workers with a high-school education, there was an increase in the equilibrium wage rate for low-skill workers, and, at the same time, there was a decrease in the equilibrium wage rate for high-skill workers. (Note that the preceding sentence uses the assumption of "all else equal". In fact, the change in the relative supply of highly skilled workers and less-skilled workers was not the only thing happening at this time. The *demand* for labor was strong enough that the wages of highly skilled workers did not actually decrease.) Therefore, the difference between high-skill wage rates and low-skill wage rates was greatly compressed. The increase in educational opportunities in the first half of the twentieth century is a major reason for the equalization of incomes that occurred, especially in the 1930s and 1940s.

The analysis shown in Figure 15.2 indicates that an increase in education will tend to make the distribution of income more equal.

By the 1950s, a large majority of Americans of high-school age were receiving a high-school diploma. Thus, our characterization of those with a high-school diploma as high-skill workers was becoming increasingly obsolete. After the Second World War, the key to being a "high-skill worker" was to have a college education. Indeed, the college-educated population has expanded rapidly in the last fifty years.

This raises a question: Why did this continuing increase in education not lead to a further equalization of the income distribution? To understand the answer to this question, it is useful to remember our assumption of *ceteris paribus*, or "all else equal". All else equal, the continuing increase in education definitely would have led to further equalization. In other words, if education had continued to increase, and if nothing else had happened, the distribution of income would indeed have continued to equalize. However, all else was not equal. At the same time that educational opportunities were continuing to expand, causing an increase in the *supply* of high-skill labor, there was also a massive increase in the *demand* for high-skill labor. All else equal, an increase in the demand for high-skill labor will tend to make the distribution of income more *unequal*.

Thus in the last few decades of the twentieth century, both the supply of high-skill labor and the demand for high-skill labor were increasing. By itself, the increase in supply would tend to *equalize* the distribution of income. By itself, the increase in demand would tend to *disequalize* the distribution of income.

Since we have observed an increase in the degree of inequality, this means that the increase in demand for high-skill workers (possibly coupled with other influences) must have been more powerful than the increase in supply.

The Lorenz Curve and the Gini Ratio

It isn't easy to use the numbers for the quintiles of the income distribution, because they are so unwieldy. It would be more convenient if we could discuss the income distribution by referring to a single number. In this section, we develop a single number that can describe the degree of inequality in any distribution.

The Lorenz Curve. We begin by graphing the entire income distribution, as shown in Figure 15.3. On the horizontal axis of this figure, the population is lined up in order of income. The lowest-income household is introduced at the far left, while the highest-income household is introduced at the far right.

With the population lined up in this way, the horizontal axis measures the "cumulative proportion of the population". For example, if we start at the left end of the diagram, and go 30 percent of the way toward the right end, we are considering the 30 percent of the population with the lowest incomes. Thus, the horizontal axis can take on a value from zero to one (that is, from zero percent to 100 percent). At the midpoint along the horizontal axis of Figure 15.3, we are considering the lowest-income 50 percent of the population. In other words, when we get to the midpoint along the horizontal axis, we have just introduced the median household.

The vertical axis of Figure 15.3 shows the "cumulative proportion of income". If we start at the bottom of the diagram, and go 40 percent of the way toward the top, we are considering 40 percent of the economy's income. The vertical axis also takes on values from zero to one.

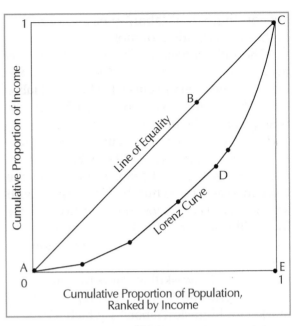

Figure 15.3 The Lorenz Curve

The Lorenz Curve for income is a graph of the relationship between the cumulative proportion of the population and the cumulative proportion of income. The Gini Ratio is calculated by dividing the area between the Line of Equality and the Lorenz Curve by the entire area under the Line of Equality. In other words, the Gini Ratio is equal to ABCD/ACE.

The *Lorenz Curve* shows the proportion of income going to each part of the population. For example, let's say that the lowest-income 20 percent of the population gets 3.1 percent of the income (as in Table 15.1). Then, one of the points on the Lorenz Curve would be 20 percent of the way from left to right, and 3.1 percent of the way from bottom to top. In other words, (0.2, 0.031) would be a point on the Lorenz Curve. Figure 15.1 shows a Lorenz Curve for the United States in 2014.

The Gini Ratio. As a standard for comparison, we could think of an economy in which income is distributed completely equally. In this hypothetical economy, if we were to take *any* 10 percent of the households, they would get exactly 10 percent of the income. In a hypothetical, completely equal economy, the

Lorenz Curve would be a straight line, slanting upward and to the right at a 45-degree angle. This is the "Line of Equality" in Figure 15.3.

There is a crescent-shaped space between the Lorenz Curve and the Line of Equality. In Figure 15.3, the area of this crescent is ABCD. If we divide ABCD by the area of the triangle ACE, we get the *Gini Ratio*, or *Gini Coefficient*, or *Gini Index*. (Gini is pronounced JEE-nee.) The Gini Ratio is the best-known measure of inequality in an income distribution.

The Gini Ratio in the United States

In a completely equal economy, there would not be any space between the Lorenz Curve and the Line of Equality. Thus, the Gini Ratio would be exactly zero. At the other extreme, if one individual had virtually all of the income, the Gini Ratio would be nearly 1.0. When the income distribution is *more unequal,* the Gini Ratio is *higher.*

We've seen that the share of income received by lower-income households has been falling in the United States, whereas the share received by higher-income households has been rising. We expect that this would *increase* the Gini Ratio, since higher Ginis are associated with more unequal distributions of income. In fact, the Gini Ratio increased from 0.397 in 1975 to 0.428 in 1990, and to 0.480 in 2014.

This may seem like a small increase in the Gini Ratio. But even a small change in the Gini is associated with a redistribution of billions and billions of dollars every year.

International Comparisons of Income Inequality

The United States has a distribution of income that is more equal than that of many countries, but less equal than that of many other countries. All of the affluent countries of western Europe have a distribution of income that is much more equal than that of the United States. In one recent study, the Gini Ratio was 0.32 in the United Kingdom, 0.30 in France, 0.27 in Germany, and 0.25 in Sweden. Canada's Gini Ratio of 0.32 means that the Canadian income distribution is also much more equal than the American income distribution. None of the other richest countries in the world is as unequal as the United States.

On the other hand, some of the poorer countries of Asia, Africa, and Latin America are *more unequal.* In one recent study, the major country with the most unequal distribution of income was South Africa, with a Gini Index of 0.63. Brazil's Gini Ratio was 0.52, and Chile's was also 0.52. However, the increase in income inequality in the United States has been so great that the U.S. is now more unequal than many of the world's poorer countries.

However, the greatest source of inequality in the world is not the inequality within countries like Brazil. Instead, the greatest source of world inequality is the disparity between the rich countries and the poor countries. The Gini Coefficient for the entire world is probably greater than 0.60, which represents a world distribution of income that is more unequal than the distribution in nearly every country.

The world's distribution of income is much more unequal than it was 200 years ago. That is because a relatively small number of countries raced ahead, with very rapid economic growth in the 19th and 20th centuries. These countries included the U.S. and Canada, Australia, New Zealand, Japan, and most of Western Europe. However, toward the end of the 20th century, the economies of China and India began to grow much more rapidly than before. This has already reduced worldwide income inequality somewhat, and it has the potential to equalize the distribution of income in the world even further, especially if other countries in Asia, Latin America, and Africa can also find ways to grow more rapidly.

THE CAUSES OF INCOME INEQUALITY

The distribution of income is influenced by an astonishing variety of forces. One example is that some of the variation in incomes is just due to luck. (For example, some of today's millionaires got rich by winning lotteries.) But much of the variation in incomes is due to other factors, which we will study now.

Differences Over the Lifetime

In Chapter 13, on labor economics, we saw that workers tend to get higher wages as they get older, because older workers have more experience. Consider Bob, who is 55 years old, and his 25-year-old son, Joe. Bob has worked his way up to a management position, and he earns $90,000 per year. Joe is just starting out as a trainee, and he earns $30,000 per year.

On the surface, it looks as if Bob is a lot better off than his son. However, Bob is at the peak of his career, and is unlikely to get any more big raises. On the other hand, Joe can expect to have rapidly rising earnings over the next several years. Joe may make just as much as his father is making (or even more), when he gets to his father's age. In other words, *some of the inequality in annual incomes is just due to the fact that people are of different ages.*

Here is another reason to think that we might get a very different picture if we look at *lifetime* incomes, rather than *annual* incomes: In any given year, some people have an unusually good year. (For example, a construction contractor might land a big project.) On the other hand, some people have an unusu-

ally bad year. (For example, a textile worker might be unemployed for a few months.) Over the lifetime, the good years and bad years tend to average out.

Because of the ups and downs in income over the lifetime, *the distribution of lifetime income for the people born in a particular year is much more equal than the distribution of annual income.* One study for Canada found that the Gini Ratio for *annual* income was 0.37, while the Gini Ratio for *lifetime* income was only 0.18. Thus about half of the inequality that we see in annual incomes could go away if we take the lifetime perspective.

Reasons for the Increase in Earnings Inequality in the Late 20th Century

Most of the nation's income is in the form of earnings in the labor market. Therefore, it's understandable that the rise in *income* inequality has had a lot to do with an increase in the inequality of labor earnings. In turn, the changes in the distribution of labor earnings have been caused by changes in labor supply and labor demand.

Changes in Labor Supply. The "Baby Boom" refers to the people who were born during the years of high birth rates in the United States, from 1946 to 1964. When the bulk of the Baby-Boom generation hit the labor market in the 1970s, there was a big increase in the supply of young workers, and especially of young work-

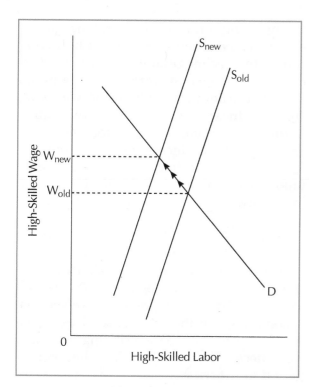

**Figure 15.4 Panel (a)
The Effect of a Decrease in the Supply
of Highly Skilled Workers**

As of 1975, the supply curve for college-educated workers is S_{old}. The demand curve is D. The equilibrium wage rate for college-educated workers is W_{old}. In the late 1970s and early 1980s, the rate of growth of the college-educated work force slowed down greatly. This can be represented as a leftward shift in the supply curve, from S_{old} to S_{new}. As a result, there was an increase in the equilibrium wage rate for college-educated workers, from W_{old} to W_{new}.

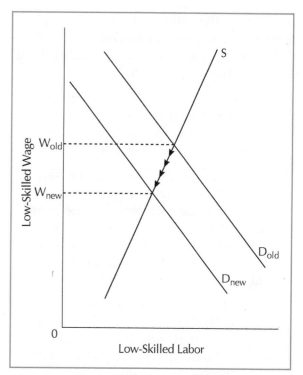

**Figure 15.4 Panel (b)
The Effect of a Decrease in the Demand
for Less-Skilled Workers**

As of 1975, the demand curve for high-school-educated workers is D_{old}. The supply curve is S. The equilibrium wage rate for high-school-educated workers is W_{old}. Since the late 1970s, as a result of technological changes and other forces, there has been a decrease in the demand for high-school-educated workers. This can be represented as a leftward shift in the demand curve, from D_{old} to D_{new}. As a result, there has been a decrease in the equilibrium wage rate for high-school-educated workers, from W_{old} to W_{new}.

ers with a college education. This meant that the wage rates for college-educated workers tended to decline. The gap in wages between college-educated workers and high-school-educated workers fell sharply in the 1970s.

By the early 1980s, most of the Baby Boomers were already in the labor force. There was a big drop in the number of new workers with a college education. This is shown in panel (a) of Figure 15.4, as a shift in the supply curve of college-educated

workers. The supply curve shifts to the left, from S_{old} to S_{new}. With fewer college-educated workers coming into the market, there was an increase in the wage premium for a college education. The supply shift increased the wage rates of college-educated workers from W_{old} to W_{new}.

Changes in Labor Demand. At the same time that the *supply* of workers was changing, there were major changes in labor *demand*.

Throughout the 1980s and 1990s, there were decreases in demand for workers with only a high-school education, and for high-school dropouts. The reasons include:

- *Technological change.* For a variety of reasons, including the increasing use of computers in the workplace, there was less demand for less-skilled workers.

- *Competition from abroad.* As we saw in Chapter 5, imports have grown dramatically in the last few decades. The American workers who were most affected were the production workers in the manufacturing industries, who tended to have only a high-school education or less.

- *The Shift from Manufacturing to Services.* Many of the highest-paying jobs for workers with a high-school education have been in the manufacturing sector. But the proportion of the economy that is devoted to manufacturing has been dropping for decades, and the service sector has been increasing. As manufacturing declines, so does the number of highly paid manufacturing jobs.

All of these forces combined to decrease the demand for less-educated workers. This is shown in panel (b) of Figure 15.4 as a shift in the demand curve for high-school-educated workers. The demand curve shifts to the left, from D_{old} to D_{new}. This leads to lower wages for these workers: Their wage drops from W_{old} to W_{new}.

Panel (a) of Figure 15.4 shows an *increase* in the wages of college-educated workers. Panel (b) shows a *decrease* in the wages of high-school-educated workers. Taken together, these changes mean that the wage premium for a college education soared during the 1980s and 1990s. This was one of the most important causes of the increase in inequality.

The Decline of Unions. As we discussed in Chapter 13, the union movement has been losing strength for many years. Since many union members have only a high-school education, the decline of unions would tend to reduce the wages of workers with a high-school education, relative to the wages of college-educated workers. The weakening of unions is probably responsible for about 15 percent of the increase in the premium for a college education. Thus the decline of unions has also contributed to the increase in inequality.

Deregulation of the Financial-Services Sector. For most of American history, the banking sector was an unregulated free-for-all. However, the Great Depression of the 1930s was so severe that it led Congress to take serious action to regulate the financial-services sector. As a result, banking became boring. This had two effects. First, it ushered in the longest period in American history without a financial crisis. Second, it reduced the incomes of financiers, when compared with those working in other parts of the economy.

This was understandably unpopular with financiers, and they fought hard to get Congress to relax or remove the regulations. In the 1980s and 1990s, the financiers succeeded in getting many of the regulations removed. This gave a tremendous boost to the incomes of a relatively small number of people who work in big banks and investment banks. One study suggests that the financial sector may be responsible for as much as one-fourth of the increase in inequality since 1980.

Reality Check: Interim Review Questions

IR15-3. Is lifetime income distributed more equally or less equally than annual income?

IR15-4. If there is an increase in the demand for more highly skilled workers, will earnings inequality increase or decrease?

THE TOP FIVE PERCENT HAVE DONE AMAZINGLY WELL

In Table 15.1 and Figure 15.1, the trends in the income distribution are shown with data for the *quintiles* of the income distribution, where each quintile represents 20 percent of the households. Since the late 1970s, the share of income going to the top quintile has increased sharply, while the shares received by the other four quintiles have all declined.

These data are useful, but they cannot show what is happening *within* quintiles. In fact, the increase in the share of the top quintile has been heavily concentrated in the hands of the top five percent of households.

As we have seen from 1975 to 2014, the share of total U.S. income received by the top quintile increased by 7.6 percentage points, from 43.6 percent of total income to 51.2 percent of total income. But the share of income received by the top five percent of households went up from 16.5 percent to 21.9 percent. That is an increase of 5.4 percentage points. In other words, the relative gains of the top 20 percent of households went mostly to the top five percent of households. The next 15 percent of households saw only a small increase in their share of total income.

In 1975, the poorer half of households in the United States received substantially more income than the most affluent five percent. By 2014, the positions of the top five percent and the bottom 50 percent of households had been dramatically reversed. By 2014, the top five percent of households were receiving about 22 percent of total income, while the bottom 50 percent of households were receiving less than 18 percent of total income.

This really is a huge shift. In order to get a sense of the massive size of this change in the income distribution, it might help to translate it from percentages into dollars. By 2014, personal income in the United States was about $14.7 trillion (*i.e.,* about $14,700,000,000,000).

As we have seen, the top five percent of American households increased their share of the total by 5.4 percentage points between 1975 and 2014. If we take 5.4 percent of $14.7 trillion, we get more than $790 billion (i.e., more than $790,000,000,000). Thus, the top five percent of American households receive about $790 billion per year more than they would have received, if the relative distribution of income had remained the same between 1975 and 2014. That's a lot of money.

Here's another way to look at it: In 2014, the average income for the top five percent of American households was a little more than $332,000 per year. If total income had been distributed in 2014 in the same way that it had been distributed in 1975, the average household in the top five percent would have received about $250,000. Thus, the shift in the income distribution favored the top five percent of households, to the tune of about $(332,000 − 250,000) = $82,000 for each of these households, every year. Any way you look at it, the last few decades have been a time of unprecedented prosperity for those at the top of the income ladder in the United States.

In the last few paragraphs, we have focused on the phenomenal increase in the share of income going to the top *five percent* of households. However, even this may give a distorted view of what is really going on. A great deal of the increase in inequality in the United States can be accounted for by changes in the incomes of the top *one-tenth of one percent* of households.

Recent research by the economists Emmanuel Saez and Thomas Piketty has shown that the top one-tenth of one percent have seen a staggering rise in their share of total income. In 1973, this group received less than two percent of all of the income in the

United States. By 2014, this had skyrocketed to about 7.5 percent of all income.

Who are these people? Economists Jon Bakija and Bradley Heim have shown that many of them are Chief Executive Officers of companies, and a very large proportion of them are Wall Street financiers.

We don't have a complete understanding of how the people in the top one-tenth of one percent were able to increase their share of income by so much. Bakija and Heim look at comparable data for Japan and France, and they do not find the same kind of pattern. In those countries, the share of income going to the top one-tenth of one percent stayed between two percent and three percent of total income. Since the trend in the U.S. is not dupli- cated in these other countries, it would be difficult to argue that the U.S. trend was caused by globalization, since all three countries have been affected by globalization in similar ways.

One possibility is that the 1980s and 1990s may have seen a change in the "social norms" governing the behavior of CEOs and Wall Street wizards. Perhaps it has always been possible for CEOs to grant themselves big salary increases, but that they once refrained from doing so. This might have occurred because it once seemed shameful for CEOs to push things to the extreme. However, if there was ever a social stigma associated with the CEO grabbing every loose dollar, it's possible that the stigma was greatly weakened during the 1980s and 1990s.

THE DISTRIBUTION OF WEALTH

So far, we've studied the distribution of *income*. A household's income is the amount that it receives *over a particular period of time.* For example, consider the Olson family's income. Members of the family earned $60,000 in the labor market in 2015, and they also received $100 of interest on a savings account. If there were no other sources of income in the year, then we would say that the family had $60,100 of income *in this particular year—2015.*

It's clearly important to study the distri- bution of income. But income isn't the only thing in which we might be interested: It's also interesting to learn about the distribution of *wealth*. A household's *wealth* is the total amount of assets that the household owns *at a particular moment in time.*

Now, consider the Olson family's wealth. First of all, the Olsons own a house. As of December 31, 2015, the net value of their stake in the house (after we subtract the amount they still owe on their mortgage) was $50,000. On that day, they also had checking and savings accounts, with balances of $20,000. Finally, the family owns two cars, some jewelry, and other household items, which were then valued at $40,000. If we add together the value of the house, the checking and savings accounts, and the household items, we get $50,000 + $20,000 + $40,000 = $110,000. Assuming that the Olsons didn't own anything else of value, we would say that their household wealth was $110,000 *at that moment—December 31, 2015.*

The Highly Unequal Division of Wealth

Wealth is distributed much *more unequally than income.* The poorest half of the American pop- ulation owns almost no wealth. (In fact, the people at the very bottom have *negative* wealth, because their debts are greater than their assets.) As we move up to the middle and upper-middle classes, we see many families who have modest amounts of wealth, much of it in homes. In 1989, the poorest 80 percent of households owned only about 15 percent of the nation's wealth.

The people at the top have an extraordinary share of the nation's wealth. In 1989, the top five percent of wealthholders had about 61 percent of total wealth. Even more astonishing is the fact that the top one-half of one percent owned more than 31 percent of the wealth!

The Gini Ratio for wealth is usually found to be around 0.8 or 0.85. This is *far* more unequal than the Gini Ratio that we saw for annual income, which, in turn, is substantially more than the Gini Ratio for lifetime income.

Real Economics for Real People 15.1 takes a closer look at the top end of the wealth distribution.

Reality Check: Interim Review Question

IR15-5. Is wealth distributed more equally than income, or less equally?

Real Economics for Real People 15.1: The Rich, the Very Rich, and the Super-Rich

We have seen that the world's income is very unequally distributed, and that wealth is distributed even more unequally than income. Thus, while most people have little or no wealth, a few are *very* rich. In 2016, the richest person in the world was Bill Gates of Microsoft Corporation, the computer software company. Gates's net worth was estimated to be $75 *billion*. In Table 15.2, we list the 20 people with the most wealth in 2016.

Some important changes in the world economy are reflected in the list of the richest 20 people. Many of these people are now from fields like computers, entertainment, and retailing, which have grown rapidly in recent years. The ranks of the very rich used to include more people from oil and heavy manufacturing, but these industries aren't as important as they once were.

The list of tycoons in Table 15.2 is just as interesting for who it doesn't include, as for who it does include. H. Ross Perot isn't on the list, and neither is Ted Turner, although it is fair to say that these gentlemen will still be able to live comfortably.

Also, most of the people at the top are *self-made* billionaires. Many of the families that got rich long ago (such as the Rockefellers, Fords, and duPonts) are still rich, but inheritance is not the main source of wealth for most of the people listed in Table 15.2. Also, three of the people listed in Table 15.2 are the Walton siblings. Most of their wealth is inherited, but it is nevertheless relatively recent wealth—they inherited their fortunes from their father, Sam Walton, the founder of Walmart Stores. Thus the list of the 20 richest people in the world is dominated by new money. If you want to become super-rich, you're more likely to do it if you start up your own computer firm, instead of waiting around for an inheritance from your long-lost uncle.

Table 15.2 The 20 Richest People in the World in 2016

Name	Residence	Estimated Net Worth	Primary Source Of Wealth
1. Bill Gates	Medina, Washington	$75.0 billion	Microsoft (software)
2. Amancio Ortega	La Coruna, Spain	$67.0 billion	Zara (clothing retailing)
3. Warren Buffett	Omaha, Nebraska	$66.3 billion	Berkshire Hathaway
4. Carlos Slim	Mexico City, Mexico	$50.0 billion	Telecommunications
5. Jeff Bezos	Seattle, Washington	$45.2 billion	Amazon.com (online retailing)
6. Mark Zuckerberg	Palo Alto, California	$44.6 billion	Facebook (social media)
7. Larry Ellison	Woodside, California	$43.6 billion	Oracle (software)
8. Michael Bloomberg	New York, New York	$40.0 billion	Bloomberg News
9 (tie). Charles Koch	Wichita, Kansas	$39.6 billion	manufacturing, energy
9 (tie). David Koch	New York, New York	$39.6 billion	manufacturing, energy
11. Liliane Bettencourt	Paris, France	$36.1 billion	L'Oréal (cosmetics)
12. Larry Page	Palo Alto, California	$35.2 billion	Google (Internet search)
13. Sergey Brin	Los Altos, California	$34.4 billion	Google (Internet search)
14. Bernard Arnault	Paris, France	$34.0 billion	LVMH (luxury apparel, liquor)
15. Jim Walton	Bentonville, Arkansas	$33.6 billion	Walmart (retailing)
16. Alice Walton	Fort Worth, Texas	$32.3 billion	Walmart (retailing)
17. S. Robson Walton	Bentonville, Arkansas	$31.9 billion	Walmart (retailing)
18. Wang Jianlin	Beijing, China	$28.7 billion	Real estate
19. Jorge Paulo Lemann	Zurich, Switzerland	$27.8 billion	Anheuser-Busch InBev (beer)
20. Li Ka-shing	Hong Kong	$27.1 billion	Diversified investments

Source: *Forbes* Magazine.

POVERTY

So far, we've talked about the *entire* distribution of income and wealth. But the people at the *bottom* of the income distribution have special problems, and they deserve special attention. When we focus on the people at the bottom of the income distribution, where people may not have enough income to meet certain basic needs, we talk about *poverty*.

In the United States, poverty has an official definition, which was developed by Mollie Orshansky of the Social Security Administration during the 1960s. The official "poverty threshold", or "poverty-line income" depends on family size, and it is updated every year to account for inflation. In 2014, the poverty line stood at $12,316 for a one-member family, $24,008 for a four-member family, and $38,953 for an eight-member family. If your family's money income is less than the poverty line (even by one dollar), then everyone in the family is classified as being poor. If your family's income is above the poverty line, then no one in the family is officially counted as poor.

These poverty thresholds probably make sense in the United States. However, it is important to remember that the people of the U.S. are much more affluent that those in most of the rest of the world. Thus a person might be officially classified as poor in the U.S., even though her income would make her quite well off in India, relatively speaking.

Changes in the Poverty Rate Over Time

In 1959, about 39.5 million Americans fell below the poverty line. This worked out to about 22.4 percent of the population. But wages grew rapidly during the 1960s, and unemployment was low. These factors helped to pull many people out of poverty. Moreover, the late 1960s and early 1970s saw an expansion of various government programs that increased the incomes of some of the poor. Social Security expanded, and this helped to create a large reduction in the poverty rate among elderly Americans. The official poverty rate fell to its all-time low of 11.1 percent in 1973.

In the 1970s, 1980s, and early 1990s, the wages of the people at the bottom of the wage distribution did not fare as well. Because of these and other forces, the poverty rate rose. The late 1990s was a time of strong economic growth, and the poverty rate fell as far as 11.3 percent by 2000. However, because of the recession of 2001, and especially the much deeper recession of 2007–2009, the poverty rate rose again. By 2014, the poverty rate stood at 14.8 percent, which is higher than it had been in all but seven of the previous 50 years. In 2014, an estimated 46.66 million Americans were in poverty, which is an all-time record.

Differences in the Poverty Rate for Different Groups

The information in the preceding paragraph deals with the poverty rate *for the United States as a whole*. However, different groups within the U.S. have very different poverty rates.

Differences by Region. Table 15.3 shows that poverty is much more common in some regions of the country than in others. In 2014, the poverty rate in Louisiana stood at 23.1 percent, and the poverty rate was 21.2 percent in Arizona and 19 percent in the District of Columbia. These rates were much higher than in New Hampshire, with a rate of 7.2 percent, or Minnesota, with a rate of 8.3 percent. Generally speaking, the highest concentrations of poverty are in the South and Southwest. Some of the States with the highest poverty rates are in a band that stretches from Arizona and New Mexico to Arkansas and Mississippi, and on through Alabama, Tennessee, and West Virginia. The lowest poverty rates are in the Northeast and the Great Plains.

Differences by Race. There are also large differences in poverty rates among the different demographic groups of the United States population. Some of these differences are shown in Table 15.4. For one thing, race plays an important role. In 2014, non-Hispanic whites had a poverty rate of 10.1 percent, whereas blacks had a rate of 26.2 percent. The poverty rate for Hispanics was 23.6 percent.

Differences by Age. Table 15.4 also shows that there are big differences in poverty rates by age. The rate for young people (below the age of 18) was 21.1 percent in 2014, which is substantially higher than the rate for the rest of the population.

The poverty rates for different age groups have changed dramatically over the years. Fifty years ago, the elderly were much more likely to be in poverty. However, the 1970s brought big increases in spending on the elderly through the Social Security programs. As a result, the poverty rate for older Americans fell sharply from the late 1960s to the middle 1980s. In recent years, poverty has been substantially lower among the elderly than among any other age group.

Differences by Family Structure. One of the biggest changes in American society in the last generation has been the increase in the number of female-headed families. These families have always had relatively high poverty rates. Consequently, the rise in the number of

Table 15.3 Poverty Rates by State, 2014

State	Percentage of Population in Poverty	State	Percentage of Population in Poverty
Alabama	17.8	Montana	12.0
Alaska	11.9	Nebraska	11.8
Arizona	21.2	Nevada	17.0
Arkansas	18.4	New Hampshire	7.2
California	15.8	New Jersey	11.3
Colorado	12.3	New Mexico	20.0
Connecticut	8.6	New York	14.0
Delaware	11.0	North Carolina	17.1
Dist. of Columbia	19.0	North Dakota	9.7
Florida	16.7	Ohio	15.6
Georgia	16.8	Oklahoma	17.3
Hawaii	10.8	Oregon	14.4
Idaho	12.4	Pennsylvania	12.5
Illinois	13.7	Rhode Island	11.3
Indiana	14.6	South Carolina	16.5
Iowa	10.3	South Dakota	12.8
Kansas	12.1	Tennessee	17.3
Kentucky	20.0	Texas	16.4
Louisiana	23.1	Utah	10.2
Maine	14.6	Vermont	9.3
Maryland	9.8	Virginia	10.2
Massachusetts	13.6	Washington	12.0
Michigan	14.8	West Virginia	20.6
Minnesota	8.3	Wisconsin	10.9
Mississippi	22.1	Wyoming	9.7
Missouri	10.4		
		UNITED STATES AVERAGE	14.8

Table 15.4 Poverty Rates for Different Demographic Groups, 2014

Group	Percent in Poverty
Entire Population	14.8%
Whites	12.7
Non-Hispanic Whites	10.1
Blacks	26.2
Hispanics	23.6
Aged under 18	21.1
Aged 18–64	13.5
Aged 65 and over	10.0
Female-headed families	33.1

female-headed families is one reason why poverty rates increased in the 1970s and 1980s. From 1970 to 1993, the number of poor people in female-headed families went up by about seven million. This is sometimes called the *"feminization of poverty"*. Table 15.4 shows that the poverty rate is still much higher for those in female-headed households than for those in other household types.

Trends Over Time in the Poverty Rates for Different Groups Figure 15.5(a) shows the official poverty rates from 1959 to 2014, for whites, blacks, and for the entire population. A number of things can be seen from this figure. First,

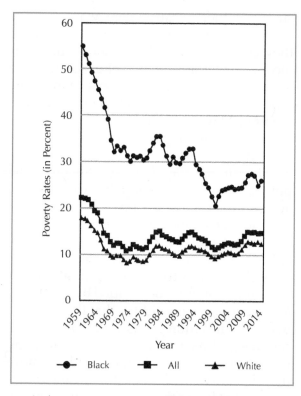

Figure 15.5(a)   Official Poverty Rates in the United States by Race, 1959–2014

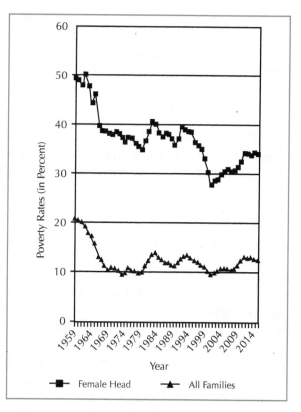

Figure 15.5(b)   Official Poverty Rates in the United States for Different Household Types, 1959–2014

the trend in poverty rates for whites is fairly close to the trend in poverty rates for the entire population. This is not a surprise, since whites make up a majority of the population.

Second (again no surprise), the poverty rates tend to fall during economic expansions, and they tend to rise during economic recessions. There were recessions in 1982, 1991, 2001, and 2008–2009. In each case, more workers were unemployed. As a result of the weakness in the labor market during recessions, the poverty rate tends to rise.

Third, in absolute terms, the gap between the white and black populations has shrunk over time. In 1959, the poverty rate for whites was about 18 percent, and the rate for blacks was about 55 percent. Thus, the poverty rate for blacks was about 37 percentage points higher than the rate for whites in 1959. By 2014, as we have seen, the poverty rate for

whites was 12.7 percent, and the rate for blacks was 26.2 percent, for a difference of 13.5 percentage points. However, even though the difference between the poverty rates for whites and blacks has decreased, it is still remarkably large.

Figure 15.5(b) shows another aspect of the trends in the poverty rate. This figure shows the poverty rate for all families, and the poverty rate for female-headed households. According to the definition used by the Census Bureau, the man is the head of household in a married couple. Thus, according to the definition, there is no husband in female-headed households. These households include women who are widowed, divorced, or never married, as well as their children. (The never-married category has increased dramatically in the last several decades, as a result of the increase in births out of wedlock.) Figure 15.5(b) shows that female-headed households are much more likely to be in poverty than other households.

Problems with the Poverty Statistics

When it calculates the official poverty rate, the government uses some problematic assumptions.

In-Kind Income. One of the biggest problems with the official definition of poverty is that it only counts *cash* income. But many low-income people receive *"in-kind"* assistance (that is, assistance that doesn't come in the form of cash). Millions of low-income families receive in-kind income such as Supplemental Nutrition Assistance Program payments (better known as Food Stamps), Medicaid, Medicare, or subsidized housing, but the government does not count these forms of assistance when it decides whether a family is below the poverty line.

By ignoring in-kind income, the official poverty rate would tend to *overstate* the true amount of poverty. Some estimates suggest that the poverty rate would fall to less than 10 percent, if we were to include income in-kind. In other words, there may be several million Americans who are officially counted as poor, but who aren't *really* poor because of their in-kind income.

We need to keep in mind that the official poverty numbers *do* include cash transfers from the government, such as Social Security, unemployment benefits, and other cash payments. If it weren't for these payments, the poverty rate would be much higher. About 15 million Americans are kept out of poverty by cash transfers.

Under-reporting. The official poverty rate is based on a survey in which people are asked about their incomes. But it appears that many people don't report their full incomes on the survey, either because they want to hide income from illegal sources, or because they've forgotten about some of their income, or because they feel uncomfortable about revealing their income. Since the official poverty rate doesn't adjust for under-reporting, it would once again tend to *overstate* the true amount of poverty.

Overstating the Rate of Inflation. The poverty-line income is adjusted each year, to account for inflation. In principle, this is a good idea. However, the adjustment is done on the basis of the Consumer Price Index (CPI). For a variety of reasons, the CPI tends to overstate the true rate of inflation. An influential commission, headed by Stanford's Michael Boskin, concluded that the CPI may overstate inflation by as much as 1.1 percentage points per year. As a result, the poverty-line income is increased by more than is really necessary. This means that a standard of living that was above the poverty line in the past might be judged to be below the poverty line now. Therefore, there is a tendency for the CPI to lead to an overstatement of the poverty rate.

Income Mobility. Consider the Jackson family, who have never been in poverty. This year, however, Mr. Jackson is laid off from his job for four months. During that time, the Jacksons draw upon their savings, so that they consume just as much as they did when Mr. Jackson was working. They stay in the same apartment, and they eat the same food as before. Their lifestyle is unchanged. According to the official statistics, the Jacksons are poor this year, because their income falls below the poverty line this year. But are the Jacksons really poor?

As a result of under-reporting and income mobility, the *spending* of some families will be more than the poverty level, even though their reported *income* is below the poverty line. In fact, many low-income families spend twice as much as their income. For the 20 percent of the population with the lowest incomes, the share of *spending* is nearly twice as great as the share of *income*. This once again suggests that the official poverty rate may *overstate* the true amount of poverty.

Missing Persons. Each of the above points suggests that the official numbers can *overstate* the number of Americans who are really poor. However, one important factor works in the opposite direction. The Census Bureau's survey does a poor job of finding homeless people. By undercounting these people, the official statistics will tend to *understate* the true extent of poverty.

On balance, it appears that the official poverty statistics may overstate the "true" poverty rate. Even if we were to adjust the official statistics to account for all of these problems, however, we would still find that more than 20 million Americans are in poverty, and many more are not far above the poverty line. The war on poverty isn't over. In the next few sections,

we will look at some of the policies that have been used to fight poverty, and we'll think about how these policies could be improved.

As we said a few paragraphs ago, the poverty statistics are influenced by homelessness. The homeless population is interesting and important for other reasons, as well. We discuss homelessness in *Real Economics for Real People 15.2*.

Reality Check: Interim Review Questions

IR15-6. In calculating the official poverty statistics for households, the government ignores in-kind income (such as food stamps). Does this lead the official poverty rate to be biased? If so, is the official rate an overstatement or an understatement of the "true" rate?

IR15-7. In which region of the country does poverty tend to be highest?

IR15-8. Is poverty among the elderly higher or lower than poverty among the young?

Real Economics for Real People 15.2: The Problem of Homelessness

The poverty of the homeless appears to be even more desperate than the poverty of others. This may explain the fact that homelessness has received more attention in recent years.

For obvious reasons, it's very hard to get a good count of the homeless population. It's easy for the Census Bureau to miss people who are living in abandoned cars. Nevertheless, government agencies and private organizations have tried to count the homeless. The best estimates are that somewhere between 200,000 and 600,000 Americans are homeless at any one time. These numbers

range from less than one-tenth of one percent of the American population, up to about one-quarter of one percent of the population.

However, the homeless population changes over time. Some homeless people find homes, while some people lose their homes and become homeless. Even though only a few hundred thousand people are homeless at any one time, it's possible that a few million may be homeless at one time or another, in any given year.

Why are these people without shelter? There are many reasons, but here is a partial list:

- Mental illness. In 1955, the public mental hospitals in the United States had 559,000 patients. However, thousands of mental patients were released in the 1960s. By 1978, only 150,000 patients were still in mental hospitals.

  The movement toward releasing mental patients was based on good intentions. The idea was that the mentally ill could receive better treatment if they were in community-based treatment centers. Unfortunately, these centers were often funded poorly, and were not always able to provide the necessary care. As a result, many people with a history of mental problems ended up on the streets.

- Drug and alcohol abuse. Some studies report that as many as 70 percent of the homeless are abusers of alcohol or other drugs. People with serious substance-abuse problems often find it difficult to hold a job. In addition, the small amounts of money that they do have may be drained away by drugs.

  When mental illness combines with drug addiction, the results can be especially frightening. One well-publicized case is Larry Hogue, the "wild man of 96th street". Mr. Hogue is addicted to crack cocaine. When he takes crack, he becomes psychotic, and terrorizes his neighborhood in New York City. He has been hospitalized for psychiatric care on more than 40 occasions. Each time, however, he returns to the streets.

- Low wages, high unemployment, and declining transfers. During the 1980s, wages fell for low-skill workers (especially for high-school dropouts), and unemployment rose. We would expect this to increase homelessness, unless incomes were supplemented by government transfer payments. But more than 80 percent of homeless people are men, and non-elderly men are the least likely to receive transfer payments, since they aren't eligible for some programs.

- Lack of low-income housing. Urban renewal projects often mean that housing units are replaced by office buildings. These projects led to the destruction of more than a million rental units across the country during the 1970s and 1980s. In addition, the housing aid budget for the Federal Department of Housing and Urban Development fell during the 1980s. This forced the government to reduce its support for low-income rental units.

It should be clear that homelessness has many causes. Because of this, any serious attack on homelessness will need to address many causes at once. More housing projects may help, but they can't be the entire solution. It's probably best not to think of homelessness as merely a housing problem. If homelessness is to be reduced very much, it will be necessary to deal directly with the problems of untreated mental illness, untreated substance abuse, and low earnings.

POLICIES TO REDUCE POVERTY

Transfer payments are payments to people who do not provide any services in return. Many transfer payments are specifically targeted at low-income people. However, even when transfer payments aren't aimed directly at the poor, they still may reduce poverty.

Governments in the United States spend more than a trillion dollars every year on transfers, which is a lot of money. Table 15.5 shows

Table 15.5 Federal Government Expenditures on Selected Transfer Payment Programs, 2015

Social Security	$738.0 billion
Medicare	$622.1 billion
Medicaid	$349.8 billion
Disability	$143.4 billion
Food Stamps	$ 76.1 billion
Earned Income Tax Credit	$ 60.1 billion
Supplemental Security Income for Aged and Disabled Poor	$ 52.3 billion
Unemployment Assistance	$ 32.7 billion

Source: Budget of the United States Government, Historical Tables.

where some of the money goes. The table shows the estimated expenditures on some of the most important federal-government programs, for 2015.

One thing stands out when we look at Table 15.5. The federal government spends much more on programs for elderly people (regardless of whether they are poor) than on programs targeted at the poor. The *Social Security* retirement program in the United States is the largest domestic spending program in the world, with more than $700 billion per year in spending. The rapidly growing *Medicare* program provides the elderly with more than $600 billion per year for medical expenses. By contrast, transfer programs for the non-elderly poor are far less generous. Therefore, it's no wonder that transfer-payment programs do far more to reduce the poverty rate for the elderly than for the rest of the population.

Effects of Transfer Programs: The Equality/Efficiency Tradeoff

In our chapter on labor supply, we saw that transfer payments may cause people to work less. This means that, when $1000 is given to a poor person, the person's income is likely to go up by *less* than $1000, because the person is likely to work less.

Let's say that the government collects $1000 of taxes from Aaron (who has a high income), and pays the money to Brian (who has a low income). As a result of this government grant, Brian works less. If Brian's earnings in the labor market go down by $333, then his income has only gone up by ($1000 – $333) = $667, even though Aaron's income went down by the full $1000.

In other words, Aaron's loss is (1000/667) = 1.5 times as much as Brian's gain. The true cost of the transfer is 1.5 times as great as the amount by which the poor person's income was increased. Economists (including the author of this book) have estimated that the loss to those who pay for transfer payments may be substantially greater than the gains for those who receive the transfer payments. However, the *form* of the transfer payment can make a big difference. A cash payment is likely to lead to a much bigger reduction in labor supply than a subsidy to labor-market earnings. The income effect on labor supply means that a cash payment will *reduce* the quantity of labor supplied. But an earnings subsidy creates a substitution effect, which can be expected to *increase* the quantity of labor supplied. The Earned Income Tax Credit is an earnings subsidy. We will discuss it in more detail, later in this chapter.

The Future of the Fight Against Poverty

How can we change American society, in order to reduce the rate of poverty? This has been a hot topic for years, and it will continue to be a hot topic in the future. Because poverty has many causes, there is no one change that will magically cure all of our problems. In the next few paragraphs, we outline some important ways of keeping the poverty rate down. Some of these involve government policies, but some also include changes in people's attitudes and behavior.

Sound Macroeconomic Policies. Low unemployment is one of the best anti-poverty programs. The poverty rate always rises during a recession, and falls during an economic expansion. No matter what transfer payments are used, it will be easier to rely on jobs to reduce poverty (rather than on unemployment benefits).

Responsible Parenting. By the early 1990s, over one million children per year were being born out of wedlock in the United States. Out-of-wedlock births now account for more than 30 percent of all births. The poverty rates for female-headed households are very high, which means that the increase in out-of-wedlock births is a sure prescription for poverty.

Throughout history, the greatest discouragement to illegitimate births was the disapproval of others in the community. It appears that the social stigma associated with out-of-wedlock motherhood has been greatly reduced. If illegitimacy is greeted with social approval, the policies of the government may not make much difference.

The last few paragraphs have focused on the behavior of mothers. Of course, fathers bear just as much responsibility. One big problem is that of the "Deadbeat Dads"—fathers who skip out on their child-support payments. In recent years, the Federal government and many State governments have tried (with some success) to increase their enforcement of the child-support laws. Still, millions of fathers are delinquent in their payments. One of the problems is that the court system is a clumsy place in which to handle child support. In the future, we can expect that child-support payments will increasingly be taken care of as an automatic payroll deduction.

Encouragement of Work. If well-paying jobs are available, most people will choose to work. Education and training are the key to getting people into good jobs.

But what about the people with the least skills, for whom good jobs are hard to find? In trying to help these people out of poverty,

American governments give them cash, food stamps, Medicaid, and subsidized housing. All of these will reduce labor supply. In fact, when we consider the incentives with which low-income people have been faced over the years, it is remarkable that they have worked as much as they have.

And yet, the political debate is often full of talk about "lazy welfare chiselers". Having given the poor a set of severe disincentives for working, it's ironic that the rest of the population seems to be upset that the poor do not work more.

From the perspective of economics, it would make more sense to provide the poor with better work incentives. Instead of giving them cash and *taxing* them at high rates, it would work better to *subsidize the wages* of the poor. In the United States, the largest attempt to do this is the *Earned Income Tax Credit* (EITC). The EITC increases the wages for people in families with low incomes.

The EITC is no magical cure-all, but it's better than most other transfer payment programs. When President Ronald Reagan signed an expansion of the EITC in 1986, he called it "the best anti-poverty, the best pro-family, the best job creation measure to come out of Congress".

Finding Better Ways to Provide for Retirement. The good news is that Social Security and other transfer payments lift millions of elderly Americans out of poverty. The bad news is that, *without* these transfers, more than half of the elderly population would be below the poverty line. This suggests that the poverty rate would continue to fall, if ordinary citizens would do more to save for their *own* retirements.

Today's policy debates include proposals to strengthen the incentives for retirement saving. These proposals include expanded tax credits for saving, as well as fundamental changes in the Social Security program. We'll talk more about some of the possibilities in the next chapter. But we must keep in mind that it isn't just up to the government. Whatever the government policies may be, individual families bear most of the responsibility for saving. To increase the saving rate by a lot, it will take more than sound government policies: It will take a cultural change toward more patience, more planning, and a greater ability to delay gratification.

Regardless of the level of saving, it is also true that our Social Security expenditures are not targeted very precisely. Billions and billions of dollars are paid every year to the affluent elderly. If we were to take the same amount of money, and aim it more precisely at those who are elderly and *poor*, we would get a much greater reduction in the poverty rate.

ECONOMICS AND YOU: WELFARE REFORM

The Aid to Families with Dependent Children program (AFDC) was created in the 1930s. It provided a Federal guarantee for female-headed households. The level of benefits varied widely from State to State, but families could not be denied benefits, as long as they met certain requirements.

In the 1960s, participation in the AFDC program soared, from less than 2 percent of the population to more than 5 percent. There was a widespread perception that the program was encouraging women to have children out of wedlock, and that it was discouraging work. Many taxpayers feared that AFDC was creating a permanent "underclass", consisting of people with little incentive to work, and every incentive to remain dependent on government assistance. These concerns led to much political pressure for welfare reform. In the early 1990s, the Federal government granted "waivers" to many of the States. These welfare waivers allowed the States to experiment with different rules for the AFDC program. Many of the waivers allowed States to require AFDC recipients to work or go to school, in order to continue to receive benefits.

This movement culminated in the passage of a new Federal law in August, 1996. The Personal Responsibility and Work Opportunity Reconciliation Act (PRWORA) removed the Federal guarantee of benefits, and replaced it with a series of block grants to the States. The total amount of the block grants was smaller than the amount previously provided by the Federal government, so it was expected that overall spending would be reduced.

PRWORA also required that, in most cases, poor adults should be required to find a job within two years of receiving aid. The law also established a five-year lifetime limit on aid coming from Federal block grants. Another important provision of the new law was a set of requirements for unmarried teenaged mothers. Those below the age of 18 are now usually required to live with an adult and attend school, if they are to receive benefits.

When PRWORA was passed, some analysts suggested that the new law would have catastrophic results, pushing a million children into poverty. At first, however, those dire predictions did not come true. The welfare rolls were reduced dramatically in the second half of the 1990s. From 1994 to 1999, the total number of welfare recipients fell from about 12 million to about 7 million. In spite of the reduced number of people receiving benefits, the poverty rate continued to fall during those years.

However, a big part of this story is that the labor market was very strong in the late 1990s. Employment surged, and the unemployment rate fell. Thus it was possible for poverty to fall, despite the reduction in welfare payments. But the first decade of the 21st century saw sluggish job growth, if any. This meant that it was hard to find a job, especially for the low-skill workers who have traditionally relied on public assistance. As mentioned earlier in this chapter, by 2014, the number of Americans in poverty was at an all-time high. To reduce poverty in this affluent country, it will be necessary to see changes in a variety of public policies and private behaviors.

Chapter Summary

1. The Lorenz Curve shows the amount of income received by each portion of the population. If income were distributed completely equally, the Lorenz Curve would be an upward-sloping, straight line. In reality, however, income is distributed unequally, so that the slope of the Lorenz Curve increases as we move from left to right.

2. The Gini Ratio is the best-known measure of inequality. If income were distributed completely equally, the Gini Ratio would be zero. If income were distributed extremely unequally, the Ratio would approach one. For the United States in recent years, the Gini Ratio has been about 0.48. The developed countries of Europe tend to have lower Ginis than does the U.S. (that is, these countries are *more equal*), while the poorer countries of Asia, Africa, and Latin American tend to have higher Ginis (that is, they are *more unequal*).

3. Part of the inequality that we observe is due to age differences. The Gini Ratio for *lifetime* income is substantially lower than the Gini Ratio for *annual* income.

4. The income distribution in the United States has become more unequal since the 1970s. A major force behind this change is that the wage premium received by workers with a college education has gone up sharply, due to changes in the supply and demand for different kinds of labor. The decline of labor unions has also contributed to the increase in inequality. The deregulation of the financial-services sector led to skyrocketing incomes for financiers, and this also contributed to the disequalization.

5. Wealth is distributed much more unequally than income. The Gini Ratio for wealth is probably in the range of 0.8 to 0.9.

6. The official definition of poverty depends on family size, and it is adjusted over time to account for inflation. The poverty rate fell dramatically until about 1973, when it reached 11.1 percent. The rate stood at 14.8% in 2014.

7. Different groups within the population have different poverty rates. Poverty rates tend to be highest in the South and Southwest. Poverty is more prevalent among blacks and Hispanics than among whites. Poverty rates for the elderly have fallen a great deal since the 1960s, so that the poverty rate among the elderly is now lower than average, and much less than the rate for young people. Female-headed families have high poverty rates, as do families with large numbers of children.

8. If we are to keep the poverty rate low in the future, it will be necessary to address a number of problems. First, it will be important to keep unemployment low. Second, we will need a productive, well-educated population, in order to get well-paying jobs. Third, it will be important to reverse the trend toward out-of-wedlock births and the growth of single-parent families. Fourth, we will need to improve our system of child-support payments. Fifth, instead of taxing the poor at high rates, it would be better to provide them with work incentives. This is currently done through the Earned Income Tax Credit. Sixth, poverty rates among the elderly can be reduced further if people will save more while they are young. Seventh, billions of dollars in transfer payments go to those who are not poor. If these dollars were to be concentrated on the poor, it might be possible to achieve further reductions in the poverty rate.

Key Terms

Lorenz Curve

Line of Equality

Gini Ratio, or Gini Coefficient, or Gini Index

Wealth

Poverty

Feminization of Poverty

In-Kind Income

Transfer Payments

Social Security

Medicare

Earned Income Tax Credit

Questions and Problems

QP15-1. We have seen that wealth is distributed very unequally. The Federal estate tax can be seen as an attempt to reduce this inequality. In fact, however, rich people can usually avoid paying very much estate tax, if they plan ahead. Should the estate tax be made stronger or weaker? Should its rates be higher or lower, or should they stay the same? If the estate tax rates are raised, do you think that people will choose to leave smaller estates?

QP15-2. One reason why the estate tax is so easy to avoid is that it is only collected once for every person, at the end of life. In an attempt to avoid this problem, some of the European countries have a small tax on wealth every year. What are the positives and negatives associated with this type of tax?

QP15-3. If you were the ruler of the world, and if you could choose any distribution of income, how much inequality would you choose? Would you want a Gini Ratio of about 0.48 or so (like we have in the United States now), or would you prefer 0.3, or 0.2, or 0.6? What about a Gini Ratio of 0.0? If the Gini Ratio were to be reduced to a very low level, it would be necessary to have much higher tax rates than we have now. What effects do you think these higher tax rates would have on the economy?

QP15-4. Birth rates have risen in the last few years. Because of this, what do you think will happen to the wage rates of new college graduates, 20 years from now?

QP15-5. Briefly list and discuss the most important causes of income inequality. How have each of these causes changed in the last few decades?

QP15-6. Beethoven, Mozart, and Tchaikowsky, as well as many other famous musicians, were supported in their work by very rich people. The same goes for famous artists, such as Michelangelo and Leonardo. If the distribution of income had been dramatically more equal, there might not have been anyone rich enough to support artists such as these. Does this imply that society ought not to pursue equality too far?

QP15-7. Should society strive to provide equal *opportunity*, or equal *incomes*? Which would be associated with a higher Gini Ratio?

Chapter 16

Public Goods, Government Spending, and Taxation

ECONOMICS AND YOU:
WILL SOCIAL SECURITY BE THERE WHEN YOU RETIRE?

The Old Age and Survivors Insurance system, better known as Social Security, was established in 1935. At first, the system was modest in size. Since then, however, it has grown into the largest program of government-provided cash payments in the history of the world. In Chapter 15, we saw that the Social Security system was paying out well over $700 billion per year by 2015.

In spite of the fact that the Social Security program is very popular, it faces a number of problems. The biggest problem is that over the long run, the scheduled tax rates aren't high enough to pay for the benefits that have been promised by law. Many people seem to believe that Social Security will stop paying benefits someday, but that's not correct. However, it is true that it will be necessary to reduce some benefits, and/or increase some taxes.

One part of the problem is that the "Baby Boom" generation (consisting of Americans born between 1946 and 1964 , during a time of very high birth rates) have begun to retire. In the coming years, this will cause a rapid increase in the number of retired people.

When there are more retirees, the financial resources of the Social Security system will be stretched. However, the funding problems will continue even after the Baby Boomers are gone. This is because life expectancies are projected to continue to increase. Longer lifespans mean longer retirements, and this puts a strain on the Social Security system.

If Social Security were to run out of funds, it would be a major political disaster. Consequently, it's likely that some changes will eventually be made in the law. But which changes should be made, and who will make the decisions? These questions are somewhat different from many of the questions that we have asked in earlier chapters. In most of this book, we have concentrated on the decisions of individual households and business firms. But Social Security is a government program, and decisions regarding this system are made by elected officials and bureaucrats, rather than by households and firms.

In this chapter, the focus is on government spending, and on the taxes used to finance that spending. You will begin by learning about the reasons for the existence of government programs. Then we discuss the actual trends in various categories of government spending. Later in the chapter, you will read about taxes. You will learn to think about the effects of taxes on the efficiency of the private market economy, and you will also learn about how taxes affect the distribution of income. At the end of this chapter, we will return to the question of Social Security's future.

WHY DO WE NEED A GOVERNMENT?

Throughout this book, we have emphasized the virtues of the private market economy. Private markets often move quickly to deliver goods and services. When the markets are competitive, consumers can attain maximum satisfaction.

If private markets are so wonderful, who needs a government? In fact, there are several reasons why it is important to have a government. For one thing, governments are needed to assure that the private economy will function smoothly. Private producers and consumers rely on contracts, and it's necessary to have a system of laws and courts, so contracts can be enforced, and so that disputes about the meaning of a contract can be resolved peacefully.

Beyond the need for a legal system, however, there are some important situations in which it may be necessary to rely on governments. First of all, there is a role for government in providing "public goods", which are consumed by many people at the same time. Secondly, the private market economy may give rise to a distribution of income that many people consider unacceptable. Thus there may be a role for government in using taxes and transfer payments to affect the distribution of income. The purpose of this section is to discuss public goods and income distribution in detail.

Public Goods

Earlier in this book, we have studied imperfect competition, which is an important type of *market failure*. In this chapter, we will study another type of market failure, known as *public goods*. We discuss the characteristics of a public good below. Whenever there is a market failure, it's possible that a government may be able to intervene, to improve the workings of the market. (However, there is no guarantee that government programs will always improve the situation, especially if the programs are designed poorly, or if they are associated with political corruption.)

What would happen if BoomBoom Corporation were to put on a fireworks show on the Fourth of July? In order to cover its costs, the company would have to charge admission. But this presents a problem: Fireworks explode high in the sky, which means that they can be seen over a wide area. If BoomBoom Corporation were to send up the fireworks over the local stadium, and charge admission to enter the stadium, who would pay? Lots of people would probably decide to sit outside the stadium. In this way, they can enjoy the fireworks without having to pay.

Because of this problem, it's very difficult for any private company to make money by putting on a fireworks show. There are some exceptions, but many of the biggest fireworks shows are sponsored by governments.

Nonrival Consumption. The fireworks show illustrates some important characteristics of public goods. First of all, the fireworks show can be enjoyed by many people at the same time. In other words, when *I* enjoy the show, it doesn't decrease *your* enjoyment of the same show. If many people can enjoy a good at the same time, consumption of the good is *nonrival*.

Nonrival consumption does not apply in the case of a *private good*. One example of a private good is a pair of socks. If I wear a particular pair of socks, there is no way that anyone else can wear that same pair of socks at the same time. For a private good like a pair of socks, we say that consumption is *rival*.

Costly Exclusion and the Free-Rider Problem. Another feature of the fireworks show is that it is hard to exclude people from enjoying the show, even if they do not pay. In a case like this, we say that consumption is characterized by *costly exclusion*, or *nonexcludability*.

In the case of a purely private good, it is easy to exclude those who don't pay. If you go to a store to buy some shirts, you have to go to a cash register to pay for the shirts. Unless you want to run the risk of going to jail for shoplifting, it's necessary to pay before you carry the item out of the store.

However, in the case of a public good, such simple mechanisms for excluding those who don't pay are not available. Thus for a public good, nonexludability is an extremely important problem. If private producers aren't able to collect money from the people who enjoy a good or service, the private producers won't be able to stay in business. If private producers can't exclude those who don't pay, private markets are certain to fail. When nonexcludable goods are produced at all, it will be necessary for governments to do the producing.

Costly exclusion leads to another problem for public goods. If people know they can see the fireworks show (even if they don't pay), then they don't have any incentive to reveal whether they really want to see the show. Let's say that private producers are unable to put on a fireworks show in the town of Jonesville, USA, because of the problem of costly exclusion. As a result, the City Council is thinking of putting on a fireworks show. The Council asks residents whether they would be willing to pay higher taxes, in order to support a show. Many residents of Jonesville may say that they *aren't* willing to pay (even when they really *are* willing to pay), because they believe that someone else will eventually foot the bill. This is called the *free-rider problem*. For a nonexcludable

public good, people have an incentive to be "free riders", by understating their true preferences for the public good. As a result, it will be hard to determine the amount of public good that would be best for society.

We can come to a better understanding of the free-rider problem, by thinking about why there isn't any free-rider problem for a pure private good. For a private good, if you want the item, you get out your wallet and pay for it. Thus people are forced to reveal whether they are willing to pay for private goods. For public goods, however, it is much more difficult to get people to reveal their preferences.

More Examples of Public Goods. Defense against nuclear attack is a classic example of a public good. If the Defense Department is able to protect you from nuclear attack, it must also be able to protect everyone within many miles of you. Therefore, missile defense is nonrival. At the same time, missile defense is also nonexcludable. It's impossible to protect Joe Jones (who paid his taxes) without also protecting Sam Smith (even though Sam didn't pay his taxes). Missile defense is a "pure" public good, because it is completely nonrival and nonexcludable.

At the other extreme are the pure private goods, such as socks. Pure private goods are completely rival and excludable. In between, there are goods that are somewhat public, but not as much so as national defense. For example, for a fireworks show, it's difficult to exclude those who do not pay, but it may not be absolutely impossible to do so. The same goes for parks, lakes, and other recreational facilities. Police protection, fire protection, and vaccination programs all have a substantial degree of nonrivalry and nonexcludability, but not as much as national defense.

Higher education has fairly low costs of exclusion, since it's hard to receive a college degree unless you enroll, and it's hard to enroll unless you pay. However, higher education is partly nonrival, since an education may provide some benefits for the entire society, and not just for the individual student.

These examples show that many goods are neither pure private goods nor pure public goods. For the pure private goods, it's best to use private markets. For the pure public goods, such as national defense, it will be necessary to rely on government. The in-between goods will have to be taken on a case-by-case basis. For example, in most States, governments pay for virtually all of the expenses of elementary and secondary education. Presumably, this is because of the belief that a large part of the benefits from a basic education are enjoyed by society as a whole, and not just by the individual. (In other words, there is a big element of "publicness" to elementary and secondary education.) However, governments pay for a smaller portion of the costs of college education. This is probably because of the belief that the individual captures a much larger part of the benefits of higher education. (In other words, there appears to be a belief that higher education is less of a public good than elementary education, even though both types of education have a degree of publicness.)

Even though we will have to rely on governments to decide on how much of a public good to provide, it does not follow that governments have to *provide* the public goods. For example, even though national defense is a public good, many weapons systems are actually produced by private contractors.

The "Demand" for Public Goods

In an earlier chapter, it was seen that the market demand curve for a private good is derived by adding the individual demand curves together. In a competitive market, every consumer faces the same price, but different consumers may choose different quantities. In graphical terms, the individual demand curves are added horizontally to get the market demand curve.

Because pure public goods are characterized by nonrival consumption, it is necessary to use a different technique to evaluate the "demand" for public goods. In the case of a pure public good, every consumer receives the same quantity. However, different consumers may be willing to pay different amounts of money for the public goods they receive.

Figure 16.1 shows the "willingness-to-pay" curves of Attila and Bartholomew, regarding the quantities of nuclear missiles. These are marked as WTP_A for Attila, and WTP_B for

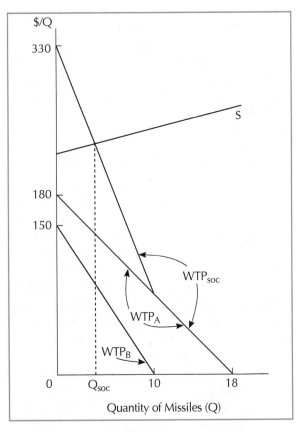

Figure 16.1 The Willingness-to-Pay Curve, or "Demand" Curve, for a Pure Public Good

Missile defense is a pure public good. Attila's willingness-to-pay curve for missiles is WTP_A. Bartholomew's willingness-to-pay curve is WTP_B. We add them vertically to get WTP_{soc}, which is the willingness-to-pay curve for the entire two-person society. The optimal number of missiles is found by locating the intersection of WTP_{soc} with the supply curve, S.

Bartholomew. For each individual, the willingness-to-pay curve for a public good shows the maximum amount he is willing to pay for one additional missile, depending on the number of missiles that are already in place. Basically, these individual willingness-to-pay curves give the same information that would be given by the demand curve for a private good. However, we refer to them as "willingness-to-pay curves", rather than demand curves, to keep in mind the fact that public goods and private goods are different in some important ways.

One important difference between private goods and public goods is that the method of adding the individual curves together is different for public goods than it was for private goods. For private goods, everyone pays the same price. Therefore, the procedure is to pick a price, and add all of the individual demands *horizontally*. For pure public goods, on the other hand, everyone receives the same quantity. The procedure is to pick a quantity, and add all of the individual willingness-to-pay curves *vertically*. It is said that society's willingness-to-pay curve is drawn by *vertical summation* of the individual willingness-to-pay curves.

In Figure 16.1, society's willingness-to-pay curve is WTP_{soc}. When there are more than 10 missiles, Bartholomew isn't willing to pay anything for any more missiles. Therefore, when there are more than 10 missiles, the willingness-to-pay curve for this two-person society (WTP_{soc}) is exactly the same as Attila's willingness to pay (WTP_A). When the quantity of missiles is less than 10, WTP_{soc} is drawn by adding WTP_A and WTP_B vertically. For example, when the quantity of missiles falls all the way to zero, Attila is willing to pay $180 for a missile, and Bartholomew is willing to pay $150. Adding these two together, we get a total willingness to pay of $330.

It is possible, *in theory*, to identify the optimal level of a public good. The optimal quantity of a public good is found at the intersection of the social willingness-to-pay curve with the supply curve. In Figure 16.1,

the supply curve is S, and the socially optimal quantity of missiles is Q_{soc}.

However, there is one other important difference between the demand for private goods and the "demand" for public goods. Demands are revealed very well in private markets. As a result, private markets tend to reach equilibrium quickly and efficiently. For better or worse, it's different for public goods. In the "market" for public goods, the free-rider problem means that people have an incentive to conceal their true preferences. Thus, *in practice*, it will be difficult for society to figure out exactly what Q_{soc} should be.

Since people don't have an incentive to reveal their true preferences for public goods, there is no mechanism that will quickly lead society to the optimal level of a public good. Instead, society has to rely on the political process. In the search for the correct level of a public good, society has to rely on politicians, voters, bureaucrats, lobbyists, editorial writers, protestors, and other such folks. There is no guarantee that the political process will find the optimal level of a public good. Depending on a number of factors, the political system might choose too much of a public good, or too little.

Income Distribution

Even if there were no public goods, and even if there were no market failures of any kind, the government might still have an important role to play. This is because there's no guarantee that private markets will produce a distribution of income that is considered "fair". Markets reward people on the basis of the resources that they own: Highly skilled people tend to earn higher wages and salaries, and wealthy people receive relatively large amounts of interest, dividends, royalties, and so on. Since markets don't account for fairness, it would be an accident if the market economy were to provide a "fair" distribution of income.

As was mentioned in Chapter 15, most countries use taxes and transfer payments, in an attempt to reduce the extent of inequality in the distribution of income. In the United States, governments spend more than two trillion dollars ($2,000,000,000,000) on transfer-payment programs every year. These include Social Security, Medicare, Medicaid, Food Stamps, welfare programs, and many other programs. Some of these transfer payments go to very affluent people, but much of them goes to lower-income people. On average, transfer payments do reduce the inequality in the income distribution.

Once again, the amount of spending on transfers is decided upon by governments, and not by private markets. Most people won't give up their incomes voluntarily. As a result, governments are in charge of paying transfer payments, and collecting the taxes that are needed to finance them.

Reality Check: Interim Review Question

IR16-1. Is there a good justification for providing weather forecasting services through the government? What about child-care services? What about retirement pensions for government workers?

TRENDS IN GOVERNMENT SPENDING

The previous section describes some of the reasons why it might be desirable to have a government. However, to understand government fully, it's necessary to know about the *actual* spending of governments. How many dollars do governments really spend? Which government programs have grown, and which have shrunk? Without an understanding of the actual spending levels, any discussion of government spending will be left in a vacuum.

In this section, we will describe some of the trends in government spending in the United States. We begin with the federal government, and we then move on to the state and local governments. Finally, there is a brief comparison between the spending levels in the United States and the spending levels in some other countries.

Many people are amazingly uninformed about the basic facts of what government does. One public-opinion survey showed that the average American believes that the government spends 28 percent of its budget on foreign aid, whereas the true figure is about one percent. Thus anyone who reads this section will be way ahead of most people!

Federal Government Spending

In 2015, the federal government in the United States spent about $3.69 trillion. (That's $3,690,000,000,000.) This works out to about 20 percent of gross domestic product (GDP).

The federal government's share of output has not always been so large. Back in 1799, the federal government spent only about 1.4 percent of national income. Even as late as 1929, the federal share of GDP was only about three percent. In the 1930s, however, the government increased its spending on domestic programs, in an effort to ease the pain of the Great Depression. Then, federal spending really soared during the Second World War. At the height of the war, in 1944, federal spending was about 44 percent of GDP! Federal spending decreased after the war, but it never fell back to the levels of the 1920s.

During most years in the 1950s, about 18 percent of GDP went to federal spending. This fraction rose to about 22 percent in the 1980s and early 1990s, before falling back somewhat in the late 1990s. GDP fell sharply during the deep recession of 2007–09. At the same time, federal spending was increased, in an attempt to reduce the severity of the recession. Thus when we calculate federal spending as a percent of GDP, we had both an increase in the numerator and a decrease in the denominator. As a result, federal spending rose to about 24 percent of GDP in 2009, before falling back to about 21 percent by 2015.

The Growth of Transfer Payments and Interest Payments. Although the overall level of federal spending has increased in the last few decades, some programs have grown much more rapidly than others. As a result, it is said that the "composition" of federal spending has changed. Figure 16.2 shows some of the changes in the composition of federal spending from 1940 to 2015. The fraction of Gross Domestic Product (GDP) that is spent by the federal government soared in the early 1940s as a result of national-defense spending during the Second World War. A smaller surge in defense spending occurred in the early 1950s, during the Korean War. Since then, the portion of GDP devoted to defense has tended to decline. Meanwhile, there has been a rapid increase in transfer payments, such as Social Security, Medicare, Medicaid, Food Stamps, unemployment compensation, and so on. By 2015, more than $1.7 trillion per year was being spent on the three largest programs: Social Security, Medicare, and Medicaid.

The Relative Decline of Defense Spending. While transfer payments were increasing rapidly, defense spending was becoming relatively less important. After correcting for inflation, the defense budget was almost exactly the same size in 2000 as it had been in 1966. Since defense spending stayed about the same, at a time when the overall size of the economy was increasing, it follows that defense spending as a percentage of gross domestic product must have decreased. Figure 16.2 shows that defense's share of GDP has fallen from nearly 10 percent to about 3.3 percent during the last 50 years.

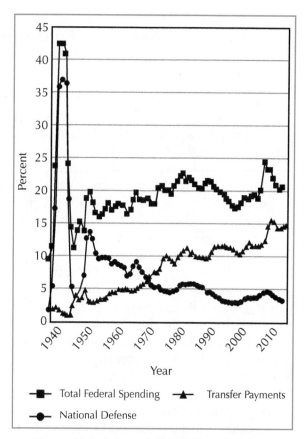

Figure 16.2 Selected Categories of Federal Government Spending, as Percent of Gross Domestic Product, 1940–2015

Federal spending surged in the early 1940s as a result of World War II. A smaller surge took place in the early 1950s as a result of the Korean War. Since then, the fraction of GDP devoted to national defense has decreased significantly. On the other hand, transfer payments have risen fairly steadily. Total federal spending has been between 18 percent of GDP and 23 percent of GDP in most of the last 50 years.

In recent years, transfers, interest, and defense have accounted for more than 90 percent of federal spending.

Of course, the government does other things, as well. The federal government regulates food and drugs, and it operates embassies around the world, and the National Park Service, and the Federal Bureau of Investigation (FBI), and the National Aeronautics and Space Administration (NASA), the

Real Economics for Real People 16.1: Budget Deficits

After the huge deficits of the Second World War, the federal government's deficits were very small for a generation. In fact, in several years during the 1950s and 1960s, the government ran a surplus, which means that taxes and other receipts were *greater* than spending. However, beginning in 1969, there was a period of three decades during which the federal government ran a deficit in every year. Moreover, as a proportion of GDP, the deficits were larger than anything that had ever occurred before, except during times of war. The deficit climbed to 4.2 percent of GDP in 1976. In 1983, the deficit reached 6 percent of GDP, which was an all-time record for peacetime. Even as recently as 1992, the deficit was 4.7 percent of GDP.

There are many reasons for these large budget deficits. One is that the economy grew more slowly in the 1970s and 1980s than it had in earlier decades. Serious recessions rocked the economy in 1974–75, and in 1982, and a smaller recession occurred in 1991. When the economy is shrinking, or growing slowly, it isn't possible to collect as much tax revenue. Another cause of the deficits is a political tug-of-war. The Democratic Party tends to favor higher levels of both spending and taxes, while the Republican Party tends to favor lower levels of both spending and taxes. Neither party is in favor of deficits, as such. However, Democratic lawmakers have been generally willing to tolerate deficits, rather than reduce spending dramatically. And Republican lawmakers have been generally willing to tolerate deficits, rather than approve major tax increases. In fact, the deficits were widened by major tax cuts passed into law in 1981 and 2001.

In the 1990s, these conditions began to change. Tax increases were passed in 1990 and 1993, and some spending reductions were made, as well. More importantly, after the 1991 recession, the economy achieved a long period of steady growth. A growing economy means that more tax revenues are coming in. The rapid growth of revenues was sufficient to bring the deficits to an end by 1998.

In 2000, there were many predictions that the surpluses would go on indefinitely. However, these forecasts were based on the assumption that the economy would continue to grow at a robust pace, and that a recession would not occur. (This seems like an odd assumption, since the economy had already had nine recessions since the Second World War.)

The budget surpluses did not last. The economy slipped into a recession in 2001. As the economy shrank, tax revenues were collected at a much smaller pace. Even when the recession ended, in November of 2001, the economy expanded very slowly.

Meanwhile, even if the recession had not occurred, the budget surpluses were an endangered species. During the 2000 election campaign, the air was filled with ideas for how to spend the surpluses. Some proposals involved more government expenditures, and some proposals involved tax cuts. Tax cuts were very important to the eventual winner of the Presidential campaign, George W. Bush, and a tax-reduction bill was passed in 2001. Spending also increased on many items, including the Iraq war and a host of domestic projects. By 2004, deficits were in the range of $400 billion per year. At the end of 2007, the economy sank into a recession, which grew dramatically worse in late 2008. The deep recession led to sharp declines in tax revenues. In an attempt to keep the recession from getting worse, Congress enacted a series of further tax cuts and spending increases. The deficit soared from $342 billion in 2007 to more than $1.5 trillion in 2009, and then slowly decreased.

Figure 16.3 shows the trends over time in national debt, as a percentage of GDP. (National debt is the accumulation of all of the deficits.) Taxes went up during the Second World War, but government spending went up even more rapidly. Thus the ratio of debt to GDP skyrocketed. However, for the next 30 years, the government ran small deficits in some years, and small surpluses in others, while the economy grew rapidly. Consequently the ratio of debt to GDP shrank. Substantial deficits returned in the 1970s and 1980s, so that the debt-to-GDP ratio rose from about 23 percent in 1974 to about 48 percent in 1993. However, the deficits shrank, and eventually disappeared, in the middle and late 1990s. As a result, the debt-to-GDP ratio fell substantially. Although no one really likes the national debt, it does not represent a crushing burden. As a proportion of GDP, the debt was much higher in 1945 than it has been recently. And yet, the economy did just fine in the late 1940s, in spite of the debt.

However, even though it's possible to survive with debt and deficits, it does not follow that they are particularly good. Even though modest deficits are no problem, large deficits are a major cause for concern. That is especially true of the deficits of the early years of the 21st century, for a couple of reasons. First, Americans are not saving enough to buy all of the new government bonds. Instead, people from other countries are buying huge amounts of American debt every day. For a country like the United States, which has long played a very important role in world affairs, there are potential dangers to being in debt to other countries. Also, with the retirements of the Baby Boom generation, the Social Security and Medicare programs are expanding greatly. This will put added strain on the budget. How Americans deal with these budgetary issues will be one of the most interesting and important stories of the coming decade.

National Weather Service, the Census Bureau, and many other agencies. In fact, these agencies provide some very important public goods. However, the amounts of money spent on these other categories are relatively small. Even if these other activities were to be reduced dramatically, the effect on the overall budget wouldn't be very great. Thus any attempts to reduce federal spending in a serious way will be doomed to failure unless they deal with the really big categories of spending, the biggest of which is transfer payments.

For most of the last 45 years, the federal government has been running budget deficits, by which we mean that its expenditures have usually been greater than its receipts. The deficits were eliminated for a few years, but by the early 21st century, they were back with a vengeance. We discuss the deficit situation in *Real Economics for Real People 16.1*.

Spending of State and Local Governments

In the previous section, we saw that federal government spending had grown to nearly $3.7 trillion by 2015. At the same time, state and local governments were spending a total of more than $2.4 trillion. Thus, the total spending of state and local governments is very substantial, although it is somewhat less than the total spending of the federal government.

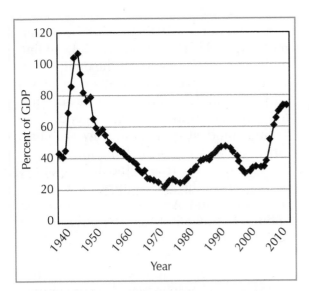

Figure 16.3 Federal Government Debt as a Percentage of Gross Domestic Product, 1940–2015

The ratio of federal debt to GDP rose dramatically during the Second World War. For the next 30 years, the federal debt increased more slowly than GDP, so that the debt-to-GDP ratio fell substantially. From the middle 1970s to the middle 1990s, the economy grew slowly and debt grew rapidly, so that the debt-to-GDP ratio increased. In the late 1990s, the ratio again began to shrink. But budget deficits returned at the beginning of the 21st century, and the debt-to-GDP ratio was on its way up again. The deep recession of 2007–09 and its aftermath led to further large increases in debt.

The federal government spends most of its money on transfer payments, interest, and defense, but state and local governments tend to spend on different activities. The biggest category of state and local spending is education, which consumes more than 30 percent of the total. Highways, hospitals, police departments, fire departments, and income support for the poor are also important spending categories for the state and local governments.

International Comparisons of Government Spending

If we add together the spending of all governments in the United States (including federal, state, and local), the total is more than $6 trillion per year. This works out to more than 30 percent of GDP. This is far more than the percentage spent by governments in the U.S. before the 1920s. However, the percentage for the United States is lower than that of some European countries. France, Germany, Sweden, and the United Kingdom devote more than 40 percent of GDP to government spending.

Until now, most of this chapter has been devoted to the spending programs of governments. These programs are important, but they aren't the whole story. If a government wants to spend money, it will have to find some way to pay its bills. We'll spend most of the rest of the chapter on the economics of taxes, which are the most important method of financing government programs.

Reality Check: Interim Review Questions

IR16-2. Describe the differences between federal government spending programs and the spending programs of state and local governments.

IR16-3. What are the three largest federal transfer payment programs?

HOW DO GOVERNMENTS PAY FOR THEIR ACTIVITIES?

Since government programs cost money, it's necessary for governments to pay for their activities. Over the centuries, governments have tried many methods of financing. These include the following:

- *Confiscation*. What would you do if a hungry soldier came to your house, pointed a machine gun at you, and demanded food? You would probably decide to feed him, even if he didn't offer to give money in return. When governments acquire resources without paying for them, it is said that the governments "confiscate" the resources. Although outright confiscation does sometimes occur, especially in wartime, it makes up a very small part of government finance in most countries.

- *Inflation*. Hundreds of years ago, most money was in the form of coins. It was common for kings to clip or shave some of the gold or silver from around the edges of the coins. The kings would then melt down this gold or silver, and cast it into new coins. This practice would lead to inflation, since a larger number of coins would be chasing the same amount of goods and services. Today, most countries engage in a modern version of coin clipping, by issuing paper money at a rate that is faster than the growth rate of the economy. In either case, we get inflation: The value of the currency will go down, and the prices of goods will rise. In recent years, the rate of inflation in the United States has been about two percent per year. However, inflation sometimes reaches much higher levels than this. For example, Brazil's inflation rate was about 7000 percent per year in the middle of 1994. In November 2008, the inflation rate in Zimbabwe briefly reached 80 billion percent per month.

- *Bonds*. Governments finance part of their activities by borrowing, which means that they issue bonds. It's common for governments to borrow heavily in wartime. For example, in 1943 (during the Second World War), borrowing by the federal government amounted to more than 31 percent of GDP! From 1970 to the middle 1990s, the federal government borrowed an average of about 3.3 percent of GDP per year. The recession sent borrowing skyrocketing to 10 percent of GDP in 2009. The federal deficit gradually receded to 2.5 percent of GDP by 2015.

- *Taxes*. Most governments finance most of their activities with taxes. In the United States, governments use a wide variety of taxes, including personal income taxes, corporation income taxes, payroll taxes, sales taxes, property taxes, and taxes on estates, inheritances, and gifts.

Since taxes are the most important source of revenue, we will concentrate on them in the rest of this chapter. We begin by describing the characteristics of a "good" tax system. We then look at the actual effects of the tax system in the United States. Finally, we will discuss some important current controversies in tax policy.

Characteristics of a Good Tax System

In order to judge whether our current tax system does a good job, it's necessary to define the goals that a tax system is supposed to achieve. Ideally, the tax system should achieve several different goals. These goals are discussed in the next few paragraphs.

Raising Revenue. If governments didn't spend any money, there would be little need for taxes at all. (Even if governments did not need to pay for roads, schools, and other things, we still might want to have taxes on air pollution, tobacco products, and alcoholic beverages, in an attempt to reduce their adverse effects. We will discuss these taxes in more detail in the next chapter. For now, it's good to understand that this type of tax is unlikely to raise anywhere near as much revenue as is currently collected in the United States.) Therefore, the first important goal for any tax system is to raise tax revenue. Consequently, a tax on toothpicks is not likely to be a very successful part of the tax system—the toothpick market is too small to yield very much tax revenue, even if high tax rates are used. In the United States, and in many other countries, most taxes fall on earnings in the labor market. This is partly because labor taxes can raise a lot of revenue.

Economic Efficiency. Every tax affects the behavior of households and/or firms. For example, the personal income tax creates an incentive for people to work less. Another example is the corporation income tax, which creates an incentive for people to invest in non-corporate businesses, rather than in corporations. In an effort to reduce their taxes, people change their behavior in many ways: They work less, save less, and change their buying patterns.

When a tax leads to changes in behavior, we say it is a *distortionary tax*. Distortionary taxes tend to mess up the workings of the economy. Economists say that distortionary taxes create *inefficiency*. Thus another important goal for the tax system (all else equal) is to minimize inefficiency. Later in this chapter, we will learn how to measure some of the inefficiencies caused by the tax system, so we can begin to think about how to keep inefficiency to a minimum.

Ease of Compliance and Administration. Every year, American families spend about two billion hours (that's 2,000,000,000 hours) keeping records, filling out tax forms, and so on. They also spend billions of dollars hiring accountants and attorneys, whose job is to help guide the taxpayer through the complexities of the tax system. Employees of businesses also spend several billion hours every year, complying with the business tax laws.

There is a real opportunity cost to this activity, since people could have done something else with their time. When the private sector has to spend real resources to obey the tax law, we say that the tax system creates *compliance costs.*

The Internal Revenue Service and the various State and local revenue agencies also spend real resources on getting the tax system to run smoothly. For example, the revenue agencies have to hire clerks, auditors, and attorneys. We refer to these costs as the *administrative costs* of the tax system. Another important goal for a tax system (all else equal) is to minimize the costs of compliance and administration.

Fairness. Another goal for the tax system (all else equal) is to distribute the tax burden "fairly". This may sound like a simple goal, but it isn't. The problem is that different people may have very different views about fairness. The next few paragraphs define some ways of thinking about fairness. However, it won't be possible to prove that one set of opinions about fairness is right, or that some other set of opinions is wrong.

Horizontal Equity. All else equal, it's probably desirable for the tax system to treat similar people in similar ways. If two families live in similar houses, and if they have similar incomes, and so on, then it would probably be good if they were to have similar tax payments. When a tax system treats similar people in a similar manner, the tax system is characterized by *horizontal equity*.

In order to understand horizontal equity, it may help to know of some situations in which the tax system is *not* horizontally equitable. One example is the way in which the income tax treats people according to their marital status. In the United States, there are separate tax schedules for married couples who file a joint tax return, and for married couples who file separate returns, and for single people. Because of these complications, the income tax is said to be "not neutral with respect to marital status". Some couples receive a *marriage bonus*, which means that the couple's total tax payments would be lower if they were married than if they were unmarried. On the other hand, some couples face a *marriage penalty*, which means that the couple's total tax payments would be lower if they were unmarried. These marriage bonuses and marriage penalties strike many people as being violations of the principle of horizontal equity.

Here is another example: Virtually all homes in the United States are subject to a property tax. However, in several States, a home is only assessed to its correct market value when it is sold. Since some families stay in the same house for many years, the property-tax assessments can become very inaccurate. Even though two houses may have the same market value, they can be assessed very differently for the property tax. When similar houses are taxed very differently, many people would say that we have another case of horizontal inequity.

Vertical Equity. Whereas horizontal equity involves treating *similar* people in a *similar* way, **vertical equity** involves treating *different* people in *different* ways. Vertical equity deals with the desire to allocate the tax burden in accordance with "ability to pay". This is usually interpreted as meaning that people with higher incomes should pay higher taxes than people with lower incomes.

At this point, it's important to define some terms that are often used to describe the degree of vertical equity of a tax system. In a **proportional tax**, everyone pays the same percentage of income in tax. For example, if Arnold has $10,000 of income and pays $1000 in tax, he pays ten percent of his income in tax. If Alice has $20,000 of income and pays $2000 in tax, then she also pays ten percent of her income in tax. Since both people pay the same percentage, the tax is proportional.

In a **progressive tax**, people with higher incomes pay a *higher* percentage of income in tax. To continue with the example from the previous paragraph, let's say once again that Arnold has $10,000 of income, and pays $1000 in tax, for a tax rate of ten percent. If Alice has $20,000 of income and pays $3000 in tax, then she pays 15 percent of her income in tax. Since

the percentage of income paid in tax is rising when income rises, this is a progressive tax.

A **regressive tax** is one that allows people with higher incomes to pay a *lower* percentage of income in tax. If Alice has $20,000 of income and pays $1800 in tax, then she pays only nine percent of her income in tax, which is less than the rate of ten percent paid by Arnold. The percentage of income paid in tax is falling when income rises, so this is a regressive tax.

Notice that a regressive tax does not necessarily mean that higher-income people pay a lower *total amount* of tax. (In the preceding paragraph, Alice has more income than Arnold has, and she pays $800 more tax than Arnold pays.) Instead, a regressive tax only means that higher-income people pay a lower *percentage* of income in tax. (Alice pays nine percent of her income, whereas Arnold pays ten percent.)

If a tax raises the same number of dollars from everyone, it is a highly regressive tax. If everyone pays $1000 of tax, this is 10 percent of income for someone with income of $10,000, but only one percent of income for someone with income of $100,000.

It's important to emphasize that reasonable people can disagree about the degree of progressivity that the best tax system might have. If person A prefers a progressive tax system, while person B prefers a proportional system, neither of them can prove that the other is wrong.

Recall that positive statements are statements about the actual workings of the economy, whereas normative statements are about what ought to be. When we are discussing whether a tax should be progressive, proportional, or regressive, we are very much in *normative* territory.

Conflicts Among the Goals

So far, you have read about four goals for the tax system. All else equal, it would be good for the tax system to:

- raise revenue,
- create a minimal amount of economic inefficiency,
- create a minimal amount of administrative and compliance cost, and
- distribute the tax burden "fairly".

One other goal that is sometimes discussed is macroeconomic stabilization. For example, tax policy might be used in an effort to keep the overall rates of inflation and unemployment under control. Even though macroeconomic stabilization is important, we will not discuss it here. Instead, this chapter is focused on *microeconomic* issues.

Unfortunately, no single tax is best at achieving every goal, because the goals conflict with each other. One important conflict among the goals is the *equity-efficiency trade-off*: Progressive taxes are often more inefficient than proportional and regressive taxes. For example, the personal income tax plays a very important role when it comes to promoting progressivity, but it also causes inefficiency. Also, the payroll tax is less inefficient than most other taxes, but it is regressive over the upper range of incomes.

Because of the conflicts among goals, it won't be possible to identify the "perfect" tax system. The best that can be done is to learn more about the inefficiencies of the various taxes, as well as their costs of administration and compliance, and their effects on the distribution of income. Then, each person can decide what kind of tax system he or she would prefer, based on his or her own beliefs about the relative importance of the various goals.

Reality Check: Interim Review Question

IR16-4. Most people fill out a form when they begin to work at a new job. After the form is filled out, payment of the payroll tax is automatic, and the employee never has to do any more paperwork to pay the payroll tax. On the other hand, many taxpayers spend dozens of hours every year filling out forms and keeping records for the individual income tax. On the basis of these facts, we can say that the payroll tax is better than the income tax in terms of one of the characteristics of a good tax system (efficiency, administration, compliance, horizontal equity, or vertical equity). Which one?

TRENDS IN TAX REVENUES

So far, very little has been said about the actual structure of the tax system. Which taxes are big, and which are little? Which have grown most rapidly, and which have grown slowly or not at all? This section provides answers to some of these questions.

Federal Taxes

In 2015, the federal government collected about $3.25 trillion (i.e., $3,250,000,000,000), in the form of taxes and other receipts. This was about 18.3 percent of GDP. Figure 16.4 shows some of the trends in federal tax revenues as a propor-

tion of GDP, from 1940 to 2015. In Figure 16.3, we saw that the Second World War had a huge effect on the federal government's debt. Figure 16.4 shows that World War II also had a huge effect on the tax collections of the federal government. To finance the war, the government issued large amounts of debt, and it also raised taxes dramatically. The biggest increases came from the individual income tax and the corporation income tax.

Since the 1950s, however, there has not been much of a trend in the total amount of federal revenues as a percent of GDP. There are some fluctuations from year to year, of

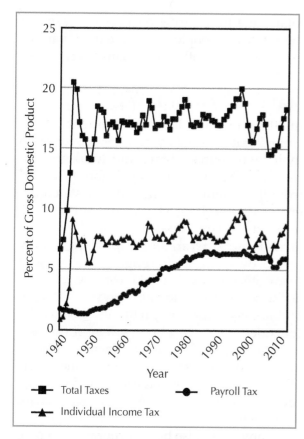

Figure 16.4 Selected Categories of Federal Revenues, 1940–2015

For most of the last 60 years, the federal government has taken in between 15 percent and 20 percent of GDP. Throughout this period, the individual income tax has been the most important revenue source. The payroll tax grew rapidly, especially in the 1960s and 1970s, and it is now the second-most-important revenue source.

course. However, for the most part, the ratio of federal taxes to GDP has stayed within a fairly narrow range. Since 1951, federal taxes have been between 15 percent and 20 percent of GDP in all but two years. Those two years are 2009–2010. These low relative levels of revenues were the result of the deep recession, combined with tax cuts that were passed in an attempt to prevent the recession from getting worse.

The Federal Individual Income Tax. In the 1890s, the Supreme Court ruled that an income tax was unconstitutional. As a result, the United States didn't get a permanent *individual income tax* until the Sixteenth Amendment to the Constitution, in 1913. As the name suggests, the income tax applies to many types of income, including wages and salaries, dividends, interest, rents, and royalties. In its early years, the income tax only collected a relatively small amount of revenue. However, the income tax was expanded greatly during the Second World War, and it has been the largest source of federal revenue ever since.

Figure 16.4 shows that the individual income tax has collected between seven and ten percent of GDP in nearly every year, for the last several decades. Year in and year out, the income tax is responsible for more than 40 percent of the revenues collected by the federal government. By 2015, this tax generated about $1.54 trillion in tax revenue.

Payroll Taxes. Many of the federal government's Social Insurance programs (such as Social Security and Medicare) are paid for by a *payroll tax*, which was instituted in 1937. The payroll tax is only applied to wages and salaries. As shown in Figure 16.4, the payroll tax has been the fastest-growing source of federal revenue in recent decades.

Most wages and salaries are subject to a flat rate of payroll tax. The payroll tax rate has increased dramatically, from two percent in 1937 to 15.3 percent today. By 2015, the payroll tax and other Social Insurance taxes collected about $1.07 trillion for the federal government. This comes to about 33 percent of federal revenues.

The Corporate Tax and the Excise Taxes. Since the Second World War, the individual income tax has brought in a fairly constant share of federal tax revenues, and the payroll tax has brought an increasing share. This means that some other taxes must have become relatively less important. The two big revenue sources that have declined are the corporation income tax and the family of federal excise taxes.

The *corporation income tax* was instituted in 1909. The corporation tax applies to the profits of corporations, although the legal definition of corporate profits is extremely complicated. The corporate tax grew rapidly during World War II. However, its share of federal revenues declined fairly steadily from 1952 to 1986. There are many reasons for the decline, but one of the biggest is that Congress enacted a number of generous deductions and credits over the years. In 1986, an attempt was made to increase the revenues from the corporate tax. This attempt was only moderately successful, however, because interest payments remained deductible from the corporate tax. As a result, many corporations increased their use of debt, which allowed them to deduct more interest payments.

The federal government also levies a number of *excise taxes* on the sale of specific commodities. As recently as 1963, there were excise taxes on playing cards, musical instruments, appliances, cameras, film, luggage, and dozens of other items. However, most of the smaller excise taxes have been repealed. Today, the major remaining excise taxes are on alcoholic beverages, tobacco products, gasoline, and other fuels. Even for some of the excise taxes that remain in effect, there has been a drop in the relative amounts of revenue raised. This is because some of them are levied in such a way that their revenues are eroded by inflation.

In 2015, the individual income tax accounted for about 47 percent of federal revenues, the payroll tax and other Social Insurance taxes were responsible for about 33 percent, and the corporation income tax brought in about 11 percent. The remaining nine percent of the total came from tariffs on imports, taxes on the estates of people who have died, various excise taxes, and other miscellaneous charges.

State and Local Taxes

In 2015, state and local governments in the United States raised about $1.56 trillion from their own sources. State and local governments also receive substantial amounts of aid from the federal government. For state governments, the biggest revenue sources are individual income taxes and *general retail sales taxes*. **General retail sales taxes** are usually levied on sales of clothing, hardware, and many other goods. Sales of most services (such as the services provided by lawyers, doctors, and accountants) are usually *not* covered by the sales taxes. In many states, food isn't taxed, either. For local governments, property taxes are the largest sources of revenue. Overall, the vast majority of the state and local tax revenues come from income taxes, sales taxes, or property taxes.

Many states also have corporation income taxes. Alaska, Oklahoma, Texas, and other oil-producing states get a lot of revenue from "severance taxes" on oil. Finally, state and local governments also get revenue from an immense variety of smaller charges, such as professional license fees, parking fines, and so on.

Reality Check: Interim Review Questions

IR16-5. Describe the differences between the federal tax system and the tax systems of state and local governments.

IR16-6. What are the two largest sources of tax revenue for the federal government?

THE EFFECTS OF TAXES ON EFFICIENCY AND DISTRIBUTION

In the previous section, you learned about a number of different taxes, including individual income taxes, corporation income taxes, payroll taxes, general retail sales taxes, excise taxes, and property taxes. The tax-revenue system in the United States certainly has a tremendous amount of variety. Which of these taxes work well, and which don't? To move toward an answer to that question, this section develops some ways of thinking about the economic effects of taxes.

The best way to analyze a tax is to look at its effects on supply and demand in the marketplace. In this section, supply/demand diagrams are used to study the economic effects of taxes. You will learn to identify the revenue generated by the tax, as well as the efficiency loss the tax generates. In addition, you will learn to think about how the burden of the tax is divided among buyers and sellers.

The Effects of a Sales Tax or Excise Tax

The simplest tax to understand is a commodity tax. You have probably had direct experience with commodity taxes, such as general retail sales taxes or excise taxes. General retail sales taxes are used in 46 of the 50 states. Excise taxes on alcoholic beverages, tobacco products, and gasoline are levied by the federal government, and by each of the 50 states and the District of Columbia.

The No-Tax Equilibrium. When we use supply/demand diagrams to study the effects of a tax, we always start by looking at the market equilibrium that would occur if there were no tax. Then, we look at the market equilibrium that would occur after the tax is imposed, and we compare the two equilibria. (This is the same technique that we used in

Chapter 5 when we studied the effects of a tariff, which is a tax on imports.) Figure 16.5 shows the effects of a sales tax on bicycles. The supply curve is horizontal in this case, which means that supply is perfectly elastic. (We will consider upward-sloping supply curves later in this chapter. For now, we use a horizontal supply curve because it simplifies the analysis.) In the absence of tax, the supply curve is S_{net}. It is called "S_{net}", to indicate that this supply curve is net of taxes. In other words, taxes are not included in the net-of-tax supply curve, S_{net}.

When there are no taxes, the market equilibrium is determined by the intersection of the demand curve with the net-of-tax supply curve, S_{net}. In Figure 16.5, the no-tax quantity is $Q_{no\ tax}$, and the no-tax price is $P_{no\ tax}$. Without any taxes, the buyers' price is the same as the sellers' price. The buyers pay a price of $P_{no\ tax}$ per bicycle, and the sellers receive the same $P_{no\ tax}$ per bicycle.

The Equilibrium with a Tax. Now, the government imposes a tax on bicycle sales. (Let's assume that the tax law is obeyed, and that people don't evade their taxes.) Because of the tax, it's now necessary to draw a new, gross-of-tax supply curve, S_{gross}.

In most of the examples in this book, only one supply curve is relevant at any one time. Now, however, two supply curves are in operation at the same time. The original supply curve, S_{net}, tells about the prices that are actually received by sellers. The new supply curve, S_{gross}, tells about the prices that are paid by buyers, when there is a tax. The difference between the two supply curves is the tax per unit: At any quantity, S_{gross} is equal to S_{net} plus the tax per unit. In Figure 16.5, the vertical distance between S_{gross} and S_{net} is the tax per unit.

With a tax, the price paid by the buyers will be greater than the price received by the

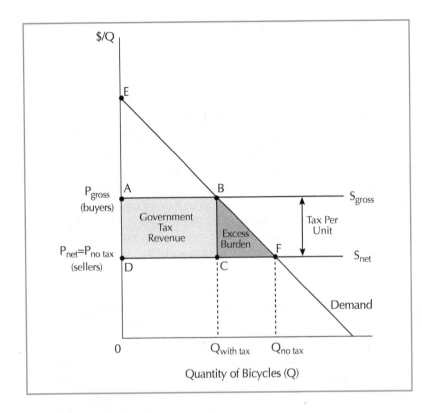

sellers. The gross-of-tax supply curve, S_{gross}, shows the prices that buyers have to pay, *including* taxes. From the buyer's point of view, this is what really counts. If you're shopping for a bicycle, and you have to pay $210, you don't really care whether the entire $210 goes to the seller, or whether the seller gets $200 and the government gets $10 of tax revenue. Buyers care about the total amount they have to pay, including all taxes.

The new equilibrium is given by the intersection of the demand curve with the new, gross-of-tax supply curve, S_{gross}. The new equilibrium quantity is $Q_{with\,tax}$.

In most of the examples in this book, the intersection of the supply and demand curves gives exactly one equilibrium price. However, when there is a tax, there are *two* equilibrium prices. The gross-of-tax price is the price paid by the buyers. In Figure 16.5, the gross-of-tax price is P_{gross}. The net-of-tax price is the price received by the sellers, which is P_{net} in Figure 16.5.

Before the tax was imposed, the sellers received $P_{no\,tax}$. After the tax is in place, the sellers receive P_{net}, which is exactly the same as $P_{no\,tax}$. Therefore, for the case shown in Figure 16.5, the tax doesn't change the price received by the sellers. The sellers' price is unchanged because the supply curve is perfectly elastic. With perfectly elastic supply, the sellers must receive $P_{no\,tax}$, or they won't produce any bicycles. Later in this chapter, we will see what happens when the supply curve is not perfectly elastic.

The Government's Tax Revenue. To calculate the total amount of tax revenue received by the government, we multiply the amount of tax per bicycle by the number of bicycles sold. The amount of tax per bicycle is ($P_{gross} - P_{net}$), or AD in Figure 16.5. The number of bicycles sold is $Q_{with\,tax}$. Thus the government's tax revenue is the area of the rectangle ABCD. If the tax were $10 per bicycle, and if one million bicycles were sold in a year, then the government's revenue would be ($10 per bicycle) (1 million bicycles) = $10 million.

The Excess Burden of the Tax. The public sector has gained revenue of ABCD, but the private sector has been made worse off by the tax. It would be good to know the size of the private sector's loss, so that it can be compared with the public sector's gain. To measure the private sector's loss, we use the concept of consumer surplus, which was introduced in Chapter 7.

Consumer surplus is the difference between the willingness to pay (given by the demand curve) and the amount actually paid (given by the price). Before the tax is imposed, the buyers of bicycles have consumer surplus of EFD in Figure 16.5. However, the tax raises the buyers' price to P_{gross}. Because of this, consumers decide to buy only $Q_{with\ tax}$ bicycles, and they get less consumer surplus from each bicycle they do buy. Buyers are made worse off by the tax, as seen by the fact that consumer surplus falls to EBA.

The loss for the buyers of bicycles is the difference between the consumer surplus they had before the tax and the consumer surplus that remains after the tax. In Figure 16.5, the consumers' loss is the area ABFD. This is the maximum amount that consumers would be willing to pay, for the privilege of having the tax on bicycles removed.

So, the government revenue is ABCD, and the consumers' loss is ABFD. The consumers' loss is greater than the government's gain. The difference is called the *excess burden* of the tax, and is shown by the area of the triangle BFC. The excess burden is sometimes also called the *deadweight loss* or *welfare cost* of the tax.

Excess burden is the best measure of the inefficiency of a tax. If efficiency is your goal, then it would be best to use the taxes that generate the smallest amount of excess burden. Later in this chapter, we will see some estimates of the excess burdens for different taxes.

It's important to understand one thing before going on. Just because taxes have excess burden, it is *not* necessarily wrong to have tax-financed government spending. After all, some government programs have great potential to improve the workings of the economy by providing valuable public goods. However, excess burden *does* mean that it's important to be careful. It's important to avoid government programs that are of little value, and it's important to avoid relying on taxes that generate unusually large amounts of excess burden.

Who Really Pays the Tax? When we think about who bears the burden of the tax, we are studying something called *tax incidence*. It is possible to distinguish between two concepts of tax incidence. *Statutory incidence* is determined by the statutes of the law. Thus if the law says that retail sellers are required to make sales-tax payments to the State Treasury, the "statutory incidence" falls on the retail sellers. However, just because the seller writes a check to the government, it doesn't necessarily follow that the seller *really* bears the burden of the tax. The true *economic incidence* of a tax falls on those who *really* pay. The economic incidence is determined by the elasticities of supply and demand. In Figure 16.5, the buyers are the ones who truly bear the burden of the tax on bicycles. The buyers lose a portion of their consumer surplus. The sellers don't lose any surplus—with perfectly elastic supply, the sellers' price stays the same after the tax is imposed. (However, this does not mean that sellers will be happy with the tax. Even though the sellers' price is unchanged, the volume of sales is reduced.)

Figure 16.5 shows that the true *economic* incidence of a tax can be different from the statutory incidence. In this case, 100 percent of the economic burden of the tax is borne by buyers of bicycles, even though the law says that the retail seller is ultimately responsible for writing a check to the government.

Revenue and Excess Burden with Different Elasticities. Figure 16.5 illustrates many of the most important concepts regarding the economic analysis of taxes. However, Figure 16.5 only deals with one special case, in which the supply curve is perfectly elastic, and the demand curve slopes downward in a particular way. How will the revenue, excess burden, and incidence be changed when different elasticities are used?

To begin our study of the effects of taxes with different elasticities, consider Figure 16.6, which is very similar to Figure 16.5. In each case, the supply curve is perfectly elastic, the initial price is $P_{no\ tax}$, and the initial quantity is $Q_{no\ tax}$. Each case also looks at the same size of tax. The difference is that panel (a) of Figure 16.6 considers the market for speedboats, which has a very elastic demand curve. On the other hand, panel (b) of Figure 16.6 shows the market for milk, which has very inelastic demand.

Panel (a) of Figure 16.6 shows what would happen if demand were very elastic: The tax would reduce the quantity of speedboats to

Q_2, which is a very big reduction. As a result, the tax doesn't raise much revenue, and the excess burden is very large. If efficiency is your goal, this is a bad situation: When a tax creates lots of excess burden but doesn't raise very much revenue, it isn't a very good tax.

From the point of view of efficiency, panel (b) of Figure 16.6 presents a better picture. With inelastic demand, the tax causes only a small change in the quantity of milk. This means that the tax on milk raises a lot of revenue, but does not create much excess burden.

The message is this: If a government wants to raise revenue in an efficient manner, it should put higher taxes on the commodities that are relatively more inelastic. However, this may create a major tension between equity and efficiency. According to the examples in Figure 16.6, efficiency considerations would mean that the tax rate should be higher on milk than on boats. Many people would be troubled by a tax system like this, because of

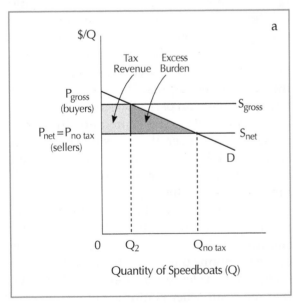 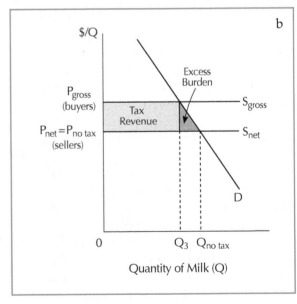

Figure 16.6 The Elasticity of Demand and the Economic Effects of a Commodity Tax

In panel (a), the demand for speedboats is fairly elastic. As a result, the tax only collects a small amount of revenue, but it generates a large amount of excess burden. In panel (b), the demand for milk is fairly inelastic. The tax on milk collects a lot of revenue, with only a small excess burden.

concerns about fairness, since milk makes up a larger part of the budget for low-income households.

Tax Incidence with Different Elasticities. In either panel of Figure 16.6, buyers bear the burden of the tax, in terms of reduced consumer surplus. When supply is perfectly elastic, the sellers do not suffer a reduction in their net selling price, although the quantity of sales is reduced. What would happen if the supply curve were upward sloping? Figure 16.7 shows that *the more inelastic side of the market will bear most of the burden of the tax.*

Panel (a) of Figure 16.7 shows the market for gem-quality emeralds, in which supply is very inelastic and demand is fairly elastic. In this situation, a tax would cause a big decrease in the sellers' price, P_{net}, but only a small increase in the buyers' price, P_{gross}. Thus the sellers would bear most of the burden of a tax on emeralds. Conversely, panel (b) of Figure 16.7 shows

the market for white bread, in which supply is elastic and demand is inelastic. In this case, a tax would only cause a small decrease in the sellers' price, P_{net}, but it would cause a large increase in the buyers' price, P_{gross}. This means that the buyers would bear most of the burden of a tax on white bread.

These results make sense when we think about the meaning of inelastic behavior and elastic behavior. If buyers or sellers are inelastic, they will not make big changes in their quantity demanded or quantity supplied, even if the price becomes a lot less favorable. In other words, if a tax is imposed, the inelastic person will bear the burden of the tax, and continue to buy or sell. On the other hand, if a buyer or seller is elastic, any attempt to impose a tax will lead to relatively large changes in behavior. For those who are extremely elastic, there is simply no way to get them to bear much of the burden of a tax: They will simply leave.

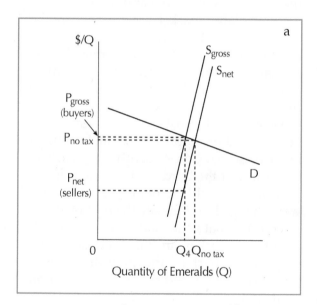 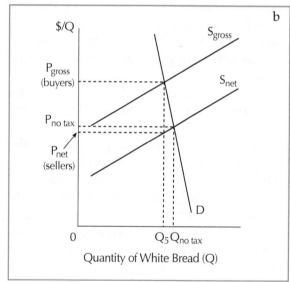

Figure 16.7 Tax Incidence and the Elasticities of Supply and Demand

In panel (a), the supply of emeralds is relatively inelastic, but demand is elastic. As a result, a tax does not raise the buyers' price very far, but the sellers' price falls by a great deal. The sellers bear most of the burden of the tax. In panel (b), the supply of white bread is elastic, but demand is inelastic. A tax raises the buyers' price by a lot, but the sellers' price only falls by a small amount. The buyers bear most of the burden of the tax. In each case, the more inelastic side of the market bears most of the burden of the tax.

If buyers are relatively more inelastic, they will bear most of the burden of a tax. If sellers are relatively more inelastic, they will bear most of the burden of a tax. These examples show that the more inelastic side of the market will bear most of the burden of the tax. These ideas are used in *Real Economics for Real People 16.2*, which looks at the incidence of the payroll tax.

What Have We Learned About the Effects of the Tax System?

In the last few pages, we have seen some of the ways in which economic reasoning can be used to understand the effects of taxes. Over the years, economists have used these ideas to come up with estimates of the effects of the tax system.

Real Economics for Real People 16.2: Who Really Pays the Payroll Tax?

Earlier in this chapter, we saw that the payroll tax is the second-largest source of revenue for the Federal government. The payroll tax is levied at a flat rate of 7.65 percent on the worker and 7.65 percent on the employer, for a total rate of 15.3 percent. Thus, the statutory incidence of the payroll tax is half on the employer and half on the employee.

It would be possible to raise the same amount of revenue, while changing the way in which the tax is divided between employers and workers. If the total tax rate is 15.3 percent, then the government could raise the same amount of revenue by putting the entire 15.3 percent on the workers, or by putting it all on the employers. The government could also raise the same amount of revenue by putting 10 percent on the employers and 5.3 percent on the employees, or by using any other combination.

Occasionally, there are proposals to change the way in which the payroll tax is divided between employers and workers. One such proposal involves putting the entire 15.3 percent on the employer. The people who make this type of proposal tend to make the argument that putting more of the tax on employers would be an advantage to the workers.

However, for better or worse, it really won't make much difference. The same effects should occur as long as the total tax rate is 15.3 percent, regardless of how much of the statutory burden goes on the employer and how much goes on the employee. The true economic incidence of taxes isn't determined by whether the government says that the employer or the worker is responsible for paying the tax. The true economic incidence is determined by the elasticities of supply and demand.

In the labor market, the workers are the suppliers of labor, and the firms are the demanders of labor. If supply is more inelastic than demand, the workers will bear most of the burden. If demand is more inelastic than supply, the firms will bear most of the burden. In fact, most of the evidence suggests that labor supply is more inelastic than labor demand. Consequently, the workers bear most of the burden of the payroll tax. This would still be true, even if the laws were changed to eliminate the portion of the payroll tax that is officially the responsibility of the worker. In 2011 and 2012, the employees' part of the payroll tax was reduced by two percentage points, in an effort to hasten the recovery from the very deep recession of 2007–2009. The analysis presented here suggests that the effects would have been about the same, if the payroll tax holiday had been divided between employers and employees in a different way.

One consistent result is that the overall tax system in the United States is roughly proportional or slightly progressive, even though the pieces of the tax system may not be proportional. Economic studies indicate that income taxes are somewhat progressive, for two reasons. First, income taxes have *personal exemptions*. The personal exemptions allow for every person to have a certain amount of income that is not subject to tax. The exemptions are especially important for the poor. Second, the federal income tax (like most of the state income taxes) has *graduated marginal tax rates*, which means that the tax rate applied to an additional dollar of taxable income is higher, for people who have higher taxable incomes.

Figure 16.8 shows the marginal and average tax rates for a married couple who file a joint return, for the federal individual income tax in 2015. For the calculations behind Figure 16.8, we assume that the couple has three children, so that they have a total of five personal

exemptions. Since each exemption is worth $4000, this means that the first $20,000 of their income is exempt from any tax.

To simplify the analysis, we assume that the exemptions are the only method used by this family to reduce their taxable income, and that they truthfully report all of their income. (Later in this chapter, we will see that the actual tax system offers many ways for families to reduce their taxable income.)

For the first $20,000 of income, which is exempt from tax, the marginal tax rate is zero, and the average tax rate is also zero. When the family's income rises above $20,000, every additional dollar of income is taxable. The marginal tax rates are shown as a "stair-step function". The average tax rates are calculated as the weighted average of all of the marginal tax rates.

For example, if the family has $50,000 of income, its marginal tax rate is zero on the first $20,000, 10 percent for the next $18,450, and 15 percent for the next $11,550. The family's

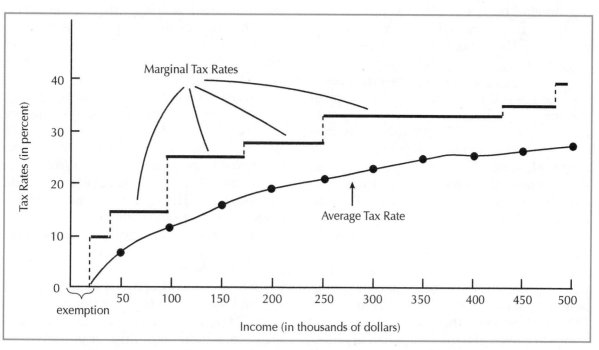

Figure 16.8 Marginal and Average Tax Rates in the Federal Individual Income Tax, 2015

tax is thus (0 x $20,000) + (0.1 x $18,450) + (0.15 x $11,550) = $1845 + $1732.50 = $3577.50. If we divide this tax liability of $3577.50 by the family's income of $50,000, we find that their average tax rate is about 7.16 percent.

Earlier in this book, we saw that if a marginal value is greater than the corresponding average value, the average value will increase. That is exactly what we see here: The marginal tax rates are greater than the average tax rates, and so the average tax rates increase as we move up the income scale. That is another way of saying that this tax is progressive.

The federal income tax is progressive for two reasons. First, at low incomes, the tax is progressive because of the personal exemptions. Second, when we move to higher incomes, the graduated marginal rates continue to impart more and more progressivity.

The top marginal tax rate is 39.6 percent. For married couples, this rate begins to apply when taxable income exceeds $464,850. Thus the top rate only applies to a fraction of one percent of households. For those with very, very high incomes, the average tax rate will approach the top marginal tax rate of 39.6 percent.

On the other hand, sales taxes are somewhat regressive. This is because sales taxes do not apply to saving, and higher-income people tend to save a higher proportion of their incomes.

The payroll tax is progressive at lower income levels, because it doesn't apply to transfer payments. The payroll tax is then about proportional over much of the income range. Most middle-income households get the vast majority of their income from labor earnings. Since the payroll tax is a flat percentage of labor earnings, it is about proportional in the middle income ranges. Finally, the payroll tax is regressive at high incomes, for two reasons. First of all, the full payroll tax of 15.3 percent is only collected on earnings below a ceiling. (In 2015, the ceiling was $118,500.) Second, the payroll tax doesn't apply to dividends, interest, rents, royalties, or capital gains, all of which are concentrated at the upper income levels. If we add up the effects of income taxes, sales taxes, and all the other sources of revenue, we get a system that takes about the same percentage of income from everyone. For example, one famous study found that the total burden of all taxes was between 28 percent and 30 percent for four-fifths of the U.S. population.

Another important result is that the tax system generates a large amount of excess burden. One study found that the United States tax system generates an overall excess burden that is probably more than 10 percent of tax revenues. If this estimate is correct, it means that the efficiency losses from distortionary taxes may be as much as several hundred billion dollars per year.

In many studies, economists have found that different amounts of excess burden are created by different parts of the tax system. For example, the payroll tax leads to relatively little excess burden, because labor supply is not very elastic. On the other hand, studies suggest that corporate taxes create a much larger deadweight loss (per dollar of tax revenue collected) than is created by the payroll tax. This implies that the overall excess burden of the tax system could be reduced, by reducing the corporate tax and increasing the payroll tax.

Since the owners of corporate capital tend to have high incomes, many studies suggest that the corporate tax is a relatively progressive part of the revenue system. On the other hand, we have seen that the payroll tax is approximately proportional over much of the income range. Thus if we were to reduce the corporate tax rate and increase the payroll tax, we might reduce excess burden, but we would also have a less progressive tax system. This is one of many situations in which tax policy involves a tradeoff between equity and efficiency. One way to increase reliance on the payroll tax, while making the tax more progressive, would be to raise or eliminate the payroll-tax ceiling.

CURRENT TAX POLICY ISSUES

Tax policy is extremely controversial, because nobody enjoys paying taxes. The political fighting over tax policies has been especially fierce since 1980, because Congress and the White House have usually been controlled by different political parties. In this section, you will read about some of the big recent controversies in tax policy. We begin with proposals to "flatten" the schedule of marginal tax rates in the individual income tax. Later, we look at some issues in the taxation of capital income, including the corporation income tax and the taxes on "capital gains".

A "Flat Tax"

The United States, like many other countries, has a system of graduated marginal income tax rates. In 2015, the first dollar of taxable income is taxed at a rate of 10 percent. For a married couple, the marginal tax rate increases to 15 percent when the couple's taxable income rises to $18,450. At higher incomes, the marginal tax rates continue to rise, until they reach 39.6 percent for couples with incomes over $464,850.

These tax rates are actually *low* by historical standards, as can be seen in Figure 16.9. In 1944 and 1945, the top marginal tax rate was 94 percent. As recently as 1981, the top marginal rate was 70 percent. During the late 1980s, the marginal tax rate on those with the highest incomes fell to 28 percent, which was the lowest it had been since 1930. Since then, the top marginal rate has been the subject of a tug of war between the political parties. Democrats tend to prefer higher tax rates on those with the highest incomes, and President Bill Clinton (a Democrat) succeeded in raising the top rate to 39.6 percent in 1993. President George W. Bush (a Republican) signed a law that pushed the top rate down to 35 percent in 2003. Under President Barack Obama (a Democrat), the top rate was pushed back up to 39.6 percent in 2013.

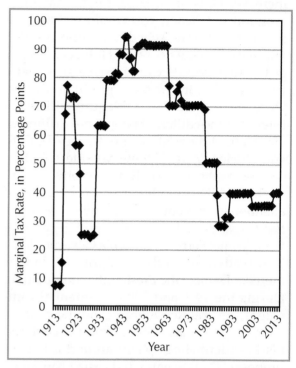

Figure 16.9 Highest Marginal Tax Rate in the U.S. Federal Individual Income Tax, 1913–2015

In Chapter 15, we saw that the distribution of income in the United States became dramatically more equal in the middle of the 20th century, and dramatically more unequal toward the end of the century. The same political forces that led to those trends in the income distribution are also clearly present when we look at the trends in the income-tax rates. The equalization of the 1930s and 1940s was achieved in large part by the policies of the New Deal under President Franklin Roosevelt, which included steeply progressive taxation. The disequalization since the 1970s was achieved in large part by the more conservative policies that have been in place over the last 40 years; these policies include a decrease in the progressivity of the tax system.

Studies by economists have found that the excess burden of the income tax tends to increase substantially as the marginal rates increase. Thus, if your goal is to maximize economic efficiency, you would want a relatively flat tax-rate schedule, without much graduation in the tax rates. However, if your goal is to have a very progressive tax system, you would want to have graduated rates. Once again, there is an equity-efficiency tradeoff. Since different people have different views about the relative importance of equity and efficiency, the income-tax rate schedule is a constant source of disagreement.

In the 1980s, the idea of a *flat tax* got a lot of attention from economists and others. Under a *flat tax*, all taxable income would be taxed at a single rate. Former California Governor Jerry Brown advocated a flat tax during his bid for the 1992 Democratic Presidential nomination. During the 1996 and 2000 Presidential campaigns, several Republican candidates made flat-tax proposals. Steve Forbes centered his Presidential campaign around a flat-tax proposal. Texas Senator Ted Cruz proposed a flat tax as part of his 2016 campaign for the White House.

Virtually all of the flat-tax proposals would give up a great deal of progressivity, in exchange for some efficiency. Many of the flat-tax proposals would reduce the tax payments of the most affluent Americans by hundreds of billions of dollars per year. However, many of the proposals would do much more than merely flatten the tax rates. Because there are big differences in the other aspects of the proposals, it's difficult to make general statements that would tell the truth about all of the plans. Still, the next few paragraphs describe some of the issues.

How Much Revenue Would Flat Taxes Collect? Some of the flat-tax proposals are designed to raise the same amount of revenue as today's income tax. However, some of the plans would collect less revenue. If the amount of revenue collected from the income tax is reduced, then one of the following things must happen: Either government spending must be cut, or some other tax must be raised, or the government must increase its borrowing.

What Would Happen to the Deductions and Exemptions? If you want to carry the idea of the flat tax to its logical conclusion, you would tax every single dollar of income at exactly the same rate. However, none of the popular proposals would go that far. In 2015, the income tax had a personal exemption of $4000 per person. The personal exemption is not taxable. Thus with a personal exemption of $4000 per person, a family of four with income below $16,000 would not pay any income tax at all. It could be said that the income-tax rate is actually zero at very low incomes. None of the popular flat-tax proposals would eliminate the personal exemptions, and some proposals would increase the exemptions by a great deal. This means that the flat-tax proposals really have *two* tax rates, instead of just one. Under these proposals, the first marginal tax rate is zero, and the other marginal tax rate is usually something like 17 percent or 19 percent.

Beyond the personal exemptions, there are hundreds of other tax breaks. For example, when your employer pays health-insurance premiums for you, or contributes to your pension fund, the income tax doesn't apply. This is an example of an *exclusion*, under which a particular type of income is excluded from the tax base. If you pay interest on your home mortgage, you get to subtract the interest payments from your taxable income. This is called a *deduction*. A *deduction* allows the taxpayer to reduce his or her taxable income, by spending money on a particular type of activity. Table 16.1 shows some of the most important deductions and exclusions, along with estimates of how much tax revenue is lost as a result.

Table 16.1 shows that the income tax system loses a tremendous amount of revenue because of all of the special tax breaks. These deductions and exclusions are sometimes called "tax expenditures", because a reduction

Table 16.1 Some Important Deductions and Exclusions in the Federal Individual Income Tax, for 2016

Provision of Tax Law	Estimated Revenue Loss in 2016
Exclusion of employer-paid health insurance	$211.0 billion
Special tax treatments for capital gains	$203.6 billion
Exclusion of pension contributions and earnings (employer plans, 401(k)s, Individual Retirement Accounts)	$191.1 billion
Deduction for mortgage interest on owner-occupied homes	$62.4 billion
Deduction for contributions to charities	$54.4 billion
Deduction for state-and-local government income taxes	$51.4 billion
Exclusion of interest on state-and-local government bonds	$42.2 billion
Deduction for state-and-local government property taxes	$33.1 billion

in taxes has the same effect on the budget deficit as an explicit government expenditure.

The biggest of these is the exclusion of employer-paid health insurance. For most American workers, health insurance is paid by the employer. Whereas salaries are fully subject to the income tax, the employer-paid health-insurance premiums are excluded from the tax. This exclusion is estimated to cost the federal government more than $200 billion per year in lost tax revenues.

If you were to add up the revenue losses shown in Table 16.1, along with all of the other revenue losses that aren't shown, you would get a total revenue loss of something like $1 trillion per year.

These revenue losses have a major effect on the tax rates. If Congress were to eliminate the deductions, exclusions, and exemptions, it would be possible to raise the same amount of revenue that is raised now, but with lower tax rates. If you want to raise today's amount of tax revenue from a flat tax, but don't change any of the deductions, exclusions, and exemptions, you would need a tax rate of about 23 percent. However, if all of the deductions, exclusions, and exemptions were removed, a flat tax rate of about 12 percent would do the job. A system with fewer tax breaks and lower tax rates would be a more efficient system.

Of course, there are problems with removing the tax breaks. Consider the mortgage interest deduction, for example. Many people have responded to this deduction by getting big mortgages. If the tax deduction were to be removed suddenly, it would probably cause bankruptcies for some people with large mortgages, and it would cause home prices to fall. The price decreases could be large in some regions of the country. All of this could put an enormous strain on the financial system. (The financial crisis of 2008 was largely caused by problems in the mortgage market.) Consequently, if we were to remove the mortgage interest deduction, it would be wise to consider phasing in the change over a long period of time, such as 15 or 20 years.

In this section, we have seen that the debate about a flat tax isn't just about the flatness or steepness of the tax rate schedule. The flat-tax debate is really about four important questions:

- How steep should the income-tax rates be?

- How much revenue should be raised by the income tax?

- How many deductions, exclusions, and exemptions should there be?

- If the tax system is to be changed, should the changes be phased in quickly or slowly?

Real Economics for Real People 16.3: What's All the Fuss About Capital Gains Taxes?

A *capital gain* is an increase in the value of a capital asset, such as a home or a share of stock. If you buy a share of stock at a price of $50, and if the price increases to $60, you have a capital gain of $(60 − 50) = $10. Similarly, if you buy a house for $100,000, and its price goes up to $110,000, you have a capital gain of $(110,000 − 100,000) = $10,000.

Capital gains are only subject to tax when the asset is actually sold. Thus, if you hang on to your corporate stock for many years, you won't pay any capital-gains tax, even if the price of the stock goes up a long way. In addition, if you hold the stock until you die, and bequeath it to your children, the capital gain is forgiven completely. This gives a powerful incentive for investors to avoid taxes by holding on to their stocks, even if the stocks aren't performing very well. The incentive to hold on to stocks in order to avoid taxes is called the *lock-in effect*.

Another important feature of the capital-gains tax is that gains are not indexed for inflation. If your stock goes up by 20 percent during a period of years when the overall price level also goes up by 20 percent, you haven't really increased your purchasing power at all. Nevertheless, if you sell the asset, you will have to pay taxes on the entire nominal "gain". This creates problems, both for equity and for efficiency. To many people, it seems unfair for the government to inflate prices, and then tax people on the resulting paper gains.

Controversy has swirled around the capital-gains tax for years. Most capital gains are received by people with high incomes. As a result, if you believe in a strongly progressive tax, you may want to keep the tax rate on capital gains fairly high. On the other hand, those who prefer a less progressive tax system may want to reduce the tax rate on capital gains.

For most of the history of the income tax, this debate has been resolved in favor of those who want a special, lower tax rate for capital gains.

Sometimes, people argue in favor of lowering the tax rates on capital gains, because of a belief that lower rates will bring about a large increase in the rate of economic growth. This is unlikely to occur, however. For several reasons, much of the capital stock is already not subject to capital-gains taxes. One reason is that very wealthy stockholders may hang on to much of their stock portfolios until they die. If they do, there is no capital-gains tax at all. Also, it is believed that many taxpayers get away with not paying their capital-gains taxes. Thus, even if the tax rate were cut in half, it would still only give a modest boost to the overall rate of return on corporate stocks. This might lead to some additional saving and investment, but the amounts are likely to be small. Consequently, the effect on the overall rate of economic growth would also be small.

Sometimes, the proposals for lower tax rates on capital gains are justified on the basis of claims that they will raise more revenue. For this to occur, there would have to be a large increase in the number of stock sales in response to the tax cut. In the short run, there might be a burst of sales. Over the long haul, however, the increase in sales is unlikely to be large enough to bring about any major increase in tax revenue.

It appears that many of the arguments that are given in favor of reducing the capital gains tax rate are fairly weak. A reduced tax rate on capital gains would have some effects, but they are unlikely to be exceptionally large. However, there is a more fundamental question: Should there be any tax on capital gains at all? Nearby, in the section on corporate taxation, you will read about a proposal that would involve complete elimination of the tax on capital gains.

It's likely that the debate over these issues will continue for years to come. The results of the debate will tell us a lot about the efficiency and equity of the tax system in the future.

Real Economics for Real People 16.3 discusses the capital-gains tax, which is another hotly debated tax-policy issue.

Must Corporate Income Be Taxed Twice?

In several countries, including the United States, corporations have to pay a tax that is separate from the individual income tax. If a corporate firm wants to pay dividends to its stockholders, it must first pay the corporate tax. Then the stockholders have to pay individual income tax when they receive the dividends. This is sometimes called the *double taxation of corporate income.*

Some people try to justify the double taxation of corporate income on the basis of their belief that "business needs to pay its fair share of taxes". This argument can be misleading. After all, businesses don't really pay taxes: The ultimate burden of a tax can only be borne by people. A tax that is levied on a corporation's profits can only be borne by consumers (as a result of higher prices), by workers (as a result of lower wages), by stockholders (as a result of lower share prices or lower dividends), or by other owners of capital. In fact, economic studies of the incidence of the corporation tax indicate that all of these groups are likely to bear at least some of the burden of the tax.

Corporations have to pay the corporate tax, but non-corporate firms don't have to pay a tax of this type. (The non-corporate sector includes much of agriculture and real estate, as well as partnerships and other small businesses.) Therefore, the tax system favors the non-corporate sector of the economy, relative to the corporate sector. The economy ends up with less than the optimal amount of corporate output, and more than the optimal amount of non-corporate output.

Another problem with the corporate tax is that it allows a deduction for interest payments. Thus the corporate tax creates an incentive for corporations to go into debt: If a corporation goes into debt, it will pay interest on the debt, and the interest payments will allow the firm to reduce its taxes.

In short, the corporate tax creates a large number of distortions. Some estimates suggest that the corporate tax creates more excess burden per dollar of revenue than any other tax. With the goal of getting around this problem, economists have suggested several proposals for *"corporate tax integration"*. The idea of corporate tax integration is to coordinate the corporate income tax with the individual income tax, to solve the problem of double taxation.

One of the best of the proposals for corporate tax integration is called a "Comprehensive Business Income Tax", or CBIT. This tax would apply equally to all businesses, regardless of whether they are incorporated. In this way, it would remove the distortion between corporate and non-corporate firms. In addition, the CBIT would not allow a deduction for interest. Therefore, it would no longer give an advantage to firms that take on a lot of debt.

Finally, the CBIT would only tax business income once. The individual income tax would not apply to business income, such as dividends, interest, rents, and so on. These incomes will already have been taxed once by the CBIT. Therefore, any attempt to tax them again under the individual income tax would lead to double taxation.

Some economists have estimated that the excess burden of the corporate tax is one-third of revenues, or even more. If a Comprehensive Business Income Tax were enacted, it would reduce the excess burden very substantially. Moreover, by eliminating the double taxation of corporate income, the CBIT would remove one important source of unfairness in the tax system. Once again, however, we should remember that a large fraction of business income goes to people with very high incomes. Thus, as is so often the case in tax policy, there is a tradeoff between equity and efficiency.

ECONOMICS AND YOU:
WILL SOCIAL SECURITY BE THERE WHEN YOU RETIRE?

At the beginning of this chapter, we saw that the Social Security System could run out of money, unless some changes are made. Since it would be a political disaster to allow the Social Security System to go bankrupt, we can expect that some changes will be made. However, no one can predict with certainty *which* changes will be made, but here are some of the possibilities:

- *Raising the retirement age.* In fact, the age at which Americans are eligible for full benefits has already been raised, back in 1983. For people born before 1937, it has been possible to collect full benefits at age 65. This retirement age is now being increased gradually. Those born after 1960 will have to wait until the age of 67 before they can collect full benefits. Whenever the retirement age is raised, there is a reduction in the amount of benefits that must be paid out. If the age for full benefits were raised to 69, the Social Security System would be much more likely to be balanced in the long run.

- *Raising the payroll tax rate.* As was mentioned earlier in this chapter, the payroll tax rate is now 15.3 percent. Most of the revenues are used to pay for Social Security, and the rest go for Medicare and the Disability Insurance program. If we were to leave benefits unchanged, we would have to rely exclusively on taxes to finance the system. This would make it necessary for the payroll tax rate to rise by several percentage points.

- *Raising the ceiling for the payroll tax.* As mentioned earlier, the payroll tax rate of 15.3 percent does not apply to all earnings. In fact, it applies to a smaller fraction of earnings than it did a few decades ago, because the ceiling is indexed with respect to inflation, but the earnings of the highest-earning workers have increased much faster than that. If the ceiling were raised or eliminated, the payroll tax would bring in a substantial amount of additional revenue.

- *Making other changes to the benefit formula.* An individual's monthly Social Security benefit amount is based on the payroll taxes that were paid when he or she was working. However, the translation from taxes paid to benefits received is based on an extremely complicated formula. Any number of minor adjustments to the benefit formula could improve the long-run finances of the Social Security system. Some proposals would adjust the formula to reduce the gap between the benefits of low-income retirees and high-income retirees.

- *More fundamental changes.* Today's Social Security System is a *pay-as-you-go retirement system*. This means that the system doesn't really do any saving. Instead, it merely taxes those who are working today, and uses the money to pay transfer payments to those who are retired today. Since the money is not invested, future generations won't do as well with Social Security as they would have done if the same amount of money had been invested in the stock market or in other investments.

Some economists have suggested that the basic character of the system should be changed. Instead of a pay-as-you-go system, the government could sponsor a system of required saving. To accomplish the transition to the new system without causing a great deal of harm to any one generation, it would be necessary to phase in the new system gradually, over a period of several decades. Since such a long transition period will be required, if it were decided to make such a change, it would be better to start sooner than later.

Economists Sylvester Schieber and John Shoven have suggested that we move to a hybrid system, which would include both a pay-as-you-go system and a system of personal accounts.

One thing is certain: If any of these changes is to be made, it will be made by government officials, rather than by the private market. For better or worse, the key players will be politicians, bureaucrats, lobbyists, and voters. Can the political system rise to the challenge? The answer to this question will be one of the most important developments of the 21st century.

In the meantime, what can you do? The most important thing to remember is that Social Security benefits won't be enough to provide a very comfortable retirement. (Today, the average Social Security beneficiary receives less than $15,000 per year.)

By themselves, Social Security benefits won't do much more than keep you out of poverty, if they even do that. (As we saw in Chapter 15, about 10 percent of elderly Americans fall below the poverty line.) If you want to have a comfortable retirement, you will have to do some saving of your own. The nature of compound interest is such that a dollar saved today will provide much more retirement income than a dollar saved ten years from now. Therefore, the earlier you start to save, the better.

Chapter Summary

1. Public goods are nonrival, which means they can be enjoyed by many people at the same time. In addition, public goods are characterized by costly exclusion, which means it is difficult to deny the public good to those who do not pay. Costly exclusion leads to the free-rider problem: People do not have an incentive to reveal their preferences for public goods.

2. Public goods are an example of market failure. Because of costly exclusion, private markets will typically be unable to provide public goods. As a result, government may have a role in providing them. The other important justification for government spending is that the private market economy may not produce a distribution of income that people consider fair. Government may be able to use taxes and transfer payments to make the distribution of income more equal.

3. Since 1960, transfer payments have been the fastest-growing component of federal spending, while the share of defense spending has declined. Education gets the largest share of state and local spending.

4. Ideally, a good tax system will raise revenue without causing a lot of inefficiency. A good tax system would also have low costs of administration and compliance, and it would be "fair". This means that the tax system would be horizontally equitable, that is, similar people would be treated similarly. A good tax system would also be vertically equitable. Vertical equity has to do with the way in which taxes are distributed across income groups. In a progressive tax, an increase in income is associated with an increase in the percentage of income paid in tax. In a regressive tax, an increase in income is associated with a decrease in the percentage of income paid in tax. In a proportional tax, the percentage of income paid in tax is constant. Reasonable people can disagree about the correct degree of vertical equity. Often, these goals are in conflict with each other. As a result, there is no perfect, ideal tax system.

5. Since World War II, the individual income tax has been the largest source of federal revenue. The payroll tax is now the second-largest source of federal revenue. The corporation income tax and the excise taxes have become relatively less important. For the state and local governments, the largest sources of revenue are individual income taxes, general retail sales taxes, and property taxes.

6. A tax raises revenue for the government, but it also makes consumers worse off. Usually, the losses for the private sector are greater than the revenue for the government. The difference between the private sector's loss and the government's revenue is the excess burden, or deadweight loss, of the tax.

7. All else equal, excess burdens are greater when at least one side of the taxed market is elastic. Thus if we want to minimize inefficiency, it is good to tax inelastic markets at higher rates than elastic markets. This is one reason why so many countries (including the United States) have relatively high tax rates on labor-market earnings—labor supply is inelastic, and so it is possible to generate a lot of revenue with a relatively small amount of excess burden. Excess burdens do not mean that government expenditure is a bad thing. Many government programs produce large benefits, so that they are valuable to society even if there is excess burden. But excess burden does mean that we should be careful when designing the tax system.

8. The study of tax incidence is concerned with determining who really bears the burden of a tax. Using supply/demand diagrams, it can be shown that the more inelastic side of the market will bear most of the burden of a tax. The true economic incidence does not depend on whether the law says that buyers or sellers are ultimately responsible for paying the tax. The true economic incidence depends only on the elasticities of supply and demand.

9. One recent controversy deals with whether the individual income tax should have graduated marginal tax rates. Some have advocated a "flat tax", under which all taxable income would be taxed at the same marginal rate. Under most flat-tax proposals, the income tax would be more efficient (that is, it would have lower excess burdens), but it would be much less progressive. Thus there is a tradeoff between efficiency and vertical equity.

10. Regardless of whether the income-tax rates are flat or graduated, many economists are in favor of broadening the tax base, by removing some exclusions and deductions. This would make it possible to raise the same amount of tax revenue, while reducing the tax rates.

11. The United States tax system has a tax on corporation income, and a separate individual income tax. This leads to double taxation of corporate income, which causes substantial excess burdens. Some economists have proposed a Comprehensive Business Income Tax, under which all business income (including corporate and non-corporate income) would be taxed once. There would then not be any need to tax business income in the individual income tax. However, a very large fraction of business income is received by those at the top of the income scale. Thus once again, there is a tradeoff between efficiency and vertical equity.

Key Terms

Market Failure

Public Goods

Nonrival Consumption

Private Goods

Costly Exclusion, or Nonexcludability

Free-Rider Problem

Distortionary Tax

Inefficiency

Compliance Costs

Administrative Costs

Horizontal Equity

Marriage Bonus

Marriage Penalty

Vertical Equity

Proportional Tax

Progressive Tax

Regressive Tax

Equity-Efficiency Tradeoff

Individual Income Tax

Payroll Tax

Corporation Income Tax

Excise Tax

General Retail Sales Tax

Excess Burden, or Deadweight Loss, or Welfare Cost

Tax Incidence

Statutory Incidence

Economic Incidence

Personal Exemption

Graduated Marginal Tax Rates

Flat Tax

Exclusion

Deduction

Capital Gain

Lock-in Effect

Double Taxation of Corporate Income

Corporate Tax Integration

Pay-as-you-go Retirement System

Key Figure

The key figure for this chapter is Figure 16.5. It uses a supply/demand diagram to show how a commodity tax can be viewed as creating a new, gross-of-tax supply curve. The new equilibrium is determined by the intersection of the gross-of-tax supply curve with the demand curve. Once the new equilibrium quantity and prices are known, it is possible to calculate the government's tax revenue and the excess burden.

Questions and Problems

QP16-1. The largest sources of federal tax revenues are the individual income tax, the payroll tax, and the corporation tax. Which of these scores best in terms of administrative costs, compliance costs, and excess burden?

QP16-2. If you consider the federal individual income tax, the payroll tax, and a general retail sales tax, which is most progressive?

QP16-3. David has income of $10,000, and he pays a tax of $2000. Amy has income of $100,000, and she also pays a tax of $2000. Is this tax regressive, or proportional, or progressive?

QP16-4. How would your answer to the preceding question change, if at all, if Amy's tax were $1000? What if Amy's tax were $20,000? What if it were $40,000?

QP16-5. Discuss the appropriate role of government in providing the following: National defense, cosmetic surgery, income-maintenance payments for poor people, streets and sewers, elementary education, higher education.

QP16-6. A kind of compact-disc player has a perfectly elastic net-of-tax supply curve: $P_{net} = \$100$. A kind of non-glare picture frame has exactly the same supply curve: $P_{net} = \$100$. In the absence of any taxes, the equilibrium quantity is the same in the two markets. A 10-percent commodity tax is imposed in both markets. The elasticity of demand for compact-disc players is 1.0, and the elasticity of demand for non-glare picture frames is 2.0. In which market will the tax create relatively more revenue, and relatively less excess burden?

QP16-7. The net-of-tax supply curve for a kind of blue jeans is perfectly elastic: $P_{net} = \$30$. The demand curve slopes downward, and is given by $Q = 100 - P$.

a. If there is no tax on this type of blue jeans, what are the equilibrium price and quantity?

b. Now, suppose that a tax of $20 per pair of blue jeans is levied. What happens to the buyers' price, the sellers' price, and the equilibrium quantity?

c. How much tax revenue does the government collect from this tax? How much excess burden is generated? (Remember that the area of a rectangle is equal to the height of the rectangle, multiplied by the base of the rectangle. The area of a triangle is equal to one-half the base of the triangle times the height of the triangle.)

QP16-8. In the market for gumdrops, the demand is inelastic and the supply is elastic. In the market for grapefruit, the demand is elastic and the supply is inelastic. Assume that a tax of the same size is levied in each of these markets. In which case would most of the burden be borne by buyers, and in which case would most of the burden be borne by sellers?

QP16-9. If you were an adviser to the President, would you advocate a flat income tax? Why or why not? If you are not in favor of a flat tax, do you think that the present income tax has about the correct amount of progressivity? Would you prefer a tax that is more progressive, or less progressive, or about the same? Why?

Chapter 17

The Environment and the Economy

ECONOMICS AND YOU:
WHAT CAN *YOU* DO ABOUT CLIMATE CHANGE?

In July of 1995, a blistering heat wave gripped the Midwest, and more than 700 people died in Chicago alone. It's possible that this scorching heat was just an isolated, temporary event. But it's also possible that it could be part of a broad trend toward a hotter Earth. In the last 20 years or so, many scientists have warned that we may be entering a period of climate change, caused by the emission of "greenhouse gases" into the atmosphere. The most important of the greenhouse gases is carbon dioxide, which is released when we burn oil, coal, or other fossil fuels.

According to some predictions, the increased amounts of greenhouse gases could raise average air temperatures by 2.7 degrees Fahrenheit (1.5 degrees Celsius) or even more. This might be good for farmers in Alaska, Russia, and other cold climates, but it could cause big problems for agriculture in regions that are already hot and dry. In addition, the warmer air would lead to warmer water in the oceans, and this could increase the number and severity of hurricanes.

In fact, a tremendous amount of scientific evidence suggests that a process of climate change is already well underway. Global average temperatures have been substantially higher in the last few decades than they were in the early part of the 20th century. Glaciers and ice caps have receded in the Arctic and Antarctic. If this melting continues as some scientists predict, it could lead to big increases in the sea level. This would mean trouble for low-lying areas in Louisiana, Bangladesh, and elsewhere.

Of course, we're not certain about how much the earth will heat up. But let's say that we can put the uncertainty aside. What if we were absolutely convinced that climate change is occurring, and that it will cause catastrophic changes. What would *you* do about it?

To slow the process of climate change, it will be necessary to reduce the amount of carbon dioxide that gets spewed into the air. So, you could stop driving your car. And you could move into a tent, so you wouldn't use any energy to heat or air condition your "home". But even if you were to take these extreme actions, you would only reduce the total amount of carbon dioxide going into the air by a fraction of one-millionth of one percent.

Clearly, no single person can do very much to solve the problem of climate change. A problem like this can only be addressed if we take *collective* action. People and governments will need to work together.

In this chapter, we will learn the economic approach to thinking about air pollution, water pollution, and other environmental problems. With this knowledge in hand, we'll begin to think about policies for reducing pollution.

THE ECONOMICS OF POLLUTION

Environmental problems occur as a result of a huge variety of human activities, and the dimensions of the problems can be staggering.

Every day, pollutants are sprayed into the air by cars, factories, and homes. In the United States in 2013, more than *five billion tons* of carbon dioxide went into the air. (That's about 17 tons for every person in the country.) The carbon dioxide was joined by about 107 million tons of carbon monoxide, along with 15 million tons of sulfur dioxide and an additional 19 million tons of nitrogen oxides. In and around the waters of the United States, there were more than 3900 oil spills in 2004. Nationwide, there were about 1300 high-priority hazardous waste sites.

Meanwhile, Americans generated about 250 million tons of solid waste, such as paper, yard waste, plastic, metal, and glass. (That's almost a ton per person.) Much of the solid waste went into landfill.

Some people believe these levels of pollution are leading us down the road to an environmental catastrophe. Others aren't so pessimistic. But nearly everyone agrees that environmental damage is a cause for concern. In this section, we will develop the economic way of thinking about these concerns.

Externalities: The Strange Case of the Missing Market

SmokeBelch, Inc., is a steel producer. In the process of making steel, the firm also pollutes the air. If we look carefully at the decisions made by SmokeBelch, we can begin to understand the economics of environmental pollution.

Labor is one of SmokeBelch's most important inputs. Since SmokeBelch has to pay a wage to each of its workers, the firm has an incentive to employ the workers efficiently, and to avoid wasting their labor. SmokeBelch also uses coal and electricity. Since the firm has to pay for its coal and electricity, it has an incentive to avoid wasting them. The firm will be better off if it uses coal and electricity wisely.

In each of the cases above, SmokeBelch has an incentive to use scarce resources wisely, because it has to pay for them.

But SmokeBelch also uses one scarce resource for which it does not pay. When the firm spews gunk out of its smokestack, it uses clean air. *Since SmokeBelch doesn't have to pay for the clean air that it uses, it has no reason to conserve clean air. Instead, the firm has every incentive to waste clean air, by sending untreated pollutants into the air.*

Thus the problem of air pollution can be seen as a problem of a *missing market*. The markets for labor, coal, electricity, and so on, tend to work efficiently. But clean air is wasted, because *there is no market for clean air.*

Market Failure

In this book, we've often talked about the virtues of the private market economy. Competitive markets tend to deliver goods and services very efficiently. Under certain conditions, the private market economy can produce the best outcome for society. But the market system can only do its job when markets exist! Unfortunately, there's no market for clean air, or for clean water, or for quiet streets. Because these markets are missing, the economy tends to be too polluted, too noisy, too crowded. Therefore, we say that pollution is an example of a **market failure**—a situation in which the private market economy will *not* tend to produce the best outcome for society.

Economists have a name for the problems of pollution, noise, and congestion that occur as a result of missing markets: We call them *externalities*. An **externality** occurs when the actions of one person or firm have an effect on another person or firm, and the effect is not directly accounted for by the system of market prices. We use the word "externality", because we are talking about effects that are *external* to the price system.

To understand externalities more fully, let's consider the difference between air pollution and the purchase of a toothbrush at a drugstore. When Paula buys a toothbrush for $2.99, the market does an excellent job. We know that this purchase makes Paula better off. After all, she has the option of *not* paying $2.99. Since she *does* pay $2.99, we know that the toothbrush is worth at least that much to her.

Similarly, the store that sells the toothbrush is better off, or they wouldn't be selling that item. The buyer and the seller are both made better off by the transaction. The market helps both parties to improve their situation voluntarily. We say that the market *internalizes* everything that is important about the transaction.

Unfortunately, this happy outcome doesn't occur in the case of air pollution. When SmokeBelch, Inc., spews pollution into the air, it causes a number of problems for Paula. Her eyes sting, and she gets lots of sinus infections. If she breathes polluted air for many years, she might eventually get emphysema. The grimy air also forces Paula to wash her windows more often than she otherwise would.

It's clear that Paula has been made worse off by the air pollution. However, she doesn't receive any payment from SmokeBelch, to compensate her for her losses. Thus, *the damage done by air pollution is* external *to the system*

of markets and prices. If the market system is left alone, it won't function properly when there is a pollution externality.

The Difference Between Private Costs and Social Costs

Figure 17.1 shows one way of looking at the economic effects of a pollution externality. In the market for steel, there is a downward-sloping demand curve (D), which represents the true social marginal benefits (SMB) of consuming

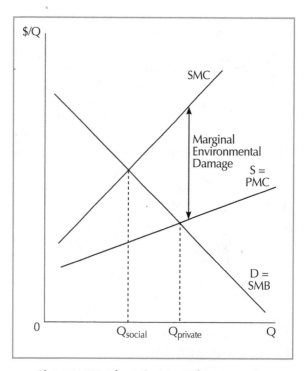

Figure 17.1 The Private Market Quantity and the Socially Optimal Quantity in a Market with an Externality

The demand curve (D) represents the social marginal benefit (SMB) of steel consumption. The supply curve (S) reflects the private marginal costs (PMC) of steel production. However, because of the pollution externality, the true social marginal costs (SMC) are higher. The quantity supplied equals the quantity demanded at $Q_{private}$, which is the private market equilibrium. However, the socially optimal quantity is found at Q_{social}, where the social marginal benefit equals the social marginal cost.

steel. In other words, the demand curve shows all of the benefits of consuming steel, for the entire society.

Figure 17.1 also has an upward-sloping supply curve (S). The supply curve comes from the marginal costs that the steel companies actually have to pay for. Thus, the supply curve depends on the wage rates of workers, the price of coal, the price of electricity, and so on.

The supply curve represents the *private* marginal costs (PMC) of producing steel. But the supply curve leaves out the damage done by pollution: It ignores the poor health suffered by people and animals as a result of breathing the smoke that's belched into the air. The supply curve also ignores the damage to crops and forests from air pollution, and it ignores the fact that fish may die when pollution falls into lakes and streams. Thus the supply curve doesn't account for all of the costs that *society* incurs when steel is produced. Therefore, the supply curve understates the true opportunity cost of producing steel.

Because of the pollution, the true *social* marginal cost (SMC) of producing steel is greater than the private marginal cost. This is shown in Figure 17.1: The SMC curve is higher than the PMC curve. The vertical distance between the two curves is the marginal damage from the air pollution.

The Private-Market Outcome and the Socially Desirable Outcome

What will happen if the private market is left to its own devices? As usual, the private market will find an equilibrium at the quantity where the supply curve crosses the demand curve. This is shown by $Q_{private}$ in Figure 17.1.

If there were no externality, $Q_{private}$ would be the best quantity for society. However, because of the externality, the private market will *not* achieve the best outcome for society. The only way to achieve the best outcome for society is to pay attention to *all* of the costs and benefits. In this case with an externality, the private market for steel takes all of the *benefits* into account, but it ignores some of the social *costs* of producing steel (such as dirty windows, sick lungs, and dead fish).

The quantity of steel that's best for society is Q_{social} in Figure 17.1. At Q_{social}, the *social* marginal benefit of steel production is equal to the *social* marginal cost. Q_{social} is less than $Q_{private}$, which tells us that the private market will produce too much steel. Private markets will tend to produce too much of any good that is associated with a negative externality.

Figure 17.1 shows that *the optimal amount of pollution is not zero*. In the figure, even at Q_{social}, the SMC curve is still above the PMC curve. (The vertical distance between the two curves is the amount of extra pollution damage from making one extra unit of steel.) This implies that a world with no pollution is *not* our goal. Just about every industrial process involves some pollution. We generate pollution when we make clothes or furniture or medicine. Automobiles create pollution, and so do buses and trains. If we were to eliminate pollution, we would be very poor. Instead of trying to eliminate pollution, our goal should be to strike the *correct balance* between the true social marginal costs and social marginal benefits of the goods that we produce and consume. We may find ways to *reduce* the amount of pollution, but it's nearly impossible to cut pollution to zero. A world with no pollution would be a world of incredible poverty.

Here's another way to look at it: If we were to reduce output below Q_{social}, we would have a cleaner world, but we would *not* be better off. Less output does mean less pollution, but it also reduces the amount of goods that can be consumed. When we go below the socially optimal quantity, the pain of giving up those goods is greater than the gain from reducing pollution and the other costs of production. (In other words, when we get below Q_{social}, the social marginal benefit is greater than the social marginal cost.)

Society's Loss from the Pollution Externality

If we don't do anything to fix the externality, we will end up at $Q_{private}$ instead of Q_{social}. What difference does it make? How much worse off will we be, because of the externality?

We can answer this question by looking at Figure 17.2. When we produce more than the optimal quantity, Q_{social}, we produce units for which the social marginal cost (SMC) is greater than the social marginal benefit (SMB). As a result, society is made worse off by *every* unit of output from Q_{social} to $Q_{private}$. Thus, for each unit of output from Q_{social} to $Q_{private}$, the loss is the difference between SMC and SMB. In order to calculate the total loss to society, we add up these losses for all units from Q_{social} to $Q_{private}$. We see from Figure 17.2 that society's total loss is the shaded triangle, BAD.

For a large country like the United States, this social loss is likely to run to the hundreds of billions of dollars per year, unless action is taken to reduce pollution.

Reality Check: Interim Review Questions

IR17-1. We have often emphasized the advantages of private markets. However, pollution externalities are an example of a situation where private markets fail. Can you name other situations in which private markets do not give desirable results?

IR17-2. If it were somehow possible to establish a market in clean air, would you expect that we could solve the externality problem?

Positive Externalities

So far, we have focused on negative externalities. In the case of a negative externality, the private market will produce more than the socially optimal quantity. However, not all externalities are negative. Consider the thoughtful neighbor who does an unusually

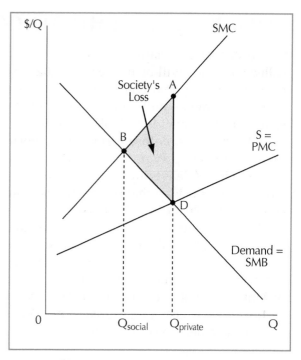

Figure 17.2 Society's Loss from Producing Too Much Output in a Market with an Externality

The socially optimal quantity is Q_{social}. If we produce a quantity greater than Q_{social}, the social marginal costs of each additional unit will be greater than the social marginal benefits. This means that society is made worse off by each unit above Q_{social}. If we add up the losses from all units of output between Q_{social} and $Q_{private}$, we get the total of society's loss. This loss is shown graphically by the area of the triangle BAD. This is the *loss* from *not* correcting the externality; it is also the gain from going ahead and correcting the problem.

good job of maintaining her house and lawn, in a way that gives a better look and feel to the entire neighborhood. We could think of this is a *positive externality*. Following the same logic that we used above, we conclude that the private market will produce *less* than the socially optimal quantity of goods that are associated with positive externalities.

In Chapter 16, we discussed public goods, which are characterized by nonrival consumption. In fact, one way to think about public goods is to see them as goods that are characterized by positive externalities.

POLICY APPROACHES TO CONTROLLING POLLUTION

At the start of this chapter, we suggested that collective action will be needed for attacking problems like global warming. This means that governments will be involved. But the economist's instinct is to look for voluntary, private solutions, before turning to government. After all, private markets can do an excellent job of delivering goods and services. Isn't there some way that private actions can solve the problem of externalities?

In the next few paragraphs, we'll see that private solutions may be successful some of the time. However, if the conditions aren't just right, the private market won't do a good job of controlling pollution. Therefore, later in this section, we will also look at government policies that can help to control pollution.

Private Negotiations: The Coase Solution

Judy and Bill live next door to each other in an apartment building. They would get along well, except for one thing. Every night, Bill bakes his own pizza. He puts 27 cloves of garlic into the sauce, and he uses extra-ripe Limburger cheese, lots of anchovies, and sauerkraut. Judy is overwhelmed by the smell.

The situation faced by Judy and Bill is a classic case of an externality. Bill makes Judy worse off, but he doesn't pay her to compensate her for the loss.

Property Right Goes to "Polluter". It's possible that private negotiation could solve the problem. In order to understand this, let's start out by assuming that Bill has the legal right to use the air however he wants. Then, if Judy wants him to bake fewer pizzas, she would have to pay him a bribe. What would happen if Judy were to offer to pay $5 for every day that Bill doesn't bake one of his pizzas? If it's worth more than $5 to Bill to eat pizza (instead of waffles or hot dogs), then he

would continue to bake the pizzas. However, if it's worth less than $5 to him to have pizza, he would accept Judy's bribe, and eat something else.

Let's assume that the first pizza in a given week is worth $6.50 to Bill. Since he gets more value from baking the pizza ($6.50) than from accepting Judy's bribe ($5.00), he will go ahead and bake at least one pizza per week.

If Bill is like most people, he has a downward-sloping demand curve for his special pizzas. As it turns out, the second pizza in a week is worth only $5.50. Even though the second pizza has less value for him than the first pizza, he will still bake the second one, because its value ($5.50) is greater than Judy's bribe ($5.00).

The third pizza in a week is worth $4.50 to Bill, the fourth is worth $3.50, and so on. For these pizzas, the value of Judy's bribe is greater than the value of the pizza, so he will choose to take the money and not bake a pizza. If the numbers given here are really a good description of Bill's demand curve, he will bake two pizzas per week, and he will accept Judy's bribe on the other five days.

If Judy and Bill can negotiate freely, they should be able to choose the "efficient" payment from her to him. In other words, they should be able to choose the payment that will exactly balance her discomfort with his benefit.

Property Right Goes to "Pollutee". Now, let's assume that Judy has the right to breathe fresh air. In this case, if Bill wants to bake pizzas, he will have to bribe *her*. What if Bill were to offer to pay $5 to Judy for every pizza that he bakes? He will only offer such a bribe if it's worth more than $5 to him to eat pizza (instead of waffles or hot dogs). If Bill's demand curve for pizzas is still the same as it was in the previous section, he would once again bake two pizzas per week.

As before, if Judy and Bill can negotiate freely, they should be able to choose the efficient payment.

The Coase Theorem

We have just stated a remarkable result. If people can negotiate freely, then they should be able to achieve the efficient outcome, regardless of who has the property right to the air! This amazing result is called the *Coase Theorem*, after Ronald H. Coase, who developed the idea in 1960. Coase says that it doesn't matter who gets the property rights—the only important thing is that the property rights must be defined *clearly*.

The Limits of Private Negotiation

There are many examples of private arrangements to protect the environment. For example, some rivers in England and Scotland have been owned privately for 800 years. This has given the owners a strong incentive to preserve the rivers, and they have succeeded in preventing over-fishing and in controlling pollution. In Maine, gangs of lobster fishermen have divided the waters into a set of informal territories. In this way, they create something that is similar to a system of private ownership. To enforce the territories, the lobster fishermen cut the lines to the lobster traps of those who would violate the agreements. As a result, the fishermen prevent the over-harvesting of lobster.

In most cases, when externalities are solved through private actions, only a few people are involved in the negotiations. But many of our environmental problems involve thousands, or even millions, of people. When an electric power plant sends soot into the air, it can hurt millions of people who live downwind. If we were to use private negotiations to solve the externality problem in a case like this, it will be necessary to have hundreds of costly meetings, and to hire lawyers, media-

tors, and other middlemen. Costs such as these are called *transaction costs*. In a case involving thousands or millions of people, the transaction costs of internalizing the externality may be very large. It's extremely difficult to get millions of people together to negotiate.

The private solution also has another limitation, which has to do with the *distributional* effects of the outcomes. In one case, Judy pays $5 to Bill, five times per week. In the other case, Bill pays $5 to Judy, twice per week. It's true that Bill ends up baking two pizzas per week in each case, but there's a big difference between Bill paying Judy and Judy paying Bill.

Private negotiation can solve many externality problems, but it can't solve them all. If we are to solve some of the more complex environmental problems, it will be hard to avoid relying on governments.

Controlling Industrial Pollution Through Regulations

If governments want to clean up the environment, they can choose among several policy options. For the most part, the United States government has chosen to rely on regulations. The regulatory approach to pollution control is sometimes called a *command-and-control approach*. The government dictates the details of the pollution-control effort. Unfortunately, this leaves little room for private businesses to develop innovative ways of fighting pollution.

The air-quality standards for industries are set by the Environmental Protection Agency (EPA), which was created by Congress in 1970. One of the most striking things about the EPA standards is that they tend to be *inflexible*. Here are some important aspects of this inflexibility:

- The law requires the EPA to set the standards *without considering what it might <u>cost</u> to meet the standards.*

- The law prohibits changing the degree of pollution control when the weather changes.

Thus industrial polluters must meet the same emissions standards, regardless of whether it's sunny or rainy, windy or calm.

Thus the EPA simply *can't* balance the marginal costs and marginal benefits of pollution controls, unless it wants to break the law. Throughout this book, we've seen that efficiency is enhanced if we can set the marginal benefits of some activity equal to its marginal costs. Therefore, we expect that the EPA's regulations will *not* be efficient.

In fact, since 1974, the EPA has actually dictated the specific pollution-control devices that must be used by some firms. The problem with this is that it removes the incentive for firms to invent new and better technologies.

Because of the law's inflexibility, the regulatory approach to pollution control has been inefficient. That is, we have spent a lot more money than we need to have spent, to achieve the amount of pollution control that we have achieved. Still, in many ways, the environment in the United States is much cleaner today than it was in 1970. For example, sulfur dioxide emissions into the air were reduced by 53 percent from 1970 to 2005, even though the economy nearly tripled in size during that period. The most spectacular success involved reducing the amount of lead in the air. Because of the switch to unleaded gasoline, the emissions of lead were cut from about 221 million tons in 1970 to about 1.6 million tons in 2002. That's a decrease of more than 99 percent!

The Inefficiency of the Regulatory Approach

If all sources of pollution could be cleaned up for about the same cost, the command-and-control approach would be efficient. However, the fact is that different sources of pollution can have very different costs of pollution control. For example, one study in St. Louis found that it cost only $4 for a paper-products factory to reduce particulate air pollution by a ton, but it cost $600 for a brewery to do the same thing.

The regulatory, command-and-control approach to pollution control ignores these cost differences. Regulators just command all firms to achieve the same standard. Let's say that the paper-products factory and the brewery are each required to reduce pollution by one ton. If this happens, then the total amount of pollution would fall by two tons, and the total cost would be $(4 + 600) = $604.

But it's possible to get the same amount of pollution abatement for a much lower cost. Instead of forcing each plant to cut its emissions by *one* ton, what if we could get the paper-products plant to reduce its emissions by *two* tons, while the brewery doesn't cut its emissions at all? In this case, the total amount of pollution would still fall by two tons, just as under the regulatory approach. Thus the air would be equally clean in either case. But the total cost of pollution abatement would be only $(4 + 4) = $8.

Thus if we could somehow get more of the pollution control to be done by the plant with lower costs for pollution control, we could remove two tons of pollution for $8, instead of $604. That comes to about a 98-percent savings.

How can we get more of the pollution control to be done by the firms for which pollution control is cheapest? The answer lies in *market-oriented approaches to pollution control*, which we discuss below.

Market-Oriented Approaches to Controlling Industrial Pollution

Even though it may be impossible to create an actual market in clean air, market-oriented policies are designed to create something *similar to* a market. The idea is to require polluters to pay a financial price when they pollute, because pollution uses our scarce environmental resources.

Pigouvian Taxes. One example of a market-oriented pollution-control strategy occurs when a tax is used to control pollution. A tax that is designed to correct a pollution externality is sometimes called a *Pigouvian tax*, after the British economist Arthur Cecil Pigou.

For the sake of simplicity, let's say that there are only two sources of pollution in the world—the paper-products plant (where pollution control costs $4 per ton) and the brewery (where pollution control costs $600 per ton). What would happen if a Pigouvian tax were levied on air pollution, at a tax rate of $20 per ton? The brewery's managers would then face a choice of whether to clean up some of the air pollution. If the brewery were to clean up one ton of pollution, it would reduce its taxes by $20, but it would also have to pay abatement costs of $600. Therefore, the brewery would lose $(600–20) = $580 by cleaning up even one ton of pollution. The brewery managers would choose not to clean up.

It's a different story for the paper plant, however. If the paper plant cleans up one ton of pollution, its taxes will fall by $20, but it only has to pay $4 for pollution abatement. Therefore, if the paper plant were to reduce pollution by one ton, it would increase the firm's profit by $(20–4) = $16. If the managers of the paper plant are smart, they will choose to clean up at least one ton of pollution. In fact, the paper plant may clean up far more than just one ton of pollution. If the cost of removing a second ton is also $4, then the firm will once again benefit from cleaning up. The paper plant will continue to reduce pollution, as long as its cost of abatement is less than the tax.

This example illustrates two big advantages of Pigouvian taxes, compared with the regulatory approach. First, Pigouvian taxes create incentives for most of the pollution abatement to be done by the firms with the lowest cleanup costs. This is exactly what we need for efficiency. Second, under the regulatory approach to pollution control, there's no

incentive for any firm to clean up *more* than the standard. With a pollution tax, however, a firm may reduce pollution far more than it would under the regulatory standard. The firm will continue to reduce pollution, as long as it makes money by doing so.

In fact, because of Pigouvian taxes, companies may find it worthwhile to engage in research, in an effort to find even more cost-effective methods of cleaning up pollution.

We've often seen that private markets can deliver goods and services efficiently. Taxes on pollution are efficient because they copy the workings of the market. A Pigouvian tax gives a sort of "price for pollution" to firms, just as other markets also convey information by using prices. A Pigouvian tax also lets the firms make their own decisions, just as firms in other markets make their own decisions. On the other hand, with the command-and-control approach, the government dictates that all firms must meet a fixed standard, regardless of cost.

Earlier in this chapter, we saw that the private market will provide *too little* of a good that is associated with a positive externality, just as it will provide *too much* of a good with a negative externality. Just as a tax can help to correct the problem of a negative externality, a subsidy can help to correct the problem of a positive externality.

One way to think about education is that education provides many positive externalities. (In the language of Chapter 16, education has a strong element of public good.) Thus it is not surprising that most societies subsidize education very heavily.

Marketable Licenses. Unfortunately, it's hard to tell whether a particular Pigouvian tax will reduce pollution by a lot or a little. This is because it's hard to predict what technologies will be used in the clean-up process. Unless the government can predict exactly how firms will respond to the tax, it won't be able to predict how much pollution will be eliminated.

Fortunately, there is a different market-oriented strategy that helps to avoid this uncertainty.

Let's say that 2000 tons of gunk are currently being dumped into the air every year. Furthermore, let's say that we decide that the optimal level of gunk emissions is only 1000 tons per year. Now, what would happen if the government were to issue 1000 licenses, each of which gives permission to spew one ton of gunk into the air? If the government can make sure that no one pollutes without having a license, then it can predict with certainty that only 1000 tons of gunk would go into the air. If this license scheme is to be effective, it is important that producers be able to buy and sell the licenses. Therefore, this type of market-oriented mechanism for pollution control is known as a *marketable-license system.*

If the clean-up technology is inexpensive, then many firms will choose to clean up, rather than buy a license. As a result, the demand for licenses will be small, and the market price of a license will be low.

On the other hand, if it's relatively expensive to clean up, many firms will decide to buy licenses, rather than clean up. The demand for licenses will then be strong, and the market price of a license will be higher.

Pigouvian taxes set the *price* of pollution, and allow firms to adjust the *quantity* of pollution. But marketable licenses set the *quantity* of pollution, and allow the *price* to adjust. Since we're probably more interested in controlling the quantity of pollution, it's worth considering the marketable-license idea.

A system of marketable licenses was used successfully in combating sulfur-dioxide pollution, under the Clean Air Act Amendments of 1990. Marketable licenses are at the heart of the "cap-and-trade" system that President Obama proposed in 2009, as part of an effort to fight climate change by reducing emissions of carbon dioxide.

Although the economics of a cap-and-trade system are well-established, the politics are very difficult. For one thing, many members of Congress deny that a process of climate change is occurring, despite the accumulation of scientific evidence. (It is difficult to know whether these members of Congress really don't believe in climate change, or whether they are just denying it out of political expedience.) Any serious attempt to reduce carbon pollution would create incentives to reduce consumption of oil and coal, and the oil and coal industries have lobbied hard to prevent this.

Pigouvian taxes can raise revenue for the government, and so can marketable licenses. This revenue-raising potential is another big advantage of market-oriented methods for fighting pollution. If a market-oriented method raises revenue, it allows us to reduce our reliance on other taxes (such as income taxes and sales taxes). In Chapter 16, we saw that these other taxes can damage the economy. If we can reduce the damaging taxes, and replace them with market-oriented methods of reducing pollution (which actually improve the economy), we'll be better off.

However, taxes on coal, oil, and other energy sources are likely to be regressive. Therefore, if we were to institute a carbon tax and use the revenues to reduce other taxes, it would make sense to include some protections for low- and middle-income households.

The Gains from Using a Market-Oriented Strategy. We've shown that we could clean up the environment more cheaply by using a market-oriented strategy to pollution control. But we also want to know whether the savings would be big enough to make much difference.

As it turns out, the savings are probably enormous. One study of sulfur dioxide pollution in Arizona, Colorado, New Mexico, and Utah found that the command-and-control approach costs 4.25 *times as much* as an efficient method of cleaning up. In a study of nitrogen dioxide in Chicago, the command-and-control approach was found to be more than *14 times as costly* as the efficient approach. It was also found that the command-and-control approach was *22 times as expensive* as the efficient approach, for controlling particulate pollution in Philadelphia and the Lower Delaware River Valley.

Our environmental laws also usually require pollution controls to be constant over time. In other words, firms usually aren't allowed to use different technologies, depending on the weather conditions. It has been estimated that constant abatement may be *five times as costly* as a strategy in which abatement can be adjusted, depending on the weather forecast.

Overall, a market-oriented strategy would probably allow us to achieve the same amount of environmental quality, while spending at least *one-third less* on pollution control. As we saw in the previous paragraphs, some estimates suggest that the savings might even be a lot more than that.

Since the nation currently spends about $200 *billion* per year on pollution abatement, a savings of one-third would be no small matter. We could achieve today's level of environmental quality for $60 billion less every year! Alternatively, we could spend the same amount that we spend now, and have a much cleaner environment.

Reality Check:
Interim Review Questions

IR17-3. Consider two situations: (a) Your neighbor bothers you by playing his polka records late at night, and (b) Air pollution from electric power plants causes "acid rain" over a large portion of the eastern United States and Canada. Which of these is most likely to be solved through private negotiation?

IR17-4. So far, we have discussed four approaches to pollution control—private negotiation, government regulations, Pigouvian taxes, and marketable licenses. Which of these has the potential to raise revenue for the government?

The Politics and Economics of Pollution Control

If we could get an environment that's just as clean as the one that we have today, and if we could pay $60 billion less for it, why don't we do it? Why would society *choose* to pay an extra $60 billion every year?

For much of the last 40 years, the environmental debate has been dominated by two groups of people. On one side have been environmentalists, who are sometimes suspicious of market-oriented incentives. On the other side have been business groups, who are sometimes reluctant to have any pollution control at all. The tide is turning, however, as more and more people are *both* eager for a clean environment, *and* eager to do the cleaning as cheaply as possible.

In fact, when the Clean Air Act was amended in 1990, the federal government took its first big steps toward using market-oriented strategies to clean up industrial pollution. Essentially, the new law sets up a system of marketable licenses. Now, many firms are trading pollution credits for sulfur dioxide and other pollutants. If a firm wants the right to emit pollutants, it will have to pay. It appears that environmental policy is slowly heading in the right direction.

It's important to understand that government must still be involved, regardless of how we decide to fight pollution. If we use Pigouvian taxes, some government agency must collect the taxes. If we use a system of marketable licenses, some government agency must issue the licenses. More importantly, a government agency must monitor the firms, to make sure they aren't illegally polluting more than they say they're polluting.

Thus, when we talk about the problems of regulation, we don't mean that the Environmental Protection Agency must be abolished. Instead, if we are to overcome the problems of regulation by adopting market-oriented mechanisms for pollution control, there are two options: Either the EPA must stay on (with a different role), or some other government agency must run the environmental programs. Except in the limited cases in which a Coase solution is possible, it will not be possible to rely exclusively on private markets. Instead, some sort of government intervention in the private economy will be essential.

What to Do in an Emergency

We have suggested that a market-oriented mechanism, such as a Pigouvian tax or a system of marketable licenses, can do a good job of dealing with negative externalities. What if we institute one of these market-oriented mechanisms, and then decide that we still have too much pollution? In that case, we can increase the level of the Pigouvian tax, or reduce the number of licenses. In many cases, it is possible to adjust our policies gradually.

However, some environmental problems do not allow us the luxury of gradually adjusting our policies. For example, consider a meltdown at a nuclear power plant. Fortunately, these situations are rare, but they have occurred. Nuclear power plants had major problems at Three Mile Island in Pennsylvania in 1979, at Chernbyl, Ukraine, in 1986, and at Fukushima, Japan, in 2011. In an emergency situation, it doesn't make sense to think in terms of adjusting a Pigouvian tax. Rather, the best policy toward an emergency is to take emergency action. The plant needs to be shut down, and people need to be evacuated.

CURRENT ENVIRONMENTAL PROBLEMS

So far in this chapter, we have looked mostly at the pollution caused by industry. In this section, we look at several other important environmental issues. We begin with the air pollution caused by automobiles. Later, we will look at garbage and recycling, and endangered species.

Two themes will emerge from our studies. First, it's very common to run into trouble by not taking *incentives* and *human behavior* into account. We have already seen that a market-oriented approach to fighting industrial pollution has some big advantages. The market-oriented approaches are more effective because they give relatively greater incentives for people to behave in ways that are beneficial to society. If we use command-and-control approaches, we usually provide fewer of these incentives. This applies in practically every area of environmental economics.

The second theme is that there is much uncertainty about the relationship between the environment and the economy. It would be nice if we could learn about the precise effects of economic activities on the environment. It would also be nice if we could place a precise value on a beautiful, clean environment. Unfortunately, in many cases, we just don't have that kind of precise knowledge. As a result, it's often difficult to develop the correct environmental policies, because we simply don't have as much information as we would like to have. The most we can hope for is to get *close* to the optimal set of policies.

Controlling Air Pollution from Automobiles

Industrial pollution is sometimes called *stationary-source pollution*, because it comes from sources that don't move. On the other hand, the air pollution from automobiles is sometimes called *mobile-source pollution*.

At this time, we don't have a cheap technology to measure the amounts of carbon dioxide and other pollutants coming from the tailpipe of every automobile. This means that it isn't yet cost-effective to impose a Pigouvian tax directly on the pollution that comes from cars. At some point in the future, it may be possible to monitor the pollution of every car. For now, however, we have to find other policies for controlling automobile pollution.

There are three basic ways to reduce pollution from cars:

- We can build cars that get more miles per gallon;
- We can use cleaner fuels, or cleaner-burning engines;
- We can drive fewer miles.

We will look at each of these strategies in turn.

More Miles Per Gallon. America's efforts to reduce auto pollution have mostly been directed at building cars that get more miles per gallon. The federal government has long required the auto companies to meet a standard for *Corporate Average Fuel-Economy* (known as CAFE). By 1994, the standard was 27.5 miles per gallon for cars, and 20.6 miles per gallon for trucks. According to a new law passed in 2009, the CAFE Standards are scheduled to rise to 35 miles per gallon by 2016.

The CAFE standards probably *have* helped to reduce the amount of gasoline burned in the U.S. However, the standards are clearly a command-and-control technique. Thus, they are likely to be inefficient. Moreover, the improved fuel-efficiency of cars and trucks was not enough to offset an increase in the number of miles driven.

Cleaner Fuels and Cleaner Engines. The Clean Air Act Amendments of 1990 also required service stations in some of the dirtiest metropolitan areas to sell "reformulated gasoline". The new fuel generates about 20 percent less pollution, but it costs about five to ten cents more per gallon.

Many of the cars built before 1982 are much less efficient at burning gasoline than the more recent models. In an attempt to clean up the "clunkers", the Environmental Protection Agency ordered an inspection and maintenance program for the 83 dirtiest metropolitan areas. Every other year, the owners of vehicles in these areas have to line up for an inspection. If their cars flunk the test, they will be liable for repairs of up to $450.

In 2009, Congress passed a "cash-for-clunkers" program, which provided incentives for people to trade in older vehicles for newer, more fuel-efficient ones. This was intended to provide some support to the automobile industry during a time of severe recession, as well as to help clean up the environment. More than half a million new-car buyers took advantage of the program. The Department of Transportation reported that the average fuel efficiency of the trade-ins was 15.8 miles per gallon, compared to 24.9 miles per gallon for the new cars purchased to replace them. However, since most old vehicles remained on the road, the overall effect on fuel economy was small.

Driving Fewer Miles. Americans have long had a love affair with the automobile. The number of miles driven continues to increase, year after year. All else equal, however, it's obvious that we will pollute less if we drive less. With the Clean Air Act amendments of 1990, Congress attempted to discourage driving in certain areas. Unfortunately, this law stuck with the old command-and-control methods in its approach to automobile pollution.

In 1995, a new set of rules began to apply to commuters in the 10 metropolitan areas with the dirtiest air, which include Los Angeles, Milwaukee, Philadelphia, and San Diego. Under the new law, an employer in these areas will have to develop plans to reduce the number of workers who drive to work alone, *if* the employer has 100 or more workers.

This command-and-control method has some serious problems. First, commuting only accounts for one-third of the total miles driven. Non-commute driving is completely unaffected by the law. Second, the law applies only to businesses with 100 or more employees, even though 88 percent of all workers are employed in smaller establishments.

If we really want to clean up automobile pollution effectively, we would rely on market-oriented methods. The most obvious method would involve increasing the tax on gasoline, so that the price of gasoline would increase. (The price of gasoline is much less in the United States than in Europe.)

A higher price of gasoline would cause drivers to demand more fuel-efficient cars, and it would gradually lead to changes in driving habits. Indeed, when the price of gasoline soared above $4 per gallon in 2008, sales of fuel-efficient hybrid vehicles increased. Of course, when gas prices fell later in 2008, people began to look again at big gas-guzzling vehicles. One advantage of a gasoline tax increase is that it could be adjusted to market conditions.

If we were to increase the gasoline tax, we could also reduce our reliance on other types of tax. For better or worse, however, the political opposition to increased gasoline taxes seems very powerful.

Real Economics for Real People 17.1, on p. 455, discusses the problems that accompanied a scheme for reducing automobile pollution in Mexico City.

Garbage and Recycling

Americans generate hundreds of millions of tons of garbage every year. This has the potential to be a mountain of an externality problem.

For many years, the most common way of dealing with the garbage has been to bury it in landfill sites. But in the late 1980s, many communities began to fear that they would run out of landfill space. As a result, communities increasingly began to turn to *recycling programs*, in which newspapers, bottles, and cans are collected by by city employees. The num-

ber of cities with curbside collection programs skyrocketed from about 600 in 1989 to about 4000 in 1992, to nearly 9000 in 1996.

The Economics of Recycling. Recycling programs have been fairly successful in reducing the amount of garbage that goes to landfill. However, they haven't been a big *financial* success. The reason is simple: Recycling programs lead to rightward shifts in the supply curves of scrap paper, glass, tin, and so on. As we saw in Chapter 4, when the supply curve shifts to the right, the price goes down.

The size of the price decrease will depend on the elasticity of demand. There is evidence that the demand for recyclable products may be very inelastic, which means that prices have fallen *sharply*.

The problem of falling prices doesn't necessarily mean that we should abandon recycling. However, it does mean that local governments will need to be very careful when they estimate the effect of recycling on their budgets.

Solid-Waste Policies for the Future. What should we do about all of our garbage? One alternative is to continue to bury it underground. Still, if we look further into the future, we can see a world in which solid-waste disposal becomes a bigger and bigger problem. How will we respond? The answer will depend on how much it's worth to us to control the amount of garbage that goes into landfill. This will involve judgments about benefits and costs. What is the value of avoiding the ugliness of more and more trash dumps? What is the value of avoiding the possibility of groundwater contamination? These questions aren't easy to answer, because we don't have a market to give us a dollar value for environmental protection.

Let's suppose that we look at the benefits and costs, and that we decide to do more to reduce the amount of garbage that goes to landfills. What policies would be best? It appears that *charging by the garbage bag will not do very much* to reduce the amount of garbage

The Pitfalls of Regulating Air Pollution in Mexico City

Mexico City has some of the dirtiest air in the world. The pollution comes from many sources, but one of the worst offenders is the automobile: The streets are clogged with millions of cars. In an attempt to reduce the number of cars on the streets, the Mexican government adopted a "Day-Without-a-Car" program.

Under the Day-Without-a-Car program, every car in Mexico City was assigned one day of the week on which it couldn't be driven legally. The illegal day of the week depended on the car's license plate number.

The government officials who designed this program had good intentions. They probably hoped that people would join carpools, or ride the bus. If this had happened, there would have been less pollution from cars. But people responded to the regulations in a way that the government officials had not anticipated: Many families decided to buy a second car. (Of course, they had to be careful to buy a car that could be driven on the day when their first car couldn't be driven.) As a result, there may have been an *increase* in the number of miles traveled. Families could now have two cars on the road at the same time.

It's expensive to buy a second car, especially in a relatively poor country like Mexico. Therefore, it isn't surprising that many people bought old used cars. These older cars often caused more pollution than the cars that were in use before the Day-Without-a-Car program began. Because of this, the driving that was being done in Mexico City became dirtier, on average.

It appears that the Day-Without-a-Car Program increased the number of miles driven, and it also increased the average amount of pollution per mile. If the goal was to reduce air pollution, the program has to be called a spectacular failure.

A lesson can be learned from the sad experience of the Day-Without-a-Car program. It failed because it was designed without understanding the ways in which people would respond to incentives. If we are to design successful policies for fighting pollution, we need to think carefully about how consumers and producers will change their behavior in response to the policies. The regulatory approach often fails because it doesn't use market incentives. If the Mexican officials had used the price system, they probably would have been more successful. For example, if they had increased the tax on gasoline, people would have had a clearer incentive to drive less.

Unfortunately, policy makers in other places do not seem to have learned from the poor experience of the Day-Without-a-Car program in Mexico City. In 2016, Delhi, India, tried the same program, and encountered the same problems.

that must be disposed of. (See *Real Economics for Real People 17.2.*) *Curbside recycling programs appear to be much more effective* in reducing the amount of garbage that goes to landfill.

An even more effective alternative is to have a deposit-and-return program. Under a *deposit-and-return program*, consumers pay a deposit fee up front, when they buy an item (such as a soft-drink can) that could generate solid waste. Then, if the item is returned, the consumer's deposit is refunded. With a deposit-and-return program, consumers have a real incentive to make sure that recyclable materials do get recycled properly.

Deposit-and-return programs have been adopted in California, Connecticut, Delaware, Hawaii, Iowa, Maine, Massachusetts, Michigan, New York, Oregon, and Vermont. In these states, the deposit-and-return programs have mostly been restricted to aluminum cans and glass and plastic bottles. However, it should be possible to apply deposit-and-return programs to all sorts of recyclable materials.

Endangered Species

What do the Colorado Pikeminnow, the Iowa Pleistocene Snail, and the Okaloosa Darter all have in common? They are all on the list of endangered species, which was begun with passage of the Endangered Species Act of 1973. Most of the species covered by the Endangered Species Act are not very well known. A few, such as the Spotted Owl, have attracted a lot of attention.

It is difficult to make sound policy regarding endangered species. For one thing, we have only a small amount of information about the *costs* of protecting the endangered species. (One estimate suggested that the cost of the "recovery plan" for the Atlantic Green Turtle might be nearly $100 million, but this estimate is controversial.)

We have even less information about the *benefits* of protecting endangered species. Just exactly how much is it worth to society to protect the Socorro Isopod? There are two distinct views of the benefits of species protection. In one view, we think of the loss of other species as a warning sign: If some other species are in trouble, it's a signal that all is not well with the environment, which may have implications for *people*. According to this view, the biggest reason to protect other species is to protect ourselves. Another view is that, because people are the dominant species on the planet, we have a moral, ethical obligation to protect other species. The second of these views would certainly suggest that species protection is extremely important, while the first view would allow more tradeoffs. In this book, it simply isn't possible to decide what is the "correct" view. It's safe to say that species protection will continue to be an extremely controversial subject, because different people can have very different ideas about the value of protecting other species.

In our discussion of the Coase Theorem, we saw the importance of establishing property rights clearly. It turns out that property rights play a key role in a variety of environmental problems. One of these is the threat to the survival of some endangered species, such as the African elephant.

In Kenya, in east-central Africa, the elephants are not owned by anyone. In other words, there is no clearly-established property right to the elephants. When the property rights to a resource are not established, we say there is a *common-property-resource problem*. Since the elephants are "common property", no one has a financial incentive to take care of the elephant herds. Killing the elephants is illegal, but killings still occur. In fact, elephants have been driven to the brink of extinction in Kenya, and in some other African countries.

In southern Africa, the rules are different. In this region, local communities are allowed to treat the elephants as private property. This overcomes the common-property resource problem. If tourists want to take pictures of the elephants, they have to pay a fee to the local people. Some hunting is allowed, but the amount of hunting is strictly limited, and the hunters also have to pay. In Zimbabwe, villagers earned $5 million in 1990 by selling hunting rights.

Because of this, the local communities have a powerful incentive to preserve and protect the elephant herds. The villagers care for sick elephants, and unauthorized hunters are shot on sight. As a result, the elephant herds in southern Africa are increasing. From 1982 to 1991, the elephant population in Botswana and Zimbabwe grew from 50,000 to 94,000.

In some cases, the establishment of property rights can go a long way toward solving our environmental problems. Unfortunately, the property-rights solution won't work as well for some species as it works for elephants. After all, elephants are unusually easy to see, and this makes it easy for the villagers to keep track of the elephants.

Common-property-resource problems are sometimes known as the *"Tragedy of the Commons"*. History is full of examples of the Tragedy of the Commons. Between 1860 and 1960, the bison population of North America was reduced by about 99.999 percent, and the species was driven very close to extinction. This occurred in large part because no one owned the bison. Thus no one had any incentive to maintain the bison herds. Instead, bison hunters had every incentive to kill as many bison as possible, as quickly as possible. If one hunter did not kill the bison, another hunter would.

During the same period when bison were driven close to extinction, the cattle population of North America was thriving. Since ranchers owned the cattle, they had every incentive to maintain healthy herds.

One thing does seem clear. The growth in the size of the human population has put tremendous pressure on many species. Two thousand years ago, there were only about 250 million people on this planet. By the year 1900, there were about 1.6 *billion,* and there were more than 7 *bil-* lion by 2012. By the year 2025, the world's population has been projected to rise to as much as 8 billion, or even more. The species *Homo sapiens* is definitely not on the endangered list.

In *Real Economics for Real People 17.3*, we discuss the plight of the African elephant.

After you read the box, you will see that things can be done to protect endangered species, regardless of the size of the human population. However, virtually all of our environmental problems are made more severe by the growth in the number of people. Unless people control their numbers, the outlook is probably fairly bleak for many species. Fortunately, the world's population growth rate is slowing down.

ECONOMICS AND YOU: SHOULD WE FIGHT CLIMATE CHANGE? IF SO, HOW?

We began this chapter by discussing the threat of climate change, caused by the build-up of greenhouse gases in the upper atmosphere. The first question to ask is whether a large amount of warming will actually occur. It would be good to give a precise answer, but, unfortunately, the correct answer is "maybe". Over the years, temperatures have fluctuated a great deal. After all, the earth has had periodic ice ages. The last major ice age (which ended about 11,000 years ago) once spread a thick sheet of ice over almost all of what is now Canada, New England, the Middle Atlantic States, and the Great Lakes States.

Average temperatures did increase by a little less than one degree Fahrenheit from 1880 to 1940. However, this increase can't be blamed on greenhouse gases, since most of the build-up of those gases has occurred more recently. Worldwide average temperatures actually *fell* from 1940 to 1970, but they have risen since then. In 1995, the International Panel on Climate Change (a group of 1500 climate experts from 60 nations) issued a report suggesting that global warming is a very real threat. In subsequent years, the International Panel has issued additional reports. Over the last few years, more and more evidence is pointing to climate change caused by human activities. Increasingly, the fact of climate change is not a controversy, although the exact magnitude of the change is still uncertain.

Early in the 21st century, technological improvements in the process of hydraulic fracturing (also known as "fracking") led to a large increase in the supply of natural gas in the United States. The carbon emissions from natural gas are much lower than the carbon emissions from coal. As a result, U.S. carbon emissions actually decreased slightly. It remains to be seen how much this will slow down the process of climate change. For one thing, carbon stays in the atmosphere for a very long time. In addition, fracking has the potential to create other environmental problems, especially in terms of ground-water pollution. It seems likely that fracking will provide only a temporary reprieve for carbon pollution, and that lots of additional efforts will be necessary to control climate change.

If a strong effort were to be made to control carbon dioxide and the other greenhouse gases, how would we do it? For one thing, trees act as a "carbon sink". That is, trees actually absorb carbon from the atmosphere. Therefore, efforts should be made to encourage the planting of trees, and to discourage the elimination of forests. Brazil's Amazon region is one of the most heavily forested regions on earth, but the forests are being cut down at an alarming rate. One promising possibility is that the Amazon may become one of the world's foremost fruit-exporting regions. Fruits with exotic names such as acerola, camu camu, and cupuacu can be grown in the Amazon, and some of these fruits are loaded with vitamin C. If the markets for these fruits can be developed, the Amazon region will eventually be a vast fruit basket, and a carbon sink, too.

However, if we want to reduce our emissions of carbon into the atmosphere, we will have to find a way to burn less of the fossil fuels, such as oil, gas, and coal. Throughout this chapter, we've emphasized that command-and-control methods do not work as well as market-oriented methods of controlling pollution. Thus if we try to reduce the consumption of fossil fuels, we would want to use a market-oriented mechanism, such as a carbon tax. A carbon tax would be placed on the various fossil fuels, in proportion to their carbon content.

What kind of carbon tax would be necessary, to stabilize the amount of carbon dioxide in the atmosphere? In all likelihood, it would take a very large tax, on the order of $100 per ton of carbon. A tax of this size would have profound effects. It would certainly raise a lot of revenue—perhaps as much as $200 billion per year in the United States alone. Unless other taxes were cut, it would be hard for the economy to swallow a tax of this magnitude without a reduction in the rate of economic growth.

Coal has a higher carbon content than oil or natural gas. Consequently, the carbon tax rate on coal would be higher than the rate on oil or gas. This would have a big effect on coal-producing regions. Since China has some of the world's largest reserves of coal, we would expect the Chinese government to be less than enthusiastic about carbon-tax proposals. What would happen if all of the world were to adopt a carbon tax, except China? In all likelihood, polluting industries would flock to China. This suggests that international cooperation will be one of the thorniest issues that we face in designing a worldwide carbon tax.

In 2015, representatives of nearly 200 countries met at Paris, under the auspices of the United Nations Framework Convention on Climate Change. They concluded an agreement that would push toward a reduction of greenhouse gases. Most countries (including the two biggest polluters, China and the United States) signed on to the agreement. Most analysts are skeptical that the Paris Agreement will do enough to stop climate change, but it may slow down the process.

What can *you* do? Plant a tree. Drive a fuel-efficient car. Don't keep your home or apartment too warm in winter, or too cool in summer. But the actions of isolated individuals are likely to have only a modest effect. The problem of climate change is ultimately a public, collective problem. Success or failure will ride on our ability to reach collective decisions, through national governments and international cooperation.

Chapter Summary

1. Externalities occur when the actions of one person or firm have an effect on another person or firm, and the effect is not directly accounted for by the system of market prices. Externalities include air pollution, water pollution, congestion, noise, solid waste, and toxic waste.

2. There is no market for clean air, or for clean water, or for peace and quiet. Thus externalities arise in cases where there is a missing market. Externalities are an example of market failure.

3. When the production of a good involves a negative externality, such as air pollution, the true social marginal cost of production is greater than the private marginal cost of production. Because of this, the private market will produce a quantity that is greater than the socially optimal quantity.

4. One way to overcome pollution externalities is through private negotiation. The Coase Theorem states that private negotiations will lead to the same efficient outcome, regardless of whether property rights are held by the "polluter" or the "pollutee". The most important thing is that the property rights be defined clearly.

5. Many modern externality problems have an effect on thousands of people. In cases like these, it will be difficult to solve the problem through private negotiation, because the transaction costs of doing so are high. As a result, there is a role for government in the fight against pollution.

6. For the most part, governments in the United States have tried to deal with pollution by using regulations. This approach has had some successes, because many pollutants have been reduced substantially since 1970. However, this approach is often much more costly than necessary, because it ignores the differences in the cost of pollution abatement for different sources of pollution.

7. Economists argue that "market-oriented" methods of reducing pollution will often be much more cost-effective than regulations. Market-oriented policies include Pigouvian taxes and marketable licenses. The advantage of these policies is that they cause most of the cleanup to be done by the firms with the lowest cost of cleaning up.

8. The federal government has tried to reduce the amount of automobile pollution. Its main policy tool has been Corporate Average Fuel Economy standards, which have forced producers to increase the fuel efficiency of their cars and trucks. The government has also mandated that drivers in some areas use "reformulated gasoline". These regulatory policies are limited in their effectiveness, because the number of miles driven has increased substantially over the years. If we were to attempt to control the growth in the number of miles driven, an increase in the gasoline tax would be one of the best choices.

9. To reduce the amount of garbage that gets buried or burned, governments have started a number of programs. Curbside recycling programs are effective at reducing garbage, and so are the "deposit-and-return" programs that encourage people to return their bottles and cans for recycling. Some communities have begun to charge residents for every bag of garbage. The effectiveness of this policy has been questioned, because people tend to stuff each garbage bag until it is very full (without actually reducing the total amount of garbage). Some people also respond by dumping their waste illegally.

Key Words

Missing Market

Market Failure

Externalities

Coase Theorem

Transaction Costs

Command-and-Control Approach

Market-Oriented Approaches to Pollution Control

Pigouvian Taxes

Marketable Licenses

Stationary-Source Pollution

Mobile-Source Pollution

Recycling Programs

Deposit-and-Return Program

Common-Property-Resource Problem

Tragedy of the Commons

Carbon Tax

Questions and Problems

QP17-1. We have emphasized the advantages of market-oriented methods, compared to command-and-control techniques. However, command-and-control techniques might be more appropriate during a very serious environmental emergency. What do you think would be the best policies for dealing with a "killer smog", or a meltdown at a nuclear power plant?

QP17-2. What is the Coase Theorem? Is it relevant to environmental problems?

QP17-3. The highway between Middletown and Centerville is badly congested from 6 a.m. to 9 a.m., and again from 4 p.m. to 7 p.m. (At other times, traffic flows freely on the highway.) When the highway is congested, each additional car creates a negative externality. This is because each additional car slows down all of the other cars. It has been suggested that a Pigouvian tax, in the form of a toll, could be used to encourage more efficient use of the highway.

a. If it doesn't cost anything to collect the toll, what would be the optimal toll at 8 a.m.? What would be the optimal toll at midnight?

b. How would your answer to (a) change, if we recognize that it is costly to collect the tolls?

c. Let's consider two ways of collecting tolls. With the first method, every car stops at a toll booth, in order to complete a cash transaction. With the second method (which has begun to be used in recent years), every car would be equipped with a bar-coded device, which could be read by an optical scanner. Each car owner would be sent a bill at the end of the month, reflecting the number of times his or her car had travelled the highway. What are the pluses and minuses of using these two methods of collecting tolls?

QP17-4. There are two bridges across the river between Bigtown and Giant City. A toll is collected on one of the bridges, in an effort to deal with the externality of congestion. However, no toll is collected on the other bridge. At rush hour, traffic flows smoothly on the bridge with the toll, but there are severe traffic jams on the bridge with no toll.

A member of the planning commission proposes that $50 million should be spent to widen the bridge with no toll, to deal with the problem of traffic congestion. Can you think of any alternative policies that might be more effective?

QP17-5. The demand curve for gizmos is given by $P = \$(10-Q)$. The supply curve is perfectly elastic, and is given by $P = \$3$. Unfortunately, the production of gizmos involves industrial pollution. The marginal damage associated with this pollution is $4 for each additional gizmo. Thus the true social marginal cost associated with the production of gizmos is $\$(3+4) = \$7$.

a. What is the equilibrium quantity that would be produced by the private market?
b. What is the socially optimal quantity?
c. What is the dollar value of the benefit from correcting the externality? (To get the correct answer, you will need to calculate the area of a triangle. See Figure 17.2 for an example.)
d. How would your answer to (b) change if the marginal damage associated with this pollution were actually $7 for each additional gizmo. In this case, the true social marginal cost associated with the production of gizmos would be $\$(3+7) = \$10$.

QP17-6. When there is no market for clean air, the firm's opportunity cost of pollution is zero. However, when marketable licenses are used to establish a market for clean air, the firm has a positive opportunity cost for pollution. What does this imply about the firm's incentives to develop new technologies for cleaning up pollution?

QP17-7. Suppose that we desire to reduce water pollution. Discuss the strengths and weaknesses of the following four approaches to achieving this goal:

a. Private negotiation.
b. Regulations mandating that all sources of pollution should meet some fixed standard.
c. Pigouvian taxes.
d. Marketable licenses to pollute.

QP17-8. There are two industries in Environmuck. Each spews a noxious substance called "gunk" into the air. The cost of reducing gunk emissions by one unit is $10 in industry A, and $1 in industry B.

a. It has been decided that gunk emissions must be reduced by 30 units. One way to do this is to require each industry to clean up 15 units of pollution. What would be the total cost of cleaning up 30 units in this way?
b. Another way of cleaning up 30 units of gunk would be for industry B to do all of the cleaning. What is the total cost of cleaning up 30 units in this way?

Glossary

Absolute Advantage: A term used to describe the relationship between the productive capacities of two people, or two countries. One person or country has absolute advantage over another person or country, if the first person or country can produce a given output using fewer resources than the other person or country. Absolute advantage can be defined with reference to one good or activity, whereas comparative advantage requires at least two goods or activities.

Accounting Cost: The sum of all of the explicit, out-of-pocket costs incurred by a firm. Accounting cost does *not* include the implicit costs that are included in economic cost, such as the normal return on investment.

Accounting Profit: Total revenue minus accounting cost. Since accounting cost does not include the normal return, accounting profit will be greater than economic profit.

Administrative Costs of the Tax System: The costs of operating the tax system that are incurred by the government. The Internal Revenue Service and the various state and local revenue agencies spend real resources on getting the tax system to run smoothly. We refer to the costs of these agencies as the administrative costs of the tax system.

Advertising: A form of non-price competition, by which firms try to push their demand curves outward or make their demand curves more inelastic.

***ALCOA* Case**: Antitrust case in 1945, in which the Supreme Court reversed the Rule of Reason by finding ALCOA guilty of violating the antitrust laws, even though the firm had not acted unreasonably.

***American Tobacco* Case**: Antitrust case in which the Supreme Court, in 1911, broke James B. Duke's Tobacco Trust into 16 smaller companies.

Antitrust Laws: Laws that make it possible for the government to break a large firm into smaller pieces, in an attempt to overcome the problems of monopoly. The antitrust laws, which include the Sherman Act of 1890 and the Clayton Act of 1914, prohibit monopolization, price fixing, tying arrangements, certain forms of price discrimination, exclusive dealing arrangements, and interlocking directorates.

***AT&T* Case**: Antitrust case, which was decided by a consent decree in 1982. American Telephone & Telegraph (AT&T) was required to divest itself of its local telephone operating companies. AT&T continued to provide long-distance telephone service. The local operating companies became known as the Baby Bells.

Average Fixed Cost: Fixed cost per unit of output. Average fixed cost is calculated by dividing total fixed cost by the quantity of output. A graph of average fixed cost will slope downward as we move from left to right. This is because total fixed cost is a constant. Therefore, as we divide total fixed cost by quantity, the quotient becomes smaller and smaller as we consider larger and larger quantities.

Average Revenue: The average number of dollars that the firm receives, per unit of sales. For a firm that does not practice price discrimination, average revenue is equal to price.

Average Total Cost: Total cost per unit of output. Average total cost is calculated by dividing total cost by the quantity of output. Another way to calculate average total cost is to add average variable cost and average fixed cost.

Average Variable Cost: Variable cost per unit of output. Average variable cost is calculated by dividing total variable cost by the quantity of output.

Backward-Bending Labor-Supply Curve: A labor-supply curve that slopes downward as we move from left to right. For a backward-bending labor-supply curve, the income effect is larger than the substitution effect, and the labor-supply elasticity is negative.

Barriers to Entry: Barriers that keep new firms from entering an industry. Significant barriers to entry are present under monopoly, and possibly also under oligopoly, but not under perfect competition or monopolistic competition. Examples of barriers to entry include patents and exclusive-franchise arrangements. As a result of barriers to entry, the existing firms in a market may be able to have positive economic profits for a long period of time.

Basing-Point Pricing: A method for facilitating collusion among the members of an oligopoly. Basing-point pricing reduces the number of prices that must be agreed upon. The Pittsburgh-Plus pricing scheme, once used in the steel industry, is an example of basing-point pricing.

Black Market: A market with illegal sales. Black markets frequently arise in response to the shortages that occur when a price ceiling is enforced at a price below the equilibrium price.

Capital: The long-lived man-made goods that are used in the production process. Capital includes machinery and equipment, such as computers, drill presses, drop forges, and circular saws. Capital also includes structures, such as office buildings, factory buildings, and warehouses. Capital also includes railroad cars, delivery vans, and other types of moving capital.

Capital Gain: An increase in the value of a capital asset, such as a home or a share of stock. The tax treatment of capital gains in the federal individual income tax has long been a subject of controversy. Currently, the top marginal tax rate on capital gains is less than the top marginal tax rate on other types of income.

Capital Investment: The process of acquiring more capital. For example, capital investment might include the creation of factories, or pieces of equipment, or computers, or office buildings.

Cartel: A collusive agreement among the firms in an oligopolistic industry, under which the firms fix prices. Cartels are a violation of the antitrust laws in the United States.

Celler-Kefauver Act: Antitrust law, passed in 1950, to close a loophole in earlier laws. Previously, it had been illegal to monopolize by acquiring *stock*, but firms were still allowed to merge by acquiring *physical assets*. This loophole was plugged by the Celler-Kefauver Act.

Ceteris Paribus: A Latin phrase that means "all other things equal".

Change in Demand: A shift to a new demand curve. A change in demand can be brought about by a change in tastes, or by a change in incomes, or by changes in the prices of other goods, or by changes in other variables.

Change in Quantity Demanded: A change in the quantity of a good or service that buyers are willing to buy, brought about by a change in the price of the good, while all other influences remain constant. In other words, a change in quantity demanded refers to a movement along an existing demand curve.

Change in Quantity Supplied: A change in the quantity of a good or service that sellers are willing to sell, brought about by a change in the price of the good, while all other influences remain constant. In other words, a change in quantity supplied refers to a movement along an existing supply curve.

Change in Supply: A shift to a new supply curve. A change in supply can be brought about by a change in the price of an input, or by a change in technology, or by changes in other variables.

Clayton Act: The second important antitrust law, passed in 1914. The Clayton Act prohibits tying arrangements, exclusive dealing arrangements, and interlocking directorates.

Coase Theorem: An idea (named for Ronald H. Coase) regarding the solution of externality problems. For example, if we consider air pollution, if people can negotiate freely, they should be able to achieve the efficient outcome, regardless of who has the property right to the air. Coase says it doesn't matter who gets the property rights—the only important thing is that the property rights must be defined clearly. However, the applicability of the Coase Theorem may be limited, because of the transactions costs of reaching negotiated agreements.

Collusion: In oligopolistic industries, collusion is the practice by which firms cooperate with each other in an attempt to increase profits. In the United States, collusion is a violation of the antitrust laws.

Command-and-Control Approach: The regulatory approach to pollution control. Under the command-and-control approach, the government dictates the details of the pollution-control effort. Unfortunately, this leaves little room for private businesses to develop innovative ways of fighting pollution.

Common-Property-Resource Problem: A type of environmental problem that can occur when the property rights to a resource are not clearly established and enforced. For example, there are common-property-resource problems in ocean fisheries. No one company owns the ocean, and firms have an incentive to harvest the fisheries too intensively.

Comparative Advantage: A term that describes the relationship between the productive capacities of two or more people or countries. A person has comparative advantage in an activity if his or her opportunity cost of that activity is lower than the opportunity of that activity for anyone else. A country has comparative advantage in an activity if its opportunity cost of that activity is lower than the opportunity cost for any other country. To calculate comparative advantage, it is necessary to compare at least two activities, whereas absolute advantage can be calculated with reference to only one activity.

Compensating Wage Differential: The extra wage that must be paid (all else equal), to attract workers to an unpleasant job. For example, night-shift workers are paid somewhat more than day-shift workers who are otherwise comparable.

Complements: A pair of goods for which the demand for one good decreases when the price of the other good increases. The cross-price elasticity of demand is negative for complements. Complements stand in contrast to substitutes.

Compliance Costs of the Tax System: The costs of operating the tax system that are incurred by the taxpayers. Compliance costs of the tax system include the time spent keeping records and filling out forms, and the expense of hiring tax accountants and tax attorneys.

Conglomerate Merger: A merger between two firms in unrelated industries.

Consent Decree: Negotiated settlement between the government and a company. If a consent decree is used in an antitrust case, it means that the case does not go all the way through the court system. The *AT&T* case and the *Xerox* case were settled by consent decrees, and were never heard by the Supreme Court.

Constant Returns to Scale: The situation that exists when the percentage change in output is the same as the percentage change in all inputs. For a firm that is experiencing constant returns to scale, the long-run average-total-cost curve will be a horizontal line.

Consumer Decision Rule, or Optimal Purchase Rule: The rule stating how the consumer should allocate his or her expenditures, in order to maximize consumer surplus. Consumers should continue to buy products as long as marginal utility is equal to or greater than price. For the last unit purchased, marginal utility will be equal to price.

Consumer Surplus: The excess of the amount the consumer is willing to pay for a good, over the amount actually paid. Graphically, consumer surplus is represented by the area of the triangle that is above the price line, but below the demand curve.

Corporate Tax Integration: A type of proposal for reforming the tax system. The idea of corporate tax integration is to coordinate the corporate income tax with the individual income tax, to solve the problem of double taxation of corporate income.

Corporation Income Tax: A tax that applies to the profits of corporations. The corporation income tax in the United States was instituted in 1909. The legal definition of corporate profits is extremely complicated, so that the compliance costs of the corporation tax are high. The corporation tax also causes a lot of inefficiency, because it applies to corporate income, but not to the income of non-corporate enterprises.

Costly Exclusion, or Nonexcludability: A characteristic of a public good. For some goods, it is difficult or impossible to exclude people from enjoying the good, even if they do not pay. In a case like this, we say that consumption is characterized by costly exclusion. Costly exclusion is also referred to as nonexcludability, or nonexcludable consumption. As a result of costly exclusion, private firms may be unable to provide the good.

Cross-Price Elasticity of Demand: The percentage change in the quantity of one good, divided by the percentage change in the price of another good. The cross-price elasticity of demand is positive for substitutes, zero for pairs of goods that are independent in demand, and negative for complements.

Cross-Subsidization: A common practice imposed by government regulatory agencies, under which some customers were charged higher prices, and the resulting revenues were used to subsidize other customers. For example, in airlines, passengers on longer flights were forced to subsidize passengers on shorter flights. In telecommunications, long-distance calls were forced to subsidize local service. These practices have been reduced by deregulation.

Deadweight Loss of Monopoly: The difference between how well off society is under perfect competition and how well off it is under monopoly. The loss in consumer surplus as a result of monopoly is greater than the monopoly profit. The difference between the lost consumer surplus and the monopoly profit is the deadweight loss.

Deadweight Loss of a Tax: The loss from a tax, over and above the amount of revenue raised for the government. For most taxes, the loss suffered by the private sector is greater than the revenue collected by the tax. The difference between the private sector's loss and the government's tax revenue is the deadweight loss of the tax. Deadweight loss is also called "excess burden" or "welfare cost".

Decreasing Returns to Scale: The situation that exists when the percentage increase in output is less than the percentage increase in all inputs. When a firm is experiencing decreasing returns to scale, its long-run average-total-cost curve will slope upward as we move from left to right. Decreasing returns to scale is sometimes also called "diseconomies of scale".

Deduction: A feature of many income-tax systems, under which taxpayers are allowed to reduce their taxable income by spending money on a particular type of activity. For example, in the federal individual income tax, if a taxpayer pays interest on a home mortgage, the taxpayer can subtract the interest payments from taxable income.

Demand Curve: A graph of the relationship between price and quantity demanded, holding constant all other influences on buyers. In other words, a demand curve is a graph of the information in a demand schedule. If buyers obey the Law of Demand, the demand curve will slope downward as we move from left to right.

Demand Schedule: A table showing the quantity of a good or service that would be demanded, at a number of different prices, holding constant all other influences on buyers. In other words, a demand schedule is a table of the information in a demand curve.

Deposit-and-Return Program: System for solid-waste disposal, under which consumers pay a deposit fee when they buy an item (such as a soft-drink can) that could generate solid waste. The consumer's deposit is given back when he or she returns the item. This gives consumers a financial incentive to recycle the item.

Deregulation: The process of removing many of the economic regulations that had previously applied to trucking, railroads, airlines, and other industries. The late 1970s and early 1980s were the most important period of removing regulatory restrictions.

Derived Demand: Term used to describe the demand for factors of production. The term "derived" demand comes from the fact that the factor of production is *not* an end in itself. Rather, it is a means to the end of making money for the firm. The demand for factors is *derived* from the demand for produced goods and services.

Diamond-Water Paradox: The puzzling fact, noted by Adam Smith, that diamonds can be sold for prices that are much higher than the price of water, even though water is essential for survival and diamonds are not. The paradox is resolved when we see that demand is determined by marginal utility, rather than by total utility.

Differentiated Product: When the firms in a market produce goods that have noticeable differences in quality, or location, or service, we say that the market is characterized by product differentiation. Differentiated product stands in contrast to homogeneous, or standardized, product. Product differentiation is a key characteristic of monopolistically competitive industries. Some oligopolies also have differentiated products.

Diseconomies of Scale: The situation that exists when the percentage increase in output is less than the percentage increase in all inputs. When a firm is experiencing diseconomies of scale, its long-run average-total-cost curve will slope upward as we move from left to right. Diseconomies of scale are also called "decreasing returns to scale".

Disequilibrium: A situation in which the quantity supplied is different from the quantity demanded. Both shortages and surpluses are cases of disequilibrium.

Distortionary Tax: A tax that leads to changes in behavior, because it changes the relative prices in the economy. Distortionary taxes tend to create inefficiency by distorting the decisions of buyers and sellers.

Dividends: A form of capital income. Corporations sometimes pay dividends to their stockholders.

Double Taxation of Corporate Income: Corporations are subject to the corporation income tax. If a corporation then pays a dividend to its stockholders, the stockholders have to pay individual income tax when they receive the dividends. Thus corporate income is subject to two levels of tax. This is called the double taxation of corporate income.

Duopoly: A special case of oligopoly, in which there are exactly two sellers.

Earned Income Tax Credit: A transfer-payment program in the United States. The Earned Income Tax Credit is only available to workers. Whereas many other transfer-payment programs encourage people to work less, the EITC encourages people to work more.

Economic Costs: The payments a firm must make, to attract resources away from other activities in which they might be used. Economic costs include the explicit, accounting costs, *and* they also include *implicit* costs. Thus, economic cost = accounting cost + implicit costs. The most important implicit cost is the opportunity cost of being in business, which is the normal return on investment.

Economic Incidence: The economic incidence of a tax is who *really* bears the burden of a tax. The economic incidence is determined by the elasticities of supply and demand. The economic incidence is not necessarily the same as the statutory incidence.

Economic Model: A stylized representation of some aspect of the real economy.

Economic Profit: Total revenue minus all costs, regardless of whether they are explicit or implicit. In other words, economic profit is equal to total revenue minus economic cost. Since economic cost is greater than accounting cost, economic profit is less than accounting profit.

Economic Regulation: A variety of laws designed to regulate the behavior of business firms. Economic regulation has been used to control prices, quantities, and entry into the industry, in industries such as utilities, airlines, and trucking. This type of economic regulation was first applied to railroads in the 19th century, and then extended to other industries in the 1930s. However, economic regulation was reduced substantially, as a result of the process of deregulation in the 1970s and 1980s.

Economics: The study of how people use their limited resources to satisfy unlimited wants. Another definition is that economics is the study of how a society chooses to use its scarce resources to produce, exchange, and consume goods and services.

Economics of Industrial Organization: The branch of economics that deals with the interactions among the firms in an industry, and the ways in which consumers are affected by industries with different market structures. For example, industrial-organization economics deals with the behavior of cartels, the effects of government regulation, and the effects of the antitrust laws.

Economies of Scale: The situation that exists when the percentage increase in output is greater than the percentage increase in all inputs. For a firm that is experiencing economies of scale, the long-run average-total-cost curve will slope downward as we move from left to right. Economies of scale are also called "increasing returns to scale".

Elastic Demand: When the percentage change in quantity demanded is greater than the percentage change in price, the own-price elasticity is greater than one. In this case, we say that demand is elastic. When demand is elastic, a decrease in price will lead to an increase in total revenue, and an increase in price will lead to a decrease in total revenue.

Elasticity: The percentage change in one variable, divided by the percentage change in another variable.

Elasticity of Labor Supply with Respect to the Wage Rate: The percentage change in the amount of labor supplied, divided by the percentage change in the wage rate. This elasticity is positive for upward-sloping labor-supply curves, and negative for backward-bending curves. It is also called the labor-supply elasticity.

Energy: A category of factor of production. The energy sector includes oil, natural gas, electricity, coal, solar, wind, and other sources of energy.

Environmental Economics: The branch of economics that is concerned with the causes and effects of environmental pollution. One of the goals of environmental economics is to find the most efficient ways to clean up pollution.

Equilibrium: The condition that exists when quantity demanded is equal to quantity supplied in a market. When the market is in equilibrium, there will not be any pressure for price to rise or fall.

Equilibrium Quantity: A term that can be used to refer to either the quantity supplied or the quantity demanded for a market that is in equilibrium, since equilibrium means that quantity supplied is equal to quantity demanded.

Equilibrium Price: The price at which quantity supplied is equal to quantity demanded.

Equity-Efficiency Tradeoff: A problem in the design of a tax system. Progressive taxes are sometimes associated with a larger degree of economic inefficiency, while proportional and regressive taxes are sometimes relatively more efficient, in the sense that they lead to a relatively smaller amount of excess burden or deadweight loss. As a result, for those who would like to increase the progressivity of the tax system, an increase in progressivity must be weighed against the possibility of increased economic inefficiency.

Excess Burden: The loss from a tax, over and above the amount of revenue raised for the government. For most taxes, the loss suffered by the private sector is greater than the revenue collected by the tax. The difference between the private sector's loss and the government's tax revenue is the excess burden of the tax. Excess burden is also called "deadweight loss" or "welfare cost".

Excess Capacity: A characteristic of monopolistically competitive industries. The firms in these industries typically produce at a level of output that is too small to minimize costs. It has been said that these firms have excess capacity, since they could reduce their average total costs by expanding.

Excise Tax: A tax on the sale of a specific commodity. The federal government and each of the 50 states have excise taxes on alcoholic beverages, gasoline, and tobacco products.

Exclusion: A feature of many income taxes, under which a particular type of income is excluded from the tax base. For example, in the federal individual income tax, when an employer pays health-insurance premiums for an employee, or contributes to the employee's pension fund, these payments are not counted as part of the employee's income for tax purposes.

Exclusive Dealing Arrangement: Business arrangement under which a dealer agrees to buy all of its supplies from one supplier. Exclusive dealing arrangements are restricted by the antitrust laws.

Exclusive Franchise: A type of barrier to entry. An exclusive franchise is a business arrangement under which only one firm is allowed to produce in a particular territory.

Export: When a seller in one country sells goods or services to a buyer in another country, we say that the selling country has made an export.

Externality: A problem that occurs when the actions of one person or firm have an effect on another person or firm, and the effect is not directly accounted for by the price system. The word "externality" refers to the fact that the effects are *external* to the system of market prices. Air pollution, water pollution, congestion, and noise are examples of externalities.

Factor Markets: The markets in which factors of production, or inputs, are bought and sold. Factor markets include labor markets, capital markets, and markets for land, energy, and materials. Factor markets are also called input markets.

Factors of Production: The inputs in production processes. The factors of production include labor, capital, land, energy, and materials.

Federal Trade Commission Act: Antitrust law, passed in 1914, creating a new agency for dealing with antitrust issues. (Previously, the Department of Justice had been the only agency involved with antitrust.)

Feminization of Poverty: Term used to describe the increase in the proportion of poor people in female-headed families, which occurred at an especially rapid rate in the United States during the 1970s and 1980s.

Fixed Costs: The costs of fixed inputs. By definition, fixed costs do not change when there is a change in the level of output.

Fixed Inputs: Inputs that cannot be changed during the time period under consideration. In the short run, at least one input must be fixed. In the long run, there are no fixed inputs.

Flat Tax: An income tax under which all taxable income would be taxed at a single rate. During the 1980s and 1990s, a number of proposals circulated, under which the federal individual income tax would be converted to a flat tax. However, none of these proposals has been passed into law.

Food Stamps: Transfer-payment program that provides low-income people with vouchers that can be used to buy certain food items. Food Stamps is an example of an in-kind program.

Foregone Earnings: The additional wages and salaries that could be earned, if a person were to go to work right after high school, instead of going to college. Foregone earnings are an important part of the opportunity cost of a college education.

Fraction: One number divided by another number. For example, one-half = 1/2 is a fraction.

Free Entry: One of the characteristics of perfectly competitive markets and monopolistically competitive markets. Free entry means that there are no substantial barriers to entry into the industry. As a result of free entry, positive economic profits will be "competed away" in these industries (i.e., positive economic profits will not persist for long).

Free Exit: One of the characteristics of perfectly competitive markets and monopolistically competitive markets. Free exit means that there are no substantial barriers to a firm going out of business and leaving the industry. As a result of free exit, an industry in which firms are suffering economic losses will eventually be restored to a situation of zero economic profits.

Free-Rider Problem: For a nonexcludable public good, people have an incentive to be "free riders", by understating their true preferences for the good. People may say they aren't willing to pay (even when they really are willing to pay), because they believe that someone else will eventually foot the bill. As a result, it will be hard to determine the amount of public good that would be best for society.

Game Theory: The study of how people and organizations interact with each other in strategic situations. A game-theoretic analysis involves identifying the "players" in the game, and the rules of the game. Then the analysis will specify the payoffs that accompany various outcomes. On the basis of the rules and the payoffs, each player will develop a set of strategies that will determine how he or she will play the game. In economics, some of the most important applications of game theory have to do with the interactions among firms in an oligopoly.

General Retail Sales Tax: A tax on purchases of a wide variety of items, which is usually levied on sales of clothing, hardware, and many other goods. Most states in the United States have a general retail sales tax. Sales of most services (such as the services provided by lawyers, doctors, and accountants) are usually *not* covered by the sales taxes. In many states, food also isn't taxed.

Gini Ratio, or **Gini Coefficient**, or **Gini Index**: The best-known measure of inequality in an income distribution. The Gini Coefficient is calculated by dividing the crescent-shaped area between the

Lorenz Curve and the Line of Equality, by the area of the entire triangle under the Line of Equality. The Gini Ratio can range from zero (which represents complete equality) to one (which represents extreme inequality).

Graduated Marginal Tax Rates: A feature of some individual-income-tax systems. Under a system of graduated marginal tax rates, the tax rate applied to an additional dollar of taxable income is higher, for people who have higher taxable incomes. The federal individual income tax has graduated rates, as do the income taxes of most states. Graduated marginal rates are a source of progressivity.

Homogeneous Product: A characteristic of perfectly competitive markets. When the outputs of the firm are homogeneous, it is impossible for buyers to tell any difference between the outputs of two firms. This is one of the reasons why perfectly competitive firms are price takers. If a firm produces a homogeneous product, and if it is small relative to the market, it will not be able to manipulate the price to its advantage, and thus it will be a price taker. Homogeneous product has the same meaning as standardized product, but it stands in contrast to differentiated product.

Horizontal Axis: One of the two axes in a two-dimensional graph. The horizontal axis extends to the right from the origin. The independent variable is often represented on the horizontal axis. The horizontal axis is also called the x-axis. The horizontal axis stands in contrast to the vertical axis, or y-axis.

Horizontal Equity: When a tax system treats similar people in a similar manner by the tax system, the tax system is characterized by horizontal equity. The income-tax system is not neutral with respect to marital status, and this is an example of a violation of horizontal equity.

Horizontal Merger: A merger between two firms that are competing with each other directly in the same industry. Horizontal mergers have the potential to reduce competition, especially if the firms involved in the merger are large relative to the market. Thus horizontal mergers are a bigger concern for economic policy than vertical mergers or conglomerate mergers.

Hub-and-Spoke Route System: Under this type of system, an airline sends a great deal of traffic through its "hubs". For example, American Airlines has hubs in Chicago and Dallas, and Delta Airlines has hubs in Atlanta and Detroit.

Human-Capital Investment: Term used to describe the investments that people make in themselves, in the hope that the human capital will pay off in higher earnings in the future. Human-capital investments can take many forms, but education and on-the-job training are the most important.

IBM Case: Antitrust case in which the government charged International Business Machines Corp. with a number of anti-competitive practices. After a very long trial, the case was dropped by the Justice Department in 1982.

Imperfect Competition: Term used to describe industries that are either monopolistically competitive or oligopolistic.

Import: When a buyer in one country buys goods or services from a seller in another country, we say that the buying country has made an import.

Import Quota: A restriction on the quantity of a particular good that can be imported from a particular country. The import quota is administered by the government of the importing country. This stands in contrast to a voluntary export restraint, which is administered by the exporting country. If the import quota is above the equilibrium quantity, it will have no effect on the market. However, if the import quota is less than the equilibrium quantity, it can lead to substantial profits for the holder of the import license as well as to higher prices for the consumers in the importing country.

Income Effect on Labor Supply: When there is an increase in the wage rate, there is an increase in the possibilities available to the consumer/worker, which is similar to an increase in non-labor income. Thus when the wage rate rises, the consumer is "richer", and there will be an increase in leisure, or a decrease in work, because leisure is a normal good. When there is a decrease in the wage rate, the consumer is "poorer", and there will be a decrease in leisure, or an increase in work. The total effect of a wage-rate change on labor supply is the sum of the income effect and the substitution effect.

Income Elasticity of Demand: The percentage change in quantity, divided by the percentage change in income. The income elasticity is positive for normal goods, and negative for inferior goods.

Increasing Returns to Scale: The situation that exists when the percentage increase in output is greater than the percentage increase in all inputs. For a firm that is experiencing increasing returns to scale, the long-run average-total-cost curve will slope downward as we move from left to right. Increasing returns to scale are sometimes also called "economies of scale".

Independent in Demand: When the demand for one good is unaffected by the price of another good, the two goods are independent in demand. For goods that are independent in demand, the cross-price elasticity of demand is zero. Goods that are independent in demand are neither complements nor substitutes.

Individual Demand Schedule: A demand schedule for a single person. An individual demand schedule stands in contrast to a market demand schedule.

Individual Income Tax: A tax that applies to many types of income, including wages and salaries, dividends, interest, rents, and royalties. The United States did not get a permanent income tax until the Sixteenth Amendment to the Constitution, in 1913. Most states and some cities also have an income tax.

Inelastic Demand: When the percentage change in quantity demanded is less than the percentage change in price, the own-price elasticity is less than one. In this case, we say that demand is inelastic. When demand is inelastic, an increase in price will lead to an increase in total revenue, and a decrease in price will lead to a decrease in total revenue.

Infant-Industry Argument: An argument that it may be beneficial to give trade protection, such as a tariff, import quota, or voluntary export restraint, to a domestic industry during the first few years of its existence. One problem with the infant-industry argument is that, once tariff protection is in place, the protected firms may push to continue the tariff protection, even after they have grown beyond infancy.

Inferior Good: A good for which demand decreases when incomes increase. Similarly, an inferior good is one for which demand increases when incomes decrease. The income elasticity of demand is negative for an inferior good. Inferior goods stand in contrast to normal goods.

In-Kind: Term used to describe payments that do not come in the form of cash. For example, Food Stamps and Medicare are in-kind transfer-payment programs.

Inputs: The productive resources used by business firms when they produce outputs. Inputs include labor, capital, land, energy, and materials. Inputs are also known as factors of production.

Input Markets: The markets in which inputs, or factors of production, are bought and sold. Inputs markets include labor markets, capital markets, and the markets for land, energy, and materials. These markets are also called factor markets.

Interest Payments: One form of capital income. Interest payments are received by people who own bonds.

Interlocking Directorates: Practice under which the same person would sit on the Board of Directors of several competing companies. Interlocking directorates are a violation of the Clayton Act.

International Economics: The branch of economics that deals with activities involving more than one country. For example, international economics deals with why one country will import some goods, and export different goods. International economics also deals with the effects of tariffs, quotas, and voluntary export restraints.

Invisible Hand: A phrase used by the 18th-century Scottish economist Adam Smith to describe the beauty of market equilibrium. Even though no one sets out with the goal of achieving market equilibrium, it is as if an invisible hand leads the market in that direction.

Job Rationing: System for determining who gets a job in a labor union. Since labor unions are often successful at increasing wages above the equilibrium level, they will tend to suffer job losses. This makes it necessary to have a system of job rationing. Seniority is a common method of job rationing.

Labor: Term used by economists to refer to the work done by workers. Labor is the most important factor of production.

Labor Economics: The branch of economics that is concerned with work, pay, and other aspects of labor markets. For example, labor economics is concerned with explaining wage differentials. Labor economics also deals with the effects of unions and minimum-wage laws.

Labor-Supply Elasticity: The percentage change in the quantity of labor supplied, divided by the percentage change in the wage rate. This elasticity is positive for upward-sloping labor-supply curves, negative for backward-bending curves, and zero for perfectly inelastic labor-supply curves. It is also called the elasticity of labor supply with respect to the wage rate.

Labor Unions: Organizations of workers, which negotiate with employers about wages, fringe benefits, and working conditions. Many labor unions are also active in political lobbying. In recent years, about 11 percent of American workers have been members of labor unions.

Land: A factor of production.

Law of Demand: A statement of the usual relationship between price and quantity demanded. The Law of Demand states that, when the price of a good or service increases, the quantity demanded will decrease, all else equal. Conversely, when the price decreases, the quantity demanded will increase, all else equal.

Law of Diminishing Marginal Utility: For virtually every consumer good, the amount of additional utility provided by consuming one additional unit of the good will eventually go down, as the consumer increases his or her level of consumption.

Law of Diminishing Returns: The Law of Diminishing Returns indicates that, when we increase one variable input, holding constant all other inputs, the marginal (physical) product of that variable input will eventually decrease. The Law of Diminishing Returns is sometimes also called the Law of Diminishing Marginal Returns, or the Law of Diminishing Marginal Product.

Law of Increasing Opportunity Cost: The Law of Increasing Opportunity Cost says that the opportunity cost of producing one additional unit of a good will increase, as we produce more and more of the good.

Law of Supply: A statement of the usual relationship between price and quantity supplied. The Law of Supply states that, when the price of a good or service increases, the quantity supplied will increase, all else equal. Conversely, when the price decreases, the quantity supplied will decrease, all else equal. In this book, we most often assume that the Law of Supply is obeyed. However, on several occasions, we consider supply curves that do not obey the Law of Supply, such as perfectly inelastic or perfectly elastic supply curves.

Leisure: One of the activities to which a person can devote time. In our model of labor supply, a fixed amount of time is allocated between working in the labor market (which we call labor) and doing other things (which we call leisure).

Lock-In Effect: The incentive to hold on to stocks, in order to avoid paying capital-gains taxes.

Long Run: A period of time that is sufficiently long that there are no fixed costs. We also use the phrase "long run" to describe the period of time that will be necessary for entry and exit to lead us to the zero-profit situation.

Long-Run Supply Curve: A curve showing the relationship between the quantity of output of the industry and the prices that will be charged (assuming zero economic profits).

Lorenz Curve: A curve showing the proportion of income going to each part of the population. The horizontal axis of the Lorenz Curve shows the cumulative proportion of the population, ranked by income. The vertical axis shows the cumulative proportion of income.

Machinery and Equipment: Types of long-lived man-made goods that are used in the production process. Machinery and equipment includes computers, drill presses, drop forges, and circular saws. Machinery and equipment are important types of capital.

Macroeconomics: The study of the aggregates for the economy as a whole, such as the overall rate of economic growth, the overall rate of unemployment, and the overall rate of inflation. Macroeconomics is one of the two broad branches of economics; the other is microeconomics.

Marginal Cost: The additional cost that is necessary to produce one additional unit of output. Marginal cost is the change in total cost, divided by the change in the quantity of output. Also, marginal cost is the change in total variable cost, divided by the change in the quantity of output.

Marginal Factor Expense: The marginal cost to the firm of hiring one additional unit of a factor of production. For example, the marginal factor expense of labor is the additional expense the firm must incur, to get one more worker to work for the firm. For a firm in a perfectly competitive labor market, marginal factor expense is equal to the wage rate. For a monopsony firm, marginal factor expense is an upward-sloping curve, which is steeper than the corresponding supply curve.

Marginal (Physical) Product: The extra output produced by an extra unit of a variable input. For example, the marginal (physical) product of labor is the additional output produced when the firm hires one additional worker. Marginal physical product is also called "marginal product".

Marginal Revenue: The extra amount of money the firm receives, when it sells one additional unit of output. For a perfectly competitive firm, marginal revenue is equal to the market price. For a firm with market power, the marginal-revenue curve is a downward-sloping curve, which is below the demand curve.

Marginal Revenue Product: The additional revenue received by the firm, when it hires one additional unit of a factor of production, and then sells the extra output that is made by that extra unit. For example, the marginal revenue product of labor is the additional revenue received by the firm when it hires one additional worker, and then sells the extra output that is made by that extra worker. Marginal revenue product is calculated by multiplying marginal (physical) product by marginal revenue.

Marginal Utility: The additional amount of satisfaction received by the consumer, as a result of consuming one additional unit of a good. In this book, we define the marginal utility as the maximum amount of money the consumer would be willing to pay to receive one additional unit.

Market: Any organized system of exchange of a good or service between buyers and sellers. Another way to say this is that a market is any institution or mechanism that allows people to interact, for the purpose of buying and selling some good or service.

Marketable-License System: A method for dealing with pollution externalities. A marketable-license system is a market-oriented mechanism for dealing with pollution, similar to a Pigouvian tax. Under such a system, a certain number of licenses would be issued for each type of pollution. Firms would be able to buy and sell the licenses. Firms with low costs of pollution abatement would be less likely to want to buy the licenses, and firms with high costs of pollution abatement would be more likely to buy the licenses. A type of marketable-license system was introduced in the United States for sulfur dioxide pollution, in 1990.

Market Demand Curve: A graph of the relationship between price and quantity demanded in a market, all else equal. If buyers take the market price as given, the market demand curve is constructed by adding horizontally the demand curves for all buyers.

Market Demand Schedule: A demand schedule for all of the buyers and potential buyers in a market. A market demand schedule stands in contrast to an individual demand schedule. A market demand schedule is constructed by adding the individual demand schedules of all buyers in the market.

Market Failure: Description of a situation in which the private market economy will *not* tend to produce the best outcome for society. Monopoly, oligopoly, monopsony, oligopsony, public goods, and externalities are examples of market failures.

Market for Loanable Funds: The market for loans with which firms make capital investments. Private households save their money in financial institutions, which then make loans to businesses.

Market Power: If a firm is able to exert some control over its price, we say the firm has market power. Monopolistic firms have a substantial amount of market power. Oligopolistic firms and monopolistically competitive firms have some market power. Perfectly competitive firms have no market power.

Market Structure: Term used to describe the way in which the firms in a market relate to each other, and to their buyers. The four market structures are perfect competition, monopolistic competition, oligopoly, and monopoly.

Market Supply Curve: A graph of the relationship between price and the quantity supplied in a market, all else equal. In a perfectly competitive industry, the short-run market supply curve is constructed by adding horizontally the supply curves for all of the individual firms.

Market Supply Schedule: A supply schedule for all of the sellers and potential sellers in a market. A market supply schedule is a table of the relationship between price and the market quantity supplied, holding constant all other influences on sellers. In a perfectly competitive market, the market supply schedule is constructed by adding across the supply schedules of all of the individual firms.

Marriage Bonus: Situation under which a couple's total tax payments would be lower if they were married than if they were unmarried. This is widely considered to be a violation of horizontal equity.

Marriage Penalty: Situation under which a couple's total tax payments would be lower if they were unmarried. This is widely considered to be a violation of horizontal equity.

Materials: A factor of production, which includes items such as bricks, paper, plastics, steel, and wood.

Medicare: Transfer-payment program that provides elderly Americans with medical insurance. Medicare is the second-largest transfer-payment program in the United States; the largest is the Social Security retirement program.

Microeconomics: The study of the behavior of households and business firms, and the way in which they interact with each other in markets. Microeconomics is one of the two broad branches of economics; the other is macroeconomics.

***Microsoft* Case**: Antitrust case brought against Microsoft Corporation for a variety of offenses, including trying to use its near-monopoly in personal-computer operating systems to establish a monopoly in internet browser software. A Federal District Court ruled that Microsoft should be broken into two pieces, but this ruling was overturned by an appeals court.

Minimum Efficient Scale: The smallest scale at which a firm no longer has increasing returns to scale. If a firm has an initial region of increasing returns to scale, this can be represented as a region in which the long-run average-total-cost curve is sloping downward as we move from left to right. When the firm reaches its minimum efficient scale, it will have reached a region in which the long-run average-total-cost curve is horizontal.

Missing Market: A way to characterize the problem of air pollution and other externalities. The markets for labor, coal, electricity, and so on, tend to work efficiently. But clean air is wasted because there is no market for clean air. Taxes on pollution and marketable licenses to pollute are attempts to resolve this problem, by creating something like a market.

Mobile-Source Pollution: A term used to describe pollution from sources such as automobiles, because this type of pollution comes from sources that move. Mobile-source pollution stands in contrast to stationary-source pollution.

Monopolistic Competition: A market structure that is similar to perfect competition, in that there are many firms in an industry, and each firm is relatively small, and it is easy to enter the industry or exit from it. The difference between these two market structures is that monopolistically competitive firms have differentiated products, whereas perfectly competitive firms do not. Monopolistic competition is widespread in retailing.

Monopoly: A market structure in which there is only one firm in an industry. In this book, we apply the same analysis to the case of a "near monopoly", in which there is more than one firm, but in which one firm has a very dominant position. If a monopoly is to be maintained over time, there must be some significant barriers to entry, which keep new firms from entering the industry. In addition, a monopoly firm cannot have close substitutes for its product. As a result of the barriers to entry, monopoly firms may be able to generate positive economic profits for a long period of time.

Monopsonistic Exploitation: Phrase used to describe the fact that the workers hired by a monopsonistic employer are paid less than their marginal revenue product. The monopsonist's market power allows it to "exploit" the workers, by paying them less than their marginal revenue product.

Monopsony: A market in which there is only one buyer or one dominant buyer. An example is the "company town", in which one large employer dominates the labor market.

Natural Monopoly: An industry in which a single firm can produce at a lower average total cost than any combination of two or three or more firms. For a natural monopoly, the average-total-cost curve will slope downward through the entire relevant range of output.

Nonexcludability, or Nonexcludable Consumption: A characteristic of a public good. For some goods, it is difficult or impossible to exclude people from enjoying the good, even if they do not pay. In a case like this, we say that consumption is characterized by nonexcludability. Nonexcludability is also referred to as costly exclusion. As a result of nonexcludability, private firms may be unable to provide the good.

Non-Labor Income: The portion of a household's income that is received from sources other than the labor market. Non-labor income includes transfer payments (such as Social-Security benefits), as well as interest income, dividend income, lottery winnings, and gifts and inheritances.

Non-Price Competition: Any of several practices by which firms try to compete with each other by means other than reducing prices. Advertising is a very widespread form of non-price competition. Other methods include contests, giveaways, and special services.

Nonrival Consumption: One of the characteristics of a public good. If many people can enjoy a good at the same time, consumption of the good is nonrival. Because of nonrivalry, the construction of the social willingness-to-pay curve for a public good involves vertical summation of the individual willingness-to-pay curves.

Non-Zero-Sum Games: In game theory, a type of game in which the sum of the gains and losses can be positive or negative. The Prisoner's Dilemma is an example of a non-zero-sum game.

Normal Good: A good for which demand increases when incomes increase. Similarly, a normal good is one for which demand decreases when incomes decrease. The income elasticity of demand is positive for a normal good. Normal goods stand in contrast to inferior goods.

Normative Economics: An approach to economics that is concerned with what ought to be. Normative statements cannot definitively be shown to be true or false, because normative economics inevitably involves value judgments. Normative economics stands in contrast to positive economics.

***Northern Securities* Case**: The first important application of the Sherman Act. In 1904, the Supreme Court used the Sherman Act to rule that two railroads (Northern Pacific and Great Northern) could not merge.

Occupational Segregation: Term used to describe the fact that many women are crowded into low-paying occupations that have typically been dominated by females (such as cosmetologists, nurses' aides, and child-care workers). Occupational segregation explains a portion of the gender wage gap.

Oligopoly: A market that has only a few sellers. Oligopoly is common in manufacturing industries, such as automobiles, breakfast cereal, aircraft manufacturing, and others.

Oligopsony: A market in which there are only a few buyers.

Opportunity Cost: The opportunity cost of one good or activity is the value of the next-best alternative. In other words, the opportunity cost of one good or opportunity is the value of what has to be given up, to get that good or undertake that activity.

Outputs: The goods and services produced by a business firm.

Own-Price Elasticity of Demand: The percentage change in the quantity of a good demanded, divided by the percentage change in the price of the good. The own-price elasticity of demand is sometimes simply called the price elasticity of demand.

Patent: A legal arrangement that gives an inventor a monopoly on his or her invention for a period of time. A patent is a type of barrier to entry.

Pay-As-You-Go Retirement System: A retirement system that taxes those who are working today, and uses the money to pay transfer payments to those who are retired today. In other words, a pay-as-you-go system does not engage in real saving. The Social-Security system in the United States is a pay-as-you-go system, although many proposals are currently being debated that would change it to a more fully funded system.

Payoff: In game theory, the payoffs are the gains and losses that will accrue to the players of the game, depending on the outcome of the game.

Payroll Tax: A tax on wages and salaries. Many of the federal government's Social Insurance programs (such as Social Security and Medicare) are paid for by a payroll tax, which was instituted in 1937. The payroll tax is levied at a flat rate on wages and salaries, up to a ceiling.

Percentage: A proportion multiplied by 100. For example, 50% is the percentage corresponding to the proportion 0.5, which is equal to one-half, or 1/2.

Perfect Competition: A market structure in which the market has many firms, and each firm is small relative to the market. The firms produce a standardized product, or homogeneous product. Therefore, perfectly competitive firms are price takers, and the demand curve for the output of a perfectly competitive firm is perfectly elastic. Perfectly competitive markets are also characterized by free entry and free exit, so that the tendency of these markets is toward zero economic profit. Perfect competition has the same meaning as pure competition.

Perfectly Elastic Demand: A special case of elastic demand, in which the demand curve is completely horizontal. In this case, we say that demand is perfectly elastic. The demand curve for the output of the individual perfectly competitive firm is perfectly elastic.

Perfectly Inelastic Demand: A special case of inelastic demand, in which the quantity demanded does not change at all when price changes. The demand curve would be graphed as a vertical line, and the own-price elasticity of demand would be zero.

Perfect Price Discrimination: The condition that would exist if a firm were able to charge the exact maximum that each customer is willing to pay.

Personal Exemptions: A feature of many individual-income-tax systems. The personal exemptions allow every person to have a certain amount of income that is not subject to tax. The exemptions give an element of progressivity to the tax.

Pigouvian Tax: A tax that is designed to correct a pollution externality, named after the British economist Arthur Cecil Pigou. Pigouvian methods have not been used as widely as command-and-control techniques.

Positive Economics: An approach to economics that is concerned with the actual workings of the economy. Positive economics is concerned with what is, rather than with that ought to be. In principle, positive statements can be shown to be true or false. Positive economics stands in contrast to normative economics.

Poverty: Term used to describe the economic situation of people at the bottom of the income distribution. In the United States, there is an official definition of the "poverty line", which is the amount of income below which all members of a household are counted as being in poverty. There is variation in the official poverty line, depending on household size.

Present Discounted Value: The maximum amount that a person would be willing to pay today, in order to receive a given payment at some time in the future.

Price Ceiling: A type of price-control law, under which there is a maximum legal price. In other words, a price ceiling makes it illegal to buy and sell at more than a certain price. Examples of price ceilings include rent controls, price controls on gasoline, and usury laws. If a price ceiling is above the equilibrium price, it will have no effect on the market. However, if a price ceiling is enforced below the equilibrium price, it will lead to shortages.

Price-Control Law: A law that makes it illegal to buy and sell at some prices. Price ceilings and price floors are examples of price-control laws.

Price Discrimination: The practice by which a seller charges different prices for the same good or service to different buyers (even though the costs of production are the same). In order to increase profits by engaging in price discrimination, a firm must not be perfectly competitive, and it must have some way of distinguishing customers on the basis of willingness to pay, and it must be difficult for customers to re-sell.

Price Elasticity of Demand: The percentage change in the quantity of a good demanded, divided by the percentage change in the price of the good. The price elasticity of demand is sometimes called the own-price elasticity of demand, to make clear that the change is in response to the price of the good in question.

Price Elasticity of Supply: The percentage change in quantity supplied, divided by the percentage change in price. The price elasticity of supply is also known as the supply elasticity, or the own-price elasticity of supply, or the elasticity of supply.

Price Floor: A type of price-control law, under which there is a legal minimum price that must be paid. In other words, a price floor makes it illegal to buy and sell at less than a certain price. Examples of price floors include minimum-wage laws and agricultural price supports. If a price floor is below the equilibrium price, it will have no effect on the market. However, if a price floor is enforced above the equilibrium price, it will lead to surpluses.

Price-Taking Firm: A firm that accepts the market price as given. The demand curve for the output of a price-taking firm is perfectly elastic. If a firm is to be a price taker, it must be small relative to the market, and it must produce an output that is homogeneous, or undifferentiated. Perfectly competitive firms are price takers.

Prisoner's Dilemma: A famous example of a non-zero-sum game. In a Prisoner's Dilemma game, the players will develop strategies that will not lead them to the outcome that would be best for the group. In economics, we use the idea of the Prisoner's Dilemma to study the behavior of oligopoly firms. Under certain circumstances, the firms in a cartel will have an incentive to cheat on the cartel agreement, so that the cartel will break down. This reduces profits for the firms in the cartel, but it is good for consumers.

Production-Possibilities Frontier: A graphical representation of the combinations of outputs that can be produced, if all of the available resources are used as well as possible. The production-possibilities frontier is always negatively sloped. Usually, the frontier is concave, or bowed outward, with respect to the origin.

Progressive Tax: A tax under which people with higher incomes pay a higher percentage of income in tax. The individual income tax is the most important progressive tax in the United States.

Proportion: A fraction expressed in decimal terms. For example, 0.5 is the proportion corresponding to the fraction one-half = 1/2.

Proportional Tax: A tax under which people with different incomes pay the same percentage of income in tax. In the United States, the payroll tax is approximately proportional over most of the range of incomes.

Public Economics: The branch of economics that deals with the causes and effects of government spending, and the taxes that are used to pay for government operations. Public economics deals with the effects of government programs, such as Social Security. Public economics also deals with the effects of different taxes.

Public Good: A good that is characterized by nonrival consumption and nonexcludability. Because of these characteristics, it is difficult for private markets to produce public goods. Therefore, in many cases, public goods are produced by governments. National defense is an example of a pure public good.

Pure Competition: A market structure in which the market has many firms, and each firm is small relative to the market. The firms produce a standardized, or homogeneous, product. Therefore, purely competitive firms are price takers, and the demand curve for the output of a purely competitive firm is perfectly elastic. Purely competitive markets are also characterized by free entry and exit, so that the tendency in these markets is toward zero economic profit. Pure competition has the same meaning as perfect competition.

Quantity Demanded: The amount of some good or service that buyers are willing to buy, at a specific price, in a given period of time, holding constant other influences on buyers.

Quantity Supplied: The amount of some good or service that sellers are willing to sell, at a specific price, in a given period of time, holding constant other influences on sellers.

Rational: Economists usually assume that economic agents are rational, which means they do the best they can with what they have. For example, it is usually assumed that consumers maximize consumer surplus, and that firms maximize profits.

Reciprocal: The reciprocal of a fraction is the number which, when multiplied by the fraction, gives one. For example, the reciprocal of 2 is 1/2, and the reciprocal of 2/3 is 3/2.

Recycling Programs: Systems for collecting newspapers, bottles, cans, and other materials. Recycling programs became much more popular in the late 1980s, as many communities began to fear they would run out of landfill space.

Regressive Tax: A tax under which people with higher incomes pay a lower percentage of income in tax. Sales and excise taxes tend to be somewhat regressive.

Regulatory Lag: A problem encountered by government regulatory agencies. Regulatory lag occurs when the prices that the regulated industry is allowed to charge do not keep pace with changing economic conditions.

Rent: A type of capital income. Rent payments are received by owners of land and buildings.

Rent-Control Law: A type of price ceiling that is used in some cities. If the rent-control law is enforced at a level below the equilibrium rent level, shortages of quality housing will occur.

Retail Sales Tax: A tax on purchases of a wide variety of items, which is usually levied on sales of clothing, hardware, and many other goods. Most states in the United States have a retail sales tax. Sales of most services (such as the services provided by lawyers, doctors, and accountants) are usually *not* covered by the sales taxes. In many states, food also isn't taxed. Retail sales taxes are sometimes called general retail sales taxes, to indicate that the tax applies to a wide variety of goods.

Returns to Scale: Term used to describe the relationship between input and output, when we allow all inputs to increase by the same proportion.

Robinson-Patman Act: Antitrust law, passed in 1936. This law was designed to protect small businesses from competition from large discount chains. Thus the Robinson-Patman Act goes against the grain of most of the antitrust laws.

Rule of Reason: A philosophy of interpreting the antitrust laws. In 1920, the Supreme Court refused to rule against U.S. Steel, because they said the firm had not acted badly. The Court thus stated the Rule of Reason, that a firm would not be found guilty unless it had behaved in an *unreasonable* way. The Rule of Reason was reversed in the ALCOA decision in 1945.

Rule of 72: Over a fairly wide range of interest rates, the number of years to double your money is approximately equal to 72 divided by the interest rate, where the interest rate is expressed as a number of percentage points.

Shared Monopoly: The ultimate goal of every cartel is to act as a shared monopoly, which means that the cartel firms would charge the same price a monopolist would charge, and the total profits of the cartel members would be the same as the profit a monopoly would make.

Sherman Act: The first antitrust law, which was passed in 1890. The Sherman Act prohibits monopolization and price fixing.

Shortage: A condition that occurs when quantity demanded is greater than quantity supplied. A shortage will occur when the price of a good is below its equilibrium level. A shortage will lead to pressure for price to rise.

Short Run: A period of time over which at least one input is fixed.

Short-Run Shut-Down Decision: The firm should go out of business in the short run if total revenue is less than total variable cost. This is equivalent to saying that the firm should go out of business in the short run if average revenue (which is equal to price) is less than average variable cost.

Short-Run Supply Curve for a Perfectly Competitive Firm: When price is greater than or equal to average variable cost, the supply curve is the marginal-cost curve. When price is less than average variable cost, the firm will shut down, and its quantity supplied will be zero.

Single-Price Monopoly: A monopoly in which the firm sells all of its output at the same price. In other words, a single-price monopoly does not practice price discrimination.

Slope of a Line: The change in the value of the variable on the vertical axis, divided by the change in the value of the variable on the horizontal axis.

The slope is positive for a line that slopes upward as we move from left to right across the diagram, and negative for a line that slopes downward as we move from left to right.

Social Security: A government-operated retirement program in the United States. Social Security is the largest domestic spending program in the world, with well over $700 billion per year in spending. The Social-Security program is a pay-as-you-go system, under which taxes on the working generation are paid to the retired generation. In other words, the Social-Security program does not generate real saving.

***Standard Oil* Case**: Antitrust case in which the Supreme Court, in 1911, broke John D. Rockefeller's Standard Oil Trust into 33 separate companies.

Standardized Product: A characteristic of perfectly competitive markets. When the outputs of the firm are standardized, it is impossible for buyers to tell any difference between the outputs of two firms. This is one of the reasons why perfectly competitive firms are price takers. Standardized product has the same meaning as homogeneous product, but it stands in contrast to differentiated product.

Stationary-Source Pollution: A term used to describe industrial pollution, because it comes from sources that don't move. Stationary-source pollution stands in contrast to mobile-source pollution.

Statutory Tax Incidence: The official assignment of tax burdens, determined by the statutes of the law. Thus if the law says that retail sellers are required to make sales-tax payments to the State Treasury, the "statutory incidence" falls on the retail sellers, even though the true, economic incidence may fall on buyers.

Strategy: In game theory, each player will develop a strategy, which consists of a set of actions to be taken in various situations as the game evolves.

Structures: Buildings, such as office buildings, factory buildings, and warehouses. Structures are an important type of capital.

Substitutes: Term used to refer to a pair of goods, for which the demand for one good increases when the price of the other good increases. The cross-price elasticity of demand is positive for substitutes. Substitutes stand in contrast to complements.

Substitution Effect on Labor Supply: The wage rate is the opportunity cost of leisure. When there is an *increase* in the wage rate, people tend to substitute away from leisure, which means they *work more*. The substitution effect of a *decrease* in the wage rate is that people tend to substitute toward leisure, which means they *work less*. The total effect of a wage-rate change on labor supply is the sum of the income effect and the substitution effect.

Sunk Cost: A cost that has already been incurred in the past, and cannot be recovered.

Supply Curve: A graph showing the relationship between price and quantity supplied, holding constant all other influences on sellers. In other words, a supply curve is a graph of the information in a supply schedule. If sellers obey the Law of Supply, the supply curve will slope upward as we move from left to right.

Supply Schedule: A table that lists different prices for a good or service, and shows the quantity that would be supplied at each price, holding constant other influences on sellers. In other words, a supply schedule is a table of the information in a supply curve.

Surplus: A condition that occurs when quantity demanded is less than quantity supplied. A surplus will occur when the price of a good is higher than its equilibrium level. A surplus will lead to pressure for price to fall.

Tariff: A tax on imports.

Tax Incidence: Term used to describe the study of who bears the burden of a tax.

Technology: Society's pool of knowledge about how to produce a good or service.

Technological Improvement: New inventions, as well as new techniques that allow us to produce more or better goods from a given amount of resources. Technological improvements are one of the ways of pushing the production-possibilities frontier outward and to the right.

Total Cost: The total of all of the costs incurred by a firm. Total cost is equal to total variable cost plus total fixed cost.

Total Expenditure: The total amount of money that buyers pay for a product. If there are no taxes, the buyers' total expenditure will be equal to the sellers' total revenue. Total expenditure is calculated by multiplying the price of the good by the quantity demanded.

Total Factor Expense: The total number of dollars that a firm pays to a factor of production. For example, the total factor expense for a particular type of labor is equal to the number of such workers hired by the firm, multiplied by the wage rate paid to the workers.

Total Fixed Cost: The total of all of the costs incurred by a firm for its fixed inputs. By definition, total fixed cost does not change when there is a change in the level of output.

Total Product: The total amount of a good or service produced by a firm. Total product is sometimes also called "total (physical) product", to indicate that we are concerned with outputs, rather than revenues. Another name for total product is "quantity of output".

Total Revenue: The total amount of money that a business firm gets from selling a product. If there are no taxes, the firm's total revenue will be equal to the total expenditure of its customers. For a firm that does not practice price discrimination, total revenue is equal to price multiplied times quantity.

Total Utility: A measure of the total satisfaction that the consumer receives from consuming a particular quantity of a good. In this book, we define total utility as the maximum total amount of money the consumer would be willing to pay to receive a number of units of a good or service.

Total Variable Cost: The total of all of the costs incurred by a firm for its variable inputs.

Trade Deficit: A situation that occurs when the value of a country's imports is greater than the value of its exports.

Trade Surplus: A situation that occurs when the value of a country's exports is greater than the value of its imports.

Transaction Costs: Costs of reaching agreements and carrying out transactions. For example, transaction costs are a reason why it may be difficult to apply the Coase Theorem. Coase suggests using private negotiations to solve the externality problem. However, in many cases, this approach will make it necessary to have hundreds of costly meetings, and to hire lawyers, mediators, and other middlemen. Costs such as these are called transaction costs.

Transfer Payments: Payments to people who do not provide any services in return. In the United States, some of the most important transfer-payment programs are Social Security, Medicare, Medicare, Food Stamps, and the Earned Income Tax Credit.

Tying Arrangements: Practice under which a seller would not sell one product unless the buyer agrees to buy some other product from that same seller. These arrangements are violations of the antitrust laws.

U.S. Steel Case: Antitrust decision, in 1920, in which the Supreme Court found U.S. Steel not guilty of violating the antitrust laws. This case was an articulation of the "Rule of Reason", under which a firm would not be found guilty unless it had behaved in an _unreasonable_ way.

Union Spillover Effect: One of the effects of labor unions on the wages of non-union workers. The wage gains in the union sector can lead to a decline in employment in that sector. As a result, workers are displaced, and forced to find work in the non-union sector, which leads to decreases in wages in the non-union sector. The union spillover effect will increase the size of the union wage gap.

Union Threat Effect: One of the effects of labor unions on the wages of non-union workers. Some non-union employers may be willing to pay higher wages, if they believe this will keep their workers from organizing into a union. The union threat effect will decrease the size of the union wage gap.

Union Wage Gap: The wage differential between union and non-union workers (while holding constant any other influences on wages). In the United States, the union wage gap is probably around 10% to 15%.

Unit-Elastic Demand: When the percentage change in quantity demanded is equal to the percentage change in price, the own-price elasticity is equal to one. In this case, we say that demand is unit-elastic. When demand is unit-elastic, total revenue does not change when the price changes.

Upward-Sloping Labor-Supply Curve: A labor-supply curve that slopes upward as we move from left to right. This will occur when the substitution effect is larger than the income effect. The labor-supply elasticity is positive for an upward-sloping labor-supply curve.

Usury Laws: Interest-rate ceilings, which make it illegal to borrow and lend at more than a specified interest rate. If the usury law is above the equilibrium interest rate, it will have no effect. However, if the usury law is enforced at a level below the equilibrium interest rate, it will lead to shortages of credit.

Utility: The term used by economists to describe the satisfaction that consumers receive from consuming goods and services.

Variable Costs: The costs of variable inputs.

Variable Inputs: Inputs whose quantity can be varied during the time period under consideration. In the short run, not all inputs are variable. In the long run, however, all inputs are variable.

Vertical Axis: One of the two axes in a two-dimensional graph. The vertical axis extends upward from the origin. The dependent variable is often represented on the vertical axis. The vertical axis is also called the y-axis. The vertical axis stands in contrast to the horizontal axis, or x-axis.

Vertical Equity: An aspect of the tax system that deals with the desire to allocate the tax burden in accordance with "ability to pay".

Vertical Intercept: The value of the y variable (the variable on the vertical axis) when x = 0 (i.e., when the variable on the horizontal axis takes on a value of zero). The vertical intercept is also called the y-intercept.

Vertical Merger: A merger between a firm and one of its suppliers.

Voluntary Export Restraints (VERs): Restrictions on the quantity of a good that can be sold from one country to another, administered by the exporting country. This is in contrast with import quotas, which are administered by the importing country.

Wealth: The total value of the assets that a household owns at a particular moment in time. A household's wealth includes the value of a home, cars, stocks, bonds, saving accounts, etc. Wealth is distributed much more unequally than income.

Welfare Cost: The loss from a tax, over and above the amount of revenue raised for the government. For most taxes, the loss suffered by the private sector is greater than the revenue collected by the tax. The difference between the private sector's loss and the government's tax revenue is the welfare cost of the tax. Welfare cost is also called "deadweight loss" or "excess burden".

x-axis: One of the two axes in a two-dimensional graph. The x-axis extends to the right from the origin. The independent variable is often represented on the x-axis. The x-axis is also called the horizontal axis. The x-axis stands in contrast to the y-axis, or vertical axis.

X-inefficiency: A characteristic of some firms that have market power. When a monopoly is wasteful, because it has a reduced incentive to use resources wisely, the waste is called X-inefficiency.

***Xerox* Case**: An antitrust case that ended in 1975 with a consent decree, under which Xerox Corporation agreed to license its photocopying patents to its competitors.

y-axis: One of the two axes in a two-dimensional graph. The y-axis extends upward from the origin. The dependent variable is often represented on the y-axis. The y-axis is also called the vertical axis. The y-axis stands in contrast to the x-axis, or horizontal axis.

y-intercept: The value of the y variable (the variable on the vertical axis) when x = 0 (i.e., when the variable on the horizontal axis takes on a value of zero). The y-intercept is also called the vertical intercept.

Zero-Sum Game: In game theory, a type of game in which the amount that is lost by some players is exactly equal to the amount that is won by other players. Poker is an example of a zero-sum game.

Answers and Discussion

CHAPTER 1:

Interim Review Questions

IR1-1. One definition is that economics is the study of how people use their limited resources to satisfy unlimited wants. Another definition is that economics is the study of how a society chooses to use its scarce resources to produce, exchange, and consume goods and services.

IR1-2. Microeconomics deals with the behavior of households and business firms, and with the way in which they interact in markets. Macroeconomics deals with the aggregate totals of the economy, such as the overall rates of inflation, unemployment, and economic growth.

IR1-3. Every society must make fundamental choices regarding what to produce, how to produce, and for whom to produce.

IR1-4. Statement (a) says that if the supply of chickens is reduced by a heat wave, the price of chicken will increase. This is a statement about the actual workings of the economy. If we have enough data, and if we analyze the data properly, we can determine whether the statement is correct or incorrect. Thus this is a positive statement. On the other hand, statement (b) is a normative statement, because it involves a value judgment, as shown by the fact that it includes the word "should". People with one set of values might agree with statement (b), whereas people with other values might disagree. It is not possible to prove whether this statement is correct or incorrect.

IR1-5. *Ceteris paribus* means "all other things equal".

IR1-6. The *ceteris-paribus* assumption allows us to concentrate on one issue at a time. If we did not do this, it would be very difficult to make sense of our complicated world.

Questions and Problems

QP1-1.

a. The overall rate of inflation is a macroeconomic topic.
b. A household's choice of how many tacos to buy is a microeconomic topic.
c. The overall rate of economic growth is a macroeconomic topic.
d. The wages paid by high-tech firms are a microeconomic topic.

QP1-2. Positive analysis is concerned with "what is". In other words, positive analysis deals with gaining an understanding of the actual workings of the economy. In principle, positive statements can be shown to be correct or incorrect. On the other hand, normative analysis is concerned with "what ought to be". Normative statements cannot be shown to be correct or incorrect, since they are based on value judgments.

QP1-3. International economics is used to gain an understanding of the pattern of imports and exports, the effects of restrictions on international trade, the exchange rates between the currencies of different countries, and so on. Labor economics deals with the determination of wage rates for workers, and with the effects of trade unions, minimum-wage laws, and so on. The economics of industrial organization is concerned with the ways in which business firms interact with each other and with their customers, and with the effects of government regulations of business.

Appendix:
Interim Review Questions

IR1A-1. If we multiply 0.37 by 100, we get 37. Thus $0.37 = 37\%$.

IR1A-2. If we divide 9 by 10, we get 0.9. Thus $9/10 = 0.9$. If we multiply 0.9 by 100, we get 90. Thus $0.9 = 90\%$.

IR1A-3. If we multiply 3/7 by 7/3, we get 1. Therefore, the reciprocal of 3/7 is 7/3. If we multiply 9/4 by 4/9, we get 1. Therefore, the reciprocal of 9/4 is 4/9.

IR1A-4. Our goal is to divide 2/3 by 3/4. The way to do this is to multiply both the numerator (which is 2/3) and the denominator (which is 3/4) by the reciprocal of the denominator. If we multiply 3/4 by 4/3, we get 1. Therefore, the reciprocal of 3/4 is 4/3, so we want to multiply the numerator (2/3) and the denominator (3/4) by 4/3. We have already seen that when we multiply 3/4 in the denominator by 4/3, we get 1. When we multiply 2/3 in the numerator by 4/3, we get 8/9. Thus, $(2/3) \div (3/4) = 8/9$.

IR1A-5. To solve the equation $y = (x/2) + 3$, we begin by subtracting 3 from both sides of the equation. This gives us $y - 3 = x/2$. Now, we multiply both sides of the equation by 2, which gives us $x = 2(y - 3) = 2y - 6$.

IR1A-6. To solve the equation $y = 10/x$, we begin by multiplying both sides of the equation by x. This gives us $xy = 10$. Next, we divide both sides of the equation by y. This gives us $x = 10/y$.

IR1A-7. We are given two equations: $y = 10 - x$, and $y = x$. If we substitute one of these equations into the other, we have $10 - x = x$. Next, we add x to both sides of the equation. This gives us $10 = 2x$. The next step is to divide both sides of the equation by 2, which gives us $x = (10/2) = 5$. We can confirm that we have worked the problem correctly, by substituting $x = 5$ into the two equations. First, we substitute $x = 5$ into the first equation, $y = 10 - x$. If $x = 5$, then $y = 10 - 5$, which means that $y = 5$. Next, we substitute $x = 5$ into the second equation, $y = x$. If $x = 5$, then $y = x$ means that $y = 5$. Since we found $y = 5$ in both cases, we have confirmed that we have found the correct solution to this system of two equations.

IR1A-8. The first point on the line is (1,3), and the second point is (2,7). To find the "rise" (the change in the vertical dimension, or Δy), we subtract 3 from 7. Thus, Δy is $(7 - 3) = 4$. To find the "run" (the change in the horizontal dimension, or Δx), we subtract 1 from 2. Thus, Δx is $(2 - 1) = 1$. The slope of the line is the rise divided by the run, or $\Delta y / \Delta x$, which is $4/1 = 4$.

IR1A-9. In this case, the first point on the line is (3,6), and the second point is (5,4). To find the "rise" (the change in the vertical dimension, or Δy), we subtract 6 from 4. Thus, Δy is $(4 - 6) = -2$. To find the "run" (the change in the horizontal dimension, or Δx), we subtract 3 from 5. Thus, Δx is $(5 - 3) = 2$. The slope of the line is the rise divided by the run, or $\Delta y/\Delta x$, which is $-2/2 = -1$.

IR1A-10. The area of a rectangle is the height multiplied by the base. When the height of the rectangle is 10 and the base of the rectangle is 8, the area is $(10)(8) = 80$.

IR1A-11. The area of a triangle is 0.5 multiplied by the height, multiplied by the base. When the height of the triangle is 9 and the base of the triangle is 4, the area is $0.5(9)(4) = 0.5(36) = 18$.

CHAPTER 2:

Interim Review Questions

IR2-1. The opportunity cost of going to a professional baseball game is the value of all the things that must be given up, in order to see the baseball game. This would include the price of the ticket, which could be $15 or $25 or $35 or more, depending on whether you sit in the bleachers, or in a box seat, or in a luxury box. It would also include the price that is charged for parking your car, and the cost of the gasoline burned in driving to the stadium. If you buy a souvenir program, or a T-shirt, or some similar items, the opportunity cost of the baseball game would also include the price of those items. The opportunity cost of the baseball game would also include the value of the time spent going to the game and watching the game. (After all, you could have stayed home and watched TV.) If you buy a hot dog and a beer at the stadium, this will *not* necessarily be a true opportunity cost of the baseball game. (You were probably going to eat *something*, regardless of whether you chose to attend the game.)

IR2-2. The opportunity cost of spending $15 on a bouquet of flowers is the value of the next-best thing that you could have bought with the $15.

IR2-3. Some production-possibilities frontiers are straight lines, because the goods on the two axes involve the *same* resources and technology. However, if the goods involve *different* resources and technology, the production-possibilities frontier will be a curved line, which is bowed outward, or concave with respect to the origin.

IR2-4. The slope of the production-possibilities frontier is the negative of the opportunity cost of the good on the horizontal axis.

IR2-5. The Law of Increasing Opportunity Cost says that the opportunity cost of producing one additional unit of a good will increase, as we produce more and more of the good. A curved production-possibilities frontier will exhibit increasing opportunity cost.

IR2-6. When a country is below its production-possibilities frontier, some resources are being wasted. In this situation, it would be possible to increase production without increasing the resources that are available— it would only be necessary to use the resources more efficiently.

IR2-7. An economy's production-possibilities frontier can expand outward as a result of technological improvements, capital investments, and increases in the size and quality of the labor force.

IR2-8. The endpoints of Arnold's production-possibilities frontier are 5A and 10B. Therefore, the opportunity cost of 5 units of good A is 10 units of good B, and the opportunity cost of 10 units of good B is 5 units of good A. This can be expressed in an equation: 5A = 10B. To find the opportunity cost of one additional unit of good A, we divide both sides of the equation by 5: (5/5)A = (10/5)B, which means that the opportunity cost of one unit of good A is 10/5 = two units of good B. Using similar reasoning, we find that the opportunity cost of one unit of good B is 0.5 units of good A, which is the same as one-half of a unit of good A. Note that the opportunity cost of one unit of A (which is 2) is the reciprocal of the opportunity cost of one unit of B (which is 0.5, or 1/2).

IR2-9. The endpoints of Lynnette's production-possibilities frontier are 15A and 20B. We can find the opportunity costs by using the same reasoning that we employed in the previous question. Since 15A = 20B, we can find the opportunity cost of one additional unit of good A by dividing both sides of the equation by 15: (15/15)A = (20/15)B = (4/3)B. Therefore, the opportunity cost of one unit of good A is 4/3 of a unit of good B, which is the same as one and one-third units of B, which is approximately equal to 1.3333 units of B. Similarly, the opportunity cost of one unit of good B is 3/4 of a unit of good A, which is the same as 0.75 units of A. Note that the opportunity cost of one unit of A (which is 4/3) is the reciprocal of the opportunity cost of one unit of B (which is 3/4).

IR2-10. Lynnette can produce as many as 15 units of good A, and Arnold can produce only 5 units of good A. Therefore, Lynnette has absolute advantage in the production of good A. Lynnette can produce as many as 20 units of good B, and Arnold can produce only 10 units of good B. Therefore, Lynnette also has absolute advantage in the production of good B. However, even though Lynnette has *absolute* advantage in each activity, she only has *comparative* advantage in the production of good A. Her opportunity cost of one unit of good A is 4/3 of a unit of good B. This is lower than Arnold's opportunity cost of good A, which is two units of good B. On the other hand, Arnold has lower opportunity cost of good B, which means that he has comparative advantage in production of good B.

Questions and Problems

QP2-1. If we only consider the money that has to be paid, then the cost of a taco at Taco Town is lower than the cost of a taco at The Taco Joint. However, the true opportunity cost of a taco involves *all* of the relevant costs, including the cost of waiting in line. The full opportunity cost of a taco at Taco Town is higher than the money cost because of the cost of waiting in line. If your time is valuable, then the cost of waiting in line may be very substantial. If this is the case, then it might make sense to switch to The Taco Joint, where there is no line. On the other hand, if your time is not very valuable, it might make sense to wait in line at Taco Town.

QP2-2. The opportunity cost of time is high for a highly paid business executive. It will make sense for such a person to get someone else to mow his or her lawn. The person who mows the lawn might be a teenager, whose time is not so valuable.

QP2-3.

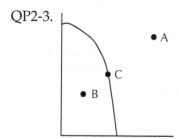

The production possibilities depicted at point A are infeasible. It might be possible to produce the combination of goods represented by point A at some time in the future, if the productive capacity of the economy is increased. However, it is not possible to produce A with the resources and technology that are currently available.

QP2-4. At point B, some resources are being wasted. Some resources are not being used in an efficient way.

QP2-5. In moving from point B (which is below the p.p.f.) to point C (which is on the p.p.f.), it is *not* necessary to increase the total available supply of resources. All that is necessary is to use the available resources in a more efficient, less wasteful way.

QP2-6.

a. Dozens of Blintzes

16

8 Gallons of Gazpacho

b. One endpoint of Jane's production-possibilities frontier is (0,16). The other endpoint is (8,0). As we move from the first of these points to the second, $\Delta y = -16$, and $\Delta x = 8$. Therefore, the slope of the p.p.f. is $(-16/8) = -2$.

c. The opportunity cost of *eight* gallons of gazpacho for Jane is 16 dozen blintzes. This can be expressed as $8G = 16B$, if we represent blintzes with B and gazpacho with G. To find the opportunity cost of *one* gallon of gazpacho, we divide both sides of the equation by 8: $(8/8)G = (16/8)B = 2B$. Thus the opportunity cost of one additional gallon of gazpacho is two dozen blintzes. Note that the opportunity cost of a gallon of gazpacho is the negative of the slope of the p.p.f.

d. If Jane were producing six gallons of gazpacho per day, the maximum number of blintzes that she could produce would be 4 dozen per day. If you draw the graph with great care, you can use the graph to determine this. Regardless of your skills with graphing, you can answer this question by expressing the p.p.f. in the form of an equation of a line. If we are to express the p.p.f. as an equation, we need to know the vertical intercept and the slope of the line. In part (b) of this question, we have already seen that the slope is –2. From the graph, we can see that the vertical intercept of the p.p.f. is 16. If we put these pieces together, we see that the equation for the p.p.f is $B = 16 - 2G$. To find the maximum number of blintzes that Jane can produce if she were producing six gallons of gazpacho per day, we insert $G = 6$ into the equation for the p.p.f. This gives us $B = 16 - 2(6) = 16 - 12 = 4$. If Jane were producing six gallons of gazpacho per day, she could also produce as many as four dozen blintzes per day.

e. No. If Jane were producing 12 dozen blintzes per day, she would not be able to produce any more than 2 gallons of gazpacho. The question asks about the point (4 gallons of gazpacho, 12 dozen blintzes), which is infeasible, because it is above the p.p.f. To find the maximum amount of gazpacho that Jane could produce if she were to produce 12 dozen blintzes per day, you could again use the equation $B = 16 - 2G$. If $B = 12$, then the maximum amount of gazpacho Jane could produce can be calculated by substituting $B = 12$ into the equation for the p.p.f. Thus $12 = 16 - 2G$. If we subtract 16 from both sides of this equation, we have $-4 = -2G$. If we then divide both sides of the equation by -2, we have $G = 2$. If Jane is producing 12 dozen blintzes per day, the most that she could do would be to produce two gallons of gazpacho per day.

QP2-7.

a.

Dozens of Blintzes — 8

6 — Gallons of Gazpacho

b. One endpoint of Samantha's production possibilities frontier is (0,8), and the other is (6,0). To find the slope of the p.p.f., we must find the "rise" (i.e., the change in the vertical dimension) and the "run" (i.e., the change in the horizontal dimension) as we go from (0,8) to (6,0). The rise is $(0 - 8) = -8$. The run is $(6 - 0) = 6$. Therefore, the slope of Samantha's p.p.f. is $-8/6$. If we divide both the numerator and the denominator by 2, we see that the slope is $-4/3$, which is minus (one and one-third), or about -1.3333.

c. Samantha can produce 6 gallons of gazpacho or 8 dozen blintzes. Thus, the opportunity cost of *six* additional gallons is 8 dozen blintzes: $6G = 8B$. The opportunity cost of *one* $(= 6/6)$ additional gallon is $8/6 =$ one and one-third dozen blintzes. Note that the opportunity cost of a gallon of gazpacho is the negative of the slope of the p.p.f.

d. To find the equation for Samantha's p.p.f., we need the slope and the vertical intercept. We have just seen that the slope is $-4/3$. The graph shows that the vertical intercept is 8. Therefore, the equation for Samantha's p.p.f. is $B = 8 - (4/3)G$. We want to know the maximum number of blintzes that Samantha can produce if she produces three gallons of gazpacho in a day. To find this, we substitute $G = 3$ into the equation for the p.p.f. If $G = 3$, then $B = 8 - (4/3)(3) = 8-4 = 4$. If Samantha produces 3 gallons of gazpacho per day, the maximum number of blintzes she can produce is four per day.

e. No. If Samantha were producing six dozen blintzes per day, it would not be possible for her also to produce four gallons of gazpacho in a day. If she were producing six dozen blintzes per day, the largest amount of gazpacho she could produce in a day can be calculated using the equation for the p.p.f., $B = 8 - (4/3)G$. If $B = 6$, then $6 = 8 - (4/3)G$. If we subtract 8 from each side of this equation, we have $-2 = -(4/3)G$. Finally, we divide both sides of the equation by $-(4/3)$, which is equivalent to multiplying both sides by $-(3/4)$. This gives $G = -2/(-4/3) = 6/4 = 3/2 =$ one and one-half $= 1.5$, as the maximum amount of gazpacho that Samantha could produce in a day, if she were also producing six dozen blintzes per day. Therefore, it's infeasible for Samantha to produce six dozen blintzes *and* four gallons of gazpacho per day.

QP2-8. For Jane, the opportunity cost of an additional gallon of gazpacho is two dozen blintzes. For Samantha, the opportunity cost of an additional gallon of gazpacho is one and one-third dozen blintzes. Since 1⅓ is less than 2, the opportunity cost of additional gazpacho is lower for Samantha. Thus she has comparative advantage in gazpacho production. Jane has comparative advantage in blintz production.

CHAPTER 3:

Interim Review Questions

IR3-1. When incomes increase, the demand curve for a normal good will shift to the right.

IR3-2. A demand curve is constructed by allowing the price to vary, while holding constant all other influences on buyers. Thus if the price changes, we move along an existing demand curve. If the price of a digital camera decreases because of a government price control, this is *not* a shift in the demand curve. Instead, this would be represented by a movement downward and to the right, along the *existing* demand curve.

IR3-3. For many consumers, a piece of furniture bought this week will be a close substitute for a piece of furniture that is bought next week. If there is a reduction in the expected price of furniture next week, consumers will reduce their demand for furniture this week. In other words, this week's demand curve for furniture will shift to the left.

IR3-4. If plastic is an input in the production of office chairs, and if the price of plastic increases, then the supply curve for office chairs will shift to the left.

IR3-5. A technological improvement will cause the supply curve to shift to the right.

IR3-6. The equilibrium price of a type of spiral-bound notebook is $2.50. At this price, the quantity supplied is exactly equal to the quantity demanded. If the price is $1, then the quantity demanded will be greater than the equilibrium quantity, and the quantity supplied will be smaller than the equilibrium quantity. As a result, at a price of $1, quantity demanded would be greater than quantity supplied, and there will be a *shortage*. If the price is $4, the quantity demanded will be smaller than the equilibrium quantity, and the quantity supplied will be larger than the equilibrium quantity. Therefore, at a price of $4, quantity supplied will be larger than quantity demanded, and there will be a *surplus*.

IR3-7. In a supply-demand diagram, the point at which the supply curve and the demand curve intersect each other is the equilibrium point.

Questions and Problems

QP3-1. As a result of the prohibition on eating meat on Fridays, the demand curve for fish was farther to the right than it would otherwise have been. When the prohibition on eating meat was removed, some Catholics probably decided to eat meat on Fridays, instead of eating fish. This would shift the demand curve for codfish to the left.

QP3-2.

a. The Law of Demand says that, when there is an *increase* in the price of a good (holding constant all other influences on buyers), the quantity demanded will decrease. Similarly, when there is a *decrease* in the price of a good (holding constant all other influences on buyers), the quantity demanded will increase. The Law of Demand refers to movements along an *existing* demand curve, holding everything else constant.

b. A demand curve is constructed by allowing the price of a good to vary, while holding constant all other influences on buyers. Thus if the price of the good changes, we move along the existing demand curve. (This is called a change in quantity demanded.) However, if there is a change in some other influence on buyers (such as a change in tastes, or incomes, or the prices of other goods), we shift to a different demand curve. (This is called a change in demand.)

QP3-3. Whenever the price of an input increases, there is a decrease in supply. In terms of the graph, the supply curve will shift to the left. Since corn is an input in the production of hogs, an increase in the price of corn will lead to a leftward shift in the supply curve for hogs.

QP3-4.

a. The Law of Supply says that, when there is an *increase* in the price of a good (holding constant all other influences on sellers), the quantity supplied will increase. Similarly, when there is a *decrease* in the price of a good (holding constant all other influences on sellers), the quantity supplied will decrease. The Law of Supply refers to movements along an *existing* supply curve, holding everything else constant.

b. A supply curve is constructed by allowing the price of a good to vary, while holding constant all other influences on sellers. Thus if the price of the good changes, we move along the existing supply curve.

(This is called a change in quantity supplied.) However, if there is a change in some other influence on sellers (such as technology or the price of an input), we shift to a different supply curve. (This is called a change in supply.)

QP3-5. It is probably reasonable to assume that American cars are substitutes for Japanese cars. If the price of one substitute good rises, there will be an increase in the demand for the other substitute good. Thus if there is an increase in the price of Japanese cars, there would be an increase in the demand for American cars. In other words, the demand curve for American cars would shift to the right.

QP3-6. "The worldwide reserves of oil are fixed, but the size of the economy keeps increasing. Sooner or later, demand will just outrun supply." At best, this statement is very misleading. The statement ignores the way in which the system of market prices can adjust to changes in demand and supply. If demand increases while supply is constant, there will be an increase in the price of the good. "Demand will just outrun supply" seems to imply that there will be shortages. However, as long as the market is allowed to achieve equilibrium, there is no reason to believe that shortages will occur. Another problem with the statement is that, while the total quantity of oil reserves is fixed, the amount of oil that is brought to market in a particular period of time is *not* fixed. The market will determine the amount that is pumped out of the ground. If prices are higher, producers will have an incentive to develop new oil fields, and to find ways to get more oil out of the existing fields. It is very appropriate to be concerned about the amount of oil that is pumped out of the ground. (One reason for this is that, when we burn petroleum products, we create a variety of types of environmental pollution. We will discuss pollution in Chapter 17.) But we are a long way from exhausting all of the world's oil reserves.

QP3-7.

a. A decrease in the price of an input will shift the supply curve to the *right*.

b. A government price control will *not* shift the supply curve or the demand curve. It will merely move us along the existing supply and demand curves.

c. A technological improvement will shift the supply curve to the *right*.

d. An increase in the price of an input will shift the supply curve to the *left*.

e. An increase in the price of a complement will shift the demand curve, but it will *not* shift the supply curve.

f. The market supply curve is the sum of the supply curves of the individual firms. This means that, all else equal, an increase in the number of firms will shift the market supply curve to the *right*.

QP3-8.

a. A government price control will *not* shift the supply curve or the demand curve. It will merely move us along the existing supply and demand curves.

b. If raisins are a normal good, and if there is an increase in consumer incomes, the demand curve for raisins will shift to the *right*.

c. If raisins are an inferior good, and if there is an increase in consumer incomes, the demand curve for raisins will shift to the *left*.

d. An increase in the price of an input will shift the supply curve, but it will *not* shift the demand curve.

e. If prunes are a substitute for raisins, and if there is a decrease in the price of prunes,

then the demand curve for raisins will shift to the *left*.

f. If raisins can be stored easily, then raisins bought this year may be reasonably close substitutes for raisins bought next year. If so, an increase in the price expected for *next* year will cause *this* year's demand curve to shift to the *right*.

g. A decrease in the price of a complement will shift the demand curve to the *right*.

h. The labor of workers at the raisin factory is an important input in the production of raisins. Therefore, the main effect of an increase in the wages of these workers will be to shift the supply curve to the left. However, there may also be an effect on the demand curve. If the workers' wages go up, they will probably have more income. If raisins are a normal good for these workers, their demand curve will shift to the right. This effect is likely to be very small, since the workers in the raisin factory are probably only a very small portion of the population.

QP3-9.

a. If the environmentalists succeed in making parents uncomfortable about using disposable diapers, the *demand* curve will shift to the *left*.

b. Most of the people who have demand for disposable diapers are the parents of babies. If there is an increase in the number of babies, we would expect the *demand* curve to shift to the *right*.

c. An improved technology will shift the *supply* curve to the *right*.

d. A decrease in the price of an input will shift the *supply* curve to the *right*.

QP3-10.

a. Lumber is an input in the production of new houses. If there is a decrease in the price of an input, the *supply* curve will shift to the right.

b. If people borrow money for a new home, and if the interest rate goes down, the *demand* curve for new homes will shift to the *right*.

c. Much of the demand for new homes comes from newly formed households. If there is a decrease in the number of new households being formed, the *demand* curve for new homes will shift to the *left*.

d. If there is a decrease in the amount of land that can be developed, we can say that the supply curve of land shifts to the left. This will lead to an increase in the price of land. Since land is an input in the production of new homes, an increase in the price of land will cause the *supply* curve for new homes to shift to the *left*.

QP3-11.

a.

Price	Caps Demanded	Caps Supplied	Surplus or Shortage	
$26/cap	70,000	130,000	60,000	(Surplus)
24	80,000	120,000	40,000	(Surplus)
22	90,000	110,000	20,000	(Surplus)
20	100,000	100,000	0	(Equilibrium)
18	110,000	90,000	−20,000	(Shortage)
16	120,000	80,000	−40,000	(Shortage)
14	130,000	70,000	−60,000	(Shortage)

b. The equilibrium price is $20 per cap. The equilibrium quantity is 100,000 caps.

QP3-12.

a. $Q_s = 5000P$, and $Q_d = 200,000 - 5000P$. At the equilibrium, $Q_s = Q_d$. If we substitute the supply equation and the demand equation into the equilibrium equation, we have $5000P = 200,000 - 5000P$. To solve this equation, first add $5000P$ to both sides. This gives us $10,000P = 200,000$. Next, we divide both sides of the equation by 10,000, which gives us $P = 20$: The equilibrium price is $20 per cap.

b. If we substitute the price of $20 per cap into the *demand* equation, we have $Q_d = 200,000 - (5000)(20)$, which means that $Q_d = 200,000 - 100,000 = 100,000$. The equilibrium quantity is 100,000.

c. If we substitute the price of $20 per cap into the *supply* equation, we have $Q_s = (5000)(20) = 100,000$. Once again, the equilibrium quantity is 100,000. Since we found the same quantity in both part (b) and part (c) of this question, we have verified that we found the correct solution for the equilibrium.

d. If the price is $16 per cap, the quantity supplied is 80,000, and the quantity demanded is 120,000. This means that the unsatisfied demand (that is, the shortage) will be 40,000 caps.

CHAPTER 4:

Interim Review Questions

IR4-1. As long as the supply curve obeys the Law of Supply, a rightward shift in the demand curve for peanuts will cause the equilibrium quantity of peanuts to increase, and the equilibrium price of peanuts will also increase.

IR4-2. As long as the supply curve obeys the Law of Supply, a leftward shift in the demand curve for cotton socks will cause the equilibrium quantity of cotton socks to decrease, and the equilibrium price of cotton socks will also decrease.

IR4-3. As long as the demand curve obeys the Law of Demand, a rightward shift in the supply curve for electric pianos will cause the equilibrium quantity of electric pianos to increase, but the equilibrium price of electric pianos will decrease.

IR4-4. As long as the demand curve obeys the Law of Demand, a leftward shift in the supply curve for aluminum will cause the equilibrium quantity of aluminum to decrease, but the equilibrium price of aluminum will increase.

IR4-5. The equilibrium price of pencils is 10 cents each. If there were a price floor at the minimum legal price of 5 cents, it would have no effect (because the equilibrium price would still be legal). However, if the price floor were at 20 cents, the equilibrium price would not be legal any longer. If the law were enforced, the quantity of pencils supplied would be greater than the quantity of pencils demanded. In other words, there would be a surplus of pencils.

IR4-6. The equilibrium price of pajamas is $20 per pair. If there were a price ceiling at the maximum legal price of $30, there would be no effect (because the equilibrium price would still be legal). However, if the price ceiling were at $10 per pair, the equilibrium price would not be legal any longer. If the law were enforced, the quantity of pajamas demanded would be greater than the quantity of pajamas supplied. In other words, there would be a shortage of pajamas.

Questions and Problems

QP4-1. Let's say that the equilibrium rental price for a video is $2 per day. If there were a price ceiling law at a maximum legal price of 25 cents per day, the equilibrium price would not be legal any longer. If the law were enforced, the quantity of videos demanded would be greater than the quantity of videos supplied. In other words, there would be a shortage of videos. On the other hand, if the price ceiling were set at $6 per video, there would be no effect because the equilibrium price would still be legal.

QP4-2.

a. If wooden boards are a normal good, and if incomes increase, there will be an increase in the demand for wooden boards. In other words, the demand curve for wooden boards will shift to the *right*. As a result, there will be increases in both the equilibrium price and quantity of wooden boards.

b. If brick is a substitute for wooden boards, and if the price of brick decreases, there will be a decrease in the demand for wooden boards. In other words, the demand curve for wooden boards will shift to the *left*. As a result, there will be decreases in both the equilibrium price and quantity of wooden boards.

c. If trees are more susceptible to disease and insects, there will be a decrease in the supply of wooden boards. In other words, the supply curve for wooden boards will shift to the *left*. As a result, the equilibrium price of wooden boards will increase, but the equilibrium quantity of wooden boards will decrease.

d. If there is an improvement in the technology of transforming trees into wooden boards, there will be an increase in the supply of wooden boards. In other words, the supply curve for wooden boards will shift to the *right*. As a result, the equilibrium price of wooden boards will decrease, but the equilibrium quantity of wooden boards will increase.

QP4-3. If the demand curve shifts to the right, the old equilibrium price will not be an equilibrium anymore. At the old equilibrium price, the quantity demanded would exceed the quantity supplied. In other words, there would be a shortage. This puts upward pressure on price. Because of the rightward shift in the demand curve, we move upward and to the right along the existing supply curve. The new equilibrium price is higher than the previous equilibrium price.

If the *supply* curve shifts to the right, it is once again true that the old equilibrium price will not be an equilibrium anymore. At the old equilibrium price, the quantity supplied would exceed the quantity demanded. In other words, there would be a surplus. This puts *downward* pressure on price. Because of the rightward shift in the supply curve, we move downward and to the right along the existing demand curve. The new equilibrium price is lower than the previous equilibrium price.

QP4-4.

a. If there is a decrease in the price of cotton (an important input in the production of cotton sweaters), there will be an increase in the supply of cotton sweaters. In other words, the supply curve for cotton sweaters will shift to the *right*. As a result, the equilibrium price of cotton sweaters will decrease, but the equilibrium quantity of cotton sweaters will increase.

b. If there is an increase in the price of wool sweaters (a substitute for cotton sweaters), there will be an increase in the demand for cotton sweaters. In other words, the demand curve for cotton sweaters will shift to the *right*. As a result, the equilibrium price of cotton sweaters will increase, and the equilibrium quantity of cotton sweaters will also increase.

c. If lots of people decide that they prefer the feel of polyester, instead of the feel of cotton, there will be a decrease in the demand for cotton sweaters. In other words, the demand curve for cotton sweaters will shift to the *left*. As a result, the equilibrium price of cotton sweaters will decrease, and the equilibrium quantity of cotton sweaters will also decrease.

d. If there is an improvement in the technology of producing cotton sweaters, there will be an increase in the supply of cotton sweaters. In other words, the supply curve for cotton sweaters will shift to the *right*. As a result, the equilibrium price of cotton sweaters will decrease, but the equilibrium quantity of cotton sweaters will increase.

QP4-5. News about the beneficial effects of drinking red wine might be expected to shift the demand curve for red wine to the *right*. In other words, the news about the benefits of drinking red wine would cause the demand for red wine to increase. As a result, there would be increases in both the equilibrium price and the equilibrium quantity of red wine.

QP4-6. If the equilibrium price is $30 per shirt, and if a price-ceiling law sets a maximum legal price of $40, the law will have no effect, because the equilibrium price will still be legal. However, if the price ceiling is set at $20, the equilibrium price would not be legal any more. If the law is enforced, the quantity of shirts demanded will exceed the quantity of shirts supplied. In other words, there will be a shortage of shifts. This could lead to black-market activity.

QP4-7. The supply curve in this question does not obey the Law of Supply. A graph of the supply curve for this type of mineral water will be a vertical line. If a price floor is set above the equilibrium price, there will be a surplus. The quantity supplied will be the same as before, but the quantity demanded will be less. The actual quantity bought and sold will be less than it was before.

If a price ceiling is set below the equilibrium price, the quantity supplied will be the same as before, but the quantity demanded will be more. There will be a shortage. However, the actual quantity bought and sold will be the same as it was before, because the quantity supplied is unchanged.

QP4-8. When a price ceiling is enforced below the equilibrium price, the quantity demanded is greater than it was at the equilibrium, and the quantity supplied is less than it was at the equilibrium. As a result, the quantity demanded is greater than the quantity supplied, and there is a shortage.

When a price floor is set above the equilibrium price, the quantity supplied is greater than it was at the equilibrium, and the quantity demanded is less than it was at the equilibrium. As a result, the quantity supplied is greater than the quantity demanded, and there is a surplus.

QP4-9. The equilibrium price of donor organs (like the equilibrium price of any other scarce commodity) is positive. If a price ceiling sets the price at zero, the equilibrium price will not be legal, and a shortage will occur. The quantity of organs demanded will be greater than the quantity supplied. As a result, people who are experiencing organ failure must wait for a long time before they can receive a donor organ. Thousands die before they can receive a transplant.

QP4-10.

a. If tastes change, so that people don't want to listen to recorded music as much as before, there will be a decrease in the demand for CDs. In other words, the demand curve for CDs will shift to the *left*. As a result, the equilibrium price of CDs will decrease, and the equilibrium quantity of CDs will also decrease.

b. If there is an increase in the price of plastic components, and if plastic components are an important input in the production of CDs, there will be a decrease in the supply of CDs. In other words, the supply curve for CDs will shift to the *left*. As a result, the equilibrium price of CDs will increase, but the equilibrium quantity of CDs will decrease.

c. As a result of an improvement in the technology of producing CDs, there will be an increase in the supply of CDs. In other words, the supply curve for CDs will shift to the *right*. The equilibrium price of CDs will decrease, but the equilibrium quantity of CDs will increase.

d. If CDs are a normal good, and if there is an increase in incomes, the demand curve for CDs will shift to the *right*. In other words, there will be an increase in the demand for CDs. As a result, the equilibrium price of CDs will increase, and the equilibrium quantity of CDs will also increase.

QP4-11.

a. The equilibrium price is $50 per vase, and the equilibrium quantity is 50 vases per week.

b. If a price-floor law sets a minimum legal price at $70, the equilibrium price will not be legal anymore. If the price-floor law is enforced, the quantity supplied would be 70 vases per week, but the quantity demanded would be only 30 vases per week. There will be a surplus of 40 vases per week.

c. If the price floor were at $30, the equilibrium price would still be legal, and the price-floor law would not have any effect.

d. If a price-ceiling law sets a maximum legal price at $80, the equilibrium price will still be legal, and the price-ceiling law would not have any effect.

e. If the price ceiling were set at $20, the equilibrium price would not be legal. If the price-ceiling law is enforced, the quantity supplied would be 20 vases per week, and the quantity demanded would be 80 vases per week. There would be a shortage of 60 vases per week.

QP4-12.

a. We have equations for the demand for mountain bikes and for the supply of mountain bikes: $Q_d = 100,000 - 250P$, and $Q_s = 250P$. At the equilibrium, quantity demanded is equal to quantity supplied: $Q_d = Q_s$. To solve for the equilibrium price, we substitute the demand equation and the supply equation into the equilibrium equation: $100,000 - 250P = 250P$. Next, add 250P to both sides of the equation, to get $100,000 = 500P$. The next step is to divide both sides of the equation by 500. This gives us $P = \$200$ per bike.

b. If we substitute the equilibrium price of $200 into the demand equation, we have $Q_d = 100,000 - (250)(200) = 100,000 - 50,000 = 50,000$ bicycles. If we substitute the equilibrium price of $200 into the supply equation, we have $Q_s = (250)(200) = 50,000$. Regardless of whether we use the supply equation or the demand equation, we find that the quantity is 50,000 bicycles. That is because we are dealing with the *equilibrium* quantity.

c. If a price ceiling is set at $500 per bicycle, the equilibrium price will still be legal, and the price-ceiling law will have no effect. The equilibrium price will still be $200 per bicycle, and 50,000 bicycles will still be bought and sold.

d. If the price ceiling is set at $100 per bicycle, the equilibrium price will not be legal anymore. To find the quantity demanded, we substitute a price of $100 into the demand equation: $Q_d = 100,000 - (250)(100) = 100,000 - 25,000 = 75,000$ bicycles. To find the quantity supplied, we substitute a price of $100 into the supply equation: $Q_s = (250)(100) = 25,000$ bicycles. Since the quantity demanded is 75,000 and the quantity supplied is 25,000, there will be a shortage of $(75,000 - 25,000) = 50,000$ bicycles.

CHAPTER 5:

Interim Review Questions

IR5-1. Over the last few decades, exports and imports have become *more* important—they have become a larger fraction of gross domestic product.

IR5-2. The most important trading partners of the United States are in North America (Canada and Mexico), East Asia (Japan, China, Taiwan, South Korea), and Europe (United Kingdom, Germany, Netherlands, France).

IR5-3. Yes, high-income countries (such as the United States) can benefit from trading with low-income countries. When two countries exploit their comparative advantages by trading with each other, *both* countries can be made better off.

IR5-4. When an import quota is imposed at a level that is *higher* than the equilibrium quantity, the quota will have no effect. There will only be an effect if the import quota is *lower* than the equilibrium quantity.

IR5-5. A tariff, an import quota, and a voluntary export restraint can all lead to a reduced quantity, and to higher prices for the consumers in the importing country. Also, domestic producers may be helped in each case, because they don't have as much competition from abroad. However, there are differences. A tariff generates revenue for the Treasury of the importing country. A quota will give financial benefits to the holder of the import license. A VER will give financial benefits to the exporting producers.

Questions and Problems

QP5-1.

a. The supply curve is given by $Q_s = 2P$, and the demand curve is given by $Q_d = 100 - 2P$. At the equilibrium price, $Q_d = Q_s$. Therefore, if we substitute the supply equation and the demand equation into the equilibrium equation, we have $2P = 100 - 2P$. Adding $2P$ to both sides of this equation gives $100 = 4P$. Then if we divide both sides of the equation by 4, we have the equilibrium price: $P = \$25$.

b. If we insert the equilibrium price of $25 into the supply equation, we find that the quantity is $2(25) = 50$. If we insert the equilibrium price into the demand equation, we find that the quantity is $100 - 2(25) =$ $100 - 50 = 50$. Thus if we use either the supply equation or the demand equation, the equilibrium quantity is 50 brupkas.

c. The new equilibrium is found by setting $Q_d = Q_s$, using the *old* import demand curve and the *new*, gross-of-tariff export supply curve. Thus, $-20 + 2P = 100 - 2P$. To solve for P, we begin by adding 20 to both sides of the equation, and adding $2P$ to both sides of the equation. This gives us $4P = 120$. Dividing both sides of the equation by 4 gives us the gross-of-tariff equilibrium price: $P_{gross} = \$30$.

d. If we substitute the gross-of-tariff equilibrium price of $30 into the old import demand curve, we find that the equilibrium quantity is $100 - 2P = 100 - (2)(30) = 100 - 60 = 40$ brupkas. If we substitute the gross-of-tariff equilibrium price into the new, gross-of-tariff supply curve, we get the same answer: The equilibrium quantity is $-20 + 2P = -20 + (2)(30) = -20 + 60 = 40$ brupkas.

e. The quantity is 40. If we substitute this value into the net-of-tariff supply curve, we have $40 = 2P_{net}$. Dividing both sides of the equation by 2, we have $P_{net} = \$20$. Alternatively, we can get the same answer by taking the gross-of-tariff price of $30 per brupka and subtracting the tariff of $10 per brupka, which gives a net price (received by the sellers) of $20.

f. The tariff is $10 per brupka. If we multiply by the equilibrium quantity of 40 brupkas, we get revenue of $(\$10)(40) = \$400$.

QP5-2.

a. The demand curve is $Q_d = 100 - 2P$. Because of the quota, $Q = 40$. Therefore, if we substitute a quantity of 40 into the demand equation, we see that the price paid by the buyers is given by $40 = 100 - 2P$. Subtracting 100 from both sides of the equation, we have $-60 = -2P$. Finally, if we divide both sides of the equation by (–2), we can solve for the price that will be paid by the buyers: P = $30.

b. The supply curve is $Q_s = 2P$. Because of the quota, Q = 40. Therefore, if we substitute a quantity of 40 into the supply equation, we see that the price received by the sellers is given by 40 = 2P. Dividing both sides of the equation by 2, we have the price that will be received by the sellers: P = $20.

  This indicates that there are important similarities between tariffs and quotas. In QP5-1, we saw that a tariff would reduce the quantity to 40 brupkas, and that the buyers' price would be increased to $30, and that the sellers' price would be reduced to $20. Here, we have seen that a quota can lead to exactly the same outcomes.

c. The equilibrium quantity is 50 brupkas. Therefore, if the quota is set at 60 brupkas, it will not have any effect. Fifty brupkas would be bought and sold, just as if there had been no quota at all, and the price would be $25 per brupka.

d. If the quota is set at only 20 brupkas, we would substitute a quantity of 20 into the demand equation to find the price paid by the buyers. We have 20 = 100 – 2P. Subtracting 100 from both sides of the equation gives us –80 = –2P. If we then divide both sides of the equation by (–2), we can solve for the price that will be paid by the buyers: P = $40. When the amount of imports allowed into the country is reduced, the price buyers will pay will increase. As the quota decreases, we move upward and to the left along the demand curve, and the buyers' price will increase.

  If we substitute a quantity of 20 into the supply equation, we can calculate the price received by sellers. The equation is 20 = 2P. Dividing both sides of this equation by 2, we have P = $10. When the amount of imports that is allowed to come into the country is reduced, the price that sellers will receive will decrease.

  A quantity of 20 brupkas will be bought and sold.

QP5-3. *Any* kind of restriction on international trade is bad for the consumers in the importing country. However, if the political pressure for trade restrictions is overwhelming, it might be better to use a VER. That is because a VER gives benefits to the producers in the exporting country. Because of this, there might not be much pressure for the exporting country to retaliate.

QP5-4. U.S. exports to Mexico are much bigger than U.S. exports to any other low-income country. This is largely because Mexico is very close geographically. Therefore, the costs of transporting goods from the U.S. to Mexico are less than the costs of transporting goods to most other countries.

QP5-5. It is not very useful to think of imports as being bad. *Both* imports and exports are good, because they allow countries to exploit their comparative advantages. There is no particular reason to think that a trade surplus is good, but that a trade deficit is bad. If a country has very large trade deficits for a long period of time, some problems can occur. However, modest trade deficits should not be viewed as a problem. Finally, it is impossible for every country to have a trade surplus. The trade balance for the entire world has to be zero. If some countries have trade surpluses, then some other countries must have trade deficits.

CHAPTER 6:

Interim Review Questions

IR6-1. The quantity demanded decreases from 4200 million pounds per year to 3800 million pounds per year. Thus, the change in quantity demanded is (4200 – 3800) = 400 million pounds per year. (We drop the minus sign.) The reference level of quantity demanded is the midpoint between 3800 million pounds and 4200 million pounds, which is 4000 million pounds. The price increases from $1.35 per pound to $1.65 per pound. The change in price is $(1.65 – 1.35) = $0.30 per pound. The reference level of price is the midpoint between $1.35 and $1.65, which is $1.50 per pound. Now we can calculate the elasticity, $(\Delta Q_d / Q_d)/(\Delta P/P) = (400/4000)/(\$0.30/\$1.50) = (1/10)/(1/5) = 5/10 = 1/2 = 0.5$.

IR6-2. If we represent the elasticity by e, the elasticity formula states that $e = \%\Delta Q_d / \%\Delta P$. We know that e = 0.5, and that $\%\Delta P = 10\%$. If we substitute these values into the elasticity formula, we have $0.5 = \%\Delta Q_d / 10\%$. To solve for the percentage change in quantity demanded, multiply both sides of the equation by 10%. This gives us $\%\Delta Q_d = (0.5)(10\%) = 5\%$, which tells us that there will be a 5% decrease in the quantity of movies rented.

IR6-3. If the own-price elasticity of demand for red-delicious apples is 1.0, we say that demand is unit elastic. In this case, total revenue does not change, even if there is an increase in price. If the elasticity were greater than one, and if price were to increase, the percentage reduction in quantity demanded would be relatively greater than the percentage increase in price, and total revenue would decrease.

IR6-4. If we represent the elasticity by e, the elasticity formula states that $e = \%\Delta Q_d / \%\Delta P$. We know that $\%\Delta Q_d = 7\%$, and that $\%\Delta P = (-)10\%$. Thus $e = 7\%/10\% = 0.7$. Therefore, the elasticity of demand is 0.7. Demand is inelastic. When demand is inelastic and price decreases, total revenue also decreases.

IR6-5. If the price of Sprite were to increase substantially, while the prices of 7-Up and Sierra Mist stay the same, we would expect many consumers to make very large reductions in their consumption of Sprite. In other words, it is very likely that the demand for Sprite is elastic.

IR6-6. A price floor that is 10% above the equilibrium price will lead to surpluses in each market. However, we are told that the demand for red-delicious apples is more elastic than the demand for eggs. Thus when the price floor pushes the price up by 10%, the percentage reduction in quantity demanded must be larger in the market for red-delicious apples, where the demand is more elastic. We are also told that the supply curves are the same in the two markets. Thus, the only difference between them is in the elasticity of demand. Therefore, the surplus will be relatively greater in the market for red-delicious apples, because of the larger relative reduction in quantity demanded.

IR6-7. If there is a rightward shift in the demand curve for a good when incomes increase, we say that the good is a normal good. In this case, the income elasticity is greater than zero.

IR6-8. If there is an increase in the price of vacations in France, the demand curve for vacations in the United States will shift to the right. In other words, the increase in the price of vacations in France leads to an increase in the demand for vacations in the United States. This means that vacations in France and vacations in the U.S. are substitutes. The cross-price elasticity of demand for vacations in the U.S. with respect to the price of vacations in France is greater than zero.

IR6-9. The elasticity of supply is the percentage change in quantity supplied, divided by the percentage change in price. There is a 10-percent increase in the quantity of bicycle helmets supplied, as a result of a 20-percent increase in the price of bicycle helmets. Therefore, the elasticity of supply for bicycle helmets is 10%/20% = 0.5.

IR6-10. Over a period of 10 weeks, apple growers will not be able to increase the quantity supplied by very much. They can hire more farm workers, and they can use more fertilizer, and so on, but the number of trees is fixed. However, if the price is expected to be higher over a period of many years, the growers may decide to plant more apple trees. As a result, the relative increase in quantity supplied may be much larger over a long period than over a short period. Therefore, the elasticity of supply will probably be larger when a longer time period is considered.

Questions and Problems

QP6-1.

a. The price of lettuce rises from $1.75 per head to $2.25 cents per head. Therefore, the change in price is $(2.25 − 1.75) = $0.50. The reference level of price is the midpoint between $1.75 and $2.25 cents, which is $2.00. If we divide $0.50 by $2.00, we see that there is a 25-percent increase in price. Since the quantity demanded goes down by 25 percent, the elasticity of demand is 25%/25% = 1.

b. The demand for lettuce is unit-elastic.

c. Since demand is unit-elastic, total revenue for lettuce sellers will not change.

QP6-2. Based on the information presented in this question, we would say that coffee and tea are substitutes. Therefore, the cross-price elasticity of demand for coffee with respect to the price of tea is positive.

QP6-3. If an increase in incomes leads to a decrease in the demand for turnips, we would say that turnips are an inferior good. If this is the case, then the income elasticity of demand for turnips is negative.

QP6-4. The price ceiling on leather belts is below the equilibrium price, and this leads to shortages. One reason for the shortages is that the quantity demanded will increase when the price is driven downward. If we hold constant the elasticity of supply, the shortage will be larger when the own-price elasticity of demand is larger. Therefore, the shortages will be more severe if the own-price elasticity of demand is 0.8 than if it is 0.5.

QP6-5.

a. The price of a programmable calculator decreases from $55 to $45. Therefore, the change in price is $(55 − 45) = $10. The reference level of price is the midpoint between $55 and $45, which is $50. The quantity demanded increases from 1000 to 1500. Therefore, the change in quantity demanded is (1500 − 1000) = 500. The reference level of quantity demanded is the midpoint between 1000 and 1500, which is 1250. The elasticity is $(\Delta Q_d/Q_d)/(\Delta P/P) = (500/1250)/(10/50) = (0.4)/(0.2) = 2$.

b. Since the elasticity of demand is 2, we say that demand is elastic.

c. When demand is elastic and price decreases, the increase in quantity demanded is so large that there is an increase in total revenue. In this case, we can actually calculate total revenue. Before the price change, calculators sold for $55 each, and 1000 were sold. Therefore, total revenue was ($55)(1000) = $55,000. After the price change, calculators sell for $45 each, and 1500 are sold. Therefore, total revenue is ($45)(1500) = $67,500. Indeed, there is an increase in total revenue.

QP6-6.

a. Ace Computer Equipment Company increases the price of its printer cables by 20%. As a result, there is an 80-percent decrease in the quantity demanded for Ace cables. If we insert these numbers into the elasticity formula, we see that the elasticity is (80%/20%) = 4.

b. Since the elasticity is 4, the demand for Ace's cables is very elastic.

c. The market demand elasticity for printer cables is probably significantly less than the elasticity of demand for the printer cables of any particular company. It is relatively easy to substitute one company's cables for another company's cables. However, it is not as easy to substitute away from cables entirely.

QP6-7.

a. Real income in Winesburg, Ohio, increases from $80 million to $120 million. The change in income is $(120 million – 80 million) = $40 million. The reference level of income is the midpoint between $80 million and $120 million, which is $100 million. Therefore, the proportional change in income is ($40 million)/($100 million) = 0.4. If we convert this to a percentage, we

get 40%. As a result of the increase in income, there is a 10-percent increase in the quantity of bread demanded. If we substitute this information into the formula for the income elasticity, we find that the income elasticity of demand for bread is (10%/40%) = 0.25.

b. Since the income elasticity of demand for bread is greater than zero, we say that bread is a normal good.

QP6-8.

a. The cross-price elasticity of demand for chicken with respect to the price of fish is 0.7. Since this cross-price elasticity is greater than zero, we say that chicken and fish are substitutes.

b. The cross-price elasticity of demand for automobiles with respect to the price of gasoline if –0.2. Since this cross-price elasticity is less than zero, we say that automobiles and gasoline are complements.

c. The cross-price elasticity of demand for oranges with respect to the price of notebook paper is zero. Since this cross-price elasticity is zero, we say that oranges and notebook paper are independent in demand.

QP6-9. When the price floor pushes the price upward, a surplus will occur. The amount of the surplus will depend on the amount of the increase in quantity supplied. If the elasticity of supply is larger, the increase in quantity supplied will be larger. Therefore, if we hold constant the elasticity of demand, the surpluses will be greater if the price elasticity of supply is 1.3, rather than 0.6.

QP6-10.

a. If the own-price elasticity of demand for raisins is 0.8, we say that demand is inelastic.

b. If we represent the elasticity by e, the elasticity formula states that $e = \%\Delta Q_d / \%\Delta P$. We know that $e = 0.8$, and that $\%\Delta P = 50\%$. If we substitute these values into the elasticity formula, we have $0.8 = \%\Delta Q_d / 50\%$. To solve for the percentage change in quantity demanded, multiply both sides of the equation by 50%. This gives us $\%\Delta Q_d = (0.8)(50\%) = 40\%$, which tells us that there will be a 40% decrease in the quantity of raisins demanded.

c. If demand is inelastic, and if there is an increase in price, total revenue for sellers will increase, because the decrease in quantity demanded is not large enough to offset the increase in price.

QP6-11.

a. If we represent the elasticity by e, the elasticity formula states that $e = \%\Delta Q_d / \%\Delta P$. We know that $e = 1.5$, and that $\%\Delta Q_d = 30\%$. If we substitute these values into the elasticity formula, we have $1.5 = (30\%) / \%\Delta P$. To solve for the percentage change in price, we first multiply both sides of the equation by $\%\Delta P$. This gives us $(1.5)(\%\Delta P) = 30\%$. Now, we divide both sides of the equation by 1.5. The price of computer spreadsheets must have fallen by $(30\%)/(1.5) = 20\%$.

b. If the elasticity of demand is 1.5, the demand for spreadsheet programs is elastic.

c. If demand is elastic, and if price falls, the increase in quantity demanded is large enough that there will be an increase in total revenue.

QP6-12. All else equal, the own-price elasticity of demand tends to be larger if it is easier to substitute for the good in question. All else equal, the own-price elasticity also tends to be larger if we allow a longer time period during which consumers can adjust. Finally, all else equal, the own-price elasticity tends to be larger for items that make up a larger portion of the consumer's budget.

QP6-13.

a. Inelastic demand and a price increase => total revenue will increase.

b. Elastic demand and a price increase => total revenue will decrease.

c. Unit-elastic demand and a price increase => total revenue will remain the same.

d. Elastic demand and a price decrease => total revenue will increase.

e. Unit-elastic demand and a price decrease => total revenue will stay the same.

f. Inelastic demand and a price decrease => total revenue will decrease.

CHAPTER 7:

Interim Review Questions

IR7-1. The Dolphins gain six yards on the first play and four yards on the second play. Their total gain from the first two plays is $(6 + 4) = 10$ yards. They gain 11 yards on the third play. Their total gain from the first three plays is $(6 + 4 + 11) = 21$ yards.

IR7-2. The slope of the total-revenue curve is called "marginal revenue".

IR7-3. If the first scarf costs $15, but Vicky's marginal utility from the first scarf is only $10, she should not buy. She should only buy if marginal utility is greater than or equal to the price.

IR7-4. Derek's marginal utility of the first grapefruit is $1. If Derek obeys the Law of Diminishing Marginal Utility, then his marginal utility from the second grapefruit will be less than $1.

IR7-5. The price of a movie ticket is $6. Catherine should buy movie tickets as long as the marginal utility is greater than or equal to the price. Thus she should buy three tickets, since the marginal utility of the third ticket is $6. The first ticket has marginal utility of $10, so it gives her consumer surplus of $(10 − 6) = $4. The second ticket has marginal utility of $8, so it creates consumer surplus of $(8 − 6) = $2. The third ticket has marginal utility of $6, so it does not create any consumer surplus. Since Catherine has $4 of consumer surplus from the first ticket, and $2 of consumer surplus from the second ticket, her total consumer surplus is $(4 + 2) = $6.

IR7-6. Since Mr. A is an accountant and Mr. B is a janitor, it is probably true that Mr. A's wage rate is much higher than that of Mr. B. Therefore, Mr. A is more likely to travel by air, and Mr. B is more likely to travel by bus, because the value of time is greater for Mr. A. Let's say it takes one hour to travel from Sacramento to Los Angeles by air, and eight hours to travel by bus, so that the time saved by traveling by air is seven hours. Mr. A is probably willing (and able) to pay more, to save those seven hours.

Questions and Problems

QP7-1. The Law of Diminishing Marginal Utility states that the additional utility from consuming one additional good will eventually go down, as more and more units are consumed. In fact, it is very difficult to think of any goods for which this Law would not hold. There are some goods for which there might be an initial range of increasing marginal utility, but marginal utility is *eventually* almost certain to go down. For example, let's say that you see "The Matrix" at the movie theater for the first time. If you go a second time, you may enjoy the movie even more, as you try to dissect its layers of meaning. You might even get more enjoyment a third time. However, sooner or later, your marginal utility is likely to decline. The Law of Diminishing Marginal Utility does *not* state that marginal utility goes down immediately. The Law only says that marginal utility goes down *eventually*.

QP7-2.

a.

Game	Marginal Points	Total Points
1	20	20
2	24	44 (= 20 + 24)
3	15	59 (= 20 + 24 + 15)
4	19	78 (= 20 + 24 + 15 + 19)
5	26	104 (= 20 + 24 + 15 + 19 + 26)

b. The graph of marginal points represents the slope of the graph of total points.

QP7-3. Since police officers have higher rates of death and injury than file clerks, we would expect police officers to have higher wage rates than file clerks, *all else equal*.

QP7-4. Time is valuable. Consumers are willing to pay higher prices at convenience stores, if they believe they will be able to make the purchase quickly. Thus if you pay a higher price for a gallon of milk at 7-Eleven, we could say that you are buying two goods at the same time. You are buying the milk, and you are also buying some convenience.

QP7-5.

a. If the price of a movie ticket is $6, Betsy gets consumer surplus of $(15 − 6) = $9 from the first movie, and $(9 − 6) = $3 from the second movie. (The marginal utility of the third movie is $6. Betsy does buy a ticket for a third movie, but she doesn't get any additional consumer surplus from it, since its marginal utility is just equal to its price.) Therefore, her consumer surplus is $(9 + 3) = $12.

b. If the price were to increase to $9, Betsy would get $(15 − 9) = $6 of consumer surplus from the first movie. She would not get any consumer surplus from the second movie, since its marginal utility is now equal to its price. Therefore, her consumer surplus is $6. When prices increase, consumer surplus falls, for two reasons. First, the consumer buys fewer units. Second, for each unit that is bought, the consumer receives less consumer surplus.

QP7-6. To go from Chicago to San Francisco by air costs *more money* than going by bus, but it takes *less time*. Therefore, the people who are willing and able to pay more money to save time are the ones who will fly. Those who are *not* willing and able to pay more money to save time will take the bus. People who have a higher value of time will be more likely to travel by air.

QP7-7.

a. $Q_d = 10 − P$, and $P = \$1$. By substituting the price of $1 into the demand equation, we find that the equilibrium quantity is $(10 − 1) = 9$.

b. In this problem, consumer surplus is represented by the area of a triangle. The base of the triangle is the quantity, which is nine. The height of the triangle is the vertical distance between the price ($1) and the vertical intercept of the demand curve ($10). Therefore, the height of the triangle is $(10 − 1) = \$9$. The area of the triangle is $(0.5)(9)(\$9) = (0.5)(\$81) = \$40.50$.

QP7-8.

a. If a tax raises the price to $P = \$2$, we find the new equilibrium quantity by substituting the price of $2 into the demand equation, $Q_d = 10 − P$. The new equilibrium quantity is $(10 − 2) = 8$.

b. Once again, consumer surplus is given by the area of a triangle. The base of the triangle is the new quantity, which is eight. The height of the triangle is $(10 − 2) = \$8$. The area of the triangle is $(0.5)(8)(\$8) = (0.5)(\$64) = \$32$.

c. Before the tax was levied, consumer surplus was $40.50. After the tax is levied, consumer surplus is $32. As a result of the tax, consumer surplus declines by $(40.50 − 32) = \$8.50$.

CHAPTER 8:

Interim Review Questions

IR8-1. A basketball team is currently averaging 68 points per game. If they score 75 points in the next game, their marginal score is greater than the average score from the previous games. As a result, their average will increase. If they score 68 points in their next game, their marginal score is equal to the average score from the previous games. As a result, their average will stay the same. If they score 59 points, their marginal score is less than the average score from the previous games. As a result, their average will decrease.

IR8-2. The average cost of the units produced so far has been $20 per smoke detector. If the marginal cost of the next unit is $22, the marginal cost is greater than the average cost of the previous units. As a result, the average cost will increase. If the marginal cost of the next unit is $20, the marginal cost is equal to the average cost of the previous units. As a result, the average cost will stay the same. If the marginal cost of the next unit is $19, the marginal cost is less than the average cost of the previous units. As a result, the average cost will decrease.

IR8-3. Average fixed cost is equal to total fixed cost divided by the quantity of output. If total fixed cost is $10, and total product is 5 units, then average fixed cost = $10/5 = $2 per unit.

IR8-4. Marginal cost is the additional cost of producing one additional unit. Marginal cost can be defined as the change in total cost divided by the change in output. Since variable costs are the only costs that change, we can also say that marginal cost is the change in total *variable* cost, divided by the change in output. If total variable cost increases from $100 to $105 when output increases from 10 to 11, the marginal cost of the 11th unit is $(105 − 100)/(11 − 10) = $5/1 = $5.

IR8-5. Fixed costs are the costs that are incurred, regardless of the level of output. Therefore, if total cost is $10,000 when total product is zero, total fixed cost is $10,000.

IR8-6. If the LRAC curve is a horizontal line, the firm is experiencing constant returns to scale.

IR8-7. If a firm can increase its output by 30 percent by increasing all inputs by 20 percent, we say that the firm is experiencing increasing returns to scale. The firm's LRAC curve will slope downward.

Questions and Problems

QP8-1.

a. Hiring a few additional workers is a short-run decision.

b. When a firm opens up a new store, it changes its scale of operations. Therefore, this is a long-run decision.

c. Applying additional fertilizer to a cornfield is a short-run decision.

d. Increasing the size of the cornfield is a long-run decision.

Quantity of Output	TVC	ATC	TC	MC
0	0	—	20	—
1	10	30	30	10
2	18	19	38	8
3	28	16	48	10
4	40	15	60	12
5	56	15.2	76	16
6	76	16	96	20

QP8-2.

In the textbook, several of the values in this table were left blank. One of these was the value of average total cost (ATC) for a quantity of 1. We calculate the ATC by dividing the total cost of $30 by the quantity of 1, so that the ATC is $30 per unit. Similarly, when quantity is 4, total cost is 60, so that ATC is $(60/4) = $15 per unit.

Marginal cost is the change in total cost as a result of producing one additional unit of output. When quantity increases from 0 to 1, total cost increases from $20 to $30. Therefore, the marginal cost of the first unit of output is $(30 − 20) = $10. Similarly, the marginal cost of the second unit of output is $(38 − 30) = $8, and the marginal cost of the fifth unit of output is $(76 − 60) = $16.

To find the total cost when quantity is 3 units, we take the total cost when Q = 2, and add the marginal cost of the third unit. Thus the total cost for Q = 3 is $(38 + 10) = $48. Similarly, the total cost when Q = 6 is $(76 + 20) = $96.

Total cost is equal to total variable cost plus total fixed cost: TC = TVC + TFC. Therefore, if we subtract TFC from both sides of the equation, we find that TVC = TC − TFC. We know that TFC = $20, because total cost is $20 when Q = 0. Thus we can find TVC by subtracting $20 from TC. When Q = 2, TC = $38, so that TVC = $(38 − 20) = $18. When Q = 4, TC = $60, so that TVC = $(60 − 20) = $40. When Q = 6, TC = $96, so that TVC = $(96 − 20) = $76.

There is also another way to calculate TVC. For example, we can find TVC for Q = 4 by taking TVC for Q = 3, and adding the marginal cost of the fourth unit. Thus for Q = 4, TVC = $(28 + 12) = $40.

QP8-3.

a. In the short run, at least one input is fixed. In the long run, all inputs are variable.

b. Fixed costs cannot be changed during the time period under consideration. Variable costs can be varied during the relevant time period.

QP8-4. If marginal cost is greater than average total cost, average total cost is increasing. If marginal cost is equal to average total cost, average total cost is constant. If marginal cost is less than average total cost, average total cost is decreasing.

QP8-5. For a season-ticket holder, the cost of the ticket has already been paid, regardless of whether the person attends a particular game. Therefore, the cost of the ticket is a sunk cost, and it should have no bearing on decisions. The decision of whether to attend the game will depend on whether the marginal benefit of going to the game is greater than or less than the marginal cost. The marginal benefit depends on the enjoyment that the fan expects to get from going to the game.

The marginal cost depends on how long it takes to get to the stadium, how much it costs to park, and other factors. Therefore, there are fewer no-shows when a championship is on the line, and there are more no-shows when there is bad weather or if construction delays make it difficult to get to the stadium. But the number of no-shows should not depend on the price of a ticket, because that is a sunk cost from the perspective of season-ticket holders.

CHAPTER 9:

Interim Review Questions

IR9-1. The four market structures are perfect competition, monopolistic competition, oligopoly, and monopoly. Wheat farming or corn farming are perfectly competitive industries. Retail stores are examples of monopolistically competitive firms. Some of the best examples of oligopoly are in manufacturing, such as commercial-aircraft manufacturing, automobile manufacturing, and breakfast-cereal manufacturing. Some electric-power utilities are organized as monopolies.

IR9-2. Perfectly competitive firms do *not* have differentiated products, whereas monopolistically competitive firms *do* have product differentiation.

IR9-3. Perfectly competitive industries have many firms, each of which is small, and the firms produce homogeneous (non-differentiated) output. These characteristics are the reasons why perfectly competitive firms are price takers. Because of their small size, the firms are not big enough to have any control over price. The lack of product differentiation is another reason why perfectly competitive firms are unable to control the price. To be a price taker, a firm must *both* be small and a producer of homogeneous output. (Free entry and exit is another characteristic of perfect competition, but this does not have a bearing on whether the firms are price takers.)

IR9-4. The firm described in this question is *not* a perfectly competitive firm. This firm is making a choice regarding the price to charge. Perfectly competitive firms merely take the market price as given.

IR9-5. For a perfectly competitive firm, price is equal to marginal revenue, and price is also equal to average revenue.

IR9-6. Economic cost is greater than accounting cost.

IR9-7. Economic profit is less than accounting profit.

IR9-8. If Joe's Burger Joint is earning an accounting profit of 6%, but the normal rate of return on an investment in the burger industry is 12%, then Joe's has a negative economic profit.

IR9-9. If marginal cost is less than price, the firm should expand output, because doing so will increase its profit.

IR9-10. Profit is equal to total revenue minus total cost. Graphically, profit is maximized at the quantity at which the total-revenue curve is parallel to the total-cost curve. Also, profit is maximized at the quantity at which marginal revenue equals marginal cost. Marginal revenue is the slope of the total-revenue curve, and marginal cost is the slope of the total-cost curve. Therefore, if marginal revenue is equal to marginal cost, the slope of the total-revenue curve will be equal to the slope of the total-cost curve, which means that the total-revenue curve will be parallel to the total-cost curve.

IR9-11. The market price is $20 per shirt, and the firm's average total cost is $24 per shirt. This means that the firm's profit per unit is $(20 − 24) = −$4. In other words, the firm is suffering a loss of $4 on every shirt. However, the firm's average *variable* cost is only $16 per shirt. Since price is greater than average variable cost, the firm should stay in business in the short run.

IR9-12. In the previous question, if average variable cost were $22 per shirt, price would be less than average variable cost, and the firm's short-run decision should be to shut down.

IR9-13. Currently, the firms in a perfectly competitive industry are earning economic profits. In the future, we expect that (a) more firms will enter the industry. Because of the increase in the number of firms, the industry supply curve will shift to the right, and (b) the market price will fall. The market price will fall until (c) the firms are earning zero economic profits.

IR9-14. At the competitive equilibrium, the marginal benefit is exactly equal to the marginal cost. If the quantity is increased beyond the competitive-equilibrium level, the marginal cost will be greater than the marginal benefit. If we consume units for which marginal cost is greater than marginal benefit, we make ourselves worse off.

Questions and Problems

QP9-1. A firm will maximize profit by producing the quantity of output at which marginal revenue is equal to marginal cost. In this question, marginal cost is $10, but marginal revenue is $12. Therefore, the firm is not maximizing profit. Instead, the firm should expand output—if the firm were to produce and sell one more unit, it would increase its profit by $(12 − 10) = $2.

QP9-2.

a. The marginal cost of the first unit is $5, and the marginal cost of the second unit is $3. Therefore, when two units are produced, *total* variable cost is $(5 + 3) = $8. To find *average* variable cost, we divide total variable cost by the number of units of output: when two units are produced, average variable cost = ($8/2) = $4 per unit.

b. Total cost is $20 when the quantity is zero, which means that total fixed cost is $20. When quantity is three, total cost is equal to $20 (the total fixed cost) plus $5 (the marginal cost of the first unit) plus $3 (the marginal cost of the second unit) plus $5 (the marginal cost of the third unit). Thus when quantity is three, *total* cost is $(20 + 5 + 3 + 5) = $33. *Average* total cost is equal to total cost divided by the quantity of output. In this case, average total cost = ($33/3) = $11 per unit.

c. *Total* fixed cost is $20, because this is the cost that is incurred, even when output is zero. *Average* fixed cost is equal to total fixed cost divided by the quantity of output. When quantity is two, average fixed cost = ($20/2) = $10 per unit.

QP9-3. The perfectly competitive firm is small relative to the market, and it produces a homogeneous output. Because of these two characteristics, the firm is a price taker. (If a firm lacks *either* of these two characteristics, it will not be a perfect competitor.) The market is characterized by free entry and exit, and we assume perfect information. The difference between a monopolistically competitive firm and a perfectly competitive firm is that the monopolistically competitive firm produces a differentiated output. Therefore, the monopolistically competitive firm is not a price taker: It can raise its price (at least slightly) without losing all of its customers.

QP9-4.

a. Boeing Corporation is an oligopolistic firm. It has a large share of a market with only two producers.

b. A corn farm is most likely a perfect competitor. Many thousands of farms produce corn, and each farm's corn is very similar to the corn produced by other farms.

c. A gasoline station is most likely a monopolistically competitive firm. The market has many firms, but the products of the various firms are differentiated, due to location, quality of service, brand, and other characteristics.

d. Some (although not all) electric-power utilities are monopolies.

QP9-5.

Quantity	Price	Marginal Revenue	Average Revenue	Total Revenue
1	$5	$5	$5	$ 5
2	$5	$5	$5	$10
3	$5	$5	$5	$15

The price is $5, regardless of the level of output. Total revenue is equal to price multiplied by quantity: TR = (P)(Q). Average revenue is equal to total revenue divided by quantity: AR = TR/Q. But since TR = (P)(Q), it follows that AR = PQ/Q. Thus average revenue is equal to price. Marginal revenue is the change in total revenue associated with selling one additional unit. We have seen the relationships between marginal cost and average cost, as well as the relationships between marginal revenue and average revenue. In each case, we found that if marginal is equal to average, average is constant. Conversely, if average is constant, marginal is equal to average. In this case, average revenue is unchanged, and marginal revenue is equal to average revenue.

QP9-6. The perfectly competitive firm produces the quantity at which price is equal to marginal cost. Therefore, for any price, we can go to the marginal-cost curve to find the quantity that will be produced (as long as the firm is in business). This means that the marginal-cost curve traces out a relationship between price and quantity supplied, which is a supply curve.

However, if price is less than average variable cost, the firm should shut down.

Therefore, for prices that are below average variable cost, the firm's quantity supplied is zero.

QP9-7. The market supply schedule, or industry supply schedule, is the sum of the supply schedules of the individual firms. If the firms are all identical, the market quantity supplied can be calculated by multiplying the firm's quantity supplied by the number of firms. Thus if there are 1000 firms,

Price	Firm Supply	Market Supply
$0	0	0
$1	5	5000
$2	10	10,000
$3	15	15,000

QP9-8. In the figure on which this question is based, at the profit-maximizing quantity (the quantity at which price equals marginal cost), price is greater than average total cost. Because profit per unit is the difference between price and average total cost, the firms in this perfectly competitive industry are earning positive economic profits. As a result, we would expect new firms to enter the industry. This will push the industry supply curve to the right, which will drive down the price. When the price falls, the firm's quantity supplied will decrease slightly, as it slides downward and to the left along its marginal-cost curve. Eventually, economic profit will be zero.

QP9-9. In the figure on which this question is based, at the profit-maximizing quantity, price is less than average total cost. Since profit per unit is equal to price minus average total cost, the firms are suffering economic losses. Since price is greater than average variable cost, firms will not go out of business immediately. However, unless business conditions improve in the short run, some firms will eventually go out of business. The industry supply curve will shift to the left, and the price will rise. When the price rises, the firm's quantity supplied will increase slightly, as it slides upward and to the right along its marginal-cost curve. Eventually, economic profit will be zero.

QP9-10.

Q	TFC	TVC	TC	MC	Price	MR	AR	TR	Profit (=TR–TC)
0	$10	$ 0	$ 10	—	$10	—	—	0	−$10
1	10	6	16	6	10	$10	$10	$10	− 6
2	10	10	20	4	10	10	10	20	0
3	10	15	25	5	10	10	10	30	5
4	10	22	32	7	10	10	10	40	8
5	10	32	42	10	10	10	10	50	8
6	10	46	56	14	10	10	10	60	4
7	10	65	75	19	10	10	10	70	5
8	10	90	100	25	10	10	10	80	− 20
9	10	122	132	32	10	10	10	90	− 42

In this table, we have included a column for total fixed cost and a column for total variable cost, even though these were not specifically requested in the question. In the question, we are told that the firm is a perfect competitor. Thus even though the table only shows a price of $10 per unit at a quantity of zero, we know that the firm faces a price of $10 per unit at every quantity. Once we know that the price is $10 per unit, we can fill in the columns for total revenue, average revenue, and marginal revenue: Total revenue is equal to price multiplied by quantity: $TR = (P)(Q)$. Average revenue is equal to total revenue divided by quantity: $AR = TR/Q$. But since $TR = (P)(Q)$, it follows that $AR = PQ/Q$. Thus average revenue is equal to price. Marginal revenue is the change in total revenue associated with selling one additional unit. Since $TC = \$10$ when $Q = 0$, we know that $TFC = \$10$. TVC is the sum of the marginal costs, and $TC = TVC + TFC$.

a. Profit is maximized by producing the quantity at which marginal revenue equals marginal cost, which occurs here when $Q = 5$.

b. The firm's profit is $8.

CHAPTER 10:

Interim Review Questions

IR10-1. Bell's Brewery is the only producer of Bell's Oberon Ale. However, it is not very useful to think of Bell's as a monopolist in the market for Oberon Ale, because many other beers and ales are reasonably close substitutes for Bell's Oberon. It's best to think of Bell's as an oligopolist in the market for beers and ales.

IR10-2. Marginal revenue is a constant for the perfectly competitive firm because the firm takes price as given. The price of the first unit sold is the same as the tenth unit and the hundredth unit. On the other hand, the monopolist faces the entire market demand curve, which slopes downward as we move from left to right across the diagram. Therefore, the monopolist faces a choice that is not faced by the competitor: For the monopolist to sell more units, it must lower the price to all of its customers.

IR10-3. If the firm's total revenue increases when one more unit is sold, the firm's marginal revenue is greater than zero. This means that the firm faces elastic demand. If total revenue is to increase, the increase in quantity demanded must be relatively larger than the decrease in price, and this means that demand must be elastic.

IR10-4. A monopolist will maximize profit by producing and selling the quantity at which marginal cost is equal to marginal revenue. This is also true for any other type of firm.

IR10-5. No, a monopoly firm does not have a supply curve. A supply curve is a *unique* relationship between price and quantity supplied. However, for a given price, the monopolist might produce a greater or smaller quantity, depending on the shape of the demand curve and the marginal-revenue curve.

IR10-6. The monopolist (like any firm) will maximize profit by producing and selling the quantity at which marginal revenue is equal to marginal cost. Marginal cost must be positive. Therefore, the monopolist will produce a quantity at which marginal revenue is also positive. Marginal revenue is positive when demand is elastic.

IR10-7. Consumers will be worse off under monopoly than under perfect competition. They will face higher prices, and will be forced to consume lower quantities. As a result, consumers will suffer a loss of consumer surplus.

IR10-8. For a natural monopoly, the average-total-cost curve will slope downward as we move from left to right across the diagram, throughout the relevant range of output.

IR10-9. No, perfectly competitive firms do *not* engage in price discrimination. To engage in price discrimination, a firm must have some ability to control its price. However, by definition, a perfectly competitive firm is a price taker, which means that the firm has no control over its price.

IR10-10. Price-discriminating firms charge higher prices to customers with relatively less elastic demand because this enables them to increase their revenues and profits.

Questions and Problems

QP10-1. A natural monopoly is protected by a barrier to entry in the form of a cost advantage. Some firms have monopoly power as a result of control over some key resource. Some firms (such as those in professional sports) are protected by exclusive-franchise arrangements. Other firms are protected by patents. If the patents encourage innovation, they may be socially beneficial, despite the temporary monopoly granted by the patent.

QP10-2. The demand curve facing a perfectly competitive firm is a horizontal line (that is, demand is perfectly elastic). The monopolist faces a downward-sloping demand curve.

The perfectly competitive firm's marginal-revenue curve is the same as its demand curve, so that the marginal-revenue curve is also a horizontal line. The monopolist's marginal-revenue curve slopes downward even more steeply than its demand curve. (If the demand curve is a straight line, the monopolist's marginal-revenue curve has exactly twice the slope of the demand curve.)

The curves are different because the perfectly competitive firm takes the market price as given, whereas the monopoly must choose its profit-maximizing combination of price and quantity.

QP10-3. If demand is inelastic, marginal revenue is negative. However, if demand is unit-elastic, marginal revenue is zero. If demand is elastic, marginal revenue is positive.

QP10-4. No, if AAAA Corporation is facing inelastic demand, it is not maximizing profit. In order to maximize profit, the firm should produce the quantity at which marginal revenue is equal to marginal cost. Since marginal cost is positive, marginal revenue must also be positive if we are at the profit-maximizing quantity. Marginal revenue is positive when demand is elastic, but this firm is currently in the *inelastic* region of its demand curve. To maximize profit, the firm would need to reduce output, so as to get into the elastic portion of its demand curve.

QP10-5.

(a) and (b)

Price	Quantity Demanded	Total Revenue	Marginal Revenue	Marginal Cost	Total Cost	Profit
$10	0	$ 0	—	—	$ 0	$ 0
9	1	9	$ 9	$3	3	6
8	2	16	7	3	6	10
7	3	21	5	3	9	12
6	4	24	3	3	12	12
5	5	25	1	3	15	10
4	6	24	−1	3	18	6
3	7	21	−3	3	21	0
2	8	16	−5	3	24	− 8
1	9	9	−7	3	27	−18
0	10	0	−9	3	30	−30

Total revenue is equal to price multiplied by quantity: $TR = (P)(Q)$. Marginal revenue is the additional revenue the firm receives as a result of selling one additional unit of output: $MR = \Delta TR / \Delta Q$.

Total variable cost is equal to the sum of the marginal costs: $TVC = \sum MC$. Total cost is equal to total variable cost plus total fixed cost: $TC = TVC + TFC$. However, in this question, it is assumed that there are no fixed costs. Thus if $TFC = 0$, $TC = TVC + 0$, so that $TC = TVC$.

c. The firm's profit-maximizing quantity of output is four zolotkas. The firm charges a price of $6 per zolotka. The firm makes profit of $12.

d. When we subtract total cost from total revenue, we find profit. Profit is maximized at a quantity of four. Comparing marginal cost and marginal revenue, we see that these variables are the same at a quantity of four.

e. In the above table, it is assumed that the firm has zero fixed costs. If, instead, the firm had fixed costs of $15, most of the columns in the table would not be changed. However, all of the numbers in the total-cost column would be increased by $15. As a result, all of the numbers in the profit column would be *decreased* by $15. The firm's maximum profit would be −$3. (The firm would stay in business, because this operating loss of $3 would be much less than the $15 of fixed costs. Therefore, the firm would lose more by going out of business than by continuing.) The most important point is that the firm's profit-maximizing price and quantity do not change. The profit-maximizing choice is determined by *marginal* revenue and *marginal* cost. Even though *total* cost has changed, *marginal* cost has not.

QP10-6.

a. Here we assume that the firm can practice perfect price discrimination. In this case, total revenue is not equal to the product of price and quantity, because each customer pays a different price. Instead, total revenue is calculated by adding the revenue for each customer. The first will pay

$9, the second will pay $8, and the third will pay $7. Therefore, when three units are sold, total revenue will be $(9 + 8 + 7) = $24. In this case, marginal revenue is equal to price, just as it was for a perfectly competitive firm!

a.

Price	Quantity Demanded	Total Revenue	Marginal Revenue	Marginal Cost	Total Cost	Profit
$10	0	$ 0	—	—	$ 0	$ 0
9	1	9	$ 9	$3	3	6
8	2	17	8	3	6	11
7	3	24	7	3	9	15
6	4	30	6	3	12	18
5	5	35	5	3	15	20
4	6	39	4	3	18	21
3	7	42	3	3	21	21
2	8	44	2	3	24	20
1	9	45	1	3	27	18

b. If the firm has no fixed costs, the profit-maximizing quantity is seven zolotkas. The firm charges $9 to the first customer, $8 to the second, and so on, down to $3 for the seventh customer. The firm's profit is $21.

c. If the firm had $15 of fixed costs, most of the columns in the table would not be changed. However, all of the numbers in the total-cost column would be increased by $15. As a result, all of the numbers in the profit column would be *decreased* by $15. The firm's maximum profit would be $6. The most important point is that the firm's profit-maximizing price and quantity do not change. The profit-maximizing choice is determined by *marginal* revenue and *marginal* cost. Even though *total* cost has changed, *marginal* cost has not.

d. The price-discriminating monopoly has a larger quantity. When compared with the single-price monopoly, the price-discriminating monopoly charges a higher price to some customers, but it charges a lower price to other customers. The monopolist makes higher profits, because it is able to extract every bit of consumer surplus. The first few customers are worse off under price discrimination: They received consumer surplus when there was no price discrimination, but when the firm is able to discriminate, all of their consumer surplus is taken away. However, some consumers are better off. These are the consumers who would not have been able to consume at all under the single-price monopoly, but who are able to consume under price discrimination.

QP10-7.

a. If the industry shown in the previous two questions were perfectly competitive, and if there were no fixed costs, the market equilibrium price would be $3, and the equilibrium quantity would be seven zolotkas.

b. The competitive equilibrium involves a higher quantity than the single-price monopoly. The competitive equilibrium involves a lower price than would be charged by a single-price monopoly.

c. The equilibrium quantity under perfect competition is the same as the equilibrium quantity under the perfectly price-discriminating monopoly. The price for the last customer is the same under competition as under the perfectly price-discriminating monopoly, but all other customers pay less under competition.

QP10-8. Just because a firm is making a large amount of economic profit, the firm is not necessarily a monopoly. Even perfectly competitive firms can make large economic profits for a while, if conditions are right. However, perfectly competitive firms cannot expect to continue to make economic profits for a long time, because they are not protected by barriers to entry.

QP10-9. The profit-maximizing quantity is the quantity at which marginal revenue is equal to marginal cost. If the firm charges the highest possible price that can be charged without driving the quantity demanded all the way down to zero, it will *not* be maximizing profit.

QP10-10. At any given show, the movie theater charges the same price to every customer. Thus the theater is not using one possible strategy for price discrimination. However, the firm does charge different prices, depending on the time of the show. This can be viewed as an attempt to price discriminate by charging higher prices to those with less elastic demand. It is entirely possible that those who come to the 8 p.m. show may have less elastic demand than those who come to the 4 p.m. show. On the other hand, it is also possible to interpret the difference in prices as a response to perceived differences in demand. Thus it is difficult to say for certain whether this is a case of price discrimination.

QP10-11. "Buy one, get the second one for half price" is not an example of price discrimination. Every customer is given the same price schedule.

CHAPTER 11:

Interim Review Questions

IR11-1. A monopolistically competitive firm is similar to a perfectly competitive firm, in that the firm is one of many firms that are small relative to the market, and there is free entry and exit. A monopolistically competitive firm is similar to a monopoly in that it faces a downward-sloping demand curve.

IR11-2. If the firms in a monopolistically competitive industry are suffering economic losses, some firms will soon shut down. As a result of the decrease in the number of firms in the industry, prices will rise.

IR11-3. Profit per unit is the difference between price and average total cost. If profit is zero, the average-total-cost curve must be tangent to the demand curve. In the case of perfect competition, the demand curve is a horizontal line. Thus when profit is zero for a perfectly competitive firm, the average-total-cost curve is also horizontal at the profit-maximizing quantity. This occurs when the firm produces at the minimum point on its average-total-cost curve. However, in the case of the monopolistically competitive firm, the demand curve is downward sloping. Therefore, at the quantity at which price is equal to average total cost, the average-total-cost curve is downward sloping. If the ATC curve is sloping downward, it cannot be at its minimum point.

IR11-4. An industry with 75 firms *might* be an oligopoly, if it is dominated by a small number of very large firms. For instance, an industry might have three large firms that produce the overwhelming majority of the industry's output, and it might also have 72 very small firms. Thus the existence of a large number of firms does not *necessarily* mean the industry is competitive. In a perfectly competitive industry, *all* firms are small relative to the market.

IR11-5. International trade is a non-zero-sum game. In everyday language, international trade is a "win-win" situation.

IR11-6. Game theory is not very useful for studying perfectly competitive industries because the firms in these industries have such a simple strategy: Perfectly competitive firms produce the quantity at which price is equal to marginal cost, and they do not need to pay a lot of attention to all of the other firms in the industry.

IR11-7. A shared monopoly is an oligopoly that succeeds at maximizing the industry's profits, by producing the same quantity that would be produced by a monopoly.

IR11-8. The scheme described in this question certainly does sound like a scheme for tacit collusion. It may be effective. In fact, in some stores, Coca-Cola products and Pepsi products are priced in exactly this way.

Questions and Problems

QP11-1. From most competitive to least competitive, the four market structures would be ranked in the following order: (1) perfect competition, (2) monopolistic competition, (3) oligopoly, (4) monopoly.

QP11-2. The demand for the output of a perfectly competitive firm is perfectly elastic. In other words, the perfectly competitive firm faces a demand curve with an elasticity of infinity. The monopolistically competitive firm's demand curve is likely to be elastic over much of the relevant range of output. (It will certainly be elastic at the profit-maximizing quantity.) However, the monopolistic competitor's demand curve is not *perfectly* elastic. The monopolist faces the entire market demand curve, which is likely to be much less elastic than the monopolistically competitive firm's demand curve. The monopolist will maximize profits by choosing a quantity at which demand is elastic, but the demand curve may have substantial portions over which demand is inelastic.

QP11-3. In some cases, it makes sense to focus our attention on the degree of industrial concentration at the national level (or even the level of the entire world). In the case of commercial airlines, it is certainly plausible to argue that we should concentrate on local routes, rather than on the nation as a whole. Much will depend on the extent to which consumers are able to choose alternative products, and on the extent to which new firms are able to enter the market.

QP11-4. The long-run price for a monopolistically competitive firm will be higher than the long-run price for a perfectly competitive firm that has the same average-total-cost curve. The monopolistically competitive firm will have a lower quantity. However, the differences may be fairly small.

QP11-5. If Coke and Pepsi were to lose market share to lower-priced store brands, there would be greater product variety and lower prices.

QP11-6. Price leadership certainly appears to be a form of tacit collusion.

CHAPTER 12:

Interim Review Questions

IR12-1. If a natural monopolist uses marginal-cost pricing, its price will be less than its average total cost, and the firm will suffer losses.

IR12-2. For a natural monopoly, profit maximization will lead to the highest prices, average-cost pricing will lead to lower prices, and marginal-cost pricing will lead to even lower prices.

IR12-3. For a natural monopoly, marginal-cost pricing will lead to the highest quantities (assuming that the government provides a subsidy, so the firm is able to stay in business), average-cost pricing will lead to lower quantities, and monopoly profit maximization will lead to even lower quantities.

IR12-4. Cross-subsidization occurs when a regulator allows firms to earn economic profits in some of their activities, on the condition that they use some of those profits to subsidize other activities. This once occurred in the airline industry. Before deregulation, cross-subsidization also occurred in the telephone industry. The telephone monopoly earned high profits on long-distance service, and provided subsidized local service.

IR12-5. Businesses will appreciate regulation if it makes it difficult for new firms to enter, and if it makes it difficult for existing firms to compete by offering lower prices. These are exactly the things that occurred when airlines, trucking, and railroads were regulated. As a result, it is not surprising that the business firms in these industries were happy with regulation, and that they fought against deregulation.

IR12-6. If an occupational safety regulation saves one life per year, and if the annual cost of the regulation is $1 million, it would almost certainly be beneficial to society. Many of the estimates of the value of saving a life are in the range of *several* million dollars. If the annual cost were $10 million, it is questionable whether the regulation would be beneficial to society, because that figure is higher than some estimates of the value of saving a life. If the cost were $100 million, or $1 billion, or $1 trillion, the regulation would certainly be a mistake.

IR12-7. The *Standard Oil, American Tobacco,* and *ALCOA* cases all involved breaking up an existing firm.

IR12-8. The Robinson-Patman Act is more difficult to justify than any of the other anti-trust laws, because the Robinson-Patman Act can actually reduce competition.

Questions and Problems

QP12-1. The economic theory of regulation stresses that legislators want to maximize their political support. Therefore, they may respond to a small, well-organized lobbying group, even though the gains to that group are smaller than the losses for the rest of society. This may explain the rise of trucking regulation in the 1930s: The trucking industry was able to put pressure on the political system. The deregulation of trucking in the 1970s and 1980s might be partly due to the decline in the political power of the trucking industry, and the rise of consumer-oriented groups. Of course, it is important to realize that regulation and deregulation are very complicated phenomena, and no single theory is likely to provide a complete explanation. For example, it is also possible that legislators in the 1930s did not understand how the proposed laws would hurt consumers, and that the legislators of the 1970s were more familiar with economic reasoning.

QP12-2. The "Rule of Reason" suggests that firms should only be found guilty of violating the antitrust laws if their behavior is "unreasonable". Thus under the Rule of Reason, it would be possible to acquit a firm that was technically violating the law, if the firm had not acted in an "unreasonable" way. (Of course, different people may have different views about what is unreasonable.) The Supreme Court applied the Rule of Reason in the *U.S. Steel* case, when it found U.S. Steel to be not guilty. However, the Court abandoned the Rule of Reason in the *ALCOA* case, when it found ALCOA to be guilty, even though it was agreed that ALCOA's behavior had been reasonable.

QP12-3. The Sherman Act prohibits monopoly, attempting to monopolize, and price fixing. The Clayton Act prohibits price discrimination that is not based on cost differences, and it also prohibits stock mergers that reduce competition substantially, tying arrangements, exclusive dealing arrangements, and interlocking directorates.

QP12-4. There is not necessarily a "correct" or "incorrect" answer to this question. However,

a. A merger between two small soybean farms does not seem to be worthy of much attention from the Justice Department. If the farms are allowed to merge, it would have almost no effect on the industry, which would still be extremely competitive.

b. A merger between United Airlines and American Airlines would seem to be cause for major concern. If these two airlines were to merge, it would create a very high degree of concentration on routes into and out of Chicago's O'Hare Airport, which is one of the busiest airports in the United States, as well as many other airports. If such a merger were proposed, the Justice Department might very well become involved.

c. A conglomerate merger, such as a merger between a potato-chips company and an auto-parts company, would not have any effect on competition. Therefore, the Justice Department probably does not need to be concerned about conglomerate mergers.

d. If Exxon Mobil were to take over 10,000 gasoline stations, it might reduce competition substantially in the gasoline retailing industry. Consequently, this might be grounds for antitrust concern.

The suggested answers to parts (a) and (c) are that there is not much reason to be concerned. These answers do not depend on economies of scale. If, in parts (b) and (d), the firms say that the merger would help them to achieve large economies of scale, it *might* change the answer. Of course, it is important to remember that the firms might *claim* they will achieve economies of scale, regardless of whether they really expect to do so.

QP12-5. All of the cases listed here could be prosecuted under the antitrust laws. Lowest priority should probably be given to the charge that Walmart is competing "unfairly" by offering lower prices. This charge is mostly the result of sour grapes from other firms that are jealous of Walmart's efficiency.

The easiest and strongest case is against the simultaneous election of the same person to the Boards of Directors of three major automobile producers. This is a blatant violation of the antitrust laws, and it should be straightforward to get the courts to rule against it.

A contract requiring anyone who buys an automobile from a dealer to get repair work done at the same dealer is also a serious violation of the antitrust laws. Meetings between the financial-aid committees at several colleges may also be a violation of the antitrust laws.

QP12-6. The *Standard Oil* case was a Supreme Court decision. The *Xerox* case and the *AT&T* case were both consent decrees. The *Standard Oil* case and the *AT&T* case both involved breaking up an existing company, whereas the *Xerox* case required Xerox Corp. to license its patents to its competitors.

QP12-7. A case can be made for strong licensing regulations for heart surgeons. The case for licensing regulation is probably somewhat weaker for social workers. For barbers and dental hygienists, the case for regulation is fairly weak. If there is to be any regulation, it should be minimal. It is difficult to make any case for licensing regulation for assembly-line workers or newspaper-delivery persons.

QP12-8. It is easy to see how the railroad industry would be in favor of regulation during the 1880s. The industry had been subject to frequent "price wars", and regulation put a stop to them. As a result, the industry was more profitable with regulation. By the 1950s, the trucking industry was also being regulated by the Interstate Commerce Commission. The railroad industry may have desired to find ways to compete more effectively.

QP12-9. It is true that the antitrust laws penalize a firm that is so successful as to become a monopoly. (This is one of the lines of argument given by the lawyers of Microsoft Corporation in its antitrust suit.) However, it is an exaggeration to say that the antitrust laws are fundamentally inefficient. The antitrust laws help to ensure competition on an ongoing basis, and not just when a firm becomes a monopoly.

QP12-10. When a regulator resigns and takes a position with a company in the regulated industry, it is easy to imagine that the relationship between the regulatory agency and the firm will become more cozy and friendly than was intended. This may reduce the ability of the regulatory agency to oversee the industry effectively. Therefore, it is questionable whether this practice should be allowed.

QP12-11.

a. Just because other medications were already on the market, it does not follow that the FDA should not allow new drugs to be marketed. Each drug is slightly different, and some drugs are more effective for some people. A good argument can be made for allowing the pharmaceutical companies to devise new products.

b. The optimal size of a pre-market test for a new drug is the size of test at which the expected marginal benefits are equal to the marginal costs. Therefore, it does not make sense to insist on trials involving hundreds of thousands of subjects. These will be very costly, and they are unlikely to produce a marginal benefit as great as the marginal cost. It is certainly possible to argue that the FDA should have insisted on a larger pre-market test, but it is *not* obvious that this should have occurred.

c. The adverse reaction to felbamate occurred in about one out of every 10,000 people who took the drug. In light of this, the FDA's decision seems reasonable. Many people can continue to benefit from the drug, if no other drug works for them. (After all, if epilepsy is left untreated, it can have very serious consequences, including death.) If someone uses felbamate, he or she can still minimize the risk of serious side effects by having regular blood tests. How-

ever, if the frequency of the bad side effects had been much greater, it might have been appropriate for the FDA to ban the drug altogether. (Of course, if the frequency were much greater, it would probably have been picked up by the pre-market test.)

CHAPTER 13:

Interim Review Questions

IR13-1. The marginal-revenue-product curve slopes downward as we move from left to right across the diagram.

IR13-2. In a competitive labor market, the marginal-revenue-product curve for labor is exactly the same as the firm's demand curve for labor.

IR13-3. The five main categories of factors of production are labor, capital, land, energy, and materials.

IR13-4. If the wage rate were to *increase*, the *substitution effect* would lead toward an *increase* in labor supply.

IR13-5. If the wage rate were to *decrease*, the *income effect* would lead toward an *increase* in labor supply.

IR13-6. When Hilary Swank established herself as a very good motion-picture actress, the demand for her services increased. In other words, the demand curve for her services shifted to the right. Movie executives would estimate that her ability to get people to buy movie tickets was increased. In other words, her marginal revenue product was higher.

IR13-7. Immigration causes an increase in the supply of labor. In other words, immigration (at least if it involves immigration of working-age people) shifts the supply curve of labor to the right.

IR13-8. Pleasant jobs should have equilibrium wage rates that are lower than the wage rates for jobs that are unpleasant but otherwise comparable.

IR13-9. In the last few decades, the ratio of women's earnings to men's earnings has increased substantially. The ratio of earnings for black men to earnings for white men has increased only by a very small amount in recent decades (although it increased substantially in the middle decades of the 20th century).

IR13-10. The union spillover effect tends to *reduce* the wages paid by non-union firms. The union threat effect tends to *increase* the wages paid by non-union firms.

IR13-11. For a monopsonistic firm that faces an upward-sloping labor-supply curve, the marginal-factor-expense curve lies above the labor-supply curve.

IR13-12. Monopsonistic exploitation occurs when a monopsonistic employer pays workers less than their marginal revenue product.

Questions and Problems

QP13-1. For the firm that is perfectly competitive in its output market, marginal revenue product is calculated by multiplying marginal (physical) product by the price of the output. For the firm that is a monopolist in its output market, marginal revenue product is calculated by multiplying marginal (physical) product by the marginal revenue. In either case, the marginal-revenue-product curve slopes downward as we move from left to right across the diagram.

QP13-2. The substitution effect on labor supply comes from the fact that an increase in the wage rate is the same as an increase in the price of leisure. When leisure becomes more expensive, the worker will substitute away from leisure by working more. Therefore, the substitution effect of an increase in the wage rate is an increase in work. The substitution effect of a decrease in the wage rate is a decrease in work.

The income effect on labor supply comes from the fact that an increase in the wage rate leads to an increase in the consumer's real income. Since leisure is a normal good, the income effect of an increase in the wage rate is a decrease in work. The income effect of a decrease in the wage rate is an increase in work.

If the income effect is stronger than the substitution effect, we have a "backward-bending" labor-supply curve, with a negative labor-supply elasticity. If the income effect and the substitution effect are of equal strength, the labor-supply curve will be a vertical line, and the labor-supply elasticity will be zero.

QP13-3. An automobile uses a very wide range of factors of production, including some from all of the major groups. The assembly line has workers, who use capital equipment. The factory runs on electricity, and it is built on land. Finally, the automobile is built with steel, plastics, rubber, paint, and a variety of other materials.

QP13-4. The labor-demand curve is probably more elastic for Joe Dokes than for Placido Domingo. It is relatively easy for firms to substitute for Joe Dokes's labor, because lots of people are able to flip burgers. However, Placido Domingo's talents are unique, or at least very unusual.

QP13-5. *All else equal*, we would expect the influx of workers in the Mariel boatlift to lead to a decrease in the wage rate for less-skilled workers in the Miami area, and an increase in the quantity of labor. However, if the increased immigration was coupled with a substantial reduction in the number of people moving from other parts of the United States to the Miami area, there might be minimal effects on wages and employment in Miami.

Overall, we would not expect the Mariel boatlift to have much effect on labor markets in the United States. At that time, for the U.S. as a whole, employment was about 1000 times as great as the number of people who came in on the boatlift. Thus the Mariel boatlift was simply not large enough to have a large effect overall.

QP13-6. For a firm that is a perfect competitor in its output market, the marginal revenue product of labor is calculated by multiplying marginal (physical) product by the price of the output. In this case, marginal (physical) product = 10 − L, and the output price is $10 per unit. The marginal-revenue-product curve is therefore $10 (10 − L) = $(100 − 10L).

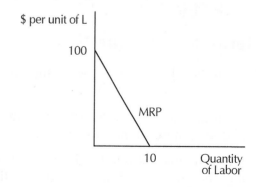

– 521 –

QP13-7. On average, workers with higher educational attainment have higher earnings than those with lower educational attainment. However, even though Sam has nine years of post-high-school education, he earns less than Zelda, who has only a high-school diploma. This can occur for a number of reasons. First, Sam might be fresh out of graduate school, whereas Zelda might have had many years of experience on the job. Second, Zelda might be represented by a union, which succeeds in pushing up her wage rate, whereas Sam might not be represented by a union. Third, Sam's work involves reading Greek and Latin in a quiet library, whereas Zelda's job involves repairing telephone lines during snowstorms. Therefore, Zelda's wage might be increased by a compensating wage differential. Fourth, Zelda might be helped by an affirmative-action program. Finally, it may be that the demand may be greater for Zelda's output: Perhaps relatively few students want to take Greek, while lots of people are willing to pay to have the telephone wires working.

This suggests that a very large number of forces have an influence on wage rates.

QP13-8. This question deals with the union spillover effect. If workers are displaced as a result of job losses in a unionized firm, many of them will eventually seek work in other industries. This can be represented by a rightward shift in the labor-supply curve in the other industries. As a result, wages will fall and employment will increase in these other industries.

QP13-9. In a competitive labor market, the firm can hire as many workers as it wants to hire, at the market wage rate. Therefore, the labor-supply curve facing the firm is a horizontal line, and the firm's marginal-labor-expense curve is also a horizontal line. To hire one additional worker, all the firm has to do is pay the market wage rate. However, in a monopsonized labor market, the firm faces an upward-sloping labor-supply curve. This means that the firm has to increase its wage rate, if it is to hire an additional worker. Since the firm has to raise its wage rate for *all* workers (and not just for the marginal worker), the marginal-labor-expense curve rises more rapidly than the labor-supply curve.

QP13-10. Should college football players be paid a salary? This is a controversial question. From the perspective of this chapter, the key point is this: If college football players are *not* paid a salary, they will be victims of monopsonistic exploitation.

CHAPTER 14:

Interim Review Questions

IR14-1. If the interest rate *increases*, the *substitution effect* will cause an increase in saving.

IR14-2. If the interest rate *decreases*, the *income effect* will cause an increase in saving.

IR14-3. If the interest rate used for discounting the future is 5%, the present discounted value of $100, to be received one year from now, is $(100/ (1.05)) = \$95.24$ (approximately). If the discount rate is 10%, the present discounted value is $(100/(1.10)) = \$90.91$ (approximately). If the discount rate is 20%, the present discounted value is $(100/(1.20)) = \$83.33$ (approximately).

IR14-4. If the interest rate used to discount the future is 5%, the present discounted value of $100, to be received *ten* years from now, is $(100/ (1.05)^{10}) = \$61.39$ (approximately). If the discount rate is 10%, the present discounted value is $\$(100/(1.10)^{10}) = \$38.55$ (approximately). If the discount rate is 20%, the present discounted value is $\$(100/(1.20)^{10}) = \$16.15$ (approximately). The examples in questions IR14-3 and IR14-4 show that present discounted values are sensitive to the discount rate and the length of time over which the discounting occurs.

IR14-5. The net present discounted value of this project is the present discounted value of the revenues, minus the present discounted value of the costs. The present discounted value of the costs is $100. This does not have to be discounted, because the costs are incurred at the beginning of the life of the project. The revenues are $110, and they are to be received in one year, so they must be discounted. If the interest rate used to discount the future is 5%, the present discounted value of the revenues is $\$(110/ (1.05)) = \$104.76$ (approximately). Therefore, the net present discounted value of this project is $\$(104.76 - 100) = \$4.76$. Since the net present discounted value is positive, the project should be undertaken.

If the revenues of $110 were to be received in three years, the present discounted value of the revenues would be $\$(110/(1.05)^3) = \$95.02$ (approximately). Therefore, the net present discounted value of this project is $\$(95.02 - 100) = -\$4.98$. Since the net present discounted value is negative, the project should *not* be undertaken.

This example shows that investment decisions will depend in an important way on the length of time it takes for projects to be completed.

Questions and Problems

QP14-1. The first installment of $10,000 is received today. Therefore, it does not need to be discounted, and its present discounted value is $10,000. The second installment arrives in one year, so it must be discounted. If the future is discounted at a rate of is 8%, the presented discounted value of the second installment is $\$(10,000/(1.08) = \$9259.26$ (approximately). The third and final installment arrives in two years, so it must be discounted twice. The present discounted value of the third installment is $\$(10,000/(1.08)^2) = \$8573.39$ (approximately). To calculate the present discounted value of the entire stream of cash flows, we add the present discounted values of the three installments: $10,000 + $9259.26 + 8573.39 = $27,832.65.

QP14-2. The net present discounted value of the project is the present discounted value of the revenues, minus the present discounted value of the costs. The costs (of $300 million) occur at the very beginning of the project, so they do not need to be discounted. The revenues (of $330 million) occur one year later, so they must be discounted. If the future is discounted at a rate of is 8%, the present discounted value of the revenues is $330 million/1.08 = $305,555,556 (approximately). In this case, the net present discounted value of the project is $\$(305,555,556 - 300,000,000) = \$5,555,556$. Since the net present discounted value is positive, the firm should undertake the project.

If the discount rate is 10%, the present discounted value of the revenues is $330 million/1.10 = $300,000,000. The net present discounted value of the project is zero. The firm should undertake the project.

If the discount rate is 12%, the present discounted value of the revenues is $330 million/1.12 = $294,642,857 (approximately). The net present discounted value of the project is $(294,642,857 − 300,000,000) = −$5,357,143. Since the net present discounted value is negative, the firm should *not* undertake the project.

The firm should undertake this project if the discount rate is equal to or less than 10%.

QP14-3. The supply curve is $Q_s = 0.1P$. The demand curve is $Q_d = 100 − 0.1P$. At the equilibrium price, $Q_s = Q_d$. Therefore, if we substitute the supply equation and the demand equation into the equilibrium equation, we have $0.1P = 100 − 0.1P$. Adding 0.1P to both sides of the equation, we have $0.2P = 100$. Dividing both sides by 0.2, we find the equilibrium price, which is $500. (This is a per-period rental price.) If we substitute the equilibrium price into the supply equation, we get $Q_s = (0.1)(500) = 50$. If we substitute the equilibrium price into the demand equation, we get $Q_d = 100 − (0.1)(500) = 100 − 50 = 50$. Since we find the same quantity by using the supply equation and the demand equation, this confirms that we have performed the calculations correctly. In either case, the equilibrium quantity is 50 cement-mixer trucks.

QP14-4. The equilibrium interest rate is 6%. If a usury ceiling is established at 20%, the equilibrium interest rate is still legal, and the usury ceiling will not have any effect on the market. However, if the usury ceiling were at 5%, the equilibrium interest rate would not be legal any longer. If the law is enforced, the quantity of credit demanded will be greater than the quantity of credit supplied, and there will be a shortage of credit (which is sometimes called a "credit crunch").

QP14-5. Using the Rule of 72, we can see that it will take approximately (72/6) = 12 years to double your money, if the interest rate is 6%. If the interest rate is 10%, it will take a bit more than 7 years to double your money.

CHAPTER 15:

Interim Review Questions

IR15-1. After the middle 1970s, there was an increase in the share of income received by the top 20 percent of households in the United States.

IR15-2. If the Lorenz Curve for country B is closer to the Line of Equality than the Lorenz Curve for country A, then country A will have a larger Gini Ratio.

IR15-3. Lifetime income is distributed more equally than annual income.

IR15-4. An increase in the demand for more highly skilled workers will raise the equilibrium wage rate for more highly skilled workers. This will lead to an increase in earnings inequality.

IR15-5. Wealth is distributed less equally than income.

IR15-6. By ignoring in-kind income, the official poverty statistics tend to overstate the "true" rate of poverty.

IR15-7. Poverty tends to be highest in the South and Southwest.

IR15-8. Poverty among the elderly is lower than poverty among the young.

Questions and Problems

QP15-1. There is no single correct answer to the question of whether the federal estate tax be made stronger or weaker. Those who believe in making a strong effort to reduce inequality will probably prefer a strong estate tax. Those for whom the reduction of inequality is a lower priority will probably prefer a weaker estate tax, or no estate tax at all. If estate tax rates were raised, it is reasonable to think that some people would choose to leave smaller estates. However, the effect might not be very large. Many people do not do much estate planning; this is at least partly because estate planning involves contemplation of death, which makes people uncomfortable. Also, the estate tax has a number of loopholes, which make it possible for people to leave substantial estates while minimizing their estate taxes.

QP15-2. An annual wealth tax would close some of the avenues for avoiding the estate tax. However, a big problem with any type of wealth tax is that it is necessary to *measure* wealth. Measuring wealth properly is difficult from an administrative point of view.

QP15-3. There is no single "correct" answer about the optimal distribution of income. Reasonable people could prefer for the U.S. economy to be more equal than it is today. However, the optimal distribution will almost certainly *not* be very close to complete equality. Since people have very diverse skills, equilibrium in the labor market will inevitably involve some earnings inequality. To reduce this inequality, it will be necessary to make use of taxes and transfer payments. As the level of taxes and transfers is increased more and more, there could be more and more of a disincentive to work. As a result, if the government tries to achieve a level of redistribution that is too great, there can be adverse effects on the economy. For example, in the 1970s, Sweden had tax rates that were in excess of 80% for many people. It is believed that these high tax rates discouraged many people from getting a college education and/or working. The Swedish political system responded to these perceived problems by reducing the level of taxation (although tax rates in Sweden are still much higher than they are in the United States).

QP15-4. If birth rates increase, there is a good chance that there will be an increase in the number of new college graduates about 20 to 25 years later. If there is indeed an increase in the supply of new college graduates, we would expect the wage rates for new college graduates to fall, all else equal.

QP15-5. Income inequality has a number of sources. The biggest source is the inequality in earnings. Those with more education and experience tend to earn more. The rates of return to education and experience have increased in the last quarter of the 20th century. This has been a major cause of the increase in inequality in recent decades. Unions also have an effect on the distribution of income. However, since unions have been in decline for many years, their effects have diminished. The distribution of capital income also has an effect on the overall distribution of income. Since the distribution of wealth has become more unequal, the distribution of capital income has also become somewhat more unequal, and this has contributed to the overall increase in inequality.

QP15-6. Once again, there is no single "correct" answer to this question. It is certainly possible that, if the distribution of income had been much more equal, there might not have been any wealthy benefactors to support creative artists. Of course, if there weren't as many wealthy benefactors, it does not necessarily mean that there would not have been any artistic creations. Still, some people have argued that inequality serves a valuable role in the development of the economy, because artistic and technological creativity is supported by the existence of wealthy people.

QP15-7. If society were to make an explicit effort to pursue the goal of equal incomes, it would probably lead to more equality than we would see under an effort to pursue the goal of equal *opportunity*. Thus, the goal of equal opportunity would probably be associated with a higher Gini Ratio than the goal of equal incomes.

CHAPTER 16:

Interim Review Questions

IR16-1. Weather-forecasting services could be provided through government, and indeed, the National Oceanographic and Atmospheric Administration provides much of the apparatus for weather forecasting. This can be justified on the grounds that weather-forecasting services have an element of nonrivalry. However, weather-forecasting services are certainly not a *pure* public good: Some people gain much more than others from having an accurate weather forecast. Some firms provide private weather forecasts to private clients (such as farmers).

Child-care services also have at least a small element of publicness. It's good for the society as a whole that children are cared for. Nevertheless, the public-goods justification for providing child-care services through government is fairly limited. There may be good reasons for governments to *regulate* child-care services, in an attempt to assure that the child-care environments are safe, but there is not much reason to think that the government needs to *provide* child-care services. On the other hand, there may be a justification for government to subsidize child-care services, especially for low-income families. Here the justification would have a tone of income redistribution.

Retirement pensions for government workers could be provided by government, but there is no particular reason to believe that government can do the job better than private financial-services companies.

IR16-2. The federal government handles national defense, which does not involve state and local governments. State and local governments are deeply involved in education, while the federal government's role in education is much more limited. The federal government spends heavily on transfer-payment programs. State and local governments also spend some on transfer payments, but they tend to spend more on highways, hospitals, police protection, and fire protection. Finally, the federal government spends a lot on interest payments on the national debt, whereas state and local governments spend much less on debt service.

IR16-3. The three largest federal transfer-payment programs are Social Security, Medicare, and Medicaid.

IR16-4. The payroll tax is far better than the income tax in the respect that the payroll tax has much lower costs of administrative and compliance.

IR16-5. The federal government raises most of its revenues from the individual income tax and the payroll tax. State governments (and some local governments) also use income taxes, but not to the same extent as the federal government. State governments rely heavily on general retail sales taxes, which are not used at the federal level. Local governments rely heavily on property taxes, which are not used at the federal level, and are only used slightly by the states.

IR16-6. The two largest sources of tax revenue for the federal government are the individual income tax and the payroll tax.

Questions and Problems

QP16-1. In terms of administrative costs, compliance costs, and excess burden, the payroll tax is better than the individual income tax or the corporation tax.

QP16-2. The federal individual income tax is more progressive than either the payroll tax or a general retail sales tax.

QP16-3. David's average tax rate is $2000/$10,000 = 20%. Amy's average tax rate is $2000/$100,000 = 2%. Since the average tax rate decreases when income increases, we say that this tax is regressive.

QP16-4. In the previous question, if Amy's tax were $1000, her average tax rate would be $1000/$100,000 = 1%, so that the tax system would be even more regressive than before.

If Amy's tax were $20,000, then her average tax rate would be $20,000/$100,000 = 20%. Therefore, her tax rate would be the same as David's tax rate, and the tax system would be proportional.

If Amy's tax were $40,000, then her average tax rate would be $40,000/$100,000 = 40%. In this case, the tax system would be progressive.

QP16-5. National defense is a classic example of a pure public good, and there is a very strong justification for providing national defense through government.

Cosmetic surgery is very close to a pure private good, and there is very little justification for providing cosmetic surgery through government.

Income-maintenance payments for the poor will generally have to be provided by government.

Streets and sewers have a substantial degree of publicness, and there is at least some justification for providing them through government. Indeed, many governments do participate in the building and maintenance of streets and sewers. However, it is possible for private companies to provide roads and bridges; when this occurs, the roads and bridges would be funded through tolls, rather than taxes.

Elementary education has a significant degree of nonrivalry, since an educated population provides significant benefits that go beyond the individual students who receive the education. Thus there is a fairly strong provision for public *support* of elementary education. However, as has been highlighted in the debate over school vouchers, this is not the same as saying that elementary education must be *provided* by government. It would be possible for government to provide funding, but to have private firms do the actual teaching.

Higher education also has a degree of nonrivalry, although higher education is believed to be less public than elementary education. This is because a substantial portion of the benefits of a college education are captured by the individual who receives the education, in the form of higher earnings. Thus there is some argument for public support and/or public provision of higher education, although the case is probably not as strong as the case for public support and/or provision of elementary education. In recent years, however, many state governments have reduced their support for higher education *drastically*. This has led to very large increases in tuition, and a large increase in the number of students who emerge from college with large burdens of student-loan debt. Even if we agree that students should have to pay a significant amount of tuition, we would not necessarily reach the conclusion that the drastic changes of recent years are justified.

QP16-6. Each market has a net-of-tax price of $100. If a 10-percent tax is imposed in each market, then each market will have a gross-of-tax price of ($100)(1.1) = $110. Thus in each market, $10 of tax revenue will be collected from each unit that is bought and sold. If the elasticity of demand for compact-disc players is 1.0, the 10-percent increase in price will lead to a 10-percent reduction in the quantity demanded. If the elasticity of demand for non-glare picture frames is 2.0, the 10-percent increase in price will lead to a 20-percent reduction in quantity demanded.

As a result of the larger change in quantity demanded, the amount of tax revenue collected will be less in the market for non-glare picture frames. For the same reason, the excess burden will be greater in the picture-frame market.

QP16-7.

a. The net-of-tax supply curve is P_{net} = $30. The demand curve is $Q_d = 100 - P$. In the absence of tax, the equilibrium price must be $30. We can find the equilibrium quantity by inserting this price into the demand curve: $Q_d = 100 - 30 = 70$. The equilibrium quantity is 70 units.

b. If a tax of $20 is imposed, the new, gross-of-tax supply curve will be P_{gross} = $50. The buyers' price will now be $50. The sellers' price will remain at $30. The equilibrium quantity can be calculated by inserting the new, gross-of-tax price into the demand curve: $Q_d = 100 - 50 = 50$.

c. The government's tax revenue is $20 per unit, multiplied by the number of units that are bought and sold. We have just seen that the new equilibrium quantity is 50 units. Therefore, the tax revenue is ($20)(50) = $1000.

The excess burden is represented by the area of a triangle. The base of the triangle is the change in quantity as a result of the tax. Before the tax was imposed, the quantity was 70 units. After the tax is imposed, the quantity is 50 units. Therefore, the change in quantity is (70 - 50) = 20. The height of the triangle is the tax per unit, which is $20. The excess burden is (0.5)(20)($20) = (10)($20) = $200.

QP16-8. In the market for gumdrops, the tax will be mostly borne by buyers, because we assume that the demand for gumdrops is inelastic, while the supply is elastic. In the market for grapefruit, the tax will mostly be borne by sellers, because we assume that the supply of grapefruit is inelastic, while the demand is elastic. In each case, most of the burden is borne by the more *inelastic* side of the market.

QP16-9. There is no single "correct" answer to this question. Those who advocate a flat tax usually point to its benefits in terms of efficiency and simplicity. Advocates of a flat tax are thus willing to accept a substantial loss of progressivity, in return for an increase in efficiency and simplicity. However, those who are opposed to a flat tax usually do so on the basis of their belief that the flat tax will greatly reduce the progressivity of the tax system.

It is important to keep in mind that most proposals for a "flat tax" involve a very substantial personal exemption, which would impart progressivity at the bottom and middle of the income scale. Thus under these "flat-tax" proposals, the schedule of effective tax rates is not really constant, even though the word "flat" would seem to suggest that tax rates are the same for everyone.

CHAPTER 17:

Interim Review Questions

IR17-1. Earlier in this book, we have mentioned a few other situations in which private markets do not work well. One of these is imperfect competition among sellers (especially monopoly). Another is imperfect competition among buyers (that is, monopsony). In Chapter 16, we dealt with public goods, which can also give rise to market failure.

IR17-2. *If* we could establish a market in clean air, it is reasonable to expect that the externality problem would be solved. Of course, that is a very big "if".

IR17-3. It may be fairly easy to use private negotiation to solve the problem caused by someone who bothers his neighbors by playing polka records late at night. However, when air pollution from electric-power plants causes acid rain over a region of millions of square miles, it is difficult to see how private negotiation can work. Instead, it will probably be necessary to use Pigouvian taxes, or other means, to improve the situation.

IR17-4. Pigouvian taxes will raise revenue for the government.

Marketable licenses have the *potential* to raise revenue, as well, if the government auctions the licenses. The Clean Air Act amendments of 1990 do establish a system of marketable licenses for some forms of air pollution, but the licenses were given to existing producers. Therefore, even though marketable licenses have the potential to raise revenue for the government, these particular marketable licenses do not do so.

Private negotiation will certainly not raise revenue for the government.

Government regulations may raise small amounts of revenue, if violators of the regulations are fined.

Questions and Problems

QP17-1. During a "killer smog", it is best to order coal-fired power plants and other sources of air pollution to shut down immediately. Similarly, during a meltdown at a nuclear power plant, the correct policy is to shut down the reactor as soon as possible.

QP17-2. The Coase Theorem states that, if people can negotiate freely and if property rights are established clearly, it should be possible to achieve the efficient outcome with respect to an externality problem, regardless of whether property rights are given to the "polluter" or the "pollutee". Coase's solution may be relevant to some environmental problems. However, Coase's solution will only work if the transactions costs of negotiating are relatively small. Thus many of the most important environmental problems may be difficult to handle through private negotiations.

QP17-3.

a. If it doesn't cost anything to collect the toll, the optimal toll at 8 a.m. would be equal to the marginal congestion cost imposed by each additional car. The optimal toll at midnight would be zero, because there is no congestion problem at midnight.

b. If it is costly to collect tolls, the case for collecting a toll is not as strong as before. The toll booth may create more congestion than it solves, by forcing cars to stop to pay a toll. It still may be best to collect a toll, even if it is costly to do so. The correct policy will depend on the relative sizes of the costs and benefits of collecting the toll.

c. When every car has to come to a complete stop to make a cash transaction, the collection of the toll can cause a great deal of congestion. If the toll is recorded by an optimal scanner, cars would not need to slow down very much. Thus the efficiency of the traffic flow might be enhanced by the more technologically sophisticated approach. Indeed, this type of system is now in use in many parts of the United States.

QP17-4. When there is a toll on one bridge, but no toll on the other, it is not surprising that traffic will flow freely on the bridge with the toll, and that there will be congestion on the bridge without the toll. We can expect that drivers will flock to the bridge without a toll, until the marginal costs of crossing the two bridges (including the explicit cost of the toll and the cost of waiting in line on the bridge with no toll) are the same.

Thus the congestion on the bridge with no toll has been *caused* by the policy of having a toll on only one of the two bridges. This suggests that it may not be wise to spend a lot of money to widen the bridge with no toll. Instead, a better choice might be to equalize the tolls on the two bridges, either by imposing a toll on the bridge that does not currently have a toll, or by removing the toll from the bridge that does have a toll.

QP17-5.

a. The demand curve is $P = \$(10 - Q)$. The supply curve is $P = \$3$. If we substitute the supply curve into the demand curve, we have $3 = (10 - Q)$. If we add Q to both sides of the equation, and subtract 3 from both sides of the equation, we have $Q = 7$.

b. The socially optimal quantity is calculated by taking account of *all* of the social costs, including the marginal damage from pollution. The true social marginal cost is $7 per unit. Therefore, from society's point of view, the correct price is $7. If we substitute this price into the demand curve, we have $7 = (10 - Q)$. Following the same procedure that was used in part (a) of this question, we find that the socially optimal quantity is 3 gizmos.

c. The dollar value of the benefit from correcting the externality can be represented by the area of a triangle. The base of the triangle is the difference between the private-market quantity and the socially optimal quantity. This is $(7 - 3) = 4$. The height of the triangle is the difference between the socially optimal price and the private-market price. This is $\$(7 - 3) = \$4$. The area of the triangle is $(0.5)(4)(\$4) = \$8$.

d. If the marginal pollution damage were $7, the true social marginal cost of gizmos would be $10. Therefore, from society's point of view, the optimal price is $10 per gizmo. If we substitute the optimal price into the demand equation, we find that the optimal quantity is zero. If the environmental damages from a good are sufficiently large, it may sometimes be best not to produce the good at all.

QP17-6. A system of marketable licenses will increase the opportunity cost of pollution for the firm. Therefore, a system like this is likely to give the firm a greater incentive to develop new technologies for cleaning up.

QP17-7.

a. Private negotiation may work to solve some kinds of externality problems. However, private negotiation is unlikely to be successful unless the transactions costs of negotiation are small.

b. Regulations can indeed help to reduce water pollution. However, they do not take into account the differences among firms in the costs of pollution abatement. Therefore, regulations may be a relatively costly way of achieving a given goal of pollution reduction.

c. Pigouvian taxes do account for the differences among firms in the costs of pollution abatement. Therefore, Pigouvian taxes are likely to be more efficient than regulations, in achieving a given goal of pollution reduction. Also, Pigouvian taxes will raise revenue for the government. This revenue can be used to reduce reliance on other taxes, so that the overall level of excess burden can be reduced.

d. Marketable licenses are similar to Pigouvian taxes, in that they account for the differences among firms in the costs of pollution abatement. Marketable licenses can raise revenue for the government, *if* the licenses are auctioned. However, if the licenses are merely given away, they will not raise revenue.

QP17-8.

a. In industry A, the cost of reducing pollution by one unit is $10. If the industry is required to reduce pollution by 15 units, the total cost will be (15)($10) = $150. In industry B, the cost of reducing pollution by one unit is $1. If the industry is required to reduce pollution by 15 units, the total cost will be (15)($1) = $15. Therefore, if each industry is required to reduce pollution by 15 units, the total cost of reducing pollution by 30 units is $(150 + 15) = $165.

b. If industry B reduces pollution by 30 units, the total cost will be (30)($1) = $30. Thus we see that the total cost of cleaning up 30 units of pollution can be dramatically different, depending on how the pollution abatement is allocated among firms. In this case, it is much less costly for industry B to do all of the cleaning up. If industry B does all of the pollution abatement, the total cost of cleaning up 30 units is only $30, whereas, if each firm is required to do the same amount of pollution abatement, the total cost of cleaning up 30 units will be $165. Since $165 is 5.5 times as great as $30, this is a very substantial difference.

Index